THE GATESHEAD GURKHAS

A HISTORY OF THE 9TH BATTALION

THE DURHAM LIGHT INFANTRY

1859 – 1967

To my late brother Tom who did not live to see the final book.

This book is dedicated to the memory of all those officers and other ranks who served with the 9th Battalion The Durham Light Infantry and in memory of all those who made the supreme sacrifice in both World Wars. It is also dedicated to the widows and families of those who served with the Battalion and are no longer with us. WE WILL REMEMBER THEM.

Text © Harry Moses, 2001
Maps © Yvonne Beadnell, 2001

Published by County Durham Books, 2001

County Durham Books is the imprint of Durham County Council
Arts, Libraries & Museums Department

ISBN 1 897585 65 9

CONTENTS

PHOTOGRAPHS & DRAWINGS

ABBREVIATIONS

Ranks

Pte.	Private
L/Cpl.	Lance Corporal
Cpl.	Corporal
L/Sgt.	Lance Sergeant
C/Sgt.	Colour Sergeant
S.M.	Sergeant Major
C.S.M.	Company Sergeant Major
R.S.M.	Regimental Sergeant Major
R.Q.M.S.	Regimental Quartermaster Sergeant
Q.M.	Quartermaster
2/Lt.	Second Lieutenant
Lt.	Lieutenant
Capt.	Captain
Maj.	Major
Lt. Col.	Lieutenant Colonel
Col.	Colonel
Brig.	Brigadier
Brig. Gen.	Brigadier General
Maj. Gen.	Major General
Lt. Gen.	Lieutenant General
Gen.	General
C.O.	Commanding Officer
G.O.C.	General Officer Commanding
W.O.II	Warrant Officer, Second Class
C.Q.M.S.	Company Quartermaster Sergeant
S/Sgt.	Staff Sergeant

Decorations and awards

V.C.	Victoria Cross
D.S.O.	Distinguished Service Order
O.B.E.	Order of the British Empire
M.C.	Military Cross
D.C.M.	Distinguished Conduct Medal
M.M.	Military Medal
B.E.M.	British Empire Medal
M.S.M.	Meritorious Service Medal
M.I.D.	Mentioned In Despatches
G.C.B.	Grand Cross of the Bath
C.B.E.	Commander of the British Empire
T.D.	Territorial Decoration

Additional

Bde.	Brigade
B.E.F.	British Expeditionary Force
Bn.	Battalion
H.M.T.	His Majesty's Troopship
K.D.	Khaki drill
K.O.S.B.	Kings Own Scottish Borderers
L.M.G.	Light machine gun
M.G.	Machine gun
N.A.A.F.I.	Navy Army Air Forces Institute
O.P.	Observation post
R.A.M.C.	Royal Army Medical Corps
R.A.O.P.	Royal Army Observation Post
R.A.S.C.	Royal Army Service Corps
R.E.	Royal Engineers
R.F.C.	Royal Flying Corps
S.A.A.	Small arms ammunition
S.H.A.E.F.	Supreme Headquarters Allied Expeditionary Force
T.T.	Tyne Tees

U.S.A.A.A.	United States of America Air Force
W/T	Wireless/telegraph

FOREWORD

COLONEL H. SELL O.B.E., M.C., T.D., D.L.

This well-written and painstakingly researched history is the story of the Durham civilian soldier who, having made his commitment in peace, fulfilled his undertaking in two world wars, twice within the span of a lifetime and returned to rebuild the life of his community with equal determination.

This 9th Battalion along with the 6th and 8th Battalions The Durham Light Infantry, formed 151 Brigade 50th (Northumbrian) Division and were recruited from County Durham. They remained together through the greater part of the two world wars, forming a unique unit of the British army that became so professionally proficient as to be welcomed and praised by all the general officers under whose command they served.

They were assigned to all the major actions in whatever theatre they were sent and to which their battle honours bear a fitting testimony. The natural character of the officers and other ranks was one of determination and dogged perseverance displayed under all circumstances of the varying fortunes of war. On the first day of mobilisation, the 9th Battalion, to a man, reported to the drill hall.

No. 151 Brigade went to France in April of 1915 and fought in most of the major battles throughout the war. The 9th Battalion marched into Germany in late 1918 as part of the Army of Occupation.

With the British Expeditionary Force to France in 1939, they were among the first to confront the German offensive in 1940 and were fighting with the last units to leave from Dunkirk. From the beaches of southern England when the invasion threat passed, the path led to Egypt, Cyprus, Palestine, Iraq and the campaigns of the Western Desert and Tunisia, the invasion of Sicily and the landings on D-Day in Europe. The battalion was involved in heavy fighting in the Bocage of Normandy and in Belgium, which fittingly ended in Berlin with the complete destruction of the Reich.

The regimental motto is "Faithful" and it could not be a more apt description of its service in both world wars and in other countries of conflict during its long history.

This history, full as it is, cannot record all the memories of those momentous events and much must be left to the conjecture of the reader. Memories of the many, many comrades who did not return must not be forgotten. Nor do we forget those who were prisoners of war, some in labour camps for five years, who continued the struggle by assisting the numerous units of the Resistance, which finally led to the collapse of the internal structure of the Reich.

Well done the 9th and the Durhams, my service with you in peace and war is one of great pride and humility.

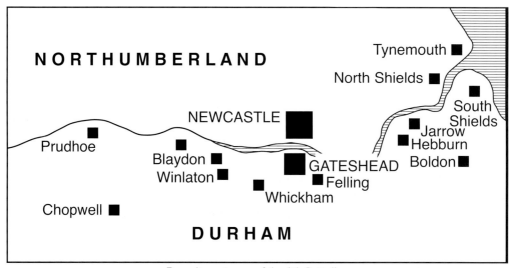

Recruitment area of the 9th Battalion

CHAPTER I

VOLUNTEERS & TERRITORIALS 1859 – 1914

On the 12th May 1859, a War Office letter to the Lords Lieutenants of Counties gave them authority to raise volunteer rifle companies. On the 24th October 1859, a public meeting was held in the Town Hall, Gateshead, chaired by Councillor Biggar of Deckham Hall. Twenty-nine names were put forward and a volunteer rifle company was formed. A committee was set up and rules were agreed so as to regulate the membership.

Companies were formed in neighbouring towns and in February 1861, the following corps were amongst the 18 active in County Durham:

Number	Place	Commanding Officer
6th	South Shields	Capt. J. Williamson
8th	Gateshead	Capt. G.H.L. Hawks
9th	Blaydon	Capt. J. Cowen
14th	Felling	Capt. W.W. Pattinson

Rifle green was adopted as the uniform and remained so until changed to scarlet with green facings in 1908. Many members of the 9th Battalion were short, stocky, strong miners and shipyard workers. Wearing the dark green uniform of the D.L.I. in the 1880s and 1890s, they appeared quite similar to the stocky men of Nepal who had served with the British army since 1816 – the Gurkha battalions. This earned the 9th D.L.I. its nickname of 'The Gateshead Gurkhas'. Throughout the book the Gateshead Gurkhas are referred to by their full regimental title of the 9th Battalion The Durham Light Infantry.

In the summer of 1860, the various rifle corps in County Durham were formed into administrative battalions and 6th, 8th and 9th Corps formed the 3rd Administrative Battalion Durham Rifle Volunteers. Headquarters was at Gateshead and the battalion was commanded by Lt. Col. G.H.L. Hawks and quickly given the nickname of 'Ha'aks Men'. By April 1862, the 9th Battalion consisted of six companies, totalling 399 rank and file. In 1880, the 3rd Durham Rifle Volunteers had a total strength of 864 of all ranks classified as 'efficients' having passed their drill and weapons tests. In this year the number of the battalion was changed to the 5th Durham Rifle Volunteers and later, on the 1st January 1888, to the 5th Volunteer Battalion The Durham Light Infantry. It retained this title until the reorganisation of the volunteers by the Territorial and Reserve Forces Act of 1907.

The first annual camp was held at Gibside in 1884 and in each successive year until 1889. Morpeth provided a site for an annual camp from 1890 to 1895 and succeeding camps were held at Monkseaton (1896), Redcar (1897), Rothbury (1898), Scarborough (1899 and 1902), Aldershot (1901), Castleton (1904), Ramsey, Isle of Man (1905), Conway (1906) and Ripon (1907). In 1899 the Boer War broke out and the 5th Volunteer Battalion sent 41 volunteers to serve in the campaign. Three men, Ptes. E. Dixon, S. Jones and R.H. Whitfield died on active service in South Africa.

In 1907, Lord Haldane, Secretary of State for War, brought in his Territorial and Reserve Forces Act, which became law on the 1st April 1908. Largely brought about by the lessons of the Boer War, the yeomanry and volunteer units throughout the country were combined into one organisation, which took the title of 'Territorial Force'. The 5th Volunteer Bn. The Durham Light Infantry was renamed the 9th Bn. The Durham Light Infantry. It was brigaded with the 6th, 7th and 8th Battalions of the regiment. The new brigade was the Durham Brigade of the Northumbrian Division, one of 14 Territorial divisions formed under the act. Later, during the First World War, these titles were changed to 151 Brigade, 50th Northumbrian Infantry Division and both were to earn undying fame in the two great wars of the 20th century.

Colour Party with Colours presented to the battalion by H.M. King Edward VII, 19 June 1090.

The routine of the new Territorial battalions in the years following 1908 changed little from that which had gone before. Khaki became the service dress. The volunteer badge was replaced by the silver bugle of the regular battalions in 1910. The Territorials were now expected to attend a fortnight's camp in midsummer with pay and allowances paid by the government. Weekend camps became popular from 1909. The 1908 annual camp was held at Ripon and, in subsequent years, it was held at Blackhall Rocks (1909), Rothbury (1910), Strensall (1911), Scarborough (1912 and 1913) and Conway in 1914. The camps came in for some criticism from the press. They were, in their opinion, a waste of money as work there could have been done at home.

On the 19th June 1909, Colours were presented to the battalion at Windsor by H.M. King Edward VII. The Colour Party comprised Lts. A. Hebron and W. de G. Martin, C. Quartermaster Sergeant Siddle, S/Sergeant Arkless, Colour Sergeants Ridley, Johnson, Dick and Kingston, Sergeants Hutchinson, Hands, Bainbridge, Wilson, Douglas and Maddison. Sergeant Maddison later became Regimental Sergeant Major of the battalion and was awarded the Territorial Efficiency Medal and two Bars. In 1911, on the occasion of the coronation of King George V, the battalion was represented along the route taken by the royal carriage by a street-lining party.

The years up to 1914 continued in the usual way. Drill nights, weekend camps and the annual camps kept the battalion on its toes. At the end of July 1914, 9th Bn. D.L.I. was in an annual brigade camp at Conway in North Wales. On the 3rd August, an advance party moved off to the battalion headquarters in Gateshead. This was followed by the battalion which, on arriving in Gateshead on the 4th August, was sent off to its various company headquarters and from there the men were sent home. This was in accordance with the provisions of the 1907 Territorial Act. Territorials were to be mobilised from their homes for the defence of the country in times of danger. The telegram ordering mobilisation was received at Burt Terrace headquarters at 7.15 p.m. on the same evening. The various companies assembled at their drill halls and, on the following day, moved to Gateshead. Out of 1,013 total strength, 996 officers and men had reported by midday. At 3.30 p.m. the battalion boarded a train for its war station at South Shields. The next three weeks were spent digging trenches as coastal defences. They then moved to the brigade camp in the grounds of Ravensworth Castle. Increasing numbers of officers and men joined in the next five weeks, sufficient in number to form a second line battalion, which moved to Salonika on the 5th November 1916. A third line battalion was also formed and this became a depot and training battalion for future drafts.

At Ravensworth the battalion began a toughening-up programme. Route marches and training exercises on the moors of north-west Durham were an addition to the usual weapon and marching drills. Trenches were dug and weapons were fired on the range at Scotts House. The battalion was accommodated in tents. The cold and wet late autumn weather turned the grounds of the castle into a morass of mud – an introduction on a very minor scale of the conditions the soldiers would meet later in France and Belgium. Early in October 1914, the battalion along with the rest of the Northumbrian Division, moved to the Newcastle area. Exercises in defence and attack continued together with route marches, bayonet drills and trench digging. Some men became guards for important communication centres such as main railway stations, goods yards and bridges over the Tyne. It was during this period that the battalion was asked to volunteer for active service overseas. The very great majority of officers and men agreed to do so. In December, the eight-company structure of the battalion was changed to mirror the four-company organisation of the regular battalions. On the 15th of the month, the battalion was brought to stand-to when elements of the German High Seas Fleet bombarded Hartlepool.

CHAPTER II

BAPTISM OF FIRE – YPRES SALIENT 1915

O rders were received in mid-April 1915 to prepare for the move to France. Equipment and men underwent interminable inspections as the day of embarkation approached. Maj. John English, Second in Command of the battalion, was to travel in advance of the main force with the transport and machine gun sections. He supervised the preparations for the movement of these sections, which were due to leave on the 17th April. It was no easy task as his diary records:

> There was an immense amount of work to be done, and only a few days to do it in. The Quartermaster's department and the transport were busy from daylight until long after dark. Mules and limbered wagons full of harness, boots and equipment of all descriptions came rolling in until the school yard was stacked high with packing cases, and all this had to be issued. The Battalion was then photographed in all its warpaint. We were drawn up in what was once a cricket ground, but which now resembled a ploughed field. It was a rainy day, our chargers did not approve of the performance and the whole thing was a fiasco.
>
> We had orders to entrain the transport on Saturday evening 17th April at the Cattle Dock. I went down to the transport lines on Saturday morning to see how things were progressing and found an apparently hopeless state of affairs and felt certain we would not be ready in time. However, Stafford, our transport officer, soon made order out of chaos and by 4 o'clock paraded the whole of the transport complete in every detail. I must say that he did this in marvellously short time, though he took it out of himself in the process as he had no grub all day.
>
> It was arranged for all the transport to parade around the field to see how it looked when in column, but this arrangement was evidently not sanctioned by the mules as they went on strike and refused to budge. Coaxing was tried and the whip was tried – all to no purpose, except that they gave us a fine display of their kicking powers. Presently two horses attached to a limbered wagon decided to run away. They tore out through the narrow gate on to the main street through crowds of people, but their driver luckily managed to regain control before any damage was done. Then the whole cavalcade was ready to march to the station. The Colonel and I went to see how his first charger looked with all her kit on. We roared with laughter as the poor little beast was simply weighed down with all the various things she had on, and gave us such a forlorn look as much as to say, 'Don't you feel sorry for me?' We had an awful game getting the transport on the move, as the mules began to jib again and when they once started it was almost impossible to stop them.

Things did not improve on arrival at the Cattle Dock at Newcastle Station:

> On arriving at the station we had another fearful time getting the wagons up a steep incline on to the platform, however after much hard work and more hard swearing it was

accomplished, and we were met there by a fussy young station transport officer, who in a la-de-da voice wanted this, that and the other done. By this time our patient and long-suffering transport officer was getting near the end of his resources, and was just on the point of consigning the station officer to the nether regions when I took the matter in hand, after which we ignored the station officer and carried on without his assistance.

Eight horses had to go in each truck and the wagons loaded in a certain way. Here I got my first lesson on how to put transport wagons on a truck with the least possible labour. The horses and mules were a big handful and after much struggling and the loss of skin both from men and horses we all entrained.

If there were sighs of relief on having got on the move, they were premature. In a letter to his wife dated 18th April, Major English described the continuing saga:

Major John English, Second in Command 9th BattalionApril 1915. His son Major I.R. English M.C. (two Bars) served with the 8th Bn. D.L.I. in World War II.

We had a most eventful journey. All went well until we arrived at York where we found two big draught horses down, and six others dancing a cake walk on top of them. We took them all out on to the platform and I found my experiences of hauling horses down the pit most useful. The two which had been down were rather worse for wear, but were not as bad as I had anticipated. We put them back again and the train was signalled away when we heard loud shouts from the platform and beheld two or three belated Tommies tearing along after the train, one without any boots. This often happens with Territorial troops, but I thought our discipline was better after the year's training. Nothing important happened until we got to Rotherham where we found a horse was down again, and sure enough it proved to be old Tom, one of the two we had so much trouble with at York. Here we had to shunt to a dock and this time I kept the old chap and put him in a truck by himself and since then we had no further trouble.

On arrival at Southampton Major English noted that, 'There were sentries everywhere to prevent the men from straying away.' Guns and wagons together with 33 troops and about the same number of horses went aboard the SS *Mount Temple*, a Canadian Pacific boat. She sailed from Southampton at about 6.30 p.m. on the 17th April. Searchlights pierced the evening sky as they passed the Isle of Wight. All lights aboard ship were extinguished by 8 p.m. Major English wrote:

I could distinguish two black masses on the port and starboard stern, which were two torpedo boats guarding us. I loved those little black blotches. The moon was new and twinkling on the water like so many fine snakes. I bowed to her majesty in a most solemn way and turned my money over; it was all very thrilling.

The transport and guns were on their way. What was happening to the rest of the battalion? Proceeded by the band the battalion marched through the streets of Newcastle to Central Station. Crowds lined the route, tears and cheers being equally in evidence. It was 19th April 1915 and the men of Tyneside were going off to war – a thrilling yet poignant moment.

The journey to Folkestone was uneventful. On arrival, the battalion went aboard the waiting ship and sailed for Boulogne. It reached France late at night and the battalion marched up the steep hill to Ostrovhe and St. Martin's Camp. The rest of the brigade joined them here. The tented camp was already quite crowded. The battalion spent an uncomfortable night. The next morning, it awoke to its first day on French soil. Battalion strength was 27 officers and more than 900 other ranks. Preparations to move and numerous inspections occupied the day. French ladies arrived in the camp eager to sell the Tommies their various wares, usually fruit. Much laughter and banter ensued as the men made their first contact with foreign people and struggled to understand the French language.

The brigade moved off from St. Martin's Camp during the 20th. The 8th Battalion left from Pont de Briques station south of Boulogne in the early afternoon. The 6th Battalion followed at 6 p.m. and the 9th left at 11 p.m. Each battalion boarded the train from Le Havre, which carried its transport and machine gun sections. These sections had reached Le Havre on the 19th April. Horses were taken from the boat and fed at nearby stables. The wagons were taken from the boat and manhandled to an allotted area of the quay. Nearby was an army supply depot from which necessary stores were obtained. Major English tried to get two additional machine guns, making a total of four for the battalion and the same as the number held by the regular battalions, but his request was refused. The sections moved to a rest camp at 6 p.m. The horses and mules gave sufficient trouble to lengthen what should have been a half-hour journey to two hours. Major English continued his story of the journey:

When I got there I told the officer in charge it was no good our going into tents as we had to move off in a short time. We outspanned by the roadside and tied the horses to the wagons, fed and watered and got a fire going. We had some tea, bread and butter and tongue. I did enjoy that meal in the dark by the firelight on the roadside, horses and men all around.

Orders to move were received shortly after midnight on the 20th April. Major English wrote:

It was 1 a.m. on the 20th when we left for the station. It was weird going along the dark streets with the rumbling of the wagons on the paved streets. A pair of mules jibbed at a red light on the canal bridge which we had to cross; after a lot of bother we unspoked them and manhandled the wagons over, then hung the mules on again…The right is the rule of the road and the men are not used to it yet. We arrived at 2.30 a.m. at the station, having taken 1½ hours to do half an hour's journey. I anticipated that, and was there in time. It was just as well as there was a ratty old fusspot Officer who had been dug out from somewhere and who was running the show as Entraining Officer. We were all dead tired but had to entrain at once, entraining the horses, wagons etc. We finished at 5.30 a.m., then went to a coffee stall which is run by the London ladies. They were charming and had been doing that for five months every night…I had a sardine sandwich and two cups of cocoa.

I gave all the men some grub at the stall as they had behaved so well…We started to the minute 6.27 a.m. as ordered. We had a first class carriage lighted by a funny old oil lamp locked to the luggage rack. Trucks with roofs on like our meat trucks and powder trucks were for the men. We had to put 43 in each truck, an awful crush. We drew six tons of rations and six men carried all that stuff and put it on the train. The men worked splendidly and were as happy as sandboys and as black as pitmen, officers also…[We] arrived at another station at 11 p.m. [Pont de Briques] where we picked up the battalion. They had had an eventful crossing as they were befogged, and lost the escort. They got into a minefield and had to drop anchor. The people ashore gave them up as lost.

Sgt. Robert Constantine. His letters home traced the increasing disillusionment with the progress of the war. He was killed in action on 15 September 1916.

The battalion joined the transport train and a long and very slow journey ensued as the train puffed its way by a roundabout route which took it close to Calais and on to a small station near Cassel. Here it detrained and marched to Terdeghem and into billets in farmhouses (officers) and barns (men). The Northumbrian Division was concentrating round the St. Omer–Cassel area. Of the Durham Brigade, in addition to the 9th Battalion, 6th Battalion was at Hardifort, 8th at St. Marie Cappelle and the 7th at

Riveld.

Cpl. Robert Constantine of Newcastle upon Tyne – later Sergeant and killed in action on the 15th September 1916 – wrote to his parents of the journey which led him to Terdeghem:

> I arrived safe and well on Tuesday morning at 6 o'clock after a rough journey from Folkestone. Instead of coming across in one and a quarter hours it took us nearly five hours, we were nearly done for, he had to make a different course on account of submarines, never mind we are here and will shortly be into the Germans. We arrived here and rested on Tuesday and moved on Tuesday night in cattle trucks into the country and we had a good long march before we arrived in our billet at a farm, where we remained for two days.

It was usual for a new division arriving in France to be gradually introduced to life in the trenches. This could take a number of weeks to complete. This sensible programme was not to be the experience of the Northumbrian Division. Within less than a week of its arrival in France it was thrown into action in a great crisis, unprepared and not having had a shot fired at it in anger.

On the 22nd April 1915, at about 5 p.m. and with a slight breeze blowing from the direction of the German lines, the enemy launched chlorine gas from both sides of Langmarke village. This strange cloud moved slowly down on two unsuspecting French divisions holding the line in front of the enemy positions. The 45th Algerian and 87th French Territorial Divisions were devastated. Panic-stricken officers and men staggered towards the back areas, gasping for breath. Many choked and died in the trenches and others collapsed by the sides of tracks and roads. A gap of several miles opened up to the advancing German troops who followed on behind the gas. The position was extremely serious. On the right, where the gas appeared to be less dense, the left flank of the Canadian division, together with those French troops alive and remaining in the line, held steady and by so doing, probably saved the salient position from total collapse. The enemy, fortunately, had no experience of his new weapon and what it was capable of doing. The German soldier did not relish following the gas too closely, though his face and mouth was covered with a gauze pad. Their slow advance gave a desperate defence an opportunity to attempt to fill the huge gap in the line. Units of the British and French armies were flung, piecemeal, into the battle. Officers and men fought to the death in counter-attack after counter-attack in an attempt to hold the enemy and form a solid defensive line.

On the 23rd April, the brigades of the Northumbrian Division were called forward. They were about to enter the Battle of St. Julian, which raged from the 24th April to 4th May. The Durham Brigade concentrated at Riveld before marching off to Steenvoorde. Here it rested in fields until a stream of London double-decker buses arrived to convey the 6th and 8th Battalions to Vlamertinghe. Brigade headquarters and the 9th and 7th Battalions marched off by the same route to the same destination. Few

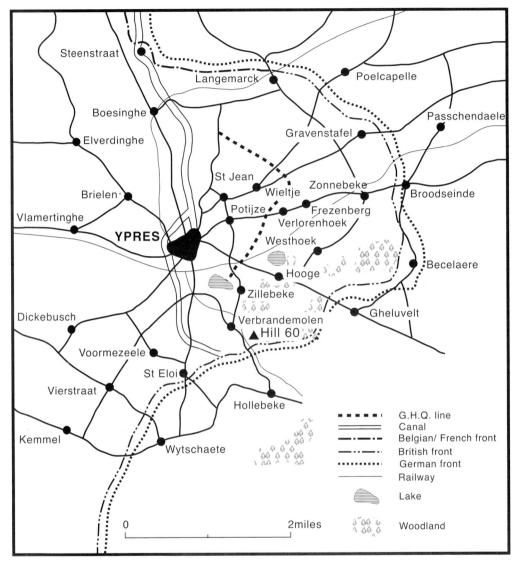

Ypres Salient – 22 April 1915

men ever forgot that march. All around them was noise and intense activity. The battalions had to march on one side of the road. The road itself was choked with crowded buses, lorries and wagons taking men and supplies towards the sound of the distant guns.

In the opposite direction, transport of one sort or another returned empty to pick up the next load. Amongst these were ambulances bringing the seriously wounded and dying to the main medical treatment centres. Bodies of cavalry moved forward up the road led by anxious officers shouting at anyone who lay in their path. Then, as they approached their destination, came the sprinkling of pitiful and terrified refugees carrying their few belongings, who gradually increased in number. So this was war! Whatever these inexperienced soldiers had thought war might be like whilst exercising on the moors of north Durham, the reality came as a shock. However, the enormous activity and urgency gripped them and they marched up the road to Vlamertinghe in the highest of spirits. They laughed and joked as they had done on their route marches in peaceful England. The fearful implications of the increasing roar of the guns ahead were suppressed and each man drew strength from his close comrades marching by his side.

The battalion reached Vlamertinghe and found itself occupying huts next to a Canadian unit. The Canadians were in a poor state, having lost most of their battalion in the fierce fighting of the previous day. Maj. John English wrote:

> They [the Canadians] saved the situation as they pushed back the Germans…They asked me to have some grub and made me some tea. They are a fine lot of men, very kind and hospitable, but very rough. I tried to go to sleep at 5.30 a.m. but never a wink as the noise of the guns was terrible. We expected to have to move at any time and everybody's nerves were on edge.

Cpl. Robert Constantine wrote in his letter to his parents:

> I am sitting in my hut writing this and listening to the guns going off all around, it is just off and on like thunder and it must be awful to be among them. It is cruel to see the refugees tramping along the road with only a small barrow and a few of their belongings on, such as bedding: one of our huts is full of refugees, from old men to very young bairns. The grub we have had up to now is cruel, noot but hard biscuits, I have a bit bread, but I had to buy it; it is different bread to what we have in England. I suppose I'll have to do without luxuries now as money has gone. We expect to be in the fighting line in a few days time and I'll write again shortly and let you know what it is like.

The scenes witnessed were viewed with sympathy and curiosity by these young men, who were new to the horrors of war. The lessons were not far away.

The strength of the 9th Battalion was 31 officers and 1,026 other ranks. The Durham Brigade was placed at the disposal of V Corps. Orders were issued to be prepared to move at short notice. However, the 23rd April passed without any movement orders being given. The following day the march continued towards Ypres, which was under shellfire. The marching troops saw their first civilian casualties as they passed the pitiful bodies by the roadside or those lying in the ruins of the buildings. Shells roared overhead and, occasionally, exploded close to the marching columns, drawing the men closer together, their bodies bent forward as if marching into a storm. Major English remembered the march:

> That night march I shall never forget as long as I live. We got along fairly well for the first four miles or so. All the time as we were marching on the right of the road, ammunition wagons, supply lorries and vehicles of every description were passing us on the

paved portion of the road, making an awful noise, and above all the booming of the guns without a second of interval. Here and there rapid musketry fire could be heard and farms were burning all around the countryside. Presently we came to the town of Ypres. The first building we came to was shattered and in ruins, then we had our first dose of shrapnel. None of the officers were mounted. I was marching along at the rear of the Battalion when suddenly the Company in front of me disappeared in the gutter and I was left standing, then I heard shrapnel bullets rattling on the pavement. I never heard the burst or probably I should have followed their example. I got them out and away again, when presently the same thing happened. They soon got tired of that however and found their 'sea legs'. We legged it through this town pretty quickly in spite of having our full kit on. You never saw such a mess as the town is in. The ruins of the cathedral and Cloth Hall near the market place we could just see. There were wagons, horses etc. lying all over the place, and houses literally blown away wholesale by the big 17-cm guns of the Germans. It was dark of course, this was the night of the 24th. I have lost count of the days of the week, let alone the days of the month. At last we were through the awful city of death. Just out of the town we had a long halt for some reason. The halt was rotten. Then we moved on and after going a mile or so, the Huns started shelling the road. We were very lucky and only lost one man wounded (he died later). Then we arrived at Potijze where we had another halt. When we moved on, one of the subalterns came back to me and said he had lost touch and could not find the rest of the battalion. I halted and sent him scouring round in the dark to try to find them. Eventually he found they had turned to the left into a wood.

It is very easy to lose touch on a road you do not know on a pitch dark night when there are thousands of other troops about, to say nothing of guns wagons etc. We were told to get into the wood and dig ourselves in. It was then 11 p.m. and it commenced to rain. I found a bit of a hole and enlarged it with an entrenching tool for the C.O. and myself. There we sat the night through sleeping fitfully, raining all the time. What a mess we were in the next morning. We had to remain close in the wood all that day and could only have bully beef and biscuits as no fires were allowed.

A battery of Canadian guns were in position very close to us, they were hammering away all night and all day, sometimes very rapidly. We dared not move about in the wood as aeroplanes were constantly overhead, apparently looking for the battery. During the afternoon the Germans started shelling the wood. A piece of stone or something of the kind hit me on the back of the calf of my left leg. It bruised the muscle so much I could with difficulty put my foot on the ground. It was frightfully painful.

Our transport were in a field behind the wood when the Huns got onto it with their guns, they did tremendous execution. We lost several men and about half our horses.

The shelling continued throughout the night of the 24/25th April. On the 25th, the battalion was ordered to advance from Potijze Chateau to occupy high ground ahead of it. Major English observed:

In the afternoon the Battalion had orders to move off to attack in a certain direction. They moved off at 5 p.m. up the road to Verlorenhoek and about half a mile beyond where a small stream crosses the road they went off half left. They got into artillery formation with two companies in the front line and two in support with their left on the small stream.

Presently an aeroplane came over and spotted them, then the game commenced...a perfect rain of shells of all sorts and sizes…One would think even a fly could not live as the air is simply full of shells…The men moved splendidly. Some artillery officers who watched the whole show, told the C.O. that it was done as if on parade. Presently they came to another stream which the C.O. was given to understand was as far as he had to go. However, he went a little further under the rise of the ridge where he judged the men would be less under shellfire, which proved correct. The C.O. was told before starting that one of our Brigades had got into difficulties and could not get back so we had to go right up on their right to draw the fire and enable them to get back. They drew the fire alright.

We had an officer, Andrew Little, and one or two men killed and a few wounded, so we were very lucky.

Pte. H. Bell, wrote to his sister and brother-in-law, Mr. and Mrs. J. Walker of New Brancepeth:

The Battalion…went into action under heavy shellfire. An advance of about one and a half miles was made but owing to the splendid formation, the casualties of the Battalion were very slight…We got to within a mile of the German trenches and drew their fire whilst our fellows executed a more important move in the front trenches. We captured two trenches at that time. Our Colonel [Henderson], was afterwards highly complemented by the Officers of the surrounding artillery on the way it was carried out.

I was amongst the first to examine Lieut. Little after he was shot. He was killed outright. We afterwards retired to a position about 2 miles further back and entrenched ourselves.

The battalion withdrew to the stream at the side of the road and dug in. In addition to Lieutenant Little, Pte. Walter Garbutt was also killed, Capt. Harry English, half brother of Maj. John English, was missing and seven men were wounded. On this day the 25th April, on another sector of the front, 8th Bn. D.L.I. was having its baptism of fire at Boetleer's Farm on the Gravenstafel Ridge. The 6th Battalion was preparing for its first action in front of Zonnebeke, which would take place on the following day. From the 26th to the 30th April, the 9th Battalion was entrenched in fields east and west of Verlorenhoek and subjected to shellfire. Enemy aeroplanes were constantly overhead and there appeared to be enemy guns all around. Heavy shrapnel fire descended on the positions from time to time but by now they were well dug in. As Maj. John English described, they were 'living like rabbits in damp holes, which smell horribly. We cannot light fires and so we have to live on bully beef and bread and jam, but no one is taking any harm and we are settling down to it wonderfully.'

C.S.M. Frederick Bousfield was awarded the Distinguished Conduct Medal during this action. His citation read:

For conspicuous gallantry. During an advance his company, coming under heavy shell and rifle fire, hesitated, but he took command and by his bravery and personal example, led them forward to the line they had been directed to take up.

C.S.M. Frederick Bousfield was given a commission later in the war. He won the

Military Cross in 1917 and the Croix de Guerre whilst serving as a major with another battalion.

The battalion was attached to 85 Brigade 28th Division, which was operating on the right flank of the Canadians. Throughout the 26th April it was heavily shelled, followed by more shelling on subsequent days. A number of men were killed during this period. Pte. Thomas Richards was killed on the 26th and Pte. Joseph Beresford on the 27th. Pte. John Brown was killed the following day. A further eight men were wounded and five were missing. Working parties were formed – a tiring and extremely stressful experience, made worse by the fact that it was easy to get lost on the battlefield. Major English wrote:

> I had orders to take 300 men to meet Engineer officers at the Moat Farm, and the C.O. had to take 300 men to meet R.E. officers near Wiltje at dusk…The Moat Farm was not marked on the map…I started off to find a farm with a moat round it in country I did not know on a pitch dark night. I sent officers to all the farms about with no result, so eventually I found my way back to Brigade Headquarters in Verlorenhoek together with Eric Dryden and an orderly. I met Captain Clayton, the Brigade Major and he told me the orders had been altered and that I would find the Engineer officers about half a mile further along the road towards Potijze…We should have met the R.E. Officer at 7.30 p.m. but it was 9.30 p.m. before we found him. We commenced at once to dig a trench on the north of the road and dug until 12.30 when we were relieved. The Huns sent a few shells near us, but our men dug like Trojans. They did put some work off their hands and I think astonished the Engineer officers.
>
> The C.O. had a similar experience. He wandered off on his own without an escort up the St. Julian road without seeing any signs of R.E. Officers or stores. He went so far that he was eventually sniped at and came back when he met a cyclist who told him that the orders had been changed. He eventually came to dig on the opposite side of the road from where I was.
>
> We were attached to the 28th Division and were under the orders of Gen. Chapman [Brigadier General Chapman – 85 Brigade]. The staff work was rotten.
>
> This same night, 'A' Company under Capt. Hebron had to go up to the trenches near Zonnebeke and had a rather rotten time. They had one killed and three wounded…Today, the 30th, we have done nothing but keep under cover…The shellfire comes from three sides. I found it very cold at nights and have not washed for two days now and have a nice beard. I have not had my boots off for a week. We cannot get water to drink, let alone to wash in.

Rest brought little in the way of relaxation. The above account was not exceptional. Tired troops wandered around the battlefield in the dark trying to find their destinations and carrying weapons, wire and an assortment of digging tools. Stooping under heavy loads, stumbling in the muddy going and negotiating shell holes taxed them to the utmost. On arrival, they had to dig quickly and efficiently, always expecting an enemy shell to arrive or a flare to drop and reveal them to the enemy who was often just in front of them. Then followed the inevitable burst of machine gun fire. At least the Durhams could dig and earned an enviable reputation amongst other units. Such tasks, however, took their toll and casualties began to build up.

Pte. H. Bell, wrote to his sister:

We were there until Sunday, May 1st when it was hell on earth again. During the week they gave us 3 or 4 periods of shelling every day and we lost a few men and some wounded. But on the Sunday it was hot, from the first thing in the morning until dusk. We made a little building into a dressing station about 30 yards from our trenches. It was our stronghold during the shelling although they put 7 shells through it. The Germans fired 151 shells in half an hour during one spell. Just as we were preparing to leave during a lull, a shell whizzed over our heads. Another piece of shrapnel went through one of our men's topcoat, tunic and two shirts and never broke the skin. It gave the fellow a rare fright. Another piece caught the lad next to me in the stomach but we could not find any wound. He was very bad however and is now in hospital. Well we got away at last and after travelling 4 miles, we were passing a place called Hell's Corner when shrapnel burst right in amongst the fellows of my company, killing 6 or 7 outright. We pulled them to one side of the road and then followed the battalion. They were buried next day.

Corporal Constantine had a lucky escape in this incident, which he described to his brother in a letter dated 3rd May:

[the shell] burst just about 20 yards in front of me and I got plenty of muck in my face but I am alright, if it had not been for some artillery passing at the time and making us stop a few minutes, I think I would have got the full force of the shell so I consider myself lucky…I heard rumours this morning that we are making a shift into the country away from the firing line for garrison duty and I do hope it is right because we have had a awful time of it since we arrived here. We have orders to rest all today as we have a 17 miles march in front of us tonight.

Shellfire was coming from three sides. Farms were on fire or already burnt out, the ruins of their walls looming against the background of flames that lit the evening sky. The nights were cold. There was little opportunity to take off boots and clothes, nor even to wash or shave as water was scarce. Destruction lay everywhere and the salient was beginning to take on the moon-like landscape it was to retain for the next three and a half years.

During any period of action, essential supplies of food, ammunition and so on, were brought forward by the transport, often under heavy artillery fire. Major English wrote:

I have the greatest admiration for them, especially men taking forward ammunition to the guns. They just gallop on and take no notice of anything. Every now and then one can see a man struggling along the road with slight wounds and then a motor cyclist rushes past with a despatch heedless of all danger…Everywhere flare lights which the Germans send up to light up the country to enable them to see, every minute or so the boom of the big guns and, occasionally, sharp bursts of musketry fire…The bombardment is gradually dying down and they have ceased shelling us. In some cases where they want to blow up a building they plump 4 or 6 Jack Johnsons right into it, a huge cloud of dust springs about 100 feet into the air and the building is no more. It is a fine sight to watch…I can hear a thrush whistling now and again when the roar dies down.

At 2 a.m. on the 3rd May, the battalion arrived at Brielen Huts. During the move, the casualties, referred to above in Private Bell's letter, occurred as they moved through Ypres. Seven men were killed by shellfire and seven were wounded. The killed were Ptes. John Lightfoot, Ralph Masterman, James Williams, Randolph Vickers, James Walker, James Longstaff and Thomas Todhunter. Ptes. George Batey and Stanley Hicks died of their wounds. The march to Brielen was described by Major English:

> That night march I will never forget, nor will any of us. We marched along the main road past Potijze and before coming to Ypres we turned to the right so as to pass through the northern border town. The road was littered with wagons and dead horses and full of shell holes. The Germans were shelling the road but, fortunately, we had no casualties until we were passing through Ypres when a shell plumped into the middle of our column killing 8 men [actually the seven named above] and wounding about 14 others. Presently we came to what appeared to be a field road and it was difficult to keep the battalion together on account of the obstacles which we had to cross, as it was very dark.
>
> We arrived in this place about 2 a.m. and found wooden huts for the men to sleep in.

A further move was made to St. Jan-ter-Biezen, between Ypres and Watou. The strain of the days spent in the Salient had taken their toll and a very tired battalion, little more than half-awake, reached its new billets in the farms around St. Jan-ter-Biezen in the early hours of the 4th May. Major English wrote:

> Now we are safe from shellfire, well back in the rear at a place called St. Jansten Biezen. Last night we started from our rest camp at 8.30 and went across country on very bad roads until we joined the main road from Vlamertinghe to Poperinghe and followed that road until we arrived here at 2 a.m…We are billeted in farms all around among the quaintest of farm people. One never sees a young man, only old men, women and children.

The battalion settled down to a few days of rest and refitting. The Commander-in-Chief, Sir John French, arrived on the 4th to talk to the battalion and other units of the brigade. Major English described the event:

> The 6th and 9th were drawn up ready in a field by the side of the road. There were about 20 red hats present and the little sunburnt man with a white moustache walked quietly through the gate into the middle of the 3-sided square, took the salute and commenced his speech.
>
> He said as Commander in Chief he wished to thank every officer, N.C.O. and man personally for the manner in which they had behaved in such an emergency. He said that

troops that first came out were always given some time to settle down and find their feet before being sent forward, but on this occasion, owing to the dastardly act of our enemies who call themselves soldiers, in spraying our troops with poisonous gases, they succeeded in denting our line. It had been necessary to send up the Northumbrian Division to help to drive them back, and that we had done very well indeed and he congratulated us and said we had every reason to congratulate ourselves…The 6th he said had lost 3 officers killed and 11 wounded and men (the exact number he mentioned I forget). This, he said was a very serious loss but they had done their duty. The 9th he said, had not lost so heavily, but he had heard excellent accounts of the steadiness of the men under shellfire as he had experienced it. He went on to say he had admired our spirit in coming out to fight for our country, as there was no reason for us to do so except the love of our country. As Territorials we were for Home defence but we had volunteered our services for foreign service and for no other reason than patriotism and he admired us very much, especially as men had given up good appointments for the purpose. He said we would be down resting for some time and he hoped that when next it was necessary to send us up we would behave in the same gallant manner. In fact he said everything nice he could possibly say. We lay for 8 solid days and nights under violent shellfire and believe me, of all the most nerve-racking things, this is the limit, as one can do nothing to retaliate…every officer and man feels he has had enough for the present. One chap who was a great grouser in Gateshead was heard to say, after lying out in the open under shellfire for about an hour, that he had no fault to find with Shipcote Schools now! [one of last winter's billets in Gateshead]

The stay at St. Jan-ter-Biezen was, in the circumstances, almost idyllic. The weather was fine and warm. The troops lay in the fields amongst the farms in peaceful surroundings with only the distant rumble of the guns to disturb the tranquillity. Spring flowers bloomed and cows grazed contentedly nearby. From time to time, a Frenchman and his wife appeared in the fields selling oranges and officers and men indulged in the rapidly learnt pastime of bargaining to get the prices down. Bivouacs were erected and washing appeared to be hanging everywhere. Spirits rose appreciably with the arrival of the first mail. Church parade was held on Sunday and, after the experiences of battle and the loss of so many friends, it was well attended. Major English wrote:

We went to the village to Holy Communion at 8.30 a.m. which our own Chaplain, that is the Brigade Chaplain, administered. It was held in a little place about ten feet wide and twenty feet long. On one side was a joiner's bench covered with bread, bacon and all kinds of food. Thick straw covered the floor under the bench for men to sleep in. Hanging all around the walls were rifles and equipment of all sorts. At the end behind the Chaplain was the telephone orderly with his instrument beside him connected up to Brigade Headquarters. The altar was a bacon box standing on two pieces of wood acting as legs. It was covered with a clean serviette and a blanket was folded and laid down for the priest to kneel on. The Chancel rail where we knelt to receive the sacrament consisted of three bacon boxes laid lengthwise along the floor and covered with clean serviettes. The floor was common brick, worn into holes in many places, and there you saw officers, NCOs and men kneeling in all sorts of attitudes during the service. The place was full and many waited outside. When a man received Communion he had to pass to the back to allow another to come forward. It was a most impressive service.

In this simple place, men came close to their God and not even the greatest cathedral in Christendom could have created a more moving and impressive service than that crowded hut on that Sunday morning.

On the 9th May, a move was made to woods just north of Brandhoek, midway between Poperinghe and Vlamertinghe. The weather was fine and warm, there were still leaves on the trees and, although the rumbling of gunfire was constantly in the background, no shells disturbed the pleasant and quiet woodland camp. No. 151 Brigade had been placed on one hour's notice to move. Meanwhile, bivouac shelters were set up under the trees and, although fires were not allowed after 6.30 p.m., the battalion settled down despite the regular intrusion of a 9.2-in. howitzer in position some 400 yards away, busily firing into the enemy lines. Working parties were found to dig communication trenches for the cavalry in the front line. This work was done, of course, after dark and often carried on until the early hours of the morning.

On the 11th May, 151 Brigade was ordered to move into the G.H.Q. line as part of a divisional move to relieve the 1st Cavalry Division. The move commenced at 7.50 p.m. The 7th, 6th and 9th Battalions, from the right, took position astride the Potijze–Menin road, from Zillebeke Lake across the road at the level crossing to a point 500 yards east of Potijze Village. The trenches in this area were in a bad state and proved to be very difficult to find in the dark. Major English described:

We marched out on to the Vlamertinghe–Ypres road and just before entering Ypres we turned to the right and skirted round to the south of Ypres until we got on to the railway. That is the line that runs from Ypres to Zonnebeke. Ypres itself was burning fiercely and the red glare lighted up the whole place. The railway was a bad place to march on, the men had to march in file instead of fours. In places the railway runs along an embankment, at other places through a cutting just like all railways. Every here and there telephone wires were lying across the line over which the men often tripped up and it was full of shell holes, rails torn up and lying across the way. All this interfered with the column getting along. The head of the column could more or less see what was coming, but all these interruptions strung out the column to a great extent until big gaps existed and they lost touch. At the rear of the column it was awful; we would move along about 3 yards then halt, and then move a few more yards and halt again and so on. Then we would come to a shell hole or some other obstruction which was the cause of all the delay. Just at one of these places a battery of our guns opened fire on our left and was replied to by a German one. So we had a bad time for a bit. My job at the rear of the Battalion was always a rotten one on these night marches, as I keep running up and down the column to try to keep things together a bit. The platoon commanders and Captains do not look after their men sufficiently. It was all very weird, the gaunt and broken telegraph poles standing up silhouetted against the red glare on our left front. The men were carrying a big load and were tired and nervous. It was an awful nightmare.

In the end there was a long halt…The guide had known nothing about the lines and, as it turned out, had only seen them from the railway. The result was we had come too far and had to scramble down one at a time off the embankment, over the gutter and through the hedge. The bank was steep and the only bridge over the gutter was a narrow plank. To bring a battalion through that on a dark night was awful. Many of the men came scrambling down the bank, flopping into the ditch, carrying a heavy pack, equipment and a rifle, until they found the gap in the hedge. There were several phone lines lying along the embankment which tripped the men up. They were getting on so slowly that I went on to the bank and stood there directing every man down and we got on a little quicker. Then when we got down into the field, they went right into a howitzer battery and got mixed up with the limbers, lorries, harness etc., and lost the men in front of them…We eventually got them together again and found the trenches. By that time it was nearly daybreak and we had to stand to arms. Each night we had to go out and dig, so eventually we came to be known as the battalion which was shelled all day and dug all night…We got quite a reputation for digging.

The G.H.Q. line ran from the north-east corner of Potijze Wood to near the stream on the Potijze–Verlorenhoek road. It then crossed and followed the Potijze–Zillebeke road as far as the station on the Ypres–Roulers railway, near to Hellfire Corner. The trenches varied in quality. Mostly built by the French, in the centre of the line it was a labyrinth of communication trenches and dugouts which made it difficult to manage the men. The trenches were subject to flooding and quickly became waterlogged. Conditions were appalling. Heavy rain and shellfire had caused great damage to the trenches. The battalion was now involved in the Battle of Frezenberg Ridge, which raged from the 8th to the 13th of May. Casualties on the 12th of May were four killed and 19 wounded, with a further four killed and 36 wounded on the following day. Amongst the dead were Ptes. Thomas Canaffan and John Hutchinson, and Cpl. George Lucas. Cpl. Robert Constantine of Newcastle wrote to his mother on the 12th May:

> I'm properly upset today as I have some awful sights among our boys this morning. I am putting my whole trust in God and I hope and trust I'll get through alright…I am sitting cramped up in a dugout writing this. It's not safe for anyone to put his head out. I have not had a wash since Sunday so you can just have a good idea what I'd be like, I'm as black as crow. I'm doing my best to cheer my wounded pals just now.

The realities of war were becoming obvious to these young men as they wrestled to come to terms with the desperate and upsetting sights that were a daily occurrence in the front line.

Corporal Constantine went on to write to his brother Jim on the 13th May:

> After having nine days' nice rest, we are back again in the trenches and it's hell all day long, shells of all sorts, bursting all about, but the German shells are not very good because I've seen a lot of them not burst at all and others are full of marbles and some of our chaps were saying that they had seen some burst that were full of nails, a nice thing to put in shells, eh! I put an awful day in yesterday, it was the longest day I've ever had and I felt properly upset…We passed a large city [Ypres] on Tuesday night on our way to the trenches and the whole place from end to end was on fire, what a sight, it's just done for

wilful destruction and nothing else…You shouldn't grumble about going to bed without a light, you should be lucky you have such a nice bed. I know I would just now.

On the 16th May, the 9th Battalion, along with the 7th Battalion, was transferred to the 4th Cavalry Brigade. The 6th and 8th Battalions had been sent back to rest in huts north-west of Ypres. Digging parties were sent forward. Major English was in command of one of these:

I took 500 men out digging…There were no end of stray bullets about, but we were fortunate as usual, as we only had one man wounded. I was looking round the work after we had got the men placed and came across Royal Scots in a brick kiln. I had a cigarette with them and a nice talk. Their trenches are only 30 yards from the Germans (Saxons) and I believe they chaff each other very much and are quite good friends, but do a great deal scrapping all the same. I was very glad when I got all the men out safely…I hope they will not keep us here much longer as the men are getting very tired as they get no proper rest and not enough food. (We have to censor their letters.) Some of their letters are pathetic and fill one's heart. I very seldom read them but cannot help seeing some of their remarks. There are some cheery ones, in fact most of them are, but some are very nervy now and several of the officers also.

Each day saw someone killed or wounded by enemy artillery fire. One man was wounded by British anti-aircraft fire, when he was hit by falling shrapnel. On the 18th May, the battalion was relieved and marched to huts west of Ypres. Pte. Archibald Stewart was killed on this march and a further five men wounded. The march was along the Ypres–Menin road, by now a notoriously dangerous area. Where there had been lovely trees along each side of the road with beautiful houses, there were now torn-up roots and trees broken and twisted in fantastic ways. The houses were wrecked and yet, in all this, nightingales could be heard singing. Major English wrote:

From time to time an ammunition train gallops along the road making an awful din. We meet a fleet of Red Cross vans. Then a great gun will suddenly boom out just on the other side of the fence and nearly scare us out of our skins. Presently the Germans reply and one sees the flash and burst in the air, then a deafening roar of the explosion of a shrapnel shell and one can hear the bullets clipping through the branches of the trees, splashing on the paved road making the sparks fly. Then the word is passed down the column for the stretcher bearers and the doctor…The nerves of the Battalion have suffered lying under all the shellfire.

The camp was a sea of mud, which added to the misery of the wet and weary men. Occasionally German shells arrived in the immediate area. Miserable though the conditions were, to be away from the front line was a great relief, as Corporal Constantine showed in a letter to his brother Jim, dated 19th May:

I've been a bit downhearted these last two days but I feel champion now and full of good spirits (not whisky you know). Well Jim we have been in those terrible trenches. We went in on the 11th and remained until the 17th and it rained the whole of the time and it's still raining. It was with being dirty and soaked through when in the trenches that made us all downhearted but now we are in huts awaiting orders to move…When we were resting the last time we all got a sub of 10 Francs and it came in very handy, it allowed us to get some good grub. The only fault out here in the villages the things are very dear.

The time was spent cleaning up and providing working parties. Water was scarce as farms refused to give it up and charged exorbitantly for everything they could sell: one franc for a loaf of bread and the equivalent of three and a half pennies for two eggs.

On the 21st May, the battalion moved into the G.H.Q. line once more and into trenches near Potijze. The brigade was attached to the 28th Division. The 9th Battalion was with 85 Brigade, now commanded by Brig. Gen. C. E. Pereira. Working parties were provided night and day, improving trenches. On the 23rd, a move was made into trenches just west of Bellwaarde, which were found to be in a very poor state and unable to hold the whole of the battalion. One company was taken into Potijze Wood and dugouts found for them. The march had been made in torrential rain and there was little shelter for the men in the trenches. It was the eve of the Battle of Bellewaarde, which was fought over the next two days.

No. 85 Brigade held the front between Bellewaarde Lake and the Ypres–Zonnebeke road. The line was held by 'A' and 'B' Companies, 7th Bn. D.L.I. and the 3rd Bn. Royal Fusiliers. Both of these battalions were south of the Ypres–Roulers railway. Two companies of the Middlesex Regiment together with 'C' and 'D' Companies, 9th Bn. D.L.I. and the 2nd Bn. East Surrey Regiment held the line north of the railway, between the railway and the Zonnebeke road.

The 24th May was Whit Monday. It was a fine and very hot day. Most officers and men were sleeping whilst sentries peered out across no man's land from the trench fire steps. At 2.45 a.m. an immense enemy barrage fell on the whole of V Corps front line, from just south of Hooge to close to Turco Farm, a total of four and a half miles in length. In addition to the hail of shellfire, the Germans opened up with rifles and machine guns. For four and a half hours the British trenches were saturated under a deluge of shells culminating with the release of a dense cloud of gas on a scale never experienced before. The enemy trenches were close to the British line and, although the line was alert, there was little time to get respirators on. Exploding shells covered the front line trenches in black smoke and dust. Trenches, already in a very bad state from the incessant rain of the previous days, collapsed. Communications were destroyed and information to the various headquarters had to be carried out by runners who braved the shells and bullets – almost a suicide mission. The bombardment and gas fell with particular violence on the front held by 85 Brigade. During the day, the 9th Battalion experienced 13 hours of shelling. The two companies along with the East Surreys and reinforced by the 8th Bn. D.L.I. at 7.30 a.m., stuck to their positions throughout the ordeal. With great tenacity and courage they denied the enemy entry

21

into their battered positions. Casualties were four officers and 51 other ranks, including Colonel Henderson who was wounded in the back by a piece of shrapnel. The ordeal of this gas attack is described by Maj. E. Hardinge Veitch M.C. in his book on the history of the 8th Bn. D.L.I.:

> …a large proportion of the shells containing poisonous gases, cyanide of potassium, was afterwards traced both by the smell and by deposits in the shell craters, but it was uncertain whether this was in the general gas cloud, or only in the shells, or in both. The appearance of the gas was that of a thick mist which varied in intensity. Whilst it lasted one could seldom see more than a hundred yards through it. It caused a choking sensation and intense irritation of the eyes, which streamed with water…the effect was more moral than otherwise, the respirators – of cotton waste soaked in phosphate, even a sock damped in urine – seeming quite effective…

The German attack petered out and over the next few days the battalion held on to its part of the line, though suffering casualties from heavy shelling.

Major English wrote of this attack:

> The next morning – 24th May – I was out at 2.50 a.m. when a most violent rapid fire commenced and bullets were flying over my head. I lay flat on my face and crawled back to my dugout. I felt my eyes smarting very much and immediately thought of gas. I groped about for the C.O. and found he was not there. I immediately got my respirator and put it on but I had had a good doze of gas before I could do this. I went out to the trench and there found the C.O. and we got the men to man the trench. The gas was coming in clouds. At about 3 a.m. the shelling started and it was absolutely terrific. The C.O. was hit a glancing blow in the back but hung on and would not be attended to. We had to get down to take cover from the shells bursting overhead and, on the other hand, we could not be in the bottom of the trench where the gas lay thickest. At the same time we had to keep a lookout over the trench in case the front line broke. So we had a merry time. Orders are difficult to issue when one's mouth and nose are covered.
>
> After a few hours the rifle fire got weaker, but the shell fire continued for 13 solid hours. I felt I was losing the use of my arms but it went off after a while when we got some fresh air, though I still had a chest irritation. We had four officers and 51 men gassed and had to go to hospital.
>
> The front line held except in one place on our right and another on our left. I was watching through my field glasses and I saw a party streaming down a field apparently dragging something and carrying a Red Cross flag. I thought it might have been a Red Cross party of ours but it was the Germans dragging two machine guns after them and protecting themselves by a Red Cross flag.
>
> We had sent 'C' and 'D' Companies into the front line trench along with the 2nd East Surreys to learn trench warfare. Though we were anxious about them, we heard they had given a very good account of themselves. They had very few gassed and when the Germans attacked they forgot their ailments with the gas. They produced a withering fire into the Germans who were driven back, only to come on again and be driven back a second time. The German never got nearer than 150–200 yards.
>
> It never pays to retire under any circumstances because as soon as you do, they catch

you in the open and you are bound to have heavy casualties. If you hang on, you can always retaliate with rifle fire and you have the protection of the trench. Moreover, when support arrives in the shape of a counter-attack the men left in the trench render them very material support. It is the old Zulu myth – 'If we go back we die, if we go forward we die; therefore, let us go forward.' If you can stand firm, you may die or be taken prisoner. Of course, it is all very well talking on paper but it takes a bit of doing in practice. Nevertheless it is only common sense. Moreover, there is a General Order that no one must retire without a written order. We were like Wellington at the Battle of Waterloo.

Over the next few days, the battalion continued its work in the G.H.Q. line, constantly improving trenches and dugouts and always under heavy shelling. This work was done at night as it was impossible to move during daylight. Officers and men had simple needs, a hot meal, cigarettes, dry clothing and, most of all, the mail from loved ones back home, which came up to the trenches with the rations each night. In the front line the two companies of the battalion spent the daylight hours sniping at the enemy and being sniped in return. As a result of this sniping and shelling there were a number of casualties each day, although many were also inflicted on the enemy facing them.

Among the dead was Pte. George Turnbull, born New Walls End, New South Wales. He was described as 'a tall, clean, open-faced lad and used to be a servant in the officers' mess at Ravensworth.' He had gone out into no man's land as a member of a sniping party. The party occupied a house and, as he cautiously stood up for a second at a window, he was hit by an enemy sniper.

On the 29th May, relieved by the 1st Bn. Northumberland Fusiliers, the battalion marched back to the wood near Brandhoek they had occupied prior to moving into the line. The march took them through a ruined Ypres, across the market square and past the Cloth Hall, now seriously damaged. The battalion turned right at the end of the Cloth Hall and marched passed the damaged cathedral. Houses were in ruins with bricks scattered across the road and fires smouldering. Finally, passing the water tower, the battalion reached the countryside, thankfully not having had a single shell fired at it. The march went on to Vlamertinghe and halfway to Poperinghe, then into the wood at Brandhoek.

The battalion machine gun section had an interesting time. Along with the machine gun section of the composite 6th/8th Battalion, it was ordered to move forward on the 4th June. They were told a guide would be waiting for them at the junction of the Menin road and Ypres–Zillebeke road to take them on to a position in Sanctuary Wood. On arrival at the junction of the roads no guide appeared. Evidently he was waiting in a totally different place and so failed to make contact, a situation which occurred quite often. Guides had an extremely difficult task. They stumbled about the battlefield on dark nights, unable to show a light, moving over shell-torn ground with all landmarks obliterated, searching for a unit to be led to the line. Even when found, leading the unit forward still had its difficulties as the guide strove to retrace his steps. A great deal of anger and frustration were heaped on the unfortunate guide as tired men, who had already come some distance carrying heavy loads, stumbled over the scarred landscape, often losing their way yet again. They had to reach the relative safety of their trenches before daybreak or be caught out in the open under the gaze of an alert enemy. It was often a close-run thing.

Without their guide the officers searched around for assistance. A nearby unit headquarters in a dugout pointed them in the direction they had to go. The route took them down the Menin road, through Zillebeke, across country and into Sanctuary Wood. Day was breaking and they just got into position as the morning 'hate' bombardment fell. Here, they relieved a gun team of the Royal Scots Fusiliers in a reserve position and were instructed to hold it 'at all costs.' Their problems were not over. The only dugouts available were already occupied by the 4th Bn. East Yorkshire Regiment, 150 Brigade. When this battalion moved to the front line, the machine gun sections dove into a vacated dugout before the 5th Bn. Yorkshire Regiment, could move in – possession was truly nine-tenths of the law.

The machine gun sections held the position for 19 days without relief. On the 23rd June, they were relieved by the machine gun sections of the Sherwood Foresters. The sections marched out to Dranoutre and then moved on to Locre and reported to 151 Brigade headquarters. One of the section gunners wrote:

> The amazing look on the Brigade Major's face was amusing. He seemingly had no idea where we had sprung from. Our appearance must have been awful, unwashed and unshaven for five or six days and with the marks of our day's march upon us.

Without any rest, the machine gun section joined the battalion in the trenches in front of Kemmel Hill.

On the 5th of June, 151 Brigade came under the command of the 50th Division, for the first time since it had marched into action in April. On the night of the 6th/7th June, the division relieved the 3rd Division in the sector lying on both sides of the Observatory Hill–Zillebeke road. To the west lay Zillebeke village and lake and the Lille Gate. Ypres was some three-quarters of a mile away to the north-west. The battalion occupied a sector in the Maple Copse area. The trenches were in a poor state and much work had to be immediately undertaken to improve them. 'B' Company went into the front line at Maple Copse for the period 6th to the 12th June and was relieved by 'A' Company for a further seven days to the 19th June. The entire area was subjected to heavy small arms and shellfire throughout the period. There could be no movement during the day and food and essential supplies were brought up at night. No fires were allowed. On the 9th, with the exception of 'B' Company, the battalion moved into dugouts at Kruistraat. These were found to be in good condition and quite comfortable. The 6th and 8th Battalions, due to heavy losses, had been combined into a composite battalion and, as a result, the 5th Bn. Loyal North Lancashire Regiment joined the brigade. On the 20th, 50th Division, now including the combined 6th/8th, was transferred to II Corps and relieved the 48th Division opposite Messines and Wytschaete.

CHAPTER III

MESSINES, WYTSCHAETE & ARMENTIÈRES 1915

On the 21st June, the 9th Battalion marched to a farm near Dranoutre, named Inkerman Farm. Here, along with the 6th/8th Composite Battalion, it was addressed by the new Corps Commander, Lt. Gen. Sir Charles Ferguson. The General welcomed them to the corps and informed them they were in a quiet area. The trenches were good and he expected them to keep them that way. The Durhams' reputation for digging and maintaining excellent trenches had obviously not yet reached the General. The enemy trenches were between 40 and 200 yards from the British front line. They followed the higher and drier ground and included a commanding strong point named Spanbroekmollen, which meant that the Germans had good observation over the British trenches and movement during the daylight hours was extremely risky. Enemy snipers were very active and casualties amongst the battalion built up over the ensuing days. The line occupied by 151 Brigade was opposite Messines Ridge and in front of Kemmel Hill. The latter was a high, steep and thickly wooded eminence, which dominated the area and gave the British a fine panoramic view of the enemy lines not only in the immediate area but also over the whole of the Ypres Salient.

Behind the trench lines the countryside was little scarred by the ravages of war. The fields were clothed in flowers, not least among them the poppy, which came to signify the sacrifice of the men locked in deadly battle only a few short miles away. Farmers worked in their fields and civilians still occupied the village of Kemmel, giving the area a semblance of normality and providing comfortable billets for officers and men. Drinks could be purchased at the Hotel de Petite Ypres, which remained open in the village. Even the trenches were an improvement on what had gone before. Corporal Constantine wrote home to his parents:

> We have moved to another part of the line now but the trenches we are now in are cushy compared with the ones we have been in. You perhaps will not believe me when I tell you we are only about 30 yards from the Germans but they don't trouble us much. We have flowers and potatoes and mint growing all round our trenches and it helps to make things more pleasant…It is now about 1.30 and I am going to make a bit dinner, roast beef, potatoes and vegetables. I mean bully beef and a few trench potatoes, it'll go down alright…

The term 'quiet area' was something of a misnomer. Every morning and evening at stand-to, the artillery of both sides opened up for a short period of intense bombardment. This was known as the morning or evening 'hate'. The ubiquitous sniper was a constant danger to men moving around in the trenches. The front line trenches were reached by a long communication trench, which stretched from the Lindenhoek crossroads. This was named on the British maps as Regent Street, with Vigo Street and

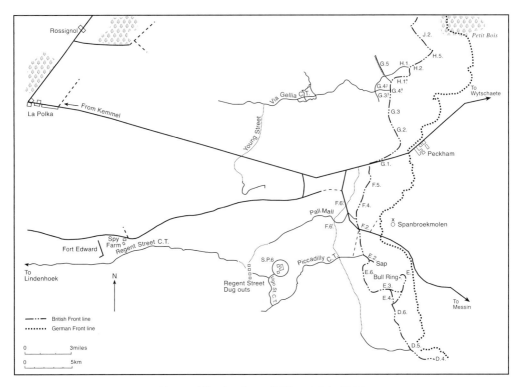

Kemmel Sector June 1915 and July 1916

Piccadilly on the right and Pall Mall on the left. On the right flank a strong point, the 'Bull Ring', was under construction. To join up with this feature, a sap was being dug out from Trench E2 across the front of Trench E1. On the left flank, the brigade position ended at a barricade on the Kemmel–Wytschaete road. There was little or no wire in front of the trenches and the Royal Engineers and working parties provided by the battalions were busy placing defensive wire in position over the first few days. Quiet area or no, the battalions quickly commenced their aggressive patrols seeking to dominate no man's land and quickly becoming a nuisance to an enemy not used to such activities before the arrival of the British.

During the first year of the war as officers and men gained experience, night firing was a regular occurrence. Sentries on the fire step stared out into the darkness towards the enemy trenches. Even on the blackest nights the varying intensity of darkness caused the inexperienced eye to see shapes, which were often taken to be an advancing enemy. Imagination played tricks constantly at night. The inexperienced soldier newly arrived in the trenches saw many a German in his imagination and fired. In addition many solitary sentries, under great stress, fired off his rifle into no man's land to relieve his feelings. An outburst of rifle and machine gun fire, occasionally supported by artillery, would be heard faintly far away. This would roll nearer and nearer, growing louder and more menacing as trench after trench along the line took it up.

26

Then it would pass and die away into the distance. As night gave way to day, troops took up their stand-to positions on the fire steps, eyes searching no man's land, ears straining to hear the approaching dixie of heavily chlorinated tea coming down the trench. A new day began. Men moved about the trenches with great care. The ever-watchful sniper would pick out any unwary soldier and the crack of the rifle often meant death or wounding. One German sniper, opposite Trench E2, could smash the small bayonet periscope whenever it was raised.

The enemy snipers remained a daily and deadly nuisance for the unwary. On the 22nd June, C.S.M. John Davidson was killed by a sniper. On the following day, 2/Lt. Alfred Haughton was killed whilst examining wire in front of the trenches. Pte. Charles Harrison was also killed on this day. On the 24th, Pte. Christopher Bowman was killed and four men wounded.

The enthusiasm and high spirits, which filled the men on leaving England, was by now wearing off. The war was lasting much longer than they had hoped. It was dirty, dangerous and uncomfortable. Friends were disappearing, killed in appalling circumstances. Rumours of moves raised or lowered the spirits. Corporal Constantine wrote to his parents on the 19th June:

> There's a great rumour out here that our Division is leaving here for England on the 28th of this month and, for all I've heard it from good authority, I can hardly believe it but, by gum, I hope it's true. A chap that is with me just now got a letter the other day and it said in it that they were busy decorating the stations in readiness for us coming home. Do you know if this is true?

Rumours of going home, victory by Christmas, and the collapse of the German army constantly made the rounds in the trenches. They were no more than expressions of the soldiers' prayers and hopes as the war became more terrible. Corporal Constantine and his comrades were again back in the trenches early in July.

The battalion was relieved by the 5th Bn. Loyal North Lancashire Regiment on the night of the 27th June. It moved into a rest area close to Bailleul. A few days were spent here, free of artillery and sniper fire. The men cleaned themselves and their uniforms, getting rid of the mud and lice always prevalent in the trenches. Bailleul had good shops and cafés where troops could relax. Some training and marching were undertaken to harden feet made soft by the stay in the trenches. A worrying situation arose on the 1st July, when 152 rifles were condemned due to the expansion of chambers brought about by faults in cartridges. Faults in some of the rifles had been a problem since the early days in the Salient and it was now that, with time to check out the weapons, identification and replacement of rifles could be organised.

The battalion moved back into the same trenches on the 3rd July. The daily casualties from artillery and sniper fire continued. Ptes. William Fettes, Hilton Gustard and Private Hailes were killed on the 4th. Brigadier General Shea, from the 6th Division, replaced Brigadier General Martin as Brigade Commander. He proved to be extremely

The front line near Houplines as sketched by Capt. R. Mauchlen M.C.

popular with both officers and men, appearing daily in the front line to inspect the conditions and to talk to the men. He was a young man with considerable organising ability and his officers always found him available for advice and assistance.

Reports from an observation post on Kemmel Hill indicated that the Germans were preparing an assault against the brigade trenches. It was thought that the enemy was placing gas cylinders in their front line and that mining was taking place. Enemy shelling of the sector increased. On the 14th July, the enemy blew a mine under a sector of trenches immediately north and very close to the battalion positions. As a result five men of the battalion were buried. Frantic digging by their comrades uncovered the bodies but it was too late, all were found to be dead. They were Ptes. George McLeay, William Towler, Charles Harris and Joseph McGuire and Cpl. John Barker. The following day, the battalion moved off to another sector of the front.

On the night of the 14th/15th July, the 50th Division was relieved and began moving to a new sector, which stretched from the Armentières–Lille road on the right, through the ruins of L'Epinette to a position near Houplines. The trenches were largely breastworks and were found to be comfortable and in good condition. Recesses in the parapet allowed men to rest in some shelter. The officers had wooden or sandbagged huts which, though more comfortable, gave little protection from shelling. On the 15th, home leave was started for the first time since leaving England and two officers and three men were selected to go off together. The march to Armentières had been a difficult one. The road was *pavé* for long distances and the cobblestones caused considerable discomfort to the men's feet, which had not recovered from the static situation in the trenches. Falling rain made the surface even more difficult, with the men slipping and slithering in their heavily studded ammunition boots. On the 17th July 1915, the battalion relieved the 2nd Bn. King's Shropshire Light Infantry in the trenches in front of Chapelle d'Armentières. These positions were served by two wide communication trenches named Leith Walk and Lothian Avenue, each of excellent construction. Each day, French civilians sold newly baked bread, eggs and butter at the entrances to the communication trenches. Vegetables could be found in the nearby fields. The enemy trenches lay some 250 to 300 yards away. It was a 'quiet' sector but not without its morning and evening 'hate' bombardments and the very active snipers. On the 18th, 2/Lt. Oliver Field was killed and five other ranks wounded. A few men were killed and wounded each day and casualties gradually mounted over the period of time until the battalion was relieved on the 24th July. It then marched to billets in Armentières.

Armentières was quite a remarkable town. Close to the front line, it was shelled daily by the Germans. Many of its inhabitants had left the town for safety, yet quite a number remained encouraged by the spending power of the troops who filled so many of its buildings. Shops and cafés were quite numerous and plied a lucrative trade. Every Sunday afternoon, those inhabitants remaining donned their Sunday best and walked up and down the road leading west out of the town to Pont de Nieppe and watched the Germans shells falling on Le Bizet. However, life in the town remained hazardous as both civilians and troops became casualties to enemy shelling. The battalion was billeted in the Blue Blind Factory. No. 151 Brigade was in divisional reserve. On the 29th July, 'A' and 'B' Companies relieved two companies of the 6th Bn. D.L.I. in the support line and Lille Post. August began with fine, warm weather, and occasional thunderstorms.

The battalion returned to the trenches on the 7th August. The 6th and 8th Battalions had their separate identities restored after this date. Flies were proving to be a considerable nuisance and a threat to good trench hygiene, which the Durhams always practised. The country around the trenches was littered with refuse, a wonderful breeding and feeding ground for these most maddening of creatures. Trenches were regularly sprayed with creosol and high standards of hygiene were set to ensure that trenches remained clean. All refuse was collected immediately when a new battalion entered the line. All items that could harbour flies and disease, such as toilet paper, empty food tins and bottles, were placed in empty sandbags and taken out of the trenches before dumping.

On the 19th August, the battalion was relieved and moved back into Armentières.

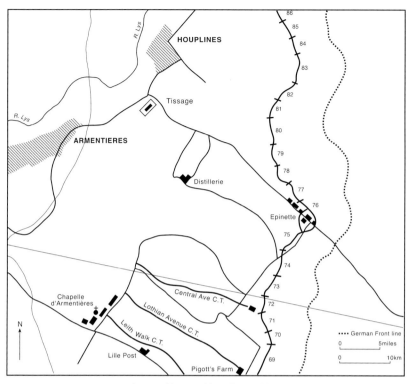

Armentières – Houplines 1915

Here on the 28th, Pte. James Bainbridge was killed by enemy shelling. On the 31st, the battalion relieved the 7th Bn. D.L.I. in the trenches. During most of the month of September, the battalion alternated between periods of rest in Armentières and in the front line trenches. Casualties were light. Cpl. John Cain was killed on the 2nd September. Amongst the wounded were Lieutenant Boys-Stones and Company Sergeant Major Wright. During the month, the new tubular pattern smoke helmet was issued. The 'P' helmet, as it was known, comprised of a flannel bag treated with chemicals, which tucked in all round the neck under the collar of the service jacket. Breathing in and out was through the material. It was intensely disliked by its wearers whose opinion was divided as to whether it was better to die from asphyxiation with the helmet on, or from gas with it off! A new version of the helmet had an improved glass eye-piece and a mouth-piece which made breathing much easier and more comfortable. The glass of the eye-piece needed constant rubbing with a paste carried in a small tin to stop fogging. On the 4th September the divisional concert party, the 'Jesmond Jesters', appeared for the first time to entertain the battalion.

The battalion was relieved in the trenches on the 23rd September by the 4th and 6th Bns. Northumberland Fusiliers and moved back to Armentières. The following day, 151 Brigade was placed in reserve to the Second Army, prior to the commencement of the Battle of Loos on the 25th September. On the 26th, the battalion moved up to trenches at Houplines in support of the brigade. Armentières was heavily shelled on the 27th. On the same day, the battalion moved to trenches at Le Tissage. It was a very wet period and constant repair work was undertaken to stop trenches from falling in or flooding. Trenches in this area were identified on the maps by numbers. One trench, numbered 99, was 45 yards from the enemy front line. On the 28th, Pte. John Raine was killed.

The battalion relieved on the 4th October and moved to Le Bizet. The following day, an order was issued that all ranks were to be trained in throwing grenades. Lectures were arranged and these were followed by throwing practice. The first 'bombs' used in practice were bully beef tins. Lieutenant Callender, however, used a live bomb in his lecture to 'D' Company. The bomb exploded in his hand, killing himself and Pte. Robert Renforth. A brief return to Armentières on the 6th was followed two days later by the relief of the 7th Bn. D.L.I. The battalion occupied Trenches 84, 85, 86 and 87. Battalion headquarters was in Chateau Houpline. The rest of the month was spent alternating between the line and Armentières. Casualties occurred through heavy enemy shelling.

Amongst the dead was Pte. Edward Holloway who was killed on the 27th October. An officer of the battalion wrote a letter to his mother who lived at 4 Elizabeth Street, Gateshead, which she would receive before the dreaded telegram.

> I have very sad news to give you. Your son was shot this morning when acting as sentry in the front line trenches and died shortly afterwards. I cannot say anything that will bring comfort to you in your present distress, but it may be a joy to you afterwards to know that he was doing his duty when the time came and he endured no suffering. Your boy had been wounded soon after coming to the Front. I delighted to pass him in the trenches, for he was always bright and cheerful and did everything with a good heart, no matter what the hardships were. All the men were very sad to lose him and, on their behalf and on my own behalf, I ask you to accept our deepest sympathy.

There were many letters to write in the ensuing months, a sad task which many officers were to find extremely difficult. Such letters from comrades did, however, help the bereaved, when compared with the terse pronouncements of the official telegram. These often answered their questions, 'Where?', 'How?' and 'Were his friends with him when he died?' The knowledge that their loved one had not died alone and was with friends was a great comfort to the bereaved family.

Also on the 27th October, Captain Dryden, Lieutenant Boys-Stones (whose injuries must have been slight) and Lieutenant Goodall, together with 56 other ranks went to Bailleul. They formed part of a composite battalion to march past King George V. The King was, 'pleased with the soldierly bearing of the troops and all he saw.'

Heavy rain at the end of the month made life in the trenches extremely uncomfortable. There was no overhead shelter, and mud and water in the bottom of the trenches was often knee-deep. Men standing for days in water-filled trenches often developed 'trench feet' – a type of foot rot. If left untreated, this affliction could cause the loss of toes and whole feet. To keep this curse at bay, officers and N.C.O.s were instructed to carry out a daily check on the men's feet. The men changed socks as regularly as possible and rubbed their feet with whale oil, which was thought to prevent dampness from soaking into the skin, but it remained a great problem in the wet conditions. Trenches collapsed, mud was thick, and constant digging and repairing went on. These conditions remained throughout November.

On the 3rd November, the battalion again relieved the 7th Battalion in the line, with the 6th Battalion on the right and the 5th Bn. Loyal North Lancashire Regiment on the left. Three platoons of the 8th Bn. Lincolnshire Regiment joined them for trench instruction. The trenches were in a very bad state due to the continuing rainfall. On the 7th, L/Cpl. W. Carr was wounded. He had a good record as a battalion sniper and was one of the most experienced patrollers. An N.C.O. of 'B' Company, he was out in front of the wire at 10 a.m. when the fog lifted suddenly. This revealed him to the enemy and he was hit when they fired. Lieutenant Palmer and Private Bell, seeing his predicament, ran out under fire and brought him in.

The 50th Division tour of the trenches in the Armentières area came to an end on the 12th November. The Division concentrated in the Merris–La Crèche area for cleaning and training. It was a farming area and, though the rain continued to pour, the battalion had a pleasant and happy stay. Football was played against neighbouring units. On the 20th November, Sergeant Major Crouch, who had been with the battalion for seven years, left to take up a commission with the 1st Bn. D.L.I. In January 1916, the *London Gazette* announced his award of the Distinguished Conduct Medal. His citation read, 'For conspicuous, good and efficient works as Sergeant Major throughout the campaign, always displaying great coolness and devotion to duty and giving a fine example to all ranks.'

Sergeant Major Crouch was a veteran of the Boer War and was to return to the battalion as Second in Command and ultimately took command in late 1917, following the promotion of Roland Boys Bradford V.C., M.C. to Brigadier.

Sir Hubert Plumer and Sir Charles Ferguson inspected the brigade on the 22nd November. The battalions marched past in impressive style, looking smart and relaxed. The rest period continued into the first half of December. This was indeed a rest period, free of digging duties and the men were able to make up for lack of sleep, boredom and the continual stress and dangers of trench life. The weather was cold. Corporal Constantine wrote to his brother on the 28th November:

> I expect you'll all be crowding round the fire now telling the tale. I am lying wrapped up in my blankets to keep warm, mind it's only about 6 o'clock. Fancy being in bed at such a time on a Sunday night, it's scandalous, what do you say? But it's the best place where we are at present as there is nothing to see, it's just like being at the North Pole. In fact, I think this must be the place where Capt. Scott lost himself, when he was on the North Pole expedition [sic]. We are having very nice dry weather, a hard frost and, mind, very

very cold. We have two blankets a man now and also waterproof capes and we were all dished out with gloves yesterday. The gloves are made with only a place for the thumbs. I got a nice Sleeping Helmet and mittens sent out to me the other day and it's nice and warm with the helmet on, but taking all our comforts into consideration, such as football etc. I would sooner be at home now to no fire…Our boots were all frozen this morning and we couldn't get them on for a bit. What price that eh?

Hopes were high that Christmas would be spent in this area and out of the line. It was not to be.

CHAPTER IV

The 5th Bn. Border Regiment replaced the 7th Bn. D.L.I. (which had become Divisional Pioneers) on the 16th December 1915. The 5th Bn. Loyal North Lancashire Regiment was transferred to the 55th Division on the 20th December. The 50th Division went into the line and into positions stretching from just south west of Hill 60 to a little short of the Menin Road. The Division had returned to V Corps. On the 19th December, the relief of the 9th Division in the front line commenced. The relative peace of a 'quiet' area was replaced by the killing grounds of the Salient. The countryside was blasted beyond recognition – evil smelling, desolate and ruined. The area had already achieved the terrible reputation for death and destruction, which it retained throughout the rest of the war.

The 9th Battalion left Steenwerke on the 18th December and arrived at Poperinghe in the late afternoon. On the following day, it marched via Basseboum and Ouderdom to Dickebusch Huts. These were old Belgian army huts sited in a small grove of trees and surrounded by fields of mud. They were draughty and cold and required a lot of work by the battalions of 151 Brigade to improve them. Huts were repaired and duckboards were laid across the muddy fields. Later a Y.M.C.A. recreation marquee appeared and brought some creature comforts to those who used the camp as a rest centre. Dickebusch village about a mile ahead, lay on the road from La Clytte to Ypres. It had suffered in the war and a number of its houses had been destroyed or damaged by shellfire. Remarkably, a number of its inhabitants still occupied the village and two or three shops remained open and sold their wares to the troops. One, for example, sold tinned food and wine. Whilst in this camp the battalion learned that General Haig had replaced Field Marshall French as Commander of the British armies in France.

The line held by 151 Brigade included Hill 60. The line ran through Sanctuary Wood to within 500 yards of the Menin Road, due west of Stirling Castle, which was held by the enemy. The distances between the front line trenches opposite Stirling Castle were some 20 yards, a few feet at Hill 60 and 200–300 yards elsewhere. The area was very wooded though few trees remained untouched by shell or bullet. Most of the trees were snapped off, leaves and many branches had gone and only the torn and twisted trunks remained. Sanctuary Wood and the area around already had an evil reputation. In the wood itself the smell of decaying soldiers, killed in previous actions, was strong and almost overpowering. Even the food seemed tainted by it. Battalions had to spend longer periods in the trenches in this area than most other parts of the front.

On the 20th December, the battalion moved into dugouts in Maple Copse and relieved the 8th Battalion who, along with the 6th Battalion, moved into the front line.

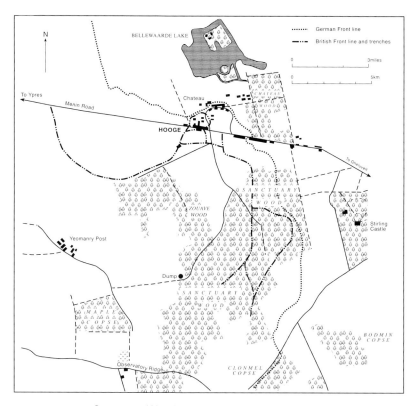

Sanctuary Wood and Hooge – December 1915

'A' Company suffered five casualties from enemy shelling, which fell on Canal Dugouts. The dugouts, though fairly comfortable, were under constant observation from enemy balloons. Over the next two days, the front line and the rear areas were heavily shelled by German artillery. To add to the misery heavy rain fell. Trenches collapsed or were blown in by enemy shells. As quickly as they were repaired the Germans blew them in again. The wooded area, which extended to the front of the trenches, climbed up to higher ground. This meant that the enemy trenches could not be seen from our B1, B2 and B3 Trenches, which were occupied by the battalions of the brigade. Strong points in the German lines were Stirling Castle and the Birdcage. The latter got its name from the wires attached between trunks of trees, which were set up by the enemy to try to give some protection from grenades thrown from the British trenches.

Everywhere there was deep, cloying mud, at least ankle-deep and in places waist-deep. The onset of winter brought snow and rain, which fell regularly. It was virtually impossible to remain dry in the trenches. Uniforms were wet and plastered with mud. Trench feet were an ever-present problem. Another ailment raised its head: scabies, thought to have been brought over from England by new drafts, claimed an increasing number of sufferers. Men ached, shivered and scratched. Lice had no respect for rank

35

or status – everyone had lice. A variety of measures were tried to contain them. All failed. Creosote was added to water at the laundries behind the lines but the women who did the work complained of discoloured hands and this practice was stopped. Appeals were made in men's letters home for anti-lice powder and potions to cover clothing and body. A lighted match or candle run along the seams of the clothing might bring a brief relief. By this means the active lice might be killed. It did not kill the eggs, which hatched as soon as the clothing was put on and the heat of the body caused a new population to be born. Men tried to accept these 'lodgers' in their clothing and live along with them, and they tried to keep them at bay by match or hunting them and squeezing those they caught between fingers. A regular change of clothing was organised out of the line when men attended baths. The relief, however, was brief as a new 'army of occupation' eagerly awaited the men's return to the line.

The 9th Battalion relieved the 8th Bn. D.L.I. in the line on the 23rd December and remained there over Christmas. On Boxing Day, the Germans tried to explode a mine in front of Trench B7, which was held by 'C' Company. It had little success and no damage was done. On the 27th December, the battalion was relieved by the 6th and 8th Battalions and moved into rest at Dickebusch Huts. Officers and men now enjoyed a delayed Christmas dinner. A well-stocked expeditionary forces canteen in Poperinghe supplied traditional Christmas food, which included plum puddings, drinks, cigars, and cigarettes. The battalion returned to the front line on the 31st December. The 8th Battalion was relieved in Sanctuary Wood. At 10.55 p.m. and 11.55 p.m., a five-minute bombardment by artillery, machine gun fire and a shower of hand grenades fell on the German trenches at the close of the old year. The only retaliation was four mortar bombs, which exploded in a trench bay opposite the enemy-held Birdcage. Pte. Edward Dixon was killed and three men were wounded. Active patrolling was carried out each night, whilst the men laboured to repair and rebuild damaged trenches and wire defences. The battalion strength was 33 officers and 824 other ranks.

On the 4th January, 1916, the battalion was relieved by the 8th Battalion and moved to Maple Copse and Canal Dugouts. It returned to the line on the 9th January and occupied trenches B1 to B7. The following day, Pte. John Tulley was killed by a sniper. The remainder of January was spent alternating between the front line, Maple Copse and Dickebusch Huts. The usual activities took place. Artillery bombardments by both sides, bursts of rifle and machine gun fire, sniping, patrols and working parties were unchanging features in the daily life of the front line soldier. Officers and men became more and more weary. Casualties occurred on most days. On the 21st January, Ptes. James Turbitt and Thomas Armstrong were killed. A draft of 175 other ranks from the 2/9th Battalion back in England joined on the 23rd January. Of the draft, some men had scabies, one man was blind in his right eye and another was missing a trigger finger!

The battalion relieved the 8th Battalion in Sanctuary Wood on the 25th January. At one point in the line the enemy could be observed moving about the trenches, usually carrying timber to improve the position. At 9.30 p.m., 2/Lt. T. Mack was struck by a stray bullet while out on patrol with two of his men. He instructed them to go back and leave him as he was 'done for'. They refused to leave him and carried him back to safety, but he died immediately upon reaching the trench. He was buried in Zillebeke Valley the following day. Brigadier General Shea took the service in the absence of the chaplain.

The battalion was relieved on the 29th January and moved to Dickebusch Huts. It returned to the line on the 6th February. This was a day of some activity. In the early hours of the morning a German working party was spotted near the Birdcage and close to Trench B4. The battalion bombarded the Birdcage with trench mortars, supported by 18-pdr. guns. The enemy immediately retaliated with rifle grenades and mortars, which fell on Trench B2 and its support trench. There were seven casualties. Two men were killed and five wounded. Second Lieutenant Stafford was returned to England suffering from shell shock. A further move to Maple Copse was made on the night of the 6th/7th February. Company positions were in Consett Dugouts, Border Lane Dugouts and Cumberland Dugouts, with battalion headquarters in Maple Copse. Working parties were sent to the support line at the east end of Sanctuary Wood. Brigade headquarters at the south-west corner of Zillebeke Lake, was heavily bombarded when it revealed its position by showing too many lights. The 8th February was a very hot day. Enemy artillery was active throughout the day. German aircraft were overhead, totally undisturbed as there was no anti aircraft retaliation. 2/Lt. G. Palmer was seriously wounded when his jaw was smashed in several places by flying shrapnel. Ptes. John Nicholson and George Turnbull were killed on this day.

On the 12th February, the Germans commenced an attack which led to the capture of the Bluff. Brigade 151 was put on half an hour's notice to move. The battalion moved into divisional reserve at Scottish Lines, near Ouderdom. During the move, Ptes. James McCrystal and Thomas Horrocks were killed at Shrapnel Corner. The Bluff fell to the enemy on the 14th February, after they had blown five mines under 57 Brigade of the 17th Division who were holding the position. On the night of the 18th/19th, the 50th Division moved into the Hill 60 sector, holding the line from Hill 60 to the Menin Road. No. 151 Brigade was holding Hill 60, which had already achieved an awful reputation. The battalion was in brigade reserve at Bedford House, about 1,500 yards from the front line trenches. The building had been damaged but the underground rooms were in good condition and well furnished with items from the upper rooms.

Hill 60 was a man-made mound built from soil excavated when the railway cutting was dug. At its highest point it was 60 metres above sea level, hence its name. It was riddled with trenches and actively mined by both sides. The opposing trenches were very close. The British trenches were reached through the railway cutting, which the Germans shelled from time to time. It was a dangerous journey and a very wet one in winter with water in the bottom. On leaving the cutting the way lay through a cov-

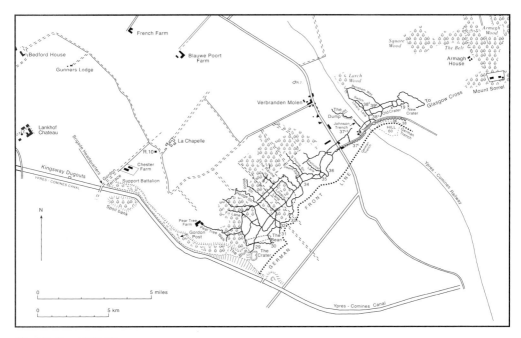

The Bluff and Hill 60

ered communication trench. Its overhead covering gave some protection against the incessant shrapnel fire from the enemy guns. This trench led to the Dump, another mound formed by rubble from the excavations. A deep dugout here provided shelter for the wounded until it was possible for them to be taken back for treatment. The final move from here was into the trenches, the most risky part of what was always a dangerous journey from reserve positions to the front line.

The battalion remained in brigade reserve from the 20th to the 22nd February. On the 20th, Lt. Rollo Atkinson, Battalion Bombing Officer, was killed. On the 22nd, the battalion relieved the 8th Battalion in the front line trenches 37–41 on Hill 60. The weather was bitterly cold and snow fell during the relief. The position was held until the 26th of the month. There were casualties on each of the days in the line, mainly due to heavy enemy shelling, mortaring and rifle grenades. Mining and counter-mining went on. The casualties included Lt. J.H. Edgar who died of wounds on the 24th February. He was a barrister from Ireland who had also been a member of the Newcastle Pen and Palette Club. Amongst the other ranks who were killed were Ptes. Frederick Baggeley, Jonathan Pearson, William Elliott and George Cook. From the 26th to the end of the month the battalion remained in support. On the 1st March, it moved back into the line in the Hill 60 sector and occupied trenches 37L to 47S. The 50th Division had been ordered to make a demonstration to draw the enemy's attention away from a proposed attack on the Bluff by the 17th Division who were to attempt to recapture ground lost to the Germans in February. Lewis guns opened up on the enemy front line and bombers threw bombs into their trenches. The divisional artillery fired shrapnel aimed at cutting the enemy wire. The enemy retaliation was quick and intense. An artillery and mortar barrage fell on the British lines. Battalion losses in this demonstration were four men killed, five wounded and one man missing. The dead were Ptes. Johnson Coxon and Daniel Graham and L/Cpls. John Drummond and Robert Edwards. The 17th Division did not, after all, attack on this day but did so on the 2nd, with another demonstration provided by the 50th Division. 'A' Company was in support in Sunken Road dugouts near the Dump. It was ordered to send two platoons to the 9th Bn. Duke of Wellington's Regiment. Despite the intense enemy shelling these platoons reached their destination without loss. At 2 p.m. another platoon from the 9th Battalion was sent to 'A' Company of the 8th Bn. D.L.I. who had suffered heavy casualties. The attack by the 17th Division was successful and much lost ground was retaken. 'A' and 'B' Companies meanwhile were attached to 149 Brigade, 50th Division

German retaliation was predictable and an intense artillery bombardment fell on the British trenches. On the night of the 2nd/3rd March, the battalion lost 10 killed, 24 wounded and 10 missing. Amongst the dead was Pte. George Condon Morris, twin brother of James Morris who was to lose his life in 1917 whilst serving with another battalion of the regiment. Four brothers of the Morris family served in this war. The Morris twins were miners from Gateshead. Also amongst the dead were Ptes. William Finlay D.C.M., James Charlton, Norman Telford and Arthur

One family's sacrifice: Twins George and James Morris, both killed in action. George dies in 1916 and James just a year later in 1917.

Fawcett. Headquarters and 'C' and 'D' Companies moved to the rest camp in Dickebusch Huts on the night of the 2nd and 3rd. 'A' Company was relieved and left 149 Brigade and rejoined the battalion on the 3rd March, leaving 'B' Company with this brigade. Five men were wounded during the relief.

The awfulness of the tour of duty in the trenches in the Hill 60 sector was almost beyond description. The weather was bad with heavy falls of rain and snow. The trenches were extremely wet and muddy with little shelter against the elements. Sleep was almost impossible with constant shelling, bombing and mining by both sides. Death was ever present. Very little movement was possible during the day. Food and supplies could only come up at night and these carried by units in support or at rest, just recently out of the line and already quite exhausted. Although wet, dirty, weary and under constant stress, the men clung to their positions under a hail of shrapnel and bombs. Yet, morale remained surprisingly high and the health of the battalion was remarkably good.

Over the next few days the weather worsened. Snow and ice conditions made life even more miserable. Battalion headquarters, 'A', 'C' and 'D' Companies remained in Dickebusch Huts. Constant work on the camp had improved the conditions considerably. 'B' Company had moved to Bleauwpoort Farm and was still attached to 149 Brigade. This position lay just over a mile from Bedford House, towards Verbranden Molen. Enemy aircraft dropped three bombs near Dickebusch Huts causing little damage and no casualties.

On the 7th March, Major General Wilkinson, G.O.C., 50th Division, wrote the following letter to Brig. Shea:

> Gen. Pilcher has written asking me to express his thanks to you and the officers of the 5th Borders and 9th D.L.I. concerned, for the quick and ready manner in which assistance was rendered to the 9th Duke of Wellington's Regiment, on 2nd March, when they were hard put to it. The officer commanding the Battalion informed Gen. Pilcher that the prompt help he received in being sent stores of different descriptions as well as troops, was of the greatest value. Will you let the troops know their services were appreciated.

A letter of thanks also came from the Officer Commanding 9th Duke of Wellington's Regiment, Maj. G.E.T. Parnell:

> Please accept my thanks and appreciation for the two platoons of your regiment that came to reinforce my Battalion on March 2nd. Your men were splendid, they came up through the barrage in perfect order and behaved throughout with great gallantry. I hope your losses were not too severe. My men much appreciated their assistance.

On the 10th March, the battalion relieved the 1st Bn. Royal Scots Fusiliers in the Bluff Sector and occupied trenches 34–38B. One man was wounded during the relief. In the most active areas carrying out reliefs could be extremely difficult and dangerous. Men struggled and cursed their way through narrow communication trenches with heavy loads, pushed and squeezed past men coming from the other direction, often meeting stretcher bearers with wounded moving down to the next medical post. All this went on whilst an alert enemy shelled and sniped at any movement. In the darkness men often had to hold on to the belt of the man in front. This was necessary to negotiate the maze of trenches, which went off at all angles and it was easy for part of a relieving force to miss a turn and lose its way. In bad weather, trenches were deep in mud and the journey sapped the energy of the relief before they had even reached the trench line. Occasionally, units would climb out of the communication trench and move across the open in order to reach the front line before daybreak. This was an extremely dangerous move and taken at great risk. It was not done frequently. In the most dangerous areas, units moving into and out of the line either as a relief or being relieved, invariably suffered casualties from enemy fire.

The soldier in winter as sketched by Capt. R. Mauchlen M.C.

The Bluff was formed before the war from soil excavated when the Ypres–Commine Canal was built. It was about 30–40 feet high and about 100 yards in length. It was covered with trees before the violence of war had broken over it. It gave good observation over the surrounding area and became an objective, which both sides strove to take and hold. Many fierce battles were fought and much blood was spilled trying to take it. It had been captured by the Germans on the 15th February and recaptured on the 2nd March. There had not been time to clear the dead of these two bitterly fought battles. The trees became stumps. The tangled undergrowth hid many putrefying bodies, German and British. Trenches criss-crossed the area, many mere holes hurriedly dug into the ground to create a shelter from the terrific artillery and mortar fire that constantly deluged its slopes. Mines had been blown and craters formed, which reeked of the smell of explosive materials and the dead who lay in them. Dugouts had been blown in along with the men who had occupied them. When they could, usually under the cover of darkness, men dug feverishly on the site of dugouts, endeavouring to reach the bodies of their comrades. A machine gun, with its team lying dead beside it, was uncovered from a blown-in sap. On the top of the Bluff the body of a Lancashire Fusilier lay crouched, one hand pressed on the earth in front of him, the other hand still held his rifle. There he faced the enemy who had killed him. This petrified figure somehow epitomised all that was glorious, yet futile and cruel in this war.

The trenches held by the battalion were in an appalling state, constantly damaged or destroyed by shell and mortar fire. Much work was carried out to repair the damage. Fortunately, during this tour of the trenches the enemy remained fairly quiet. Snipers, though, were always a nuisance. Pte. John Rawson was killed and one man was wounded on the 13th March. On the 14th, the battalion was relieved by the 4th Bn. East Yorkshire Regiment and moved into close support at Bedford House, Sunken Road and Swan Chateau. Three men were wounded during the relief. The usual working parties were organised to work under the supervision of the Royal Engineers. A draft of 30 other ranks was received on the 17th March. The following day, the battalion moved to rest billets at Scottish Lines and, for the next four days, company training was carried out. A further draft of 94 men arrived from England on the 19th. The next move, on the 23rd of the month, was to trenches 34–37R in the Bluff sector. The usual enemy shelling and mortaring was experienced during the tour. L/Cpl. Thomas Carmichael was killed on the 24th March. A draft of 63 men arrived from England on the 26th March.

On the 27th, six mines were blown in the St. Eloi Sector under German trenches to the right of 151 Brigade positions. This heralded an assault by the 3rd Division. The artillery duel in this area was intense and involved most of the enemy guns facing 151 Brigade. The Germans concentrated on the 3rd Division's attack and the Durhams' front had a quiet spell, not before Pte. Felix Kelly was killed. An observation post was set up in a position that gave a clear view of a part of the enemy communication trench and his support and rear lines. The unsuspecting enemy lost six men to the Lewis guns of Lieutenant Spencer's Section, all killed by one burst from his guns. These Lewis guns made it virtually impossible for the Germans to continue vital work on their trenches. The enemy remained reasonably quiet for the rest of the month. During the period, three men were wounded, one of whom, Pte. Robert Atkinson, died of his wounds.

On the 11th March 1916, the *London Gazette* announced the award of the Distinguished Conduct Medal to C.S.M. William Snowball Ridley. Company Sergeant Major Ridley was later commissioned on the battlefield. He was born at Felling and had served previously with the Rifle Volunteers. He went to South Africa with the volunteers for the Boer War. At a ceremony in Victoria Square on the 26th March 1916, the Mayor of Gateshead presented him with a sword.

In the same issue of the *London Gazette*, Ptes. W.R. Laskey and H.F. Lee were also awarded the Distinguished Conduct Medal. Private Laskey also won the Military Medal later in the year.

On the 30th March 1916, the *London Gazette* announced several awards to members of the battalion who had carried out courageous acts whilst serving in the Salient. Amongst these was the award of the Distinguished Conduct Medal to Pte. Ernest Davison whose citation read:

> For conspicuous gallantry. He is always one of the first to volunteer for any dangerous work and is always cheery. On one occasion he went out under fire to look for two missing signallers. He has often carried messages under fire. Once he volunteered and went out to assist a bombing post of another battalion.

Private Davison was a company bomber, trained in the skill of grenade throwing. Amongst his friends he was known as 'Happy Days'. His medal was presented to him by the Mayor of Gateshead, Alderman W. Wardill, in a ceremony outside the Town Hall on the 26th June 1916. He had been employed by the Newcastle upon Tyne Co-operative Wholesale Society who also gave him a silver cigarette case.

Ptes. W. Dixon and W. Finlay, the latter from Swalwell, were both awarded the Distinguished Conduct Medal for attempting to rescue a buried miner. This brave act was carried out whilst under heavy shellfire and the additional danger of the collapse of the tunnel on top of them. The miner, when released, was found to be dead.

Pte. S.J. Sterry of Bensham was also awarded the Distinguished Conduct Medal for rescuing three wounded men under fire. He also won the Military Medal later in the year.

The quiet period lasted until the 2nd April. On this day the line was bombarded by enemy artillery. Brigade headquarters, in Gordon Trench, suffered heavily from the shelling and there were many casualties. That night the battalion was relieved by the Canadians and moved into brigade reserve and into dugouts at Ridgewood, near Vierstraat. It was a difficult relief carried out in dense fog and considerable enemy fire, from which two men were wounded. One later died of his wounds. A further move to another front was in the offing.

CHAPTER V

VIERSTRAAT & WYTSCHAETE 1916

T he 50th Division had been moved to the Wytschaete Sector following its efforts around Hill 60 and the Bluff. This was considered a quiet area, which would allow the division to recuperate. Brigade 151 held the line from near Byron Farm to Bois Confluent, occupying trenches M1 to O4. On the 4th April 1916, the 9th Battalion moved forward to trenches M1 to N2, with the 5th Bn. Northumberland Fusiliers on the right and 5th Bn. Border Regiment on the left. Trenches M and N ran north and south along the slopes below Wytschaete. To the front lay the Grand Bois and Bois Quarante. Trenches in this area were light breastworks. Kemmel Hill lay behind the front line. In the rear areas local people still occupied their farms and cultivated land. Out of the line, officers and men enjoyed a quiet and relatively untouched countryside. In the line snipers were a persistent nuisance. On the 5th April, Pte. John Collins was killed and two men wounded by sniper fire. On this day, a Special Order of the Day was received from Brigadier Shea, commanding 151 Brigade. It read:

> The G.O.C. wishes to thank the officers, NCOs and men of the Brigade for the good work done while the Brigade was in the Ypres Salient and to congratulate them on the good name which they have made for themselves. He particularly wishes to thank the men in the ranks for the soldierly and cheerful spirit in which they faced many difficulties and much discomfort. He is very proud to command such men.

On the 7th, the British launched an attack on Hill 60 and retook it. The battalion's positions were heavily bombarded by shrapnel and high explosive shells and five men were killed and nine wounded. Amongst the dead were Ptes. E. Edwards and William Cawthorne. Further casualties were claimed by enemy shellfire on the following day and during the relief carried out that night. The battalion moved to billets at La Clytte and into divisional reserve. To the battalion's delight, hot baths were available and clean underwear was issued. Refitting was carried out until the 11th of the month when it moved back to Ridgewood and into brigade reserve. Six men were wounded by shellfire during the relief. Each night a working party of 300 men was supplied for essential tasks. Ridgewood lay just over 2,000 yards from the front line and, remarkably, had suffered very little from shelling. The trees gave good cover from enemy observation. Dugouts in the wood were clean and comfortable. The Y.M.C.A. occupied a large dugout in the centre of the wood, making a wider range of items available to supplement the basic rations. Included in these were chocolate, cigarettes, tobacco and writing materials. At that time, it was indeed a haven in the midst of the war which lapped all round it.

On the 14th April, a draft of two officers and 41 other ranks was received. On

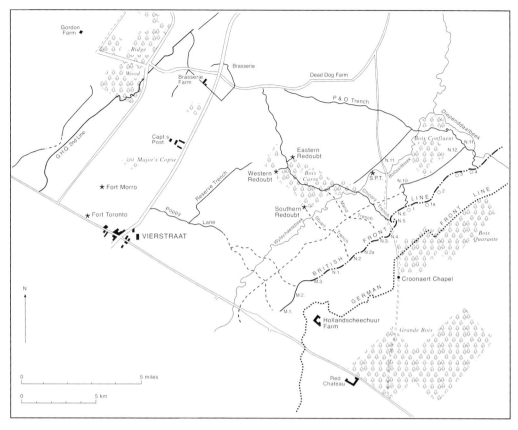

Vierstraat Sector 1916

returning to the line in the left sub-sector of the Vierstraat area, one man, Pte. William Parkin was killed and three men were wounded. On the 18th, Capt. Mark Bettison of Queen's Road, Jesmond, who had returned from leave the previous evening, was killed in a rifle grenade attack on the trenches held by the battalion. He was buried in Ridgewood Military Cemetery, Voormezeele, Belgium. On the anniversary of the battalion's arrival in France, total casualties for the year were 50 officers and 1,264 other ranks, the equivalent of full battalion strength. On the 21st of the month, 50th Division was relieved and marched to billets near Westroutre to become part of the corps reserve and to a well-earned rest.

On the 28th, Sir Douglas Haig inspected 151 Brigade. The brigade stayed in this area until the 4th May. During this period, Maj. Roland Boys Bradford joined the battalion as Second in Command with the rank of temporary Major. The Battalion Commander was Lt. Col. W.B. Moir. Bradford's association with the battalion lasted until October 1917. This exceptional soldier took command of the 9th Battalion in summer of 1916, at the age of 24. He won the Victoria Cross in October 1916 and became the youngest Brigadier General in the British army at the age of 25. He was killed at the end of November 1917. More of him later.

From the 4th to the 7th May 1916, the battalion provided working parties for the Vierstraat defences. On the 8th, it moved back to Westroutre and into rest billets. On the 17th of the month, Brig. Gen. 'Jimmy' Shea left the brigade to take command of the 30th Division. He had the greatest regard and affection for his brigade whose officers and men he called his 'tigers'. They equally held him in the very highest esteem. One eyewitness account of the Brigadier galloping off after his final speech to the brigade spoke of tears streaming down his face. He was always visiting his battalions in and out of the line, in quiet and active times. Wherever he led his men would follow – the hallmark of true leadership. He was succeeded by Brig. Gen. P.T. Westmorland.

The rest period came to an end on the 26th May, when the battalion moved to Ridgewood and into brigade reserve. The following day, it relieved the 7th Bn. Shropshire Light Infantry in the left sub-sector in the Vierstraat area and moved into trenches M and N. Pte. Thomas McKenzie was killed during the relief. During the seven-day tour of the trenches, both sides hammered away at each other with heavy mortar bombardments. German Minnenwerfers, in particular, made the left of the battalion's positions almost unsafe to hold. It took a week of fierce retaliation to quieten the enemy mortars. Casualties were remarkably light, being three killed and 12 wounded. Active and aggressive patrolling took place to gain control of no man's land. On the 2nd June, when relieved by the 6th Bn. D.L.I., the battalion moved into divisional reserve. The following day, a ferocious enemy attack was made on the Canadians holding Sanctuary Wood. The Canadians were driven out of most of their trenches from Mount Sorrel to Trench B4. This night battle could be seen from the battalion's rest billets. The sky was lit up with Verey lights, rockets and bursting shells, causing a fantastic pyrotechnic display. Any enjoyment of the scene was lost in the knowledge that men were dying beneath it. For the rest of the month, the battalion moved between front line and reserve and suffered a small numbers of casualties due to enemy mortaring and shelling. Amongst the casualties was Lt. Alfred Haughton who was killed on the 23rd June. Whilst out of the line the usual exhausting working parties were found to repair roads and trenches.

Sgt. Robert Constantine wrote to his brother on the 2nd July:

Received parcel safe and in good order and I guess I'll enjoy my tea today before we again proceed up the line. We have been out for our usual six days but sure it's not been a rest for the boys because they have been out working every night up to 4 a.m. in the mornings but still the good old boys of the D.L.I. can always do their bit.

Since many of the Durhams were from a mining background, they became first choice for digging projects. Many were sent to work in mines, which were burrowing under the enemy positions. Conditions under which the men worked must have been bad enough to cause one Company Commander to protest. Lieutenant Boys-Stones, commanding 'D' Company, wrote:

> In accordance with instructions from H.Q. we are supplying working parties of 14 men every six hours for work in mines. The first party have just arrived back. They are soaking wet from head to foot and covered in a beastly green slime – uniforms are ruined. Can this please be laid before the Brigade immediately and either proper and efficient overalls (with which sappers are clothed) be supplied or the party be discontinued. My whole company will be soaked by tomorrow morning. We have no means of drying clothes nor blankets for men who are soaked.

The protest did reach Brigade and Brigadier General Westmorland wrote the following reply to Lieutenant Colonel Moir who was commanding the 9th Battalion:

> Reference attached – I have issued the necessary orders. No work will be done in the mine unless overalls and gumboots are provided. Will you kindly explain to your officers that (while thoroughly sympathetic with Lt. Boys-Stones' just indignation), I must insist that all military correspondence must be *absolutely polite*.

Some relaxation whilst in reserve was provided by the divisional concert party, the Jesmond Jesters.

The battalion returned to the line on the 2nd July. The War Diary for the following day has this entry:

> Enemy fairly lively with Trench Mortars, Bombs and larger Minnenwerfers, but by keeping careful look out men are mostly able to avoid the large bombs. Very amusing to watch them playing Hide and Seek round the traverses and paradoses dodging these large Rum Jars [large mortar bombs] and Bombs.

On the 19th July, the 50th Division extended its frontage and 9th Battalion moved into E and F trenches in the Kemmel sector. This was the same area held by the battalion in June and July 1915. Snipers were very active, otherwise normal trench activity prevailed. Both sides resorted to heavy shell and mortar fire. Several men were wounded by snipers and shellfire.

The 9th Battalion patrols were active and kept the British policy of dominating no man's land by driving off enemy patrols seeking to do the same. Patrol work, though vital, could be incredibly dangerous. On the 23rd July, an officer patrol made up of 2/Lt. D.A. Brown, Corporal Kelly and Private Pearson went out to reconnoitre no man's land. They failed to return. Two search patrols were sent out but failed to find any trace of them. 2/Lt. D. A. Brown died in enemy hands shortly after capture. Kelly and Pearson survived as prisoners of war.

On the 26th, several men were shot in the head but were saved from serious injury by their recently issued steel helmets. On this day, the battalion moved into reserve near Kemmel Hill. The importance of the new steel helmet was demonstrated on the 5th August when Capt. T. Ridley had a miraculous escape. His helmet deflected a bullet which only slightly grazed his head. The War Diary stated: 'These steel helmets are very valuable and have saved several men during this tour of duty.'

Sgt. Robert Constantine, in a letter home on the 6th August, was showing signs of discouragement:

Well you are all well at home after your canny holiday? I got your postcards…and when I received them I was wishing I was there as I am properly fed up, but I am keeping well in myself. We are now in part of the line we have never been in before but quite close before and the country round about is champion…we are expecting being relieved tomorrow or Monday and according to rumours we are under orders for right down south. I expect you will have an idea where I mean. We had one officer and two men taken prisoners the other day…you will guess what a putting up we will get marching about this weather, it's far hotter than in Blighty. When we are in the line we never have our coats on, just go about in our shirts with sleeves doubled up, ready for Fritz you know…We are in amongst some Australian sappers just now and what a carry on they make with the Geordies, as they call us. They think we are the hardest lot they have ever come across and sure we have some hard cases in our crush – don't care for anything…We are now into the third year and it seems no further forward.

On the 8th August, the division was relieved and marched to Dranoutre Huts. Preparations were now put in hand to commence the march south to the Somme.

CHAPTER VI

THE SOMME 1916

Over the next few days, the battalion marched to Godewaersvelde, where it boarded a train for Candas. From the 12th to the 27th August, it marched a total of 35 miles from Prouville to Baizieux via Vignacourt and Raineville. The Brigadier praised the battalion as being the best marching battalion in the brigade. At Baizieux, the men set up bivouacs of waterproof sheets, branches and brushwood in the wood. Officers camped in tents. Heavy rain fell making the conditions very bad indeed. Everywhere men crouched in their little shelters beneath the trees whose drips added to the rain, soaking everything and everyone. Daily training exercises were organised based on the early lessons of the battle and were carried out until the rain made the conditions impossible for such activities. The stay in the wood lasted seven days.

An interesting diet sheet was drawn up by Capt. and Adjutant R. Boys-Stones. It read:

> In future a diet sheet will be drawn up weekly by Company Commanders. Pudding cloths
> will be provided. Suggest items for Diet Sheet:
> Fried biscuits, Rissoles, Pea Pies,
> Steak Pies with crust, Roly Poly Jam Puddings,
> Bread Puddings with fruit, Broken Bread, Onion Pudding,
> Irish stew, Welsh rarebit.

In the battles that followed, it is doubtful that the men obtained such meals in the front line. Captain Boys-Stones' list seems to be a more realistic diet when out of the line.

The battalion remained in Baizieux Wood (named 'Bazooka Wood' by the troops) until the 9th September. Training was carried out, mainly to do with assaulting trenches and holding them against the inevitable counter-attack, which was the usual German response on losing a position. After a long period of relatively static duty in the trenches of the Salient area, officers and men were not as fit as they could be. Energetic training exercises were organised and the level of fitness improved considerably. Lt. Col. Roland Boys Bradford was now commanding the battalion, having succeeded Lieutenant Colonel Moir. He demanded peak physical fitness and, if the men grumbled at the increased numbers of physical exercises and long route marches, they soon recognised the need for them in the gruelling fighting which was to follow.

In his final letter home to his younger brother Jim before his death on the 15th September, Sgt. Robert Constantine wrote:

> By we haven't half been getting put through it lately. We have now been out of the line
> about three weeks, but we are training heavy to take part in the push and I am only wish-
> ing the war was finished before we go up, but no such luck. Never mind I'll just have to

take my chance the same as all the other boys. I expect you will have an idea what part we are at now, let us know and I'll write and tell you if you are right. There's an awful bombardment raging while I am writing this, so some poor chaps are going through it hot…We are getting awful grub just now and I don't know how I am sticking it and the small place we are in at present can hardly buy anything…the sooner this is over and I'm back home the better. I am getting properly fed up and sick of the damned job, but it's no use grumbling, I'll have to stick it.

The stress of the war was beginning to tell on the Sergeant, as can be seen from his letter. There were, undoubtedly, many more like him who were, 'properly fed up and sick of the damned job' and were beginning to wonder when the war would end.

On the 10th September, the brigade marched to Bécourt Wood near Albert. One member wrote:

The day was heavy with mist and perhaps for that reason there was no shelling of Albert or anywhere on the way. The outskirts of Albert did not appear to have suffered greatly and there were still civilians living in their houses but the centre was a second Ypres. The way lay by the ruined Pilgrimage Church of Notre Dame de Brebieres where our 'Lady of Pity' looked down on the men as they passed.

Clear of the town, the road divided to the left, leading to Contalmaison and Bapaume but the Brigade kept straight on up the hill into Bécourt Wood. It was amazing to find there, only such a little way behind the Old Front Line of July 1st, a chateau now used as a Dressing Station, standing almost unharmed in gardens, which had once been gardens but were now the last resting place for many men. Here, even between the graves, bivouacs were pitched. East of Bécourt Wood the hill fell sharply down into Sausage Valley, beyond lay the old Front. Line after line of trenches scarred the downs. The Somme was a chalk country and one looked as though at a troubled sea frozen to a sudden stillness.

On the 14th September, the battalion moved to Mametz Wood and bivouacked in the south-west corner of the wood. Mametz Wood was torn by days of heavy bombardment and was the scene of bitter fighting between its German defenders and the British who had striven for some days to capture it. It was now in British hands but constantly under enemy artillery fire. Losses in the taking and holding of the wood had been enormous. Wrecked trenches criss-crossed the wood. Many of the dead of both sides lay in the undergrowth awaiting discovery and decent burial. Beneath the stumps of the trees, men had dug holes or crouched in hastily erected bivouacs. No fires were allowed, no lights could be shown. It was the eve of 50th Division's entry into the Battle of the Somme.

The Battle of the Somme commenced on the morning of the 1st July 1916. Before the day was out 57,470 British officers and men became casualties. Of these 19,240 had lost their lives. No British army before had lost so many men in one day for so little reward. North of the Albert–Bapaume Road there had been very little progress. South of the road some progress had been made and the 30th Division, commanded by

Maj. Gen. 'Jimmy' Shea, along with the 18th Division had reached their first-day objectives. For the following fortnight, progress was exceptionally slow and losses amongst officers and men remained high. On the 14th July, the British army picked itself up and carried out a brilliant night attack against the German second line of defences. These were breached on the Longuval–Bazentine Ridge. High Wood was found to be empty and ready for the taking. The opportunity was lost as orders were received to halt and consolidate what had been won. High Wood was reoccupied by the Germans. It would take two months of bitter and bloody fighting to force the enemy out of the wood and off the ridge.

On the 7th September, the 50th Division had received orders to take over the right sub-sector held by the 15th Scottish Division. This move commenced on the 10th September. The 15th Scottish Division held a line south-west of Martinpuich. On the right was the 50th Division and on its right, the 47th London Division. At this time about half of High Wood was in the hands the British. It was the task of the 47th Division to take the remainder of the wood. The 50th Division held a salient between its two flanking divisions. In this position it was threatened by enfilade fire and flank attacks from the Germans. On the right, the divisional line rested on Sutherland Trench, a communication trench running north and south, which joined Clarke Trench where it met the Bazentine-le-Petit and High Wood Road. The line then ran westward along Clarke Trench and Swansea Trench to join up with the right flank of the 15th Division. The ground occupied by the 50th Division was a tangle of trenches, roads and tracks, which were difficult to negotiate by day or night. The ground was in an appalling state. The huge expenditure of shells had wrecked the land. Innumerable shell holes and craters covered the ground. Trenches and dugouts had been blown in. Two brigades were in the front line, 149 on the right and 150 on the left. No. 151 was in reserve.

The enemy positions facing 50th Division comprised three lines of trenches. The first was Hook Trench. The second line comprised Martin Trench, the Bow and the Starfish Line. The third line was a continuation of the Starfish Line and Pru Trench, running east and south-east from Martinpuich. The Flers Switch Line, a strong German position, ran from the rear of High Wood and along the high ground from the north-east of Delville Wood and Ginchy on the right, to south of Martinpuich on the left.

The Battle of Flers–Courcelette was fought between the 15th and 22nd September. The three British divisions were to attack together. A small number of a new secret weapon – the tank – would be used for the first time in history, though none was available to assist 149 Brigade. The opening artillery and mortar bombardment of the enemy line commenced on the 12th September. At the time of the attack, 47th Division on the right was about 300 yards to the rear of the 50th Division's right flank. The 15th Division on the left was 250 yards to the rear of this division. Major General Wilkinson, G.O.C. 50th Division, had a difficult decision to make. Should he wait until the 15th and 47th Divisions attacked on his open flanks and came up level with him?

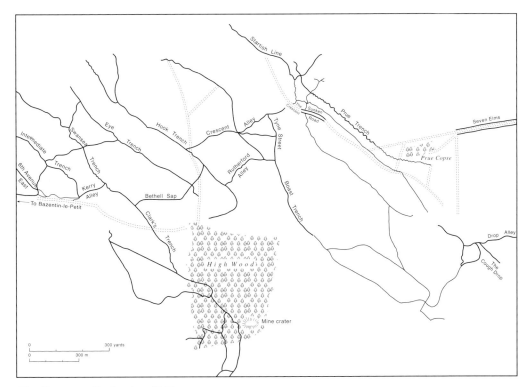

The Somme – September 1916

Or should he attack at the same time when he could greatly assist the two flanking divisions by threatening the enemy rear? He decided to attack immediately. By so doing there is little doubt that the 50th Division did assist their comrades on each flank by threatening the enemy rear. Neither histories of the 15th and 47th Divisions refer to this undoubted assistance given to them by Major General Wilkinson's decision. It was, however, a decision that made the 50th's task much more difficult.

At 6.30 a.m. on the 15th September, the three divisions assaulted the enemy positions. No. 149 Brigade, on the right of the 50th Division, attacked with two battalions, the 4th Bn. Northumberland Fusiliers on the right and the 7th Battalion of this regiment on the left. The first objective was Hook Trench and this was captured about 7 a.m. It was the 50th Division's first experience of a creeping barrage. The divisional artillery was firing from Caterpillar Valley and the valley west of Bazentin-le-Grand Wood. The initial barrage of 18-pdrs. came down 150 yards in front of the divisional front line. It crept forward at 50 yards per minute to a point 200 yards from the first divisional objective. Here the barrage fell for one hour, then it moved on at the same rate to within 200 yards of the second objective, which was Martin Trench, the Bow and part of the Starfish Line. Again it stayed here for an hour and then moved on to the final objective, Pru Trench and the left of the Starfish Line.

After taking Hook Trench in the first half-hour of the attack, 149 Brigade moved on to its next objective, which was part of the Starfish Line. Enemy fire was intense; shell, bomb and bullet fell on the advancing lines of Fusiliers. The 47th Division was locked in deadly conflict in High Wood and was unable to move. Enfilade fire added to the storm of artillery, which fell on the attacking battalions of 149 Brigade. Casualties were very heavy. To gain shelter from the attack, the two battalions frantically dug in. The start of 149's advance towards the Starfish Line was timed for 7.20 a.m. It was late in starting. With the 47th Division still held up in High Wood, the plan was to push ahead and so threaten the enemy rear as to cause them to pull out of the wood. Clouds of thick dust from the dry ground added to the smoke of the exploding shells and bombs, which made vision difficult and did not help the units to maintain direction. The sunken road, south of the Bow, was reached by men of the 7th Bn. Northumberland Fusiliers. They were few in number and very exhausted.

Lieutenant Colonel Bradford led the 9th Battalion from its position in Mametz Wood at 6.20 a.m. on the 15th September. It was attached to 149 Brigade at 12 noon. Two companies were moved to Mill Street and two companies to Chalk Road. The whole battalion moved to Hook Trench at 3 p.m. Battalion headquarters was in Clarke Trench. High Wood was, by now, in the hands of the 47th Division, assisted in no small measure by the action of 149 Brigade. The orders were to assault the Starfish Line and Pru Trench at 6 p.m. The attack was to be made by the 5th Borders and 6th and 9th Bns. D.L.I. This was delayed until 9.40 p.m. Even then the 5th Borders were late in starting due to the appalling destruction of the ground and trenches leading to the line, which caused its guides so much difficulty in locating the jumping-off trenches. Both Durham battalions went ahead in four waves and were met by a storm of rifle and machine gun fire from the flanks. Survivors of the first two waves crossed the Starfish Line and got to within 30 yards of Pru Trench where they dug in. Gradually these small parties were killed, except for four wounded men who managed to crawl back to rejoin the battalion. The men who had reached the Starfish Line were driven out by heavy bombing and rifle fire. The surviving Durhams dug in behind the sunken road south of the Bow, which was held by the Northumberland Fusiliers.

This was Lieutenant Colonel Bradford's first action as commander of the 9th Battalion. His Second in Command, Major Crouch, wrote that Bradford had received a nasty facial wound from a piece of shrapnel:

> But the tenacious spirit of the C.O., which would not be denied the honour of leading his battalion into action, kept him at duty. What he suffered physically by this noble act, he alone knew, but I do know that two months later it was still necessary for the M.O. to dress the wound.

The professional relationship between Bradford and the older and experienced Crouch was quite exceptional. Bradford, young and enthusiastic, was filled with a religious zeal. To him the war was a religious crusade, good against evil, and God was certainly on his side. Crouch was an old experienced soldier who had come up through the ranks. He was more dour and solid, and exercised restraint on his young Commander's more ambitious schemes. The one complemented the other and this successful partnership was founded on a mutual respect of each other. There is no doubt that Bradford was a brilliant soldier and Commander, but he owed much to the support and wise counsel of the experienced Crouch, who was to prove to be a good Battalion Commander when he succeeded Bradford in November 1917.

Bradford quickly stamped his authority and his personality on the battalion. He was a hard taskmaster, particularly to his officers. Any dereliction of duty would bring immediate retribution. Officers who did not measure up to his high standards were quickly removed. Those who did meet his standards earned his complete support. His policy was that the officers' first duty was to the welfare of their men and this endeared him to almost every man in the battalion. His strong personality and quick mind did not always meet the approval of his senior officers. He always spoke his mind and was not shy to give his opinion to senior commanders at brigade and divisional level.

At the end of the first day of action, plans were made for attacks on the following day, the 16th September. A Commanding Officer of another battalion wrote:

> At a meeting of the C.O.s at 8.30 p.m., on that day [15th September], Bradford was present and said very little. A plan of attack was being drawn up by the Brigadier and the hour he had first fixed was, I think 10 a.m. At this point Bradford spoke and said he thought it was too early. It was put off until, I think, 10.30…Bradford during this attack was up in the front line of his battalion and back in Clarke Trench and continually moving about with most surprising vigour. He went forward with one attack and carried a wounded man back under heavy fire to the assembly trench.

This officer's memory of the times of the attack quoted above was somewhat faulty as, according to the battalion War Diary, the attack made by the battalion and the 5th Borders commenced at 9.30 p.m. The assault made on the Starfish Line was again held up by heavy machine gun and rifle fire from the front and flanks.

On the 17th September, two parties of about 50 men, each under the command of Second Lieutenants Bowdery and Thompson, made another attempt to reach the Starfish Line but they too met a wall of murderous machine gun and rifle fire. They did establish a number of shell hole posts about 100 yards in front of the line. Second Lieutenant Bowdery was awarded the Military Cross for his intrepid leadership in this action. On the 18th, in a similar action with about 100 men of the battalion and Captain Oswald's company of the 8th Bn. D.L.I., a further assault was made on the Starfish Line with the same result as the previous day. At 8 p.m. the 9th Battalion was relieved by the 8th and withdrew to Clarke Trench.

Casualties during the period of action were Capt. Robert Rutherford and 2/Lts. Eric Walton and Alfred Lawson; 2/Lt. James Tyler died later of wounds. Another nine officers were wounded. Of the other ranks 44 were killed, 27 were missing (most of these would be dead), and 219 were wounded. This was about 44 per cent of the battalion strength. The battlefield was, by now, a gruesome sight. Shell holes covered the ground, and were quickly filling with mud and water as the rain poured down. Trenches collapsed and men struggled to rebuild them. The bodies of soldiers lay in the open mud with smashed equipment and torn clumps of wire. The great majority of the wounded lay alongside their dead comrades on the soaked battlefield and many died where they lay. The pitiful cries of the wounded preyed on their comrades' nerves as they could not be reached until nightfall. To attempt to reach them during daylight would have led to certain death. Yet stretcher bearers and comrades did try to reach them, attend to their wounds and bring them in to safety. Miraculously some succeeded but many became casualties themselves. Ration parties found it extremely difficult to get to the front line where men were cold, wet and hungry. No fires could be lit to warm body and food.

On the night of the 20th September, 151 Brigade was relieved by 149 and moved to the south-west corner of Mametz Wood and into divisional reserve. A draft of 23 was received whilst in the wood. The battalion remained here until the 25th where it was reorganised and, as usual, according to the War Diary, 'furnished strong working parties'. The 26th and 27th of September were spent in the sad and often unpleasant task of clearing ground and burying the dead on the battlefield.

The 9th Battalion moved into the line again on the 28th, and relieved the 4th Bn. East Yorkshire Regiment. Lieutenant Colonel Bradford's intelligence report for the period 9 a.m. 28th to 9 a.m. 29th September, outlined the day's activities:

> Last night a fire trench was dug from M22d 1.3 to M22c 7.3 [map reference] and a communication trench from M22d 1.3 to M28a 9.6. The fire trench I have called Blaydon Trench and the communication trench Chopwell Avenue. It is regretted that the fire trench was not dug in the position ordered but the officer in charge of the work was wounded when proceeding to the site and the party was very much hampered by artillery and rifle fire. We have Advance Posts at M22d 0.5 and M22d 2.8. We did not get in touch with 8 DLI. At 7.30 a.m. today a party of bombers under an officer [Second Lieutenant Wilson] worked forward along the tramline and endeavoured to effect a lodgement at M22b 2.2. At the same time a party of fifty men under an officer [2/ Lt. W.E. Scott] worked forward and endeavoured to effect a lodgement at M22 1.1. Both parties were discovered and met with heavy machine gun fire and rifle fire and had to retire.
>
> The officers report the line to be very strongly held. They saw about thirty Germans and heard them shout out the alarm. Some of the noblest men in the battalion were killed. A prisoner [21st Bavarian Reserve Regiment] was captured in a shell hole at M22d 1½.3, he was evidently a sniper and was about to fire his rifle when captured. Rutherford Alley from M28b 1.2 was cut through to our line at M28a 9.6. Block built in Crescent Alley at M28b 3.8. The first line of wire about 100 yards in front of enemy trench [Flers Line] is badly damaged and of no account. The second line of wire about 10 yards in front of his trench is very little damaged and is quite formidable. There is a small gap however at M22b 0.1. The enemy has thrown up a lot more earth in front of his parapet during the night. Pru Trench and Crescent Alley were shelled intermittently throughout the night by 7.7-cm and 15-cm [guns]. Our men who dug Chopwell Avenue came in for heavy

shelling throughout the night. Among a large amount of other enemy material in the trench has been found a Fishtail Bombs machine and a box of Fishtail Bombs. We are in telephone conversation with Blaydon Trench.

Six men were killed during these activities including Ptes. George Forbes, Henry Hampton and L/Sgt. James Gregory. 2/Lt. William E.O. Scott went missing and was later reported killed.

The intelligence report for the next 24 hours included the following:

Operations: At 5.57 p.m., a strong officer's patrol endeavoured to effect a lodgement at N22b 2.1. They found the enemy line manned and were unable to enter. A badly wounded German of the 24th Bavarian Reserve Regiment, who had been shot by one of the snipers, was captured by a patrol at M22 3.5. New fire trench was dug from M22d 2.7 to M22c 8.7. Germans made a bombing attack on this trench at 5 a.m. this morning but were driven off…The communication trench, Chopwell Avenue, was continued to fire trench. Blaydon Trench was improved and communication trenches deepened…A machine gun fired on us frequently…The enemy shelled Blaydon Trench heavily from 6 p.m. to 6.30 p.m. with 7.7-cm shells. The whole area between Pru Trench and Blaydon Trench was intermittently shelled throughout the day and night. Our own artillery, both heavy and field, was firing short last evening. It is essential that the F.O.O.[Forward Observation Officer], proceed to our new fire trench about M22 d0.7 to observe the wire cutting of Flers Line wire. The enemy was sending up large numbers of various coloured lights during the night and threw a number of bombs into his own wire at intervals. He was undoubtedly very nervous.

On the 1st October 1916, an assault by four divisions was made on Eaucourt L'Abbaye and the enemy line east and west of that hamlet. The divisions involved from right to left were the 47th, 50th and 23rd Divisions and the New Zealand Division. Zero hour was 3.15 p.m. On the 50th Division front, 149 Brigade was in support and 150 Brigade was in divisional reserve. The attacking 151 Brigade had the 6th Bn. D.L.I. on the right with a composite battalion on the left, made up of companies of the 8th Bn. D.L.I. and the 5th Bn. Border Regiment. The 9th Bn. D.L.I. was in close support behind the 6th Battalion.

On 30th September the divisional artillery commenced a bombardment with the intention of cutting the enemy wire. The enemy artillery retaliated quite vigorously. During the night 30th September/1st October, the divisional artillery switched to a heavy bombardment of the enemy trenches and communications. After darkness, pioneers and infantry completed digging and improving the jumping-off trenches, which were North and South Durham Trenches, Blaydon Trench and Rutherford Avenue. Dumps of ammunition, bombs, water and other essential stores were built. The attacking battalions formed up in their trenches at 6 a.m. There was a nine-and-one-quarter-hour wait ahead of them, a very worrying and stressful time for both officers and men. The enemy artillery retaliation was awaited with some trepidation. Crammed together in the narrow trenches, men were lost in their own thoughts. Conversation was quiet and on any subject but that of the impending attack. N.C.O.s and officers moved amongst the men, checking weapons and equipment. As the time for the attack grew nearer, the tension rose. It was more difficult now to keep thoughts of the action out of the mind. What would it be like? Would the artillery cut the wire and quieten enemy retaliation? Many men wondered whether they would survive or sustain a terrible wound. Many thought of what their loved ones back in England would be doing at this time. The German artillery did not remain inactive, but had quietened during the night. From 10 a.m. to noon it opened up with a heavy bombardment of the front line trenches. Had the Germans suspected that an attack was about to start? Did they know that the trenches opposite were crammed with men? The crouching infantry feared the worst. At noon, the enemy guns slackened and by 3.15 p.m. were quiet. There had been casualties amongst the waiting infantry but not as many as were feared.

At 1.30 p.m. Major Wilkinson, commanding the 6th Bn. D.L.I., was wounded and made his way back to the casualty clearing station for treatment. The Major later wrote:

> On my way back, I went in and saw Colonel Bradford and his Adjutant at his headquarters at Seven Elms and told him of the situation and I suggested to him that he should go up and take command of 6th D.L.I. in addition to the 9th. I told him that it was imperative to have a senior officer up to control matters, as I had no one in my battalion except Lieutenants and 2nd Lieutenants.
>
> I, then, proceeded on my way back and met the Brigadier and his Brigade Major two miles behind, coming up to their Battle Headquarters and I told him what I had arranged with Colonel Bradford and he immediately approved my action.

The British heavily bombarded the German wire and trenches, held by the 17th Bavarian Regiment, from 7 a.m. on the 1st October. This shelling gradually intensified until 3.15 p.m. When the infantry left their trenches, they followed a wall of exploding shells. The advance was made in good order. The 6th Battalion took the first line of German trenches but failed to gain touch with the 47th Division on its right. This division had dropped behind its barrage, which was now well ahead of the advancing infantry and was now suffering heavy casualties from the German counter-fire. The advance slowed and it was unable to reach its objective, Eaucourt L'Abbaye. The 6th Battalion had its right flank exposed due to the failure of the 47th Division to reach its objective. It was now subjected to intense enfilade fire from enemy machine guns and suffered heavy casualties. It had a precarious footing in Flers Trench. At this critical stage, Lieutenant Colonel Bradford appeared having crossed no man's land under heavy enemy artillery fire. He rallied the battalion and ordered and supervised the building of a block in the right flank trench. Two companies of the 9th Battalion were ordered forward to reinforce the 6th and they reached the front line about 9.30 p.m. The reinforced Durhams moved forward and took the second line of trenches. This was accomplished by 1 a.m. on the 2nd October and another trench block was built to

Lt. Col. Roland Boys Bradford V.C., M.C.

counter enemy attacks and enfilade fire. The brigade position was, as it had been on the 15th September, a salient with its right flank up in the air. These two blocks were subjected to vicious bombing attacks from the enemy as they strove to drive the Durhams out who, in their turn, met bomb with bomb and would not be moved. The 9th Battalion War Diary states:

> The 47th Division did not gain their objectives on our right and the enemy is holding the trenches strongly. Bomb fighting of a severe nature raged round our blocks on our right

flank for 24 hours but all attempts to eject us were repulsed.

A German breakthrough on this exposed flank would have had the most serious repercussions. Certainly 151 Brigade front would have been rolled up. This, in turn, would have opened up the rest of the British line to enemy enfilade fire and attack. That this failed to happen was due to the obstinacy and fierce fighting qualities of the 6th and 9th Battalions, led by their young Commander. Lieutenant Colonel Bradford was everywhere and conspicuous in the very centre of the action, giving out orders, firing the men's spirits and confidence with his presence, and leading very much from the front. Major Veitch, 8th Bn. D.L.I., visited Bradford's headquarters soon after the battle. He wrote:

> Lt. Colonel Bradford was first recommended for the D.S.O. by Brigadier Gen. Cameron [151 Brigade] but as full details of this action became known, this recommendation was withdrawn and he was recommended for the V.C. instead. On the 1st October, immediately after the successful attack, I went to his headquarters at 'Seven Elms', about half a mile in front of High Wood. Colonel Bradford had only a short time before returned from leading the attack and I was astonished to find him looking as though he had just stepped out of his tailors. Looking at him it was difficult to realise that less than an hour before he had been in the thick of the fighting. It was all in keeping with his strong belief in the moral effect of his presence and appearance on those he came in contact with. He certainly inspired confidence in everyone who saw him at that time when things were decidedly uncomfortable and very uncertain. It was a little thing but I came away feeling that everything was alright. In other words, 'It did us all good to see him.'

Roland Boys Bradford was awarded the Victoria Cross to go with the Military Cross he had won when serving with the 2nd Bn. D.L.I. earlier in the war. The citation appeared in the London Gazette on Saturday, 25th November 1916:

> Lt. (temp. Lieut. Col.) Roland Boys Bradford M.C., Durham Light Infantry, for most conspicuous bravery and good leadership in attack, whereby he saved the situation on the right flank of his brigade and of the division. Lt. Col. Bradford's battalion was in support. A leading battalion had suffered very severe casualties and, the commander being wounded, its flank became dangerously exposed at close quarters to the enemy. Raked by machine gun fire, the situation of the battalion became critical. At the request of the wounded commander, Lt. Col. Bradford asked permission to command the exposed battalion in addition to his own. Permission granted, he at once proceeded to the foremost lines. By his fearless conduct under fire of all description and his skilful leadership of the two battalions, regardless of all danger, he succeeded in rallying the attack, captured and defended the objective and so secured the flank.

His popularity with his men was considerable. When the award was announced the battalion lay at Mellincourt on the Somme. He was cheered and carried shoulder high and all of his appeals to be put down were drowned in the cries, 'Speech, speech!' In a short speech to his officers and men, he said that he did not look upon this as an

IN MEMORY
OF THE GALLANT OFFICERS N.C.O,
AND MEN OF THE 9TH BATTALION
THE DURHAM LIGHT INF.TRY
WHO FELL IN ACTION SEP.15TH 16TH
OCT 1ST 1916

DULCE ET DECORUM EST.
PRO PATRIA MORI.

ERECTED IN AFFECTIONATE REMEMBRANCE
BY THEIR FRIENDS WHO FOUGHT WITH THEM AND
WHO WILL EVER KEEP THEIR MEMORY GREEN.

THIS IS A DRAWING OF THE CROSS WHICH WE ERECTED TO OUR
FRIENDS WHO WERE KILLED DURING THE GREAT ADVANCE.

Roland Bradford.

COMMANDING 9TH BATTALION
THE DURHAM LIGHT INFANTRY.

award to him personally but in recognition of the work of the whole battalion.

The front line of the 6th and 9th Battalions made contact with the composite battalion of the 8th Bn. D.L.I./5th Bn. Border Regiment on the left. Two uncommitted companies of the 9th Battalion were working with great energy on the communication trench, and Rutherford Alley was extended through to the second objective. Lt. E.R. Heslop was wounded during this work. The right flank of the Durhams' line had now exposed the enemy trenches to enfilade fire. The British now fired two Stokes mortars in addition to Lewis guns and Vickers machine guns into enemy positions with deadly effect. The battalion snipers were very active and recorded 50 hits between 7 and 9 a.m. on the 2nd October. Four wounded and six unwounded prisoners were taken, all belonging to the 17th Reserve Bavarian Regiment. However, it was impossible to push patrols forward due to enemy snipers firing from the Le Sars area, which made any movement in the open virtually impossible. No further progress could be made and the heavy bomb fighting around the trench blocks continued throughout the day. At 6.20 p.m., the Germans were seen to be assembling with a view to launching a counter-attack. This was broken up by a heavy artillery bombardment and by fire from all arms. The enemy made a further attempt to rush the blocks at 8 p.m. but was again driven off. Heavy rain fell throughout the 2nd October turning the trenches into channels of deep mud. Enemy artillery and mortar fire caused extensive damage to trenches. The conditions were, by now, quite appalling.

Enemy bombing attacks against the blocks eased as the day drew to a close.

During the night of the 2nd/3rd October, the communication trench from North Durham Trench to the front line was deepened and widened. There was little rest for the already exhausted troops. Damaged trenches had to be repaired before the morning light. Supplies of food and other necessities were brought up. The battalion War Diary stated:

> Enemy artillery was active throughout the day and night. He did not, however, attempt to shell our captured lines – perhaps was content to let our own heavy artillery do this. He shelled Blaydon Trench, North Durham Trench, Rutherford Alley…

It was obvious that the heavy British artillery was unaware that the Durhams now held the enemy front line. Frantic communication to the rear ultimately informed the artillery of its error and the firing ceased. Fortunately no casualties due to this 'friendly fire' were reported.

At 5.30 a.m. on the 3rd October, the battalion was relieved by the 7th Bn. Northumberland Fusiliers (149 Brigade). The journey, made by the relieving battalion from Pru Trench to the front line, took eight hours, for a distance of under a mile. This was due to the dreadful weather, which had turned the ground into a sea of mud and waterlogged shell holes. Progress was painfully slow and sapped the energy of the heavily laden troops. Enemy artillery, which was very active, did not help matters. It was 6.30 in the evening when the 9th Battalion reached Pru Trench on its way out of the line.

The battalion's casualties were not as heavy as expected, though, it must be remembered, only two companies were involved in the most severe fighting at Eaucourt L'Abbaye where the brunt of the action fell on the 6th Battalion. Between the 1st and 3rd October, seven other ranks were killed and 48 wounded. The dead included Ptes. Patrick Corcoran, James Turpin and Norman Edminson.

Amongst the awards won during this action was the Distinguished Conduct Medal to Cpl. C.T.A. Campbell who, 'held a block alone for one hour against several enemy bombing attacks. Later, he greatly assisted in repelling an enemy counter-attack.' Pte. S.J. Sterry, who had won the Distinguished Conduct Medal earlier in the year, was awarded the Military Medal 'for devotion to duty and capable handling of the wounded during three days of battle. During these three days, he was without food and sleep and weakened by his strenuous work and suffering from three wounds.' The Distinguished Conduct Medal was also awarded to L/Cpl. M. Lee. Capt. Robert Mauchlen won the Military Cross in the Eaucourt L'Abbaye action. He designed the Memorial Cross, which was erected on the Butte de Warlencourt to those who had fought and died in that action in November, 1916. This very same cross can now be seen in the regimental chapel in Durham Cathedral.

At 12 noon on the 3rd, the 9th Battalion left Pru Trench for Bécourt Wood. The following day, it moved to Hénincourt Wood for a few days' rest. Whilst they were here an order of the day was received from Maj. Gen. P.S. Wilkinson, C.B., C.M.G., commanding the 50th Division:

> Nobody could be prouder than I am at commanding such troops as you of the 50th Division.
>
> Within a few days of landing in this Country you made a name for yourselves at the Second Battle of Ypres. Since that battle you have gained a great reputation on account of your magnificent defence of a portion of the Ypres Salient during the worst months of the year.
>
> From the 15th September to October 3rd, you have had another chance of showing your qualities in attack and it is not too much to say that no Division in the British Army has, or could have, done better.
>
> You have advanced nearly two miles and have taken seven lines of German trenches. Your gallantry and determination on every occasion since you joined in the Battle of the Somme has been worthy of the highest traditions of the British Army.
>
> I deplore with you the loss of many of our intimate friends and comrades.
>
> I thank you for the excellent and cheerful way in which you have undertaken every task put to you.

As the battalion approached its wooded camp, it heard the battalion band playing the regimental march in the distance. As occurred in peacetime England, the band met the troops a short distance from camp and led them in. Backs stiffened and shoulders were thrown back and these tired yet determined men pushed their weary legs to the beat of the light infantry pace. Their regimental pride was undiminished. The band had recently been formed from those bandsmen still with the battalion and the numbers were made up from other ranks who had played with their local Salvation Army band prior to the outbreak of the war. Lieutenant Colonel Bradford had pressured higher authority to get permission to form a battalion band and had received instruments and music from the home county. An unnamed witness wrote:

> Incidentally, the band that night was conducted by the then R.S.M. (name not remembered) under the light of a hurricane lamp, an occasional shell explosion or crump giving an extra percussion to the aid of the big drums and cymbals.
>
> Subsequently augmented by bugles and drums, the band played a great part in the training and morale structure of the Battalion.
>
> On one occasion when the Battalion was somewhere near the town of Cassel, headquarters of Gen. Plumer who commanded the Second Army, the battalion marched through the streets of this small hillside town. With the Band and Drums playing, Companies marching to attention at the trail it must have done Second Army Headquarters good to behold such a well-trained Battalion with Roland Boys Bradford at its head mounted on his famous grey charger.
>
> The Band was not a separate detachment but were stretcher bearers in the companies collecting together when the Battalion was 'out of the line'. Those at Battalion Headquarters during operations were also used as working parties to take up rations to the

companies.

Lieutenant Colonel Bradford was also instrumental in forming the battalion concert party, The Green Diamonds, which put on concerts for the officers and men of the battalion.

Hénincourt Wood was an excellent camp with canvas huts and tents erected amongst the trees. Over the next week, training, refitting and reorganising took place. On the 11th October, the 9th Battalion received sudden orders to move up to the south-west corner of Mametz Wood to another tented camp. For the following three days, the battalion was put to work on maintaining and repairing roads around Contalmaison. On the 14th, it returned to Hénincourt Wood. Here, drafts were received and a hard training programme commenced. On the 23rd, it moved to Bécourt Wood. It rained heavily over the next two days.

The battalion was now up to full strength with 41 officers and 1,011 other ranks. However, of these, 32 officers and 870 other ranks were actually present in the battalion; the remainder were elsewhere with working parties. Orders were received on the 25th October to move to Bazentin-le-Grand and relieve a battalion of the 9th Division. It was not an easy relief as, after marching towards this village across the battered and soaking ground, it was ordered to retrace its steps and relieve the 7th Bn. King's Own Scottish Borderers in Mametz Wood. The 50th Division had, by now, relieved the 9th Division in the front line. No. 151 Brigade was in divisional reserve in the wood; 149 and 150 Brigades were in the front line. The divisional line ran from the Martinpuich–Warlencourt road on the left, to a boundary north of Eaucourt L'Abbaye on the right. Incessant rain and shellfire had turned no man's land into a quagmire of knee- and even thigh-deep mud. Any troops attempting to cross it under enemy fire would, almost certainly, be going to their deaths. On the 27th, the whole battalion was employed working on the road from High Wood to Bazentin-le-Petit. The weather and ground conditions were awful. The War Diary for the last few days of October stated:

> Same Place [Mametz Wood]. Working parties everyday. In spite of wretched weather and very poor quarters (tents and dugouts – both soaking inside), the spirits of the men are high and their keenness undismayed. There is every prospect of being in battle again in the course of the next few days.

On the 30th and 31st October, the weather was warmer but heavy rainstorms and gale force winds, particularly at night, were soaking the ground over which the attack would be made and deepening and thickening the mud. In such conditions no attack could be made and it was postponed.

During the 1st and 2nd November, working parties of the whole battalion were sent to repair Rutherford Alley. On the 3rd, the battalion moved into the front line to relieve the 5th Bn. Yorkshire Regiment. This relief was completed by 9 p.m. The attack on the Gird and Gird Support Trenches and the Butte de Warlencourt was fixed to start

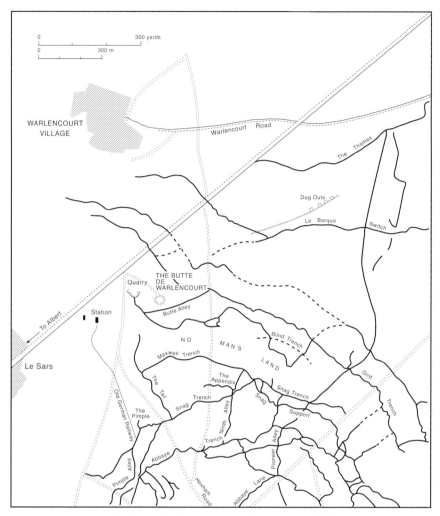

The Butte de Walencourt – 5 November 1916

at 9.10 a.m. on the 5th November. The attacking battalions from right to left were 8th, 6th and 9th Bns. D.L.I. They were to assemble in Snag Trench, Snag Support, Maxwell Trench and Tail Trench. The 6th and 8th Battalions were to take Gird and Gird Support and the 9th was to take the Butte. The 151st Machine Gun Company provided two guns with each attacking battalion with a further six guns in support and four in reserve. The 28th Australian Battalion was to attack on the right of the 8th Battalion. By now the trenches were some two feet deep in mud and water and were without trench boards.

The Butte de Warlencourt was a raised mound about 40 feet in height, reputed to be an ancient burial place. It had lost its vegetation in the shelling during the weeks prior to the attack. Now it stood out, as a conical shaped hill, chalk white against the surrounding mud covered countryside. Whilst the Butte provided the enemy with good observation of the ground towards High Wood and Martinpuich, it was not, at this time, considered of great military value. It did, however, lie in the path of the advance and, it seems, no one had given consideration to going round it and isolating it, leaving the enemy forces dug into the Butte to be mopped up later. It was to be taken by frontal assault.

Lieutenant Colonel Bradford planned to attack with 'A', 'B' and 'C' Companies in four waves, 30 paces between each wave. The objectives included the Butte and the quarry lying in front of it and parts of Gird Trench and Gird Support. These companies assembled in Maxwell Trench. 'D' Company was in The Tail and would move forward to Maxwell Trench as soon as the other companies left it. Battalion headquarters was in Hexham Road.

The night before the attack was dreadful. Heavy rain and gale force wind made the move up to the assembly trenches a nightmare. The men were heavily laden and moved through mud in some parts thigh deep. They stood in the trenches soaked through, shivering with cold and covered in mud waiting for zero hour. Twice the enemy put down a heavy barrage on Maxwell Trench and The Tail. By 6 a.m. on the 5th November, all companies were in position. Unknown to the British, the enemy was about to relieve the 24th Bavarian Division in the line with the 1st Guards Reserve Division. At the time of the action, both of these divisions would be in a position to meet the assault.

At 9.10 a.m. the three battalions of 151 Brigade commenced their assault, along with the Australian battalion on the extreme right. The mud was so deep and the ground so slippery that the first men out had to turn and pull those that followed them out of the trench. The lines of attacking infantry formed up and, at a slow walking

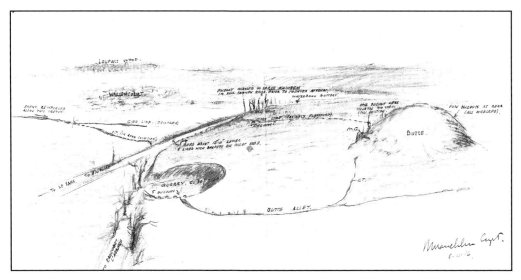

Capt. R. Mauchlen's sketch of the Butte and surrounds

pace, forced their legs through the clinging mud and moved towards the enemy lines some 250 to 300 yards away. Both the 8th Battalion and the Australians quickly became bogged down and suffered heavy losses from murderous machine gun fire from the right flank. Both of these battalions were soon back in the jumping-off trenches. The right company of the 6th Battalion suffered a similar fate. The left company, alongside the 9th Battalion, had some success and passed over two lines of German trenches and established a block in the Gird Line. Its right flank was now up in the air due to the failure of the 8th Battalion and the Australians to come up alongside.

Lieutenant Colonel Bradford described these events in his report:

> On the left the 9th D.L.I. met with less opposition and succeeded in gaining all its objectives without suffering heavy casualties. The German barrage came down at about four minutes after [the start of the attack].
>
> At 10 a.m. the 9th D.L.I. was disposed as follows: Four Posts were established in the Gird Front Line, the left one being on the Albert–Bapaume Road. There were four Posts in the space between the Butte and the Gird Front Line. The front edge of the Quarry was strongly held and two Company Headquarters were situated in the Quarry in telephonic communication with Battalion Headquarters. Each of the assaulting platoons had a reserve platoon in Butte Alley, the trench running immediately South of the Butte. Two machine guns were sited in Butte Alley and a 2" Stokes Mortar in the Quarry. Two Battalion Observers were on the Butte. The Reserve Company of the Battalion was in

Attack on the Butte de Warlencourt, 5 November 1916 as sketched by Capt. R. Mauchlen M.C.

Maxwell Trench. Eight Bavarian prisoners had been sent back to Battalion Headquarters. Some other prisoners who were on their way back had, together with their escort, been annihilated by the German artillery fire. The Germans were still holding a dugout on the north east side of the Butte. The Parties who should have 'mopped up' the Butte dugouts had either gone forward without completing their work, carried away in the enthusiasm of the assault, or had been shot by German snipers while at their work.

The Germans had now realised the scope of our attack and many of their batteries concentrated their fire on our new positions. Snipers from Warlencourt–Eaucourt were subjecting our men to a deadly fire and it was almost impossible for them to move.

The Germans in the dugout on the north east edge of the Butte had brought a machine gun into position and were worrying us from behind. Many gallant attempts were made throughout the day to capture this dugout but without success. All our parties, who tried to rush it were destroyed by the German machine gun fire and the large number of snipers in Warlencourt. However a party did succeed in throwing some Mills grenades into the dugout and this made the Boche more cautious.

The first German counter attack was made about 12 noon. It was a half hearted one and was easily stopped. During the afternoon the enemy launched several bombing attacks but these too were repulsed.

The initial task had met with success. Despite the mud the assaulting companies had moved over and round the Butte and broke into the German line beyond. One of the long remembered incidents in the early stages, as the men advanced up and over the Butte, was the sight of a solitary figure of a member of the 9th Battalion on the top of the mound. Here, he paused for a moment, looked back (some eyewitnesses said that he waved) and then disappeared down the other side. A further amazing sight was of a drunken German soldier staggering down the Albert–Bapaume Road and into the British positions. Evidently, he had had enough and gave himself up.

The heavily reinforced enemy counter-attacked after 3 p.m. Gradually the battalion was forced back. At 3.30 p.m. it held a line which stretched round the north of the Quarry to Butte Alley, south of the Butte, and then by shell hole positions to where the 6th Battalion had its block. At 5 p.m., Lieutenant Colonel Bradford reported to brigade:

We have been driven out of Gird Front Line. I believe my Posts there were captured. I have tried to get back but the enemy is in considerable force and is still counter attacking. It is taking me all my time to hold Butte Alley. Please ask artillery to shell North of Bapaume Road in M10d and M11c as Germans are in considerable force there. Enemy is holding Gird Front Line strongly on my right. In my opinion strong advance to the right of the Butte would meet with success.

Have a small Post in a shell hole at the North West corner of the Butte but the enemy still has a Post on the Butte on the North side. I am just going to make another effort to capture this Post.

This was obviously the machine gun post referred to above, which gave considerable problems throughout the day and was never taken. Desperate hand-to-hand fighting took place during the afternoon. The officers and men of the 9th Battalion were now extremely weary and had suffered heavy losses. After four hours of sustained and heavy bombardment from the enemy artillery, a final counter-attack was launched against the battalion positions. Lieutenant Colonel Bradford's final report included:

> At about 11 p.m. Battalions of the Prussians delivered a fresh counter attack. They came in great force from our front and also worked round from both flanks. Our men were overwhelmed. Many died fighting. Others were compelled to surrender. It was only a handful of men who found their way back to Maxwell Trench and they were completely exhausted by their great efforts and the strain of the fighting.

A final message from Brigade at 12.20 a.m. on the 6th November spelled out the position:

> We have been driven out of Butte Alley by a strong attack and 9 D.L.I. and 6 D.L.I. are now in Maxwell Trench. Enemy are in great force and we cannot get back to Butte Alley. All our Posts are captured or driven back.

The task set 151 Brigade had all the ingredients of failure. Once again the brigade was attacking a powerful enemy position with both of its flanks in the air. The British division on its left was not attacking. The failure of the troops on the right meant that that flank also lay open to enemy enfilade fire and attack. The failure of the flanks meant that the battalions attacked a small area only. The Germans, who had better observation posts, could concentrate all their firepower over this area, and they could intensify their fire as the situation developed. The terrific enemy artillery response cut off the attacking force from its reinforcements as a wall of shells descended on the support and reserve trenches. Also, some 400 yards to the rear of the Butte, the Germans had the advantage of a steep bank behind which they could assemble counter-attacking forces relatively unseen and undisturbed. In addition to all this, the deep clinging mud exhausted the troops and made it too difficult to dig in or consolidate captured ground.

Lieutenant Colonel Bradford, ever willing to voice his opinions, had the final say in his report to Brigade and division after the battle:

> It is wonderful, when one considers the difficulties under which our men were working and the fearful fire to which they were exposed, that they held on for so long as they did. And it makes you proud to be an Englishman.
>
> On looking back to the attack of the 5th of November, it seems that the results which would have been gained in the event of success were of doubtful value, and would hardly have been worth the loss which we would suffer. It would have been awkward for us to hold the objective which would have been badly sited for our defence. The possession of the Butte by the Germans was not an asset to them. From our existing trenches we were able to prevent them from using it as an observation point.
>
> The Butte itself would have been of little use to us for purposes of observation.
>
> But the Butte de Warlencourt had become an obsession. Everybody wanted it. It loomed large in the minds of the soldiers in the forward area and they attributed many of

their misfortunes to it. The newspaper correspondents talked about 'that Miniature Gibraltar'. So it had to be taken.

It seems that the attack was one of those tempting and, unfortunately at one period, frequent local operations which are so costly and which are rarely worthwhile.

But perhaps that is only the narrow view of the Regimental Officer.

Bradford had made his point in his usual forthright manner.

At 4 p.m. on the 6th, the enemy opened up with a heavy bombardment on Maxwell Trench, which sheltered the 94 officers and men who had come out of the battle and the many wounded who could not be moved. Enemy snipers made movement across the ground virtually impossible. At 11 p.m., the 9th Battalion was relieved by the 5th Bn. D.L.I. (150 Brigade) and moved to the camp in the north-east corner of Mametz Wood, arriving there at 3 a.m. on the 7th. The relief, made in darkness, was very difficult. Enemy shelling was so heavy that the relieving battalion had to take cover in Pimple Alley until it subsided. The ground was a morass of mud, water and shell holes.

During the day and evening of the 5th November, the Germans had lost heavily, a great number being killed. The battalion losses were very high also: six officers killed, eight wounded and three missing, 36 other ranks were killed, over 220 were wounded and 154 missing. Many of the missing were later found among the dead. Total brigade casualties numbered 38 officers and 929 other ranks. Amongst the dead officers were 2/Lts. C.E. Higginbotham and Samuel Paxton. Some of the dead are buried in the nearby Warlencourt Military Cemetery on the Albert–Bapaume Road.

There would be many letters to be written to bereaving families after the action. Lieutenant Colonel Bradford wrote personally to the family of 2/Lt. Thomas E. Coulson, whose award of the Military Cross was announced in

2/Lt. Thomas E. Coulson M.C.

the *London Gazette* on the 10th June 1920:

> Dear Sir,
>
> You will have heard that your son is missing. On November 5th my battalion carried out an attack on the enemy positions near Warlencourt.
>
> Your son led his men with the greatest gallantry to the objective and was wounded shortly after gaining it. The wound was in the shoulder and was thought by those near him not to be serious.
>
> The Prussian guards made a strong counter attack and drove us out of the captured lines. Your son fell into enemy hands.
>
> A great deal of heavy bomb fighting took place prior to our retirement and it is quite likely that he was killed. I sincerely hope that he is alive and a prisoner.
>
> He was a very brave and efficient officer and had acquitted himself nobly during the severe fighting my Battalion has been through during the last three months. His men loved him and would have done anything for him. I was very fond of the boy and had decided to make him my Adjutant. I know what anxiety the news will have caused you and you have my utmost sympathy.

Fortunately for this family, the son was taken prisoner and survived the war. Lieutenant Coulson was from High Spen and commanded 'C' Company in the attack on the Butte. He was actually wounded by a bullet through the left lung, the results of which he suffered throughout the rest of his life. He had also been Mentioned In Despatches on two earlier occasions.

The battalion stayed in Mametz Wood until the 15th November. The tents stood in a sea of mud amongst the

From the top of the Butte de Warlencourt, officers survey the ground over which the 9th Battalion attcked on 5 November 1916.

desolation and destruction of that sad place. Officers and men already exhausted by the severe fighting they had experienced were still put to work, building huts and repairing roads. They were also subjected to occasional outbursts of enemy shelling. On the 15th November, Pte. Albert Nelson was killed. The first winter frosts appeared on the 9th of the month. The period of 'rest' had not been enough to lift the exhaustion from which the men suffered. On the 16th, the battalion marched off to Millencourt, a camp with good tent accommodation. It left behind a working party which had been sent to Meault to unload ammunition at the railway siding. The party remained at Millencourt until the end of the month. New drafts arrived amounting to five officers and 219 men. Company and battalion training commenced and working parties were supplied every Wednesday and Saturday.

On the 1st December, the 9th Battalion arrived at Warloy for a longer period of rest and was billeted in old, dilapidated barns on farms in the area. The weather was cold and wet and the men were most uncomfortable. The period until the end of December was largely taken up with a rigorous training programme. 2/Lt. C.H. Wade organised an inter-company football competition. On the 13th, a brigade football league commenced. The first game against the 151st Machine Gun Company resulted in a 1–0 defeat for the battalion. The team found its feet and defeated the 151st Trench Mortar Battery 6–2. 'H.Q.' Company won the league. Sport continued and the battalion cross-country team won the brigade competition, which was held on the 24th December. Turkeys were not available for the Christmas Day dinner but pigs were an acceptable replacement. Extra Christmas items were received from home – puddings, cigarettes, sweets and so on.

Pte. Jack McCutcheon wrote a letter on Christmas Day, to his mother at 3, Buddle Terrace, Hendon, Sunderland:

> We are still lying at the same place and we are having a holiday today. We are having a special dinner cooked for us and there are football matches on. Just after I had posted my last letter to you I received a small parcel from my aunt Maggie, there were a pair of mittens and a bit tobacco in it, which were the very things I wanted and they were welcome…Well mother I have just come from dinner and a right good one it has been. We had pork and apple sauce, potatoes, Christmas pudding and nuts and a pint of beer.

The battalion moved to Albert on the 28th December. On this day, the 50th Division relieved the 1st Division in the right sector of the line held by III Corps. The billets in Albert were very good and comfortable. On the 29th, a concert was held in the cinema hall, which the troops thoroughly enjoyed. On the 30th, the battalion moved to Bazentin-le-Petit, which was by now a village of Nissen huts occupied by the army as all civilians had fled and their homes had been totally destroyed. The huts were very cold, especially at night. Snow had fallen and the days were bright and invigorating. On the following day, enemy shells fell on the camp and surrounding area. At midday, one shell landed outside a hut occupied by members of 'C' Company. Pte. Albert

Jackson was killed and five men were wounded.

At 4 p.m., the battalion went into the front line trenches at Factory Corner. It occupied a line of 16 posts in an old trench with 30–80 yards between each. The trenches were wet, muddy and cold. Shelters provided were crudely built and not weatherproof. The 2nd Australian Infantry Battalion was on the right and the 5th Bn. Northumberland Fusiliers on the left. The line lay opposite La Barque. Battalion head-quarters were at Factory Corner. Here the 9th Battalion saw in the New Year, 1917.

The weather for the start of January was warm and damp. The countryside was covered with a blanket of snow in which tree stumps stood out as did the occasional wooden cross marking a grave. This was no Christmas Card view. Patrols wore white clothing as camouflage as they moved about no man's land. The great danger was of footprints, which could reveal the presence and direction of a patrol to the enemy. Pte. Robert Bryce was killed on the 3rd January. On the 4th, Capt. P. Boynton and battalion Medical Officer Capt. J.A.C. Scott were awarded the Military Cross for bravery during the November fighting. Conditions in the line were very uncomfortable and trench feet began to affect the men. The usual treatment immediately commenced, namely, whale oil, dry socks regularly issued and thigh-length gumboots. The gumboots were not par-ticularly effective, as they were not too comfortable and the mud tended to cling to them and make movement more exhausting than it was in boots and puttees. On the night of the 4th/5th January, the battalion was relieved by the 8th Bn. D.L.I. and moved to Camp Site 1 at Bazentine-le-Petit.

On the night of the 8th/9th January, the battalion moved into the support trenches where it relieved the 6th Battalion. The following day, 124 reinforcements arrived at Baizieux Training Camp. Further smaller drafts of officers and other ranks were received during the month. On the 12th/13th, the battalion moved to High Wood West Camp. The camp was shelled on the 16th January and one shell fell on a hut occupied by men of 'B' Company. Nine men were killed, 16 wounded and taken to hospital and five were wounded but remained on duty. Pte. Jack McCutcheon described the condi-tions in a letter to his mother dated 13th January 1917:

I received your parcel in the trenches on the 11.1.17 and I thank you very much for it. The pipe and pouch are just the very thing. I have just had a bath and I am going to rub myself with the pomade and if it is all right it will take a load off my back as the beggars [lice] have trunks on them like elephants. Well dear mother I have just come out of the trenches for the second time and I can tell you it is very rough and it is marvellous how a chap escapes being knocked out. One night there were six of us standing together when a shell dropped at our feet but it did not explode being what the lads call a dud but you can guess we all thanked God for our escape. We were not so fortunate this time up as we had sev-eral killed and a lot injured from shellfire. When in the trenches it is a case of working day and night and when you do get a chance of a sleep you get into a dug out which is about seven or eight inches deep in mud, so that you will have an idea what it is like…Well dear mother I don't know whether we are getting the best of it, but I do know when he sends one shell our artillery send six over. We are getting very fair grub but at the same time your loaf came in extra. Well dear mother as I have no more news I will have to close hoping it is God's good grace to allow me to return home all right when it is all over, which I hope will be soon.

The pomade sent to Pte. McCutcheon by his mother seems to have alleviated the problem of the lice as he wrote in a following letter that, 'I gave your pomade a trial and I have not been bothered with the lice since using it.'

The battalion moved to the front line trenches on the night of the 16th/17th and relieved the 6th Battalion. 'B' Company occupied eight posts on the left and 'D' Company was in eight posts on the right. 'A' Company was in support with 'C' Company in reserve. Battalion headquarters was at Factory Corner. During the relief heavy enemy shelling killed one man and wounded four others. 2/Lt. T. Hall was wounded and evacuated to hospital. Lieutenant Colonel

Pte. Jack McCutcheon, later killed in action

Bradford and Capt. J.A.C. Scott (R.A.M.C.) were both wounded but remained on duty. After a short spell in the support trenches, the 9th Battalion was relieved by the 6th Australian Infantry Battalion (1st Australian Division) and moved to Camp Site 4 at Bazentin-le-Petit. On the 27th of the month, it moved to Camp Site 'C' at Bécourt. Two days later it moved to Ribemont and into poor and overcrowded billets, and stayed here until mid-February. During the stay further reinforcements arrived and training continued. On the 3rd February, Distinguished Conduct Medals were awarded to Sgts. J.W. Goffin and W. Craig for devotion to duty and gallantry during the recent fighting.

On the 10th February, the battalion moved to Hamel. Two days later it moved to Foucaucourt, a village that had been destroyed but had good shelter in huts and cellars. The 50th Division had relieved the 35th and 36th French Divisions on the right of the British line. The British front had been extended on the request of the French. The trenches were some four miles from Foucaucourt where 151 Brigade lay in reserve. They were approached along the road to Peronne, through the village of Estrées to near Berny. The French communications trenches were deep but, as they were without revetments, collapsed in heavy rain. As a result, all movement had to be made over the open – a decidedly risky activity. The front line trenches faced Genermont, Sucérie, St. Christ and Marchelepot. They were not far away from the banks of the River Somme. At Foucaucourt battalion training continued.

On the night of the 19th/20th February, the battalion moved into the support trenches at Berny to relieve the 4th Bn. East Yorkshires. Although these trenches were very wet and muddy due to a winter thaw, the dugouts were in good condition. The enemy artillery was active, alternating with a few shells on the trenches to quite lively but short bombardments. German snipers were, however, a constant problem and care had to be taken in moving about during the day.

There was light enemy shelling during the 21st February. The highlight of the day was the capture of a German Sergeant Major of the 41st Regiment, 221st Division. He had, evidently, been on a trench mortar course and had lost his way in the mist and walked into the battalion's trenches. Clean and smartly dressed, one can only imagine his dismay on being 'invited' to stay. Rumours began to reach the trenches that the Germans were retiring further to the north. This was the German retirement in February and March 1917 to the Hindenburg Line. This retirement must have been particularly galling to the officers and men of 151 Brigade who had sacrificed so much and lost so many comrades in November of 1916 trying to take ground which the Germans now gave up without a fight.

Two men were killed on the 23rd of the month; Pte. Harry Wray and Pte. William John Kew. The 9th Battalion relieved the 8th Bn. D.L.I. in the front line on the night of the 23rd/24th. The trenches had collapsed in places and much strenuous and urgent work had to be carried out to make them passable. The wet and muddy conditions were affecting the men's health and many were reporting sick. Uniforms were soaking and trench feet virulent. The common treatment for trench feet – whale oil – was proving to be of little use in combating this scourge. Abandoned as a cure, a further use for whale oil was found: frying potatoes in a mess tin over an alcohol stove. This gave the potatoes a strong flavour which, evidently, some of the men seemed to like.

Though the enemy was now retiring to the Hindenburg Line to the north, the 50th Division was not involved as no retirement was taking place on its front. Patrols went out regularly to the enemy front line to find out whether any retirement was taking place, but the Germans were still in occupation and very alert. On the 28th February, relieved by the 8th Battalion, the 9th Battalion moved to the Camp Des Pommiers at Foucaucourt. On arrival the rest of the day was spent in cleaning clothing and equipment.

The battalion was back in the front line on the night of the 3rd/4th March. 'A', 'B' and 'C' Companies occupied the front line trenches with 'D' Company in support. The War Diary entry for the 4th March reads:

> 2.35 a.m. A party of two officers (2/Lts. J.R. Thompson and J.T. Bailes) and 70 ORs left our line at T9.c.3.0 [map location] with the intention of raiding the enemy's trenches on the northern edge of Dragon Wood. The party crossed No Man's Land without being noticed. Zero hour was at 3.45 a.m. At this time the party had just reached the Sunken Road at T15.a.5.5, artillery and machine guns opened up with deadly accuracy on the boundaries of the portion to be raided. The noise drowned any sound which the raiding

party might have made as they rapidly cut a way through the wire obstacles and stealthily crossed the remaining 15 yards. They entered the enemy's trench at T1.5.a.55.40 without being observed. The party broke away then, half going to the right and half to the left. One German was found on sentry duty and five others were taken, some of whom were found in a dugout. At 3.55 a.m. the party withdrew and rapidly made their way along the tape which had been laid on the outward journey, entering our trench at the starting point.

Casualties NIL.

The six prisoners revealed a certain amount of valuable information. They belonged to the 3rd Coy, 1st Bn, 10th Grenadier Regt, 11th Division. The enemy trench was dry, trench boarded, deep and well revetted. No hostile artillery or machine guns replied. At dawn this morning, stretcher bearers were observed behind the enemy line carrying wounded which pointed to the fact that our artillery must have inflicted several losses upon the enemy. Maj. E.J. Crouch had returned, a few hours prior to the raid, from the 6th D.L.I. and [was] instrumental to a marked degree in bringing about its success.

This carefully planned raid had all of the hallmarks of Roland Bradford's training methods. This party had been withdrawn from the battalion a few days earlier to practice the raid over ground carefully marked out to represent the enemy positions. Nothing was left to chance. Everyone was briefed as to what he had to do and the role he had to play. There were to be other occasions when Bradford's attention to detail would lead to other successes.

Was the 2/Lt. J.R.Thompson, referred to in the above account, the same officer who appears in the following anecdote written by an anonymous observer?

In March/April before the Battle of Arras 1917, the 50th Division were in XVIII Corps [a Corps du Chasse commanded by Lt. Gen. Sir Ivor Maxse] the plan being this Corps would march through to Berlin…this anecdote tells the story of recently arrived Lieut. Thompson who was afterwards known as 'Thompson the Raider'. Actually he was, I believe, a lecturer at Durham University, and ended up as a professor.

The story is a simple one. Thompson was sent out on a quiet sector of the front line as night patrol. He got up with his men to the German trench where he was challenged. Speaking perfect German – he came back with the German sentry as prisoner. Education always pays!

The battalion was relieved by the 5th Bn. North Staffordshire Regiment on the night of the 6th/7th March and moved into billets in Foucaucourt. At 2 p.m. on the following day, it moved to Méricourt-Sur-Somme. For the rest of the month, the battalion was put through a strenuous training programme, when lessons learnt in the fighting of the last six months were tried out on the practice grounds. Many of these lessons were conceived in the mind of the battalion's brilliant young Commander and were to be used in the next action of the River Scarpe. Though the work was hard and physically demanding, attention to the men's leisure needs were not forgotten. Concerts were organised and a surprising array of talent discovered amongst the companies. Inter-company sport commenced with football and boxing competitions. Each company fired on the ranges and live grenades were thrown and new attacking formations practised. Each week ended with a church parade.

On the 16th, Military Medal awards were announced for L/Cpl. W.E. Guy and Pte. D. Varty. Lt. Gen. Sir W.P. Pulteney, K.C.B., K.C.M., D.S.O., who was G.O.C. III Army Corps, inspected 151 Brigade. He thanked it for the good work it had done whilst serving with his corps on the Somme. He announced that they would be moving to XVIII Corps in the Arras area. On the 31st March, 1917, the battalion moved by motor lorry to Talmas, via Amiens and then marched to Naours where billets were found in the convent. The 50th Division was concentrated in the Talmas–Villers–Bocage–Molliens area. Officers and men were not sorry to leave the Somme behind.

CHAPTER VII

The 9th Battalion moved to Gézaincourt on the 2nd April. Heavy snow fell during the march and the wet and weary men were both disappointed and dissatisfied to find the billets in very poor condition. Fortunately, the stay was for one night only. At 7 a.m. on the following day, the battalion set off for Sibiville and billeted there with the exception of 'A' Company, which stayed overnight in Séricourt. Dinner was provided whilst on the march. On the 4th, the battalion reached Croix and stayed for a few days in much improved billets. The award of the Military Cross to 2/Lt. J.R. Thompson and the Distinguished Conduct Medal to Sgt. D. Shepherd were announced. At 10 a.m. on the 7th April, the battalion marched to Averdoingt in the Rollecourt area. The 50th Division was now concentrating in and around Avesnes, 10 miles west of Arras. A conference was arranged at 151 Brigade headquarters. Lieutenant Colonel Karslake, 50th Division G.S.O.1, outlined the coming operation in front of Arras.

The Battle of Arras was part of a greater Allied plan to attack simultaneously on several fronts. The French were to assault further south in the Rheims sector – the ill-fated Nivelle offensive – whilst other offensives would commence in Italy and Russia. Revolutionary troubles in Russia caused the offensive there to be cancelled and Italy was not ready to act on the agreed date. The French attacks were delayed. The British attacks were planned to go ahead on time with one of the objectives of pulling German reserves away from the French front prior to that attack starting. The main objectives of the British assault were to take Vimy Ridge and Monchy-le-Preux. Everard Wyrall in his book, *The History of the 50th Division* describes the strength of the enemy trench system to be assaulted:

> The front attacked by the Third and First Armies on the morning of the 9th of April extended from just north of the village of Croisilles, south-east of Arras, to just south of Givenchy-en-Gohelle at the northern foot of the Vimy Ridge, a distance of nearly fifteen miles. It included between four and five miles of the northern end of the Hindenberg Line which had been built to meet the experience of the Somme Battles. Further north the original German defences in this sector were arranged on the same principle as those which we had captured further south. They comprised three separate trench systems, connected by a powerful switch line running from the Scarpe at Fampoux to Lievin, and formed a highly organised defensive belt some two to five miles in depth.

The British artillery bombardment of the enemy front positions, communications, strong points and wire, commenced three weeks prior to the attack starting on the 9th April 1917. By this stage of the war the artillery was both accurate and effective. The enemy must have suffered considerable discomfort. Their very deep dugouts may have protected them from the worst effects of the barrage but it was almost impossible for supplies to reach the front line and the constant explosions must have caused great suffering to their nerves.

On the 8th April, the battalion marched to Izel-les-Hameau. On the 9th, when the Battle of Arras commenced, platoons were on a route march. The next day, a sudden move was made to Agnez-les-Duisans, where 151 Brigade was concentrated. On the 11th April, the battalion occupied the reserve line near Beaurains, having marched there in a blinding snowstorm. The division had now been transferred to VII Corps.

The 50th Division relieved the 14th Division on the 12th April. The division held the line along the ridge east of the villages of Wancourt and Héninel, with the left flank resting on the River Cojeul, which flowed past the villages. The right flank rested on Wancourt Tower. The village of Chérisy, which lay to the south-east beyond the right boundary of the division, was still in German hands. Ahead and in the German lines was the village of Vis-en-Artois. Guemappe, also in German hands, was north of the River Cojeul and beyond the division's left flank. This village contained a number of enemy machine guns sited to bring down enfilade fire on any move forward by the division. The 56th Division was on the right flank and the 3rd Division was on the left.

The 9th Battalion moved into the front line on the evening of the 12th/13th April and relieved the 8th Bn. Rifle Brigade in trenches recently captured from the Germans. Patrols were sent out immediately and discovered that the nearest enemy trenches were some 500 yards ahead. Lieutenant Colonel Bradford's report for the following 24 hours stated:

> At 9 a.m. on the 13th April, I sent forward two strong patrols to establish themselves on the ridge near Wancourt Tower. These patrols met with considerable opposition but by 12 noon one Post was established on left of Tower at N.24. d.2.2 [map reference] and another in road at N.24. d.1 1½.
>
> At about 2.30 p.m., an attempt was made but without success to drive enemy from position near N30. b. 1.9. where there was a very active machine gun. We then occupied the house at N.24. d.1. 11/2 and brought rifle fire to bear on enemy position from there. The house was soon rendered untenable by shellfire. At about 3 p.m. enemy intensely shell [ed] our Post in the road and we had to withdraw lower down the road.
>
> At dusk on the 13th, Posts were pushed forward close to the Tower. At 10 p.m., the enemy blew up the Tower. On the night of the 13th/14th, a trench was dug twenty yards from the tower from N.30. b. 0.9 to N.24. d. 1. 1½. The enemy undoubtedly intended to counter-attack the position but was prevented from so doing by the activity of our patrols. Our position was intensely shelled on the 14th but as the men had dug an excellent trench few casualties were suffered.

Casualties, due largely to heavy shelling and machine gun fire, were one officer and 13 other ranks killed, three officers and 39 other ranks wounded. The officer killed was 2/Lt. Richard Greenland. Amongst the other ranks killed were Ptes. John Kelly, James Wilson, Joseph Conlon and George W. Benson and Lance Corporal Emmet. On the night of the 13th April, the battalion had two companies holding the line at Wancourt Tower and northwards for about 600–700 yards. The other two companies were in a sunken road just east of the River Cojeul. The 3rd Division had carried out an attack on Guemappe at 7 p.m. that night, which failed.

On the 14th April, the 56th Division was to attack Chérisy whilst the 50th Division was to cover its left flank by making an advance alongside. The 50th would then form a defensive flank facing northwards along the high ground and with its left on Wancourt Tower. The 9th Battalion was ordered to stand firm as a protection against any enemy counter-attack from Guemappe. The advance was made by the 6th and 8th Battalions D.L.I. and the 5th Bn. Border Regiment. The 6th Battalion advanced abreast of the 56th Division followed by the 8th Battalion; both eventually became mixed with units of the 56th Division. The final result of the action was that the ridge fell to the British assault but only after hard fighting against a resolute enemy. The task of the 9th in holding fast whilst these actions took place was not an easy one. Lieutenant Colonel Bradford's report stated:

> During the morning of the 14th, enemy machine guns raked our position in the Bank in N.23. d. and N. 24 c. and the valley just east of Wancourt. Our Lewis Guns [and] machine guns replied and eventually succeeded in making the enemy cease his fire. On the night of the 14th/15th, the Battalion with one company of the 5th Borders attached dug a continuous trench from the Tower northwards to Cojeul River. This trench was handed over to the 6th N.Fs at 2.30 a.m. on 15th and the Battalion proceeded to Ronville Caves.

Lieutenant Colonel Bradford's report, as usual, had a sting in its tail. Never one to miss the opportunity to ensure that lessons learnt in an action came to the attention of his seniors, his report on the events of the 13th/14th April terminated with the following remarks:

> Lessons: As stated above before dawn on the 13th April, our patrols found that there was no enemy within 500 yds of our line. Our relief was completed too late to enable us to push forward then. The enemy must have moved back towards our line at dawn and this shows us the importance of the principle 'advance your line while ye may.'
> The old maxims were burnt into our souls:
> 1. Consolidate with all possible energy so as to provide protection from shellfire.
> 2. Protect yourself against counter-attack by energetic patrolling.
> 3. When moving up to dig trenches be quiet and stop all jangling of equipment and tools.

Ronville Caves were part of a complex of underground shelters dug out of the solid chalk when the Arras area was part of the Netherlands held by the Spanish Duke of Alva. Later, they were used as cellars and storehouses. From 1914 the French had used them as shelters for their troops and they were completely impervious to the heaviest enemy shell. The British now held them and improvements had been made to the caves with the installation of ventilation shafts and electricity. Tunnels had also been dug under the German lines from which the assaulting units emerged on the 9th April. These caves were so extensive that several thousand troops could be sheltered in them. Safe they were, but very uncomfortable. Maj. Hardinge Veitch M.C. in his book, *Eighth Battalion The Durham Light Infantry* wrote:

> The roofs, from which an oozy slime with a dank fetid smell ceaselessly dripped, were supported only by pillars of chalk left for that purpose. No dry place existed throughout them, and the clothing of the men became quickly daubed with the grey slime, and, as they huddled together for the sake of warmth, resembled nothing so much as a flock of sheep. Apart from the factor of safety, not a single word can be said for their use. The atmosphere was that of a dense fog and unpleasantly affected the breathing, whilst on emerging into daylight, it was some minutes before the eyes could accustom themselves to the light and glare of the snow covered ground.

The battalion remained in the caves until the 23rd April. At 7 a.m. on this day, it marched to the Harp, a complex of captured German trenches protected by belts of wire, which in appearance resembled this instrument. After midday, it began to move to Nepal Trench where it was in support of 150 Brigade, which was coming under an enemy counter-attack. During this move the battalion received orders to proceed to the front line trenches and take part in an attack timed for 6 p.m. The Second Battle of the Scarpe was about to commence. Casualties were expected to be heavy. Since the set-backs of the First Battle, the Germans had brought reinforcements forward and had strengthened their positions. Wyrall gave his opinion of the situation in *The History of the 50th Division*:

> That we should have been compelled in April, 1917 to continue the operations east of Arras, after the objectives laid down by Sir Douglas Haig in the First Battle of the Scarpe, was one of the tragedies of the War. The British lines had been rolled four miles further east – all the dominating features considered necessary had been captured from the enemy – we were in a fine position on the heights looking eastwards; our casualties had been light and the enemy's heavy.

Haig felt compelled to continue operations as he awaited the delayed French offensive in the Rheims area. This offensive, due to commence on the 9th April, did not get underway until the 16th. The French had little success and exceptionally heavy casualties, which ultimately led to a serious breakdown in the French morale.

The Second Battle of the Scarpe was fought over a nine-mile front from Croisilles to Gavrelle. The 50th Division had the 15th Division on its left and the 30th Division on its right, the latter commanded by an old friend, General Shea. No. 150 Brigade was to make the initial attack with 151 Brigade in support. The first waves of infantry ran into their own artillery, which was moving forward too slowly. Despite heavy losses the troops pushed on. Enemy opposition was strong and counter-attacks drove the British right flank back, in some cases to the original front line. The left had more success. It reached and held the German front line and took many prisoners.

The 9th Battalion, as part of 150, had its part to play. Lieutenant Colonel Bradford wrote:

> At 3.30 p.m. the battalion was attached to the 150 Infantry Bde. and orders were received that at 6 p.m., the 5th Borders on right and 9th D.L.I. on left were to deliver a counterattack to win back the first objective.
>
> At 4 p.m. the Battalion moved in artillery formation to the Bank in N.24. a. & b. and then formed up for assault behind our line in N.24. b. – the line which we had dug on night of 14th/15th April. Two companies were leading, each with three platoons in first wave and one in company reserve. The two remaining companies were in support – one on right and one on left – both to follow at 100 yds distance from last line of the company in front of them. At 6 p.m. the barrage came down about 20 yds in front of our trench and remained there for 10 minutes. This caused great anxiety and one or two casualties were suffered. At 6.10 p.m. the barrage moved forward and we advanced close up to it. After an advance of about 200 yds an enemy machine gun on the railway opened fire. Our right flanking company fired several rifle grenades at this gun and the team then surrendered. About four hundred yards from our original trench, the German line was encountered very strongly held and with several machine guns in position. From this point our advance was continued in section rushes and the supporting companies which were in artillery formation were compelled to extend. Accurate rifle and Lewis Gun fire was kept up on the enemy trench, and the Rifle Grenadiers when they had rushed forward within range opened an effective fire on enemy trench. The left company which did not meet with so much opposition as the right company, penetrated enemy trench and delivered a bombing attack on the Germans. Directly the latter perceived that we were on their flank they surrendered. They were escorted to the Aid Post by several of our slightly wounded men.
>
> The advance continued without very great opposition for another 300 yds when several enemy machine guns opened heavy fire at close range into us. A short tussle took place in which our sections employed the principle of 'mutual support' most effectively, and the teams of six enemy guns were either destroyed or captured. The enemy was now in a panic and we were able to advance to the objective troubled only by long range machine gun fire from about St. Rohart Factory. We poured fire into the retreating Germans and inflicted heavy casualties on them.

An advance had been made of 1,600 yards on a frontage of 500 yards. Both flanks were in the air and these were drawn back as a defensive measure. The final enemy trench was occupied and consolidated. Throughout the action the attacking companies showed great determination and enthusiasm. It had been by any standards a brilliantly conceived and executed counter-attack that incorporated lessons learnt in previous attacks. There was no walking in long straight lines across no man's land with rifles and bayonets held across the chest. As the battalion advanced, it constantly fired its rifles at the enemy positions. Lewis guns were operated from the hip and in one case, from the shoulder. Rifle grenadiers had been trained to creep forward under the supporting fire of rifles and Lewis guns, bombing any enemy strong point or machine gun position that threatened to hold up the advance. When heavy enemy fire was encountered, the advance was made by rushing forward in sections from shell hole to shell hole, each section giving the other mutual support. Time and again the enemy was outflanked causing them to surrender or beat a hasty retreat. Major Crouch, Second in Command of the battalion, later wrote:

> By its [the battalion's] quick delivery, led by the Colonel in the front wave, it outflanked the enemy, who immediately surrendered. This action was one of the most successful carried out by us. Having regard to the results obtained, casualties were extremely small. The line was re-established and remained firmly in our hands. We captured over 300 prisoners, two large howitzers, which the enemy had destroyed, and many machine guns, thirteen of which were serviceable. The most important work of consolidating our position prevented us from salving the whole fruits of this success, and much booty had to be left. The enemy dead was thickly strewn about the area.
>
> This action would have gladdened the heart of the stoutest martinet, the value of 'training, training, training' being forced home to the most casual observer. The men under their section, platoon and company commanders worked as though on an ordinary practice attack.

Contact with the flanking divisions was made on the 24th April. Active patrolling took place on the night of the 23rd/24th April and advanced posts were set up. These posts made it impossible for the enemy to organise any counter-attack. Rations and supplies were carried up to battalion headquarters by pack ponies and distributed amongst the companies only a short distance ahead. Ration parties, therefore, had to make no long, dangerous and tiring journeys to supply points. The British now held the whole of the ridge east of Wancourt Tower, facing Chérisy.

Amongst the casualties of this fighting was Pte. Jack McCutcheon who died of wounds on the 25th April.

The battalion was relieved by a battalion of the Oxford and Bucks Light Infantry on the night of the 25th/26th April. The 50th Division was transferred to VII Corps and, on the 18th May moved to the area of Monchy-au-Bois. The battalion had more training here until moving to St. Amand, near Souastre, on the 23rd of the month. On the 31st May, a number of awards were announced for courageous acts during the recent fighting. Capt. M. Jolley, 2/Lts. H. Hall, W.W.B. Thompson and W.G. Wylie received the Military Cross. Capt. J.A.C. Scott (R.A.M.C.) and Capt. C. Bowdery both were awarded a Bar to the Military Cross

Captain Scott's citation read:

> For conspicuous gallantry and devotion to duty. He behaved with great courage and coolness in attending the wounded under heavy shellfire. For two days he worked continuously with an utter disregard for his own safety. By his efforts he was able to ensure the rapid

evacuation of the wounded and undoubtedly saved many lives.

Captain Scott was also awarded the Croix de Guerre by the French.

Sgt. A. Caldwell, M.M. was awarded the Distinguished Conduct Medal. His citation read:

> For conspicuous gallantry and devotion to duty. He led his platoon with great courage and skill. He went forward and captured an enemy machine gun and eleven prisoners. His prompt action removed a very serious obstacle.

Military Medals were awarded to Sgts. E. Waugh, S. Gibson, W. Storey, J. Greenwell, W. Goffin D.C.M. and J. Appleby, Cpls. T. Bilton and T. Varty, L/Cpls. C. Balls, J. Jones, M. Herron, E.R. Bell, C. Kenny, C.S. Reid, R.S. Britton and J. Wildish, and to Ptes. C. Bryant, T. Adamson, J.W. Stanton and R. Davison. L/Sgt. J.E. March and L/Cpl. J. Bell were awarded Bars to the Military Medal.

The battalion remained at St. Amand until the 15th June. On the 16th, it marched to Hénin-sur-Cojeul – a long and tiring march in the hot summer sun. There were more rests than usual but it was still a very tired battalion that reached its destination. The 50th Division had taken over the front line which faced Chérisy on the right and extended to the Arras–Cambrai road on the left. In the reserve position the battalion provided carrying parties to the front line trenches and still found time for more training. Casualties still occurred and 2/Lt. Charles Dixon was killed on the 22nd June, along with L/Cpl. Joseph Easterbee. On the 24th, the battalion moved to Boisleux-au-Mont for more training. On the 2nd July, it returned to Hénin and prepared to move into the front line. No. 151 Brigade took over the left sub sector of the division. The 5th Borders and the 9th Battalion were in the front line trenches and the 6th Battalion was in support. The trenches occupied were fairly comfortable had little protective wire in front.

A great deal of hard work had to be undertaken at night when it was safe. Rations were brought up at night by pack ponies, two of which were killed and the drivers wounded. Active patrolling was carried out in accordance with the usual British army policy of dominating no man's land. The battalion occupied Jackdaw and Ape Trenches. It was relieved by the 6th Battalion on the night of the 7th/8th July and remained in support from the 8th to the 11th, with 'B' Company in the caves at Marlière and the other three companies in trenches with the delightful names of Egret, Curlew and Duck. Large working parties were supplied each night. The band gave a concert for 'B' Company in the caves on the 10th July.

On the 11th July, the battalion relieved the 6th Battalion in the front line with three companies in the front trenches and 'D' Company in support. 'C' Company displayed a daily menu in its trench, which showed what food was available to the men:

Breakfast: Tea, Bacon, Bread. *Dinner*: M & V Pressed Meat Stew, Potatoes, Porridge.

Tea: Tea, Cold Meat, Bread, Jam & Cheese. ½ pint of water per man per day.

Large working parties were formed for the Royal Engineers for work on digging and improving dugouts and shelters in the support trenches, and to erecting wire defences in front of the posts that had been established. Active patrolling went on throughout the period in the front line. On the 15th, 200 men were on working parties. On the same day, the 6th Battalion relieved the 9th but, before this was carried out, a German patrol of 10 men launched a raid on one of 'A' Company's posts. This failed and the enemy was driven off without loss to the company. One of the Germans was killed. The battalion moved into brigade reserve at Neuville Vitasse. Casualties during the 12 preceding days included Pte. Walter Pitcher who was killed. Eight other ranks and one officer were wounded. The usual working parties were organised during the stay at this village. On the 19th July, the battalion moved to Mercatel and a period of training and finding working parties commenced. On the 25th July, Pte. Joseph Hillery was killed. On the 27th, the battalion moved to the front line and into Swift and Martin Trenches. No. 151 Brigade was the right-hand brigade on the 50th Division front. The trenches were bombarded occasionally by enemy mortars. Some of the bombs contained a new type of gas. This activity resulted in five casualties, one of whom, Pte. Charles P. Driver, died of his wounds two days later.

No man's land was a very active area at night. Enemy patrols were increasingly evident and clashes occurred with British patrols. 2/Lt. C.A. Marshall led one of the patrols into an enemy sap. At first this was found to be empty but on moving along it for some distance they encountered a strong enemy force and were forced to withdraw. The night of the 30th/31st July was one of considerable enemy activity. A large number of fish-tail bombs were fired into the British trenches. Another clash occurred in no man's land when a patrol led by 2/Lt. Hall met a larger enemy patrol. Although outnumbered the enemy was attacked with grenades and two were wounded before our patrol withdrew. On returning to the trenches a patrol was immediately sent out to find the enemy wounded and bring them into our lines but no trace was found. They had obviously been carried back to their own lines.

On the 31st, the 6th Battalion provided the relief force and the 9th moved into the support position. Total casualties for the month were three killed, one of whom died of gas poison, four more were gassed and survived and seven men were slightly wounded and remained on duty. The dead included Ptes. Thomas Davison and John Renforth. Three companies occupied Egret Trench and Egret Loop Trench. 'D' Company and headquarters were in the Nest. Poor weather continued over the next few days making everything wet and muddy. Nevertheless, the well built trenches were comfortable. The usual working parties were employed at night in improving trenches and digging new ones. Occasional enemy shelling occurred.

After an uneventful spell in the front line from the 4th to the 8th August, the battalion moved to Hénin. On the 9th, the award was announced of the Military Medal to

Sgt. B. Gillings. An interesting entry appeared in the War Diary on the 11th August: 'Rest and baths. Supplied 30 men for haymaking at Ervillers and Avette.' The 30 men must have enjoyed their non-military duty and the envy of their comrades who were engaged in much more dangerous tasks. On the 12th, the battalion moved to Mercatel. It stayed here until the 20th, most of the time being taken up with working parties and training. On the 18th, 12 officers and 60 other ranks went to the corps horse show at Bihucourt. Pte. Innes was awarded the Military Medal.

The 5th Bn. D.L.I. was relieved opposite Vis-en-Artois on the 20th August. During the relief, one single shell fired haphazardly by the Germans caused six casualties. Three men were killed: L/Cpls. Thomas Bevil and James Kelly, and Pte. Joseph Howarth. On the 24th, the battalion was relieved by the 6th Battalion and moved into support. Three companies were in Egret, Lion and Duck Trenches and 'B' Company was in Marlière Caves. Daily working parties and training followed until the 28th August, when the 6th Battalion was relieved in the front line. It was a very quiet tour of duty with repairing trenches and wiring taking up most of the time.

The 6th Battalion again relieved the 9th on the 1st September and the latter moved to Wancourt and Neuville Vitasse and into brigade reserve. A period of rest and cleaning both themselves and their equipment followed. Route marches were undertaken led by the band. On the 5th, the battalion moved into Durham Lines, a winter camp near Boisleux-au-Mont, where the accommodation proved to be very good. The following day, a conference was held to discuss the raid to be held in the middle of the month. Immediately replica trenches of the German lines to be assaulted were built and the battalion commenced to practice its moves. Intensive practice continued for the next few days. On the 11th September, the whole battalion carried out a practice attack watched by the G.O.C. Third Army (Gen. Sir Julian Byng), VI Corps Commander (Lt. Gen. J.A.L. Haldane), G.O.C. 50th Division (Major General Wilkinson), and 151 Brigade Commander (Brigadier General Cameron). This high-ranking audience at a rehearsal would seem to indicate that this was to be no ordinary raid. 'A','B','C' Companies and battalion headquarters moved up into the front line opposite Chérisy during the afternoon of the 14th.

Trench raids were a not uncommon tactic in the front line. The objectives were to seek information about the enemy units opposite, their strength, morale, quality, and intentions. Useful information was often revealed by prisoners. Other objectives were to kill Germans, destroy dugouts and strong points and, always the aim of the British, to keep the war on an active footing in quiet areas. What made this raid somewhat different from most other raids was the extremely careful planning and preparations at all levels. The fact that such high-ranking officers watched the battalion in training points to a special interest in the way the raid was to be conducted. The men were well aware of this top-level interest and strove to create a good impression, particularly the young Commanding Officer of the 9th Bn. D.L.I., Lt. Col. Roland Boys Bradford V.C., M.C. Another point of interest was that, unlike most raids, this one was to take place in

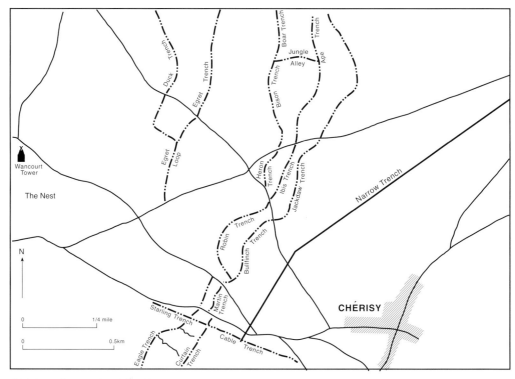

Chérisy – September 1917

broad daylight. Orders for the raid appear to have come from Division and were issued by Lt. Col. Henry Karslake G.S.O.1, Chief Staff Officer to the 50th Division.

The objective of the raid was Narrow Trench, a short distance in front of the village of Chérisy. This trench was somewhat unique in that it was a straight, without any curves and bays or traverses. As such, it was not a properly made front line fire trench. It is possible that it was started as a support trench and the advance of the British to within 250 yards of the enemy had made it the next line to be assaulted. Surprisingly in spite of its weakness, the Germans seemed to be prepared to hold this trench. It was occupied by units of the 76th Reserve Infantry Regiment, which contained many men from the Hamburg area. The raid was to be carried out by three companies of the 9th Battalion commencing at 4 p.m. on Saturday 15th September. Some time after the 9th had raided and returned to British lines, a company of the 8th Bn. D.L.I. were to assault the trench, hoping to catch the Germans off their guard as they tended to their dead and wounded and repaired their damaged defences. A detachment of Royal Engineers under the command of 2/Lt. W.H. Rebbeck of the 7th Field Company prepared explosive devices for the destruction of the deep dugouts they expected to find.

For several days before the raid the companies taking part practised over the replica trenches. An artillery fire programme was drawn up, and very impressive it turned out to be. The division's mortars were to break down the enemy's defences prior to the assault. These comprised 2-in. mortars, 3-in. medium mortars and 9.45-in. heavy mortars; their task was to literally blast away the enemy wire in front of Narrow Trench. This commenced on the 3rd September. A general bombardment of the Chérisy area by the divisional artillery commenced four days later. Shells fell along the German line as usual but rather more on the trenches west of Chérisy. Aerial photographs of the objective were taken and some German activity to strengthen Narrow Trench seemed to be taking place. A machine gun post was identified in a sap – opposite the position where 'A' Company would run into no man's land on leaving the British trenches. On the 10th September, the divisional artillery switched to bombarding Narrow Trench whilst 2-in. mortars continued with the wire cutting task. On the 11th, both artillery and mortars commenced a fire programme aimed at cutting the wire in front of Narrow Support Trench. As the divisional artillery was now fully involved in this task, the VI Corps artillery joined in by shelling Narrow and Night Trenches and arrangements were made for the guns of the 16th and 12th Divisions to bring enfilade fire on Narrow Trench. Spotter aircraft would follow the raid and photograph its progress from the air.

The three companies of the 9th and 'C' Company of the 8th Battalion (led by Capt. B.M. Williams) trained over the replica trenches intensely, until they knew every element of their task. Eight additional stretcher bearers from other battalions in the brigade were allocated to the raiders and joined on the morning of the attack. Arrangements were made to place dummy troops out in no man's land on the northern and southern flanks of the attacking force. A dummy tank, built by the 7th Field Coy. Royal Engineers, was dragged out in front of the trenches. The deception worked well as German artillery bombarded these targets. Smoke was to be fired from British guns to cover the SOS flares that the enemy would fire when the attack commenced. In addition, officers with Verey pistols were placed along the front line trenches to fire flares that would duplicate the German signals – an attempt to confuse the enemy and cause their artillery to fall on the area beyond both flanks of the attack. The flanks of the raiders were to be covered by a Lewis gun team, two rifle bombers and two snipers.

On the afternoon of the 14th September, 'A', 'B', 'C' Companies and battalion headquarters moved into the front line, relieving the 8th Battalion. It was a cold day with intermittent squalls of rain. The British artillery continued its bombardment, particularly aimed at completing the destruction of the enemy wire and ensuring that the Germans were unable to repair and replace these defences. The 8th Battalion still provided the patrols during the night. A patrol of the 9th went with them to reconnoitre the ground and, on its return, cut gaps in the British wire to allow access to no man's land on the following day.

The morning of Saturday the 15th was cold, misty and wet. The rain stopped and the weather cleared at about 10 a.m. The three companies prepared themselves for the raid. The usual fighting order was worn. Gas masks, haversacks, water bottles and entrenching tools were left behind. Every platoon had a special section of bomb throwers, each member of which carried 10 Mills bombs. There was also a special section of rifle grenadiers each carrying six rifle grenades. One man in each section carried a smoke bomb. The final element in the artillery fire plan was to concentrate six batteries of 6-in. howitzers and one of 60-pdrs. on the enemy lines. This would cordon off the area under attack on three sides and hold back German reinforcements. On the fourth side of the box, immediately in front of the attackers, a creeping barrage would move ahead of the advancing troops on a frontage the width of Narrow Trench. The final addition to the plan was a machine gun barrage from 72 machine guns, each firing 250 rounds a minute over the heads of the raiders and into the enemy positions. At 4 p.m., the whole weight of this artillery would crash down on the enemy with a mixture of high explosives and smoke. After two minutes, the guns were timed to lift from Narrow Trench and the barrage was to creep forward at 100 yards per minute.

Promptly at 4 p.m., the artillery and machine gun barrage crashed down on the enemy front line, which disappeared in clouds of smoke, earth and debris. 'A', 'B' and 'C' Companies climbed out of the trenches and advanced into no man's land. The two flank parties moved out under the command of 2/Lt. A. Hall M.C. and 2/Lt. Inman. The companies had practised this time and time again until they knew precisely every move

Aerial view of the Chérisy raid. The light dots in Narrow Trench and in the entrance to the communications trench in the bottom left are 9 D.L.I. men, not in possession and working toward the next objective. German troops are seen retreating n the bottom left.

they had to make. 'A' Company was on the left, 'C' Company in the centre and 'B' Company on the right. The advance was made in platoon waves, each led by its Commanding Officer in the centre and with the N.C.O.s on the flanks. After the first wave had moved 15 yards the second wave left the trench, to be followed by a third and fourth wave at intervals of 10 yards. The lines had not moved far when they were fired on by a German machine gun. The companies had prepared for this event as well. The bombers in the advancing lines moved quickly towards the machine gun position, throwing bombs and crawling towards the target. The gunner was killed and the gun brought back to the British lines. The advance across the pitted ground was made as a series of rushes from shell hole to shell hole. The attackers moved forward firing their rifles and Lewis guns from the hip as they advanced. This kept down enemy fire and caused casualties amongst the defenders. The Germans, confused by the surprise attack and the measures used by the British to blind their artillery counter-barrage, were unable to retaliate for a vital few minutes. When their artillery did open fire it proved to be somewhat ragged and much of it fell on the dummies worked by small parties of men under Lieutenant Leatherbarrow. Overhead the attack was observed by an R.E.8 of 12 Squadron (12 Wing), flown by Capt. D.F. Stevenson M.C., with Lt. J. Webster M.C. as his observer. They saw the British box barrage as a wall of fire with no stray shells and completely enclosing the attack area. After two minutes, the deluge of shells falling in front of them, the attacking companies moved forward as a creeping barrage. Shortly afterwards the British infantry arrived in Narrow Trench, with one casualty only.

The trench was defended by the German 6th Coy. 2/76th Reserve Infantry Regiment, 17th Reserve Division. Many were trapped in their deep dugouts by the artillery barrage and the speed of the infantry advance. The smoke bombs launched by the attackers forced some to the surface to surrender. Those who refused were buried and killed by the explosive devices thrown into the dugouts by the demolition party. An attempted counter-attack, carried out by the 5th Company of this regiment, was destroyed by British shellfire with heavy losses. The 9th Battalion War Diary states that about 70 Germans were killed and 25 taken prisoner. Total battalion losses, largely due to enemy counter-fire, included: 2/Lt. Hugh Hall M.C. and L/Cpl. John Colgan M.M., Ptes. W. Brownless, R. Hibbs, W. Miller, H.Westwood, A. Williams and W. Winchester, all of whom were killed. Two officers and 10 other ranks were wounded. Of the latter, Pte. James Dennis died of his wounds on the 15th September and Pte. Thomas Butt died the following day. Eleven dugouts were blown in and the machine gun mentioned previously captured. At 4.30 p.m., the raiders returned to the British lines through a lively enemy artillery barrage.

Later in the evening, a raid was carried out by 'C' Company 8th Bn. D.L.I., with the loss of one man killed and 11 wounded. A number of Germans were killed and three prisoners taken. Only one of the prisoners survived the crossing over no man's land to the British trenches. Two of these were killed by British artillery fire. Two wounded members of the 9th Battalion were found and brought back. Lieutenant Colonel Bradford wrote to Lieutenant Colonel Martin, commanding the 8th Battalion:

> The kindness you showed us and the assistance you gave us in getting in and out of your trenches, and all your efforts after the Raid in collecting our dear boys who were killed, are deeply appreciated by all Ranks of the Battalion which I command. Your Company in carrying out their Raid in the evening had an infinitely more difficult task than we, and all of us are full of admiration for the splendid way in which your men executed the Raid.
>
> The mutual admiration and friendliness between our Battalions will do a great deal to build up that Esprit D[e] C[orps] in the brigade which is so important for success in the larger operations.

Lieutenant Colonel Karslake, G.S.O.1, 50th Division, watched the raid and wrote to Lieutenant Colonel Bradford:

> In case it should interest you, I should like to tell you what I saw of your gallant lads on Saturday.
>
> Almost simultaneously with the first burst of artillery fire, they were swarming out of the front line.
>
> They went forward slowly, I could see some men shooting from the hip.
>
> Officers walked about slowly as they directed the men to the various gaps in the Boche wire. Once through that, they appeared on top of Narrow Trench. The men on the right were the first to arrive and they immediately began to fire from the shoulder standing up, at what I imagine were Boches running away on the left.
>
> Very soon most of them had disappeared, but some, including an officer, spent the whole time walking up and down on top of Narrow trench as if nothing imminent was happening.
>
> Then about three Boche and two of our men came back towards Lone Sap and were followed at once by two Boche and one of our men from the direction of Brown Mound.
>
> From that direction also came what I thought to be a runner carrying a board. He jumped into our front line just short of Short Alley.
>
> About 4.22 p.m., I saw four fellows coming back slowly; an officer, standing on the parapet at Narrow Trench, waved to them with his helmet, evidently directing them to the gap in the wire.
>
> I only saw one man move out of a walk, and he came from the extreme left some minutes after most of the front lines had got back from the wire. He doubled along towards Byker Sap and suddenly dropped. I was afraid he was hit, but he picked himself up and got in safely, having evidently been tripped up by the wire.
>
> I was greatly relieved to see two stretcher bearers returning with the stretchers over their shoulders. Then I left, having seen one of the finest examples of discipline that anybody could wish to see.
>
> Please accept my sincerest congratulations.

A letter to the battalion was also received from 151 Brigade:

> With reference to the raid carried out by the 50th Division on the 15th instant, the following remarks of the Third Army Commander are forwarded for the information of all con-

cerned, 'An excellent raid, full of originality and thought. The conduct of all who took part is most praiseworthy.'

Thus ended a raid which attracted much interest from the higher command and must have influenced the appropriate authorities who had earmarked Lieutenant Colonel Bradford for further promotion. All of his immense skills as a leader and trainer of men were shown in this action. Within some two months he was promoted to Brigadier General at the age of 25 and sent to command 186 Brigade, 62nd West Riding Division. It is also of interest that, shortly afterwards, Brigadier General Cameron of 151 Brigade was promoted to Major General.

On the 16th September, the 9th Battalion was at Neuville Vitasse enjoying a well-earned rest and baths. Over the next few days it spent periods of time in the front line or at rest. The usual working parties were provided to carry trench mortar ammunition and for work in Hindenburg Tunnel. On the 25th, the battalion was subjected to heavy enemy shelling prior to moving forward to relieve the 6th Battalion. Pte. William Birkett was killed.

At 10.15 p.m. on the 27th September, 2/Lt. E.S. Gibson and 21 other ranks carried out a raid on the enemy trenches in front of 'D' Company positions. There was nothing exceptional about this raid. However, the operational orders for it have survived and give a good impression of the detail that went into planning a raid. The objectives of the raid were to capture prisoners, kill Germans and to gain information. The raiding party was organised into a number of small groups with specific duties. No.1 Block Party comprised four other ranks and was commanded by Corporal Charlton. No.2 Block Party comprised seven other ranks commanded by Private Mullen. The Clearing Party of four other ranks was commanded by Corporal Wetherill and there was a Covering Party of three other ranks. Immediately prior to the raid, members of the battalion patrolled no man's land to ensure that no enemy force would be met whilst crossing this ground. Once in the enemy trench, No.1 Block Party was to move along to the right and establish a block at a junction with a communication trench. Meanwhile No.2 Block Party was to work along the enemy trench to the left for a distance of 50 yards. It was followed by the Clearing Party, which would bomb any dugouts it came upon. If any prisoners were taken whilst these movements was carried out, these parties were ordered to return to No.1 Block. When all the raiders were accounted for and present, they were to return to their own lines. In the event of no prisoners being taken, No.2 Block Party were ordered to advance for another 25 yards and await the Clearing Party. Again, if prisoners were taken the raiders would report to No.1 Block and return to the lines. If there were still no prisoners, one more advance of 25 yards was to be made. This would be the final advance and the raiders were ordered to return whether prisoners were taken or not. The orders continued:

> 2/Lt. Gibson will direct operations from the enemy parapet and the Covering Party will remain on the parapet with him, prepared to give rapid fire on any enemy crossing over

the open. No.1 guarding the right flank, No.2 the area behind enemy trench, and No.3 guarding area on the left and keeping up to No.2 Block Party.

Should the enemy place a barrage on our trenches, cover will be found in No Man's Land and the return delayed.

Dress & Equipment of Raiders:

Fighting order less P.H. Helmet, Steel Helmet, Haversack, Water Bottle and Entrenching Tool.

Soft caps will be worn.

Faces will be blackened.

Each raider will carry 3 Mills Bombs, one in left side pocket and two in the right.

Rifles will have 9 rounds in magazine, 1 in breech.

No.2 of Clearing Party will carry 6 M.S.K. bombs [smoke] for clearing enemy dugouts.

Bayonets will be covered with sacking.

Nos. 1 and 2 of the No.1 Block Party will carry two light mats for crossing obstacles.

2/Lt. Gibson and Cpl. Charlton will each have wire cutters.

No.3 of Covering party will tape out the route across No Man's Land.

All identification marks, badges and identity discs will be withdrawn from Raiders. If captured they are only to divulge their rank and name.

2/Lt. J. Dick, with a Lewis Gun Section and a Rifle Bombing Section from 'D' Company, will take up a position in Wood Trench, about V1.b.69 at 9.15 p.m. From there he will manoeuvre his party so that, in the event of the enemy opening fire on the Raiding Party, he will be able to fire his Lewis Gun and volleys of rifle grenades at the place which the enemy fire is coming.

The raid achieved its objectives as six Germans were killed and one wounded,

1917 – Lt. Col. R. Boys Bradford V.C., M.C. (centre middle row) with the officers of 9 D.L.I. 2/Lt. C.H.R. Gee is seated on the ground, second from the right.

who was brought back as a prisoner. The raiding party had one man slightly wounded by British artillery, which fired a brief salvo at the outset of the raid. 2/Lt. Gibson was described 'as a fine officer' by the battalion Adjutant, 2/Lt. C.H.R. Gee. (later Lieutenant Colonel Gee who died in 1998 at the age 100).

On the 29th September, the battalion was relieved by the 4th Bn. Northumberland Fusiliers and moved into Durham Lines, Boisleux-au-Mont. The final day of the month was taken up with baths, church parades and working parties.

On the 2nd October 1917, Lieutenant General Haldane, the Corps Commander, presented awards won by other ranks for the 15th September raid. A second Bar to the Military Medal was awarded to Sgt. J. March M.M. A Bar to the M.M. was awarded to Cpl. E.R. Bell M.M. and Sgt. W. Goffin D.C.M., M.M.

L/Cpl. J. March (later Sgt.) seated on the left; one of a small number of other ranks awarded the Military Medal and two Bars.

The following gained Military Medals: Sgts. W. Chapman and R. Stark, Cpls. J. Crozier, W. Park and T. Williams, L/Cpls. F. Ashard, E. Gill, F. Fairnington, B. Nimmo and R. Poskett and Ptes. E. Hindmarsh, J. Jackson, J. Waitt and H. Wilkinson.

The battalion moved to Gommecourt where, on the following day, the Corps Commander conferred the Military Medal on Pte. Hamill and L/Cpl. Johnson, both of 'D' Company. On the 8th, the award of the Military Cross was announced to Capts. T. Harker, J.O.Innes, E. Marshall and E.C. Palmer. The Military Medal was awarded to C.S.M. E. Maddison and Cpl. R. Williams. Training was carried out over the next few days and a number of drafts were received. On the 13th, 2/Lt. E.S. Gibson was awarded the Military Cross.

On the 17th, the battalion boarded a train at Bapaume and travelled via Esquelbecq and Boëseghem to reach Saragossa Farm Camp at 5 p.m. on the 24th of the month. Here 200 men were employed carrying trench boards and a further 210 carried rations for units in the front line. Working parties for a variety of tasks formed over the next four days. During this period seven men were killed and 20 wounded. The dead included Ptes. L. Donaldson, David Hedley, Harold Alderson, Robert Slater, and

Ephraim Syrett. The battalion moved to Marsouin Camp on the 28th where more working parties were organised and these suffered casualties amounting to one officer and seven other ranks killed and 20 other ranks wounded. Amongst the dead were 2/Lt. James Dick and Ptes. James Parkin, Mark Raine, Harry Sharples, William Swift and Joseph Waite. With this sort of casualty record, membership of a working party was no soft option to being in the front line. The month of October ended with light training and a break from working parties.

The battalion moved into the line in front of Houthulst Forest in the Salient on the 4th November and relieved the 6th Battalion. The 50th Division relieved the 34th Division in this sector of the front. The Third Battle of Ypres, which quickly assumed the emotive title *Passchendaele,* had commenced on the 31st July. It was now entering its final phase, and the land certainly had been through four months of hell. The line held by the 9th Battalion comprised waterlogged shell holes. As far as the eye could see, the ground, was one mass of flooded shell holes, almost lip to lip, smelling of gas, cordite and putrefied human flesh. Hulks of tanks, tractors and guns were half-buried in the mud. Enemy concrete pillboxes rose out of the morass, so strong that only a direct hit from the heaviest shells could put them out of action. They were sited so that their machine guns dominated the ground around them and reaped a heavy harvest amongst the attacking British soldiers. In this hell-hole no enemy could be seen from the British lines, yet death lurked everywhere. The great fear of the soldier was of slipping off the muddy duckboards whilst carrying his heavy load – many men had lost their lives by drowning in the water filled holes. The only benefit of the soggy conditions was that the worst effects of enemy shelling were reduced as the shells ploughed deeply into the ground before exploding. Constant day and night long shelling by both sides added to the dreadful discomforts and dangers of the soldiers. In these shell holes men lay and lived during their tour of duty, usually four days, in the water and the thick oozing mud with only a wet blanket and plastic ground sheet to cover them.

The 9th Battalion's tour of duty was greeted with a heavy barrage from the German guns. The 8th Battalion was on the right; 'B' and 'D' Companies of the 9th were in the front line. Battalion headquarters was at Egypt House, a captured enemy pillbox which became a favoured enemy artillery target. On this day, which proved to be his final visit to his battalion in the line, Lieutenant Colonel Bradford was wounded in the cheek. He was in a forward post when a German machine gun opened up. An eyewitness described what happened:

> About the third bullet pierced the Company Commander's steel helmet and the splinters from it wounded the Colonel in the face. He simply got up and said to the Company Commander, 'Are you hurt? What an idiot I was not to get down when I heard the first shot.' Being satisfied that his companion was alright he walked back to get his wound dressed.

The following day, Bradford learned of his promotion to Brigadier General and the command of 186 Brigade, 62nd Division. This outstanding leader left the battalion, not without regret. On the 8th November, he made his final address to his officers and men drawn up in a shell-holed field:

> Comrades, we have endured many hardships together, and it is against my wish that I leave you, but as a soldier I must obey orders. I asked permission to stay with you until the end of the war and no honours nor promotions can ease the ache in my heart on leaving you. When the war is over, I hope we may meet again and talk over days when we fought together.

His wish was not to be fulfilled. On the 30th November 1917, he was killed by a stray shell whilst resting out of the line near the Canal du Nord.

The new Battalion Commander was Lt. Col. E.J. Crouch, D.S.O., D.C.M. who was Bradford's Second in Command.

Lieutenant Colonel Crouch was quite a remarkable Commander in his own right. He joined the Durham Light Infantry on the 10th November 1891 and served with both the 1st and 2nd Battalions. During the Boer War he served as a Section Sergeant with the mounted infantry. He rejoined the 2nd Battalion of the regiment at Aldershot on the 8th January 1903 and was promoted to Colour Sergeant and posted to the 9th Battalion as an instructor. In 1913, he was further promoted to Regimental Sergeant Major with this battalion. He was commissioned in 1915 and appointed Adjutant in the 9th Battalion in 1916, and shortly afterwards to Second in Command to Lieutenant Colonel Bradford. For a few months in 1917, he commanded the 5th Bn. Border Regiment and in November of that year he succeeded Bradford in command of the battalion. He was awarded the Distinguished Service Order, the Distinguished Conduct Medal, the French Legion d'Honneur and was Mentioned in Despatches four times. 2/Lt. Gee, then 19 years old and

Lt. Col. E.J. Crouch D.S.O., D.C.M. This is probably a post-war photograph when he reverted to the rank of Major.

Adjutant to the battalion, described Lt. Col. Crouch as 'elderly…a Sergeant Major type of person with a bristly moustache…He was a good officer.'

The intense enemy shelling continued throughout 1st and 2nd December. The battalion was relieved by the 8th Bn. Suffolk Regiment on the 6th but merely side-stepped to take over from the 8th Bn. D.L. I. on its right. A quiet relief was completed by 9.50 p.m. though Ptes. George Dixon and Cecil Young were killed during the day. The battalion was relieved by the 6th Bn. Northumberland Fusiliers on the 7th, and moved to Moulle on the 10th November. Here the men had a long period out of the line, in training and at rest, until the end of the month. On the 25th, the award of the Military Medal was announced to L/Cpls. B. Davison, J. Lange, J. Wilkinson and B.Wood and Ptes. W. Anderson, J. Goundry and T. Vallans.

Lance Corporal Wood's citation read:

> For conspicuous gallantry and devotion to duty. When the enemy was annoying his men with machine gun fire from an advanced sap, he went out alone under very heavy fire and took up a position, and bombarded the sap so effectively with rifle grenades that the enemy was forced from his position. He showed fine courage and initiative.

Training continued till the 11th December. On the 8th of the month, Major Wilson of the 7th Bn. D.L.I. was appointed Second in Command of the 9th. The battalion moved by train from Watten to Brandhoek on the following day. Toronto Camp, near Brandhoek, was a good tented camp. During its stay the battalion furnished working parties for the 14th and 8th Divisions, improving roads in the forward area and a variety of other tasks. At the end of the day's work on Christmas Eve, the battalion band played carols and as they sang the men must have thought of loved ones at home and wondered whether they would ever again spend a Christmas with them. On Christmas Day, church parade was held at 10 a.m. The battalion dinner was served in the Y.M.C.A. hut, a traditional dinner with the officers serving the men. A concert was held from 3.45 to 6 p.m., and the officers' dinner was held in the evening. It snowed during the night. The battalion continued in working parties until the end of the month. and moved to Whitby Camp near Potijze on the 29th December. The following day, it moved to Seine Support. On New Year's Eve, Pte. John Clarkson was killed. The year ended with preparations to move into the front line.

The battalion relieved the 7th Bn. Northumberland Fusiliers on the evening of the 1st January 1918. The 49th Division was on the right and the 5th Bn. Border Regiment was on the left. An irregular outpost line was held by three companies with 'D' Company in close support. The ground was frozen and covered with snow which hid much of the battlefield's ugliness. The field, again, was a line of shell holes that were very cold and wet, and so cramped that little movement could be made. Shelters were cut into the walls of the shell holes, and ground sheets provided the only cover against the elements. Wooden floor boards were available which provided some comfort, but mud, which slipped constantly down the sides of the holes, made any attempt at revetment impossible. The troops shivered in these holes wet and numb with cold. Many of the shell holes around the positions were occupied by the dead in various stages of decomposition. The battalion was kept busy wiring and strengthening the positions. They also sent out patrols and set up observation posts so that the enemy lines could be watched throughout the day. On the 5th January, the battalion was relieved by the 20th Bn. Royal Fusiliers and moved back to Huzzar Camp near Potijze. It was announced that Lt. E.J. Hampton and R.Q.M.S. Taylor had been awarded the Military Cross. The next move on the 6th was to Eecke, near Steenvoorde and into corps reserve. Daily training followed until the 17th January. On this day, the battalion moved to Boisdinghem. On the 29th, the War Diary had the following entry: 'Battalion to become a Pioneer Battalion.'

CHAPTER VIII

PIONEER BATTALION 1918

The news that the 9th was to become a pioneer battalion was received with much dismay by all ranks. 2/Lt. Gee stated that, 'We loathed it. We reckoned that we were far the best battalion in the division. We did not want to be made pioneers...We thought we had been disgraced a bit.' In fact, the changeover was due to a major reorganisation in the British army resulting from an acute shortage of reinforcements. It was decided, at the highest level, to disband a number of infantry divisions and battalions and transfer officers and men to units which continued to be operative. Furthermore, the number of infantry battalions in a division were reduced from twelve to nine. The order for the change came from the Secretary of State and was quite independent of the reputation and experience – good or otherwise – of the unit or division concerned.

On the 1st February, Maj. Gen. P.S. Wilkinson, G.O.C. 50th Division, visited the battalion to say farewell. Until the 12th February, when the battalion moved to Cambligneul to join the 62nd (West Riding) Division (under Major General Braithewaite) as pioneer battalion, the 9th provided working parties for tasks in the forward area. The division the battalion was joining was the same one in which Boys Bradford had served so briefly as Brigadier General. Whilst now a pioneer battalion its fighting experience would also be called upon in the hard days ahead. Lieutenant Colonel Crouch had foreseen this. 2/Lt. Gee recorded:

> Crouch...said very quickly, 'We will have more fighting to do this year than we've ever had before and we have to train.' He said it so often...He was right...We had to train as best we could by lying steadily about the amount of other work we had to do, i.e. putting up barbed wire and digging trenches and so on.

On the 22nd February, Sir Douglas Haig, Commander-in-Chief, passed through the village and inspected the battalion guard, which he complimented on its smart drill and turnout. Capt. T.B. Jameson commanded the guard of honour, also provided by the battalion, for the visit of French president Monsieur Clemenceau to St. Pol. The battalion was reorganised on a three-company basis. It commenced a hard training programme, which it carried out for the rest of February. The first contact with units of the 62nd Division was not without humour. The following story was told by an anonymous witness:

> An amusing incident took place during a relief in February 1918, when the 9th Bn. had been transferred to the 62nd (W.R.) Division. The following dialogue took place at night when two platoons proceeding in opposite directions met. 'Halt – who are you?' 'The

West Ridings; and who are you?' Came the quick reply, 'The ruddy Durhams walking!'

On the afternoon of the 3rd March, the battalion marched to Écoivres where it left on a light railway for Roclincourt. The 62nd Division, of which the 9th was now a part, was in the line in the left sector of XIII Corps front. No. 187 Brigade held the line on the right in the Arleux sector and 185 Brigade held the Écoivres sector, while 186 Brigade was in reserve. The 9th Battalion headquarters were in Flanders Camp. Over the next few days, the battalion was employed in improving trenches, erecting wire defences and unloading supplies.

On the 21st March, the Germans commenced their major offensive aimed at splitting the French and British armies and driving the British back towards the coast. Reinforced by divisions released from the east now that Russia was out of the war, this offensive, and those that followed over the next few weeks, were the last and greatest threat to the Allied cause. The 62nd Division held the Arleux–Acheville sector with 186 and 185 Brigades in the line. These positions were heavily shelled and mortared but the main weight of the enemy offensive fell on the Fifth and Third Armies. On the 23rd March, the division was relieved by the 3rd Canadian Division and moved to reinforce XVII Corps of the Third Army. The battalion moved to Ronville Caves on the 24th. With help from the field companies of the Divisional Engineers, the men dug a trench on Telegraph Hill from 3p.m. till 10 p.m. The hill was familiar territory to the 9th as it was part of the Arras battleground of the previous year. The 9th moved to Bucquoy the following day. It was a long, tiring march with many stops due to roads heavily congested with military transport, guns, lorries, staff cars and ambulances. The division, which had also moved to Bucquoy, now came under the command of IV Corps. The desperate situation can be measured by the fact that the battalion was now pushed into the line to fill a gap on the right flank of 186 Brigade on high ground north-east of Puisieux-au-Mont. Here the men consolidated the line. No. 185 Brigade was positioned between Longeast Wood and Achiet-le-Petit; 186 Brigade was east of Achiet-le-Petit and 187 Brigade was in Bucquoy.

The German assault against 62nd Division's positions commenced at 8 a.m. on the 26th March. Fierce artillery and mortar bombardments saturated the front line and supports. The enemy captured Pusieux and threatened the right flank. 'A' Company of the 2nd/5th Duke of Wellington's Regiment was sent to take up positions facing south towards Pusieux to protect that flank. The 9th Battalion under Major Wilson, Second in Command, was sent to support in old trenches between Fork Wood to Box Wood, some 300 yards west of the Pusieux–Bucquoy road. These trenches were found to be too deep and, therefore, too difficult to fight from. There was no time to improve them as the men had marched 12 miles to take up their positions in the line. They had worked continuously for 26 hours, having only one brief halt for food and drink. Under intense pressure from the enemy the Duke of Wellington's were driven back until, with 'D' Company of the 9th Bn. D.L.I., they took up position just north of the

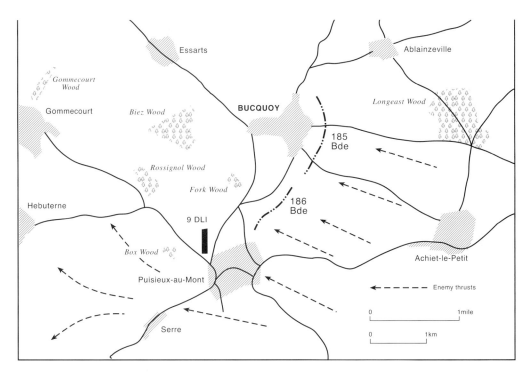

The Defence of Bucquoy – March 1918

Gommecourt–Pusieux road from the south-east corner of Rossignol Wood. The 9th Battalion was now in the front line. 'Notes on Operations' contained in the War Diary for this period described the situation:

It was a fine morning, with a sharp frost and a slight ground mist which, clearing about 8 a.m. revealed the first signs of the enemy.

On the right, some 3,000 yards away, at least a full regiment was marching in file along the farther slopes of the Puisieux Valley, accompanied by transport and what appeared to be Mountain Batteries strapped on mules.

The right flank was in the air, no resistance was offered to their advances, our artillery was not yet in position, besides which there was no sure means of communication with it. Again, Lewis Guns the only available weapons, were outranged.

At last the enemy gave an opening. He was evidently uncertain as to whether Miraumont was occupied and he halted while a whole battalion was pushed into the valley to invest the village. Four Lewis Guns were now placed in position on the right of the Battalion. The enemy attack was a fine piece of work showing careful previous rehearsal and copying of our methods, but the guns, opening fire simultaneously, spread confusion in his ranks and to one wave at least, heavy casualties were caused; the remainder were completely out of range and their advance unimpeded.

A strong battalion was now detached from the main body of the enemy and pushed by sunken roads and dead ground behind Puisieux, thus menacing the right flank which rested in Box Wood. The situation began to develop in front at this moment and our

100

advanced lines were seen withdrawing on to their supports, with the enemy in considerable force behind them…

Retreat must inevitably weaken morale, but on seeing a situation firmly held, the men from the advanced lines checked their withdrawal and came into line with the Durhams…With the exception of one minor readjustment on the right, necessitated by the fall of Rossignol Wood, this was the line held continually through the succeeding week. It lay completely in the open with a trench behind it and had a good field of fire.

West Ridings and Durhams were now hopelessly mixed up together but the men realised the position and now they had once more a definite line, they determined to hang on to it. Officers and N.C.O.s were untiring in their efforts to cheer their men, and throughout the whole day such a constant fusillade was kept up that, try as he might, the enemy was unable to advance.

At dusk the situation was obscure, especially on the right where the possession of Rossignol Wood was debatable. However orders were received that the line must be held at all costs and it was decided to reorganise as soon as darkness fell.

By this time the enemy had got machine guns in position and, diverting them on to the crest held by us, caused considerable trouble and made movement impossible. The effectiveness of his machine gun barrage, arranged in so short a time, was extraordinary and the men who had gone through a whole day without food and water, and were now tired after great physical and mental strain, were in great danger of becoming demoralised. Ammunition was short, transports were completely out of reach, dumps were not known. An attack was rumoured and the flanks fell back. The centre, however, made up of a mixture of both regiments, held, encouraged by a few officers who grasped the situation and were able to keep control. For a few minutes it was a question whether the day's work would be in vain until the swift appearance of four tanks, which, having withdrawn in the morning from Bucquoy, were now lying in the valley in the rear of our position, saved the situation. Seeing them move forward, the men who had broken fell in behind them and returned to the line. The tanks put new heart into the men as they rolled over to the enemy firing their 6-pdrs. and machine guns. For the rest of the night the enemy gave no trouble, he was evidently disorganised if not demoralised.

Capt. W.D.B. Thompson of 'C' Company won the Distinguished Service Order for the gallant way in which he led his men in this action. In spite of relentless enemy pressure at Bucquoy, he held the line. He constantly moved about in the open encouraging his company and directing their fire on the advancing enemy. He went into the action with five officers and 117 men. Only Captain Thompson and 17 men survived this action. He had already been awarded the Military Cross when leading a successful attack in the fighting of April 1917.

The fierce fighting continued over the next few days with the division grimly holding on to its positions and inflicting very heavy losses on the enemy. Pte. George Atkinson, Cpl. Arthur Hall and L/Cpl. Robert Poskett were killed on the 26th March. Casualties over the next few days included Ptes. C.S. Loades and Laurence Taylor who were both killed on the 27th. Concentrated fire from the British artillery broke up any enemy attempt to attack in force on the 27th March. At 8.45 a.m. on the 28th, the enemy opened up with a heavy bombardment on the front line. Fortunately the shooting was very inaccurate and the front line trench suffered very little, though the support areas were deluged with shells. At no point was the enemy able to reach the British line. In the centre about 25 Germans were able to advance to within 50 yards of the front trench. An officer and a number of Durhams went out to meet them and attempted to take them prisoner. The majority surrendered but one of the enemy in the rear shot the officer and a N.C.O. The 'Notes on Operations' further described the day:

> After this only four of the twenty-five remained alive and they were brought into our lines. They were guardsmen, 'The Kaiser's Own'…There was that morning [29th March] a great shooting of Germans…This attack was what the men needed as a tonic. If they fought they could remain awake, otherwise they almost slept as they stood in the trench. It was now a simple question of endurance – the men were almost worn out but by a supreme effort kept on the alert allowing no enemy movement to pass unnoticed…There was much deliberate firing at stretcher bearers and their great devotion to duty won the admiration of all.

Two officers were killed on the 28th March: 2/Lt. Arthur Bell and Lt. William Wylie M.C. and Bar. One of these was the officer shot by the enemy referred to above. Also included in the dead on this day were Cpl. Russell Stoddart and Ptes. Joseph Anderson, Frederick Philps and James W. Smith. Fourteen other ranks lost their lives over the next three days. Total battalion casualties for this period were three officers and 23 other ranks killed and two officers and 86 other ranks wounded. The third officer killed was Capt. R. E. B. Lisle. The 62nd Division held on until relieved by the 37th Division on the night of the 31st March/1st April.

One act of great courage stood out during this period of intense enemy pressure. Many wounded men lay out in no man's land, their cries for food, water and help carrying to their comrades in the font-line trenches. To attempt to help them under the alert gaze of the enemy and his rifles, machine guns and shellfire was suicidal. One man made this journey, not once, but on nine separate occasions. Pte. Thomas Young was a stretcher bearer. He went out to search for the wounded as they lay in shell holes in no man's land. He dressed their wounds and, if they could be moved, he carried them back to the trenches always under constant enemy fire. Private Young was awarded the Victoria Cross, the second one won by the battalion in the Great War. The *London Gazette*, when announcing the award on the 4th June 1918, stated, 'for conspicuous gallant conduct in the face of the enemy'. Thomas Young was a hewer in the colliery at High Spen, County Durham when he enlisted in the battalion in 1914, at the age of 19. On returning to his home on leave after winning the award he was received with great excitement. Public subscriptions had been raised by the High Spen Patriotic and Distinction Fund. At a special service held at Saltwell Park and attended by the Mayor of Gateshead, the Earl of Durham, Lord Lieutenant of the County and between 10,000 to 15,000 people, Thomas was presented with war bonds, a gold watch, a silver cigarette case, a gold albert and a medal from the inhabitants of High Spen. His reply to the presentation was typically modest:

> I am not much of a speaker. There's not a man of the Durhams who wouldn't have done what I did; it was just what any one of them would have done if he could. The thing happened to come my way and I did it. That's all.

A number of other medals were awarded for the action carried out between the 26th to 31st March. L/Cpl. Edward Hindmarch was in charge of a Lewis gun section. As the enemy pressed forward, he kept his gun in action despite very heavy enemy gunfire from close range. With the right flank in danger of being turned by an enemy flanking movement, he remained in action whilst adjustments were made to meet the threat. He continued to execute heavy casualties amongst the enemy over the

Pte. Thomas Young V.C.

next few days until he was wounded. He died of these wounds on the 29th April 1918. He was awarded a Bar to his Military Medal, which he had won in the previous year.

Cpl. Charles Bickerton took out a four-man patrol into no man's land. Moving quietly and with great care in the darkness the patrol crossed the shell-torn ground. Suddenly, the sound of an approaching enemy patrol was heard. With great personal courage and initiative Corporal Bickerton charged the enemy, firing his weapon as he ran. He killed two of the Germans and three more quickly surrendered and were brought back to the lines as prisoners. Over the following days, Corporal Bickerton set a fine example to his men and remained in constant action against the enemy. He, too, was awarded the Military Medal.

Pte. W.J. Lowes was a company stretcher bearer. During the heavy fighting at the end of March, he continually went forward under intense machine gun, rifle and shellfire to evacuate the wounded. Capt. T. Blandford James wrote, 'He laboured with unremitting energy and skill and set a fine example of self-sacrifice to the company.'

He was awarded the Military Medal.

One further award of the Military Medal, to L/Cpl. R. Timothy, is worthy of mention. He had already come to the notice of his officers by the skilful way he had handled his section under severe pressure from the enemy. Ammunition was running dangerously low and Lance Corporal Timothy volunteered to go to an ammunition dump at the far end of the valley. As he moved down the valley he was constantly sniped at by enemy machine guns. He was successful in bringing a supply of ammunition to his company. In the words of Capt. Blandford James, 'He continued to show the same contempt for personal danger and in so doing set a magnificent example to the remainder of the company.'

The Commanding Officer, Lieutenant Colonel Crouch, presented Military Medals to Sgt. E. Pallant, Cpls. M. Garrity, A. Outram and W.H. Scorer, L/Cpls. W. Baxendale, R. Carmichael, J. Fenwick, T. Henderson, T. Nicholson, R. Quinn and W. Stirling, Ptes. G. Chambers, A. Flodden, J. Glanville, A.E. Laws, J. McCoy, F. Taylor and W. Wishart.

On the 2nd April, the battalion moved to Souastre and, on the following day, to Vauchelles. It had now returned to pioneering duties – digging new trenches and defences. It moved back to the Souastre area on the 8th of the month. 2/Lt. Muir McKenzie, Sgt. Ralph Lowdon of High Spen and Pte. Thomas Taylor were killed by enemy shellfire on the 13th April and a further six men were wounded. On the same day a draft of 98 men was received, the average age of which was 18 and one-half years. Further drafts were received over the next two days. On the 17th, the battalion moved to Fonquevillers and was given the duty of defending the village. During the following week the battalion concentrated on improving the defences of the village. When relieved on the 23rd by the 9th Bn. North Staffordshire Regiment, the defences comprised two rows of wire, trench systems and several houses that had been turned into strong infantry positions, plus stores of small arms ammunition, bombs and rations. When relieved, the battalion moved to Bois Laleau near Authie. The 62nd Division moved back to Authie and into corps reserve. The remainder of the month was spent digging trenches, completing a brigade rifle range and training when the fairly constant rain permitted.

The next move on the 4th May was to Bois de Warnimont near Bus les Artois. Training and work alternated during the first half of the month. It was back to front line work on the 16th May when the battalion relieved the 9th Bn. North Staffordshire Regiment (37th Division) in the Souastre area. Over the next few days both sides subjected each other to heavy artillery and mortar bombardments. The battalion tasks included digging communication trenches in the left and right sectors of the line held by the 62nd Division. Further awards for bravery were announced.

One of these was Lt. Herbert Johnson, who was awarded the Military Cross. The advancing enemy was threatening his position, which was also under heavy rifle and machine gun fire. At this critical moment he stopped four machine guns and their crews, which were retiring through his position. He turned the guns around to fire on the advancing enemy, causing great mayhem amongst the Germans. Throughout this Lieutenant Johnson was moving about in the open, encouraging his men. The German advance was held until dusk, when another enemy attack developed under a very heavy machine gun barrage. Fierce fighting developed as the enemy strove to force the Durhams out of their positions. Lieutenant Johnson's Commanding Officer wrote, 'The initiative of this officer and the fine example which he showed his men until the line was restored were again largely responsible for the enemy being checked.'

Maj. T.B. Jameson and Lt. J.G. Weightman were also awarded the Military Cross. Sgt. T. Mason of Chopwell was awarded the Distinguished Conduct Medal.

The battalion work continued, much harassed by enemy artillery and mortar fire that added to the mounting casualties. Three men were killed on the 2nd June and one the following day. Six men of 'B' Company were wounded on the 9th whilst working on Misty Trench. L/Cpl. Henry Wilkinson M.M. was killed on the 16th. On the 24th June, the battalion was relieved and moved to Doullens by bus and into very good billets, much appreciated after the dangerous and dirty work of the last few weeks. The following two days were spent in cleaning and refitting. For the remainder of the month, companies worked on building a firing range at Authieule.

The first two weeks of July 1918 were taken up with a heavy training programme. All companies fired on the range. On the 14th, the 62nd Division began to move to the Marne where, along with the 51st Highland Division, it became part of the XXII British Corps under the command of the French Fifth Army. The 9th Battalion began its move on the following day and entrained at Doullens at 12.30 p.m., each man carrying three days' rations. The battalion reached Flavigny on the 17th and bivouacked in a wood at nearby Bury.

The German onslaughts, which had commenced on the 21st March, were nearing their end, although this was not known at the time. The Allies had been badly shaken but had held together despite losing a lot of ground and suffering heavy casualties. In the final stages of these offensives the Germans attacked on the Marne. The Second Battle of the Marne was fought between the 21st and 26th July 1918, although the French were in action as early as the 15th of the month. The French Fifth Army was on the right of the Italian Corps and it had succeeded in holding Nanteuil in the valley of the River Ardres. The Germans had some success at the junction of the French Fifth and Sixth Armies and had penetrated down the valley of the Marne towards Epernay. On the 18th, the French counter-attacked between Chateau Thierry and Soissons and took the Germans completely by surprise. The 62nd and 51st Divisions were put into the line on the Rheims flank of the German salient. Along with the 15th and 34th Divisions, who were between the Oise and the Aisne, they were given the task of pinching off the German salient between Rheims and Soissons.

At 5 a.m. on the 19th July, the 62nd Division assembled. No. 185 Brigade was at St. Imoges, 186 at Germaine and 187 at Ferme D'Eceuil. The division was to attack up the valley of the River Ardres, with the 51st Division on its left on the other side of the river. The 62nd attacked with two brigades up, 187 on the right and 185 on the left. No. 186 Brigade was to pass through these two brigades and on to the final objective, which lay about four and a half miles ahead.

The attack was made through thick forests. There were no trenches. The 62nd Division's history states:

> Guerrilla warfare would aptly describe much of the fighting…The valley of the Ardre varied from 2,000 – 3,000 yards in width. Much of it was gentle, undulating cornland with the crops ripe for cutting and of sufficient height to act as excellent cover for attacking or defending troops. The villages of Marfaux, Chaumuzy and Bligny lay on the slopes of the river, bordered by steep ridges and spurs, heavily wooded on the crests, whilst Cuitron, Espilly and Nappes were perched high up on the steep sides of the hills.

On the 19th July, the 9th Battalion was ordered to march to St. Imoges, where it arrived at 12.30 p.m. At 1 p.m. it moved off to Courtagnon Wood and into divisional reserve. Pte. James Charlton was killed during this march.

The attack began at 8 a.m. on the 20th July. It was a beautiful sunny morning. The attacking troops had had little rest and guides led them stumbling and quite exhausted through the forests. The cornfields in the valley and the vineyards on the slopes hid the waiting enemy from view. An enemy barrage commenced as soon as the troops moved and numerous machine guns opened up. Casualties were very heavy. A creeping barrage by French and Italian guns commenced 1,000 yards ahead of the advancing British. This was too far ahead to protect them and also failed to deal with many of the machine gun posts. Both the 187 and 185 Brigades lost heavily, and by 3 p.m. the attack halted.

All day on the 20th the battalion lay in this wood under enemy shellfire. Pte. Willie Ramsden was killed and two men were wounded. At 10.30 p.m. orders arrived for a move to Eceuil Farm as reserve to 187 Brigade. On the 21st, 187 Brigade was ordered to attack and capture the Bois de Petit Champ and the Bouilly Ridge. This attack was carried out by the 9th Battalion with the 5th Bn. King's Own Yorkshire Light Infantry in support. A creeping barrage, which was to lift 100 yards every 10 minutes, preceded the advance. The attack was to commence at 10.30 a.m. and the battalion moved off at 8.30 a.m. to enable it to reach the start line in time. Guides were provided to lead the battalion to the forming-up line. An error was made and the Durhams found themselves more than 600 yards farther back than was intended. The real trouble was that their protective barrage was that much farther ahead of them when they started the attack. At the appointed time of 10.30 a.m. the battalion attacked, downhill. 'B' Company was on the right, 'A' Company was in the centre and 'C' Company was on the left. On leaving the shelter of the woods the advancing troops ran into a storm of machine gun fire. Pressing on, the battalion reached the wood across the valley but were held up by what the War Diary describes as 'hundreds of machine

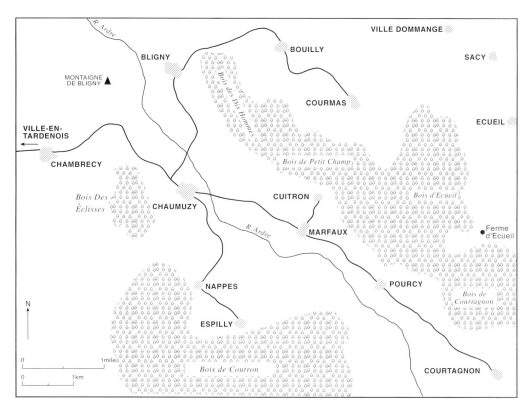

The Valley of the Ardres – July 1918

guns'. It had advanced 600 yards on a wide front but could go no farther. The captured ground was consolidated. Casualties had been very heavy. Capt. Harker M.C., Lieutenants Strachan, Tesseyman, Brenton and Chisholm and 2/Lts. A. Gibson and Dawson were wounded. Lt. Henry Strachan died of his wounds on the 29th July. Casualties amongst the other ranks were 28 killed, 131 wounded and 11 missing. Amongst the dead were L/Cpl. Frederick Chipchase, Sgt. Michael Hann M.M., Pte. Samuel Hampton and Cpl. William Park M.M. Amongst the missing and later confirmed as being killed in this action was L/Cpl. Matthew Barnes. The battalion was relieved on the 22nd July but there was to be no rest.

At 10 a.m. on the 22nd, the battalion received orders to prepare for an attack to be carried out on the following day. The 5th Bn. Duke of Wellington's Regiment was already involved in fierce fighting in the Bois de Petit Champ. The 9th Battalion was transferred to 186 Brigade. Its objective was to attack and take the village of Cuitron on the right flank. It formed up for the attack at 1 a.m. on the 23rd and came under heavy enemy shellfire, suffering 70 casualties; 60 from 'C' Company and 10 from 'A' Company. The battalion withdrew into the wood and reorganised. 'B' and 'C' Companies were formed into one composite company for the attack. At 6 a.m. the battalion moved out to attack. 'A' Company had suffered a further 30 casualties before moving out of the wood. Rushing forward, the battalion broke into the village of Cuitron and completed its capture, taking 85 prisoners. Driven out of the village in some disorder the enemy had left considerable quantities of equipment and other material lying about. The British took nine machine guns and recaptured eight French 75-mm guns. The battalion casualties were one officer wounded – 2/Lt. A. Sanderson – 15 other ranks killed and 93 wounded with eight missing. Amongst the dead were Ptes. Joseph Bellis, Frederick Davies, David White, Joseph Charlton, Walter Preston, William Wright and L/Cpl. George Wilkinson M.M. The positions taken were consolidated.

On the 24th, 'C' Company positions were bombarded by gas shells. Five men were wounded or suffered from the effects of gas. The battalion was relieved on the night of the 25th/26th July by the 2nd/4th Bn. Duke of Wellington's Regiment and moved into brigade reserve. There were no trenches and the men occupied a number of shell holes in front of the village of Pourcy. These positions were heavily shelled through the 26th with a mixture of high explosives and gas. Pte. Walter Derrick was killed and two men wounded. A draft of 200 other ranks and five officers arrived to supplement the battalion strength. On the 27th, the battalion moved forward to occupy shell holes near Chaumuzy, a village now in British hands. Subjected to heavy enemy shelling on the following day, Medical Officer Capt. J.A.C. Scott M.C. was wounded along with five other ranks. On the 29th, the battalion bivouacked in the wood north of Pourcy, and moved to St. Imoges the following day. A large cross was erected at Cuitron to commemorate those who had given their lives in the actions of the preceding days. A few days' rest could now be expected, and time to reorganise and clean up. German attacks began to slacken until, in early August, the enemy went over to the defensive. The enemy had shot his bolt. Though not realised at the time the end was but three months away.

The battalion's efforts in the fighting for Cuitron had not gone unnoticed. The Divisional Commander, Major General Braithwaite, wrote to the chairman of the Durham Territorial Association on the 2nd August 1918 that the 9th Battalion had been used as a fighting battalion and had captured the village of Cuitron. He went on to say, '…they fought magnificently as Durham men always do…and throughout the engagement their gallantry and devotion to duty was beyond praise.'

On the 4th August, the battalion was in camp near St. Léger. The 62nd Division was now part of IV Corps. On the 8th August, the great Allied offensive commenced which would in time knock Germany out of the war. The 62nd Division really needed a good rest after its recent labours. The men were tired and reorganisation was essential. For the next two weeks the 9th Battalion, along with the rest of the division, was resting and training. The award of the Military Medal to Pte. A. Simpson was announced on the 13th August.

At 10 p.m. on the 21st August, the battalion marched off to Doullens where it arrived at 3 a.m. On the 24th, it moved to Ablaizenville. The 62nd Division had been ordered to relieve the 3rd Division in the valley east and west of Courcelles. These orders were cancelled, but at 1 p.m. the division was ordered to relieve the 2nd Division, west of Mory and in front of Ervillers. No. 186 Brigade occupied a position on the ridge between Achiet-le-Grand and Gommecourt, with orders to support an attack on these two villages by the 5th Infantry Brigade. The 9th Battalion was back to its pioneering duties and was set to work on the Courcelles–Ervillers road. The division went into action on the 25th, attacking over ground which had been destroyed in the German March offensive. The objectives were Vaulx, Vraucourt, Longatte and Écoust St. Mein. The ground taken carried the line close to Ervillers and was held against heavy enemy counter-attacks. The battalion took no part in this action but carried on working on roads in the area.

On the 1st September, awards were announced for gallantry displayed during the July fighting. Capt. James A.C. Scott M.C. (R.A.M.C.) was awarded a second Bar to the Military Cross, Lt. H. Johnson was awarded a first Bar to the M.C. The Military Cross was awarded to Capt. C.H.R. Gee, Lt. W.E. Meikle and 2/Lt. L. Dodds. Sgt. W. Wilson was awarded the Distinguished Conduct Medal and Pte. C. Reid M.M., a Bar to his Military Medal. The Medical Officer, Capt. James A.C. Scott M.C., had been with the battalion since his attachment in June 1914. His citation noted that:

> He attended a very large number of wounded in the open, under heavy fire from machine guns and artillery and it was largely due to his skilful arrangements that the casualties were rapidly evacuated. Later on, while performing these duties he was severely wounded by shellfire. Throughout the whole of the operations, his courage and his example of self-sacrifice were worthy of high praise.

Captain Scott was actually wounded on two occasions, was twice mentioned in despatches and was awarded the Croix de Guerre by the French. He was promoted to Major in 1926, Lieutenant Colonel in November, 1933 and Acting Colonel in 1940.

Cpl. E. Gill M.M. was a member of a platoon in action at this time. He quickly found himself in command when the Commanding Officer and senior N.C.O.s had become casualties. He rallied his men and led them to the attack and successfully occupied the objective. He was awarded the Distinguished Conduct Medal.

L/Cpl. J. Masters of Gateshead was awarded a Distinguished Conduct Medal in the same action. When his officer and senior N.C.O.s became casualties he led the platoon with great dash and gallantry.

On the 1st September, the battalion moved into the line ready to take part in the attack by 187 Brigade, which was to be carried out on the following day.

No. 187 Brigade attacked at 5.30 a.m. on the 2nd September. Half an hour later the 9th Battalion moved forward to the ridge east of Vaulx as a support battalion. At 2.30 p.m., 'C' Company attacked Vaulx Wood and Vaulx Trench. These two trenches had been recaptured by the enemy in a successful counter-attack. The company's attack was a complete success and both objectives were taken with few casualties. Ptes.

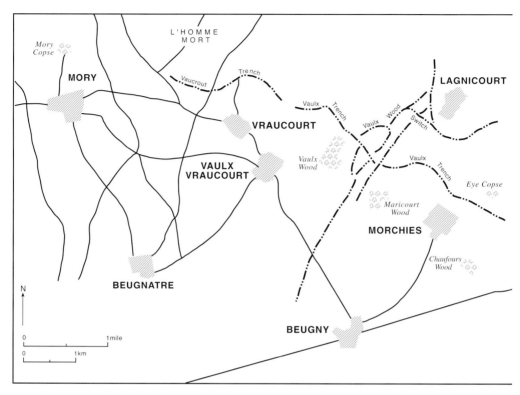

James Black and Alexander Cameron were killed. For some time now drafts to the battalion had been coming from a cross-section of the British army, such were the losses inflicted upon the Durham men during years of fighting. One man, Pte. Leonard Jones, who was killed on the 7th September, was born in Jerome, U.S.A. and lived in Bonnymean, Swansea. He had enlisted at Swansea and had joined the battalion from the Army Service Corps.

Pte. J. Horan won the Distinguished Conduct Medal during the action of the 2nd September: His citation described his actions:

> At Vaulx Wood on the 2nd September, 1918, he was acting as a stretcher bearer, and attended to the wounded under heavy fire with fine disregard of his own safety. On reaching the objective, finding the flank of the platoon exposed, he took a rifle and single-handedly attacked a machine gun, dispersing the team and capturing the gun, which he brought into our lines. He then brought in a wounded man whom he had observed lying in the open. His conspicuous gallantry and self-sacrificing devotion to duty were a splendid example to all.

On the 9th September, the battalion was attached to 186 Brigade. At 7 p.m. on the 10th, it moved up to the south-west corner of Havrincourt Wood. It billeted in old Nissen huts and remained there until early morning on the 12th. Strict orders had been issued that no movement was to take place outside the wood during daylight, except

110

for essential reconnaissance parties. This was to prevent the enemy seeing any activities that would inform them of the assembly of a large body of troops preparing an attack. The 9th Battalion was present in support of 186 Brigade. Its role was to follow the attacking battalions onto the first objective. From this position it was to attack the second objective, which was a trench system stretching from the Femy Front and support line to Keating Lane in the south.

The battalion paraded at 4 a.m. on the morning of the 12th and moved to the assembly position, which it reached at 5.15 a.m. The 62nd Division commenced its attack at 5.25 a.m. The battalion remained where it was until 6.25 a.m. when it moved forward towards the first objectives, which were now in British hands. At 8.05 a.m. 'C' Company established itself in the Hindenburg Line. The Officer in Command was unsure that the support line had been captured. He was ordered to attack this feature, which when reached was found to be in British possession. 'A' Company had a much tougher time. It arrived late at the jumping-off place due to the fact that both Commanders of the leading platoons had become casualties. The Sergeants left in command had not pushed their men forward with sufficient energy. The result was that the company had lost its barrage, which had moved forward in accordance with the timetable laid down.

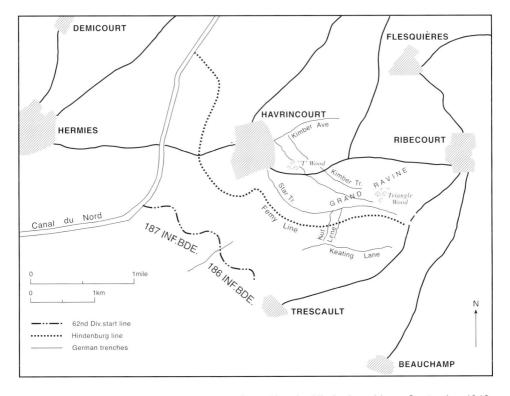

Breaching the Hindenburg Line – September 1918

'C' Company advanced behind the barrage and, in spite of considerable enemy machine gun fire, captured 60 prisoners and 10 machine guns in the sunken road running from the south-east corner of the village. The leading platoons, showing great dash, reached and took their final objectives, the Kimber Support. The enemy immediately launched a counter-attack from 'T' Wood and Triangle Copse. The first counter-attack was beaten off with heavy enemy losses. This success left the two platoons with only 14 to 16 survivors capable of fighting. When the Officer in Command saw the Germans preparing yet another counter-attack, he ordered a withdrawal down the ravine. 'C' Company was now down to about 50 other ranks and took up a position in the sunken road. 'A' Company was held up after an advance of about 200 yards and could do no more than establish contact with the flanking companies. Later, 'C' Company was subjected to enemy enfilade fire and had to make a further withdrawal to the Hindenburg Support Line and Star Trench.

Later, when darkness fell, night patrols found the final objective unoccupied by the enemy. Another patrol of two men captured 11 Germans and brought them back to British lines. Orders were received to occupy the objective and strong fighting patrols went out at dawn with this intention, only to find that the enemy had moved back in force. 'A' Company was able to occupy the sunken road with two platoons and gained touch with the 37th Division on the right. 'B' Company was now on the left with 'C' Company in support.

Casualties during the day's fighting were 2/Lt. S. Aberdeen who was wounded. Of the other ranks 13 were killed, 69 wounded and 17 missing. 2/Lt. W.R. Forest was killed, and his grave is one of a row of 10 Durham Light Infantry graves in Hermes Hill Cemetery, close to Havrincourt. The remaining nine graves are for men killed with him on the 12th September: Ptes. G.A. Parry, A. Harper, A.E. Stonehouse, A. Innes M.M., J.W. Hayes, A.W. Ball, A. Ford, W. Laybourne and L/Cpl. J.R. Taylor. In the small Hermes Cemetery opposite also lie the remains of Brig. Gen. Roland Boys Bradford V.C., M.C.

On the 13th September, 'B' Company attempted to bomb down the Hindenburg Line but could get no farther than Kut Lane. During the day four other ranks were killed, six were wounded and one was missing. The dead included Ptes. Samuel Harmsworth, Horace Jagger, Clayton Bradford and L/Cpl. Arthur Williams. Ptes. Harmsworth and Jagger are also buried in Hermes Hill Cemetery. The following day, 'A' Company took two officers and 49 other ranks prisoner. The battalion was subjected to very heavy shelling throughout the day and lost five men killed and two wounded. The dead were Ptes. Frederick Booth, Joseph Croney, George Hutchinson, George Knight and William Oxborrow. At 5.25 p.m., an urgent message was received from the Commander of No. 6 Platoon, 'B' Company, asking Company Commander Capt. W.D.B. Thompson to inform the supporting artillery that its shells were dropping short and onto his position. No attack developed on the 15th September and, that night, the battalion was relieved by the 13th Bn. Royal Fusiliers 3rd Infantry Division. The battalion moved off at 9.45 p.m. and marched to Bertincourt where a drink of hot cocoa awaited them. It then moved on to Beugny where billets were provided in huts and bivouacs. During the move, Pte. John William Rayner was killed and eight men were wounded, presumably by enemy shellfire. Total battalion casualties for this period in the line amounted to four officers and 122 other ranks.

Lieutenant Colonel Crouch, commanding the battalion, made the following observations in his report on the action:

> The telephonic communication was very bad for the first 36 hours but improved considerably. I was unable to use the pigeons owing to the Sgt. Signaller, who had all the necessaries, being killed early in the advance and a good deal of work had to be done by runners…
>
> Lewis guns, I am at a serious disadvantage to any ordinary unit being of a lower establishment in manpower and have only 12 Lewis guns against the increased establishment of an Infantry Battalion.
>
> The organisation of 3 coys. system in Pioneer Battalions does not appear to me to be so suitable and elastic for offensive operations and I would recommend a 4 coy. organisation to be adopted by all Pioneer Battalions.
>
> The supply tank proved a great success as Stores etc. were dumped at Boggot Hole almost as soon as the Village had fallen.

As usual, there were a few awards for the period of the 12th to the 15th September. Sgt. C.W. Caygill and Pte. J. Gundry were already holders of the Military Medal. For their courage and devotion to duty, they were both awarded the Distinguished Conduct Medal. Their citation read:

> For magnificent conduct at Havrincourt 12th to 15th September, 1918. When forward platoons of their company were heavily counter-attacked and pressed back by the enemy, leaving many casualties on No Man's Land, they went forward and rescued the wounded in the face of heavy machine gun and sniper fire. They made nine journeys and brought in 16 of their wounded comrades, whose lives they undoubtedly saved.

On the 16th of the month, the battalion moved to an old camp near Vaulx. It remained here resting, refitting, and training until the 26th September. At 9 p.m. on the 26th, the battalion paraded and marched off in the rear of 186 Brigade. The battalion occupied shallow trenches and officers and men spent a miserable night without cover as the rain sheeted down. The Third Army attacked at 5.20 a.m. on the 27th. The 62nd Division's role in the attack was to leapfrog through to the second objective at Rumilly. The 9th Battalion, now in its pioneering role, was to turn the dried-up bed of the Canal du Nord into a plank roadway and to repair the Havrincourt–Ribecourt road. Work in the area of Ribecourt and Marcoing continued over the next few days. Pte. Anthony West was killed by enemy shellfire on the 1st October, 1918 and was the last other rank soldier to be recorded as killed in action in the Durham Light Infantry section of 'Soldiers Died in the Great War'.

The following awards were announced on the 1st October. A second Bar to the Military Medal was awarded to L/Cpl. G. Landreth M.M. A Bar to the same was awarded to Pte. G. Waitt M.M. Military Medals were awarded to Sgt. F. Noble, Cpls. H.S. Clay and A. Jones, L/Cpls. L. Farrow, J. Hudson, A.E. Jones, J.E. Moore, T.W. Robson and T. Waters and Ptes. A. Fortune, G. Skilbeck, H. Tebb, J.H. Williamson, C. Wood and F. Wright.

The following letter was written to the chairman of the Durham Territorial Association on the 9th October 1918, by Maj. Gen. R. Whigham, G.O.C. 62nd Division:

> I have succeeded Lt. General Sir W.P. Braithwaite K.C.B, now commanding IX Corps, in command of the 62nd (West Riding) Division on the 28th August and I am sure you will be glad to have further news of the deeds of the 9th Battalion Durham Light Infantry.
>
> The Division has been engaged in the great offensive since 25th August and the Battalion has not only carried out its normal role as a Pioneer Battalion but has twice been called in to take part in heavy fighting.
>
> On 2nd September it was attached to the 187 Infantry Brigade and recaptured Vaulx Wood, which the enemy had wrested from us by counter attack.
>
> Again in the 'Second Battle of Havrincourt' the 9th Battalion Durham Light Infantry was attached to the 186 Infantry Brigade and did splendid work.
>
> The Battalion has a magnificent spirit and I cannot speak too highly of its value to the Division.

The battalion continued its work on roads until the 9th October. On this day it moved to Masnières for more work on the roads around Rumilly, Séranvillers, La Targette, Wambaix and Cattenières. Further awards were announced on the 16th and 17th October. The Distinguished Conduct Medal was awarded to Pte. J. Horan. A Bar to the Military Medal was awarded to Cpl. H, Williams M.M. The following received the Military Medal: Sgt. J.F. Carr, L/Sgt. S. Hammond, Cpl. P. Holborn, L/Cpls. M. Fenwick, J. Nichol, J. Norris, R. Otley and H. Wiseman and Ptes. T.E. Atkins, F. Byrne, R. Edwards, C. Holmes, W. Jackson, H. Kitching, P. Munt, F. Newton, J.W. Purvis and J. Radford. A Bar to the Military Cross was awarded to Capt. C.A. Marshall. Capt. J.D. Rickaby and Lts. H.C.B. Plummer and F.R. Armstrong were awarded the Military Cross.

On the 18th October, Major Jameson M.C. led a party of eight officers and 250 other ranks to a camp near Quiévy where it worked alongside the 460th Coy. Royal Engineers. The task was to bridge the River Selle. The remainder of the battalion was employed on roads near Cattenières. The battalion moved to Bevillers on the 19th and to Quiévy on the following day. No. 186 Brigade attacked Solesmes, and the bridging of the River Selle by the engineers and the battalion party enabled the operation to go forward with great success. The remainder of the battalion followed up the attack and was employed in clearing and repairing roads on the western edge of Solesmes. Casualties were 2/Lt. F.W. Cowling and two other ranks wounded. Working on roads continued until the 24th October, when the battalion moved to billets in Solesmes. 2/Lt. Edgar Frankland was killed on this day.

More awards were announced on the 26th October. Bars to the Military Medal were awarded to Sgt. C. Hutton and L/Cpl. W. Sterling. Military Medals were awarded to Sgts. F. Graham and W.J.H. Wilson, L/Cpls. A. Burnside, C.J. Cobb, J. Hardy, P. Henary, T. Leadbitter, G.E. Smith and J. Taylor and Ptes. M. Annable, P. Cranney, J. Crass, G. Dempsey, T. Forbes, E. Galley, T. Gill, W.R. Hewitt, J.W. Howe, C. Johnson, J.W. Moore, S. Morgan, J. Morris, C. Nobes, J. Parker, J. Slack, D. Slater, J. Smith, T. Timothy, W. Todd, J.W. Waterworth, J. Watts and S. Whittaker.

Whilst the 62nd Division continued to attack the enemy, the battalion continued its work on roads. This work was vital as it enabled the movement of men and supplies to reach the attacking forces and maintain the advance against what was now quite clearly seen as a demoralised enemy. This work continued into November. On the 4th, the battalion moved at 4 a.m.to Escarmain. The 62nd Division attacked at 5.30 a.m. and advanced five miles. The battalion moved to Orsinval and continued to work on the roads in the area. On the 6th, a move was made to Gommignies. The division advanced nine and one-half miles and took 800 prisoners and a number of guns. On the 8th November, the battalion moved to Bavisiaux and worked on the Bavisiaux–Quene au Loup road. On the 10th, it moved to Sous-le-Bois. Billets were good and the band played for the village inhabitants in the evening. The following day, the last day of hostilities, work was being done on filling craters when the cease-fire was announced. Charles Gee, now Captain and still Adjutant, remembered:

The note came that armistice was at 11 o'clock. I took it to the Colonel who said, 'I don't believe it.' Nor did I. I hadn't had time to read the intelligence reports that had come in. I did lose 10 shillings to somebody who said there was an armistice. He had read the intelligence reports and I hadn't. I said to the Colonel, 'What do we do?' He said, 'Carry on.' The companies were working. We realised the armistice was on and I had a glass of wine.

Captain Gee wrote to his elder brother serving with the 13th Bn. Durham Light Infantry. The excitement on learning of the armistice was shattered when he was informed that his brother had been killed in action on the 8th November.

The battalion was given a bouquet and an address from the civilian population of the village. This small, yet touching gesture, must have meant a great deal coming from a people who had spent four years under German dominance.

This terrible war was now at an end. The officers and men who had set out from Newcastle over three and one-half years before had suffered much. Many of their friends and comrades were dead, many more had suffered grievous wounds both to body and mind. If there was excitement and enormous relief when the end was announced, it must have been tinged with many sad memories of those who were with them no more. The battalion had fought in many fierce battles and earned great praise from the highest-ranking Generals. They had served under four Commanders, namely

Lt. Cols. A. Henderson C.M.G., W.B. Moir, R.B. Bradford V.C., M.C. and E.G. Crouch D.S.O., D.C.M., all of whom had impressed their personalities on the officers and men during their tenure of command. The battalion had earned many awards – a total of 328, which was claimed to be the highest total given to any battalion during the war. Now the men wanted to get back home to their loved ones. This was to take time, as there was another duty awaiting them – the march into and occupation of Germany.

CHAPTER IX

T he war was over but the work of the battalion continued. On the 12th November, 'A' and 'B' Companies spent the day filling in craters. 'C' Company cleaned itself up and went out to do some training. More awards were announced for bravery in action. Military Medals were awarded to Sgt. J. Munro, Cpl. E. Edmundson and Ptes. G. Bolam, T. Burton, J.T. Coombes, J. Cooper, W. Jackson, P. O'Neil and T. Prudham.

Work and training continued until the 14th of the month. On the 15th, final preparations were made for a move to start on the following day. This move fired the imagination and curiosity of all ranks. At last they would see their enemies up close – the battalion was to move into Germany as part of the advanced guard of the 62nd Division, now earmarked as one of the occupation divisions. How would they get there? How else? The battalion was to march, over 200 miles entirely on foot. The local people of Sous-le-Bois gloomily told the troops that, due to the winter weather, they would never make it.

On the 16th November, the battalion commenced its long march through eastern France and into Germany. It arrived in Komhern on Christmas Day, 1918. The War Diary's final entry for this day was, 'No facilities for festivities.'

The battalion's stay in Germany was relatively short. Its role was to guard sensitive and vital installations such as major road and rail bridges and administrative buildings. This was not the Germany of 1945. There was little destruction. The blockade had brought acute food shortages and this required urgent attention. The battalion was one of many, however, who had seen much action and was looking forward to being replaced by battalions of young conscripts new out from England. In 1919 it returned to England and to demobilisation.

Reformed in 1920, the battalion settled into its peacetime activities. These included the usual weekly training nights, weekend camps and annual camps. The first annual camp was held at Scarborough and, in the following years, at Ripon, Pwllheli (North Wales), Catterick, Marske, Ravensworth, Whitby, Alnwick and Shilbottle. Commanding officers of the battalion during the inter-war years were Lieutenant Colonels Henderson, W.de G. Martin, H. Saddler, K. Dunn and W.F. Simpson. A large number of men who had served in the First World War paraded at Saltwell Park, Gateshead on 11th August 1920, and received gallantry medals from the Divisional Commander. The battalion soccer team was defeated in the final of the Territorial Army football championship. Permanent staff of the battalion included R.S.M. Lister and Sergeants Cooper and Hawkins. The winter training season commenced in January and continued until the end of April. There were courses covering all aspects of military

Annual Camp, Scarborough 1920 – the first camp after World War I. Colonel Henderson is seated third from the right with Major Crouch D.S.O., D.C.M. on his left. Capt. James A.C. Scott M.C. & two Bars (Battalion Medical Officer) is third from the right, back row. Others identified are Capt. Hugh Swinburne, standing far left, and Capt J. Porter (Q.M.), centre back row.

skills, which included those for section leaders, signallers, and for improving proficiency with the machine gun, Lewis gun and rifle. There were annual sports meetings and shooting competitions. Route marches strengthened legs and stamina, though marching immediately behind the officer on his horse could have its less pleasant moments. Sgt. John L. Williams (later commissioned into the Royal West Kents Regiment) wrote of one such route march when on night manoeuvres:

> If you were a Lance Corporal in charge of a section, you marched at the head of the section…I remember marching in the moonlight at the head of my section and the officer's horse was in front of me and it was breaking wind in my face all the way.'

On the 19th December 1926, the battalion led by the band and Colours marched to St. Mary's Church, Gateshead for the unveiling of the wooden cross, originally erected near Le Sars on the Somme battlefield, in memory of those who fell in action in the area of High Wood. It was made under the instructions of Lieutenant Colonel Bradford, whilst he was with the battalion and was designed by Captain Maucklin. The cross was unveiled by the honourary Colonel, Col. F.R. Simpson T.D. Wreaths were laid by Lt. Col. E.G. Crouch D.S.O., D.C.M., and ex-Sergeant E. Mitchell, both of whom had fought in the Somme in 1916.

The life of the battalion continued to prosper over the following years. In 1934, it took part in the Northern Command Tattoo at Ravensworth. Company Sergeant Major Morris was selected as a reserve for the Territorial Army inter-services shooting team. An Old Comrades Association had been formed and reunion dinners and dances were well attended.

In the 1938, war clouds formed yet again. Belatedly, much new transport began to arrive. The Bren gun made a first appearance. The new weapon was not available in sufficient numbers to equip the companies initially, but one or two were provided to enable lectures to take place on stripping and assembling them. In one training session the following was an interesting comment on current military thinking:

> The Attack Demonstration made clear an important principle, 'Fire and Movement' in the old sense is, in the face of modern defence weapons, as dead as the cavalry charge. The crux of the Attack plan is the Fire Plan, and smoke is a fundamental part of the Fire Plan. We should all remember the sensation of waiting, in a thick blinding pall of smoke, for the appearance within yards of us, of the helmeted figures with bayonets.
>
> One observer of the Bren Gun demo said it was, 'A wonder they did not make it lay its own aim and fire itself'. In any case, the new weapon impressed us all with its powers and its simplicity and we are all anxiously waiting an opportunity of becoming 'riflemen trained as Bren Gunners'. The tactical handling of the gun is part of present training but

Battalion parade at Burt Terrace, Gateshead, inspected by Brig. Jackie Churchill. Lt. Scott-Batey is third from the left. Brig. Percy commanded 151 Brigade 1939–40. The date of the parade could be 1938 to clelebrate the accenssion of King George VI.

such training will become twice as realistic when the actual weapon is in our hands.

The 50th (Northumbrian) Division was selected as a motorised division and, in the months immediately prior to the outbreak of war, Lt. Gen. Sir Giffard Le Q Martel K.C.B., K.B.E., D.S.O., M.C., set about training his officers in this new role. This was not an easy task as much of the work was undertaken in T.E.W.T.s – Training Exercises Without Troops! Martel's theories were taken on board by the officers in quick time. The division was fortunate in the appointment of General Martel as he was a tank enthusiast and well versed in the theories of mobile warfare. As a motorised division, the 50th comprised two brigades, 150 and 151, with a reconnaissance unit, the 4th Bn. Royal Northumberland Fusiliers. Supporting arms comprised artillery, engineers, medical services and the Royal Army Service Corps. No. 151 Brigade was commanded by Brigadier Jackie Churchill who had served with distinction in the First World War. As the T.E.W.T.s took place, vehicles to make the division mobile were arriving.

In 1939, the battalion formed the guard of honour for the visit of King George VI to the region. This guard was mounted at the Team Valley Estate. Lt. J.J. March carried the Colours. Maj. H.L. Swinburne was in command.

Training intensified as the weeks passed and September 1939 approached. Headquarter company, with Maj. R.C. Kelly commanding, comprised No.1 Platoon (signals), No.2 Platoon (anti-aircraft and bugles), No.3 Platoon (mortars), No.4 Platoon (carriers), No.5 Platoon – (pioneers) and No.6 Platoon (motor transport section). The rifle companies were 'A' Company (Capt. V.H. Jackson), 'B' Company (Capt. W.S. Olleson), 'C' Company (Capt. A.C. Ritchie) and 'D' Company (Capt. J.C. Slight). On the 1st September, the battalion was embodied. Its strength was 50 officers and 1,234 other ranks.

Key men had been called up on the 24th August. Their task was to prepare to receive the full battalion when mobilised. Sgt. John L. Williams was one of these key men. He recalled the general mobilisation:

> I was playing darts with the Sgt. Maj. when the telephone rang and the code name came through [for general mobilisation]. The Sgt. Maj. said, 'We'll finish this game then gan and caal oot the lads.'

Shades of Sir Francis Drake!

CHAPTER X

THE SECOND WORLD WAR

MOBILISATION & THE COTSWOLDS 1939–40

On the 3rd September 1939 at 11 a.m., Prime Minister Neville Chamberlain announced to the nation that we were at war with Germany. The battalion, which had been mobilised on the 1st September, was on church parade. Lt. Ken Wood, who was to win the Military Cross with the 6th Battalion in 1944, remembered the event:

> At morning church service, Padre Lindsey informed us at the end of the service that we had declared war on Germany. We paraded outside as the air raid sirens sounded for the first time and were galvanised into action. The streets were suddenly deserted and the odd small child snatched indoors as we doubled, in three ranks, up the hill to our billets. Steel helmets were donned, respirators fixed and we were on parade for action with rifles and bayonets as the all clear sounded.

Pte. G. Lambert, a member of the Militia training in Fenham Barracks, Newcastle, remembered the declaration of war:

> On the Sunday morning that war was declared, we were all lined up ready to go down Barrack Road, to go to the Baths, because that facility was not in the barrack room. All the people, or quite a number in Barrack Road, came out to watch us going down with tears running down their faces.

Pte. Richard Atkinson, who had joined the Territorials in March, remembered how life changed for him on mobilisation:

> The first thing they said to me, I can remember plain as anything, PSI [Platoon Sergeant Instructor] Rigg said, 'Atkinson, you're no longer a Territorial.' On your shoulder in those days, you wore a 'T' for Territorial. He says, 'You're no longer a Territorial soldier, take that 'T' down, Territorial brass off your shoulder. You're now a regular soldier.'

On the 4th September, changes were made in the composition of the battalion. A second line battalion had been formed when, in June 1939, the Government ordered that the size of the Territorial Army should be doubled.

> Permission was received for the 2nd Ninth – later to be called by the pleasing title of 'Duplicate Battalion' by the authorities and 'Gestetner Gurkhas' by the ribald – to receive the name of the 'Tyneside Scottish' and the following officers were posted to the new unit: Lt. Col. H.L. Swinburne T.D., Capt. C.W. Oxley, Lts. G.D. Harker and J. Dempster

and 2/Lt. A. Walton.

A number of men who had joined the 9th Battalion were transferred to this second-line battalion and were far from happy with the move. Originally given the title of 12th Bn. The Durham Light Infantry, it had its title quickly changed to the 1st Bn. the Tyneside Scottish, and ultimately became part of the Black Watch. It was brigaded with the 10th and 11th Battalions D.L.I., which had been formed in similar circumstances from the 6th and 8th Battalions of the regiment and went to France in 1940 – partially trained and badly equipped. Its role was that of a labour battalion, working on roads and airstrips. It suffered grievous losses in the German offensive of late May 1940.

Further changes were due since the battalion had been trawled to transfer skilled workers back to civilian employment vital to the country's war effort. In addition, men who were too old or too young for active service overseas and those unfit for the rigours of warfare were taken out. Their places were taken by conscripted men. These had completed their basic training at centres such as Willington, Esh Winning and New Brancepeth.

Remembering his training days some 50 years later, ex L/Cpl. Fred Welsh, commented on his treatment and what the army came to mean to him. His sentiments were far from uniquely held.

> I'll never understand the treatment of recruits. I'll never understand it. Somebody cursing at a young lad who is homesick, a young lad who does not know where he is. I can't see how calling him a 'Bastard' and all the rest of it, I can't see how it makes a man a better soldier. There were some thirty-three of us always together. Your officer was a friend, your sergeant was a friend and even the R.S.M., though he sometimes lost his temper when you were on guard. When you were in a fighting unit, life was so much different...I was called up and was there to fight and from being the youngest in a family of seven, all of a sudden I had to be a man – [you were] put on your own and dependent on those around you. I would say that every platoon in the army would be made up of the same thirty-odd people: the boozer, the person who wouldn't buckle down, those who wanted to try, those who were interested in the war. There would be the same people in every platoon. 'Barrackroom Lawyers' as they call them – big mouths, drunkards. We had them all. Wherever you went there was the same guy, only he had a different name. Whoever you met you stuck to during the war. You found your own level, your own friends. We shared cigarettes, parcels. That is how you lived your life. If you had ten cigarettes, you had five each. If you had a bar of chocolate, you had half a bar of chocolate each...The word is 'comrade'.

As the Territorials of the battalion drilled, went on route marches and dug trenches, the conscripts who would join them trained on the surrounding areas of Willington, Esh Winning and New Brancepeth. Pte. Joe Clark remembered some of the innovations experienced in his training:

> There used to be a drift mine at Esh Winning and the set [group of small-wheeled coal

carrying tubs] would come out of the bankside. One of the officers used to use it as though it was a tank. He would give a word of command. He used to say, 'Armoured vehicle passing your front. Go into action,' and it was the set coming out.

The battalion War Diary for the 11th September 1939 stated that intensive individual training commenced. Training Exercises Without Troops (T.E.W.T.) for officers emphasised the drills and technique for movement and deployment of a motorised division. Officers and N.C.O.s were sent on a variety of courses. A two-week course in tactics, weapon training and drill was organised for Corporals and Lance Corporals of the battalion. There were junior leadership courses for officers and N.C.O.s and courses covering many aspects of military skills.

Pte. Fred Welsh and his platoon were sent to dig trenches the army way:

> We went onto the hilltop at New Brancepeth to learn how to dig trenches. I always remember a miner from Ryhope. I suppose it would be the first time he'd ever spoken to the sergeant. 'I'm sorry sergeant,' he says. 'You can teach me anything you like but do not try to teach me how to use a shovel.' He came from Oxford, this sergeant. You picked and shovelled to numbers. You didn't dig a hole…You pick, rake and pull and then you shovel. You dig in, you pull out, then throw it out. These men were telling you what to do with a shovel and this lad was in the next trench, sat and finished and this sergeant had just got the sods off the grass…It was good digging on top of New Brancepeth, it was like a peat place, it was good digging and this lad said, 'No! If I'm digging for my life, I'm digging my way.'

On the 27th September, companies were moved. 'A' Company went to Gateshead, 'B' Company to Sunderland and 'D' Company to South Shields. At the beginning of October, Major Kelly left for Oxfordshire to seek out billets for the battalion's move to Shipston-on-Stour, Long Compton and Little Compton. On the 16th October, 88 militiamen were posted to the battalion. On this same day, the battalion proceeded to Whitburn Camp to fire on the ranges. Pte. Joe Clark was one of the militiamen:

> Eventually they took us to Brancepeth Station and put us on a train. We didn't know where we were going, all of us Militia lads and we finished up back at Gateshead Station. We wondered what was happening and we were put on buses and then the buses started up and we went off. We still didn't know where we were going. Part of the way on the journey, we saw these soldiers marching. We thought it was great, we [were] on a bus. Little did we know that we were going to join them at Whitburn. When the bus got to Whitburn, we all lined up at the entrance to Whitburn Range and these soldiers all marched in. We had to stand to attention when they came in. That was the beginning of joining the 9th D.L.I. They'd marched all the way from Gateshead. We were all broken up into platoons…Some were taken out to learn to drive transport. I was put into 9 Platoon and I was part of 'A' Company.

Pte. Fred Welsh remembered the Whitburn Ranges for a different reason:

We went to Whitburn Firing Range to learn to shoot…[this] was the first place I ever saw a man shot. You had to take your turn in the Butts, which means you were sat in a dugout watching the scores and you marked the scores for the soldiers firing. This man was hit by a ricochet in his arm and badly injured. There was an officer with us. He and another lad were versed well enough in first aid to treat the lad and stop the firing and get him to hospital at Sunderland. So, after the firing, at night when everything was finished, somebody said to this lad, 'It's your mate that's in hospital, phone up to see if he's all right.' A true story this, true. He phoned the hospital and he came back and we said, 'How is he?' He said, 'He must be all right as he's just gone to Sunderland Empire to the theatre with his sister.' He'd been going to the hospital theatre to have his arm taken off! He'd lost his arm and this man thought he'd picked his sister up and was going to the theatre to the Sunderland Empire.

On the 19th October, there were more transfers of officers and men to the 12th Battalion. Most of the men transferred were too young for active service overseas. The end of an era was signalled when Lt. Col. J.A.C. Scott M.C., T.D., R.A.M.C. exchanged places with Capt. R. Rutherford of the 12th Battalion. Lieutenant Colonel Scott had served with great distinction with the battalion during the First World War and the years between the wars.

Maj. J.C. Slight with six officers and 18 other ranks left with the transport on the 22nd October for the new station in Oxfordshire. At 11p.m. on the same day, the battalion boarded busses at Whitburn for Newcastle. Here it joined a train at Newcastle Central Station in the early hours of the 23rd and proceeded to the Cotswolds. Battalion headquarters and headquarter company were billeted at Kitebrook House, near Moreton-in-the-Marsh. 'A' and 'B' Companies were at Shipston-on-Stour and 'C' and 'D' Companies at Long Compton. At first nervous of these men from the far north, the civilian population of the area quickly warmed to the friendly Geordies.

Pte. Joe Clark described his encounters with the locals:

There were three or four of us. We met a man called Dick Dunsby. He had a sister who was a good age, I should think. Anyway, he took us along one night and we had a good feed at the house, in Mill Street it was. I think he was connected with the butchery trade somehow. We used to go along regularly after that. They called her Gladys Dunsby and she was a great woman, great woman. I remember even when I went abroad, I used to write to her. She used to say, 'Let us know where you go', and I used to write back to her. She was like a mother to us. We were just young lads. She was very good, that woman…There used to be a workhouse on the outskirts of Shipston. They used to march us up there to the showers.

This friendliness established with the civilians made up for what were, on the whole, far from comfortable billets and pretty basic army food. Pte. Fred Welsh, it appears, was not quite as fortunate as Private Clark and his friends:

We were at Kitebrook Hall, which was a great big hall. There was no lighting. There was no hot water. We had field kitchens to make the grub. Beds of a type, which were a double tier and lattice with like metal tapes and you had a palliasse [and] I think three blankets. It was getting around Christmas time by this and it was freezing cold and there was nowhere to go. You just had to sit in your room with candles and chat and talk…The food was pretty grim. It was adequate…We had a concert party came to us at Christmas. We made them cry as well. At the end of the show, we sang our 'Abide With Me'. They were standing on the stage with tears running down their cheeks.

Lt. Ken Wood described conditions for the officers:

'C' Company settled down in Long Compton with company HQ happily in the Red Lion Snug. I was O.C. 13 Platoon…'A' Company was in Shipston-on-Stour commanded by George Dunn and officers V.H. Jackson, my brother George and Jasper March, joined later by Norman Henderson, Geoff Pettinger and Tony Hartnell. Wives were allowed in the area and my wife and I had a comfortable three-roomed suite in a farmhouse. Saturday nights were often spent at Stratford-on-Avon where there was always a stage revue to be seen…We were to be the proud chosen members of an elite unit; a motorised division which would strike its way through enemy defences in the vanguard of a victorious British Army! Rommel had the same idea and better equipment.

Our citizen army was indeed badly equipped despite the efforts to improve things in the last months prior to the outbreak of war. Equipment and vehicles were beginning to come through in increasing numbers but it would take time to complete all requirements. Not all the battalion even had the latest battle dress. Lieutenant Wood wrote:

Some battledress was filtering through and was issued as it arrived – none for the officers yet…The Brigade Anti-Tank Company was formed. I was not surprised to be selected. Capt. Jackson from 'A' Company was to command. The three platoon commanders were myself 9 DLI, Maurice Kirby 6 DLI, Chris Beattie 8 DLI and we assembled with our platoons from each battalion at Bledington, a small, sleepy village. Of course, there were no guns or equipment of any kind except three 15cwt trucks and four 8cwt pickups. Our W.O.II was a regular reservist who had his work cut out but stuck to it with a will.

Fortunately, Maurice Kirby went on a course and came back full of knowledge. We practised for hours loading non-existing 2pdr guns onto non-existing portees [a specially equipped low loader from which the guns could be fired], stacking non-existing ammunition, kneeling round the 'gun' carrying out the proper 1, 2, 3 and 4 operatives, 'loading,' 'aiming' and 'firing' until we were all completely efficient in all positions…We continued this day after day without protest while we got to know each other and settled in.

Gradually the equipment arrived and the battalion, under its active Commanding Officer, Lt. Col. W.F. Simpson, began to reach the level of efficiency, discipline and skill that enabled it to serve with such distinction during the active part of the war. On the 1st November, a draft of 70 other ranks was received from the 12th Battalion. Transfers out of the battalion were still taking place due to the demands of industry for the return of key men and continuing medical examinations were finding men not yet fit for active service. A further draft of 50 men was received on the 16th of the month from the infantry training centre (I.T.C.) at Brancepeth. During the month, Lt. Harry Sell was transferred to 151 Brigade headquarters as brigade Motor Transport Officer and Capt. W.S. Olleson left for 50th Division headquarters to take up the position of Chemical Warfare Officer. The training became more concentrated as the end of the year approached. In December, leave parties were sent off and rumours began to surface of an impending move overseas.

Training continued into the New Year. On the 6th January, 'A' and 'C' Companies fired a weapons course on the Kingsbury Ranges at Castle Bromwich. On the same day, a further 33 other ranks classed as 'immatures' – too young for active service abroad – were transferred to the 12th (Tyneside Scottish) Battalion. These were replaced on the following day by a draft of 48 other ranks from the I.T.C. Brancepeth. 'B' and 'D' Companies replaced 'A' and 'C' Companies on the Kingsbury ranges. On the 10th of the month, 2/Lt. R.H. Forbes set off to reconnoitre the motor transport route to Southampton, the port from which the battalion would leave for France. It was a bitterly cold winter and snow and ice made road journeys difficult. Even at this late hour prior to leaving this country, vehicles and equipment were still arriving to complete the battalion's needs. The rest of the carriers arrived on the 10th and it was as late as the 15th January when the battalion was completely equipped with the new uniform and equipment and the 1908 clothing and boots dispensed with. On the previous day, Capt. W.J.R. Scott and a road advance party had left for Southampton.

The intense cold was such that the vehicles had to be started up every hour overnight and the engines run for two minutes. During the day, any vehicle not in use had to be started up every two hours and run for 10 minutes. Anti-freeze was in short supply and was allocated to aircraft, tanks and ambulances only. On the 17th January, 151 Brigade was inspected by His Majesty the King at Chipping Norton. At 9.45 a.m. 'A' and 'B' Companies were carried in transport from Shipston-on-Stour, whilst 'H.Q.' Company marched from Kitebrook and 'C' and 'D' Companies marched form Long Compton. For the King's inspection, the battalion paraded 29 officers and 756 other ranks. Lt. Ken Wood wrote:

> The King was to inspect the Division in Chipping Norton before we went to France. Without transport, we set off in a severe snowstorm, in greatcoats and small packs, to march the ten miles or so to Chipping Norton. Luckily our place of inspection was alongside a colonnaded porch where we were able to take refuge, in shifts, to dry out and warm through the several hours we had to wait our turn.
>
> Again and again, we rehearsed getting 'On Parade' and front rank dressing until it was perfect. Unfortunately, the King and entourage emerged from an adjacent side road without warning – no time to right dress – was my face red – I was right marker. It was not commented upon.

A mortar demonstration was given for the King. An entry in the War Diary states that 'owing to an error of judgement, three smoke shells fell among a flock of sheep in lamb. There were no casualties.'

An interesting entry in the War Diary for the 19th January stated that 12 officers and eight N.C.O.s attended a confidential lecture at 50th Division headquarters, on 'escaping from Germany'! As the move to France approached, 55 men were confirmed on the 21st January in Long Compton Church by the Bishop of Coventry. At 7 a.m. on the 23rd, the battalion transport left Kitebrook for Southampton. It was not an easy move. Some of the trucks had frozen radiators in spite of all protection against the extreme frost. The carriers' tracks were frozen with snow and took a lot of moving, although engines had been run every half hour throughout the night and five braziers had been burning around these vehicles. On the 28th January, buses arrived to pick up the battalion and take it to Moreton-in-the-Marsh railway station. The battalion left Moreton in two trains, arriving at Southampton by 11.30 a.m. By 1 o'clock in the afternoon, it was onboard the SS *Prague*, which sailed at 4.20 p.m.

CHAPTER XI

FRANCE & BELGIUM 1940

It was not an uneventful journey. The S.S. *Prague* ran aground and 30 minutes had elapsed before she got underway again. At 8.30 a.m. on the 29th January 1940, the boat berthed at the quayside in Cherbourg. The 9th Battalion was back in France about to face the same enemy as its forebears in 1915. There were no bands or excited, cheering civilians to welcome them. It was raining and there were few Frenchmen in sight. Within the hour disembarkation was complete and the battalion proceeded to the railway station where hot tea was available. At 1 p.m., hot stew was served and this was followed by town leave. Officers and men set off to satisfy their curiosity and make their first contact with their allies. Drinking places and cinemas were searched out along with, for some, the first intimate contact with certain French ladies. Pte. Bill Ridley remembered his first experiences in France:

> It was miserable and it was raining. It was cold and it was dark and we went into the town of Cherbourg. I said to Bob, 'Howay, let's go to the pictures.' So we saw this big, long queue and he says, 'Look at that queue there.' I says, 'We gotta go somewhere for the night. At least it will be warm in the cinema.' We joined the queue and I said to one of the lads, 'What's on? What's the picture that's on?' He said, 'What do you mean?' I says, 'What's the picture we're standing to see?' He says, 'This isn't a picture queue, it's a queue for the brothel!'

Private Ridley and his friend beat a hasty retreat. At 8 p.m. the battalion reported back to the railway station, complete except for one unnamed deserter discovered when the roll call was taken. The train left for La Hutte at 10.06 p.m. The battalion travelled under the same conditions as their fathers in the Great War; officers in draughty carriages, the men in trucks marked, '8 *chevaux*, 40 *hommes*'. On arrival at La Hutte the following morning, Major Kelly and 2/Lt. J. Browne, who had been in France arranging billets, reported back. The battalion was taken by trucks to the following billets:

Headquarters:	Sougé le Ganelon
'A' Company:	Fresnay sur Sarthe
'B' Company:	Douillet le Joly
'C' and 'D' Companies:	Assé le Boisnes

The battalion quickly settled in for what was expected to be a short stay in this area. However, the severe winter blocked the roads with ice and snow, and the battalion stay was longer than planned. The reaction of the French civilians towards the officers and men seems to have been mixed. Many of the men found them somewhat aloof and the locals did not encourage close contact. The officers seemed to have been more

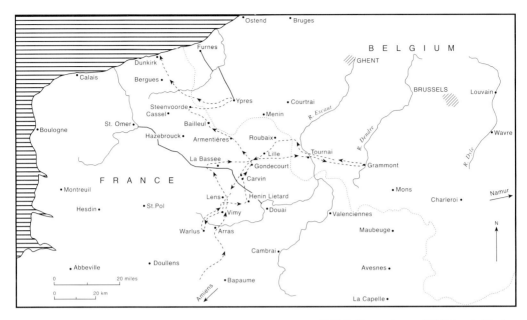

B.E.F. Campaign – 151 Brigade Routes

readily accepted and a number of them were invited into civilian homes. Prices in the local estaminets increased on the arrival of these new customers. However, this did not stop the battalion from sampling the wine – a drink which the great majority of them had never consumed before. It had a remarkable effect and led to some drastic punishment, as 2/Lt. Dick Forbes described:

> If on the other hand you got someone who drank an awful lot of beer, French wine was so cheap. The troops used to buy it like beer and drink it like beer. But, of course, what they did not realise was the alcoholic content was far in excess. So invariably, some of them got not only drunk but violently drunk and caused a lot of trouble and damage, not only to themselves and others in the Battalion but also sometimes to civilians. So something drastic had to be done apart from the normal ticking off and withdrawal of privileges…We could give them Pack Drill. Now this was hard going. The man was fully kitted out with his rifle and with his pack. His pack was either filled with sand or logs of wood. There was also a sergeant or a corporal in charge and he had to walk, march or double march round a specific area for several hours, depending on how he was standing up to the punishment or how the sergeant felt. Then, at the end of the day, he would be examined by the medical officer. If the M.O. felt he was capable of standing more he would do more the next day. That had a really salutary affect on those chaps, who did not know how to control themselves and drank too much alcohol…On the whole they [the battalion] behaved themselves.

'A' Section, 12th Troop Carrying Company, R.A.S.C., commanded by Captain Drysdale, arrived on the 2nd February. This unit provided the transport essential to a mobile unit.

129

Officer Group – 15 May 1941
Back row (left to right): 2/Lt. R.G. Girdwood, 2/Lt. P.O. Johnson, 2/Lt. D.E. Forster, 2/Lt. G.H.E.
Lewis, 2/Lt. L.E.V. Rumble, 2/Lt. A.H. Braggs, 2/Lt. L.F. Davidson.
Third row: Lt. G. Pettinger, 2/Lt. T.H. Thomas, Lt. K.M. Wood, 2/Lt. N.E. Ince, Lt. A.J. Hoskins, 2/Lt. L.J.
Kennedy, Lt. A.E.C. Hartnell, 2/Lt. A.E. Hooper, 2/Lt. G.H.B. Towns.
Second row: Capt. A.R. Haythornthwaite (R.A. Chap.D.), Capt. C.F.R. Goulden, Lt. J. Robinson,
2/Lt. G.R. Campion, 2/Lt. T.H. Thackrah, 2/Lt. G.B. Beattie, 2/Lt. A.R. Pollard, 2/Lt. M.H. Jackson,
Lt. A.C. Young, Capt. W.B. McKenna (R.A.M.C.)
First row: Capt. D.E. White, Lt. & Q.M. A.E. Love, Capt. V.H. Jackson, Maj. P.B. Robinson, Maj. J.
C.Slight (2/i.c.), Lt. Col. J.E.S. Percy (C.O.), Capt. H. Scott-Batey (Adj.), Maj. W. Robinson, Capt.
W.J.R. Scott, Capt. F. Beedom, Capt. F.W. May.
Absent: Capt. G.L. Wood (M.C.) Remained with Home Details: Capt. F.W. May

Training commenced on the 3rd February. The first exercises involved boarding
and deboarding busses in full marching order. With all troop movements postponed
until the weather improved, training was extended to include moving by road through a
23-mile route and firing weapons. On the 19th February, road conditions improved and
the battalion moved to Mortagne au Perche, a distance of 43 miles. 'A' Company was
billeted in a hall of L'Hotel des Voyageurs on the Alencon road. 'B', 'C' and 'D'
Companies and part of 'H.Q.' Company were billeted in huts at the Hippodrome. The
Signal and Motor Transport Platoons were in the Chocolaterie. Training continued over
the next few days.

On the 27th February, the battalion moved to the area west of Amiens, a distance
of 97 miles. Lt. H. Scott-Batey led the advanced billeting party. Battalion headquarters,

'H.Q.' Company and 'D' Company were billeted at Bougainville. 'A' and 'B' Companies were in Saisseval and 'C' Company at Briquemesnil. The billets were poor. Rain fell throughout the day and the essential tasks included digging latrines, working on a cookhouse and showering. The area had been occupied by their forefathers during the First World War.

On the 2nd March, Maj. Gen. Le Q Martel, the 50th Division Commander, visited the battalion. Lt. Ken Wood remembered the visit:

> Waiting in my truck with my gun sergeants, we saw three figures coming down the tracks towards us in, of all things, smart service dress with Sam Brownes, breeches and gaiters and sporting fascinating row upon row of medal ribbons with scarlet flashes on service caps and epaulets. The only things lacking were swords and scabbards. They were engrossed in discussion of the exercise. At this unbelievable sight, one of the sergeants breathed out heavily, 'Jesus Christ, Freeman, Hardy and f***ing Willis.' We all smothered our laughter and I said, 'Steady on sergeant, f***ing Willis is my brother!' I don't know if he believed me, a lowly 2nd Lieutenant. The three were General Martel, Brigadier Churchill and Lt. Colonel R. Wood TD, commanding the 4th Bn. R.N.F. [Colonel Wood was indeed Lieutenant Wood's brother.]

Training commenced immediately at company, battalion and brigade level. On the 4th March, 'A' and 'C' Companies marched to new billets in Ferrières and 'D' Company moved to Briquesmesnil. On the 17th March, a visit to the First World War Somme battlefields was arranged and this took in the Butte de Warlencourt and Chérisy

A draft was received on the 19th March. 2/Lts. J.L.S. Oliver and M.H. Jackson and 100 other ranks joined the battalion from No.2 Infantry Base Depot at Sotteville. All was not well. The paucity of modern weapons, which the cutbacks of the inter-war years had brought about, was still very much in evidence. Lt. Ken Wood experienced the problem at first hand:

> We were soon warned to collect our guns and etceteras, which evidently awaited us at Army H.Q. in Arras. [Lieutenant Wood was commanding the Anti-Tank Platoon].
> I was selected and with the gun sergeants, drivers and number ones, we left full of hope towards Arras and our full armoury of vital weapons…We sat round in the canteen and examined literature. Then it dawned on us. We were being offered inferior French pieces and equipment. I stormed in hot pursuit of a responsible officer but such were difficult to find being in conference or having stopped out for coffee and the like – so frustrating. Eventually a Warrant Officer was sent to calm me down. He explained that he understood there were no 2 pounders or portees; even anti-tank regiments had to go short.
> We had to be satisfied with what we got; not much more powerful than anti-tank rifles with split-tail mountings. One of the Sergeants, 6 ft. tall and weighing 14 or more stones, boasted he could pick the bloody thing up and fire it from the hip. We hoped we could demonstrate this before we left but his boast proved ineffective but not by far…We hardly dared hope we could penetrate armour but then 2 pounders were not that proficient either. Perhaps the noise might be enough to deter armoured cars and thin-skinned vehi-

cles.

Training continued here until, on the 29th March, the battalion moved to the Lille area. Headquarters, 'A' and 'B' Companies were at Allennes-les-Marais, 'C' Company was at Carvin and 'D' Company was billeted at Annoeullin. The 50th Division was given the task of digging defensive positions as part of II Corps Reserve Line. These comprised an anti-tank ditch and trenches linking concrete pillboxes. This line was sited along the Belgium border with France as an extension of the Maginot Line. The divisional sector ran from Loos, through Seclin to Wauvrin, a distance of eight miles. Brigade 150 dug the northern sub-sector and 151 Brigade the southern sub-sector of the Division's allotted area.

Occasionally high-ranking visitors visited the working site. These included politicians as well as Generals. On one such occasion a group visited Capt. John March's platoon:

> They came to visit my platoon and here we have these Durham miners digging their trenches. They dig so quickly and before you know where you are, they've disappeared. But, of course, when a miner digs coal he only lifts his pickaxe up a few inches and goes very, very quickly, up and down, up and down, up and down and disappearing all the time. Now I remember one of these visitors saying to me, 'March, do you realise your men are not digging the army way. It should be, 1, 2, 3, 4, 5, 6.' 'Excuse me, sir. They're Durham miners, used to hewing coal.' 'March, I'm sorry, forget about it.'

On the 1st April, the first group of 100 men was sent to Martinsart to work on the anti-tank ditch. This work was to take up a great deal of the battalion's time over the next few weeks. The work was hard, often wet and muddy but most men were used to it. Usually the work was done between 9 a.m. and 6 p.m. Some training was organised. On the 2nd April, the battalion moved to Dannes to fire their weapons on the ranges. Here, they were billeted in two empty seaside hotels at Plage St. Cecily. The battalion returned to continue working on the anti-tank ditch on the 8th April. 'A' Company was billeted in Allennes-les-Marais along with battalion headquarters and 'H.Q.' Company and 'D' Company. 'C' Company remained at Carvin.

Work continued on the anti-tank ditch until the 11th of the month when the code 'Birch Six' was received. This code placed the division on six hours' notice of a move into Belgium to counter a German invasion. The Allies had agreed Plan 'D' with the Belgians under which, in the event of a German invasion, the French and British forces would move into Belgium and take up defensive position on the line of the River Dyle. The 9th Battalion's role in this event, along with the 4th Bn. Royal Northumberland Fusiliers (the divisional reconnaissance unit), was to take up positions along the route into Belgium and control traffic, thus enabling the advancing British forces to move quickly into position. Immediately after the code was received, Maj. J.C. Slight and the road regulation personnel left for Loos to commence their tasks. All digging on the anti-tank ditch was stopped.

On the 12th April, a message was received from II Corps to the effect that the battalion was to be ready to move at 4 p.m. 'A' and 'B' Companies marched to billets in Faubourg Des Postes-Lille. 'C' and 'D' Companies moved to Croix and billeted in the factory, Isaac Holden et Fils. On the following day, battalion headquarters and 'H.Q.' Company moved to Hellemmes-Lille. The battalion's specific task as a road control unit was to regulate the movement of refugees. This flurry of activity proved to be a false alarm and the battalion settled down to the previous routine of digging and training, with the emphasis on the former. A move to new billets was carried out on the 20th April. Battalion headquarters, 'H.Q.' and 'B' Companies were in Attiches, with 'A' Company at Petit Attiches. 'C' and 'D' Companies were billeted in Le Croquet. Leave was being organised and on the 24th April, the first party left for England. The II Corps Commander, Lt. Gen. A.F. Brooke C.B., D.S.O. visited the battalion and watched work on the corps reserve line.

On the 9th May, a divisional intelligence exercise was held and, in the evening, a boxing tournament took place. It was the eve of the German invasion of the Low Countries, though no one knew of it at the time. At 7.30 a.m. on the 10th, the brigade again received the code 'Birch Six'. This time it was not a false alarm. German air activity had increased, though none of it disturbed the battalion. Plan 'D' was put into operation and the battalion moved to carry out its traffic control duties. Major Slight with 2/Lts. R.H. Forbes and J.W. Beaumont moved to No. 4 Post, II Corps at Mecheren. With them were 12 other ranks: the three officers' servants and Privates Munn and Petherick ('D' Company) and Harrison ('A' Company), who were clerks. Four despatch riders of 'H.Q.' Company were included in the party: Privates Bird, Scurfield, Adgar and Dixon. The party was completed by the drivers of 8-cwt vehicles, Privates Thorburn and Francis, both of 'D' Company. The remainder of the battalion provided road control parties in the areas of Roubaix, Gruson, Fretin, Templemars, Wattignies, Faubourg des Postes, Lezennes, Hellemmes and Croix. The main task was to keep the II Corps route into Belgium clear of refugees. The 50th Division was in G.H.Q. reserve.

On the 10th May, Lieutenant Colonel Simpson M.C., T.D. was succeeded by Major J.E.S. Percy M.C. Colonel Simpson, with a small detachment of the battalion, was moved to traffic control duties at Berg. Here the party experienced bombing and shelling and became part of the defence of the town. Sgt. John L. Williams, a member of the party, was flung into the canal by the blast of a Stuka bomb. Under attack they joined a platoon of Welsh Guards commanded by a Platoon Sergeant Major. Ultimately they withdrew to Bray Dunes and were evacuated to England.

It was not an ideal time to find oneself in command of the battalion. Lieutenant Colonel Percy wrote:

That afternoon, I received orders to take over command of the 9th Bn – not the best of circumstances to do so, when it was spread over such a wide area. I was, later, given the acting rank of Lieut. Colonel – this is rather an unstable rank, as if I go sick, or go on a course for over three weeks, I lose it.

Rumours were rife of enemy parachutists being dropped behind the Allied line. On the 14th May, the brigade was informed that 40 enemy parachutists wearing French uniforms or peasant dress had landed at Monsen Bareouil. A detachment of 'H.Q.' Company with carriers was sent out but no parachutists were found. By now refugees were appearing on the roads and control measures had to be taken to ensure that the main routes required by the B.E.F. remained open. Refugee routes had been established and these unfortunate civilians were directed onto the selected side roads. Fortunately at this time the numbers of refugees were manageable and had not reached the endless columns which appeared on the roads within the next few days. The early refugees were, by and large, the better off of the civilian population, travelling by car and other vehicles. Shortly, these were swollen by the mass of the population fleeing in the path of the advancing Germans and every conceivable means of transport was in evidence on the roads – horses and carts, hand carts, prams and pedestrians carrying pitiful small bundles of possessions on the back or under the arm. Keeping main routes open became virtually impossible and bodies of troops, advancing and then withdrawing, found it extremely difficult to push on at any speed.

The German invasion of the Low Countries had its desired effect. As the enemy pushed into Holland and Belgium and drew forward the B.E.F. and its French allies, the main hammer blows fell to the south. German panzer divisions erupted from the Ardennes and raced to the River Meuse. Once across this river they advanced rapidly across France and reached the coast at the mouth of the Somme within a few days, on the 20th May. This brilliantly conceived and executed plan destroyed France's ability to hold and defeat its invader. However, as the 50th Division awaited the call to move forward into Belgium, little or nothing was known of what was to befall it and its fellow French and British divisions.

On the 16th May, the division, now under the command of II Corps, was bussed in vehicles of the Troop Carrying Companies, R.A.S.C., to take up positions in the area of Grammont. Its role was to protect the bridges and the crossings of the River Dendre which were being prepared for demolition. The 9th Battalion's dispositions for the first night were in the woods east and south-east of Grammont. Battalion headquarters was at Saarladinghe. The battalion was on the right with the 8th Battalion on the left – both with the task of defending the bridgehead across the river. The 6th Battalion provided guards on the bridges. Digging defences took up most of the time. The 259th Anti-Tank Battery R.A. had been placed under the command of the battalion to defend the area against enemy armoured fighting vehicles. During the 17th, Belgian troops and civilians withdrew across the bridges in the battalion area. Rumours and counter-rumours flew around. One message received from the division stated that bridges had been captured from the French by German troops dressed as refugees, who had crossed the bridges and then attacked the defenders from the rear. Orders were received to take the greatest precautions against enemy forces crossing the bridges who might be dressed as refugees. At 11 a.m., information was received from the brigade to be prepared for the possibility of an enemy attack with tanks during the afternoon. In the evening, a passing motorcyclist had informed the 8th Battalion that the enemy were within four and one-half miles of the bridgehead. Both 8th and 9th Battalions sent out carrier patrols to reconnoitre their immediate front. No enemy was seen and it was considered that the report was false and, probably, started by fifth columnists in Grammont.

During the evening of the 17th May, 151 Brigade received a warning order from the division to prepare to withdraw after midnight to the line of the River Escaut. News of this withdrawal was received with considerable disgust by both officers and men. No enemy had been seen. The Durhams had had no chance to bloody the German noses. How could they withdraw without a fight? What they did not know was that a critical situation was developing on both flanks. Heavy German attacks on the French positions, the Belgians on the left flank and on the B.E.F. on the River Dyle had caused a number of withdrawals. The 2nd Battalion of the regiment had been in action on the Dyle on the 15th and 16th of the month and 2/Lt. Richard Annand had won the Victoria Cross, the first soldier in the British army to win the coveted award in World War II. The Dutch had capitulated to the Germans on the 15th May. The greatest threat was developing on the River Meuse where the French 9th Army had crumbled under the assault of the German panzers, who had attacked through the Ardennes. The withdrawal of the B.E.F. was to conform to moves by the French armies on either side.

The march to the River Escaut commenced at 9 a.m. on the 18th May. It was a long march, as the R.A.S.C. vehicles had been removed for other urgent duties. The route was via Nederbrakel, Audenarde, Kerkhove and St. Genois, a total distance of 37 miles. Lieutenant Colonel Percy wrote:

> We were ordered to dig in and make a bridgehead east of Grammont. This was a lovely bit of hilly country, covered with very fine crops. During the day [17th May] we could hear the battle coming closer and there were various alarms and a lot of horsed Belgian Artillery retreated through us. That night, [we] went to a conference at Brigade H.Q. to receive orders – we all hung about till 3 a.m. when orders came through to withdraw that morning to St. Genois, 35 miles away, on our flat feet. My unfortunate men had to do most of the march on empty tummies, as owing to traffic blocks and refugees, our cooks' lorries could not reach us. It was a very hot day and the road was choked with refugees and, as you could imagine, it was a devastating march – the last company fetched up at about 2 a.m. next morning.

The men received no breakfast because of problems with the cooks' vehicles. It was very hot weather. The roads, very often, were cobbled and not kind to the men's feet which, because of digging anti-tank ditches and travelling in trucks, were soft and not prepared for such long marches. The fact that so few dropped out is evidence of their grit and stamina. That stamina was threatened by the lack of food. Lieutenant Colonel Percy searched for food:

> It was essential to get some food for the men and going through Nederbrakel, which had been pretty well bought up by the refugees, I was lucky enough to find a baker and gro-cer's shop, tucked away up a side street. Here, I bought his entire batch of big round Belgium loaves, straight out of the oven (about 40 of them), so hot you could not hold them. These were put into the back of my big Humber car (with utility boiler), also dozens of big slabs of chocolate and biscuits, etc. We then drove off to catch up the Battalion but only got a mile or so when we had to stop as the heat given off by the loaves was so colossal as to be un-endurable. However, by opening all the windows and the back of the car, we were able to get on and dish the stuff out. Going through Audenarde, which had been heavily bombed, there was a very bad traffic jamb where two dense columns of transport converged. I went forward to clear this (it took an hour) but all the time huge French transport lorries kept coming through and double-banking on the road, making the conditions worse. Nothing could stop them until I put three of my carriers, which were at the tail of the Battalion, across the road to form a block. After passing through the town, the troops were so exhausted I decided to take a long halt in a field, well clear of the road and, providently, the cookers turned up and the troops had a hot meal before we pushed on.

It was a long march. Refugees crammed the roads with all their misery and fear. Enemy aircraft attacked the civilian columns causing panic and dreadful casualties. Pte. Bill Ridley remembered:

> We were absolutely shattered. Everything was a dream…It was about this time that I saw my first dead. We were getting stukared and machine gunned and I came across some French people or Belgians and they were loading this truck with bodies that had been killed with aeroplanes. It was pathetic really…When there was a crowd, the Stukas used to find us and used to dive-bomb…The most fantastic thing about Stukas, although they say they weren't as dangerous as what we thought, it was the fact that they used to come down and they were screaming down. It seemed that it was only you that they were aim-ing for…To me it was the most terrifying thing I had experienced….I was truly, absolute-ly terrified…I used to always pray, 'Please give us courage.' We stopped for a brief meal and we had a rest. We had a pep talk from our Colonel…I was very proud. That was the time that I started to respect the Durhams. We were on our knees, no doubt about it, we were actually on our knees when we got to that place. They gave us some grub and we marched out. We were in this huge field and we marched out of that field and they started to sing and the arms started to come up and I think that was the birthplace of my respect for the Durhams…It was fantastic.

The last units of the battalion arrived at St. Genois at 5 a.m. on the 19th May. It was a short stay. A few hours' snatched sleep was followed by a march to Lannoy, which commenced at 1 p.m. The route followed Coyghem, St. Léger and Leers Nord and the roads were choked with refugees. Lannoy lies south-east of Lille and not far from the original starting point on the 16th May. Lieutenant Colonel Percy's bitterness was revealed in his comment that they had 'accomplished nothing, except such exhaustion to the men that they never really got over it.'

At 1 a.m. on the following day, transport was laid on for a move to Meurchin on the La Bassée Canal. On arrival, Company Commanders carried out a reconnaissance of the positions to be taken up on the canal. These orders were cancelled at 4.15 a.m. and the brigade was ordered to await the arrival of vehicles which would carry them to another location. The division was again under the control of G.H.Q. No. 25 Brigade, who had been given to the division earlier, was ordered to rejoin the 50th Division on the line of the canal. Orders were received from G.H.Q. that the division, less 151 Brigade, was to move to Vimy to take offensive action against the enemy. No. 151's task was to guard the bridges over the La Bassée Canal, from La Bassée itself to the Carvin–Lens road. Shortly after midnight on the 20th May, this order was changed. As the 25th Infantry Brigade had difficulty obtaining the transport to get to its new location, 151 Brigade took 25's place on Vimy Ridge. No. 25 Brigade took over the protection of the La Bassée Canal bridges. The stage was set for the only serious counter-attack undertaken by the British forces in France in 1940.

The Germans had reached Cambrai. They had bypassed St. Quentin and taken Peronne on the 18th May. Arras was held by the 1st Bn. Welsh Guards and base troops, commanded by Maj. Gen. R.L. Petre. General Rommel's 7th Panzer Division, part of the armoured thrust, was directed on Arras. On the 20th, the enemy advance units bumped into the city's defences. Maj. Gen. Sir George Franklyn K.C.B., D.S.O., M.C. in command of the 5th Division, was charged with the overall defence of Arras and was ordered to prepare for an attack south of the city aimed at cutting the advancing enemy forces in two. The French would take part in the attack and, at the same time, their forces south of the enemy thrust would attack northwards to meet the British advance from Arras. There is no doubt that given sufficient strength and support an Allied attack across the narrow German front would stand a good chance of success. It would cut off the armoured head of the advancing panzers from the infantry and supplies following behind. This was certainly a fear among the higher German staff as their maps showed their forces strung out on long, narrow fronts as they raced for the sea. Unfortunately, the British had neither the strength nor support available to crash through the enemy and meet the expected French advance northwards. The French advance never materialised and the British attack was made by two battalions, the 6th and 8th D.L.I. supported by the 1st Army Tank Brigade and reconnaissance units of the 4th Bn. Royal Northumberland Fusiliers, all under the command of Maj. Gen. Le Q. Martel, G.O.C. 50th Division.

The story of the counter-attack at Arras on the 21st May, made by the two battalions of 151 Brigade, has been told in detail in this author's *The Faithful Sixth* and *Into Battle with the Durhams* written by Maj. P.J. Lewis M.C. and Maj. I.R. English M.C. Both battalions followed the tanks of the 1st Army Tank Brigade into action. The 8th

D.L.I. on the right, followed 7th Bn. R.T.R., reached Duisans and Warlus, taking prisoners and inflicting heavy enemy losses in men and tanks. The 6th D.L.I., led by 4th Bn. Royal Northumberland Fusiliers, advanced to Agny and Beaurains, taking numerous prisoners and inflicting heavy casualties on the enemy. Initial success was followed by strong German counter-attacks by tanks supported by Stuka dive-bombers. All four battalions, badly mauled yet defiant, withdrew at the end of the day. The attack, whilst a failure due to being too weak in numbers and having no forces available to follow through and build on the initial success, caused a ripple of concern throughout the German high command. This type of attack across their long, slender lines of advance was what the German Senior Commanders had dreaded. It probably had some influence in their decision to delay the German tank advance for a vital two days. This temporary relief from German pressure gave the Allies a tiny breathing space and assisted the defence of the perimeter, which enabled the withdrawal through Dunkirk to succeed.

The role of the 9th Battalion in this counter-attack was to follow the 8th Battalion on the right and prepare to support with whatever action was necessary. Lieutenant Colonel Percy wrote:

Our role was to follow 8th D.L.I. and protect the right flank of the advance with a view to doing a special job later, which never came off.

I had under my command, for this role, a battery of Anti-tank guns, some sappers and a company of 4th Royal Northumberland Fusiliers (Motor Cycle Bn.). These latter, during their reconnaissance round our right flank bumped some heavy German tanks and suffered rather heavy casualties. My orders were to advance by stages, under the direction of Bde. H.Q., and we remained some time, at first in a village called Neuville St. Vaast, where we were bombed. Here we saw some of our heavy tanks, which had been damaged, coming out of action. They seemed to have stood up to direct hits by German Anti-tank guns very well. Orders came to move to the next village, Maroeuil, a few miles east of Arras. The road ran along a ridge overlooking the area in which the other two battalions were advancing and it was a clear, sunny afternoon. We marched along the road, very opened out and soon after starting the Germans put in the most spectacular air attack imaginable. It was so terrific as to suggest they were showing off and was rather like the air attack in H.G. Wells's film *Things to Come* or more so. They put in 200–300 planes of all sorts and kept it up for an hour and a half while we walked slowly along the road. They were dropping salvoes of heavy and lighter stuff. The crescendo of sound was extraordinary and continuous with detonations and the scream of dive-bombers. The attack, of course, was mainly on the two battalions in front, who had a hell of a time as they were almost simultaneously counter-attacked by heavy tanks and the attack was brought to a standstill. In the initial stages, however, it was quite a success, and about 300 prisoners were taken. This was the only offensive operation carried out by the BEF and, if only it had been put in on a bigger scale and if the French had co-operated properly, the course of the campaign might have been different. The German display of air power was certainly impressive and there was no British air resistance, as it was at the time that the R.A.F. was bombed out of their aerodromes and were transferred to England – in fact we saw no British planes until we got to Dunkirk, about 10 days later.

Lieutenant Colonel Percy went on to describe the situation in the village of Maroeuil where the 9th arrived at 8 p.m.:

> On first arrival in the village, which was a big one, it was possible to dispose of our mass of transport under cover but after the arrival of the 8 DLI, another battery of anti-tank guns and some more of the Northumberland Fusiliers, it was impossible to put away any of their vehicles under cover and the streets of the village were crammed with transport. Incidentally, in the village when we arrived, was a petrol point, consisting of a number of large lorries carrying several thousand gallons of petrol and an ammunition point with many tons of shells and high explosives. The prospects for the next morning were thus not very rosy if the Boche had elected to turn on the sort of air attack we had seen during the afternoon.

At 11.30 p.m., Lieutenant Potts of the 8th D.L.I. arrived at brigade headquarters to report that his battalion was under heavy attack at Duisans and the situation there was deteriorating. Brigadier Churchill ordered Major McLaren, who was commanding the detachment of the 8th Battalion at Duisan, to withdraw through the 9th Battalion. Lieutenant Colonel Percy was ordered to provide cover by sending out his carriers and some anti-tank guns to assist with the withdrawal. Major McLaren's group arrived in Maroeuil at 1 a.m. on the following morning. Shortly after, the battalion was ordered to withdraw to Vimy Ridge and this was carried out successfully. The brigade, with both the 6th and 8th Battalions much depleted in numbers, was to hold the area of Givenchy Wood and village, and the old Canadian stone trenches. Initially the position was held by 4th Bn. Royal Northumberland Fusiliers on the left and 9th D.L.I. on the right. Later the 8th Battalion came in on the right of the 9th. The 8th D.L.I., with guns of the 260th Anti-Tank Battery, held the position on the right from Bois de la Folie Wood to the cemetery. The 9th D.L.I. held the centre with guns of the 260th Anti-Tank Battery, along with 151 Brigade Anti-Tank Company holding the Lens–Arras road. On the left were the 4th Bn. R.N.F. The 6th D.L.I. was in reserve. Lieutenant Colonel Percy wrote:

> On arrival back at Vimy we were told to put the position in a state of defence. It was a strange situation – my Battalion was holding the North West half of the Ridge on which stands the Canadian War Memorial. We were facing the opposite direction to the last war and one of my companies occupied the Canadian Memorial stone trenches as their defensive position.

The brigade was bombed quite heavily throughout the 23rd May but no casualties were reported. At 10.30 p.m. that dreaded order, feared by all soldiers, arrived from Brigade: the ridge was to be held to the end – at all costs. There was to be no withdrawal. Preparations were made to carry out this order. Necessary stores were unloaded and transport was sent five miles to the rear. The quartermaster went to Avion to draw rations but met enemy tanks on the way and had to return empty handed. Fortunately, the order was countermanded within a short time and new orders were received to begin to withdraw behind the La Bassee Canal. Lieutenant Colonel Percy remembered:

> That evening the Boche put in a heavy attack round our right flank but we got definite orders to hold the position to the last. Consequently, with the troops I had, we got down to it and did the best we could on a wide front…I dumped all the stuff off the transport which we needed for a protracted defence and sent the vehicles back…During the day, there were streams of refugees and a swine of a Messerchmidtt caught them on the road leading down from the Ridge and the result, which I was glad to say I did not see, was a shambles, including women and children.

It was a difficult withdrawal that now faced Lieutenant Colonel Percy:

> About 1 a.m. [24th May], after an urgent summons to Brigade H.Q., I was told the line was to retire and that I had to withdraw my Battalion forthwith to 20 miles behind the La Bassée Canal. Here was a nice situation. Owing to having been told several times that there would be no withdrawal, I had no transport for all the stuff I had dumped and, under the conditions, it was impossible to get the vehicles back in time. There was no time to organise the withdrawal properly in the dark but we managed to get some of our equipment and stores put on vehicles of attached units but the men had to carry all the Bren guns, anti-tank rifles and small mortars, plus ammunition, back a distance of nearly 20 miles. We got clear of the Ridge just before dawn but, although the enemy did not follow up, it was a desperate march for the wretched men carrying such heavy loads. However, they stuck to it amazingly well and all got back over the Canal before the bridges were blown. We had to leave a lot of stores and equipment on the Ridge – also, incidentally, a party of about six cooks were also left, as they had gone off somewhere to sleep in a shell hole in the trees and could not be found before the withdrawal – they must have had a surprise awakening in the morning – we have since heard they are prisoners of war.
>
> On the way back, we had to pass through a large mining town, Billy Montigny, which had been heavily bombed during the night. The town was an unpleasant sight and the streets were ankle deep in broken glass. In the main shopping centre, many of the shops stocked with goods had their fronts blown out and some of the few inhabitants who remained were misguided enough to hand bottles of wine to the exhausted troops as they went by, which did not help matters.
>
> In the afternoon, we arrived at a village called Provin, near the Canal, which was then intact, for a so-called rest.

It was a very warm day and the troops had been without sleep and had had very little food. The brigade's new positions were brigade headquarters in Ancoisne, Anti-Tank Company at Herrin and the 6th D.L.I. at Don. The 8th D.L.I. was in woods near Carvin and 9th D.L.I at Provin. On the morning of the 25th, rations were cut by 50 per cent. There was to be precious little rest. The first shock was the receipt of verbal orders at brigade for a proposed attack south with the 5th Division and the 1st Army Tank Brigade, under the command of III Corps. The French would also attack from the south as well as the north. The plan aimed at splitting the enemy front. The attack involved the crossing of the River Somme in the face of the enemy. The brigade had never practised a river crossing and this was not viewed with confidence. Fortunately, events overtook the orders and they were cancelled.

Provin was heavily shelled on the morning of the 26th May. 'C' Company's billet received a direct hit causing heavy casualties including C.Q.M.S. Stonehouse and the C.S.M. W.N. Thompson. The French 2nd North African Division was defending the line of the canal. The Germans made strenuous efforts to cross the canal using barges that had not been destroyed. The Commander of the French division called for assistance as the pressure upon his troops increased. 'A' and 'B' Companies of the battalion were sent as reinforcements to hold the crossings at Bauvin. Whilst this was going on, orders were received which placed the brigade in G.H.Q. reserve and warned it to be ready to move to the west of Armentières. It was becoming increasingly obvious that the Belgians were on the verge of collapse. If this happened – and the Belgian army did lay down its arms on the 28th – a wide gap would be opened on the left flank of the B.E.F which, if not filled, would result in disaster and the certain destruction of the British and French armies. Finding out how desperate the situation was becoming on the French front, Brigadier Churchill ordered the battalion to hold on till it received further orders. Increasingly, as the day went on all companies of the battalion became involved in the desperate fighting on the canal front. The 8th Battalion was also involved in severe fighting in and around Carvin and could not be disengaged. The 9th Battalion's 'D' Company was deployed south of Provin, with 'C' Company on its left and part of 'H.Q.' Company protecting its left flank. The Carrier Platoon was engaged in dismounted action against enemy troops trying to cross the canal on barges.

At 9.30 a.m., Major Slight went to the French headquarters at Bauvin. He was told that the enemy had crossed the canal between Bauvin and Meurchin. On reporting back to the battalion, 'D' Company was sent forward with orders to restore the situation and drive the enemy back over the canal. This the company endeavoured to do. The two forward platoons suffered heavy casualties in the advance and found it impossible to reach the bank as the ground was under severe enemy machine gun fire. They did, however, occupy a commanding position overlooking the canal. In the fighting of the 26th, many brave deeds were performed, most of which went unrecognised. Pte. William Wilson Saul of 'D' Company was awarded an immediate Military Medal for carrying three wounded men to safety whilst under heavy enemy fire. Major Slight, attempting to return from the forward positions, was wounded. 'D' Company held onto these positions till dark. The right forward platoon could not be contacted and was lost. Many were taken prisoner.

A similar situation developed north of Bauvin and 'C' Company sent out patrols to make contact with enemy elements who were reported to have crossed the canal in that area. No enemy was found. A withdrawal had been carried out by the French and, with the enemy across the canal, 'A' and 'B' Companies had to fall back to the western outskirts of Bauvin village where they came under heavy mortar fire. It was increasingly obvious that the canal bank could not be held as the enemy were making good use of the barges moored between the banks. Heavy shelling of the Provin area continued and casualties mounted. General Curtis, G.O.C. of the hard-pressed British 46th Division, requested that Carvin, which was now in enemy hands, be retaken by the 8th Battalion and the 9th Battalion to hold on to Provin. At 6 p.m., the 8th and 9th received orders to stay in the village for the night and prepare to defend it. The carriers were sent out to collect the wounded lying in the open. An hour later, heavy bombing attacks commenced.

The 9th battalion suffered heavy casualties. Captains Dunn and Ritchie and Second Lieutenant Cunningham were mortally wounded. Second Lieutenant Young was also wounded but less seriously. Of the other ranks, 28 were killed on this day. There were no ambulances available to take away the wounded to safety. Instead, they were removed in 3-ton lorries. The village of Provin was much destroyed and set on fire. At 8 p.m., the brigade was ordered to withdraw to Steenvoorde in Belgium. As there was a delay in issuing the orders, Brigadier Churchill took it upon himself to issue his own orders to withdraw to Steenvoorde. Second Lieutenant Walker was sent off to find a route, only to return with the news that he had been unable to get through as French troops and transport were cramming the roads and would not allow him to pass. In the early hours of the 27th May, the battalion marched to Annoeullin where it picked up transport to convey it to Steenvoorde.

At 8 p.m. on the 27th, the 9th Battalion moved via Elverdinghe and Brielen and took over positions on the Yser Canal from a French D.L.M. division. 'B' Company was on the right, 'D' Company in the centre and 'A' Company on the left. No. 150 Brigade was on the right of 151 Brigade. The 6th Battalion was on the 9th Battalion's left, with the 8th in reserve. The line held lay between Ypres and Boesinghe. On the 28th, the brigade was informed that it was to embark for the United Kingdom. Before this could take place there was some severe fighting to be done. During this day, Belgium capitulated. By mid afternoon, there were reports that the enemy had got across the canal. They were found to be untrue but some enemy had got into Ypres. A gap was opened between the 6th and 9th Battalions when the French withdrew before the arrival of the 9th Infantry Brigade [3rd Infantry Division]. This was covered by rifle fire until the arrival of the latter brigade. It was a memorable day for Lieutenant Colonel Percy:

> The next morning [28th May], the Coy on the Canal bank were in touch with the enemy and I got glimpses of German infantry moving N.W. the other side of the Canal. They had with them the unfamiliar sight in these mechanised days – officers on horseback. There were several attempts at preparations to cross the Canal but I was able to get our artillery on to them and nothing developed. Ypres itself, on our right, was being attacked and things there were rather obscure and we blew some of the bridges. That night, I attended a conference at Brigade H.Q. and on the way back in the car, fell asleep (this was about 1 a.m.) and was awakened by my driver saying he thought he had lost the way.

I looked out of the window and saw the twin spires of the Ypres Memorial Hall silhouetted against the sky about 50 yards away. In fact, to my consternation, we were in the middle of the town which, as far as I knew, was in German hands. It was very dark and there was a few shadowy figures floating about. However, we asked no questions and turned the car round and drove out alright. About 3 a.m. we withdrew from the Canal and took up a rearguard position about 7 miles back, where we dug in and remained all day. The Boche followed up delayed by our carriers, who again did good work. The Carrier Officer was seriously wounded and we managed to evacuate him but nothing has been heard of him since.

2/Lt. Richard H. Forbes was the carrier officer who was severely wounded. He was taken prisoner when the casualty station was overrun by the Germans. He was awarded a Military Cross for his actions over the three days from the 26th to the 28th May. His citation read:

Capt. Richard H. Forbes M.C., T.D. A post-war photograph.

> For outstanding work with the Carrier Platoon at Provin, Ypres Canal and at the intermediate position between Ypres Canal and the Bergues–Furnes Canal position.
>
> During the latter action, he delayed the enemy advance and, in spite of being severely wounded, extricated his command successfully.

Orders were received from Division on the 28th May that all mortars and signal equipment were to be destroyed before the position was vacated. This unexpected order was received with great chagrin by the 3-in. Mortar Platoon and the men manning the 2-in. mortars in the rifle companies. Some release of their anger was obtained when all mortar bombs were fired off into the enemy positions in one exciting bombardment. In the early hours of the 29th, the brigade moved back a few miles and took up new positions. The battalion moved to the Woesten–Poperinghe road. The position was held with 'B' Company on the right, 'C' Company in the centre and 'A' Company on the left. 'D' Company was in reserve. Brigadier Churchill made a quick reconnaissance of the brigade positions to ensure that his battalions had arrived safely. At first, the 9th Battalion could not be found. It had evidently taken up a more forward position than the Brigadier had intended. During the day, the movement of enemy troops and tanks was observed in front of the battalion's positions. These were engaged by medium artillery and the enemy made no attempt to advance. At 8 p.m., the battalion received orders to retire behind the Bergues–Furnes Canal. It was a difficult withdrawal as Lieutenant Colonel Percy described:

> At dusk we withdrew again in M.T. to take up our position on the final main position covering Dunkirk. This was a very ticklish business, as it was about 20 miles along an intricate route. The Battalion column was many miles long and I had the only map available at the head of the column and found it difficult enough to find the way, even with a map. We were told the route would be policed for us but this was not the case. The Boche were all round us, as the motor column pushed along through the dark. By some miracle, all the Battalion eventually turned up and we prepared to take our position on a 300-yard front on the canal near Bulscamp but before we could dig in Jerry appeared on the opposite bank and, for the next 48 hours, we had to hold the position under very difficult conditions as the Boche were able to overlook the area we were holding.

The 6th and 9th Battalions held the line of the canal, with the former on the right and the latter on the left. The 8th Battalion was in reserve on the Ringsloot Canal to the rear. Brigade 150 was on the right of the 6th Battalion and a battalion of the King's Own Scottish Borderers was on the left of the 9th Battalion. Two days' heavy fighting lay ahead of the battalions. The 9th Battalion, as Lieutenant Colonel Percy has stated, was caught in the open and immediately subjected to heavy mortar and machine gun fire. On the 30th May, orders were given for the destruction of all transport. This decision was taken by higher authority to ensure that the roads leading into the restricted beachhead were kept as open as possible as well as to deprive the enemy of valuable transport. It was vital that the enemy be held as long as possible on this line to enable the withdrawal by sea of the troops in the beachhead.

Under the heavy mortar bombardment put down by the enemy, casualties within the battalion mounted alarmingly. Second Lieutenants Duffy and Robinson were wounded. Battalion headquarters was established in a chateau south-east of Moeres. The 9th Battalion held the left of the brigade line opposite Bulscamp village. The village, together with a low ridge east of the canal, was held by the enemy and overlooked the whole of the ground behind the brigade front line. It was a most difficult position to hold. The 9th, along with the other battalions of the brigade, had been fighting and withdrawing almost continuously since the 21st of the month. Officers and men were extremely tired, almost exhausted, yet they were now called upon to make their most essential contribution to the campaign – to hold the bridgehead in this crucial area to enable others to get away.

During the day, the Germans dropped leaflets showing the dispositions of the B.E.F. surrounded by their forces. The message on the leaflets read, 'The game is up. The innings is over! There is no alternative but to surrender.' These caused some amusement at the time but, of all German leaflets dropped during the war, this one was nearest to the truth. It was just as well that its message caused disbelief rather than concern.

The fighting grew in intensity. It was during this action that Sgt. A. Hall won the Distinguished Conduct Medal. His citation read:

> For conspicuous gallantry, leadership and coolness under fire. At Bulscamp on the 30th May, 1940, Sergeant Hall's platoon occupied a position in a rearguard action, which it was essential to hold to ensure the safety of other troops. Under heavy shell fire, enemy bombing and machine gun fire, he kept a grip on the situation and, by his fine example and resource steadied his own and neighbouring troops at a critical moment. Having completed his task, he withdrew under orders and occupied another position in perfect order.

Lieutenant Colonel Percy was soon faced with a desperate situation:

> They very soon got busy with their mortars and artillery, both of which were extremely accurate and, by nightfall, casualties in the rifle coys were so heavy that I had to form a rifle coy. from the details of H.Q. Coy. and push them into the line. They consisted of transport drivers, signallers, mortar personnel etc. At this stage, we started to destroy some of the transport and had had orders to destroy most of the signal and mortar equipment, as far back as Ypres. The absence of the latter, incidentally, was not exactly helpful in conducting the rear-guard actions we subsequently had to fight.

The brigade was supported by two companies of the 2nd Bn. R.N.F. and two companies of the 4th Bn. Cheshire Regiment – both were machine gun battalions. In addition, the 91st and 92nd Field Regt.s R. A. were in support. At 4 p.m., The 3rd Bn. Grenadier Guards were placed on call for the purpose of counter-attacking should the canal be crossed. Lieutenant Colonel Percy described the day's events:

> Early on the 31st May, the Boche crossed the Canal on our left and my left Coy. fell back to conform with the Battalion next to us. However, we organised a counter attack with the reserve Coy. covered by artillery fire and regained the Canal bank without much difficulty. Sammy Battiscombe, my 2nd in Command, did very good work at this time and was most helpful in appearing in forward Coy. areas when things were rather dicky. All the morning the enemy shelling and mortar firing increased and our chateau also began to cop it. About 3 p.m., the Boche began to attack my right 'C' Company who were in a rather isolated position. It appears they [the Germans], somehow got across the Canal and through standing crops and came at the Coy. with Tommy guns from the rear. About 25 men came back but the two officers I had posted to the Coy., after all the

officers had been wounded at Provin, were lost, also the C.S.M. [C.S.M. Rigg] and all the senior N.C.O.s. So, for the second time, this unfortunate Company had heavy casualties, and lost all its officers. At the same time, part of the H.Q. Coy., who were in the centre, also came back and things generally were looking pretty desperate. There were no reserves behind us and the continuation of the embarkation and our own chances of getting away depended on the general line of the Canal being held until early next morning. I had only one attenuated Coy. 'A' in reserve and it was not strong enough to counter attack, so I used it to take up the position along a small subsidiary canal [Ringsloot Canal] to fill the gap, together with some machine gunners and, thank goodness, the Bosche did not press their advance and the position was stabilised. About 4 p.m., I went up to see how 'A' Coy. was getting on in their new position when Jerry put down a terrific artillery strafe. He put down heavy and very accurate concentration on every house and hamlet, every wood, cross road and other piece of cover. It was a remarkable sight to see from where I was on the fringe and went on for over an hour. It was the heaviest artillery fire I had ever seen, except for the elaborate artillery barrage both sides used on the Somme in 1916 and which used to take weeks to prepare.

It was at 9 a.m. on the 31st May that 'D' Company on the left had had to withdraw to the line of the railway to conform with the King's Own Scottish Borderers [9th Infantry Brigade, 3rd Infantry Division], who had been forced out of their positions. Second Lieutenant Milnes and a Platoon Sergeant Major of the K.O.S.B. remained behind in the Bulscamp position and turned a 20-cm anti-tank gun that had been abandoned onto the advancing enemy. This withdrawal also enabled the 92 Field Regt. R.A. to bring artillery fire down on the bridge at Bulscamp and the farm lying to the southwest. At 10 a.m., the K.O.S.B. with two companies of the 9th Battalion – 'A' and 'D' – counter-attacked and regained their original positions on the canal bank, which they had vacated earlier. Capt. George Leslie Wood, who was later to serve with great distinction with the 6th Battalion, was awarded the Military Cross for organising and leading a successful counter-attack and holding the objective until the rearguard position was finally evacuated. Captain Wood was later awarded a Bar to his Military Cross and the Distinguished Service Order whilst serving with the 6th, which he commanded at the end of the war. C.S.M. J.P. Kemp was awarded the Distinguished Conduct Medal for courageous leadership during this action.

Heavy enemy shelling fell on the chateau and its surrounding area throughout the day. All the headquarters of the three battalions of 151 Brigade had used the chateau, and suffered heavy casualties as a result of the shelling. At 4 p.m., the right flank of the battalion was forced to withdraw to the Ringsloot Canal. Brigadier Churchill ordered the 6th Battalion to conform with this withdrawal so as to maintain contact with 150 Brigade on the right. Casualties and exhaustion were taking their toll. Enemy pressure was intense and shell and mortar fire rained down on the weary defenders. At 7 p.m., the transport parked around the chateau caught fire. Ammunition trucks exploded and added to the general conflagration. The overall scene in the Bulscamp area was described by Lieutenant Colonel Percy:

The whole of the Bulscamp area, as was also the area of our approach to it, was an incredible sight with thousands upon thousands of destroyed and sabotaged vehicles in every direction, as far as the eye could see. A sight I would never have thought possible, just like a bad dream with literally tens of millions worth of equipment and vehicles and ordnance sabotaged and abandoned.

Early in the evening the 3rd Bn. Grenadier Guards were called forward to fill the gap between the left of the 9th Battalion and the right of the K.O.S.B. of the 9th Infantry Brigade. At the same time this battalion covered 'A' Company as it withdrew from its isolated position at Bulscamp Bridge.

Earlier, orders had been given that the line of the Ringsloot Canal be held at all costs. This was the second 'all costs' order issued during this campaign. However, as before, the order was rescinded and a new one issued to move to the seashore near Dunkirk. The withdrawal was to take place during the night. The 2nd Bn. R.N.F fired off its surplus ammunition to prevent any enemy advance under the cover of darkness.

Amongst those killed in the defence of the Bulscamp position were Ptes. R. Carson, S. Letherbridge, T. Lunam, G.W. Miller, E. Nicholls, F. Sharpe and R.E. Walker.

The battalion arrived on the beaches at 4 a.m. and dug in immediately to obtain shelter from bombs and shells. Everyone was exhausted and many fell asleep. Their ordeal was by no means over. At 1.30 p.m. Brigadier Churchill warned his Battalion Commanders to stand by for further offensive action. The plan was to divert the attention of the enemy away from the beaches, enabling the final stages of the embarkation of the remaining troops to be completed. There was no doubt that this was a suicide mission with little hope of getting away themselves. To these exhausted officers and men who had fought so manfully and against such considerable odds, it seemed like the final straw. Fortunately, the order was cancelled and embarkation went ahead. Lieutenant Colonel Percy wrote:

As usual, Jerry did nothing during the night and about 3 a.m. on 1st June, we withdrew and marched to the sand dunes North of Dunkirk. This was a march of only about 7 miles but by this time the troops were pretty well done and it was a very trying few miles. The dunes were choked with our own and French transport and French troops were floating about all over the place, without their officers...also the day before, a lot of French horsed artillery had arrived on the beach where they had panicked and cut their traces, with the result that hundreds of loose horses were ranging over the dunes and beaches to add to the confusion. While waiting in the dunes we were fairly heavily shelled but the bursts were not very effective. Some of the transport was on fire and an ammunition lorry blew up near where I was standing. It was a pretty hefty explosion and I was hit on the arm by a large chunk of very hot metal – I think it was just not hard enough to break the bone but caused a larger bruise and small wound which healed after a week or so. There were terrific air battles overhead and a lot of bombing and it was pleasing to see a Boche plane come down with one of its wings which had been shot off, fluttering down beside it. About mid-day there was a conference at Brigade H.Q. to take stock of men,

147

weapons and ammunition available, as it was expected we might have to go into the line again but at 2 p.m. we got sudden orders to destroy our remaining vehicles and get all our weapons and move forthwith down on the beach, towards the Mole…The beach is very wide and we had to march completely exposed for several miles along it. I opened the Battalion right up but we had a few casualties from dive-bombers, which skimmed just over our heads and opened up as they passed.

As a result of this dive-bombing the following men were killed: Ptes. F.L. Bowater, W.J. Miller, R.Minto, D. Stewart, J.E. Templeton and W. Wade. Lieutenant Colonel Percy went on:

The beach was a remarkable sight and was littered with discarded arms and equipment and bits of aeroplanes. There were also a dozen torpedoes and mines which had been washed up, also, at least, three destroyers and a cross-channel steamer which had been beached, after being practically blown in half by heavy bombs. Dunkirk was almost completely wrecked and there were huge oil fires burning. On reaching the end of the Mole we had to wait until dusk and then marched along it in batches of 50 to the ships. We were shelled going along the Mole and had casualties, also, some men were hit actually going up the gangway. The ship I got on was of the Channel Island variety and we were there for an hour or more before sailing, with shells landing all round. I believe the funnel was knocked off before we left but, at that time, one was past caring and after some of the most welcome cups of hot tea, I found a cabin and dossed down and did not wake up until we were in Dover harbour next morning.

Pte. Bill Ridley remembered his arrival at Dover:

I got up and I saw Dover harbour. We pulled into Dover harbour and the boat turns round and I thought, 'God! We're going back,' and tears came into my eyes. I didn't know that the boat had to turn round to get into Dover harbour. If you were to ask me what me feelings were, I must say I was relieved not to be going back to say the least.

On arrival in Dover, the survivors were put on trains and dispersed to various rest camps.

Capt. Harold Scott-Batey wrote to his wife on the 3rd June 1940:

We sailed from Dunkirk at 10 p.m. on Saturday and old Jerry gave us a grand farewell, shrapnel was flying all over, bless him. However, all was well and we landed at Dover about 7 a.m. on Sunday. We were sent to Camberley Rest Camp and here we still are awaiting orders as to where we are to go for refitting. I have lost everything except a shirt, pair of socks, shaving tackle, a towel and a pair of pyjamas. I am feeling fine now after a grand bath, a few good meals and a good night's rest. We are under canvas here and it is good. Weather is gorgeous and, as it is a little chilly at night time I have 8 blankets and a camp bed for sleeping purposes. We are all hoping fearfully that we are going to get some leave even if it is only 48 hours. Rumours hold that it will be 7 days but we live and hope for 10 days and very soon at that…When I do come on leave I shall have to wear that old grey suit because I have lost my service dress during my troubles.

Feelings of relief at being safe at last competed with the shame of defeat. Pte. Bill Ridley recalled:

> We got in the train and sat on the floor. We were utterly ashamed. We were utterly and absolutely ashamed at what had happened and it wasn't until we were passing through stations and there were oranges coming through the windows and cigarettes and all sorts. I lifted my head up and, I can remember, there was a warehouse with a slate roof and on it was written in whitewash, 'Welcome to the Dunkirk Heroes'…
>
> Despite all the things that had happened to us, despite the disasters, despite the loss of men, despite everything. Despite the fact that we had nothing to fight with. It never crossed our minds we would lose. We never thought we would get beat. We always had confidence we would win the war and when you think of what we had, that was called, 'Super-optimism'.

If the men of the B.E.F. who arrived safely in England believed that they had let themselves and their country down in a campaign which had ended in defeat, their welcome from the civilian population was tremendous. At every station there were gifts and cups of tea. Cries from the ladies crowding the platforms were of encouragement. It seemed that no longer encumbered by a defeated ally, the British could now fight the war their way and it would end in ultimate victory. Strange in its reasoning it was typically British.

CHAPTER XII

SOUTH-WEST ENGLAND – DEFENDING THE COAST

The battalion was scattered throughout camps in southern England. Lieutenant Colonel Percy, his H.Q. staff and about 150 men arrived at Barossa Camp, just above Camberley. Over the next few days, 48 hours' leave was given to officers and men. Most used their brief time to see their loved ones before returning to Rugeley in Cheshire. There was a war to fight and a powerful enemy lay just across the Channel. He could invade at any time. Joined by the rest of 151 Brigade, the 9th Battalion was reorganised and received drafts to make up the losses sustained in France and Belgium. Lieutenant Colonel Percy commented:

> Altogether, I lost about half the men and rather more than half the officers, which might have been worse, considering we had held four successive rearguard positions under difficult circumstances. We lost a very high proportion of Senior N.C.O.s, nearly all during the last day at Bulscamp, including the Regimental Sergeant Major, Regimental Quartermaster Sergeant, Orderly Room Sergeant and two Company Sergeants. These have been very difficult to replace. The Battalion did very well throughout and I was very proud of the way they stuck at it.

On the 20th June, a draft of 249 men arrived from the King's Shropshire Light Infantry. Although somewhat upset at leaving their county regiment, they quickly settled down and became proud 'Durhams'. On the 21st, a further draft of 200 men arrived from the 50th Holding Battalion. Second Lieutenants Sharpe, Mullins, Nixon, Pollard, Rumble, Heskins, Sparks, Braggs, Lavender, Lewis and Bushby joined the battalion. Captain May arrived to take over the command of 'C' Company on the 22nd of the month and the battalion moved by train from Rugeley to Sherbourne. The following day, the battalion left for Lyme Regis to take up a coastal defence role under the command of V Corps. It was accompanied by the 65th Anti-Tank Regt. Royal Artillery. V Corps consisted of the 4th, 48th and 50th Divisions. The entire area covered by these divisions stretched from Bognor to Bristol. Whilst each man had a rifle there was a serious shortage of everything else. Buses were requisitioned as transport. In the absence of anti-tank weapons, Molotov cocktails were provided. Bren guns were in short supply and some of the artillery support weapons dated from before World War I. This was the perilous state of the British army at a time when the country's very existence was threatened. A Tank Hunting Platoon was formed with motorcycles as transport to make it mobile.

There were other problems which General Martel had to face. He considered that demands for skilled personnel to return to civilian occupations and to units outside the division were affecting efficiency. Every unit was short of trained and experienced leaders and instructors and it was often men who were capable of becoming these that were being transferred. A total of 112 officers and 636 other ranks were transferred from the division during July, August and September 1940.

On arrival on the beaches of South-West England the 9th Battalion began digging and wiring slit trench defences. It was a huge programme and, at that time, demanded a great deal of the battalion's energies. It was not without its frustrations. L/Cpl. Fred Welsh remembered:

> In charge of all the defences, putting the wiring up, was a Scotch Major from the R.Es., who would set up a series of barbed wire fences. On the beach was an old hut that was used by the coastguard. One coastguard said to this Major, 'You're wasting your time there, son, 'cos that's no good at all.' The Major replied, 'You do your job and I'll do my job.' 'Why,' he says, 'I'm only telling you.' So we went ahead and put this barbed wire fence up, then a dannet wire, then another barbed wire fence. The next day, when we went down it was all washed away. This Major came down and he said, 'What's happened?' and this man said, 'I told you but you wouldn't listen. Last night was the high spring tide, which flooded all what you've done and you'll have to move it about twenty yards further back', and he had to. You couldn't tell some of them anything. We had to start all over again.

On the 28th June, 'B' Company moved to the reserve area of Bridport. 'C' Company moved to St. Albans, near Lyme Regis. The battalion's task was to send out patrols to warn of an enemy approach. Over the next few weeks, weapons and equipment began to arrive. On the 1st July, the Carrier Platoon moved to Morecombe Lake. Eight Bren guns were received and found to have faulty return springs, and the Quartermaster Sergeant reported that the battalion now had its full complement of respirators. Reports were received of enemy parachutists landing in or near the battalion area and 'B' Company sent out anti-parachute patrols. None was found. However a tragic event occurred at 12.40 a.m. on the 8th July. A patrol challenged a man dressed as a civilian who was riding a cycle. Challenged five times, he failed to stop and was shot and fatally wounded. The police were unable to identify the body. Unsubstantiated reports of parachute landings and of the activities of fifth columnists and spies were made from time to time. Invariably without foundation, they did cause the battalion to send out patrols on fruitless missions, which were not well received by officers and men.

On the 10th July, a report was received from Brigade that enemy craft were approaching Portsmouth. All positions were manned. The Local Defence Volunteers – later the Home Guard – were in position on the right flank. Excellent relations had been established with the L.D.V. who were seen as first-class guerrilla forces working on the flanks and rear of an advancing enemy. There was considerable air activity over the battalion positions and many exciting dog-fights were observed as the weeks went by. As mines became available, minefields were laid on and just off the beaches. These were also laid at Burton Bradstock, West Bay and Charmouth. On the 8th August, eight enemy bombs were dropped in the sea off Charmouth. It was a difficult and demanding time, as Lieutenant Colomel Percy recorded:

> On arrival at our Coast Defence Sector, I was allotted a stretch of about 15 miles, most of which was cliff. There were no defences and we had to get down to it immediately. It has been pretty hard for the men working all day and on guard in the defences most of the night. Gradually the works began to develop and take shape and now the defences are pretty strong. It has been a pretty trying period, with the threat of the balloon going up at any moment. The weather has been the redeeming feature, with week after week of the most wonderful clear sunny weather ever known – if only things had been different so that one could enjoy it. German bombers come over every night but no bombs have been dropped near us, except that the other night they dropped about 100 incendiary bombs on the village we are now in – one landed outside my bedroom window but did no damage…The people are very kind and helpful.

The people were indeed kind and helpful. Members of the battalion were received with great kindness wherever they went. During the following weeks, companies and platoons moved around the area. Battalion headquarters moved to Morecombe Lake on the 16th July. 'A' Company was at Bridemouth on the 23rd, 16 Platoon moved to Bridport and 18 Platoon to Bridemouth on the 30th July. Moves such as these continued for some time.

The work on the beach defences went ahead at full speed. An enemy invasion was expected at any time. Work was undertaken during the day and the slit trenches on the beaches manned at night. As the defences were completed more time became available for training. Brigade exercises were held on the 23rd and 26th August. Meanwhile, the battalions of the brigade continued to rotate between beach guard and reserve, which was a short distance inland. Lt. Jim Kennedy joined 'A' Company. He wrote:

> …nights were spent with my platoon on the reverse side of the long, shingle Chesil Bank, where the rats came prospecting among the sleeping men while the sentries on the coast watch were forbidden to chase them away. Silence at night was essential.

As the Battle of Britain reached a climax, so the threat of invasion increased. The fate of this country hung on the result of this battle. On the 1st September, the code name 'Cromwell' was received. This code placed the whole of the southern and eastern defences of the country on a high state of alert. A German invasion was imminent. Beach defences were manned. Fortunately no invasion came, and on the 19th of the month, the order to stand down came through. On the 30th, the battalion relieved the 6th Battalion at Litton Cheney.

Weapons and equipment were gradually improving. Military transport replaced the requisitioned buses. The emphasis was now on training and this included working with the Home Guard. General Montgomery had replaced General Auchinleck as

Corps Commander and a tough fitness programme was commenced. Physical training had to include all officers as well as the other ranks.

On the 19th October, the battalion moved to Sherborne, Dorset. In this area much larger exercises could be carried out at brigade and divisional level. Winter was coming and weather conditions on the moors became extreme. Lt. Eric Hooper remembered one such exercise carried out in appalling weather:

> We had one exercise which was on Exmoor…We went on the Friday afternoon and we got there, somewhere, just before dark and we went into a lot of positions and what we had to do was to dig ourselves in. In other words, get ourselves underground by daybreak because we were going to be attacked. The East was going to attack the West. They were sending planes across in the morning to see what we looked like. We started digging our holes and it absolutely teemed and as we were digging, the slit trenches were filling up. We did get underground but we were sometimes up to our knees in water. The next morning it was called off…It caused a bit of havoc because some of the boys went down with flue…We had the rum ration, which was given to each platoon commander and you had to go round your sections…On the moors at that particular time it was absolutely dark. It was finding where the hell they were…We used to issue it with a spoon, it was ridiculous…The bloke who brought the rum round asked how many men you had and he dished it out into your billycan, so many spoonfuls…You went round and made sure that they took it, to make sure they didn't store it. You had to make sure that one who didn't drink, didn't give it to the other fellow.

On the 2nd November, the battalion moved to Tiverton in Devon. Training exercises continued and the weather worsened. Snow fell and the temperature plummeted. The people of Dorset and Devon were kind and welcomed officers and men into their homes. Dances were held to which civilians, particularly the young ladies of the area, were invited. Some of the officers' wives rejoined their husbands and were accommodated in local houses and inns. Sporting activities, particularly football, were held between platoons, companies and battalions.

The moors were a very good training area. Often the exercises could be dangerous if great care was not taken. Lt. Jim Kennedy wrote:

> In the early days, the Battalion had an exercise in company and artillery co-operation. Unfortunately, the gunners had lost their 25 pounder guns at Dunkirk and had not received new ones. They had borrowed some old 75mm French guns. My platoon had to advance behind the exploding shells of four of these guns. At the rehearsal, the four guns dropped four shells in a straight line across the line of advance. So the advance started. The gunners raised their sights a little so the next line of four shells would be fifty yards ahead of the advancing soldiers. Shells exploded – one, two, three, in a straight line. Number four fell where the original shell had exploded. Fortunately, the advancing men had not moved into the danger zone but the incident had been too close to tragedy for comfort. So everyone agreed to wait for the 25 pounder guns before the next lesson on

advancing behind a moving barrage was repeated.

Individual training continued alongside that of the larger units. L/Cpl. Fred Welsh commented:

> We had to march 10 miles and do a firing test on a big range on Exmoor, which was fire at 500 yards, run 100 yards and fire again, until you got within 100 yards. The reason for this was that to fire a rifle, the most important thing was stillness and if you ran with all your equipment on you were out of breath and you had to learn to lie down and not pant when you were firing your rifle.

Not all the training was of a high order. Pte. Joe Clark was appointed batman to Lieutenant Pettinger. Amongst his duties was that of a runner:

> Sometimes he could use you as a runner. If he had a message and he wanted to pass it on quickly, he would give you a message and you had to take it, and bring the answer back. Sometimes they did train you. Initially, they didn't give you a written message so that when you did go into action, you weren't carrying information. They would just give you a verbal message to take and bring one back. Sometimes it went a bit haywire…It often went wrong. They got a group of lads together, maybe say, half a dozen and the officer would take one away and give him a message. Only the officer knew it and that man and he would have to take it to the next man and give him the message. Believe me, by the time it got back to the officer from the last man, it was nothing like it, nothing like it at all. It was a different message coming back.

Christmas followed the usual army pattern of officers and senior N.C.O.s serving the men their dinners. Within a few days six officers and 43 other ranks joined the battalion. Exercises were carried out at Oakhampton Camp, Minehead and Dulverton. Brigadier Churchill left the brigade and was replaced by Brig. H. Redman, who visited the battalion for the first time on the 18th February. The training programme continued throughout March and April. On the 2nd April, King George VI visited Wells and watched training activities of some of the units of the battalion. These included demonstrations by the Battle Patrol commanded by Lt. J. Robinson and the Anti-Tank Platoon under the command of Second Lieutenant Ince. A camouflage demonstration was given by 14 Platoon, 'C' Company, commanded by Second Lieutenant Campion. The King was so pleased with what he saw that he asked that Thursday 3rd April be declared a holiday for the battalion.

Rumours were now circulating about a movement abroad. Clues as to the whereabouts in the world the battalion might be moving became more obvious with the issue of tropical kit. It was not the most comfortable of uniforms. Lt. Jim Kennedy recalled:

> No one was enamoured of the tropical shorts, which had a large turnup so that the knees were exposed during the heat of the day. In the evening, when warmth is required, or mosquitoes were about, the turnups could be turned down and tucked into stockings

below the knee. When turned up there were buttons between the legs, high in the crotch, which were uncomfortable, needless to say.

The advance party of motor transport and carriers left on the 19th April. The battalion had had its seven days' embarkation leave. It left Tiverton by train on the 18th May 1941 for the embarkation port of Gourock, Glasgow, where it arrived on the following day. With very few exceptions, this was the first time any man had been on an ocean-going ship. Most of the men were filled with curiosity and excitement. L/Cpl. Fred Welsh described:

> We landed in Scotland, in Gourock and I was going to sail. I didn't know then I was booked on a ship called SS *Orduna*, which couldn't get into the docks. It was out at sea and we were put on these little steamers who took you out and put you on the ship. We were so well educated, we thought we were going abroad in these little steamships. Our knowledge of the world was very poor. You didn't have TV. You just had a wireless. Even London was just the name of a city, capital of England. But everybody thought, 'Ba, it will be rough in here with these wooden seats in these little paddle steamers!'

CHAPTER XIII

EGYPT – CYPRUS – IRAQ 1941 – 42

The battalion sailed in convoy on the 20th May 1941. The troop ship was packed and very uncomfortable for the men who were crammed into the lower decks. L/Cpl. Fred Welsh recorded:

This had been converted from a meat carrier, [which travelled from] Buenos Aires to England. I don't know how far we were down we were taken and there was a table fastened onto the side of the ship, towards the inner. Sixteen of you sat on one side and sixteen of you sat on the other. Above where you sat was a hook and there was a hook at the other side. The man sat opposite you had the same sort of two hooks. That was where you slung your hammocks and that's about the amount of room you had, about a square yard. It was absolutely crowded. You couldn't move down on those mess decks, where you ate, slept and had lectures, because they had to keep some sort of training going all the time…It was never comfortable because at 10 o'clock lights were put out and it was as black as Whitby Jet till 6 o'clock in the morning. You couldn't even find your way to the toilet during the night you had to wait till the morning. You couldn't find your way to anything. People vacated the hammocks and slept on the tables, slept under the tables, slept on the benches what you sat on to try and get more comfortable. A cartoon appeared on the ship's notice board one day, of a space they'd found on this ship of about six square yards. The officer is saying, 'Damn it! I could get another two battalions in that corner.'

It was not an uneventful journey, certainly in its early stages. On the 24th May, a lone enemy bomber attacked the convoy. Bombs were dropped but there were no hits and the convoy sailed on its zig-zag course out into the Atlantic before turning south-east to head for the African coastline. The *Orduna* was having problems with its steering and, as the ships of the convoy changed direction on the night of the 26th/27th May, an inevitable collision occurred with a neighbouring vessel. Both vessels were able to continue on their journey.

A few days into the journey the escort disappeared, with the exception of HMS *Exeter*. The *Bismark* had just sunk the HMS *Hood* and all available ships were pulled out to try and catch her, which they were successful in doing and she was destroyed.

The journey, on the whole, was boring. On the crowded ship, space was at a premium. Some physical training was carried out when possible. Much time was spent on stripping and assembling Bren guns and other weapons. Lectures and discussions took place on a myriad of subjects, not all military. Groups of men could be found in small corners gambling with cards and bingo was played almost every night. The power of King Neptune prevailed on crossing the equator, an experience much enjoyed by all as it broke the monotony of the journey. Fortunately, the food was good and there was a

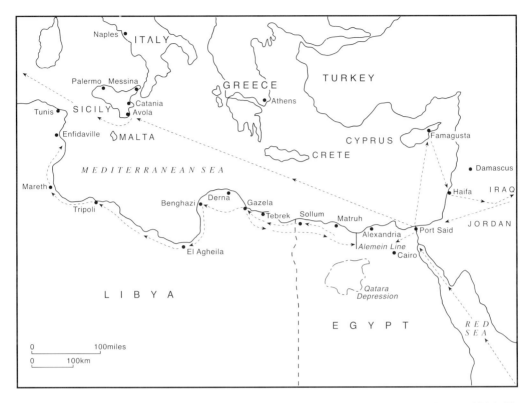

Mediterranean Theatre – 151 Brigade Routes 1941–43

wet canteen aboard. On arrival at Freetown, the men received the disappointing news that there would be no shore leave.

Anchored in Freetown harbour, the men enjoyed great fun watching and sometimes baiting the occupants of the bumboats who came out to meet them. Much bartering took place as the natives offered fruit in exchange for money and even articles of clothing. Bartering was an activity the battalion entered into with great energy, though, to be honest, the natives seemed to have the best of most bargaining encounters.

Another incident occurred whilst at Freetown. On the day of arrival, the 4th June, a plane, believed to be Vichy French, attacked shipping in the harbour. Little damage was done. The convoy left Freetown on the 6th June and reached Durban, South Africa at 9.30 a.m. on the 20th. The civilian population gave them a great welcome and provided transport and opened their homes to both officers and men and took them sightseeing. On the 22nd, a parade was held in which all the troops of the various regiments on the *Orduna* took part. The salute was taken by the Lord Mayor of Durban. The battalion, marching at light infantry pace, set off 10 minutes after the other regiments and caught them up towards the end of the parade.

The convoy left Durban on the 23rd June and sailed up the Red Sea. It arrived at Aden on the 4th July. It had been a long journey and the heat of the Red Sea was particularly oppressive. The men were hoping for the opportunity for a break ashore. The disappointment was, therefore, quite intense when orders were received that there would be no shore leave. They would have willingly accepted this as long as it included officers as well as other ranks. When they saw officers going down the gangway to board small boats to take them ashore, an angry reaction broke out. Pte. Richard Atkinson took part:

> We arrived in Aden harbour. No one was allowed ashore. By the way, this was the 5th July 1941. It was my 21st birthday…The next thing we knew, bumboats were alongside and officers were going ashore. Murder! Why can't we go ashore? Anyway, we weren't allowed and as the officers came back, we got the hoses out and turned them on them…It wasn't military discipline, it was 'mutiny'.

2/Lt. Eric Hooper was one of the victims:

> We stopped at Aden for twenty-four hours to take on water and oil. The officers got ashore much to the dislike of the troops. As we were going ashore, going down the gangway, the troops were swearing, throwing things at us. When I look back, it was all wrong really but the point was that there were too many troops. If they had got ashore, they were

Battalion Group refill water bottles at a water turck, Cyprus 1941. Note the censor has removed cap badges and helmet flashes. The sun helmets proved to be unpopular and were soon discarded.

only allowed ashore for two or three hours. I'm sure they would never have got back in time.

It seems as though no disciplinary action was taken even if any of the angry culprits could have been identified. The men were quite willing to accept the traditional difference in status between themselves and officers. They could accept the fact that officers had cabins on the upper decks and did not have to sleep in the overcrowded conditions of the steamy lower mess decks. They were, however, soldiers recruited from the civilian population and not regulars. They respected officers who were willing to respect them and their feelings. No doubt, the boredom of the voyage, the heat and unpleasant conditions on the mess decks, had much to do with this reaction. However, it came as a salutary lesson to the officers on acceptable treatment of these men under their control. The anger, once expressed, soon disappeared and normal relationships returned.

On the 17th July 1941, the battalion arrived at Port Tewfik, Egypt and disembarked and moved to Camp 17 at El Qassassin. First impressions of Egypt were not encouraging. The intense heat, the all-pervading smell and the abject poverty of the natives made a considerable impression on everyone. El Qassassin was a very large transit camp. Some tents were available but a number of men had to sleep in the sand until tents were erected on the following day. That unpleasant illness known as 'gyppy tummy' quickly appeared and almost every man suffered from it to some degree. It was the troops first encounter with the flies, the ubiquitous pests that became the bane of their lives when serving a longer spell in the desert in the following year. With the exception of several marches into the desert to help get rid of their sea legs, little training was done. Camp facilities included an open-air cinema and canteen. Ten men slept in each tent and three officers to each of their tents. The stay at El Qassassin was a short one. Crete had fallen to the Germans and there was considerable concern that Cyprus would be the next enemy objective. The 50th Division was rushed to reinforce the defences of this island.

On the 23rd July, the advance party under Second Lieutenant Thomas left El Qassassin for Port Said, to be followed on the 24th by Lieutenant Colonel Percy with 'A', 'B' Companies and details of 'H.Q.' Company. Following the severe losses in ships in the defence of Crete, the Royal Navy was sensitive to the possible danger to any of its vessels. It insisted that journeys to Cyprus be made at full speed, to ensure that its ships were able to return to port before daylight. The time allowed to the brigade to board the ships was extremely brief and equipment was hurled onboard whilst the troops embarked. On the 25th, Lieutenant Colonel Percy's group boarded H.M.N.Z. cruiser *Leander* and left Port Said for Famagusta, Cyprus. Anchored off Famagusta, this group was taken into the harbour on H.M. destroyer *Jaguar*. On this same day, the second group comprising companies 'C', 'D' and the balance of 'H.Q.' left El Qassassin under the command of Major Slight, the Second in Command. This group left Port Said and arrived in Famagusta on the 26th. Both groups were concentrated at Kato Lakkatamia on the 27th. On the 30th of the month, the battalion took over the defence of Nicosia Satalette Aerodrome from the 1st Bn. Sherwood Foresters. The initial role of the battalion was to improve the airfield defences. The battalion dug slit trenches and erected wire, and company and platoon positions were prepared. It was also prepared to take instant action against any enemy parachutists, should they appear.

It was not all work and no play. Nicosia town was quite close and it had the usual drinking places and young ladies, though the Cypriots could be very protective of their female population. Trucks were laid on after tea to take men into the town. Some local drinks were quite strong. L/Sgt. Joe Clark was in the medical room (the Medical Officer was Capt. W.B. McKenna):

> There was some stuff they used to sell there. If you got two or three drinks of it, it would send you round the bend…I remember one time a company was paraded for the doctor's inspection. He got an old petrol tin, empty. He had a little bottle [of this local drink]. He just told them to take notice and he poured this bottle out into the petrol tin and he set fire to it. He said, 'That is what some of you have been drinking. It's just like methylated spirits.'

Relationships with the Cypriots were mixed. Some were friendly; others obviously saw the troops as an occupation force. Second Lieutenant Hooper spoke of an order, which was issued at the time: 'Troops had to refrain from referring to the natives as "those f***ing Cypriots".'

On the 14th September, Capt. W.J.R. Scott, rejoined the battalion with 20 other ranks who were posted from No.3 Company, infantry base depot, Egypt. As the defences were completed, training exercises were arranged, much of it done at Pera and firing was carried out on the ranges. On the 6th October, an attempt was made to steal petrol from the dump at Pano Lakkatamia. Two Cypriots were involved and the battalion guard opened fire after receiving no answer to its challenge. Both men escaped as, due to the danger of firing in a petrol dump, the men aimed high. Captain Scott took command of 'H.Q.' Company.

The stay in Cyprus, on the whole, was a very pleasant one. The weather was kind and enabled the troops to adjust to the Mediterranean climate. It was not to last.

On the 2nd November, orders were received to prepare to move from the island within 24 hours. This move commenced on the following day. Transport and heavy baggage were left on the island; only personal weapons were carried. The battalion embarked from Famagusta on two destroyers and sailed for Haifa, Palestine. Here, it moved to Assib and into a tented camp. Replacing the 5th Indian Division also meant accepting its transport and heavy equipment. The transport had seen better days. It was old, worn out and in much need of repair and maintenance. The battalion fitters, working around the clock, did a marvellous job in preparing the transport for the long journey to Iraq. The battalion set off on the 14th November 1941. The route lay through Palestine and Jordan.

At first, the journey was through fertile and pleasant countryside, over the River Jordan and on to Mafraq, a distance of 125 miles. On the ensuing days the long column of trucks followed the line of telegraph poles, which ran along the length of the oil pipeline. The countryside changed and became more arid and rocky. Two days were spent at Habbanniya airbase and then on through Baghdad and Diltawa to a concentration area seven miles north-west of Kirkuk, a journey of over 800 miles. Throughout the journey the battalion fitters and recovery vehicles travelled at the rear of the column to deal with any breakdowns, which were remarkably few. The battalion spend a few days here and it proved to be a far from comfortable period. The battalion War Diary has this entry for the 21st November:

> At this period, the Battalion was very short of tentage and when orders were received to camp outside K1, near Kirkuk, the greater part of the Battalion slept in the open air. The weather, at this period, was very cold after the heat experienced in Cyprus.

At the beginning of the journey, all ranks had been warned that the natives were skilful thieves. Their main targets were the weapons carried by the men. Orders were issued that each weapon was to be fastened to its owner by its sling, before going to sleep. Sentries were active, moving around the camp with loaded rifles. The battalion lost no rifles.

On the 5th December, the battalion marched via Erbil to the River Khazir, 25 miles south of Mosul. It was a march of 90 miles, which took 10 days in all. Three days were spent at Altun Kupri owing to the bad roads, heavy rain and sleet. On reaching the River Khazir, a camp was erected two miles south of the river. 'B' Company was on the north bank of the river where it dug defensive positions. The movement of 50th Division (less 150 Brigade) to northern Iraq was due to Allied concern that the Germans might advance through the Caucasus and threaten Iraq and the vital oilfields.

At the Kahzir river, training involved platoon, company and battalion exercises in fighting in hilly country. One of the courses organised was a gas course for N.C.O.s under 2/Lt. T.M. Thomas. Capt. H. Scott-Batey went on a junior staff course held at Sarafand, Palestine. All the while, defences were being dug to protect the river crossing. Sport, as usual, was organised including inter-platoon, company and battalion football matches. The countryside had plenty of wildlife, ideal game for enthusiastic officers to shoot and even provided training in stalking for specialised units. L/Cpl. Fred Welsh remembered:

> An officer called Jackson from Gateshead, he formed a fighting patrol which I was nominated to go on. In one of his exercises, we set off into Iraq, round the hills. We took a tin of corned beef and a few biscuits and we were going to be self-sufficient. The idea was that we would try and stalk a gazelle, which was a small deer. We did this for two days

but we never got anywhere near them to shoot them, until one of the best shots in the Battalion, a man called Charlie Sollis, a gamekeeper in civvy street, said, 'We cannot chase them, let me have a go from farther back.' He did manage to shoot a gazelle, injure it so we could manage to catch it and kill it. We had a meal out of that.

As the winter came in, it became bitterly cold. The tents were dug in so that the men were sleeping a little below the ground. Keeping warm during the evening and the long nights was a priority. Each company was given one larger marquee to act as a social tent, where men could meet and play cards, write letters, talk and read. The intense cold usually meant that the men stuck to their own smaller, crowded but warmer tents. There was certainly plenty of crude oil available for heating purposes. In addition there was an issue of charcoal. L/Cpl. Bill Ridley recalled:

We could get a bit of petrol and put it in tins but you couldn't take it inside the tent. So we got issued with charcoal. Well we didn't know how to work charcoal and we couldn't get it to light. When we did get it to light, it was just smoke and I remember once I had to go out on a guard. When I came back after me stint and I goes into the tent where they had charcoal burning. The lads were all sitting around with their gasmasks on, trying to keep warm.

The snow arrived and the camp disappeared under a blanket of freezing whiteness. Recently promoted Lt. Eric Hooper froze along with the rest:

It was pretty miserable. The snow was that heavy that you had to have fatigue parties going round during the night, to knock the snow off the tents, otherwise they would collapse with the weight of the snow. The rivers, which were very, very quick flowing, froze. Most men [in tents] got a primus stove and had that burning overnight…You could buy the fuel from a village not very far from where we were encamped and it was pretty reasonable for they almost made the stuff there. It was crude oil…There was a lot of smoke from it. Never mind, it kept us warm.

Christmas Day dawned and was very cold and wet. Though the surroundings were miserable, the Christmas dinner was good and served in the usual British army fashion, with officers and senior N.C.O.s serving the troops. Food was plentiful and comprised turkeys and fowl that were purchased locally. Numerous parcels had been received from the ladies of India. These contained a small plum pudding, sweets and cigarettes. Each man received an issue of half a pint of beer. Nearby Mosul had a cinema, shops and a bazaar and visits for all ranks were organised. After the festivities, it was back to the long, boring daily grind but a change of scenery was not far away.

On the 25th January, Brigadier Redman was appointed G.S.O.I, 8th Army and was succeeded by Brig. J.S. Nichols D.S.O., M.C. Rumours of a move turned to fact when, at 9 a.m. on the 7th February 1942, the battalion left its camp by motor transport and proceeded to Kirkuk. It was heading for Syria. Over the next few days, it retraced its steps with stops in the same camps as those on the journey up. On the 14th, on arrival at Mafraq, the orders were changed and the battalion moved to Beit Lid Camp, Palestine, 141 miles away. It left this camp at 5 a.m. on the 17th. One party, under Major Slight, travelled by rail whilst the second group, under Lieutenant Colonel Percy, moved by motor transport. The latter party arrived at Beersheba at 3 p.m. and camped there for the night. Major Slight's rail party arrived at El Kantara on the east bank of the Suez Canal at 3.15 p.m. and crossed by ferry to the other bank. Lieutenant Colonel Percy's party with the transport arrived at Aslut on the east bank of the canal. The 19th February was spent in vehicle maintenance and camouflaging the transport for desert conditions. On the 20th, the canal was crossed on ferries and the Colonel's party proceeded to Mena Camp, close to the Pyramids, having journeyed through Cairo. The following day, the transport moved to Mersa Matruh and from there to within 30 miles of M'Sheifa. Bir Thalata was reached on the 23rd. The rest of the battalion arrived in lorries from the railhead at 3.30 p.m. on the 24th February.

Lieutenant Colonel Percy together with Company Commanders and representatives from the specialist platoons went forward to reconnoitre the positions to be taken over from the 4th Indian Division. Sgt. Jim Hawkins was one of the party:

> We eventually moved back to Palestine and then prepared to move up the desert. I was with a small advanced party with the C.O., Lt. Col. Percy and other officers. We travelled to Gazala and, that night, I was in No Man's Land on patrol with a section of Sikhs from the 4th Indian Division. How well they operated and how that night's experience was to prove useful at a later date.

The battalion followed on the 25th, under the command of Major Slight. It travelled across the Egyptian frontier at Sheferzen and into Cyrenaica. On the following day it moved by convoy to the assembly area west of Acroma and on the 28th February, it relieved the 3/1st Punjab Regiment in the central sector of the Gazala Line.

CHAPTER XIV

THE GAZALA BOX & BREAKOUT 1942

Genneral Auchinleck's successful but hard-fought campaign the previous November had ultimately relieved Tobruk and drove the enemy back to El Agheila. This new line was held by greatly reduced forces and the enemy almost immediately took advantage of this and drove the British back to the Gazala Line. Here both sides lay and watched each other and reinforced their armies prior to making another attack. Who would be ready first? The answer to that question lay in the future.

Meanwhile, the 50th Division found itself holding a part of the line in this waiting and watching period. On the British side the line was a series of self-contained 'boxes', each holding a brigade. To the north lay the South African Division with its right flank on the sea. In the centre lay the 50th Division, each of its brigades – 150, 69 and 151 – holding a box with some distance between each. To the south the Free French held Bir Hacheim. Each box was surrounded by a minefield and wire, with well marked gaps at both the western and eastern sides to enable movement into and out of the box to take place. The western edge, nearest the enemy who lay some 20 or more miles away, was wired as well as mined. Within 151 Brigade box, the 9th Battalion was on the right, the 6th Battalion in the centre and the 8th on the left. Also in the box were brigade headquarters, the 74th Field Regt. R.A., the 505th Field Coy. R. E., 'A' Coy. 2nd Bn. Cheshire Regt. Machine Gunners, a battery of the 65th Anti-Tank Regiment (Norfolk Yeomanry), a battery of Bofors of the 25th Lt. A.A. Regiment (Nothumberland Yeomanry), a battery of the 149 Anti-Tank Regiment and 'B' Coy. 149 Field Ambulance.

The theory was that each box was capable of all round defence with sufficient supplies of ammunition, food and water buried in the ground in the rear to maintain it should the enemy cut it off from support units. These supplies were expected to last for about two weeks, which would give the army time to mount a counter-offensive. Everything was dug in and camouflaged, guns, infantry positions, dressing station, vehicles and so on. 'B' Echelon was located some 15 miles to the east of the box and here the battalion Quartermaster and Motor Transport Officer had their headquarters. Companies were dug in on the periphery, in positions that would enable them to respond to any situation. Lt. Jim Kennedy described some of the activities in the box:

> All the troops were in tactical positions, well dug in and camouflaged as well as possible. Most of the infantrymen were in pairs in slit trenches and all the platoons could support each other with fields of gunfire but were well dispersed so that no significant target for the enemy fire was apparent. Aircraft flew overhead and occasionally dropped bombs. During the worst heat of the day, there was little movement and no matter what direction

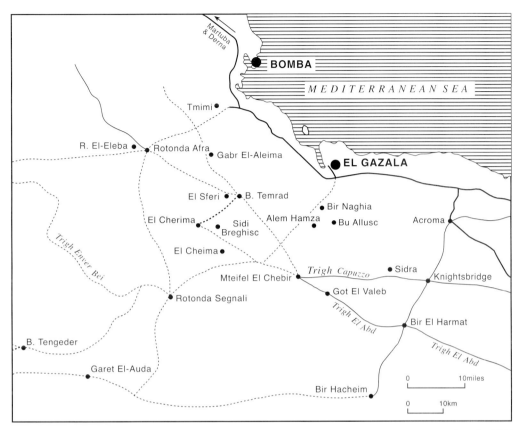

Gazala 1942

you looked the desert seemed empty despite the fact that each division comprised fourteen thousand men. At night the supply vehicles approached but their routes were carefully chosen so that the wheel tracks in the sand did not reveal much about the location of troops and stores. Track marks were sometimes brushed over.

Work proceeding on defences, patrols went out beyond the Box defences. Minefields with both anti-tank and anti-personnel mines were laid around in such a way that enemy could not easily make plans for their breaching. Barbed wire was strong in some special places but in the main the only wire problems were the ankle high wires marking minefields, some of which were dummies. There were gaps in the minefields for vehicle as well as personnel access but such were always covered by weapons nearby.

Slit trenches were dug at about shoulder depth. As time passed every attempt was made to make such primitive accommodation more habitable with shelves and steps. Camouflage was usually a tarpaulin covered with sand to make it difficult to spot from the air. Outposts were constructed in front of the wire and minefields and manned by a rifle platoon, a section of carriers, the Gunner Observation Officer and a section of machine gunners. Their task was to warn of the approach of an enemy and break up any initial attempts to attack the box.

165

The great Libyan Desert is about the shape and size of India. Whilst there are rolling sand dunes, the desert is largely made up of plateaux of broken grey stones, areas of brown pebbles and occasionally the desert traveller comes across flat topped hills of black and white rock. From Cairo to Tunisia, the desert stretches for 1,200 miles. To the south it stretches about 1,000 miles to the Sudan. For many miles the desert is fairly flat. Motor transport would bump and grind its way over stones and pebbles until, suddenly, vehicles ran into soft sandy patches. The wheels caused the sand to rise in clouds of dust, which could be seen quite easily by an observant enemy or his reconnaissance aircraft. This brought down artillery fire and one of the early lessons the troops learned was to avoid such clouds of dust.

Steep escarpments along the coastal region and sand dunes deep in the desert together with deep craters with steep cliffs, made movement by fighting vehicles extremely difficult. Most of the fighting occurred on the wide plains of the desert where manoeuvrability was much easier. The road, which followed the Mediterranean coastline, was the only one capable of taking heavy vehicles. From the Egyptian frontier to Tripoli, the Italians had provided a tarmac surface. Communications in the desert were difficult. Ancient caravan tracks crossed the interior. These were to become well known as the fighting continued, for example, Trigh Capuzzo, Trigh el Abd and the Rahman Track at El Alamein. A single-track railway line ran from Alexandria to Mersa Matruh and was extended westwards during the course of the war. Towns were only on the coast and many of these became famous during the campaigns, Tobruk and Benghazi being probably the most well known.

The climate of the desert was extremely harsh. The baking sun during the day sapped the strength of the fighting men. At night it could become quite cold, sufficiently so as to cause the troops put on warmer clothing. Battledress was worn in the winter period from December to March. In the summer the Khamseen occurred from time to time. This was a strong, hot wind from the south, which blew the sand and dust into dense storms which penetrated everything and got into eyes and mouths. There was little protection from the heat as vegetation was sparse, usually isolated clumps of scrub with the odd tamarisk tree.

Along with the heat were the flies – hordes of them. They covered the food, settled on the rims and surfaces of the mugs of tea or water. Many attempts were made to deal with them but to no avail. In the end, man and fly shared the desert day, each putting up with the other. Nightfall brought release from the flies and the troops enjoyed this freedom before the pests returned the following morning. Lt. Jim Kennedy described the conditions:

> It was a difficult situation for the best of men but most were healthy and could exercise in the cool of the night under the starry sky. Discipline was, of necessity, extremely strict in 'housekeeping' in general and in sanitation in particular. Fortunately, there was ample space and entrenching tools carried by infantrymen who could dig a latrine hole quickly. Letters from home did arrive from time to time and there was ample time to reply to them

when off duty. Food was simple and primitive but, being in a static position, Ted Lowe the Quartermaster, could deliver regularly and the ration included a tin of fifty cigarettes each man each week. The non-smokers had a valuable asset…The almost complete lack of vegetation was depressing. A few small thorn bushes provided cover for the occasional tiny animal. For some time at stand-to, just before dawn each morning I was entertained by a jerboa who seemed to come to the edge of the slit trench to say good morning.

Water was strictly rationed and brought to the rear areas by R.A.S.C. water tankers. Here battalion water trucks were filled and took the water into the box. The ration was half a gallon a day for each man. Half of this was handed over to the cooks to prepare the meals. The remaining two pints had to fill each water bottle and was used for washing and shaving. Hardly a drop was wasted. In the first few weeks, food was invariably the basic soldier's diet of bully beef and hard tack biscuits. Here again, the soldier's ingenuity knew no bounds. Hard biscuits were crushed to form a porridge or cooked with the bully beef. Whilst adequate it remained a very dull diet later; on occasions, tinned food would arrive to form a delicacy. Tins of mixed meat containing steak and vegetables together with tins of peaches and pears supplemented the diet. Bottles of Canadian and, later, American beer were supplied by the N.A.A.F.I. stores. It averaged about one bottle per man per week. To keep them cool, they would be buried in the sand for a few days before being consumed. A free issue of cigarettes was issued weekly to each man. Every vehicle that went out into the desert carried sealed cans of food and water in case of emergency.

L/Cpl. Fred Welsh spoke of some of the problems:

The main sickness was desert sores…scratches to your elbows and knees when you were kneeling on the sand attracted the flies and would easily turn to sores. Some got ulcers in their ankles, which were difficult to heal. I suppose looking back now, it was the food. You didn't get the variety of food. You had plenty to eat, biscuits and bully and you tried everything. One delicacy we thought about was, we learnt to do was, 'biscuits burgoo'. Where the name came from I don't know. You broke up as many biscuits as you had, because nobody could bite these biscuits that you got in the Army. They were like doorstops and you boiled them and you put as much Nestlés Milk as you could find and that was the only sweet thing you got.

Mobile baths appeared from time to time. L/Sgt. Joe Clark described:

They used to rig this tent up with pipes and they used an 80 gallon or 40 gallon drum of water and a pump. There was maybe, eight or ten men at a time, who undressed and would take their positions underneath the shower. Those in charge would say, 'Right!' and start pumping. You rubbed the soap in. They timed you, 'Half a minute!' And then, 'Minute! Right! Slush it off!' Two minutes we were in. That was it. If you didn't get the soap off it dried on you.

Lt. Jim Kennedy wrote about life in the desert:

Petrol was supplied to the British in flimsy, square tins, which were disposable. Soldiers would cut a can in two then use the lower half to make a fire and half fill the container with sand and pour some petrol onto it. The petrol burnt slowly and was admirable for frying – the pan could be held or rested on the sides of the half can.

Petrol had another use. Clothes, the khaki drill shorts and shirts mainly, got sweaty and lice could lodge in them. Normal washing could be infrequent so as a precaution men put petrol on the seams. Water was precious.

Dust was a problem. The mass of army vehicles loosened it from the ground and it was all pervasive. It was also revealing of moving men and vehicles. Ground, which stretched indefinitely in all directions, seemed quite flat at first but my eyes could soon detect the slight undulations and could take advantage of slight depressions to hide from view. But a dust cloud inevitably drew attention. Infantry, during the day, had to walk like cats and the desert boots helped admirably for this…In my early days of the desert, I concentrated therefore on learning to use my compass with precision by day and by night; absolutely essential where the only identifiable objects in the desert were man-made – a pile of petrol tins full of sand, a post (brought from Egypt!) driven into the sand, an old wire fence.

At night, to answer the call of nature, a man had to take his trench shovel and walk away from his slit trench and dig a hole. During the day, because the enemy was so far away and movement was possible, men could use the constructed toilets. These were usually a hole in the sand with a pole for a seat erected along it. When filled, the hole was filled in and the area marked clearly that it was soiled ground. The 'desert rose,' which appeared at this time, was described by L/Sgt. Joe Clark of the medical room staff:

A lot of people don't know what a desert rose is. You dug a trench. It needn't be very wide, maybe a yard at the most. An empty petrol tin was made it into a funnel, about four feet long. A lot of gravel was put into the bottom of the hole. The funnel was sank into the middle of the hole and then it was filled it up with gravel and sand up to the level of the desert. Another petrol tin had holes put in it and it was stuck on top of the pipe, which was sticking out of the desert. If you needed to urinate, you went to the 'desert rose' and that did not stop on the ground level, it went down through the sand and gravel into the desert. And this kept the area in good condition.

Though harsh, the desert left a lasting impression on those who served in its arid wastes. The nights were calm, often clear with superb star-lit skies. The setting sun was a beautiful ball of fire, which painted the horizon in amazing colours. L/Cpl. Bill Ridley recalled:

I loved the desert. It was great. I could have lived in the desert. It was harsh and it was beautiful. It's a funny thing to say but it had its peace about it…It was all stone and gravel where we were. The worst thing was the water…The desert was beautiful, with the most wonderful skies and wonderful sunsets. You wouldn't believe the beauty of it.

It rained very little but when it did, and this was usually near the coast, the desert floor became carpeted with an array of wonderfully coloured flowers, soon to disappear when the rain stopped.

As usual, the first task of the battalion was to improve the defences and clean up the area. Whilst this was going on, the outpost outside the wire was garrisoned and patrols went out to explore no man's land and discover the whereabouts of the enemy, who lay more than 20 miles away to the west. Each day started with stand-to, which was repeated at dusk. Reasonable movement during the day was possible. The only interference came from enemy aircraft on reconnaissance or making a hit-and-run raid. On the 2nd March, two enemy fighters machine-gunned the positions without causing any casualties or damage. This was repeated two days later when 20 Italian fighter aircraft carried out a similar raid on the forward positions with a similar lack of success. These raids were, on the whole, mere nuisances and the daily routine settled down to work and patrolling. Navigation was by compass or by the stars. Lieutenant Kennedy wrote:

> The desert skies are clear and the stars to be used can be learnt even if their names are not known, so if the bearing of the target is taken before sunset it is relatively easy to determine the direction which a patrol will move. The next problem is distance so maps need to be used, even though they might not be entirely reliable. Sometimes, of course, ground can be covered partly by day…When the men going out on patrol were notified, they would practice by day. If an officer and eight men were going, the officer and two men would be in the centre and the six would be in night sighting distance around them. By counting paces the two men with the officer could tell him the distance walked – some coins in the pocket helped. The real art is in getting back, for it is folly to return on the same outward track – you might have been seen and an ambush prepared or your return. The return route is, therefore, a dogleg one.

The duties in the box were also described by Lieutenant Kennedy:

> Duties in the Box were rotated of course. Sometimes a platoon was well inside the Box resting, i.e. getting cleaned up and doing housekeeping type work. Officers could safely leave their men in [the] charge of the Sergeant so that they could go and be briefed or trained in some new technique. For instance, there were several engineers attached to companies who lifted mines and these men were always ready to teach mine laying and lifting, particularly if they found new enemy mines. One job, which always required an officer, was guarding of what might be called, 'the gates' of the Box. There was a clear need for entrances and exits through the minefields. The 'gate' was merely a wire about the foot above the ground across the 'road' leading through the mines – there could be a belt of them ten or more yards wide. Nearby there were defences, i.e. manned slit trenches with machine guns ready for action. Here would be the officer in charge. Most men using the minefield gap would be known and the vehicles would normally be ready identified but there were occasions when unknown vehicles visited, so security had to be tight

and the officer on duty had to be aware of all who might enter or exit. Needless to say when battle was joined, the minefield gap duty was a most responsible one. If necessary, mines had to be relaid and wires removed so that the gap no longer existed. I did not like this duty at all because, if battle started, the gap guard has usually to stay to reopen if necessary.

Patrols varied depending on the task set. A fighting patrol would seek out the enemy and put in a lightning attack to try and capture a prisoner. A reconnaissance patrol set out to find the enemy and discover what he was up to and report back to battalion headquarters. A listening patrol usually went out at night and laid up close to the enemy and listened to his activities. Lieutenant Kennedy took out a reconnaissance patrol:

One night, I was asked to do a patrol merely to locate the enemy. I had to approach the suspect area by truck during the day and fortunately found a shallow wadi [dry river bed] where the truck was half hidden. There I left it with two men, did my examination of the terrain just before sunset and made my plan. All went well. The enemy were seen and heard and seemed to be digging in but the patrol was heard and we withdrew, then started the long dog-leg journey back to the truck. It couldn't be located. The enemy was alert and was within range, so quiet was essential. I had been told what to do – stay put under cover if possible and await sunrise. Every patrol man was alert and at first light one spotted the truck. The two truck men had seen us and got on board. The patrol then ran in the open order to avoid giving a single target to the enemy and were on the truck before shots were fired. Then, in zigzaging to avoid the bullets now coming our way, the truck got us safely from the scene.

The battalion organised a battle patrol. Sgt. Jim Hawkins was a member:

I was transferred from my Platoon to take over the Battle Patrol. This consisted of twenty picked men, ex-poachers and tough guys, with three sergeants as section leaders. All good solid men trained in compass and map reading and the art of survival. We had an officer, Captain Robinson [later affectionately christened 'Mad Robbo'], who was in command. Our duty was night patrols, collecting any possible information or prisoners.

It was essential that patrols were carefully monitored. Moving about no man's land at night could be a very dangerous activity. Contact with the enemy was always possible and a patrol had to stay alert. If other patrols were out it was vital to know in which area they were operating in and at what times. It was essential that this knowledge was passed to everyone involved. In the dark, it was difficult to recognise friend from foe. Sgt. Jim Hawkins had a close experience:

As battle patrol sergeant, it was my duty to take out each night a recce patrol of five men in star formation. We would leave the Box after instruction from the intelligence as to what distance and compass bearing we must take. At all times, we must be across the minefield and back in our lines before first light. Never must two patrols operate at the same time on the same front. This could be fatal as one only expects to meet the enemy. However, my story is an occasion when this actually happened.

I called for volunteers and we set off through Mr. Campion's positions, through the minefield and took our bearings from the stars and headed towards the enemy positions. No word of command was ever given once in No Man's Land. Our system of communication was the snap of thumb and finger. That signal was made and we got down to investigate. A patrol had been seen. From experience, I knew that they had also seen us. I noticed that they had closed ranks as if to discuss their action. I positioned my patrol with the instruction not to fire until ordered to do so. As this patrol advanced towards us, I knew that they would meet with certain death or serious wounds. Instinctively, I challenge them. Imagine my surprise, when in reply to my challenge, the voice of one of the sergeants of this patrol replied, 'It's us, Sergeant.'

The wide open no man's land encouraged the British to make the enemy aware of their presence, not only by aggressive patrolling. 'Jock' Columns were organised. These were named after Brig. 'Jock' Campbell V.C. who had first used them in earlier days as a means of attacking the enemy. They usually comprised a company of infantry, a section of carriers, two detachments of 3-in. mortars, a battery of 25-pdr. field guns, a battery of 2-pdr. anti-tank guns, a platoon of Vickers machine guns and a troop of Bofors anti-aircraft guns. These columns would move out into the desert between the lines for periods of several days. At night they would laager near the enemy positions and send out patrols to observe and pinpoint targets. These would be attacked where possible by a concentrated bombardment of artillery and mortars, which would last only a brief time. Then the column would be pulled out before the enemy could react. In the early days, whilst officers and men gained experience, the battalion practised moving in desert formation and working with supporting arms.

Elsewhere in the war, the gallant defence of Malta was reaching a climax. To ensure that the island's resistance was sustained, a convoy of vital and urgent supplies was due to arrive at the beleaguered island towards the end of March. To draw the attention of the enemy air force away from the convoy, columns from the three brigades of the 50th Division planned to attack the airfields at Martuba and Tmimi. Column 'A' which was assigned to attack Tmimi, included 'A' and 'C' Companies of the 9th Battalion and specialist and support units. Martuba was the objective of 150 Brigade.

The main element in this operation against Tmimi airfield, code-named 'Full Size,' included 'A' and 'C' Companies of the battalion, along with other units and tanks of 'B' Squadron, 8th Armoured Brigade. The companies set off on the 20th March to carry out the attack. At 9.50 p.m. on this day they reached Bir El Sferil. At 11.30 p.m., 'A' Company advanced on foot to a ridge two and one-half miles north of Bir El Sferil, where it dug in and covered the advance of the remainder of the column. 'C' Company passed through 'A' Company positions at 1.30 a.m. on the 21st and advanced to a ridge 2,000 yards south of Gabre El Aleima. The rest of the column advanced in turn with the objective of supporting 'C' Company. After advancing 6,000 yards, no contact had been made with 'C' Company. 'A' Company moved on to within 400 yards of Gabre El Aleima and towards a feature called 'the Pimple'. At 5.50 a.m., the company was engaged at close range by enemy guns when within a short distance of the Pimple. Return fire was withheld until visibility improved and the position of the other British infantry could be clearly seen. The artillery battery experienced difficulty in setting up observation posts. At 9 a.m., 'A' Company supported by tanks moved off to attack the Pimple. Led by the tanks, the infantry advanced over the final 600 yards and overran the enemy positions. Many of the enemy surrendered. 'A' Company dug in, covered by carriers and a platoon of machine guns and a troop of 25-pdrs. moved up in support. The attack had been a complete success with no losses to the tanks. Infantry casualties were slight, except for a carrier, which received a direct hit. Sgt. A. Whistance and Ptes. J.S. Hogg, J.Rowan and T.H. Wright were killed. A total of 90 prisoners were taken along with several anti-tank guns, machine guns and motor transport vehicles.

The enemy was now fully roused. Heavy artillery fire fell on the Pimple and attacks were carried out by enemy fighters from the airfields. This retaliation lasted for some eight hours but, well dug in, there were no casualties. Between the column and Tmimi airfield lay the high ground at Ras Chechiban. This would give excellent observation of the enemy airfield. However, between the column and this feature was about six miles of open ground, which was devoid of cover and the whole of it overlooked by the Ras Chechiban. Any advance during daylight would have been suicidal. Artillery fire was brought down on Ras Chechiban with the aim of drawing the enemy fire away from the column's motor transport. During the night of the 21st/22nd, the column was withdrawn to Sidi Breghisc without further enemy interference. There is no doubt that this action served to attract the attention of the enemy away from the vital British naval convoy, which reached Malta. This action, so early in the battalion's occupation of the Gazala box, served as very useful experience in moving about the desert and fighting in this new terrain.

Sgt. James Howe was awarded the Military Medal for his part in this action. His citation read:

> During the consolidation of the Gabre El Aleima feature on the 21st March, a direct hit by a 105 m.m. shell was sustained by a carrier in Sgt. Howe's section, killing the No.1 and fatally wounding the driver. Shelling at the time was continuous and accurate. Sgt. Howe ran to the damaged carrier and inspected the damage. He realised that the prospects of extricating the wounded men were small, unless the carrier was removed to another and more covered spot. He obtained another carrier, his own, and personally fixed the tow rope and towed out the damaged carrier to the south side of the feature. Assisted by others, he then extricated the wounded man from the carrier and arranged for his removal in an ambulance. Returning to the damaged carrier with another member of his section, he worked on it until it was in a condition to be driven and then ordered its removal to the area in the rear of the column. Throughout the event the whole area was being continually shelled by 105 m.m. guns. Sgt. Howe during this time and, in fact throughout the day, showed outstanding coolness and decision, acted throughout with a complete disregard

for his own safety and exhibited qualities of leadership and command. The Carrier Platoon Commander states that Sgt. Howe was an inspiration to him and to all ranks in the Platoon.

One humourous incident described by an anonymous writer completed the day:

We had three or four 'naughty' boys doing Field Punishment at this particular time for various breaches of military law…All I know, they were really hard cases.

Despite the fact we were in the front line, their punishment had to continue…Everything was done 'at the double' from the time they got up till the time they went to bed, from 'Stand To' pre-dawn, to 'Stand Down' at night, with the additional hardship of full marching order and with the temperatures hovering around 100 degrees, it was not a pleasant way to spend the day…

On the day of the raid, these 'Janker Wallahs' were busy digging some trenches or other, not far from the track that the returning column had to take to use the 'Gap' to take the German prisoners to the rear area…The first thing I noticed was the Colonel, 'Joss' Percy, having what I took to be an epileptic fit. His 'tash' was bristling, his gammy foot was pawing the ground like a stallion waiting to be mated. I knew it could not be that, because he was not that type of gentleman, apart from that he should be so lucky. It was not until I spotted the 'Janker Wallahs' all lined up giving the Nazi salute and shouting 'Seig Heil' and the whole German column, thinking that they were some of their comrades, returned the salute to the strains of 'Deutschland Ubba Allis' [sic] much to the amusement of everyone but the Colonel.

On the 22nd March, Second Lieutenant Mitchell arrived with a draft of 12 other ranks, all of whom were posted to 'A' Company. The Brigade Commander, Brigadier Nichols, congratulated 'A' Company on its performance during the raid.

Experience brought novel ideas, one of which was to be of considerable value. Sgt. George Lambert of the pioneer platoon recorded:

We had a Major Robinson who had the bright idea of using a carrier with the 3 inch mortars. So we had to concoct something up for him. What we did was, briefly, to get a railway sleeper and cut it to the size of the base where the Bren gun normally goes and it was cut diagonally to give it an angle of 45 degrees. Then there was a hole taken out to take the base of the 3 inch mortar. There were two straps, fastened either side of it so it wouldn't come out and would have flexibility in movement. Then that was strapped into the bottom of the carrier, on the back of it and the base. It took quite a while. Anyway, we got that made up and the day came when old Robbo came and said, 'We're going to try it out.' And, of course, off we went with it. We fired it and it was OK. He was quite pleased with it.

Further drafts of officers and other ranks were received during the period 14th to 28th April. Patrolling continued daily. Capt. J. Robinson, commanding the battle patrol, was earning a considerable reputation as an aggressive leader. Patrols were sent out commanded by Capt. W.J.R. Scott and Capt. K.M. Wood, both of whom reported no enemy in the area. Some patrols had a measure of success. Lt. Jim Kennedy led one of these:

> The eight men section I took out just before dawn was soon out of sight of the defence line, moving up a slight slope of the barren, stony desert. Here and there were odd patches of scrub, which gave us cover and we could move individually in a leapfrog fashion so that no more than two were ever visible. Across our front it was possible to see some considerable distance ahead from the occasional slight ridge. It was when the two men in advance reached such a ridge that I saw them freeze, then signal the enemy in sight. The patrol was soon in rough line, hidden along the ridge looking west, the rising sun behind them. To our front were four Germans moving around, apparently preparing to move back to their own lines. Well drilled, my men were immediately ready to fire. A quick signal all rifles together. The Germans had fallen and there was some movement where they lay on the ground. No where else was there any sign of movement. My sergeant continued to direct individual shots for a brief moment while I and one man cautiously but speedily approached what turned out to be four bodies. Quickly, taking from the breast pockets the identity documents of the four bodies, while my companion kept on the alert. I studied the ground satisfied myself that the four had been nothing more than an ordinary patrol, then returned to my men.
>
> We had obtained some information. There seemed little point in going further forward so the patrol withdrew as cautiously as it had advanced. On return to the Battalion Headquarters, I handed over the identity documents to the Intelligence Officer. The German officer was not as old as me and his photo seemed to be that of a boy. I went to the latrine and was sick.

Killing was not easy, even in war.

Active patrolling continued. On the night of the 27th/28th April, Lt. C.E. Robson and 10 other ranks moved to within 300 yards of the enemy positions and opened fire with rifles, light machine guns and 2-in. mortars. The patrol was able to withdraw without loss and they were clear of the area before enemy shelling descended upon it. On the 28th, a draft of 19 men arrived from the infantry base depot. The battalion War Diary entry for the night of the 29th/30th April stated:

> 2/Lt. G.R. Campion and a party of 8 O.R.s succeeded in laying mines on tracks used by the enemy at Sid Breghisc. They subsequently engaged a party of officers and men, standing round a staff car, with 2" mortar, Bren, Tommy Guns and rifles, causing the enemy to scatter. The enemy opened fire upon the patrol with m.g. and rifles but the patrol suffered no casualties and withdrew safely to its own lines.

On the 27th April, a new company was formed in place of 'D' Company and was named 'S' Company. It comprised one platoon of 2-pdr. anti-tank guns, and carrier and mortar platoons under the command of Maj. V.H. Jackson. The following day, Lt. C.E. Robson and 10 other ranks went out of the box and, unseen, crept to within 300 yards of the enemy. They opened fire with rifles, light machine gun and a 2-in. mortar. As soon as their ammunition was exhausted, they withdrew before the roused enemy plastered the area with a heavy artillery barrage. The active patrolling continued.

Whilst life in the box went on as usual, companies were taken to the rear areas for training for an offensive role. However, the British were unable to take to the offensive as Rommel struck first. Enemy activity increased during the first half of May and it was obvious that he was moving his lines nearer to the British. On the 23rd May, 'C' Company established a new outpost north of Heinkel Post. Patrols and columns continued their activities but the enemy was found to be in greater strength and more alert than in the past.

The German offensive commenced on the 26th May. The enemy plan was to hold the attention of the British by frontal attacks on the boxes, invariably using his Italian troops, whilst his armoured and mobile forces hooked round the open desert flank and moved on to engage the British armour in the area of Knightsbridge. The French at Bir Hacheim were quickly surrounded and cut off but they put up a splendid defence and remained a thorn in the enemy side for longer than expected. The Italian Brescia and Pavia Divisions carried out the frontal attacks on the Gazala Line. Attacks were made on the brigade outposts, which held out despite the heavy enemy pressure. Stukas carried out bombing attacks, though at this stage these aircraft did not have the affect on the battalion they had had when first met in France. Experience and the relative safety of the slit trench meant that there were few casualties. The battalion had no intention of sitting still and allowing the enemy to gain the upper hand. A raid was organised and carried out successfully against the Italians who suffered casualties and a Battalion Commander was captured. Capt. John Robinson (Mad Robbo) was awarded the Military Cross for his leadership in this raid.

Sgt. John William Jobson was awarded the Military Medal. According to his citation:

> On 27th May, Sgt. Jobson was in charge of his carrier section, which took part in an advance on a position held by an enemy company. He led his section with great determination and destroyed an m.g. post. When some enemy infantry jumped from their trenches and started to run back, Sgt. Jobson circled to cut them off and, in doing so, his carrier received two direct hits at close range, from an A/Tk gun and burst into flames. Sgt. Jobson got his crew out and led them under heavy fire until they were picked up by another carrier.

Battalion outposts were coming under increasing attack. 2/Lt. Alexander Robe was awarded the Military Cross for his leadership during one of these actions. His citation read:

> On the 29th May, 2/Lt. Robe was in charge of his platoon, which was holding an isolated outpost position. About 0200 hrs., the position was attacked by a greatly superior force. Although no M.G. or Artillery support was available for the first half hour, the attack was beaten off with considerable loss to the enemy. As a result of the action the Colonel Commanding the attacking force was captured together with 3 other officers and 12 ORs. 6 Breda guns and a considerable amount of other equipment was captured. The successful

defence of this position was largely due to the coolness and determination of the officer concerned.

Whilst the enemy was now in the rear, the brigades stood firm as planned and awaited the British army to counter-attack which would drive the enemy against the boxes. Losses on both sides had been heavy. Rommel was becoming increasingly worried about his supply situation. These had to come to him by making a wide sweep around the Free French at Bir Hacheim. The French were fighting with considerable courage and skill. Unless Bir Hacheim fell quickly, and there was little indication of this happening, the enemy faced a critical supply situation. Rommel met the challenge with typical boldness. He decided he would have to shorten his supplies route by taking out one of the boxes. He chose 150 Brigade box, which lay between that of 69 Brigade and the Free French in Bir Hacheim. He would concentrate his armour to the east of 150's box and seek to destroy the British armour in the area, which came to be known as the 'Cauldron'. Attacked on all sides and with no hope of assistance from the other boxes who had strict orders not to become involved, 150 Brigade finally fell on the 1st June after four days' bitter and gallant fighting. Rommel now had the direct supply route he wanted and proceeded to carry out his intention of destroying British resistance.

The 9th Battalion was ordered to move from its present position in 151 Brigade box to form a new defensive position to the north of the Cauldron area. This was eventually called the 'Percy Box' but disaster struck when the initial move was carried out on the 1st June. The battalion column was caught in the open by 21 Stuka dive-bombers and suffered heavy casualties. 2/Lt. A. Robe was killed. Capts. W.J.R. Scott, J. Robson and W.B. McKenna (R.A.M.C.) were wounded, and 70 other ranks were wounded or killed. Those killed were C/Sgt. L. Brennan, L/Sgt. F. Thorburn, L/Cpl. W.T. McVittie and Ptes. W.L. Banks, T. Bennett, J. Boxer, H.J. Crookham, W.A. Dunford, W.R. Elliott, A. Halliwell, A. Hogg, J. McNally, A.S. Milburn and A.E. Price.

L/Cpl. Bill Ridley was in this attack by enemy aircraft. He remembered:

I was in the back of a 30cwt truck which was crammed full of gear, also the Regimental Police were on with me...I saw nine Stukas crossing...I shouted to the sergeant, 'Stukas, Andy!' He says, 'They're on their way back, they must be empty.' I says, 'They must have seen us.' We were right in the open...I looked up and the nine Stukas were coming towards us. I shouted, 'Andy, Stukas!' He shouted, 'Get off! No, stay on!' I was off...I jumped on top of this R.A.S.C. guy. He went down. The thing you learn when you're a front line soldier is never get up when there is a bombing raid on. You lie or try to dig into the ground as fast as you can or you lie and hope to God they will miss. That's what I done and I could feel this guy panicking. He struggled and I shouted, 'Keep still!' I couldn't hold him and he was away. At that moment the whole world came to an end. The whole lot went up. After a few minutes I looked up and it was total darkness, it was just like night. In the dark I could see little red flames coming from different things. Actually it was the ambulances on fire. I waited because the Germans have always got one up their sleeves. I waited for another few minutes and then I poked my head up. First thing I done was to go round the trucks to see what had happened, to see if any of the lads were O.K. The sergeant must have got off and he had no eyes. His eyes were there but were just eyeballs. His pupils were up in his head somewhere…I smacked him across the face, belted him backwards and forwards. Eventually his eyes came down. A lot of the lads had gone under the truck. One lad, Mike Kelly, was covered with blood. It wasn't his. The Provo Sergeant had had his leg blown off…You never forget it I can put it in army language as the best way, I think: 'You poor bastard. But thank God it wasn't me.' We accepted the fact that this is what happens…You were deeply sorry in a way. You didn't dwell on it. It would affect you, you wouldn't go out again.

L/Cpl. Bill Ridley. He was severely wounded at Gazala 1942.

On reaching the new defensive positions, the battalion spent the night of the 1st/2nd June, feverishly digging in and laying mines. Patrols were quickly organised and sent out. There were casualties. L/Cpl. N.V. Jupp and Ptes. W.B. Atkinson and A. Winter were killed on the 2nd June. On the following day, Ptes. J. Ord and A.C. Place were killed. Pte. A. Rigby was killed on the 6th of the month and Pte. A.H.H. Robson on the 8th. Sgt. F.A. Rasen, of the battle patrol, was killed by a mine on the 9th June. Shelling and straffing of the battalion's positions continued over the next few days. Pte. J.A. Appleby was killed on the 11th June.

By the 14th June, the situation had become critical. Rommel had succeeded in what he had planned. The British armour had taken a terrible beating around Knightsbridge and the Cauldron and was pulling back. Rommel did not intend to allow Tobruk to become a fortress held against his lines of communication as it had done the previous year. He turned his attention to its capture and moved towards the coast. The chase was on. The order was given for the Gazala Line to be evacuated. The race was between the enemy cutting the coast road west of Tobruk and the South Africans and British pulling out of the Gazala positions in time to get away. As it developed, the South Africans took the coastal route and the 50th Division devised a plan for a memorable breakout, which took the enemy by surprise by its very audacity. General Ramsden, G.O.C. 50th Division, decided that his two remaining brigades – 69 and 151 – would break out to the west by attacking through the enemy positions in front, turn south into the desert beyond Bir Hacheim, then a turn eastwards to concentrate on the Egyptian frontier at Fort Maddalena. This was planned to take place on the night of the 14th June. The 8th Battalion was given the task of creating a corridor through the enemy lines and holding this until the rest of the brigade got out. This it successfully carried out and the 6th and 8th Battalions broke into the desert as planned and reached the concentration area.

The 9th Battalion was expected to follow the same plan and route. It had the farthest to travel from its new positions east of the old box. In case of problems,

2-pdr. anti-tank gun on portee with crew. This gun had little effect on enemy tanks unless engaged at very close range.

Lieutenant Colonel Percy had been given permission to use his own judgement on deciding the final route he would follow. The battalion was organised into three columns commanded by Lieutenant Colonel Percy, Maj. J.C. Slight and Major Duffie, the latter of the 74th Field Regt. R.A. These columns left the box at dusk on the 14th. It soon became quite obvious that the route to the west was out of the question. Following the 6th and 8th Battalions would have been folly as the enemy was, by now, very alert and heavy machine gun, artillery and anti-tank gun fire was pouring into the corridor. Lieutenant Colonel Percy decided to turn away and head for the coast road and attempt to get out through Tobruk. The columns had been joined by the 6th Battalion outpost party under the command of Maj. Mike Ferens.

The battalion moved northwards towards two passes in the escarpment leading to the coastal plain. Lieutenant Colonel Percy's column was preceded by two South African armoured cars that, on arrival at its pass, were fired on by South African artillery. On being recognised, the column filed down the pass only to be dive-bombed whilst on its way and several guns were lost. The other two columns, now under the command of Major Slight, made for the Gazala Pass. They reached it just in time, as South African sappers were about to block it with mines. The coastal plain was reached and the combined columns moved eastwards towards Tobruk, now under heavy enemy artillery fire from the top of the escarpment.

Lieutenant Colonel Percy M.C. was awarded the Distinguished Service Order for his leadership of the battalion throughout the period 27th May to 14th July. His citation read:

> During the attacks on the Gazala position on 27/29 May, Lieut. Col. Percy commanded his Bn. with great vigour and skill and displayed the very highest standard of personal leadership.
>
> On those days the outpost positions were attacked several times. Not only did he succeed in promptly driving off these attacks, but he organised two successful counter-attacks inflicting considerable loss on the enemy and destroying some guns.
>
> On 1 June, Lieut. Col. Percy was called upon to move his Bn. Group rapidly to another area to meet enemy attacks from the rear. In spite of heavy enemy air attacks and a difficult night move, Lieut. Col. Percy constructed rapidly and successfully a strong point that blocked the enemy advance.
>
> On 14 June, when the Brigade was ordered to break through the enemy's position and move back to the frontier, Lieut. Col. Percy's Bn. Group had to move via the coast road to Tobruk. He found the road blocked in the vicinity of Mrassus by enemy forces including tanks. Lieut. Col. Percy after a daring personal recce decided that he must attack although the enemy had tanks and he had none. The attack was skilfully handled and entirely successful. After seven tanks had been knocked out the enemy withdrew and Lieut. Col. Percy was able to pass his Group safely through to Tobruk and on to the frontier. All these successful operations were mainly due to the ability, personal courage and fine leadership of Lieut. Col. Percy.

On arrival at the coastal plain, it became obvious that the enemy had cut the route to Tobruk. The two columns left the coast road and headed into the sand dunes near the coast. If it came to a fight, this rough terrain would suit the infantry better than the open road. Mrassus was reached about 16 miles west of Tobruk. Here, the Germans lay across the battalion's route, dug in and supported by tanks and artillery. Lieutenant Colonel Percy put together what forces were available from the lorries nearest the head of the column and sited anti-tank guns to protect the rest of the stationary group. The attack itself was commanded by Major Slight and, in addition to the infantry, he was supported by a battery of the 74th Field Regt. R.A. and two South African armoured cars. Maj. Mike Ferens' 6th Battalion carriers led by Lieutenant Boys-Stones also played a major part in the attack. Lt. Jim Kennedy took part in the action. He wrote:

> Campbell [Slight] met me and told me there is probably a company of enemy infantry blocking the way to Tobruk…We debuss and extend to the right of 'B' Company who are going with their left flank trailing along the seashore…As we advance I hurry to catch up with Campbell who is walking grimly towards the enemy…He is magnificent. He ducks only once to a shell…
>
> We get to a knoll, which is under long range machine gun fire…There is little to see but I get some Brens to cover our advance…An occasional odd whistle proves we are observed. Range is too great for accuracy so there are no casualties. The carriers whipped up by John Willie [Robinson] catch up and I jump on one to go ahead to encourage 'C' Company to get up in line with 'B'.
>
> Far to the left, black on the white beach, I see two men and am about to engage them when I see one stagger and fall. Later I found out they were Braithwaite [Lt. R.] and a private who had got too far ahead. Braithwaite died the next day in Tobruk hospital. He had two days' married life before he left England.
>
> There is a long wadi parallel to the beach. As we swing along the seaward crest, I notice Bedouin tents in a re-entrant. Crawling between two is a uniformed figure…I point out the target to a [armoured] car and swing as many men as I can to the right…I point out a slight ridge, halfway to the tents as a first objective and rush there. A Bren gunner follows, gets into action and shoots through the head a German mortar man as he is rushing with his mortar to get into position. A rear Bren gunner covering the rush gets the German machine gun crew, as we lie under his fire. This gives us our opening…I grab the automatic of the German officer as he rises from his trench to surrender. I am croaking, 'Hand hooken!' fiercely and the unwounded Germans come out of their tents. We destroy mortar and sights, the M.G. and enemy rifles; water bottles are collected and I order them to be filled before we move off with the wounded. There are five enemies who need help. The papers from the dead are handed to me…

The attack was successful and the block was cleared. The enemy artillery firing from the escarpment caused problems as the column tried to get moving again. Major Slight got in touch with a South African battery of 25-pdrs. in position about 3,000 yards to the east. These guns opened fire on the escarpment artillery and put down smoke. The enemy fire lessened and so enabled the column to move on. The danger had not passed. German tanks attacked the rear of the column. Fire was brought to bear on them from a 2-pdr. anti-tank gun, Bofors and 25-pdrs. and the attack was beaten off with the loss of several enemy tanks. In addition, according to the battalion War Diary, 60 of the enemy were taken prisoner in the action. Battalion losses were 47 other ranks wounded or missing and three killed, namely, Ptes. D. Bainbridge, E. Hartley and G. Morris. Capt. C.E. Robson, Adjutant, and A.F. Murray R.A.M.C. were taken prisoner.

Maj. Campbell Slight was awarded a well-earned Distinguished Service Order. Sgt. Laurie Thompson was awarded the Military Medal. His citation described:

> On the 15th June, the withdrawal of the Bn. Group along the coast to Tobruk was held up by an enemy force. An infantry attack was hastily organised and Sgt. Thompson's Platoon formed part of it. In the early stages of the advance there were casualties and the Platoon Commander was wounded.
>
> Sgt. Thompson immediately took over and led his men with great coolness and resolution. They captured an enemy post together with one German officer and 17 ORs in a bayonet charge. Subsequently Sgt. Thompson continued the advance for a further 200 yards and captured two enemy M.G.s. Sgt. Thompson showed great courage in the face of heavy fire and a threat from enemy tanks and was an inspiration to his men in a difficult situation.

Pte. Alfred Norman Aldridge was also awarded the Military Medal:

> On the 15th June when the Battalion Column was held up during the move to Tobruk, an infantry attack was hastily organised against the enemy blocking its way. Aldridge took part in the advance with his platoon, which was held up by a German Spandau post. Pte. Aldridge rushed ahead of the remainder of his platoon to a fire position within 250 yards of the enemy and in full view. In spite of enemy fire, he got his Bren into action and knocked out the enemy post. This determined action by Pte. Aldridge enabled his platoon to advance and capture the position without further casualties.

Pte. John Edward Dunn received the same award for determined and aggressive action against the enemy.

Lieutenant Colonel Percy's column passed through Tobruk on the night of the 15th June and laagered up in the defence perimeter. Major Slight's column settled for the night at Gambut. Both columns united again on the following morning and made their way to the Sheferzan Gap on the frontier where further orders were received to proceed to Bir Thalata, the 50th Division assembly area. This was reached without further mishap. Lieutenant Colonel Percy and Capt. Ken Wood went to hospital and Major Slight took over command of the battalion. Lt. Jim Kennedy and his platoon did not have such a trouble free journey:

> We are two – a carrier in the rear and my troop carrying lorry to the fore. Both are overloaded. Eight were on the carrier, one a coloured South African. Twenty-eight, half a platoon's stores, a drum of petrol and a drum of water on the lorry. In the seat is a man with both a damaged arm and a wound in his leg. I ride on the step, guiding Stan at the wheel and, alternatively, driving the men when we push the lorry and cheering them on when

we can ride. All the time this damned gun trailing on behind.

From about 1800 hrs., we have been towing the 25 pounder gun, which had been left by some gunners who must have panicked during the tank attack. We saw no ammunition near it, which gives reason for the haste but the gun was left complete and undamaged. The twenty-eight men were three infantry sections I had kept as a guard to a battery covering our withdrawal against the persistent tank threat and some odds I'd collected off the beach. More were left on the seashore and in the dunes but they would have to take their chance…The Battalion had drawn ahead and now would be almost into Tobruk. The carrier was a lame duckling and was as slow as we were…Our goal was not in sight for flat-topped hills were in the way. They were intersected by steep-sided wadis, which proved most hindering. Going down meant all brakes and the ever present danger of an over-turned truck or gun. Uphill meant we all walked at least. Usually we had to push as well.

Eventually we saw through the glasses, in the dim light of dusk, a truck, thick wire and two men. We slithered happily down the next gully, the engine stalled and we came to a stop. The carrier waited on the crest for us to push on. 'Aircraft!' Our lookout pointed. We looked up.

There we see bird-like shapes, which are circling slowly. Ours? The danger we have passed through unscathed and the weariness made us careless. I looked through my field glasses. Boche! 'Debus!' I yell and all scatter down the wadi sides. Stan keeps close to his truck. I get the disabled man out of the seat and into a trench. There is no cover left for me. The Messerschmidtts have broken circle and are in flat dives. I dash a few yards and flop down in the very bottom of the wadi. A man lies five yards ahead. God! I have no helmet. Down, down they scream. One takes the carrier on the crest. Two take us in the hollow. They almost scrape their noses down the wadi. Stone splinters fly. The buttock of the man in front spurts blood…My right arm bleeds and is swollen. I bend it and find only a stone splinter puncture in the forearm. The men slowly rise…A man puts a dressing on the buttock where the bullet entered and inside the leg where it left. It is Regan. Seven have stone splinters in them. One has one between the eyes and cannot see for the blood but both eyes are safe. We move slowly up the hill to the carrier and put in it two men who had bad body wounds. I sent the carrier to Tobruk for an ambulance for Regan and discovered the coloured chappie in a hole. An explosive bullet had removed his shoulder. He eventually stayed the whole night, as the ambulance could not get back through the blocked minefield gaps.

We think maybe the ambulance will not come so we put Regan high on the lorry with all the blankets beneath him. He lies on his stomach without a murmur. On we go. The light has gone. The gap is reached as the ambulance pulls out. Grim voices challenge. We eventually enter. Safety. Grim are the voices no longer. We are in need and despite war, Christian feelings exist and all help those who can no longer help themselves. At 2 a.m. when Regan gets to a hospital we are asleep. A few days later [having left] we hear the fall of Tobruk.

The German success appeared complete. For the British, the future looked bleak.

CHAPTER XV

MERSA MATRUH – A VICTORIA CROSS

Shortly after the battalion had concentrated at Bir Thalata, Tobruk fell. There would be no more thorns in Rommel's side during this advance. The 50th Division now withdrew to Mersa Matruh. Only four per cent of the officers and men had not rejoined after Gazala but losses in supplies and equipment were heavy. The division took up defensive positions on the escarpment south-east of Mersa Matruh. No. 151 Brigade was moved after two days to positions in the Gebel Shaquqa area of the escarpment, due south of Mersa Matruh and west of the previous positions. The battalion laboured to construct defensive positions as the enemy was only a few miles away. They worked throughout the night, only to receive orders the following day to move along the escarpment to a position about 15 miles south-west of Garawla at a place named Raqabet El Sikka. The objective was to ensure that Mersa Matruh was not cut off by the enemy and so trap the 10th Indian Division who were garrisoning the town. The brigade task was to protect the left flank of the divisional line. Again the battalion worked all night on preparing defensive positions and was ordered to lay a minefield. The problem was that no mines were on hand and none arrived.

The enemy quickly followed the retreating British. On the 27th June, he bumped into the Matruh defences and was held up for a short while. Rommel's armoured columns swept around the town and on to the coast road running eastwards. The 10th Indian and the 50th Divisions were now cut off as the rest of the Eighth Army withdrew towards El Alamein. No. 151 Brigade soon felt the brunt of the enemy attacks. At 2 a.m. on the morning of the 27th, 12 Cruiser tanks entered the brigade perimeter and brought information that German armour and mechanised vehicles were drawing close. Within a short period of time, a platoon of 'B' Company was attacked by a German patrol. During the remainder of the night, there was no enemy attempt to attack although intermittent shelling and small arms fire broke out. At 5.15 a.m. the 9th Battalion was attacked by superior numbers of infantry, supported by tanks and heavy shelling and mortar fire. This frontal assault was carried out with grim determination and fierce hand-to-hand fighting took place with heavy casualties to both sides. By 7.30 a.m., the three forward rifle companies were isolated from each other and from battalion headquarters and they were eventually overrun. The Germans now turned their attention to the positions held by 'H.Q.' Company and battalion headquarters itself. Although two enemy tanks were destroyed, the remainder of the battalion was soon in a very precarious position and almost totally surrounded. At 9 a.m., orders were given for the survivors to withdraw.

Many were the gallant actions carried out on the 27th June. First amongst these was that of Pte. Adam Wakenshaw. Early in the action a German tracked vehicle approached 'B' Company's positions. Private Wakenshaw was one of the 2-pdr. anti-tank gun team positioned ahead of the company front. A report written by Capt. A.E.C. Hartnell described:

On the 27th June, south of Mersa Matruh, Pte. Wakenshaw was a member of a 2 pdr. A/Tank Gun crew sited on the forward slope of 'B' Coy. front.

Shortly after dawn the enemy attacked and a tracked vehicle towing a light gun was brought within short range of the position. The A/Tank crew opened fire and succeeded in putting a round through and immobilising the engine of the enemy tracked vehicle.

Another mobile gun then came into action. All members of the crew including Pte. Wakenshaw were either killed or seriously wounded and the 2 pdr. silenced. In this respite, the enemy moved forward to get the light gun into action against our infantry.

Realising the danger to his comrades, under intense mortar and artillery fire, which swept the gun site, Pte. Wakenshaw crawled back to his gun. Although his left arm was blown off above the elbow, he loaded the gun with one arm and fired five more rounds. He succeeded in setting fire to the tractor and damaging the light gun. A near miss then killed the gun aimer [Pte. E. Mohn] and blew Pte. Wakenshaw away from the gun, giving him further severe wounds. Undeterred, he slowly dragged himself back to the gun, placed a round in the breach and was preparing to fire, when a direct hit on the ammunition killed him and destroyed the gun.

This act of conspicuous gallantry prevented the enemy from using their light gun on

The Wakenshaw 2-pdr. anti-tank gun in position after the action on 27 June 1942.

184

'B' Coy, which was only 200 yds. away. It was through the self sacrifice and courageous devotion to duty of this infantry A/Tank gunner that the Company was enabled to withdraw and embuss in safety.

Private Wakenshaw's courageous act was outstanding and fully deserved the ultimate award of the Victoria Cross. The remainder of the crew of the gun must not be forgotten, amongst whom were Ptes. Eric Mohn and Pat Murray. They, too, played their part and lost their lives but received no tangible awards. Maj. A.B.S. Clarke, Second in Command of the 8th Battalion, wrote '…in the evening after the action, I found the body of Pte. Wakenshaw stretched out on the back of the breech block beside the ammunition box.'

Adam Wakenshaw was born in Newcastle. From a poor family, all his life he had had to

Pte. Adam Wakenshaw V.C.

struggle against the odds. He had helped to eke out the family earnings by fighting in the boxing booths and the size of the opponent did not matter – he would take on anyone. He was an incorrigible character who had more than his share of clashes with authority, particularly in the army. But officers and men of his battalion knew that there was no more loyal a comrade and one they could rely on in a fight, whether it was against soldiers of other regiments when in base camps or against the enemy. Lt. Jim Kennedy wrote:

> Private Wakenshaw was a Geordie…I found him to be a kind, friendly man. During the hard times pre-war, Wakenshaw earned a meagre living as a 'boxers chopping block', i.e. he was prepared to get into the boxing ring with more talented professional boxers for small fees.
>
> Before the Battalion moved overseas, boxing contests were held in the cold winter

evenings and to complete each evening's entertainment, Wakenshaw and a man called Lush, a professional boxer, fought a three round bout. There was always some skilful boxing in the first round, less in the second and in the final round the combatants stood toe to toe and slugged each other, with their supporters cheering them on. However good or bad had been the previous bouts, everyone was satisfied as the evening concluded with Lush and Wakenshaw standing on either side of the referee who would be holding a hand of each high in the air to proclaim a draw…

When I heard the story, I said to myself that he fought as he boxed: toe to toe, blow for blow. Needless to say, he was killed…I certainly had respect for him.

Capt. Ken Wood told of an earlier act of courage shown by Adam Wakenshaw:

Adam Wakenshaw was a notable member of a gun crew…I soon found out he was popular and coveted for specialist work with both the Battle Patrol and the Carrier Platoon…an incident occurred involving Wakenshaw…The incident was about a fire in the Company Cookhouse, which naturally was a 12ft. x 12ft. hole in the ground covered with a camouflage netting and scrim cloth, which is what ignited, probably through injudicious use of petrol. Wakenshaw, in his normal pursuit of the constantly available mug of strong tea, attacked the blazing netting with bayonet and bare hands, enough to free the cooks from an unpleasant grilling. A very commendable action…

His gallant, stubborn refusal to give in against greater odds and his fanatical desire to kill the enemy, came as no surprise to me…

After the war, an article appeared in the *Egyptian Mail*, written by Capt. Hugh Sutherland (Military Observer) on a visit to El Alamein war cemetery:

In the centre of the cemetery was a two pounder anti-tank gun painted with the familiar dun-coloured camouflage of the Eighth Army but now twisted and shell shattered…Against the shield, rested a wreath of withered white roses and purple bougainvillea. The ribbon fluttered and the dry petals rustled in the freshening wind.

Some souvenir hunter had taken the card but I was told that it bore the words, 'To the heroes of Alamein, from Turkish Officers.' It was the gun served by Private A. Wakenshaw of the Durham Light Infantry when he won the Victoria Cross…Originally buried beside his gun on the scene of the action, his body had been taken to Alamein.

The gun now resides in the Durham Light Infantry regimental museum in Durham City.

What had happened on the other areas of the front held by the battalion? Lt. Jim Kennedy wrote:

…we, left of the line of infantry, proceeded southwards down the line of the telegraph wires until we reached a small escarpment running East-West. On the line of the wires was a wadi taken over by H.Q. and the support company. 400 yards to the west was a half-saucer shaped basin occupied by us. Another 1,000 yards west was a longer basin cut into the scarp with 'A' and 'B' Companies. Our front was south and west. We had to get cover from possible shelling and bombing and fire positions dug before we slept. There were positions at the southern head of the basin, large enough for a platoon. These were excellent and were eventually extended and taken over by Jeff, his platoon and two more sections. Two sections were then to N.W. and a similar reduced platoon were to the N.E. H.Q. were on the western edge of the wadi…About 3 a.m. there was turmoil. Vehicles from the north-west dashed through our wadi and away. One driver had joined the rush with seventeen of our men aboard. We got them back but this event gave me a shock. A little later, one vehicle and 20 men came in from the same direction…Fateful dawn arrived. A little previous, our 2-pdr. had reached us. It could not come off its portee and was only a target for the enemy in such a position. We, therefore, only depended upon our small arms. To the north, on the track down the telegraph line, we could see a mass of vehicles. Ours, we thought. Within 10 minutes we were disillusioned. The visibility was very poor, with low rising sun but soon traced the slight shelling, which had begun to a Mark IV which was where the second battalion of our Brigade ought to have been. We were baffled. Later we found out that the main German column had moved in during the night. Advanced infantry had penetrated the gap between us and the next battalion [8th D.L.I.] and grabbed our supporting 25 pounders. Another large enemy infantry patrol had completely surprised and killed or taken one platoon of 'B' Company on our extreme left.

There we lay, though we knew it not, half-saucer bowl open to the full might of the enemy artillery. Soon we became aware of trouble starting. Anti-tank shells whizzed up our wadi at the tanks to our rear and what was now our right flank. The tanks rumbled away about 6 a.m. During the next two hours we were shelled and mortared unceasingly. Our vehicles were scarcely damaged, our casualties few…The sun, dust and smoke made it impossible to see the enemy or our own H.Q., which was only four hundred yards away.

A man dashed into the rear position, 'Withdraw or surrender!' This was upsetting. The shelling was now intense when, through the smoke I saw a huge Boche advancing, throwing stick grenades. He waved on a machine gun team who settled on the crest and begin to pepper us. I put old Mac onto the Boche and he shot him. To the right I heard Sgt. Rees calling fire orders as coolly as if on training.

Suddenly, the Sergeant Major cursed and it slowly penetrates my dazed brain that the left forward sections were standing up, hands above heads…Enemy fire was coming from right and left – both flanks seemed to have gone. We therefore said, 'Follow us those who care to break.' After fifty yards the M.G. fire made it obvious that our men would suffer too much. We stopped and said almost together, 'What shall we do?' I said, 'There is nothing else to do.'

Lieutenant Kennedy was taken prisoner along with many others of the battalion but was amongst a group of these who escaped during the trek to the prison camp. He rejoined the battalion. Amongst those who were wounded and taken prisoner was Maj. Campbell Slight D.S.O. He too continued to display the courage he had shown many times during the campaign. L/Cpl. Bill Ridley witnessed this during the action at MersaMatruh:

He [Maj. Slight] stood on the ridge in full view of everybody and he was scanning the front and the sergeant was standing beside him and he said to the sergeant, 'Sergeant, get them onto that point there.' A machine gun opened up, the sand spurted up just by his feet. He didn't take the slightest bit notice…The Sergeant went down on one knee and Major Slight and continued giving instructions to him…He took the binoculars off. He opened his pouch for his binoculars. He put the binoculars in the pouch, clipped the pouch closed, put his cane under his arm, slowly turned round and walked off the ridge. The sergeant, he got up and began to sing, 'The Blaydon Races' and halfway through he got a bullet which took both his eyes out.

Major Slight had left on one of the last two vehicles from the position. The other vehicle became bogged down in the soft sand. He jumped out and went to help push but before the truck got going the German armour arrived and he became a prisoner.

Lt. C.P. Donoghue [killed later in 1952 in Korea] was awarded the Military Cross. His citation read:

On the 27th June, [19]42, while the Bn. was engaging the enemy south of Matruh after his Company had been overcome by the enemy, Lieut. Donoghue took over command of the remnants of 'A' and 'B' Coys. and organised them into a defensive position. He walked about under heavy fire with extreme coolness collecting weapons from the forward positions, which had been evacuated distributing them among his men, enabling them to successfully engage the enemy. He then arranged transport for the remaining men and successfully withdrew them under fire.

Lieut. Donoghue's complete disregard for his own safety acted as a steadying influence on his men who had previously been shaken by the fire.

Lance Corporal Ridley was certain he would be captured:

I thought to myself, 'We're going to get put in the bag here.' So I took me watch off me wrist. I took me gaiters off and put me watch round me ankle and fastened me gaiter back on. Took me wallet out of me pocket, put it round me other ankle and put me gaiter back on. I thought, 'If I'm going to get taken prisoner, they're not going to get any loot off me.'

Though he wasn't taken prisoner, later he was severely wounded in the arm:

The strange thing about the army was, they never taught you First Aid. Fortunately, I'd been a Boy Scout and I knew at least one artery had gone. As it happened, two or three had gone and I knew I'd got to stop the bleeding. I put the heel of my hand into the wound…

Many of the battalion, particularly from the rifle companies, were taken prisoner. Sgt. Jim Hawkins was one of them:

As first light broke, so did the shelling and mortaring. We were pinned down, men getting killed all around us. About 11 o'clock, a huge German with a revolver drawn, stood over our foxhole and ordered us out. We were unable to pick up our small packs and were marched away to a small clearing where we found a number of other P.O.W.s. No food, no water and only the K.D. clothing we stood up in. Eventually about 5 to 6 o'clock, we were marched away under armed guard – half-track vehicles full of German guards. We marched into the desert and, at dusk, an armoured car appeared over the ridge – one of our own. The Germans scattered. We picked up a truck and headed down the coast road towards our own lines…

It was a brief interlude of freedom as the enemy had already cut the coast road running east from Mersa Matruh. Sergeant Hawkins and his comrades were recaptured and completed the remainder of the war in a P.O.W. camp. Several officers and about 100 other ranks had taken the opportunity to get away and although some were recaptured, others were successful and rejoined the battalion. Amongst these were Capts. A.C. Young and S. Pettinger and Lts. Jim Kennedy, G.R. Campion and D.K. Sleep. Young, Pettinger and Sleep were later recaptured when the division broke out from encirclement at Mersa Matruh. Pte. Jim Maddison had also escaped. He and his older brother, Joe, had continued a long family tradition of membership of this territorial battalion. This breakout through the enemy positions was not as successful as the one carried out at Gazala. The division broke up into columns, which sought to find their own individual routes across the desert towards Alamein. Some succeeded, some failed. Fuka was found to be occupied by the enemy and some columns were taken prisoner here. The division, much reduced in numbers and equipment, collected at Ikingi Maryut and Amiriya on the 1st July. The 9th Battalion was decimated. Most of its survivors were from battalion headquarters and 'H.Q.' Company. Stragglers came in over the next few days. Sergeant Edward Gallon had an interesting journey, which did not end on reaching Alamein:

Sgt. Gallon found an abandoned Bren Carrier on withdrawing from the Mersa Matruh Box and having repaired it as well as they could proceeded to Alamein, arriving 29th June 1942. By this time Sgt. Gallon was very weary and the carrier was breaking down every half mile. Eventually at Alamein, they ran into heavy shelling and the carrier was repaired again by Sgt. Gallon with complete disregard for his own safety. He had just withdrawn from the shelling area when he was asked if he could tow a serviceable 3 ton lorry, which was out of petrol, from the centre of the shelling area so that it could be refuelled and used for evacuating the many troops needing transport. Without a moment's thought, Sgt. Gallon and L/Cpl. Ferguson drove their carrier straight to the lorry. The rate of shelling increased immediately but Sgt. Gallon dismounted and affixed a tow rope to the lorry and towed it to safety where it was refuelled and used to evacuate troops. Sgt. Gallon proceeded a few hundred yards when he observed that the path of a ration convoy coming up the line was blocked by four immobilised 3 ton lorries, which were a direct target for heavy enemy shelling, which was very heavy. Sgt. Gallon at once drove his carrier to the four trucks and, one at a time with his life in immediate danger, he affixed a tow rope and managed to tow out all four lorries, thus allowing the ration convoy to make its effort to get through the barrage. The complete disregard for his own safety under heavy and continuous shelling, his devotion to duty under these conditions and in his tired state and, above all, his rapid appreciation of the urgency of clearing the way for the ration convoy regardless of his personal cost, his patience in the successful evacuation of the abandoned Bren Carrier, all showed most distinguished conduct and inspired those who were privileged to see him.

Sergeant Gallon was awarded an immediate Distinguished Conduct Medal. Among the dead on the 27th and 28th June were Sgts. H.S.W. Jones, C. Lockett and T.H. Mason, Cpls. L. Howard and F. Marshland and Ptes. J.H. Blakesley, P. Crane, M. Duffy, G. Lawton, A.S. Nellist, S.L. Onions, R. Simm and J.T. Tubmen. On the 2nd July, the battalion moved to Camp 3 at Mareopolis. Maj. W. Robinson was commanding the battalion, which comprised 10 officers and 283 other ranks.

CHAPTER XVI

THE ALAMEIN LINE 1942

Drafts began to arrive to make up for the heavy losses. Pte. Ernie Kerens recalled his first encounter with veterans of the battalion:

> We just sat there – Harold Hardman, Arthur Stapleton, Jimmie Bridges, Bill Jones, the last three all 'Scousers' and Eric Welsby.
>
> It was not until we gasped for a drink and went under a groundsheet to tell a bloke of our need, we made even a little contact – a sort of monster with matted hair, sand matted, sweat soaked shirt. Lips, nostrils and eyebrows thick with the stuff, sat up and pointed towards some 'Jerry cans' and said, 'Shake them, there will be some in one of them. As for food, hunt around you'll find some "hardtack" somewhere,' and went back under his groundsheet.
>
> For two days, we were just sat there getting 'hardtack' and water where we could, then the Brigade realised we were there…Bill Jones and I were told to pick up our kit and go to the 9th D.L.I…Bill to the anti-tank and I to the 'I' Section. After extensive enquiries, I found all that was left of the 'I' Section. It consisted of two grand blokes, Bob Redshaw, a Geordie, and Ken Foster, a very religious chap from Liverpool.

The Eighth Army was back in the Alamein Line. It had been foreseen that should Rommel threaten the Delta, a strong defensive line would be essential if he was to be stopped. Alamein was the chosen area for this defensive line. It had the advantage of protection from flanking assaults, which were a favoured method of attack by Rommel as he had already shown at the Gazala Line and Mersa Matruh and he would show again at the Battle of Alam Halfa at the end of August. The right flank of the line rested on the Mediterranean coastline. The left rested on the Qattara Depression where steep cliffs fell to the desert floor. The latter was covered with deep quicksand considered to be totally unfavourable for the movement of vehicles and tanks.

On reaching the Alamein Line, Rommel was already at a disadvantage. His lines of communication were stretched to breaking point. His men were tired after their incredible advance over many hundreds of miles, as were the British in retreat. It was quickly made obvious to him that the British intended to stay and fight. His initial attacks were driven back. He went onto the defensive and withdrew his precious armour for refitting. He placed the Italian infantry in the line supported by a screen of his deadly 88s. As at Gazala, the race was on. Rommel was refitting and strengthening his forces prior to an attack in force. The British began to see the arrival of their strong infantry and armour reinforcements, which would in time lead to the utter defeat of the Axis. General Auchinleck now went onto the offensive though his forces were much depleted and exhausted. Counter-attacks were launched on the 9th/10th July against the

Ptes. Ernie Kerens (left) and Perce Webb, Cairo
1942

enemy by the 9th Australian Division and the reorganised South African Division. On the 20th of the month, 69 Brigade was involved but, as could be expected, neither achieved a great deal. It then became the turn of 151 Brigade, which was in process of essential reorganisation.

No. 151 Brigade was now commanded by Brig. J.S. Percy D.S.O., M.C. He had succeeded Maj. Gen. J.S. Nichols D.S.O., M.C. who had taken over as G.O.C. 50th Division from Major General Ramsden. The battalion command structure was reorganised following the arrival of new drafts:

Commanding Officer   L t . Col. A.B.S. Clarke (from 8th Bn.)

Second in Command   Maj. W. 'Big Bill' Robinson

Adjutant   Capt. G.B. Beattie

O.C. 'A' Company   Maj. W.J.R. Scott

O.C. 'B' Company	Capt. J. Robinson
O.C. 'S' Company	Capt. K.M. Wood
O.C. 'H.Q.' Company	Capt. C.F.R. Goulden
Quartermaster	Lt. A.E. Love
Carrier Officer	Lt. G.R. Campion
Motor Transport Officer	2/Lt. D.J.S. Hirst
Mortar Officer	2/Lt. F.W.G.Worrall
Signals Officer	2/Lt. G. Hill
Intelligence Officer	2/Lt. R.W. Henley

The new drafts included 58 other ranks from the Durham Light Infantry; 42 from the North Staffordshire Regiment; 57 from the Oxfordshire and Buckinghamshire Light Infantry; 32 from the Shropshire Light Infantry; 10 from the Essex Regiment; 13 from the Welsh Regiment; 6 from the Duke of Cornwall's Light Infantry and 9 from the Worcestershire Regiment. In addition the following officers were included in the draft: 2/Lts. T.R. Thomas, G. Massie, G. Hill, F.W.G. Worrall, J.R. Blezard, R.W. Henley. J.F. Allan and J.C.L. Bainbridge.

On the 26th July, the battalion provided a composite company under the command of Capt. A.E. Hartwell. Other officers in this company were Capt. C.P. Donoghue M.C., Lt. G.R. Campion, 2/Lt. R. Massie and Company Sergeant Major Wood. The company joined a composite battalion under the command of Lt. Col. C.R. Battiscombe of the 6th Battalion. Both the 6th and 8th Battalions provided one company. The composite battalion, in turn, was part of a larger force, which included the 5th Bn. East Yorkshire Regiment and the 24th Australian Brigade. Tanks and artillery would be in support.

The objective of this attack was to gain more advantageous ground for the defence of the line in the central sector and, if the attack went particularly well, a possible breakthrough might lead to a general retreat from the enemy who would be pushed back into Libya. This was a most optimistic objective for units who had just come through a traumatic retreat and were busily reorganising with new drafts. The immediate objective was Sanyet el Miteiriya and the ridge running north-west from it. The composite battalion's objective was a prominent ridge, which had been given the name 'Ruin Ridge' because of the many attacks that had already failed in attempts to capture it. The enemy were well dug in and protected by extensive minefields.

Following an officers' conference held by the Commanding Officer at El Dakar, east of El Alamein Station, orders were issued. Each Bren gun was issued with 15 magazines of ammunition. Each rifleman was to carry 100 rounds of ammunition, one grenade and four empty sandbags. The composite battalion was ordered to attack the south-eastern slopes of Ruin Ridge. An Australian battalion was to attack the ridge from the north-east. Lieutenant Colonel Battiscombe attacked with the 6th Battalion contingent on the left, the 8th Battalion on the right and the 9th Battalion in reserve. South African engineers were detailed to clear a gap through the minefield.

The author's books *The Faithful Sixth* and *Into Battle with the Durhams* give fuller accounts of the action as it involved the 6th and 8th Battalions. Suffice to say that, despite the heroic fighting of the officers and men taking part that enabled them to break into the enemy positions, the action ended in disaster. Tank support was not forthcoming and the composite companies became trapped and cut off from the British lines. Most became prisoners of war. Among the dead were Ptes. F.C. Buck, J.T. King, E.H. Parry and L. Poole. Sgt. G.H. Forster was also killed. So many of the officers and other ranks had been through the Gazala campaign and the retreat to Alamein. Their experience would have served the battalion better had they been spared for the major battles to come, rather than be a casualty of what was considered by many at the time to have been a fruitless exercise.

On the 28th July, 2/Lts. G. Wilkes, W. Muir and E.C. Medway and Sgt. Pennock arrived from the infantry base depot. The whole of August was taken up with receiving drafts and commencing initial training of these new reinforcements. Pte. Ernie Kerens (intelligence section) wrote:

> During the day we were training 'un-armed' combat – how to kill your enemy with your bare hands. How to creep up behind a man and using his chin-strap for a lever, break his neck. It was so easy and effective and those taught forever more wore theirs over their tin hats and never under the chin. Bayonet practice point, lunge, withdraw or, if your enemy had the same idea, use of butt-stroke. We dug trenches, as under fire, lying on your stomachs, using the entrenching tool. We were taught to pinpoint enemy guns by back bearings from one's compass and to draw maps – a compass bearing and 120 paces counting as 100 yds. To find our way by varying compass bearings, our only light at night, the luminous dial of our compass. Soon it was second nature BUT the first time I finished up in 8th Battalion's latrines! After a while I could travel miles and finish up within feet of my objective…We were taught grenades, to hold the grenade for the first three seconds after pulling out the pin, or you might get it thrown back at you or it would at least give your foe time to dive for cover. We easily cut and wriggled over a body of a mate lying on 'Dannet' wire and find mines with a forty-five degree sloping bayonet. To render them safe with a nail in the hole of its detonator and, for that purpose, to keep at least an odd nail in your pocket…
>
> There were always tips from the desert warriors themselves, veterans. When in convoy and attacked from the air, to get as far as possible from the vehicles and not to shelter under them…To lie with arms round the head, this not only protects the eyes but gets your body as close to Mother Earth as possible. Explosions go up not down. Not to clench the teeth or tighten the muscles, to let the jaw sag. With tight muscles and concussion, the least that will happen is that you will have to wash your underpants. Taught that lying at the bottom of a two- or three-foot slit trench, it would need a direct hit to kill you but if you are crouching it might take your head off…To wash in a mug full of water, to shave in it, then filter it through a handkerchief, then save it to wash your under-clothes and socks. Taught that the monotony of hardtack could be alleviated somewhat by soaking them the night before and frying the biscuits for breakfast. On the very rare occasions one got a bottle of beer, to keep it in a damp sock in a cool place or buried in the sand, until ready to be enjoyed. Right from the start we were told to ignore Blighty soldiering. No blancoed webbing, no polished brasses. At the front at least, dirt was camouflage, it is smart not to be smart.

On the 28th August, the battalion moved from Mareopolis to Alam Shaltut close to the Cairo-Alexandria road. The Eighth Army was now under the command of Gen. Sir Bernard Montgomery who had succeeded General Auchinleck. General Montgomery quickly made his mark on the army. The word "retreat" was banned. His orders were that the Eighth Army would stand and fight where it was and if necessary die there. However, he promised increased reinforcements, better equipment, tanks and guns. Rommel would be kicked out of Africa. He knew that Rommel planned to attack in the future but, given time to prepare, he would be defeated. He did get the time he wanted and Rommel was indeed defeated. But that lay in the future. The effect of Montgomery on the morale of the Eighth Army can best be measured by the remarks of L/Cpl. John C. Rogers, who had arrived in the Alamein Line after the retreat:

> I was depressed there [the Alamein Line]. I reconciled myself that I wouldn't see home again. Until things started to brighten up. We got messages that they weren't going to put in any attacks unless we had the stuff to do the job...Monty told you what was going to happen. Before we were never told what was going to happen.

Meanwhile, Montgomery replaced the Corps Commanders he had inherited and Maj. Gen. Sir Oliver Leese replaced Major General Ramsden commanding XXX Corps and Gen. Sir Brian Horrocks took over XIII Corps.

The Axis attacked on the night of the 30th/31st August. As expected the main thrust came through the southern sector of the Alamein Line. The key enemy objective was the Alam Halfa Ridge. All this had been anticipated by General Auchinleck and by his successor, Montgomery. The ridge had been carefully prepared and the defences were strong. Montgomery gave strict orders that this was to be a purely defensive battle aimed at smashing Rommel's thrust. He was not yet ready for the offensive. The German attacks were crushed. Rommel found himself in a vulnerable position, his fuel supplies running short and under continuous pounding from the R.A.F., British armour and guns. He was forced to withdraw having suffered very heavy casualties. It was his last opportunity to take the Delta. The men, tanks and equipment he lost in this battle were never really replaced. Whilst there was still plenty of fight left in his forces, Rommel had passed the advantage to the British.

The 50th Division was not involved in this battle. No. 151 Brigade was involved in protecting airfields in the back area. The 9th Battalion was defending the landing grounds at Amariya where parachute landings were expected. Whilst parachutists never arrived, the enemy air force was very active until the R.A.F became strong enough to gain complete air control. Several air raids were made and much bombing took place but there were few casualties.

On the 4th September, 151 Brigade moved into the southern sector of the Alamein Line, taking over from the 2nd New Zealand Division. The three battalions of the brigade were in the line with the 8th on the right, 6th in the centre and 9th on the left. The 9th Battalion's position was in the locality known as El Mrier. Each battalion was supported by a detachment from the 505th Field Coy. R.E., a battery of the 74th Field Regt. R.A., a troop of the 57th Anti-Tank Regiment and a platoon of the 2nd Bn. Cheshires machine guns. The 149th Field Ambulance provided the medical services. Most of the troops were sited on a reverse slope with a well dug in observation post on the crest and in telephone communication with company headquarters. At the forward edge of the protecting minefield, each company manned a listening post, also with a telephone. Lt. W.S. White described the positions:

The crest was an observation post line. We had observation posts there and a standing patrol down the forward slope at the front edge of the wire. They were well dug in, with telephone communication and they acted as forward sentries.

They could see the ground, which rose away from the point to a small hill...The enemy were on the hill. They'd sown mines. They'd wired it up to stop us rushing them and we'd laid a lot of mines on our side of the hill to stop them rushing us. That hill was a very strong point that we'd have to attack sometime or the other, sooner or later.

Each night, brigade ordered the 9th Battalion to provide recce and fighting patrols down into no man's land, where the minefields were infested with anti-personnel as well as anti-tank mines. Patrolling and raiding became the norm. The Italian Folgore Division was opposite. This division had earned the respect of the British by the fighting qualities of its soldiers.

On the 5th September, 15 dive-bombers dropped bombs on battalion headquarters. Four other ranks were killed and five wounded. The dead were Sgt. C.E. Pennock and Ptes. L. Palmer, J. Robinson and A. Smallman. Capt. D.J.R. Parker arrived and

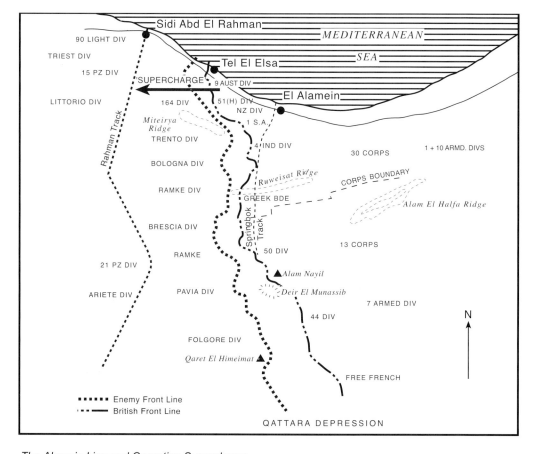

The Alamein Line and Operation Supercharge

assumed command of 'A' Company. Capt. G.H. Lohan took over command of 'S' Company from Capt. Ken Wood who had been sent to hospital.

Night exercises were carried out on the 9th September. During these, Lt. G.R. Campion, commanding the Carrier Platoon, lost his right leg when his carrier ran over a mine. On the same day, Lt. G. Eldridge arrived from the infantry base depot with 15 other ranks and he was posted to 'B' Company. No. 151 Brigade was placed under the temporary command of the 44th Division. On the 13th, a Greek brigade took over on the right of the 8th Battalion. These proved to be fine soldiers with a bitter hatred of the enemy and they took every opportunity to come to close quarters with them. On the 12th, Lieutenant Hynes led a patrol that located an Italian working party but was unable to capture a prisoner. Pte. J.T. Horton was killed by enemy artillery fire on the 14th September. The following day, leave restarted and parties were sent to the 50th Division rest camp at Sidi Bishr, near Alexandria.

Life in the box was described by Lt. W.S. White who was commanding the 11th Platoon of 'B' Company:

> Life in the Box was relatively pleasant. The occasional mortaring and shelling were tolerable but a raid of a single German aircraft did cause a bit of a stir as it flew in at zero feet. We all opened up and for a few minutes bullets flew in all directions. On the other hand a N.A.A.F.I. truck appeared at the rear of the box and, in turn, we all made our purchases. Tinned fruit was my delight and I can still remember that juice. Weapon cleaning and inspection formed a daily vital task and there was plenty of time for resting. This was essential because night time always brought work of some sort, patrolling and wiring being the main tasks.
>
> Food was adequate though monotonous but it did arrive regularly. Most evenings a hot meal appeared. Usually it was stew! We had enough to drink – tea or water. The new Company Commander [Capt. E.W.H. Worrall] soon got a grip and amongst his first orders was one saying that, for the Company's benefit, the officers loo would be sited in full view of the Company personnel so that 'regularity' could be witnessed by all!

As usual, stand-to started and ended each day at dawn and dusk. This was always considered as the time when an enemy might launch an attack. Water, though rationed, was of a better quality than at Gazala due to the proximity of fresh water supplies in the back areas. Pte. J. Everett wrote, 'We had a method. When we got our water we pierced a hole in the cork of our water bottles and instead of gulping it out, we used to sip it out.'

Casualties were caused by shelling and mortaring and, occasionally, by stumbling onto mines. On the 25th September, four men were killed trying to pull in a small enemy gun which was booby trapped. The four men killed were Ptes. J.A. Clemmett, E. Grice, D. Higgins and G. Lomax

September passed into October with very little excitement. Patrols brought information on enemy movements. Most patrols were carried out without incident and, very often, without seeing the enemy. However, occasional contact was made. On the 14th

October, Captain Worrall and Lieutenant Wilkes took out a fighting patrol of 25 other ranks, all carrying automatic weapons. Enemy patrols had been heard moving about no man's land. An ambush was organised and the patrol lay up for a time and observed an enemy patrol approaching. The latter was about seven strong. The battalion's patrol opened fire from a range of about 50 yards and inflicted two casualties on the enemy. The Germans made their escape when mortar fire descended on the British patrol. The patrol returned to the box having sustained no casualties.

Plans and preparations for the forthcoming assault at El Alamein were already well advanced. In an effort to deceive the enemy into thinking the main attack would come around the southern flank of the line, dummy concentrations of vehicles and tanks were placed behind this area of the front. They did not go unnoticed by members of the battalion. Pte. J. Everett described:

> I turned to one of my comrade and I said, 'Bah, we've got some transport down there.' He said, 'What do you mean?' I said, 'Look at them trucks. There's a fellow sat on a toilet over there!' He said, 'No, they're all canvas them.' And that's what they actually were. Made of canvas and you'd swear they were trucks and everything, even a fellow sat on the toilet!

The 17th October dawned with a cold wind and heavy dust storms. Lieutenant Eldridge and Second Lieutenant Slade took out a patrol of eight men, which split into two equal parties. Second Lieutenant Slade's party came under heavy fire and an N.C.O. was wounded in the shoulder. This patrol withdrew when the moon went down. After a short distance, the N.C.O. became too weak to go on and was left in a slit trench with one of his comrades, whilst the patrol leader went back for stretcher bearers. These were brought out and the N.C.O. was taken to safety. Meanwhile, Lieutenant Eldridge's patrol was caught in the minefield and blown up. They were spotted by a member of Second Lieutenant Slade's patrol who had become detached from his party. He returned to the lines and reported the whereabouts of the stricken patrol, lying dead or wounded in the minefield. A rescue party of carriers and an ambulance went out immediately and although they found the locality in which the patrol lay, they could not reach them before daybreak. Heavy artillery, mortar and machine gun fire drove the rescue party off. It was thought, by this time, that only one of the party was alive.

Lt. John Arnold had just joined the battalion from England. He knew Lieutenant Eldridge and that he was with the 9th Battalion. On reaching the railhead he was collected by R.S.M. Chris Armstrong. Lt. J. Arnold remembered:

> I asked him whether Lieut. Eldridge was with the Battalion and he said he was. When I tried to press for more details, the R.S.M. clammed up and would say nothing at all. So when I arrived at Battalion HQ, I pressed the matter further and I discovered that Eldridge, whom in England we had called 'Prince' because of his astonishing good looks, had gone out the night before on a foot patrol and had been wounded and was lying in the minefield between the Italian lines and our own. The Italians were resisting every effort to

rescue Eldridge, whether by armed force or by using Red X ambulance vehicles. Whatever happened, they shelled it and the upshot was that he died through loss of blood out in the minefield.

On the following day, Captain Worrall and Second Lieutenant Medway set out in carriers to try to recover the bodies. Furious artillery, mortar and Breda fire prevented them from approaching the minefield. In the afternoon the same two officers took their carriers out and charged the Italian positions and succeeded on quelling the enemy fire, whilst the bodies were removed. One man, Lance Corporal Coil, was still alive abut died shortly afterwards. The bodies of Lieutenant Eldridge, Private Thornett and Sapper Graham could not be removed. Lieutenant Hill and the sappers of the 505th Field Company under the cover of a protective patrol attempted to open a gap in the Italian minefield but enemy patrols, very active in the area, made this impossible. After all this, the battalion was in no mood to deal leniently with the Italians opposite.

2/Lt. Edward C. Medway received the Military Cross for his part in this action. His citation stated:

A few hours before dawn on 18th Oct. a small patrol of one officer and three O.R.s was discovered injured in the centre of a minefield, only five hundred yards from a strong Italian post. The minefield was known to be full of booby traps and anti-personnel mines.

At dawn it was seen by the rescue party that only one O.R. was still alive. Early efforts to reach this man were impossible owing to the intensity of enemy small arms fire. Later efforts were nullified by a full regimental artillery concentration around the men. At about 1500 hrs., Lieut. E.C. Medway led three volunteers to reach the wounded man. They dashed 170 yds. into the minefield, searched the bodies of the dead for any identification marks, picked up their weapons and the officer's compass, and 2/Lt. E.C. Medway carried away the badly wounded man on his back.

Throughout this rescue, enemy S.A. fire was fired at them from the enemy post and towards the finish enemy shellfire commenced. 2/Lt. E.C. Medway showed great personal bravery throughout the efforts to extricate the wounded man and set a fine example of courage in the face of the enemy.

Events were now moving rapidly. On the 19th and 20th October, General Montgomery spoke to officers of the Eighth Army down to the rank of Lieutenant Colonel. He outlined his plans for the Battle of El Alamein and the part he expected everyone to play. His plan envisaged a feint attack in the southern sector of the Alamein Line, which would deceive Rommel in the belief that the main British effort would follow the similar pattern he had used in his major attacks on previous occasions – around the open southern flank. Part of the elaborate deception was to build dummy vehicles and tanks behind the southern positions. The major blow of the attack would fall in the northern sector. The XXX Corps was given the task of opening a corridor through the enemy positions to enable the tanks of X Corps to pour through and defeat the German panzers in the open desert beyond. Montgomery envisaged a battle of attrition, a 'killing match', that would last about 10 days, and he impressed upon his audience that all troops should be fired with drive and enthusiasm and the aim of killing the enemy. The feint attack in the south would be made by the 44th Division, which would attack in the Munassib area and aim to break through the minefields and enemy positions and enable the 7th Armoured Division to move through and roll up the Axis defences in the rear. This attack would start on the 23rd October, at the same time as the main assault in the north. It was hoped that it would draw the German panzer divisions down to the southern sector and away from the main attack.

No. 151 Brigade's involvement in these plans was to send the 6th Battalion to a position on the plateau north of the Munassib Depression where it could dominate the depression. The 9th Battalion was to mop up any enemy positions on the north side of the depression in co-operation with 69 Brigade. Raids undertaken by the 8th Battalion and the Greek Brigade would keep the enemy fully occupied in front of their positions. No. 151 Brigade attacks were not to be carried out until the 7th Armoured Division was established in the rear of the Munassib Depression. In the event the 44th Division was unable to breach the enemy minefields and the 7th Armoured Division was unable to break through and take up its planned position, 151 Brigade's plans were considerably toned down and only raids and patrolling were carried out.

In the days immediately prior to the assault at El Alamein on the 23rd October, the battalion continued with its aggressive patrolling. Lieutenant Wilkes took a fighting patrol down to the western edge of the Italian minefield. He heard sounds of a working party. The patrol worked its way forward to within 300 yards and opened fire with 2-in. mortars and three Bren guns. The party scattered but it was too dark to observe whether the enemy suffered any casualties. On the 21st, a draft of 8 officers and 90 other ranks was received from the infantry base depot.

No patrols were sent out on the 22nd as the battalion prepared for an important raid. This raid had three objectives: first, to obtain the identification of the enemy unit holding the position; second, to destroy enemy weapons; and third, to blast two holes in the minefields and wire to enable their use on the following night. The raiding party was commanded by Lieutenant Wilkes and comprised Lt. John Hutchinson and 24 other ranks from 'A' Company. There were also four sappers with the raiders from the 505th Field Coy. Royal Engineers. They carried Bangalore torpedoes, used for blowing a gap through wire. The other raiders carried eight Thompson sub-machine guns plus grenades, wire gloves, torches, tapes and a success rocket to be fired if the enemy position was overrun. Two stretchers and four stretcher bearers would be sent out by 'A' Company to rendezvous with the raiding party on the west side of the minefield. The position to be attacked was on North Point and the raid took place at 12 midnight on the 23rd October. A full moon lit the battlefield and the distant sound of the tremendous barrage that had opened the Battle of Alamein at 9.40 p.m. could be clearly heard.

The raiders reached the protective wire in front of the enemy position without incident. At this point they were spotted and the enemy poured small arms fire in their direction. Lieutenants Wilkes and Hutchinson were both killed and the raiding party withdrew. Two other ranks were captured. Lieutenant Bamford with a patrol from 'C' Company had formed a covering base on the edge of the Italian minefield and their presence and support enabled the rest of the raiding party to withdraw without loss.

The failure of the 44th Division and the 7th Armoured Division in the tasks given to them brought about a change in the plans for the involvement of 151 Brigade. Fresh orders were issued on the 25th October. The 9th Battalion, supported by the 74th and 154th Field Regts. R. A., was ordered to attack North Point and the Twins (code names given to Points 98 and 94) from the east. This attack was dependent on the successful assault by 69 Brigade on the Moor and the Cape (Points 92 and 101). Gaps through the Danube Minefield had been made by the 7th Bn. Green Howards. The attacks were to be made on the 26th October. The machine guns of No.4 Platoon, 'A' Coy. Cheshire Regiment were with the battalion. The whole action was code-named Operation Lightfoot.

At 3 a.m. on the 26th, the battalion moved up to the forming-up point in the area held by the 7th Green Howards. The attack by 69 Brigade was only partially successful and, an hour later, the 9th Battalion was ordered to return to its lines. Lt. W.S. White remembered what happened:

Our company ['B'] of the 9th Battalion, were given the job of neutralising this strong point…where the Folgore [Division] were positioned and it was the most peculiar sort of business all together…On the evening, our company was going to leave its positions and go down to a starting point, a taped position…The code word, which I think was 'Chicken' would be given and we, on the start line, were to charge up the hill, through the mines, wire and all…My platoon was going to lead the charge. So the night came. 'Chicken' was the code for attack, 'Goose' was the code for 'Hold it, it's not tonight!'

So we walked out onto the tape and laid down. My orders were to get up the hill as far as I could when I got the command and if I couldn't get through the wire…I [and my men] were to fling ourselves on top of it and the rest of the men and supporting platoons coming up the hill behind me would run over the top of us and get in at the enemy. I thought, 'That's a nice how do you do!'…So we walked down to the start line and got the OK signal 'Chicken'…We lay down. Strange enough, looking back, I had no sense of this as a foolhardy affair…We were lying down, minutes off the start. The 'Goose' code word for operation off. So we toddled back…We were going to do it the following night. Down we went again. We'd had a bit more time to think about it. I thought, 'I hope it's going to be worthwhile.' Then, again, a few minutes before, it was cancelled again.

Indeed the operation was moved to the following night and was then cancelled. By now the men were exhausted from a combination of lack of sleep, intense stress and a long march to the start line. Great events were unfolding in the north of the Alamein Line for which the battalion had played a minor though important role.

CHAPTER XVII

THE BATTLE OF ALAMEIN – OPERATION SUPERCHARGE

The Battle of Alamein had started as General Montgomery had planned. The infantry given the task of breaking into and through the enemy lines followed the huge barrage, which commenced at 9.40 p.m. on the 23rd October. In the days that followed, bitter fighting took place and by the end of the month it was apparent that the corridor had not been opened for the tanks of X Corps. A final thrust was needed. Operation Supercharge was born. Montgomery planned to make one final effort to break through by attacking on a relatively narrow front with two brigades of infantry supported by a huge artillery barrage. The latter comprised 13 field and two medium regiments of artillery – about 350 guns – firing a creeping barrage, which the infantry would follow closely. He called forward 151 Brigade and 152 Brigade (51st Highland Division). This attack was to take place on the night of the 31st October/1st November; it was later postponed for 24 hours. The plan was for 151 Brigade to attack on the right and 152 Brigade on the left. A corridor would be punched through the enemy minefield with the object of advancing as far as the Rahman Track, about 5,000 yards from the start line. The attack was divided into two phases, the first to an intermediate objective, 3,500 yards forward of the start line. When this was reached the brigades would pause for half an hour to reorganise before pushing on to the final objective. The Germans and Italians opposing them had received a severe mauling in the previous days' attacks but were far from defeated and fought with great tenacity.

The barrage was timed to advance 100 yards every two and one-half minutes in front of the advancing troops. The 8th Royal Tank Regiment provided support with its Sherman tanks, together with a platoon for each battalion from the 4th New Zealand Machine Gun Company and a troop of Northumberland Yeomanry Anti-Tank Guns. The terrain was flat and open but rose slightly toward the Rahman Track. The forward minefield received the attention of the Royal Engineers who opened a corridor, but a suspected minefield beyond that had not been marked. It was thought that this was an anti-tank minefield and the infantry was ordered to march through it with the hope that there would be few casualties. This proved to be the case but at the time it was largely wishful thinking! The enemy positions were strong, and dug-in tanks and self-propelled guns gave considerable support to the their infantry. The famous 88s dominated the area to be attacked. The location of the operation was west of Tel el Eisa Station in the northern sector.

To assist the infantry in keeping direction, Bofors guns firing tracers marked the boundaries between the two brigades and the flanks of the attack. No. 151 Brigade came under the command of General Freyberg V.C. G.O.C., 2nd New Zealand Division. The 28th (Maori) Battalion of this division was designated to attack an enemy strong point on the northern flank of the brigade attack. Brigadier Percy's plan was for the 8th Bn. D.L.I. to attack on the right, supported by the 8th Royal Tank Regiment. The 9th Battalion was on the left supported by the 3rd Hussars. The latter had two squadrons of Sherman tanks and one of Crusaders. The 6th Battalion followed about 500 yards behind the 8th, mopping up isolated enemy posts. At a given point, the 6th had to wheel at right angles to the line of attack and face north, so creating a strong northern flank. The start line was marked with a line of cairns or oil drums. Forward elements of Australian infantry were withdrawn to allow the attacking brigades to form up on the start line. Each attacking brigade would move forward along a frontage of 2,000 yards.

When the infantry had reached their objectives, the 9th Armoured Brigade (also under the command of 2nd N.Z. Division) and, later, 1st Armoured Division would pass through. The opening barrage would fall in its full fury, just ahead of the waiting infantry. After five minutes, the medium guns and a proportion of the 25-pdrs. would lift to fire upon the known locations of enemy guns. As the infantry moved off, a curtain of shells 12 yards apart rolled ahead. Beyond this there was another curtain of shells and beyond this one a further curtain of heavier guns. These moved forward in bounds of 100 yards every two and one-half minutes. After the pause for reorganisation, the barrage would move ahead and creep up to the final objective, which lay some 5,000 yards from the start line. This barrage concentrated in so small and narrow an area was estimated, by some, to be as violent as any barrage since 1918.

On the 28th October, orders were received to leave the southern sector and proceed into G.H.Q. reserve in the north. This was done in troop-carrying vehicles and an area east of Sydney Road and north of Ruweisat Ridge was reached at 2 a.m. on the 29th. Close to the sea, bathing parties were organised and general maintenance of equipment and weapons was carried out. The sea bathing was most welcome as it was the first total immersion in water the men had had for several months. The following day the battalion moved forward along Z Track beside the railway line to a position two miles east of Tel El Eisa Station. The track was lit in places but it was a long and slow journey in the lurching trucks. Clouds of dust cut down observation to a minimum. The area allocated was already occupied by some Australian transport and it was only with great difficulty that space was found for the battalion to bivouac for the rest of the night. To make conditions even more uncomfortable enemy aircraft bombed the area and, though there were no casualties, it did not help the battalion to relax. On the morning of the 31st, the battalion awoke to find itself in the middle of elements of the 51st Highland Division – tank workshops and gun lines. Lt. Col. Andrew Clarke attended a conference held by the Brigade Commander, Brigadier Percy, along with the Commanding Officers of the other battalions. The attack was postponed for 24 hours until the night of the 1st/2nd November.

On the 1st, the Commanding Officer received orders to attack with the intention of clearing an approach through the enemy minefield. This would enable the armoured

X Corps to follow through into the open desert and engage the enemy armour. The march along the Diamond Track to the forming-up area was one of seven miles and was reached at about 5.30 p.m. It was an energy-sapping march through ankle-deep dust. The enemy forward defence line lay about 2,000 yards ahead. Pte. Ernie Kerens wrote:

> In the afternoon of the 1st November, the Battalion began its long march to the starting point of the bridgehead attack, Supercharge. At 1600 hours, we halted for the evening meal, a tin of M and V, not much to die on. An hour later we continued, not so much as a column, as an untidy 'crocodile'. Thick layers of sand clung to our skin, rags wrapped round the bolts of our weapons to ensure they would work when needed. The last few yards was through a wired-off gap in a minefield. It was lined with Aussies, who watched us in silence or quietly cheered us on in half whispers. One slapped me on the back and whispered, 'Sick 'em for me Limey.' I got the queer feeling we were going to a dangerous sort of football match. The continuous growling of the guns and whining of the shells seemed unreal. We arrived at the starting tapes at 2000 hours but zero hour was not until 0105 hours and we had to take cover for a while.

Lt. W.S. White further illustrated the action:

> When we got to the forming-up place, I paired the lads up because we still had an hour or two to wait…As far as I can remember, we were in K.D. summer kit. It was a very cold night and that was why I said, 'Get together in pairs. One can sleep but take turns.' Teddy [Worrall] came up and said, 'I like that, well done!' He said, 'What do you think of the wire in front of you?' I said, 'What do you mean, what wire have I got in front of me?' He said, 'I told you to see the bloody wire. Haven't you been?' Of course not, because he didn't tell me. He said, 'Well get yourself off and see.' It was a single strand wire across our front, which one of the allies, Aussies or New Zealanders, had put up during the preparation. Obviously it was an obstacle we had to cross and Teddy wanted to be sure that we knew what we were going to do. So I walked off with my batman and found the wire. It was about two hundred yards ahead of where we had formed up. I snipped the wire but I didn't pull it apart and about thirty yards along I snipped it again. Should we ever find it again it would be easier for us to cross. Back at the forming-up point, we rejoined the platoon. At about midnight, we opened the thermos flasks, each containing a gallon of cocoa and rum and thoroughly enjoyed a generous sip. It was warming. Ten minutes before Zero we stood up, checked our equipment and fixed bayonets. The enemy were about two thousand yards away.

The cold of the night had been anticipated and hot cocoa and rum was provided for the shivering men. The sounds of battle were now farther away and behind and around them there was almost silence. This is the time when strain gets to men and thoughts of what might lie ahead break into the mind. The close proximity of friends and comrades takes on a new meaning. They draw strength from each other, neither wanting to show the other the fear growing inside. Many wish for the action to start as then fear subsides and training, discipline and professionalism takes over. They can do the job they are trained to do. All along the frontage of the two brigades, each Durham and Scot prepared in his own individual way.

Capt. Jim Kennedy prepared his men immediately prior to the commencement of the attack. He recalled:

> I had my men in fighting patrol formation. In the centre of my own group were two men who could count paces so that they could estimate distance and not run into our own barrage. I stressed that they had to work fast to clear the area of enemy as they advanced, for the time they had until dawn was limited; and by dawn they had to be in slit trenches. On my left and just five paces behind me was my batman.

The battalion formed up with 'B' Company (Capt. E.W.H. Worrall) on the right, 'C' Company (Capt. A.H. Dunn) in the centre and 'A' Company (Capt. A.R.F. Hynes) on the left. 'B' Company was in touch with the 8th Battalion. On the left, there was some consternation when it was realised that the 5th Bn. Seaforth Highlanders of 152 Brigade had not started to advance from their expected forming-up place. A number of stray Highlanders were seen in the attack but the whereabouts of the main force was not known. However, on the following morning, information was received that the Seaforths had reached and held their objective. Tank-hunting parties had been organised by the companies of the battalion to deal with the dug-in tanks, which had been identified by air reconnaissance.

At 1 a.m. on the morning of the 2nd November 1942, 151 and 152 Brigades moved forward and followed the barrage ahead of them. Members of the intelligence section moved off with the forward infantry. Private Kerens noted:

> In our case as members of the 'I' Section, we might be ahead of them with our compasses, making sure they were on the right bearing. Though not keen, that and the rum made us proud.
>
> Zero hour. Mr. Henley, Charlie Sollis, his batman, Ken and myself led. The Signal Officer and his gang over to the left, the odds and sods behind. The moon was now up. Slowly we walked forward, circulation returning to frozen limbs, now beginning to tingle with excitement. A single strand of wire nine inches off the ground crossed our path. We checked and double-checked our bearings, it could be marking a minefield. If it was it could be set for troops or tanks. This was our bearing, it had to be crossed. Our barrage from behind was bursting on the ground to our immediate front, it was time to go. On our right, a rifle fired, then another and another, the Brr Brr of a Spandau, half a dozen of them. The barrage was literally raising the dust and through it I could see the explosions of shells and grenades and hear the rapid fire of scores and scores of Spandaus and other machine guns. My Alamein was in full swing.

This huge and noisy barrage whistled over the heads of the advancing infantry. Its power was awesome. It lifted the spirits of the troops; how could anyone live through it? It made up for what had been dished out to them in the past: at last the Germans were on the receiving end. Capt. Jim Kennedy described:

At 0105 hours, the barrage started and from then on every word said had to be a shout; more often a hand sign replaced the word. Soon the fumes of cordite and explosives mingled with the blinding dust so that when the advance started it was through a dry fog as thick as the wet ones at home. S.O.S. rockets fired by the enemy…arched into the sky and from then on the battle was joined.

Lt. W.S. White also remembered:

Zero Hour came – the silence was shattered by the crescendo of the artillery. We turned and looked behind us, to the east, to see the flashes of the guns. An awesome sight.

A shout of 'Forward', the sound of [Major Worrall] the Company Commander's hunting horn and the advance started. We came to the wire but had to cut it again and then we had a slight delay. The O.C. had lost his hunting horn! The delay was minimal and on we went. Time was vital…

The noise was terrific – gunfire, shell bursts, mortars, rifle fire, machine gun fire, the skirl of the bagpipes, the shouts of our charging infantry, and above the noise of battle we could hear, from time to time, the call of our Commander's hunting horn. It made us feel rather special and somehow comforted us.

Now that we were moving forward we no longer felt cold. The men seemed in good heart, the adrenaline was flowing and, as far as I could ascertain, we were not suffering casualties at this stage. We had not reached the actual enemy position, although we were coming across enemy slit trenches. For me, these were the most exciting moments of my life to date.

The terrific barrage had killed many of the enemy and sent a number of them into a severe state of shock but more remained untouched and, as the battalion advanced, the opposition stiffened. Visibility was down to a few yards as smoke and dust filled the air. Hand-to-hand fighting was enjoined and survival took over from reason. It was now a case of kill or be killed. Officers pointed out targets and the men charged in and finished off the opposition. In the thick, dust-laden air, some slit trenches were missed. The enemy in them waited until the infantry had passed and then fired into the rear ranks. The follow-up companies finished them off. The enemy retaliatory barrage began to fall on the advancing lines. Casualties began to mount. At the head of the advance, Private Kerens and the intelligence section peered at their compasses and tried to keep direction. Private Kerens recorded:

Glancing behind and to the left, I could see nobody except Mr. Henley and Charlie to my immediate left and Ken on my right. Bullets were now plucking at our sleeves in large numbers. The bullets and bits of shrapnel came like a shower of deadly hailstones and we had to throw ourselves down to live. On the right a vehicle burst into flames and by the light I could see company men trying to advance. We were ahead of them but some of them were still on their feet, others were falling or had done. There were tracers amongst them and explosions all around them. Over the sounds of the barrage and the small arms could be heard cursing and cries of the wounded. Someone in a pitiful voice was crying for his mother. From everywhere, 'Stretcher bearers, stretcher bearers!' and always the continuous noise. Sight had gone but the screams and curses mixed with the chatter of the machine guns and explosions of shells, continued. We hugged the ground and bullets skimmed over our heads. Ken took a bullet in his shoulder.

Suddenly, Mr. Henley said, 'I'm going forward to see what's happening, that's all I can do.' It seemed obvious to me what was happening but it was not up to me to reason why. He gave me his compass, his maps and binoculars, sent Charlie to contact the company on the left, made some little remark and walked towards the tracers. That was the last Ken and I and, no doubt anybody else, saw of him.

In Alamein cemetery today is the grave and the records: Henley, Capt. Raymond Wilfred, 187076. The South Staffordshire Regiment. Seconded to the 9th Battalion The Durham Light Infantry. 1st/2nd November 1942. Aged 27. Son of Francis Austin Henley and Julia Henley of Cheapside, LONDON.

Lt. W.S. White recalled:

At about 0230 hours, casualties were still very slight. We were all going well, when suddenly within a few yards in front of us four or five shells exploded. I'm not sure whether it was our guns dropping a few short or whether it was enemy fire but when the dust cleared, five men had been wounded and my left leg had been hit just below the knee. The platoon carried on under Platoon Sergeant Jordon and stretcher bearers checked the injured men. Fortunately none were seriously hit. My wound was not too bad but it was bleeding badly and I could not walk. Stretcher bearers bound the wound and then I asked them to bring the wounded to me so as I could keep an eye on them…

Shortly afterwards at about 0400 hours, the Field Ambulance appeared and the wounded were loaded in and off they went. A South African Nurse picked me up. Put me into her van and we were off to the Regimental Aid Post.

Many positions were charged with the bayonet and about 400 prisoners were taken. Many of these had been badly shaken by the barrage. The dug-in tanks were met and dealt with by the tank-hunting groups. Little quarter was asked or given. The fighting was bitter and casualties on both sides were heavy. Pte. J. Everett was involved in helping the wounded. He described:

We were helping, going out of our dugout, carrying badly wounded [tank and infantrymen] to our field ambulance…Captain Stone, he was American and he was walking about as if he hadn't a care in the world. I don't think he had a tin hat on and he was just moving about. To me, I've always maintained, if anybody should have been decorated, he should have been. The bravest man I've ever seen.

Private Kerens also saw Captain Stone go about his dangerous duties:

The American M.O. and his Sergeant, Bill Ryle from Gateshead were killed by a shell. The M.O., Captain Stone, had done wonders for the wounded from a hastily dug trench. When it was suggested that he take some cover he said, 'When is this darn war going to start anyway?' The same shell that caught him also killed his sergeant.

The number of prisoners coming forward increased. They came with hands raised high, many of them hysterical. The forward troops could not stop to secure them and indicated, with a wave of the rifle, to move to the rear where follow up units would deal with them. The battalion reached its objective at about four in the morning on the 2nd November. In fact some elements pushed on a further 700–800 yards and had to be recalled. Before first light, the battalion had to get below ground level. Capt. Jim Kennedy wrote:

> My batman digging an old slit trench deeper and another close by for me meant I could go around checking. There had been a lot of casualties…As the sun rose over the horizon, it was difficult to imagine how many men were in various holes in the ground around us. Only a few with uncompleted work were visible. The wounded had been evacuated; the dead lay where they had died or nearby. The prisoners had gone…
>
> So there in our holes we hid, eyes looking around as the sun rose and, then from behind us came the rumble of tanks advancing, widely spaced and guns at the ready. I thought how cold we had been in our desert uniform at midnight a few hours earlier; now we awaited a roasting while the tanks did their fighting.

The tanks indeed had a hard fight ahead of them. Rommel had 88s dug in just beyond the Sidi Rahman Track and these put up a final fierce resistance before the eventual breakthrough arrived. The forward troops of the battalion watched much of what was happening. Captain Kennedy was a witness:

> There was constant action. At one time a tank within a hundred yards was moving forward when, suddenly, there was a whiplash crack of an 88 and the tank stopped. There was a movement under the tank – someone was coming out the escape hatch and it was clear he would not walk far without help. A man leaves his slit trench and runs zig-zag forward and gets near the tank and goes to ground. In time the man from the tank is helped back behind the front line.

A battalion newsletter to the regimental depot at Brancepeth stated:

> When first light came, the 8th R.T.R. and 3rd Hussars had deployed in front of the Brigade as instructed. However, silhouetted against the dawn sky, they were met by a withering fire from 88 mm A/Tank Guns at close range and 50 mms firing from tanks further off. The 3rd Hussars suffered badly with tanks hit and both Regiments pulled back on top of the Battalion who were now furiously digging in. A much appreciated forethought had been the carriage of 6 empty sandbags by every man. They saved many lives during the day. Soon the remainder of the 9th Armoured Brigade arrived followed closely by the Support Group who placed many of their A/Tank Guns among our Companies.
>
> It was thus that the Bn. spent Nov. 2nd, taking cover in its trenches in the middle of a Tank Battle; the longest day anyone in the Bn. will ever remember. The German artillery used captured 25-pdrs, in addition to all kinds of A/Tank Guns. Their intense fire never stopped throughout the hours of daylight. They were actually firing more intensely at

1700 hrs. notwithstanding our heavy return fire and the hourly bombing by a squadron of Bostons and Baltimores.

Towards midnight on the 2nd November, the battalion was relieved by the 5th New Zealand Brigade. The relief was completed by 2 a.m. on the 3rd, and a hot meal of stew and tea was provided at battalion headquarters. Lieutenant Colonel Clarke was hit in the shoulder by a sniper's bullet, just as he led off the remnants of the battalion. It was the last round fired at the battalion in the Battle of Alamein.

Casualties included Capt. E.R. Stone (R.A.M.C.), Capt. R.W. Henley and 2/Lt. Handasyde-Dick, who were killed. Lts. R.W. Gammage, W.S. White, R.C. Rothwell and Farrant were wounded. Of the other ranks 25 were killed, 28 were missing and 75 were wounded. The dead were named as Sgt. W.N. Ryle, L/Sgt. D. Thompson, Ptes. F.W. Jones, G. Allen, A.E. Carlisle, G. Davison. A.E. Fennon, J.P. Fox, E.H. Fuller, P. Gouch, L.S. Heron, W. Hey, T. Holt, G.C. Knapper, J. Monks, W.A. Morgan, W. Nicholson, T. Pollitt, T. Potter, E.T. Rourke, C. Stevenson, S. Tams, S.J. Taylor, B. Todd and E. Whittingham.

Once the German line of 88s had been broken, the X Armoured Corps was out into the open desert. Hitler had ordered Rommel to stand and fight. Rommel knew that to do this would entail the complete destruction of the Afrika Corps. He ordered a retreat. His German units had first call on the depleted transport now at his disposal. The Italians, largely without transport, had to try and get away on foot. Many were taken prisoner. The long retreat, which would end in the fall of all enemy troops in North Africa, had begun. The 50th Division and 151 Brigade would not take part in the withdrawal from Egypt and Libya. It was a time to take stock. On the 3rd November, the 9th Battalion spent the day checking equipment and personnel. Lts. H.A.C. Vicsher. J.A. Wilson, G.W. Alward and W.G. Deacon joined with a draft of 55 other ranks. Citations were prepared and forwarded to higher authority for some of those who had carried out deeds of considerable gallantry. As always, a far higher number would go unrecognised. Capt. (Temp. Maj.) Edward W.H. Worrall was awarded the Military Cross. His citation read:

On the early morning of Nov. 2nd during the attack on enemy positions between the 300–301 grid lines, Capt. Worrall shewed great gallantry and leadership, leading his men through heavy M.G. fire, and rallying them with a hunting horn, going forward alone on several occasions with a 'Tommy Gun' to clean up M.G. nests.

On the final objective, he rallied his men against mobile enemy tanks and a coy. position, and blowing on his hunting horn ordered the charge, successfully capturing the position, and taking many prisoners.

He then led a small recce. party forward 500 yards, and despite the opposition, selected his coy. position for consolidation.

During the day, despite intense shelling, mortaring and machine gunning, he visited his dispersed men – giving them courage.

When casualties became heavy through the constant shelling, Capt. Worrall left his

German P.O.Ws of the renowned Afrika Corps captured at El Alamein

slit trench, and personally attended and organised the evacuation of the wounded, shewing a complete disregard for his own safety during the heaviest mortaring.

Capt. Geoffrey B. Beattie was also awarded an immediate Military Cross for his courageous leadership, which included a single-handed bayonet attack on a dug-in Italian tank that compelled its crew to surrender.

Cpl. Patrick B. Jordan was awarded the Military Medal. His citation ended, 'he was always the first man of his section to attack enemy strong points and gave his platoon a fine example to work under.' Another winner of the Military Medal was Pte. Charles William Swatten. His citation read:

Area El Alamein: This man is a company stretcher bearer and was attached to No. 12 Platoon during the attack on Nov. 2nd on the area 300–301 grid lines.

During the operation this man was a prisoner for 2 hours gaining valuable information about a counter-attack and the layout of enemy positions. He escaped, then decided to go back and try to obtain a marked map of whose existence he was aware. He was unsuccessful in this but succeeded in escaping again by pretending to be looking after German wounded.

Subsequently on return to the Platoon, he performed numerous deeds of gallantry in bringing in and attending to our own and enemy wounded, under heavy mortar and MG fire – at all times shewing a complete disregard of his own safety.

He set a fine example of brave and unselfish devotion to duty to all who saw him.

He was finally severely wounded after giving his slit trench up to a wounded man whom he was attending.

There was one unexpected change at the end of Operation Supercharge. Brig. J.E.S. Percy D.S.O., M.C., was replaced by Brigadier Beak V.C., D.S.O., M.C. as Commanding Officer of 151 Brigade. This was unexpected. In a letter to Capt. V.H. Jackson dated the 22nd January, 1943, Brigadier Percy wrote:

This was a great disappointment to me especially as the Brigade had done extremely well and finished up with a successful attack on the 1/2 November when after a hard fight all objectives were captured, with nearly 800 prisoners mostly Boche…

It seemed as though the army hierarchy had not dealt kindly with Brigadier Percy. The reasons for the change in command are not known. One thing is certain, the brigade had performed extremely well under the command of Brigadier Percy in a vital operation, which saw the final breakthrough that General Montgomery had always planned for and set in motion the long pursuit of the Axis forces.

On the 4th November, the battalion moved to Tel El Eisa Station where it was picked up by Australian transport. The intention was that the brigade would clear up pockets of enemy lying between the coast road and the sea. The transport conveyed the battalion to El Daba Station and moved into Italian positions that had recently been evacuated. As the transport moved in one direction, many thousands of Italian prisoners moved in the opposite without any escort, obviously pleased to be out of the war. El Daba proved to be a large Italian stores dump, which created some interest amongst all ranks. Capt. F.W.G. Worrall of the Carrier Platoon brought in five German officers and one other rank plus an Italian artillery officer.

The next few days were spent in cleaning up and salvaging material from the battlefield. On the 9th of the month, Brigadier Percy arrived to say farewell to the battalion and, in the afternoon, Brigadier Beak arrived on his first visit. Since the wounding of Lieutenant Colonel Clarke, Maj. W. 'Big Bill' Robinson was in temporary command until the Colonel recovered. Leave was granted and small parties headed to Sidi Bishr for a few days' rest. Lieutenant Hurst, the Motor Transport Officer, was evacuated to hospital on the 11th of the month and was succeeded by Lt. John Arnold. On the 13th, the battalion moved in trucks to a new area approximately 60 miles away. This was Lieutenant Arnold's first test as M.T.O. He wrote:

We had to move about thirty 3 ton truckloads but, alas, we only had twenty trucks and the normal way to handle that would be to send the trucks with one load, then let them come back to fetch the balance, which would mean that some people would be left behind to guard the stuff that was left there. I had an idea, which I discussed with the Quartermaster, Capt. Ted Lowe and he thought it might be a possibility. My idea was to very carefully load the trucks with everything we had which meant, of course, that a tremendous strain was placed on the springs but then we moved at a slow rate indeed…but the upshot was that we made it in one go.

In this new area originally occupied by the Greek Brigade, training was recommenced. Lieutenant Colonel Clarke rejoined the battalion on the 19th November. The weather was worsening with sandstorms and high winds. On the 21st, a concert party arrived to entertain the troops and three days later an E.N.S.A. troupe gave an excellent show to the brigade. On the 25th, a draft of 249 men arrived from the infantry training depot. Officers included in this draft were Lieutenants Williams and E.R. Lacey, both of the South Wales Borderers; Lt. K. Whittaker, Somerset Light Infantry; Lt. H. Sanderson, Manchester Regiment and Lt. W.J. Muir who returned from hospital.

On the 1st December, Brigade received a telegram from the Mayor and townspeople of Stockton-on-Tees. It read, 'Heartiest congratulations and thanks for the magnificent service you are rendering to our beloved country.' On the 3rd, the battalion moved via the New Zealand box, Diamond Track, and Alamein Station to Galal. The journey was made in heavy rainfall. On the following day the battalion moved to an area near Mersa Matruh, which enabled some soldiers to visit the grave of Pte. Adam Wakenshaw V.C., where they found that the body was still exposed. It was obvious that no one had visited the site since the action had taken place. A proper burial was organised. Sgt. George Lambert of the Assault Pioneer Platoon recalled:

> Somebody had the bright idea of us going back to the wadi at Mersa Matruh…The P.R.I. money, supposed to be around £600 was dropped or buried by Lt. Pickering…We wanted to see if there was a possible chance of finding it though it would be like looking for a needle in a haystack. When we got there, there was Arthur Thompson, Len Green, I think Dai Jones was with us, and myself, along with the driver of the vehicle. That's when we came across Adam Wakenshaw. He hadn't been buried, he was still lying exposed, half buried. So we buried him and two more lads beside him just where they were. Of course that put us off trying to find the money…After we had done that and went back to the Battalion, I got a cross made. Normally, any numbers or anything put on a cross were just transfers, stamped on by transfers but for that particular cross, I got a lad called Dave Walton, who was a sign writer in the platoon. He was an old T.A. lad from Blaydon or Dunston…I got him to paint everything on and he painted the D.L.I. badge on the top and 9 D.L.I. and his name and we took that back and put it where he was buried.

On the 7th December, the battalion moved via Mersa Matruh and Bir Thalata into Cyrenaica, arriving at a point on the Trigh Capuzzo near El Adem on the 10th. Here the battalion stayed and training recommenced. Training continued and was followed by a 50th Division exercise, which commenced on the 16th and ended on the 18th. Brigade exercises followed. Christmas Day was enjoyed in the traditional way. Training continued till the end of the month. On the final day of the year, preparations were being made for a further move forward.

CHAPTER XVIII

THE BATTLE OF MARETH

No. 151 Brigade continued to follow the victorious Eighth Army as it advanced towards Tripoli and Tunisia. This time, the enemy failed to make a stand at El Agheila and the advance continued. The 3rd of January was a day of torrential rain, which caused delays in the brigade column. Fort Msus and the aerodrome were passed on the 6th of the month. It rained again on the 7th. The heavy rain caused the brigade to be rerouted to Benina, which it reached on the same day. It camped south of the aerodrome. Although the town of Benina had suffered war damage some places for recreation were still active, and the native population seemed friendly. Parties were organised and visits into Benghazi were arranged. The mobile bath unit was located in the town and regular bathing could take place.

A very serious situation arose at this time. Benghazi harbour had been very badly damaged during the recent storm and seven supply ships had been sunk as a result. Supplies to the forward divisions of the Eighth Army had to be cut and General Montgomery had to make the decision to reduce the forces in the forward areas to one corps. The 50th Division was grounded and its transport was used to ferry vital supplies to the forward units. On the 10th January, Lieutenant Parker of 'A' Company left with the battalion transport to carry supplies from Tobruk to Benghazi.

Training exercises were organised, which included street fighting in the damaged parts of Benghazi. On the 11th, a message was received from the chief constable and members of the Gateshead Borough police force: 'Heartiest seasonal greetings. Proud of your achievements. Hope for an early return.' Lt. Gen. Sir Brian Horrocks visited the battalion on the 18th January. On the 21st, a draft of four officers and 23 men joined from the base depot. The Rev. R.W. Kerr was posted to the battalion as chaplain. There was time for organised sport and a rifle meeting was held, which was won by 'B' Company with 'H.Q.' Company in second place. Training continued for the next few weeks.

The following entry appeared in the battalion War Diary for the 16th February:

The C.O. has received a letter from the Officer Commanding the Graves Registration Unit in Mersa Matruh, informing him of the re-interment of the body of Pte. Wakenshaw V.C. in the cemetery there. The Garrison Engineer constructed an excellent wooden coffin.

A funeral with full military honours was organised by the units stationed in the area. The coffin was covered by the Union Jack, loaned by the Royal Navy Two of the six bearers were D.L.I. men. The Firing Party and Bugler were provided by the local Light A.A. Regiment.

The Commanding Officer has sent his grateful thanks on behalf of all ranks for the

great respect shown to the body of Pte. Wakenshaw by the units stationed in the Mersa
Matruh area.

He has requested that the last shell case be forwarded to the Regimental Depot
Museum at Brancepeth Castle. He also asked that the 2pdr gun be placed beside the
cemetery with a suitable plaque on it.

Both shell and gun are now in the regimental museum in Durham City.

Training included night exercises in assaulting strong positions and defending
these when captured. On the 2nd March, the battalion moved off in troop-carrying
vehicles of the 524th Coy. Royal Army Service Corps. The destination was Tripoli. The
division was now part of XXX Corps along with the 2nd New Zealand, the 51st
Highland, the 4th Indian and the 7th Armoured Divisions. A staging area 12 miles
south of Tripoli was reached on the 9th of the month. During the journey the battalion
experienced its first contact with the Ghibili, the Tripolitanian equivalent of the
Egyptian Khamseen and equally unpleasant. Visits into the town of Tripoli were organised. The Tunisian border was crossed on the following day and Ben Gardene was
reached at 6.45 p.m. On the 11th, the move was by the coast road to Zarzis and then to
Medenine. The sound of gunfire was now clearly audible. Stand-to was ordered.

Rommel had counter-attacked the Eighth Army at Medenine but was repulsed.
The Eighth Army approached the Mareth Line. This powerful defensive position had
been built by the French a few years before the war, as a defence against any offensive
incursions by the Italians from Tripolitania. The line stretched for some 22 miles,
almost from the sea to the Matmata Hills, which rose to a height of 4,000 feet. Both
flanks of the line were protected: on the coast by salt flats and on the opposite flank by
the hills. Both were almost impassable to wheeled vehicles. The largest and deepest of
the many wadis in the area was the Wadi Zigzaou and the main defences had been constructed along this feature. The height of the wadi banks, which were perpendicular,
varied between 8–20 feet and could only be approached by vehicles in a few places.
The average width of the bed of the wadi was between 60–70 feet with a stream running through the middle. At the time of the assault it was thought that this stream was
about 30 feet wide and about eight feet deep near the coast and shallower further
inland.

The French had constructed a series of forts along the Wadi Zigzaou. Each was
made up of four or five concrete pillboxes and blockhouses and held about half a battalion of troops. A second line of forts were built on top of the ridge behind the wadi,
these covered the first line and the rear. The forts were sited so they could cover the
wadi by enfilade fire from machine and anti-tank guns along its whole length, and also
cover the forward slopes leading down to it. Around the forts was a network of deep
trenches and, in some cases, forts were connected by underground tunnels. The enemy
on the opposite bank had not been idle, but had further improved and strengthened
defences. A deep minefield had been laid on the south-east bank, and anti-tank ditches
had been dug all along the banks except where they were too steep to cross. In front of

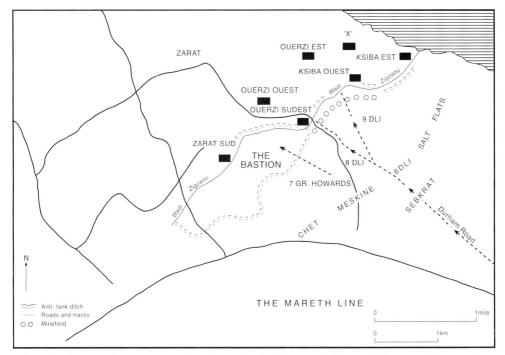

THE MARETH LINE

Anti-tank ditch
Roads and tracks
Minefield

151 Brigade attack was an anti-tank ditch sited about 100 yards beyond the wadi; yet another formidable obstacle. Additional minefields and wire protected the enemy posts. It was estimated that about 19 miles of the front were covered by wire obstacles, and that 100,000 anti-tank and 70,000 anti-personnel mines had been laid.

The fort nearest to the sea was Ksiba Est, which protected about 300 yards of the bank. Moving inland, the next fortress was Ksiba Ouest, located in a very strong position on a 12-foot bank of the wadi. Ouerzi and Zarat Sudest were also on the far bank of the wadi. Behind these near the top of the ridge was an unnamed post referred to as 'X', plus Ouerzi Est and Ouerzi Ouest. On the near side of the wadi, the enemy had built a new strong point named the Bastion. This commanded the whole area to the coast. Enemy observation of any movement during daylight stretched for 15 miles, so troops and supplies could only move up by night. The strength of these defences was known to the Eighth Army. Air photographs had revealed much and the knowledge of French officers had been passed along, particularly by Capt. Paul Metzan, the garrison engineer of Mareth.

The plan was for the 50th Division to make a frontal attack across the anti-tank ditches and the Wadi Zigzaou and smash its way through the enemy defences. The attack was to take place on the night of the 20th/21st March when the moon was full. At some point the 4th Indian Division would pass through the bridgehead and aim for the main Mareth–Gabes road with a view to cutting off the enemy holding the strong positions around Mareth and Arram. Meanwhile, the New Zealand Division, the 8th Armoured Brigade and General Leclerc's force from Chad would move secretly into the desert west of the Matmata Hills with the aim of cutting off the enemy's line of retreat.

General Nichols, G.O.C. 50th Division, was not happy with the task his division had to carry out. He was informed of this task on the 3rd March. His division had not yet reached him so that his experts, particularly his Commander Royal Engineers whose role was crucial, could not be consulted. General Nichols had no opportunity to view the enemy positions at that time. He understood that the enemy defences included scattered minefields containing many anti-personnel mines. He was allocated the Valentine tanks of the 50th Royal Tank Regiment and a battery of the new 17-pdr. anti-tank guns together with a company of Scorpion tanks. The Scorpions had metal chains on the front which rotated and, by so doing, exploded mines lying in their path. The machine guns of the 2nd Bn. Cheshire Regiment were in support. General Nichols asked for bridging material but was told that there was none in the Eighth Army. Therefore, he arranged for fascines to be prepared for the attacking brigade and to be carried on tanks of the 50th R.T.R. No. 151 Brigade was chosen to carry out the frontal assault on Wadi Zigzaou. The 7th Bn. Green Howards of 69 Brigade was given the task of dealing with the bastion before 151 Brigade assault, and this they did immediately before the Durhams attacked.

On the 13th March, the Commanding Officer and Intelligence Officer carried out a reconnaissance of the Mareth Line. The battalion was camped on the coast opposite Djerba where it practised cliff climbing, which was of value when scaling the anti-tank ditches and Wadi Zigzaou. The Carrier and Mortar Platoons rejoined the battalion here. They had been left at El Adem while the battalion moved across the desert. Training also included a minefield breaching exercise in co-operation with tanks.

On the 17th March, the battalion moved towards the Mareth Line. The line was held by the Italian Young Fascists Division, the best of the Italian troops, with the Trieste Division on its right and the German 90th Light Division, veterans of the desert war, to the right of the Trieste. In reserve, some seven miles behind the line was the 15th Panzer Division and supporting units. It was clear that the enemy intended to defend the Mareth Line to the uttermost.

The plan of attack for Operation Pugilist – the breaching of the Mareth Line devised by General Nichols – was to be carried out in three phases. Phase 1 (code word 'Hawk') was to attack and capture the Bastion and secure 151 Brigade flank from enemy enfilade fire. Phase 2 (code word 'Eagle') was the capture of Ksiba Ouest and Ouerzi and seize a bridgehead. The 8th and 9th Battalions were given this task along with tanks of the 50th Royal Tank Regiment and a battery of anti-tank guns of the 107th Anti-Tank Battery. Phase 3 (code word 'Falcon') was to use the reserve battalion of the brigade – the 6th Battalion – to capture and hold the high ground at Ouerzi Ouest, Ouerzi Est and the unnamed position 'X'. During the days immediately prior to the main attack, the enemy outposts in front of the Wadi Zigzaou were overrun.

Adequate reconnaissance remained a problem. The enemy held perfect observation from the high ground over the approaches to the Wadi Zigzaou. Some of the defences were visible from positions held by the 5th Bn. East Yorkshire Regiment but these did not give a broad view of the enemy forts and trenches. On the night of the 18th/19th March and the following night, two reconnaissance patrols were sent out by the 9th Battalion. These were led by Lieutenants Lacey and McLoughlin. Both came back with vital information relating to the position and depth of the minefield in front of the wadi, and they had even got into the wadi and tested its width and depth of water. Lt. W.S. 'Scotty' White of 'B' Company accompanied Lt. McLoughlin's patrol. He recorded:

> On the night of 19/20th March, I went out on a recce patrol led by Lt. McLoughlin to locate positions and types of mines and to find the nature of the wadi bed. We searched by bayonet, prodding right down to the edge of the wadi where we located anti-tank mines. In the wadi itself we could clearly see running water, a stream at least 20 yards wide. This we reported on our return from patrol.

The brigade formed up in the area of Chet Meskine. At 9.45 p.m. on the night of the 20th March, the whole of XXX Corps artillery opened up. This comprised 13 field and three medium regiments. Its initial task was to attempt to deluge the enemy gun positions, but this had only marginal success as a strong defensive fire was returned. Following the counter-battery work, the guns were to provide a timed barrage to cover the infantry advance. Phase 1, the assault and capture of the Bastion, started half an hour before the main attack. The 7th Bn. Green Howards took their objectives after severe fighting in which its Commanding Officer, Lieutenant Colonel Seagrim, was awarded the Victoria Cross.

In Phase 2, the 8th Battalion attacked on the left and the 9th Battalion on the right. Due to congestion and the enemy minefields, the forming-up and assembly areas for the 9th Battalion were one and the same, an area known as Palm Grove, so called because a few trees grew there. This attack commenced at 11.15 p.m. behind an artillery and machine gun barrage, the latter provided by the 2nd Bn. Cheshire Regiment. Ahead of the attacking infantry, the Scorpions flayed a route through the minefield. They were immediately followed by a route-marking party under the command of Captain Pollard who had already been wounded in the head by an 'S' mine. The Captain continued to lead his men. Sgt. George Lambert recalled:

> We, the Pioneer Platoon, had to assist the R.E.s opening the minefield out and that was for the boys to walk through. The R.E.s lifted the mines and we marked it off with a white tape to form a passage and nobody had to step over the other side of that white tape. But, unfortunately for me, somebody did. He stood on an anti-personnel mine and, of course, I got hit in the arm and the leg and, I think, four of us were wounded and two died.

The enemy, obviously aware that an attack was about to begin, shelled the forming-up area. Fortunately, casualties were light but amongst them was the whole of the

Royal Engineer party that was designated to go in with the infantry. Phase 2 was for 'C' Company (Capt. C.F.R. Goulden) to rush the wadi, cross it and the anti-tank ditch, and establish an initial bridgehead. 'B' Company (Maj. E.W.H. Worrall M.C.) was to follow, move through 'C' Company and attack and capture Ksiba Ouest. 'A' Company (Capt. A.R.F. Hynes) was to stay in reserve until needed to thicken the bridgehead. Battalion headquarters moved behind 'A' Company but remained on the near side of the wadi where better observation was obtained.

'C' Company led the way. Some of the men carried scaling ladders to enable them to climb the steep bank and cross the anti-tank ditch. The minefield had been marked by two lights that hung on the wire, a task carried out by Lieutenant Lacey and a small patrol half an hour earlier. The Company Commander, Captain Goulden, sent a report on the action to the regimental newsletter:

> The Company arrived in the F.U.P. about 2000 hrs. 20th March (Palm Grove in Chet Meskine). There were plenty of deep holes about and everybody was tucked away without difficulty. No fire was encountered moving in. By 2100 hrs. some mortar and shellfire was brought down on the Grove and from then on it steadily increased. M.G.s had the Grove taped and fixed lines kept us moving about…Rum and tea were given out at 2245 hrs., in one gallon containers. The men were more concerned with the heavy shelling and very few men got a drink…Heavy enemy fire made it quite impossible to set out in an orderly fashion. My officers led, the men followed them very well and my second-in-command and I went round calling men out of their holes. The noise was too much for shouts to be heard far. The Company sorted out as it advanced and by 2330 hrs. I had three complete platoons and an H.Q. moving behind Scorpions in their correct places.
>
> Some shelling was experienced during the approach to the enemy minefield. Lt. N.A. Sharpe was hit by shrapnel, lost a finger but walked back calmly by himself. Lt. Muir was hit in the leg by shrapnel but carried on. We contacted the lights which Lt. E.R. Lacey had placed on the forward edge of the minefield beforehand. The Scorpions split here. 13 Platoon led by Sgt. Randall followed the right vehicle and very shortly afterwards this Platoon became incorporated in 'B' Company…
>
> Remainder of Company followed the left vehicle, some fixed-line M.G. fire thickened the enemy defensive fire in minefield but we had no casualties until reaching the far side. Lt. E.R. Lacey was leading 15 Platoon, he went ahead very quickly and we lost touch with his Platoon. 14 Platoon with Lt. Muir and Coy. H.Q. had crossed the minefield and left the Scorpion by midnight.
>
> We went down a gap between two small hills towards the wadi. Strong M.G. fire came down from our right and wounded two men. The whole of 14 Platoon fired in return and when an assault party reached the hill top, it was found that the enemy had cleared out…We got down into the wadi by 0015 hrs. 21st March…Wadi and A/tk. ditch were crossed in a series of rushes and our momentum carried us through the water and up the steep bank. By good fortune, we found a footpath across the A/tk. ditch. Shelling at this point (0030 hrs.) was very light but the wadi was full of smoke and visibility about 20 yards.
>
> Lt. Lacey and 15 Platoon had crossed the Wadi, 50 yards to the right of our path. They cut footholds in the A/tk. ditch and climbed out. As soon as the first four men were

out, Lt. Lacey dashed on until he met enemy wire. He turned left and ran along it looking for a break. An enemy M.G. caught the whole party at a range of 50 yards. Lt. Lacey, L/Cpl. Burns and two men were killed instantly.

Cpl. William A. Shearer took command of 15 Platoon and led them along towards Ksiba Ouest. When about 200 yards from the Company axis they found a weak spot in the wire, rushed it and then proceeded to come back through the enemy trench system. Three enemy posts were wiped out including the one which had killed their Platoon Commander. This was their position at 0045 hrs. They were scattered, disorganised and had some wounded – they started to consolidate in these positions and tried to contact Coy. H.Q.

Meanwhile, 14 Platoon led by Lt. Muir, crossed the A/tk. ditch by the path, rushed the enemy wire and found themselves in the enemy trench system on the forward slope. They landed right in an enemy M.G. Post and the four occupants (Panzer Grenadiers) promptly surrendered. Lt. Muir pushed on with about 15 men, he had left 4 or 5 wounded in the A/tk. ditch. Coy. H.Q. took over the prisoners. Lt. Muir pushed on, 3 enemy posts were definitely cleared, some enemy surrendered but got away when others opened fire and threw grenades. Finally, Lt. Muir attacked a Post, which was evidently an H.Q. of some kind. The enemy put up a lot of fight, wounded 8 of our men, including Lt. Muir and then made off…[Lieutenant Muir was awarded the Military Cross for these actions.]

About 0115 hrs., Coy. H.Q. having explored the trench system, some good patrol work being done by C.S.M. Thompson, a real concentration from our own guns, meant for some fort or other, came down between us and 14 Platoon. A lot of shells also fell in the Wadi. My F.O.O. [Forward Observation Officer] agreed that a lot of shelling was our own, his wireless was useless, so I sent him back together with my 2 i/c, with the object of giving both my C.O. and the Gunners a picture of the position at 0200 hrs…Lt. Watts of 'A' Coy. arrived, was given the position and went back to bring up assistance…

A patrol led by L/Cpl. Lowe was sent up the road. It met a party of the enemy who called out, 'Is that you Jock?' Four enemy then surrendered to the patrol but two more opened fire on it. The enemy made off and the patrol returned. Another patrol, under C.S.M. Thompson went off right, contacted the Intelligence Officer and 15 Platoon and brought in about 10 prisoners…

We had 12 wounded and one dead at Coy. H.Q. and only about 7 men left. The odd enemy post was still firing. I decided that further advance would be futile and consolidated on the slopes of the hill 200 yds from the objective.

As referred to above, Corporal Shearer took command of the platoon on the death of Lieutenant Lacey. He had assisted his Platoon Commander to set up the lights on the edge of the enemy minefield. He was awarded the Military Medal for his dash and determination in successfully leading his platoon in the subsequent action and withdrawal.

'B' Company under Maj. E.W.H. Worrall M.C. followed closely behind 'C' Company. Its objective was the capture of Ksiba Ouest. Major Worrall's report on the action was printed in the regimental newsletter:

Left Forming Up Place about 2320 hrs., minus some of our Sappers, who disappeared [Most of these were killed by enemy fire]…advanced in the order of Coy. H.Q., 11 Pln.

'B' Coy. of 9 D.L.I. re-enact for the cameras the crossing of the anit-tank ditch, Mareth Line.

(Lt. W.S. White), 10 Pln. (Lt. Sanderson), 12 Pln. (Lt. Collyer) Reserve. Fire not too heavy at the beginning. Met Bill Lacey at the top of the rise, who showed me the right-hand lamp – poor Bill, I wished him luck and thanked him – he had done his job well [Lieutenant Lacey, 'C' Company, was killed later]. I then got the Company across the minefield in behind Sharpe's Pln., 'C' Coy, through the right-hand gap. The advance was slow as the Scorpion Tank exploded at least 8 'S' mines…

Lt. W.S. 'Scotty' White at the head of the 11th Platoon followed his Company Commander. He wrote:

We proceeded steadily up a slight slope, along the path cleared by the Scorpion. Our artillery barrage was thundering ahead on the enemy fortifications.
    From time to time we heard the Company Commander's hunting horn urging us forward, an inspiring sound to the Company. By about 00.30 hrs. we were late, so he led us ahead of the Scorpion and through the minefield. We were beginning to move down the slope to the Wadi when Maj. Worrall was wounded, a bullet had gone through his left breast. I asked the Medical Orderly to do what he could for it was obvious that the he was determined to carry on.

Before his wound, Major Worrall rallied his company and those at the rear of 'C' Company moving just in front of him. Major Worrall recorded:

About halfway through the minefield, Sharpe ['C' Company] was wounded and went back. I then went up to the head of his Pln. and kept dodging backwards and forwards between them and my Coy. I used my hunting horn to blow my Coy. on here and signal each advance (i.e. when Scorpions moved forward). Finally at 1235 hrs. approx. as we were well behind time, I went forward to Sgt. Randall of 'C' Coy. and told him I was going to chance the last fifteen yards of the minefield and not wait for the Scorpion. I went back and told Pat Smith the same information. He agreed that it was getting late.

I was hit about this time but decided to patch it up after we had taken the objective. From now on firing became really intense from the pillboxes – particularly the prominent one on the right. I then ran forward into and across the Wadi, followed by 'Scotty' White who was magnificent throughout the whole battle…

Lieutenant White takes up the story:

We moved forward again and began to cross the Wadi. Enemy rifle and machine gun fire steadily increased and we suffered casualties. I kept close to Maj. Worrall as we dashed across the Wadi, barely noticing the stream. On reaching the far side of the Wadi, I got my platoon to form a pyramid against its side and somehow we got the Company Commander up it and the rest of the platoon followed. We were out of the Wadi and then tackled the anti-tank ditch in much the same way. It must have been hell for Teddy Worrall – but he seemed to enjoy it!

Major Worrall:

I was rather a helpless member of the Pyramid, got out of the Wadi, up over the anti-tank ditch. Here, the fire was quite 'bloody'. I told Cpl. Bell, 11 Pln., who was N.C.O. i/c my Coy. H.Q. 'Thug Party' and damned good all night, to crawl forward and cut the wire. 'Scotty' White, Sgt. Randall, Cpl. Daly and myself lay beside two palm trees and tried to cover him – we couldn't have taken those pillboxes unless somebody had cut that wire and the bullets were missing by inches here. My horn had got bunged up with sand, so I couldn't blow the Company on. A lot of them had temporarily stuck and slowed down crossing the Wadi and getting up the A/tk. ditch.

At last Bell said, 'I've cut the wire, sir.' We made a dash for it and by sheer luck got into their trenches 50 yards beyond the wire. We went up these. When we got near the pillboxes, I put Randall and Daly with two Brens to fire in the slits, while White and I led a party up the trench towards them, throwing '36' grenades at each corner. To my joy, suddenly about 50 Italians appeared with their hands up. I then saw that the Bren guns had set the pillboxes on fire, at least the two left hand ones…

These Italians were not the last taken in this trench system. Lieutenant White:

It was about this time, as I was lying firing a rifle which I had acquired, that I was hit by a bullet or piece of shrapnel and was slightly wounded. My right foot had been hit just below the ankle joint. The boot was gashed and ruined but the wound was trivial, especially compared with Teddy Worrall's…

Maj. Worrall and I, plus a section of my platoon closed in on the Fort. As we moved along the trench, Maj. Worrall and I used grenades as required.

Suddenly a party of Italians appeared with their hands up and surrendered to us. A little further on we arrived at the entrance of Ksiba Ouest. There was a door to the fort and, guess what? It wasn't locked! So I gave it a thump. 'Come out.' The door opened and about a hundred came out. Fantastic! They were ready. They'd had enough…They included a Major and a Captain.…We had achieved our first objective.

The platoon in reserve, meanwhile, had run into difficulties. Major Worrall:

I was on the road, being strafed by the Italians, when 'Gunner' Hanson, my R.A., O.P., came up and said would I come back to the right-hand pillbox as there was some delay going on about attacking it. I sent Randall and Daly off to contact 'C' Coy. and left 'Scotty' White in charge of the road with most of his Pln. and some of Coy. H.Q. I went back with Hanson to see what was happening. It was then 0400 hrs. I found George Collyer had been wounded, also Sgt. Howe M.M. and Cpl. Stimpson. This had rather shaken them. I was in a bloody awful temper through a very painful and bleeding breast, but I couldn't help laughing when I heard one of them say, 'We're alright now, the Boss is here, we can sit back, he'll look after things.' I certainly didn't feel like looking after myself, let alone anyone else! However, luck was once again on my side. I put a Bren on one flank and told it to fire for EVER and then took the large 'Army' up the trench, the same tactics as last time. The Italians came rushing out in our faces. I tried to make one put his hands up but found I was unarmed. I had lost my revolver and, worst still, my hunting horn. However, no Italian fired! This time I determined there would be no need to

'B' Coy re-enact the caputre of an enemy pillbox.

go back and we swarmed over all three strongpoints quickly. We took about 80 prisoners and pushed them out of the Fort along the trench to the road.

'B' Company had taken Ksiba Ouest but Major Worrall's difficulties were not over:

I tried to fire the three-pronged success rocket. We had lost the stick and it would not go off properly. The 18 W/T set. as usual, was a wash-out…and told Pln. Commanders to get their Plns. dug-in astride the road before dawn. It was then 0445 hrs. – 10 Pln. right, 11 Pln. left, 12 Reserve – Coy. H.Q. centre…

From dawn onwards, except for a brief visit to No. 11 Pln. about 0700 hrs., when I had a shoot through a Bren, I was not much use to anyone as my wounds were stiffening up and I felt weakish.

The chaps were grand and I wouldn't be human if I was not proud we got that Fort – Alamien was a tea party compared to it.

Major Worrall was awarded the Distinguished Service Order for his courage and leadership that resulted in the capture of his company's objective.

By 3.30 a.m. on the 21st March, 'A' Company (Capt. A.R.H. Hynes) had moved up on 'C' Company's left and strengthened the position. One platoon of medium machine guns of the 2nd Bn. Cheshire Regiment was manhandled across the wadi and sent forward to 'A' Company. Three 3-in. mortars were also carried across and placed behind the anti-tank ditch. These additions were of considerable value as the day wore on. On its flank, the 8th Battalion had taken its objective, Ouerzi, after fierce fighting.

We need to look at what had been happening in the Wadi Zigzaou, as events there were to influence the outcome of the battle. The Valentine tanks of the 50th Royal Tank Regiment were to cross the wadi, nearly opposite Ouerzi Ouest. The 9th Field Squadron Royal Engineers cleared a path through the minefield for the tanks to follow. The tanks were to cross ahead of carriers towing anti-tank guns. It was here that a major mistake was probably made. Subsequent events proved that efforts should have been made to get the anti-tank guns across before the tanks. These would have enabled the infantry to withstand the enemy counter-attack, which came in on the 22nd March. The Valentine tanks that did cross over the wadi and fought with great gallantry, but were no match for the enemy tanks and anti-tank guns. The infantry, without anti-tank guns and armed with only grenades and anti-tank rifles, were faced with a desperate situation.

Without bridging equipment, the Valentines carried fascines, which measured 10 feet long and eight feet wide, to drop into the wadi and form a bridge. Some of these fascines caught fire from the hot exhausts of the engines and some delay ensued as more were brought forward. Under the most dangerous and difficult conditions, the sappers worked flat out to build a crossing. The wadi was under heavy enfilade fire and the sappers suffered considerable casualties. Eventually a crossing was completed and four tanks were able to cross before the fifth stuck and blocked the passage. It was quite obvious that the delay could not be cleared before daybreak and the Brigade Commander, Brigadier Beak V.C., decided to withdraw the 50th R.T.R. and try the following night. The 6th Battalion, which had been waiting in the forming-up area and was being subjected to heavy artillery and mortar fire, was ordered to return to the assembly area to await their involvement on the following night. No anti-tank guns could cross the wadi.

Conditions in the wadi itself were not good. Private Kerens remembered the scene as members of battalion H.Q. moved down towards the wadi:

> Now through the 'Gap' gasping at the large numbers of dead and badly wounded R.Es. that lined its sides…we dug in on the near side. Right away I made an O.P. in the wadi's bank as bullets whistled round like angry bees. By its side was a narrow gap, through which the wounded were helped. When this occurred it seemed for a second or two, the 'bees' ceased. A prisoner, we took later, swore the machine gunner was shot dead by the sergeant, because he refused to shoot at wounded…
>
> Near the O.P. was a short, steep slope down to an almost non-existent ford across the wadi. A gang of R.E.s were working on it, getting large casualties for little results. A tank tried to get across but only got stuck, which increased the shelling. At the top of the slope, what happened to be a single manned anti-tank 6 ponuder gun, was firing. I went across. It was Bill Jones, another 'Scouser' pal of my Blighty soldiering days. His arm was wrapped in a dripping, blood-stained rag but it did not stop him firing…
>
> An armoured car dashed in and out with the wounded until it was hit by a shell and burst into flames. We were smothering these with sand from tin helmets, filled with our entrenching tools, when a dozen or so Italians, their hands in the air, came rushing past. Nobody took any notice of them except the Germans, who let them get halfway up the hill, then mowed them down with machine guns.

In the forward positions held by 8th and 9th Battalions, the daylight hours of the 21st March were spent in consolidation and strengthening their positions. They were subjected to shelling, machine gun fire and sniping. Lieutenant White wrote:

> I collected my platoon and took up defensive position astride a road about one hundred yards beyond the fort…11 Platoon now totalled about eighteen men, one sergeant and two Corporals. We had two light machine guns but very little ammunition left after the assault. The Brens were sited on the flanks and the riflemen pooled some of their ammunition to feed them. The men were still in good form, tired and hungry but adrenaline was still at a high level…
>
> Artillery fire, machine gun fire and sniping went on throughout the day. It was barely possible to move and very difficult indeed to deal with the wounded. Of great help to us at this time was the presence of Capt. Hanson R.A., a Forward Observation Officer attached to 'B' Company to give us artillery fire support when demanded. The ground was fairly flat and gave little cover except to enemy snipers. But the ridge about 600 yards ahead was obviously occupied and we had managed to spot at least one machine gun post. This ridge was continually plastered by Capt. Hanson's guns. I shared a slit trench with him for most of the day. Enemy snipers and riflemen who tried to filter forward were dealt with by the Company and Sergeant Jordon M.M. must be credited with

Mareth Line after capture. Note the anti-tank ditch and the strong enemy emplacements.

chasing and killing many of them. Regrettably, Sgt. Jordon, L/Cpl. King and Pte. Eason were killed by our own guns firing short. A great loss.

The situation was much the same on the front held by the other two companies. Heavy shelling, mortaring and machine gun fire in addition to sniping meant that movement was greatly restricted. Wounded were sent back when safe to do so. The regimental aid post had been set up in the forming-up position in the Chet Meskine and dealt with a steady stream of wounded. The stretcher bearers continued throughout the battle to risk their lives to bring in the wounded. As the battalions held their positions under enemy fire, the vital need was to get a crossing operating by nightfall on the 21st March. Three crossings were ordered to be prepared and it was emphasised by XXX Corps that at least one of these crossings had to be completed, 'without fail'. This was done but the Royal Engineers suffered heavy casualties from shelling and machine gun fire that poured down the wadi.

During the 21st, the 5th Bn. East Yorkshire Regiment (69 Brigade) was moved across the wadi to strengthen and broaden the bridgehead. Orders for the night of the 21st/22nd March were issued for an attack in three phases. In the first phase, the 6th Bn. D.L.I. would cross the wadi at 10 p.m. and attack and capture Ouerzi Ouest. At 1.30 a.m. on the 22nd, the 9th Battalion would attack and capture Ouerzi Est. In the third phase, the 5th Bn. East Yorkshires would attack and capture Ksiba Est, starting at

1.45 a.m. Three hundred guns would give support, together with the machine guns of the 2nd Bn. Cheshire Regiment. Ominously, the Italian Young Fascists were being reinforced by a battalion of the 200th Panzer Grenadier Regiment and anti-tank guns and artillery of the 15th Panzer Division. The latter 15th Panzers were ordered to be ready to counter-attack. By mid afternoon, the British forward troops were subjected to increasingly heavy enemy shell and mortar fire. Whilst casualties were not heavy due to the shelter provided by the deep trenches, little sleep was possible and officers and men were becoming very tired.

Two objectives were given to the 9th Battalion. Each lay about a mile beyond the first objectives, which were now held. One, code-named 'Susan', was an unnamed enemy defensive position of about a company strength. 'B' Company, on the right, was given this objective. The second was Ouerzi Est, which was to be captured by 'A' Company operating on the left. Ammunition and rations were in short supply and needed replenishment before any attack could take place. Lt. C.W.S. Smith was in command of 'B' Company after Major Worrall was evacuated due to his wounds. His report was quoted in the regimental newsletter:

> At 1730 hrs. Lieut. Smith left for Bn. H.Q. for orders…
>
> About 2130 hrs. Lt. Smith arrived back with rations, a small amount of S.A.A. and orders for the night attack on 'SUSAN'. Lt. Smith organised the men for the attack. This was a difficult task in the dark, in the crowded trenches. Heavy shelling (enemy) choked up the automatic weapons. This shelling continued until our own barrage began. Fortunately, the deep zigzag trenches gave us good protection and no casualties occurred. Enemy aircraft also flew over and strafed us with M.G. fire.
>
> 0130 – 0145, 22nd March – Our own Barrage.
>
> At 0145 hrs. Company left trenches under Lt. Smith. There was heavy enemy gunfire for a few minutes, just as we left, but it soon died down…The only opposition to our advance was given by two or three M.G.s to our front and L.M.G.s on each flank. The Coy. took up positions with 10 and 11 Plns. forward on an isolated hill and 12 Pln. and a small party of 'C' Coy. on the forward slope of the high ground over which the road ran. Between the two halves of the Coy. was a shallow wadi with palms and banks in it. This wadi ran parallel with the road and had a dense wood across it about 800–1,000 yds. away on our left. Cpl. Frankum was outstanding for his leadership and dash in this action. His section had been under the worst of the shelling all day and it was his coolness which gave them the will to hang on. He showed great strength of character in making such an effort at night.
>
> After consolidation in this position, Lt. Smith sent for Lt. White but this officer was not to be found. In his stead, about 0330 hrs., Lt. Sanderson went back with Pte. Edney to the old position and contacted Capt. Hanson R.A., who wirelessed a message back to Bn. H.Q. asking for ammunition, water and food to be brought up by carrier before light. This was promised…By dawn, the carrier had not arrived. We were being sniped at with M.G.s and Rifles from both flanks…The R.A.O.P. W/T set was found to be useless owing to the battery being down…

Lt. 'Scotty' White had ran into trouble. He described:

Orders came that we were to attack the ridge that night. It was difficult to sort out and line up the Company for the attack. There was no natural spot to line up for the start, it was very dark and the shelling was continuous. At one stage I led my platoon into some trenches only to be turfed out immediately by the 6th Bn. D.L.I., who were already in possession.

At 0145 hrs. on 22nd March, our barrage started and I moved forward with my platoon on the left flank. Enemy gunfire lessened but there was machine gun fire from the flanks.

As I approached the ridge I spotted the position of the machine gun, which had been firing at us all day. The axis of our advance meant that we would miss the weapon post but leave it on our left flank, giving it a perfect enfilade shoot at the Company. There was little time in which to take action, so I waved my platoon to continue the advance and made a dash towards what I thought was the machine gun post.

The dash was no more than a quick hobble as my slightly wounded right ankle was now causing some discomfort. At the top of the ridge I went through a gap in the enemy wire, pushed on a little way and reached a deep communication trench running across my line of advance. I felt it could lead me to the gun post, so I dropped into it. It was about seven to eight feet deep – I landed heavily on my wounded foot. I realised at this stage that the machine gun had not been firing during my dash towards it and this signified two important points: 1. Our Company would now be safe from its fire, 2. The machine gun was no longer manned or had been withdrawn.

Lieutenant White decided he had to make sure that the machine gun was no longer capable of any further part in the action. Pushing on along the trench he came across the gun post. Observing carefully from a distance for some time, he could see no movement. He recalled:

I spent a long time observing and could see two or three bodies but there was no movement. I moved carefully to the gun position itself, fired my pistol and shouted for them to come out. There was no reaction and, after some time, I entered. There were four Italian machine gunners lying in various positions in the chamber, all were dead, and two machine guns on tripods, both on fixed lines and sited to cover our Company advance. It was not possible to see how the enemy had been killed.

One member of his platoon had accompanied Lieutenant White and was now found to be missing. The officer spent some time looking for him but without success:

The search eventually took me to the end of the ridge overlooking a small wadi. It was now quite light and enemy fire, artillery, mortars, machine guns and rifles had started once more and seemed to be getting heavier.

There was no sign of 'B' Company's position but I had a reasonable idea where they might be and headed slowly towards them. On the way I met a Lieutenant of the East Yorks who was out on a recce and, a bit later, a Lieutenant from our 6th Bn. I discussed the general situation with both of them and gave them my details. From them I learnt that a counter-attack was expected, with tanks, at any time.

'B' Company reached its objective about 600 yards ahead with not too much difficulty. 'A' Company (Capt. A.R.F. Hynes) had a more difficult task. Its objective was Ouerzi Est, which lay about 800 yards ahead. A very powerful position held by the Italian Young Fascists, a frontal assault was decided against; instead, the company would move round the flanks and attack from the rear. It was hoped that the Italians, subjected to the heavy British bombardment, would quickly surrender. This did not prove to be the case and the Italians fought with considerable resolution and courage. Every yard of trench had to be fought for. Fierce hand-to-hand fighting took place as the company inched its way forward. Captain Hynes (later awarded the Military Cross) wrote the following report, which was printed in the regimental newsletter:

> At about 1130 hrs., I moved Coy. H.Q. and the Reserve Platoon (Lt. McLoughlin's) up to our forward platoon localities. The attack of the 6th D.L.I. had gone through and things were quieter. Enemy shells were still screaming overhead towards the Wadi Zigzaou and enemy M.G.s and 47mms were pouring out spasmodic streams of tracers. Richard Pollard, wearing his huge head bandage, was helping the C.S.M. to move men into positions. I was worried about the fire coming from my left as I faced Ouerzi. The 6th Bn. should have been there. I talked it over with Richard and we decided it was necessary to make contact. Richard took my compass and went. I spoke briefly to Watts, White, McLoughlin and the C.S.M. (Diston). Watts knew the route so I put him in the lead...I walked round the men, they were in great spirits. I told them they were now going to get the snipers who had worried us all day.
>
> The moon was very bright at 0100 hrs...I called out, 'Get into your trenches, 10 minutes to go.' Five minutes later the first shells of our concentration screamed overhead. Imperceptibly the noise grew until this devil's overture made our eardrums hurt. Two guns were firing short. We lay flat in our trenches and strained our ears for the different note of these two. One was bursting just above my Coy. H.Q. trench, sending showers of sand upon us. I lay on top of the C.S.M. watching the luminous hands of my watch. I could hear the shells bursting in the Coy. area. Suddenly the noise ceased. I got up. White [J.A.] came to me crying, 'Skipper, my men are killed!' I said, 'Nonsense, how many?' 'Durkin's section,' he replied. I shouted, 'Come on 'A' Company – Let's get those B****rds.

'A' Company moved forward towards its objective, the fort at Ouerzi Est. Machine guns opened up on them, firing furiously. Moving at the double, the company reached the enemy wire. Bren guns fired at the fort in an attempt to keep down the enemy fire as a gap was made in the wire. Captain Hynes' report continues:

> Things were going very well. Suddenly Watts cried, 'O.K. Come on' – he had made the gap. His platoon poured through. Coy. H.Q. tore after him. I got up to him, crying, 'Take it slowly – look out for grenades.' We walked along the trench system, shooting into dugouts, throwing grenades round corners. An Italian appeared and was shot down, then another. I pushed up beside Watts – a bunch of three or four enemy appeared from a gun

position. I shot one, Watts the other. No rounds left in my Luger now, so rushed the next one and used the butt. C.S.M. shot him as he rocked back.

The men were grand, pushing on grimly, searching every crevice. Suddenly, some-one cried, 'Mr. Watts is hit!' I pushed on and found Watts dazed and his batman lying on the ground. 'Grenade' he told me. On again we went. I called a halt. We looked over the parapet and were fired at from the right. I decided to have a dash at this and we got ready – pins out of the grenades – Over the Top – grenades away – down! A solid sheet of flame burst upon us. Shouts of, 'Vincere, Udire, Mouri.' I realised there was quite a num-ber there. Back to the trench again. 'Keep firing – I'm going to get them with the other platoons.' I tore madly along the trench collecting stragglers as I went. I shouted for White and Mac, firing recognition tracer. I heard the reply. Then, as I ran towards them a battle started just by them, I heard Mac shout, 'Come out you B****rds.' Swarms of Italians filed out of the trenches as our two platoons (now about 20 men) closed upon them from the rear. I heard someone say, 'Shoot the B****rds' and [I] rushed towards them shouting, 'No shooting, line them up.' We herded them into the trench system. I ordered stand-to – all round – look out! After a search C.S.M. found a Verey Pistol and we fired the success signal…I sought a safe place for the wounded and made the Italians get blankets.

Watts was in great pain. Mac gave him morphia. I was anxious about a counter-attack and kept lookouts in pairs around the sector. Sgts. Lester and McDonough kept going the rounds. Mac and White were reorganising their men.

The enemy replied with a terrific bombardment but no counter-attack was made at this time. During a lull in the shelling, Captain Hynes sent the prisoners back along with his wounded. As dawn broke, it was found that another part of the fort contained enemy, who were still firing. Covered by the firing of his own men, Captain Hynes, Lt. J.A. White and a small band of other ranks advanced across the open. With one last furious barrage from his own troops, a white flag appeared and the garrison gave up. Seventy Italians, including a captain surrendered. The action was not yet over. Captain Hynes described:

I saw some men moving towards us from the trees, 500 yds. away. White and I went towards them. One shouted, 'Aventi.' I saw they were carrying arms and raised my glass-es. They were Boche. We both fired together and ran – they towards the trees and me to the Fort. For some time we exchanged shots, many claims were made for hits…Soon we saw the Huns were withdrawing…The targets were grand. How we prayed for Guns, Aircraft, Tanks!

Three 47-mm guns were knocked out in the fort and more than 120 prisoners taken, mainly Italians and a small number of Germans. Many of the enemy had been killed. However, the company's losses had not been light. Captain Pollard was dead and Lieutenants Watts and J.A. White were wounded. Lieutenant Watts later was killed in action. The company strength was down to about 35 officers and men and ammuni-tion supplies were very low. Ouerzi Est and the nameless post were now in British hands. The 6th Battalion had captured Ouerzi Ouest and Zarat Sudest. Could they be held?

During the night, a causeway had been constructed over the wadi and 42 Valentines of the 50th Royal Tank Regiment had crossed into the bridgehead. The sound of their approach had a heartening affect on the beleaguered Durhams. All that was now required was to get anti-tank guns over the crossing and much needed food and ammunition. Tragically, this was not to happen. Early in the morning of the 22nd, heavy rainfall caused the water in the wadi to rise. This same rainfall made the R.A.F. support impossible, as planes could not take off from the landing grounds. The crossing ultimately collapsed under the weight of the tanks and anti-tank guns were not able to cross. The wadi remained under heavy artillery, mortar and machine gun fire and all of the efforts of the gallant engineers to repair the damage failed. By now the sappers were exhausted by their continuous efforts and much depleted in numbers due to casualties. Communications were breaking down as wireless batteries gave out and telephone lines were broken by the intense shellfire. Runners were the only means of communication between the forward troops and H.Q. and these suffered heavy losses in attempting to cross the fire-swept ground. The tired troops, who had just taken their objectives and had their spirits uplifted by the appearance of the Valentines, knew little of the acute problems in the wadi behind them. Their questions as to the whereabouts of the anti-tank guns and replenishment of rations and ammunition were about to be answered. The enemy was about to counter-attack. This commenced at 1.40 p.m. on the 22nd March and was led by the 15th Panzer Division with its superior tanks and gunfire and, without anti-tank gun support, the Valentines had no chance and were virtually destroyed.

'C' Company lay behind the two forward companies of the battalion. Captain Goulden wrote:

> Morning of 22nd…my strength had risen to nearly 40 all ranks. About 0900 hrs. I took a section up, crossed road and looked over 'A' Coy. and 6 D.L.I. positions ahead. Our tanks were in the area. I crossed and they were drawing quite a bit of enemy fire, chiefly his 88 mms.
>
> I returned and reported to C.O. that a move from present position up to reinforce 'A' Coy. in daylight – and under enemy observation – would be quite costly. I got permission to remain in the present position.
>
> From 1000 – 1500 hrs. 22nd March, we got the heaviest enemy concentration I have ever experienced. The shells were of very heavy calibre and screamed down In 6's and 12's without much respite. We were also mortared.
>
> About 1600 hrs. we became aware that there was a pretty big tank battle in progress; we had received news of enemy tanks as early as 1000 hrs. At last light an 'A' Coy. Officer called in and said that his Company was hemmed in by enemy on three sides and that tanks and infantry were approaching our position. I sent him back to Bn. H.Q. with word that I intended to stay where I was. About 1930 hrs., one of our tanks, 150 yds. to my left, burst into flames. By its light, I could see bodies of our men marching back towards the A/tk. ditch; our forward troops had held on until ordered back, although they

had run out of S.A.A. and were nearly surrounded by enemy infantry and tanks.

My position, right in front of the A/tk. ditch and masking our own fire, would have hindered rather than helped our defence. I withdrew the Company in good order to the A/tk. ditch, met Maj. Lidwill of 8th D.L.I. and fitted myself into the general scheme…We held the line until after 0440 hrs. 23rd March – 8 hrs. of 100% stand-to. Enemy tank fire was terrific but not very accurate. All the fire seemed to go over our heads. Enemy infantry were good targets in the moonlight and our narrow front and density of S.A. fire made us confident of holding off the infantry. Most dangerous fire was from enemy L.M.G.s. These fired at all our flashes, got Pte. Coates right through the head, hit two of our Brens, putting five holes in one Bren Magazine and hit C.S.M. Thompson's fingers as he was firing his rifle.

Finally came the order to withdraw and sometime before 0500 hrs., 23rd March we emptied our magazines at the enemy and, as the men fired their last shots, they came down and went back along the track. Enemy shelling and M.G. fire was very heavy but the men seemed surfeited and just walked back – helping anyone who fell. Two of our men trod on mines, Pte. Beynon was killed outright and Sgt. Bedford wounded. L/Cpl. Lowe found three men hit by M.G. fire – he made three journeys back to the track to get them lifts on carriers.

'C' Company's total casualties were eight killed (including one officer and one N.C.O.), two missing and 36 wounded – six of whom were unaccounted for.

L/Cpl. Albert Edward Lowe was awarded the Military Medal. His citation read:

He assisted the Platoon Commander successfully to cut the wire protecting several enemy machine gun nests and then led his section with great dash and skill against the enemy posts, which he succeeded in wiping out in the face of heavy fire. After most of the section had been wounded, he personally pressed on the attack and succeeded in silencing the posts, capturing four gunners.

When his platoon was held down by heavy artillery fire, he recced enemy positions and brought back valuable information for the subsequent attack on these positions.

When an enemy patrol of four men endeavoured to attack a party of 12 wounded men, L/Cpl. Lowe singly attacked them with grenades and succeeded in scattering the patrol thus enabling the wounded men to be evacuated.

L/Cpl. Lowe by his courage, unfailing enterprise and determination to duty, considerably helped towards the successful attack of his Company.

Meanwhile, 'A' and 'B' Companies in the front line were facing their ordeal as the enemy counter-attack developed. Lt. 'Scotty' White was still searching for his company when the enemy counter-attack came in. He recalled:

Shortly afterwards the counter-attack was in full swing, supported by heavy shelling. At least a company of German infantry came moving up the ridge and passed within twenty or thirty yards to my right. I duly took careful aim and fired the two remaining shots from my pistol. Unfortunately, I could not claim any hits. About the same time, two very large enemy tanks passed on my left along the small wadi and headed down towards the Wadi

Zigzaou.

The enemy infantry had overrun the area where I had thought the Company were situated and the fact that I did not see any of the Company moving about led me to believe that they had been withdrawn. I decided that my best option was to lie low until dusk and then make my way back to the Wadi Zigzaou area.

Unfortunately for me two German officers suddenly arrived along the communication trench where I was and I became a Prisoner of War.

Lieutenant White met Capt. Ian English M.C. of the 8th Battalion who was also a prisoner and both were interned in Italy. They escaped together when Italy surrendered and made their way back to the British lines, which they reached on the 23rd December 1943 after spending three months walking down the spine of Italy.

'B' Company could see the enemy preparing to counter-attack. Tanks and infantry were seen concentrating in a wood to the left of the company's positions. Shelling, mortaring and sniping increased during the afternoon. The weather had grounded the R.A.F. and no air support was forthcoming. The company returned the enemy fire with rifles. It was found that most of the Bren guns were clogged with sand as a result of the first day's action and no oil was available to keep them working. It was obvious that the company could not hold its positions in the face of the overwhelming enemy tanks and infantry. Lieutenant Smith decided to withdraw to the old positions now held by the 5th East Yorks. He recorded:

10 Pln. was ordered to give covering fire, whilst the company withdrew in the order – 12 Pln. and 'C' Coy. remnants, 11 Pln., 10 Pln.

12 Pln. were seen to leave their position and go back, picking up some of 'C' Coy. (9 D.L.I.). 11 Pln. followed but some were hit as they crossed the wadi among the trees. Lt. Smith followed with the last few of 11 Pln. and Coy. H.Q. Half of 10 Pln. then got out, while the remainder kept up rifle fire on the enemy M.G.s. Pte. Crole of 10 Pln. was outstanding for his coolness and devotion to duty in this precarious position. Finally Lt. Sanderson ordered the remainder of 10 Pln. to get back. While 11 Pln. were withdrawing, a force of 3 enemy tanks and other vehicles was seen working its way from the wood along the wadi, with the intention apparently of cutting off our force isolated on the forward hill.

The enemy fire was very intense and everyone had to make his own way across 600–700 yds. of open ground. C.S.M. Schonewald was among those hit, as was Pte. Williams. They were both left in slit trenches. Lt. Smith collected the remains of the Coy. in the zigzag trench, took them back to the A/tk. ditch and stayed there until dark. We rejoined the rest of the Bn. early next morning.

'A' Company was also under attack. Captain Hynes wrote:

Mortars became very active and reports came in of tanks working round our right. We took a heavy toll of enemy infantry trying to filter forward on our front. Several daring snipers got quite close but were picked off one by one. Our own tanks went back and squatted behind us, firing great, long burst of M.G. fire across our flanks. It soon became apparent to me that a number of our tanks were out of action. Enemy tanks were working round both flanks and infantry infiltrated behind them. Mortar fire became very accurate and soon the right of the Fort became untenable as M.G. fire and snipers raked the trenches. I worked our little band towards the left and our tanks. Sgt. McDonough was wounded covering our move with one of his Spandau guns. We lay 'doggo' in the trenches, using our last Bren and with our men sniping at enemy movements. I passed along a box of Italian grenades and gave the order, 'Last man – last round.' The men only smiled grimly. The Bren was cracking away and my heart sank at the continued cry for more ammo. Our stocks were running low. The men continued filling magazines. The enemy came forward three times from the bushes below us and each time a volley from every weapon sent him back. A sniper crawled forward to the trenches on our left. C.S.M. Diston got him as he crossed the parapet. A tremendous avalanche of mortar shells was now falling. The Bren was hit and put our of action. I called for an ammo check. Five rounds was all we could raise among the twenty of us. The Valentines were now edging back and away from us. I decided to contact the nearest Tank Commander. He was some 300 yds. away. I stripped off my heavy equipment, pack, water bottle, glasses, revolver and ran for it. The luck was with me. I got to him and pressed his bell, spoke. He told me he was pulling back. I asked him to give us some smoke and we would try and get out too. As I went back to the fort, his smoke came down. I gave the order to get back. The men came out fast, in one's and two's. C.S.M. came last and shouted, 'All out.' C.S.M., Sgt. Young and I went for it together. Young staggered and said, 'I'm hit, Sir!' He hung on to us and we kept going to the Wadi Zigzaou.

C.S.M. Ralph Foster Diston was awarded the Distinguished Conduct Medal for his gallantry throughout the attack and withdrawal of 'A' Company. His citation stated:

> Throughout the attack, C.S.M. Diston showed a complete disregard of danger and magnificent leadership. He personally led many an assault on enemy fortified positions, clearing the numerous trenches and hideouts in the huge redoubt. His inspiring leadership rallied the dwindling numbers of his Company on numerous occasions before the final surrender of the redoubt and the capture of 120 prisoners had been obtained.
>
> At about 1300 hrs. 22nd March, German infantry and tanks approached the redoubt at 200 yds. range on three sides. C.S.M. Diston went round the defenders with great coolness, urging them to greater efforts. Finally, their ammunition expended, they were ordered to withdraw.
>
> C.S.M. Diston guided them through the only safe exit from the redoubt back to the anti-tank ditch, where he obtained more ammunition and reorganised them.

During the course of the late afternoon of the 22nd March, the three battalions of the Durham Light Infantry, much reduced in numbers, had been forced back to the anti-tank ditch. Of the 42 Valentines which had crossed into the bridgehead, 30 had been destroyed or knocked out. On the right, the 5th East Yorkshires still held Ksiba Est. The three battalions of the D.L.I. were on the left and lining the anti-tank ditch. This was the situation as night fell on the 22nd. Enemy infantry attacks were beaten off. Enemy tanks lined the top of the ridge but made no effort to move against the ditch. Orders were received from XXX Corps for a further attempt to attack the ridge using the 6th Bn. Green Howards and the 8th D.L.I. The latter had sustained heavy losses in the bitter fighting and the men were very tired. However, common sense prevailed. The enemy had reoccupied the strong Mareth positions; his tanks and anti-tank guns had destroyed the bulk of the British tanks. There were no crossings over the wadi to enable reinforcements to cross over. Strong German reserves had been drawn into the battle. It would have been suicidal to attempt another frontal assault. The order to counter-attack was cancelled and permission given for the 50th Division to withdraw.

Casualties in 151 Brigade had been very heavy. In the 9th Battalion, Captain Pollard and Lieutenant Lacey were dead. Lt. 'Scotty' White was a prisoner. Maj. E.W.H. Worrall D.S.O., M.C., Captain Partridge and Lieutenants Sharpe, Muir, J.A. White ('A' Company) and Second Lieutenant Collyer were wounded. Of the other ranks, 23 were killed and 120 wounded. Amongst the dead were L/Sgt. J.A. Jones, Sergeant P.B. Jordon, L/ Cpls. A.E.G. King and J. Burns and Ptes. J. Bradley, R. Priestley, H. Thompson, A.G. Baldwin, H. Benyon, T. Hall, D. Ivison, F.L. Williams and G. Mayers.

Lieutenant Colonel Clarke, commanding the battalion, was awarded the Distinguished Service Order for his leadership and devotion to duty throughout the attack and withdrawal. Other awards included Cpl. David Kennedy, who received the Military Medal. He commanded a carrier that became bogged down in the Wadi Zigzaou. He joined a forward company and helped some wounded men hold an important post. He personally attacked and silenced enemy opposition and silenced enemy automatic fire and snipers. As the enemy shellfire increased, he went out and collected six wounded men.

Pte. Charles Sollis also was awarded the Military Medal. His citation described:

Pte. Sollis on March 21 and 22 volunteered to act as runner between forward companies and Bn. H.Q. in the Ksiba Est area when the wireless communications had broken down. He moved between the three forward companies continuously over open country which was constantly under heavy mortar and m.g. fire, returning across the fire-swept wadi to Bn. H.Q. with vital information. He was a constant source of encouragement to all his comrades wherever he went during these two days.

When the Panzer attack came in on the afternoon of the 22nd March. Pte. Sollis lay in the open on the top of the parapet by the anti-tank ditch acting as sniper-observer, completely ignoring the hail of fire directed at the ditch. Pte. Sollis seized the Bren guns off our wounded and kept firing them from the top of the parapet until the ammunition was exhausted and he was ordered to withdraw…

Pte. Sollis by his sustained coolness, determination and cheerfulness was a great inspiration to all his comrades defending the A/tk ditch throughout the night of 22/23 March.

L/Sgt. Joseph B. Gray of 'H.Q.' Company was awarded the Military Medal. His citation read:

On March 21st 1943, at the Battle of the Mareth Line, L/Sgt. Gray heard at dawn that there were some badly wounded men lying in the open in front of the Company holding Ksiba Ouest. They had been unable to evacuate them owing to intense enemy shelling and mortar fire. L/Sgt. Gray went forward alone, individually dressed the wounds of all the men and got them under as much cover as possible. He then improvised stretchers, organised stretcher bearer parties and evacuated them. He then moved along the front to the neighbouring Company and did the same courageous work there.

L/Sgt. Gray's great devotion to duty and personal bravery had saved the lives of many wounded men on every occasion when the Battalion has been in action in the past six months.

Major General Nichols, G.O.C. 50th Division, wrote in the regimental journal in April 1950:

It is probable that the attack on the Mareth Line was the stiffest task which had been allotted to any one Division in this war. The Division almost single-handedly had to attack a defensive position built at leisure in peace-time on ground carefully chosen and carefully sited. A position containing concrete fortresses, extremely formidable wire obstacles, and possessing great natural strength, and subsequently protected by a continuous line of formidable anti-tank ditches and mine fields of great depth. Added to this the enemy had complete observation over practically the whole ground in front of the position and had ample time to register accurately every important feature and fold in the ground…

By this attack the Division eventually caused the enemy to employ nearly the whole of his reserve, thereby weakening the forces opposing the New Zealand Division, and so opened the way for 10 Corps to reach Gabes through El Hamma.

This indeed was what had happened. General Montgomery, on the night of the 22nd/23rd March, had changed his plan. Realising that the frontal attack had failed and aware that the German reserves, particularly the 15th Panzer Division, were committed to the counter-attack at Mareth, he reinforced the outflanking manoeuvre and sent the 1st Armoured Division post haste after the New Zealanders. The result was that the enemy just got his forces clear before this outflanking attack cut his line of retreat deeper into Tunisia. Major General De Guigand, Montgomery's chief of staff, in his book *Operation Victory* wrote:

50th Division were most unfortunate, for the support we had hoped to give them was not forthcoming. They had to withstand the full weight of the German counter-attack, with few supporting weapons and no air support…the attack had attracted the enemy attention and tied down one of the Panzer Divisions (15th) as well as 164th and 90th Light German Divisions…The 50th Division…had forced the enemy to reinforce the sector with German troops. This was excellent, for it would provide a great opportunity for the outflanking of the Mareth Line.

At 5.30 a.m. on the 23rd March, orders were received for the withdrawal of 151 Brigade beyond the Chet Meskine area. The surviving troops were moved at dusk by motor transport to the Medinine road. On the following day, the battalion was rested and swam in the sea. On the 25th, Major General Nichols and Lt. Gen. Oliver Leese, G.O.C. XXX Corps, arrived to congratulate the 9th Battalion for the part it played in the battle. Over the next few days, the battalion occupied various positions in the Mareth Line – the enemy had withdrawn – and in the outskirts of Mareth itself. Some salvage work was carried out to clean the area of the materials of war but little was found as the enemy had done quite a thorough job of cleaning up as he withdrew.

On the 1st April, a draft of 78 other ranks arrived form base, together with Lts. J.L. Kennedy, L.E.V. Rumble and Whittaker. The following day, parties from the battalion visited the Wadi Zigzaou battle area. Great care had to be taken as the enemy had left many mines and Company Sergeant Major Diston was wounded by one of these. A further draft of 47 other ranks arrived from base transit camp. A concert party was organised by Lieutenant Davies. On the 4th of the month, the battalion moved to El Mdou, six miles south of Gabes. Parties from 'A' and 'D' Companies were sent to unload ships in Gabes Harbour. These returned to the battalion in the early evening.

An interesting item appeared on routine orders:

> The shell-case stated to be the last loaded into the gun by Pte. A. Wakenshaw V.C., in the action in which he was killed and for which he was awarded the V.C., was received at this H.Q. a few days ago.
> It has been handed over to Brig. Lysaght Griffin, who is proceeding to U.K. and who will personally arrange for it to be handed to D.L.I. Depot on arrival in England.

The final, strong defensive position before the plains of Tunisia lay ahead of the Eighth Army. The Wadi Akarit position lay 15 miles west of Wadi Zigzaou. At this time of the year it was a dry watercourse with the sea on one flank and a large inland salt marsh on the other. The latter, named Sebret El Hamma, was impassable. The wadi was overlooked by high, steep hills through which the route to the plains lay. The enemy occupied a powerful position on these hills. The plan was for XXX Corps to breach the defences, and X Corps to follow through with its armour and break out onto the plain. The 51st Highland Division on the right was given the task of attacking the hill called Djebel Roumana – 500 feet high, very steep and impassable to wheeled vehicles. The 4th Indian Division on the left was detailed to attack Djebel Meida and Mesreb El Alig. The attacks were timed to take place on the night of the 5th/6th April. The Indians planned a silent attack and the 51st Division would attack with artillery support. Between the two hill features, a low ridge connected the hills and was crossed by a track at the Djebel Roumana end. In front of the ridge ran an anti-tank ditch and minefield. Brigade 69 of the 50th Division was given the task of attacking this ridge. The 6th Bn. D.L.I. was in reserve for this attack. Lieutenant Lloyd, 'A' Company', of the 9th Battalion was attached to 69 Brigade with carriers and a platoon to protect the Royal Engineers during the action. Captain Medway, with the Carrier Platoon, was ordered to bring up 6-pdr. anti-tank guns to support the 5th East Yorks when a bridgehead was secured. The remainder of the battalion was not called upon.

The assault began and initially a speedy advance was made. However, 69 Brigade was held up until Djebel Roumana and Djebel Meida fell to the attacking divisions. A wide gap opened astride the track between the 6th Green Howards and the Highlanders and the 6th Bn. D.L.I. was ordered forward to fill it. At some stage Lieutenant Lloyd and Captain Medway became involved. Unfortunately, the War Diary has no entry to tell us what that involvement was, except to say that the casualties in the Carrier Platoon were one killed (Cpl. T. Smythe) and two wounded. One carrier was destroyed. On the 8th April, parties went to clear the battlefield. A great deal of abandoned enemy equipment lay about. The battalion rested over the next few days. On the 11th of the month, a memorial service by Rev. R.W. Kerr was held to commemorate the Mareth battle. On the 13th, the battalion moved to the X Corps area west of Sfax. On the 17th, it had reached Hergla, south of Enfidaville, having travelled via Sfax and Kairouan. A draft of 47 arrived the previous night. Night patrols were sent out. The New Zealand Division attack on the enemy positions commenced on the night of the 19th April. The following day, a carrier patrol under Lieutenant Gardner moved up the coast track east of Enfidaville with the intention of observing and harassing enemy movements. Whilst it was clearly seen that the enemy was withdrawing from his positions, ground obstacles made it impossible to engage him. On the same day, orders were received that 50th Division was to be withdrawn from Tunisia and would be relieved by the 56th Division. On the 21st, the 9th Battalion moved off at the rear of 151 Brigade column on the long road and rail journey to the Nile Delta and the new experience that lay ahead.

CHAPTER XIX

OPERATION HUSKY – THE INVASION OF SICILY

The journey to Tobruk was a distance of more than 1,450 miles. It followed the coast road and the usual procedure was for the troops to debus from troop carrying vehicles each day and march the last five miles or so to the next staging point.

This journey placed a great responsibility on Lt. John Arnold, the battalion Motor Transport Officer. He had to ensure that the transport kept rolling and he and his section of transport fitters and drivers were kept very busy during the journey. Lieutenant Arnold described the trip:

> So there began for me one of the worst journeys I've ever experienced. Our vehicles, as I said before, were decrepit. The job was to get them along the coast of Tunisia, Libya and Egypt to Alex or to be precise, Sidi Bishr, just outside Alex. During the trip we had every kind of vehicle breakdown. We had sandstorms, which totally blocked our view. It was so hot that the radiators were boiling and some of our number tried running along in reverse, trying to keep the front cool. Fortunately, all of our vehicles arrived safely, albeit tied up with wire and string.

On the 27th April, the troops reached Tripoli and a draft of 47 other ranks arrived from base. Benghazi was reached on the 4th May and Tobruk three days later. Orders were received for the remainder of the journey to Sidi Bishr, near Alexandria, to be made in two parties: one by road the other by rail. On the 8th of the month, the road party consisting of Captain Sommerville, Lt. J. Arnold and 245 other ranks left for Sidi Bishr. The remainder of the battalion under the command of Major Robinson boarded trains at Tobruk station for the same destination. Both parties arrived on the 10th May, and leave to Alexandria and Cairo commenced immediately. Routine orders on the 14th May contained a letter from the secretary of the Dean and Chapter Colliery Pit Production Committee:

> I have been instructed by the Dean and Chapter Pit Production Committee to convey to you their great admiration of the splendid service rendered by the DURHAMS in the fight for world freedom.

The battalion moved to Kabrit for its combined operations training on the 22nd May. H.M.S. *Saunders*, a naval training base, was located here. A number of drafts were received during this period. Combined operations training included embarking and disembarking on L.C.A.s (landing craft assault). An exercise called 'Dredger', at the end of May, involved a practice assault on the Sinai coast. Exercise 'Duchess' commenced on the 3rd June. On the 6th of the month the battalion embarked on L.C.T.s (landing craft tanks) for Ataka in the Suez area.

In camp at Ataka the battalion prepared for exercise 'Bromyard'. Maj. E.W.H. Worrall D.S.O., M.C. left the 9th Battalion to join the 6th as Second in Command. On the 9th June, all personnel embarked on H.M.T. *Orantes* and joined the convoy taking part in the exercise. 'Bromyard' was a full-scale invasion exercise off the coast in the Gulf of Aqaba. The landing was 'opposed' from the shore with guns firing live ammunition and the 'attacking' troops had to breach wire obstructions on the shoreline. An overnight stay on the coast was followed by embarkation and a return to Ataka Camp. General

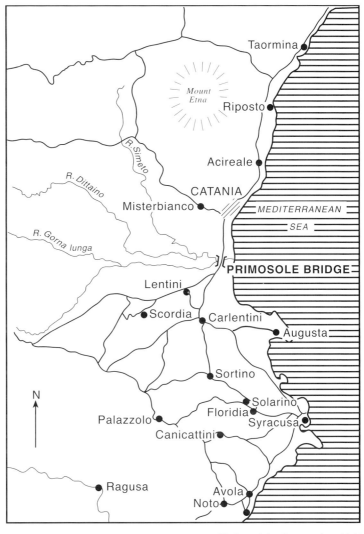

Sicily – July–September 1943

Montgomery gave a lecture to officers on the 24th June and visited the battalion on the following day. Officers were introduced to the new Divisional Commander, Maj. Gen. S.C. Kirkham O.B.E., M.C. on the 27th. On the 30th, the battalion embarked on the *Orantes* and the ship left on the following day for Port Said.

Port Said was reached on the 1st July. On the following day, Maj. Gen. S.C. Kirkham spoke to all ranks about the forthcoming operations, without mentioning the destination. Rumours, as usual in such situations, were rife, with the invasion of Greece, Crete and Italy the favourites. On the 4th of the month, Brig. A.H. Senior D.S.O., who had replaced Brigadier Beak V.C. after the Battle of Mareth, lectured all ranks on the task ahead. The following day, the ship left Port Said in convoy. Once out at sea, the ship's Captain announced the destination as being Sicily. The convoy was one of several sailing from north African ports, Malta and the United Kingdom, all carefully planned to converge and meet south of Sicily for the final leg of the journey to the island.

The invasion of Sicily had been planned for some three months. The initial plan was for landings on the Sicilian coast to be made at several points on the north-west and the south-eastern corner of the island. General Montgomery, in particular, was against such dispersal of forces and felt the landings should be concentrated on the south-east coast. This was agreed to and plans laid accordingly. The British Eighth Army (General Montgomery) and the American Seventh Army (General Patton) would be supported by airborne landings and strong naval and air support. It was important that a port was captured early in the operation together with landing sites for the air support. Syracuse and the airfields of the Pachino Peninsula were Eighth Army objectives, and the port of Licata and the airfields of Comiso were the immediate targets of the American Seventh Army. It was planned to take Syracuse, Augusta and Catania at the earliest opportunity, as these were considered vital objectives with their ports and airfields, which lay in the line of the Eighth Army's advance up the east coast of the island.

The British force comprised two corps. The XIII Corps, with the 5th and 50th Divisions, would land on the south-east corner of the island in the Gulf of Noto, south of Syracuse. Immediately prior to the landing, airborne troops would drop west of Syracuse and capture and hold an important bridge, which if destroyed or held by the enemy in force, might seriously delay the quick capture of the port. The commandos would assault and destroy enemy coastal batteries. XXX Corps, consisting of the 51st Highland Division, 231 Brigade from Malta and the 1st Canadian Division would land south of XIII Corps on both sides of the Pachino Peninsula, capture the airfields and relieve XIII Corps to enable the latter to advance towards its main objectives. At the same time, XXX Corps would link up with the Americans landing in the Gulf of Gela. It was known that the enemy forces on the island comprised two German divisions and five Italian, with a further six Italian divisions of doubtful quality whose duties were to protect the coastline.

The 50th Division was on the left of XIII Corps front with the 5th Division on the right. No. 151 Brigade was to make the initial landing on 'Jig Sector' and establish a bridgehead. No. 69 Brigade would follow up and take over the area captured by 151 Brigade and consolidate. The brigade plan was for the 6th and 9th Battalions to establish the initial bridgehead. The 8th Battalion would follow through and capture the vital high ground, which dominated the coastal area and had to be denied to the enemy. The landings were on the coastal plain in the area of Avola. This town of about 20,000 inhabitants lay some 1,000 yards inland from the coast. The coastal plain stretched for about one and three-quarter miles inland to the foothills of the steep escarpment about 1,000 feet above sea level – the objective of the 8th Battalion. Beyond the coastal road, a railway line ran parallel to the shore. The plain was cultivated with vineyards, orchards and olives in small fields. Each field was surrounded by a drystone wall. On the coast lay a small fishing harbour, Lido d'Avola, its position easily recognised by the two pillars and circular concrete platform which jutted out into the sea. The enemy defences comprised a series of concrete pillboxes and entrenchments, wired in but with few mines and no underwater obstacles, though this was not known at the time of the assault. The coastal defenders were the Italian 206th Coastal Division with Italian and German divisions in strategic positions inland.

No. 151 Brigade was supported by the following:

> 98 Field Regiment (self-propelled guns known as 'priests')
> 107 Anti-Tank Battery and 102 Anti-Tank Regiment (6-pdr. guns)
> Reconnaissance Party, 3rd Survey Regiment
> 505 Field Company, Royal Engineers
> 'A' and 'C' Companies, 2nd Bn. the Cheshire Regiment (machine guns)
> Detachment of the 149 Field Ambulance
> 34 Beach Brick (beach organising unit), including the 18th Bn. D.L.I. that had been raised in Egypt.

The 9th Battalion was to land on 'Jig Green Beach' of the 'Jig Sector'. On the left, the 6th Battalion was to land on 'Jig Amber' between the marina and the lido. The initial objective was to become established on the coast road east of Avola, and then move to the railway embankment. The 9th Battalion would then turn south and mask the exits from Avola, prior to taking the town itself. Thereafter, Avola town would be taken and the 8th Battalion would pass through to carry out its phase of the plan.

All the troop ships in the convoy were dry, that is, no intoxicating drinks available. Whilst this may have been a disappointment to those officers and other ranks who liked a drink, it was more important to land sober and fit men on the beaches. No enemy aircraft appeared over the convoy although there was a rumour of a reconnaissance aircraft above at one point of the voyage. If one such aircraft had appeared, it was not spotted and the convoy sailed on without mishap. During the 6th to 9th July, lectures were held, officers and men were thoroughly briefed, intelligence summaries were carefully scrutinised and operational orders were issued. Every man was to know his role and that of his unit. Air photographs of the invasion area were available and accurate sand models of the invasion beaches were crafted and studied. Commanding Officers explained the final plan in great detail to their battalions and companies. The weather for the first few days was ideal. On reaching the final concentration area, onlookers saw an incredible scene. As far as the eye could see ships of all sizes and types filled the sea to the horizon. Troopers and supply ships sailed in the middle whilst destroyers fussed about at top speed, surfing in and out of the ships. Cruisers and larger ships sailed on the outer edges of this great convoy.

On the 9th July, the weather began to change for the worse. The wind rose considerably and large waves roughened the once calm sea. The wind dropped towards the end of the day but an unpleasant swell would obviously make disembarkation difficult. A postponement of the attack was considered if conditions did not improve, but reason dictated that it would be almost impossible to turn such a huge fleet of ships when so close to its objective. The ships sailed on. Shortly after midnight on the 10th July, the signal was given to the awaiting infantry to assemble on deck and prepare to embark on the landing craft. This was done in silence except for the scraping of boots on the deck and the metallic clinking of equipment as the men moved to their pre-arranged places. Operation Husky, the invasion of Sicily, was about to begin.

It was not easy to climb into the landing craft, which were then lowered into the heaving sea. It was even more difficult and dangerous for those who had to climb down the sides of the ships on ladders and leap out onto the pitching landing craft, all whilst laden with equipment, ammunition and weapons. There were surprisingly few injuries and by 1.40 a.m. the landing craft had formed up and moved onwards the distant shore. Distant it was indeed. The ships should have brought the assault forces to within seven miles of the coast. Instead they were disembarked onto the landing craft about 12 miles from the shore. This meant a run of more than three hours to the beach in heavy seas, pitching and tossing first on top of a swell and then crashing down into deep troughs. Everyone on the open landing craft was quickly soaked and all, with very few exceptions, were weakened by appalling seasickness. It was virtually impossible to keep station and landing craft were soon out of position, split up and mixed with the craft carrying other units. It appeared that craft were going in every direction. There was a great deal of shouting by the coxswains as each sought to identify nearby boats and direction. The result was that the battalion was scattered and landed wherever their craft touched the beaches. Fortunately, little opposition was met as the battalions approached the shoreline. No craft were lost and only slight shelling fell on the beaches. The weather and inexperience of the glider pilots had also caused problems with the airborne landings. Gliders were scattered by anti-aircraft fire, and many were unable to identify landing areas. Many ditched in the sea with the resultant loss of life. Those who did land were widely scattered and fought many individual battles before reaching the main force.

The troops had been issued with a 48-hour ration pack, to be used over the first two days. It consisted of:

9 oz. service biscuit	3ozs cheese
3 oz. sweet biscuits	2ozs dripping spread
8oz. raisin chocolate	5oz. tea, sugar, milk mixture
4.5oz. boiled sweets	12g. preserved meat
1 box safety matches	

The first units of the 9th Battalion landed on the beaches at 4 a.m. but it took one and a half hours for the full battalion to land. The first troops ashore were 10 and 11 Platoons of 'B' Company and they landed at Marina d'Avola. The rest of the battalion landed on different areas of the shore, some on the 5th Division beaches to the north and others mixed with the 6th Battalion to the south. The latter were also widely scattered. The 6th Battalion headquarters with Lieutenant Colonel Watson landed on the 9th Battalion's beaches.

Men of the 9th Battalion moving up from the invasion beaches along a typical Sicilian lane – far differerent conditions from the Western Desert.

Several of the battalion's carriers became involved in the attack by 'D' Company of the 6th Battalion on the Avola–Noto road bridge, which crossed the Mammeledi River. Units were so mixed up that the password issued to all troops, 'Desert Rats', and the reply, 'Kill Italians!' was shouted and saved many possible mistaken identities and confrontations. Gradually companies and platoons sorted themselves out and concentrated around battalion headquarters.

An interesting paragraph in *Operation Instruction No.3* dealt with the possibility of the town of Avola being held by the enemy and reinforced from the interior of the country. It suggests that if such were to happen the civilian population be 'encouraged' to leave the town for Palazzolo, thus impeding the advance of enemy reinforcements coming into Avola along that road. As it happened none of these situations arose as the town was quickly taken with little opposition.

At 7.15 a.m. 'D' Company commenced the attack on Avola and moved into the suburbs of the town. The battalion War Diary records that Avola was captured by 'C' and 'D' Companies at 10 a.m. The Union Jack was raised above the town hall. The 6th Battalion had taken the railway station and raised the flag there. Once they had realised that the attacking troops were not Germans but British, the local Sicilians became very friendly. It appeared they had little love for the Germans and Mussolini's Italy.

The battalion moved to the Noto area at 1.50 p.m. Two M.E. 109s attacked battalion headquarters in mid afternoon but caused no damage or casualties. The day ended with the battalion preparing to attack Noto on the following morning. Casualties during the landings and actions that had followed were two killed or died of wounds and four wounded. The dead were Ptes. H.E. Robertson and F. Vickers.

At 8.30 a.m. on the 11th July, the attack on Noto began. Two priests reported that the town was empty. On receipt of this information the Commanding Officer, Adjutant and Intelligence Officer entered the town followed by carriers after the Royal Engineers had blown a roadblock. 'A' and 'D' Companies mopped up and approximately 140 prisoners were taken, almost all from the 206th Coastal Division. The battalion made contact with the 51st Division. Early on the following morning a warning order was received for a move to Floridia. Enemy planes were active over the coastal area and were engaged by Spitfires. Floridia was reached by 5 p.m. and the battalion was deployed outside the town. Ahead lay Primosole Bridge, which was seen as the doorway to the Catania Plain and was a vital objective. If the Germans could block the advance at the bridge, the whole of the eastern side of Sicily would be denied the Allies. It was a point not lost on the enemy as he fought for time to enable an ordered withdrawal from Sicily via Messina.

CHAPTER XX

PRIMOSOLE BRIDGE – THE END IN SICILY

Syracuse had fallen to the 5th Division on the night of the 10th July, aided by the capture intact of the Ponte Grande Bridge by glider-borne troops of the 1st Airborne Division. No. 151 Brigade was ordered to move to Floridia, whilst 69 Brigade moved ahead to Sortino. In the beginning the battalion moved in trucks to an area south of Floridia. This was reached on the morning of the 14th July. The battalion was on the move again, this time on foot, by 11.30 a.m. A desperate situation was unfolding at Primosole Bridge, which crossed the River Simeto, 15 miles south of Catania. This bridge carried the main coast road over the river and onto the plain south of the city. As we have seen, the Germans were well aware of its great value to the Allies and fully intended that its passage be contested.

No. 69 Brigade led the advance towards Sortino and Lentini. It encountered severe opposition from German troops of the Schmaltz Battle Group, Herman Goering Division. The terrain, through which the 69 and 151 Brigades were advancing, was entirely opposite to what they had experienced in North Africa. The open spaces of the desert had given way to narrow, winding roads lined with drystone walls. These roads ran through slender valleys bordered by steep hills, again divided by drystone walls. Small fields, orchards and vineyards filled the narrow valleys. As they fought their way forward the brigades had to adapt to these conditions and the new fighting techniques they demanded. At intervals down the road, the brigades encountered small towns and villages whose narrow, winding streets were barely wide enough to allow the passage of a tank or large vehicle. Fired on from the hills, the troops had to scale a series of drystone walls whilst climbing the steep sides to chase off the opposition. Around every sharp corner lay the possibility of an ambush laid by the retreating enemy. It was ideal defensive country. From Lentini the ground fell away towards Primosole Bridge and was open and without cover.

On the 12th July, the first elements of the German 1st Airborne Division were beginning to land at Catania airfield. They had flown in from the Avignon area of southern France where they were resting after serving on the eastern front. These were tough, well-trained and experienced troops and formidable opponents. First to land were the 1st Parachute Machine Gun Battalion of the 3rd Parachute Regiment and the 1st Parachute Signals Company of the 1st Parachute Communications Battalion. The 3rd Parachute Regiment reinforced the Schmaltz Battle Group, which was opposing the advance of 69 Brigade.

On the night of the 13th/14th July, No. 3 Commando landed from the sea with the objective of capturing Malati Bridge which crossed the River Leonardo about one and three-quarter miles north of Lentini. The 1st Parachute Brigade of the British 1st

Airborne Division dropped in the area of Primosole Bridge with orders to take the bridge, remove the explosives and hold it until the 50th Division relieved them. Malati and Primosole Bridges were taken. Unfortunately, the parachutists dropping on Primosole Bridge were widely scattered and only a small force took the bridge and removed the explosives. During the whole of the 14th July, this small group of parachutists held the bridge against severe attacks by the enemy supported by tanks. These highly trained troops of both sides fought with rare distinction. Capt. Franz Stangenberg of the German 1st Parachute Division was in command of the advance party landing at Catania as the British took the bridge. He organised the first counterattack using the 1st Signals Company and a mixed force of the Herman Goering Division. They fought with considerable skill, discipline and fanaticism. Two hundred strong, this force included signallers, clerks, mechanics and drivers, all well trained in the use of their weapons. On the night of the 14th/15th July, the 1st Parachute Battalion of the German 1st Parachute Division landed at Catania and strengthened the force trying to recapture the bridge.

Major General Kirkman's orders to 151 Brigade were to march flat out to reach the bridge as soon as possible and relieve the hard-pressed British parachutists. The 9th Battalion was at the head of the brigade, followed by the 8th and 6th Battalions in that order. The brigade passed through 69 Brigade and pressed on knowing full well that the paratroops were relying on them. It was a gruelling march in the heat of the day but despite considerable efforts to reach the paratroops in time, the 9th arrived just too late. The Schmaltz Battle Group had done a good job in slowing the advance through the difficult terrain. At about 7 p.m. on the 14th July, the British paratroops had been driven off the bridge. They held the south bank and the enemy were unable to replace the explosives. A mobile column of tanks, carriers, anti-tank guns and machine guns under the command of Major Robinson arrived about two hours later. The battalion was exhausted. Pte. Ernie Kerens wrote:

> Well before 0600 hrs. the Battalion was on the move, in single file each side of the road…The Battalion had its Bren-carriers and its ammunition trucks, nothing at all for the men to ride on. Nobby, our C.O., had his own jeep but chose to march with the men. The sun rose higher and higher. The only action was provided by two low flying M.E. 109s. We marched each side of the road…At first sign of the two planes, everybody shouted at once and vanished, as if by magic, into the fields that edged the road and any cover there was. From it they sent a shower of bullets at the aircraft. The Bren-carriers and ammunition trucks were not always so lucky. An ammo truck was hit and a danger to everybody in the area. I suppose the driver could have jumped off and ran like hell but instead he drove it up the hillside as far as he could before it exploded, killing him, poor blighter.
>
> We marched on and on and on, mile after mile over dusty, rough Sicilian roads, nursing precious contents of our water bottles…A tank went through to deal with them [the Germans]. We followed it down into Lentini. Italy was still at war with us but while we waited in the town…the villagers lined the main street, cheering and clapping and plying us with water, vino, oranges and of all things, pickled olives. One old chap kissed me

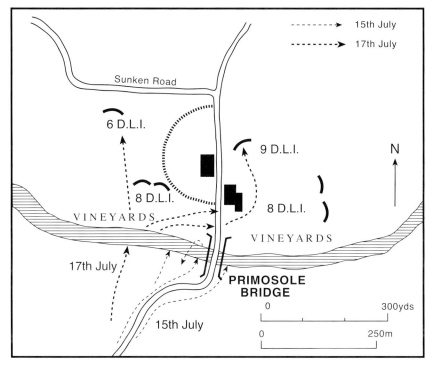

Primosole Bridge – July 15–17 1943

on both cheeks and hugged me like a long lost son. It was very noticeable that the only females were either very old or very young but fluttering bedroom curtains showed where they hid the others…

   We were off again, down to the bottom of the hill and along the road to Primosole Bridge. There was a hell of a long way to go and no transport…Darkness fell, still we marched. The column straggled, the strong carried the rifles of the weak…Less than two miles from our objective, the Primosole Bridge, Nobby had to call a halt to his weary column and said food would be provided and we would sleep here…

The exhausted men were in no fit state to launch an immediate attack on the bridge and certainly some preparation and reconnaissance would need to be carried out. It was now very late. Brigadier Senior gave permission for the battalion to be fed and rested prior to an attack to be made on the morning of the 15th July at 7.30 a.m. A hot meal was served and the tired battalion sought sleep where they were.

   It was not to be a restful night. Firing could be heard ahead of them as the para-troops fought to stop the enemy from replacing the explosives on the bridge. At 3.30 a.m., a number of Italian armoured cars approached the battalion's position from the direction of Lentini. Warned by the sound of the vehicles, the battalion prepared to receive them. Capt. Jim Kennedy described what happened:

   The Battalion had gone to ground at the end of the day at either side of the road, which was beginning to descend towards Primosole…During the night, 7 armoured cars (later found to be Italian commandos) drove as silently as they could up the road. Everyone lay silent waiting for the officer near the anti-tank gun in defilade and he waited till all seven had passed. When the last one was alongside where the battalion H.Q. was lying, the anti-tank gun fired and at close range it couldn't miss. The car stopped dead in its tracks. The other cars began to try to move off the road…Two managed to drive uphill off the road and away (they probably knew the country) and the others were dealt with. No prisoners were taken.

L/Cpl. Stanley Seymour Rose was awarded an immediate Military Medal for his role in this action. His citation read:

> On the night of the 14/15th July 1943, whilst the Battalion was resting preparatory to making a dawn attack on the Primosole Bridge near Catania, seven Italian armoured cars succeeded under cover of darkness, in penetrating to Bn. H.Q. area. Here, one 6 pdr anti-tank gun, of which L/Cpl. Rose was the layer, was sited in an open position on the side of the road. In great danger of being hit by the enemy Oerlikon guns who were firing in every direction, Lance Corporal Rose held his fire until the nearest armoured car was only 30 yards off. With his first shot he knocked it out. Then he was wounded. In great pain, he continued to fire his gun until a second armoured car was destroyed and the remaining ones routed. L/Cpl. Rose had shown exceptional coolness and bravery in most difficult circumstances. It was greatly due to the successful handling of his gun that the enemy force was beaten off before they could inflict real danger to the Battalion.

The terrain over which the battalion had to move to reach the bridge was flat and open. The road from Lentini followed a ridge and then about 1,000 yards from the bridge, it descended onto the plain. Primosole Bridge was 400 feet long and crossed the sluggish, reed bordered River Simeto. It was a structure of iron girders, not unlike a British Bailey bridge. North of the bridge were two small farms, each comprising two or three buildings and a barn. The road to Catania divided the two farms. Immediately north of the river were thick vineyards and a number of olive groves, covering a depth of about 400 yards. Beyond lay the open country towards Catania. Unknown to the attacking British troops, a sunken road ran parallel to and a few hundred yards north of the river. The combination of vineyards, olive groves and sunken road provided excellent cover for the defending Germans. The attack would have to go in over the open ground, devoid of cover. Once again, as at Alamein and Mareth, 151 Brigade was being called upon to make an attack on a narrow front and against a strong position well defended by first-class enemy troops.

At precisely 7.30 a.m. on the 15th July 1943, the 9th Battalion moved towards the bridge. At the same time, an intensive barrage from the two supporting field regiments of artillery fell on the positions of the concealed enemy. A squadron of Sherman tanks of the 44th Royal Tank Regiment was in support. Immediately, the advancing troops came under heavy fire from German machine guns, rifles and mortars. The 1st Company of the German 1st Parachute Engineers Battalion, commanded by Lieutenant

Primosole Bridge, Sicily, 1943. The bridge has now been replaced by a modern bridge that carries the main east coast motorway.

Cords, was in defensive positions on the southern bank of the River Simeto. It inflicted heavy losses on the advancing 9th Battalion. The enemy withdrew to the north bank and the Durhams advanced to the southern bank of the river. As they reached the river-bank, German troops hidden in the vineyards and lining the sunken road opened up and more men fell. Many were shot and drowned attempting to swim the river. By 9.30 a.m., one platoon from 'C' Company had managed to cross the river and bitter hand-to-hand fighting broke out. None of the other companies succeeded in crossing and these established positions south of the river and, as the paratroops had succeeded in doing the previous day, stopped the enemy from destroying the bridge. Attempts by the Sherman tanks to cross the bridge failed completely as the enemy had an 88 firing in an anti-tank role straight down the road and the bridge.

Sgt. Patrick Daley was awarded the Military Medal. He crossed the Simeto with 13 Platoon of 'C' Company. His citation described the action:

> …as soon as they reached the far bank, enemy automatics and snipers opened up on all sides from the reeds and vineyards at very close range. Sgt. Daley showed splendid leadership and great courage in the hand-to-hand fighting.
>
> Further counter attacks by the enemy forced the platoon back into the river where the water was deep. Soon three men were shouting for assistance from drowning. Sgt. Daley quickly threw off his equipment and re-entered the water in the face of close aimed small arms fire on the bank and regardless of danger endeavoured to rescue the drowning men. He remained in the water for fifteen minutes and succeeded in bringing ashore two of the men under constant fire of automatics. Throughout this day Sgt. Daley had inspired all

members of his company by his great personal valour and magnificent leadership.

Lt. W.J.H. Muir ('C' Company) was awarded a Bar to the Military Cross he had won at Mareth, for his daring leadership of his platoon. On reaching the river, he plunged straight into the water and led his men to the opposite bank, which was reached with few casualties. Lieutenant Muir was later wounded and evacuated.

Casualties were heavy. Lt. W.J.R. Hoyte was killed. Maj. C.F.R. Goulden, Capt. C.C. Ridley, Lts. W.J.H. Muir and H. Sanderson and 2/Lts. L.J. Pleavin (who later died of his wounds), C. Smith, D. Boulton and L. Thompson were wounded. Of the other ranks 33 were killed, 40 wounded and 27 missing. The dead included Sgts. I. Lloyd and L.G. Smith, Cpls. D.E. Kennedy M.M., J.H. Kennedy and T. West, L/Cpls. J.E. Smith and J.M. Taylor and Ptes. H.H. Crutcheley, T. Dawson, R. Degg, T.G. Green, W. Howells, H. Longden and C. Robinson.

In the early hours of the 16th July, it was the turn of the 8th Battalion. After bitter fighting this battalion was able to establish and hold a small bridgehead on the north bank of the river. The final attack by the 6th and 9th Battalions took place at 1.00 a.m. on the 17th. The 6th Battalion crossed the river behind the artillery bombardment. The 9th followed at 2 a.m. The enemy fought for every inch of ground. Each lane between the rows of vines was covered by automatic weapons firing on fixed lines. The troops could move only with the greatest difficulty as the thick vines caused men to lose direction. The severity of the fighting caused the battalion to change direction and make for the 8th Battalion bridgehead. At 4.30 a.m., battalion H.Q. reached the north end of the bridge and linked up with 'C' Company, which was pinned down. H.Q. was established in a ditch but found this untenable due to heavy enemy small arms and machine gun fire, and a further move was made under smoke laid down by the 8th Battalion to a shell hole about 100 yards to the rear.

'A' Company had a difficult time also. After the exertions of the 15th, it was down to two platoons. Heavy enemy fire and ground entangled with telephone cables and barbed wire made the going tough. However, the company persevered and advanced towards the main road where it captured a machine gun and three prisoners. It then crossed the road and attacked a farmhouse, capturing a further nine prisoners. At this time, the Company Commander Captain Hudson was left with 15 men. These survivors were attacked from the right rear and had to withdraw. An enemy post on the road itself joined in. Captain Hudson signalled to the Commander of a company on the other side of the road to attack the post. This, too, failed. 'A' Company now comprised only the Commander and seven unwounded men and was running short of ammunition. Captain Hudson ordered a withdrawal to battalion H.Q., but was wounded and taken prisoner.

The German counter-attacked at about 6 a.m. but this was broken up by accurate and heavy artillery fire. Shortly afterwards the 6th and 9th Battalions advanced and moved well beyond the bridge. Enemy resistance was broken. With the removal of the

88s, Sherman tanks crossed the bridge and crashed through the vineyards shooting up everything and everyone they saw. Sgt. Stan Ferguson of 'S' Company recorded:

> I and others of the 9th Battalion were crouched in a ditch on the Catania side of the bridge. We were pinned down. A tank came alongside but refused to go any further because of an 88 mm gun round the bend which, incidentally, had been knocked out. A high-ranking officer (I believe a Brig.) came forward and laid the law down to this tank commander in no uncertain terms. The tank moved forward level with Stink Alley, turned left and faced its gun down the lane. First one pair then another, hands were raised. I jumped into my Bren carrier and drove up to the tank. As the Germans came out they piled all kinds of weapons into my carrier. I then escorted them back to H.Q.

The enemy left in the sunken road surrendered. It was so full of German dead that the British troops named it 'Stink Alley'. The scene around the bridge was described in David Rissik's book *The D.L.I. at War*:

> The area round the bridge was a regular hell's kitchen; it was littered with smashed rifles and automatics, torn pieces of equipment, bloodstained clothing, overturned ammunition boxes and the bodies of British and German dead. It was a scene of terrible destruction and telling evidence of a bitter struggle in which neither side had asked or given quarter. There could have been few better German troops in Sicily than those who held the bridge. They were Nazi zealots to a man, but they fought superbly well and as their Battalion Commander was led into captivity Colonel Clarke of the 9th Battalion quietly shook him by the hand.

Capt. Jim Kennedy (promoted to Major after the action) wrote:

> German paratroops…They were fanatics…Another German camouflaged and up a tree was located and told to come down and surrender. He had no ammunition and just spat at two men who had crawled across to speak with him. He just spat at them, so was shot and his body stayed there…

By 10 a.m., the enemy were surrendering to the battalion and 60 prisoners were taken. A total of 150 Germans were taken prisoner in the action and over 300 dead lay on the battlefield.

The fighting had been bitter and prolonged. Many of the veterans who had seen action in France and the desert thought that Primosole Bridge was the worst by far. Many were the great deeds though few were recognised. C.S.M. Frederick Thompson was awarded an immediate Distinguished Conduct Medal. His citation read:

> C.S.M. Thompson, 'C' Coy. 9 D.L.I., crossed the River Simeto during the daylight attack on the Primosole Bridge, on July 15th with Coy. H.Q. immediately behind the leading platoons. As soon as they set foot on the far bank they were attacked by Germans on all sides. During the hand-to-hand fighting the Coy. Commander disappeared and both Platoon Commanders became casualties. C.S.M. Thompson took charge. He organised

The memorial at Primosole Bridge erected after the battle. Graves of those who died in battle are all around. This memorial was replaced by another to 151 Brigade which is istuated by the side of the motorway leading from the bridge across the River Simeto to Catania.

the platoons so that they fought off all efforts of the enemy to overrun his Coy. Finally, realising that they could not hold their ground, he skilfully arranged their withdrawal back across the river so that they suffered minimum casualties. During the night attack on July 16th/17th on the same position, C.S.M. Thompson took charge of his Company, who became very split up owing to well hidden enemy strong points in the vineyards. When dawn came, his small party was taking cover with most of the Bn. H.Q. in a ditch only 100 yds. from an enemy strong-point in No Man's Land where they were being shot up badly on both sides. C.S.M. Thompson volunteered to crawl 200 yds. back to get a smoke screen put down. So successful was the smoke screen that all the forces got back without further loss. C.S.M. Thompson has at all times shown most distinguished and brave conduct in the field. Always cool, calm and full of zeal, he is an inspiration to the Battalion in battle.

No. 151 Brigade was withdrawn across the River Simeto and into reserve. At 4.30 p.m. on the 18th July, the battalion reached the area from which it had moved prior the attack on the bridge. Casualties sustained on the 17th were very heavy. Capt. W.G. Deacon and 2/Lt. R.K. Carr were killed. Capt. J.H.W. Hudson was wounded and a prisoner. Lts. G.P. Wakefield and H.A.C. Vischer were wounded and Capt. G.W. Smith and Lt. C.F. Slade were missing. Other ranks' casualties were 22 killed, 36 wounded and 36 missing. The dead included W.O.II R.F. Diston D.C.M., L/Cpls. R. Carter, H.P. Kaufman and R.H. Wild, Ptes. J.C. Andrews, E. Awford, T.C. Brown, F.

Dyke, H. Holden, W. Holden, E. Moxon and L. Mullen.

A total of 94 reinforcements were received on the 19th and 20th July. On the 21st, a further draft of 147 other ranks was received. This draft included Lts. G. Lanning, C.B. Barnett, J. Brett-James and 2/ Lts. R.A. Lear, J.R. Brooker, J.D. Reid, and D.S.Taylor.

At 9.30 p.m. on the 21st, the battalion moved off to take over a reserve position from the 5th Bn. East Yorkshire Regiment. No. 151 Brigade relieved 69 Brigade in the front line. There was very little activity except for slight shelling from the enemy. In the distance towards Catania airfield, explosions could be heard and it was presumed that the enemy was destroying his bomb dumps. The battalion suffered a serious loss on the 23rd July. Lt. Col. Clarke D.S.O., and his Second in Command Maj. 'Big' Bill Robinson, had left to arrange a relief of the 8th Battalion. Pte. Les Fallows of the Carrier Platoon wrote:

> Later, on the other side of Primosole Bridge, Colonel Clarke and Maj. Bill Robinson stopped to have a word as we lay in a water duct and in the distance, from the foothills of Etna, came the sound of a 210mm as they moved into No Man's Land to recce. The salvo from the Nebelwerfer that kept our heads down, claimed their lives.

They were observing the situation from rising ground, the enemy launched a mortar attack and one of the bombs killed the two officers. Both were extremely popular with the officers and men of the battalion and the loss was strongly felt by all. Lieutenant Colonel Clarke had always led from the front and there is little doubt he would have reached higher rank had he lived. Major Robinson was equally well liked. Tall and well built, he was easily recognisable and had built a fine reputation within the battalion. For the next few days, the battalion was commanded by Maj. W.J. Scott and Capt. Jim Kennedy, the Adjutant, assisted by the visits of Brigadier Senior. Lieutenant Colonel Clarke was succeeded by Lt. Col. Humphrey Woods D.S.O., M.C. He had a reputation for courageous leadership and quickly became a popular and skilful Commander.

The 8th Battalion was relieved on the 24th July. The bridgehead over the River Simeto was now well established. Ahead lay Catania, its harbour and airfields. The Germans were not prepared to give them up easily. The Catania–Mt. Etna position was extremely strong and favoured the defence. Observation of movements towards the city from Mt. Etna was excellent and, as the mountain swept down close to the coast, the line of advance from Catania onward was narrow. Demolition of roads and bridges slowed the advance and there was a constant danger of ambushes from a determined enemy. The positions taken over from the 8th Battalion lay west of the Catania road and in front of a farmhouse called Mass della Palma. The enemy was 900 yards away across open ground. Their positions were in the Fossa Bottaceto, a strong position comprising section posts and pillboxes well stocked with machine guns. The enemy also made skilful use of any farm buildings and shell craters, which became strong points. Mortar positions behind the Fossa constantly moved, thus making them difficult to identify. Amongst the mortars the Germans had a number of Nebelwerfers – multi-rocket mortar weapons that were very unpleasant and deadly. The positions taken over by the 9th Battalion were in a ditch that ran parallel to the Fossa. The ditch was seven feet deep and was a good natural defensive position.

There were no major attacks by either side during this period but active patrolling was carried out. The battalion's positions were heavily mortared, and each dawn and dusk the enemy fired sporadic bursts of machine gun fire, which caused little damage and no casualties. Primosole Bridge was subjected to shelling from time to time from artillery positions on the lower slopes of Mt. Etna. On the 25th of the month, a draft was received which comprised Lts. J.R. Blezard and J. Bannister and 2/Lts. C.M. Casey and R. Griffiths, together with 25 other ranks. On the 27th, the battalion was relieved by the 7th Green Howards of 69 Brigade and moved into a reserve area. Here, time was spent reorganising and resting.

On the 30th July, Maj. J.R. Scott reverted to the command of 'H.Q.' Company as Major Kneale arrived to take over as Second in Command of the battalion. The companies were reorganised and were commanded by the following:

'A' Company	Captain Lowe
'B' Company	Captain Rumble
'C' Company	Captain Russell
'D' Company	Captain Medway M.C.
'H.Q.' Company	Major Scott

At 11.30 p.m. on the 30th, the battalion relieved the 1st Bn. London Scottish of 168 Brigade in the right-hand sector of the front. Patrols were sent out and the usual enemy mortaring and shelling continued. In a further reorganisation, Captain Medway returned to command the Carrier Platoon and Lt. George Lanning took over 'B' Company from Captain Rumble who, in turn, went to 'D' Company.

On the 4th August, the enemy began to withdraw. The 8th Battalion followed them with the 9th in reserve. On the evening of the 4th, the two battalions exchanged positions. The outskirts of Catania were reached on the morning of the 5th August and Lt. Roy Griffiths was ordered to take a patrol into the city ahead of the battalion. He wrote:

> The following morning I was summoned to Battalion H.Q. and there was given orders to take a larger patrol, together with an official photographer, to gain entry into Catania. The patrol, which was substantial, consisted of myself, Lt. John Reid as my 2 i/c and 12 riflemen and NCOs. We took the same route as my former night patrol but diverted ½ mile or a mile distant from the roadblock. This was a comparatively good road into Catania and we attained the outskirts without contact with the enemy. The area was considerably damaged and the official photographer enjoyed his travels with us. I got to a

9 D.L.I. carriers enter Catania on 5 August 1943.

point in Catania where I decided to stop and report my location. The Battalion then entered the town and Capt. Brian Gardner was officially handed the keys. (The film of my entry into Catania was seen on *Gaumont British News Review* for 1943 – photographs of which can be seen at the D.L.I. Museum – and very much later in *The World at War, No.13.*)

'A' and 'C' Companies entered Catania at 8.30 a.m. on the morning of the 5th August, followed by battalion H.Q. and the remaining companies half an hour later. The civilians gave them a good reception. Cpl. Bob Cork of 'A' Company remembered the event:

5th August, we moved across the plain and through Catania. A great deal of looting (by civilians) was going on. I was given what turned out to be six boxes of 3-hole razor blades, they were shared out. The wine flowed.

Pte. Jim Ratcliffe entered Catania with 'C' Company. He recalled:

When we entered Catania, Jerry had just pulled out and we must have been a bit close on his heels because an armoured car suddenly appeared at the end of the street. I don't know who was more surprised, them or us. I know at the time I was busy smashing up some Italian rifles when there was a shout for all Bren guns to the end of the road. There was a wall at the end and across the open hillside we could see a few troops running about, so we rested our guns on the wall and had a high old time having a go at them. Bob (Lord) was by my side jumping up and down with excitement saying, 'Let me have a go', which I did.

The stay in the city was brief as it was imperative to clear the northern suburbs as soon as possible. The 6th Battalion had entered Catania about the same time. Battalion headquarters was established north of the city by mid afternoon. It was shelled during the move and Capt. Jim Kennedy, Adjutant, and Lieutenant Farrant were wounded and evacuated. Capt. 'Slim' Somerville took over as Adjutant. A number of civilians were also wounded and received attention at the regimental aid post. Battalion casualties were three killed and eight wounded. Amongst the dead were Ptes. J. Clarke and S. Johnson.

General Montgomery decided to shift the weight of the attack to the left flank. XXX Corps, reinforced by the 78th Division which had newly arrived from North Africa, was given the task of working its way around the west side of Mt. Etna and threaten the rear of the enemy forces defending the coast, a plan somewhat similar to that used at Mareth. The 50th Division would continue to slog its way up the narrow and easily defended coast road. A quotation in the *Times* newspaper of August 25th, 1943 seems appropriate. The correspondent wrote:

> I always had the feeling that the sheet anchor of the Army was the 50th Division. They had the hard, dirty work at Lentini and Primosole Bridge and the long slog up the coast from Catania, past Etna, through cruel country. They got less public mention than some of the other divisions because theirs was the unspectacular flank of the front. They plugged on, learning the new warfare the hard way, taking their punishment and coming on for more. Tyne and Wear may well be proud of them, for they are a grand division.

The Catania Plain had been left behind. From this time till the end of the campaign, the 50th Division slogged its way up the coastal road towards Messina. This road clung to the coastline and the edges of the mountains that swept down to the sea. It was ideal defensive country – extremely narrow, where manoeuvrability was virtually impossible. The road crossed many mountain rivers and streams by narrow bridges, which the retreating enemy destroyed. It was at these points and along the narrow, twisting road that the rearguards laid their ambushes, placed mines and laid booby traps. Many of the steep hillsides were terraced for the growing of vines and lemons. The enemy was fighting for time to allow the evacuation of the island across the Straits of Messina to continue. He had to be careful to ensure that his forces were not cut off by XXX Corps fighting its way around the west of Etna, but this was also desperately difficult terrain to fight and move in. Small and determined rearguards made clever use of the terrain to slow down the British advance and their success ensured the successful withdrawal to Italy before Messina was reached.

The 9th Battalion was ordered to take the crest of the hills north of Aci Castello. The advance began at 10 a.m. on the 6th August. 'A' and 'B' Companies moved astride the coast road and 'C' and 'D' Companies astride the Ficarazzi–Aci Castello road. 'C' Company attacked enemy

Cpl. R. Cork and three of his section in Acireale, Scily. Cpl. Cork is sitting on the ground with his left elbow propped against the step. L/Cpl. Bill Knox is by the door. He was killed in action by Cpl. Cork's side in Normandy.

pillboxes. The company came under severe mortar fire during this action and 30 casualties were suffered. Pte. Jim Ratcliffe had a lucky escape. He recorded:

> In Sicily, the hillsides are cultivated in huge terraces with vines and lemons growing in profusion. 'C' Company was climbing up these terraces to what looked like an anti-aircraft battery. All was going well until the enemy on the top came to life. I think they were actually pulling out. One of them came to the ledge above and saw us. He threw a grenade at me. I fired the Bren but the damned thing jammed and only let one off. It must have had some effect because the bomb missed us and went off harmlessly.

The enemy was driven off and a number of prisoners were taken. A civilian informed 'B' Company that the Aci Castello–Aci Trezzo road was mined and had an 88-mm gun positioned on it. The companies were making slow progress as they came under heavy mortar fire. By nightfall 'C' Company was held up. 'D' Company moved forward to a position on the right of 'C' Company. 'A' and 'B' Companies were astride the road south of Aci Castello. Further casualties were Second Lieutenant Casey and 25 other ranks wounded. Four other ranks were killed. During the night 'C' Company reported hearing detonations from the enemy positions and it was presumed that dumps were being destroyed. Aci Castello was reported clear. On the morning of the 7th, patrols were sent out as 'A' and 'B' Companies moved towards the town. Cpl. Bob Cork of 'A' Company was a member of one of these patrols. He wrote:

> Sgt. Bill Dimond was asked to go forward to check German positions on the hill in front...he asked me to accompany him and with my section Bren Gun we moved down through vineyards, across the railway lines and steadily made our way up the hill, getting whatever cover we could, covered each 20 yards or so by our Bren. Finally at the top we had to make a decision, had we been lucky or had Jerry gone?
>
> Suddenly, civilians appeared from the pink house at the top, rushing to greet us and feeding us with luscious fruit, cheese and wine. The men all kissed us, the women shook hands. After finding out that the enemy had really withdrawn, we asked them about the little village, Aci Castello I believe it was called, at the base [of the hill] and out of sight of the Company. They didn't really know if Jerry had left, so we thought, 'Well our luck's held this far we might as well check it out.'...When we got to the village, the population seemed jubilant and came across the crossroads, through some mines which had been laid. On the other side there was a very smart German soldier, spotlessly dressed. He turned out to be an Austrian who had been conscripted and had stayed behind when the Germans had withdrawn. With girls on either side we marched down to the mayor, the German included, the wine again flowed.
>
> Back then to give our C.O. our report. He remarked that he had watched us being kissed. Also he told us that the machine guns of the Middlesex Regiment had covered us all the way up the hill. Nice if he had told us before...

Enemy resistance stiffened as the British approached Acireale. Sherman tanks were called forward to support the infantry, whilst the Royal Navy shelled enemy troops north of the town. Corporal Cork and his section moved at the head of 'A' Company. He described:

> Further on the road curved and as we rounded this bend we came under fire from German Spandau gunners and had to dive for cover in a house and each time we tried to move the Germans opened up. Mortars were also falling and in amongst all this there was a civilian turning over and over a big wooden crate of shoes he'd looted. Every time a mortar dropped, he stopped and dropped down beside the crate...this same civilian tried to flog us shoes later. During the night the Germans, I suppose rearguard machine gunners and mortar troops, withdrew, for the next day we were able to move freely forward and take up positions on the other side of town. Then a civilian came up to me and said that some Italian soldiers wanted to give themselves up down in a railway tunnel. So, taking a couple of the lads with me, we went down and out they came loaded up with machine guns, grenades, rifles etc. There was quite a pile of these by the time they all came out, 86 of

them.

The enemy pulled out of Acireale during the evening of the 8th August. Battalion casualties included Lieutenant Burnett wounded and Ptes. G.E.L. Speight, T. Fox, A.E. Friend, E. Goddard, H.T. Miles and A.A. Summerfield killed. The advance continued on the 9th. 'C' Company relieved 'B' Company and advanced along the main Messina road. 'A' Company moved along the coast road. 'C' Company was ordered to push onto Puzzilo and 'D' Company was ordered to move along the coast road to the right of the main Messina road to Puzzilo Soprano. The Italians, in particular, were giving themselves up to the advancing troops. Pte. Tony Colgan's platoon captured a number of them. He recalled:

> The [railway] line went from going over the bridge straight into a cutting. Jerry spotted us and started shelling the cutting. It was pretty accurate shooting too. A civilian just behind me was hit and killed. We made a dive for cover and on looking up saw a cave on the other side of the track with a door and, who should be peeping from behind the door, but an Italian soldier who had a number of his mates as back-up…As soon as they saw me looking, they poked a little white flag out of the door. So that was all right…Off the platoon went and I kept the prisoners in the cave for a while. Until I threatened to shoot them all if they tried to get out, then left them to their fate and walked off to rejoin the platoon.

A total of 71 Italians were taken prisoner on the 9th August. Lieutenant Brett-James was killed and buried by the side of the road. Captain Russell was wounded along with two other ranks. W.O.II F. Thompson D.C.M., Cpl. B. Turner and Ptes. S. Bates, H.J. Daglish and W. Peel were killed or died of wounds. The battalion was relieved by the 6th Bn. D.L.I. on the 10th. The 9th relieved the 8th Bn. D.L.I. on the 12th August. Battalion headquarters was shelled by a 105-mm gun but no casualties were inflicted. No. 69 Brigade relieved 151 Brigade and the battalion moved back to the Puzzilo area. Orders for a further move were cancelled and 151 Brigade moved into reserve. 'C' Company was dissolved and its personnel transferred to the other three rifle companies to make them up to strength. No. 151 Brigade and the 9th Battalion were now resting and reorganising. On the 17th of the month, news arrived of the American entry into Messina just ahead of the British and confirmation that resistance on the island had ended. For the remainder of the month, the battalion followed a routine training programme. At 9 a.m. on the 22nd, a memorial service was held for comrades lost during the campaign. The service ended with the singing of the regimental hymn, 'Abide with Me'. General Montgomery spoke to all ranks on the 30th August. In his speech he praised the division for its efforts during the Sicilian campaign and made reference to the forthcoming invasion of Italy. It seemed that the division would not be taking part in early phases of this campaign. The question on everybody's mind was, 'Are we going home?' The General ended his speech by stating, 'Never forget, wherever I go I shall send for my 50th Division.' The groans of disappointment were clearly audible to the General. He quickly replied, 'You never know, I may be going home.' Cheers burst out from the assembled troops.

During the ensuing weeks training continued based on the experiences gained during the campaign. Training Directive No.1 was issued by Lieutenant Colonel Woods on the 14th August. Its opening remarks were:

> Recent and most valuable experience has been shown us that we have encountered in practice a new and extremely difficult form of warfare. We must expect to continue fighting under these conditions in the future, i.e. in very close country and in close contact with a retreating enemy…
>
> Lessons must be studied and we must…endeavour to ensure we achieve continued success with light casualties.

The directive goes on to emphasise the need for speedy decision making and aggressive action. It continues:

> I am convinced that it is the efforts of the Junior Commanders and individuals that must produce the successful penetration and maintain the momentum of the offensive….The maximum effort will therefore be made to improve the knowledge and training of the Junior Commander, in the hope that he will cultivate the sense of individual responsibility essential to the general success of his formation.

The directive lists the aims the training would accomplish. These included initiative, the making of rapid decisions, knowledge of enemy methods, the problem of rapid movement in close country, the use of ground and the saving of time. It ended with these remarks:

> I feel that if we all put the maximum effort into this very valuable two months ahead, we shall have derived the greatest benefit from it and be fully prepared to embark on our next and perhaps final operation of the war in Europe.

This directive seems to fly in the face of those critics of the 50th Division who claimed it was still steeped in wide open desert tactics after D-Day, which affected its performance in Normandy. The experience of Sicily and the training which followed would indicate that western desert tactics were being left behind and the new lessons learnt. Nevertheless, more training in fighting in close country would have been beneficial before D-Day.

At this time malaria was prevalent among Eighth Army troops. In fact this disease caused more casualties in Sicily than the actions of the enemy. Warnings were issued about improving the precautions against catching malaria and the dosage of mepacrine tablets was increased to six a week, one for every day except Sunday, and to be given with the evening meal.

The battalion was now based in the Giardini area. Italy was invaded by the Eighth Army on the 3rd September. A divisional concert was given on the 7th of the month with a performance by George Formby. This was attended by the Divisional

Commander, Maj. Gen. S.C. Kirkman O.B.E., M.C. and Brigadier Senior D.S.O. On the 20th September, preparations commenced for exercise 'Primosole' without revealing any details of the objective of the exercise. On the 23rd, Brigadier Senior lectured to the battalion and informed all ranks that 'Primosole' was the code name for a return to England. An excited brigade attended a concert by Gracie Fields on the following day.

Meanwhile training continued, whilst leisure activities organised were quizzes, tombola, whist and football along with a service club, the Hotel Moderto, which opened in Giardini. On the 9th October the immediate award of the Military Cross was announced to Capt. K.II. Whittaker. On the 12th, 32 other ranks rejoined the battalion from the 46th Division in Italy where they had been sent as replacements. On the 16th of the month the battalion moved to Augusta and embarked on the *Sibajack* the following day. The ship left for England on the 23rd October. It was almost two and one-half years since the battalion had left England, during which it had fought three major battles – Alamein, Mareth and Primosole Bridge – and lost many of its original members.

The end of the war in Sicily, 1943. Officers of 9 D.L.I. pose together prior to leaving for England.

CHAPTER XXI

PREPARATIONS FOR D-DAY

The journey to England was uneventful. The ship stopped at Algiers on the 25th October and left on the 27th. It passed through the Straits of Gibraltar on the 29th. The battalion was inspected in battledress on the 1st November. The convoy arrived at Gourock, Scotland on the 4th of the month. An advance party left the boat on the 6th to arrange for accommodation, which turned out to be at Wimbish Camp in Essex. The remainder of the battalion left the ship on the 7th of the month. Pte. Jim Ratcliffe recalled the return:

> We dropped anchor in the Clyde…We were taken off in lighters and put on trains. There were kids stood alongside the train offering to post letters for us. Many of us took them up on this offer and, to their credit, they posted them. My parents received the letter I sent reassuring them that I was uninjured and home. On the way to Saffron Walden, the train stopped at Newcastle and some of the lads could see their homes…You can imagine the language when the train pulled out.

The trains arrived at Saffron Walden at 5 a.m. on the 8th November. Trucks took the battalion to Wimbish Camp where hot tea was served on arrival. Lt. Donald Taylor remembered:

> We arrived in a thin drizzle and under grey clouds – both were as welcome as the green of the hills after the hot yellows of the Mediterranean.
> A long train journey and thence to a camp on the outskirts of Saffron Walden. The first night bitterly cold, piling on greatcoat and any other available extras. A warmer welcome home was provided by the local Girls' High School where senior scholars invited us to a dance. On arrival at the school, some sought Dutch courage, some turned into instant wallflowers, some took to the floor with adeptness and some of us just wracked our brains for what little elementary training we might have had in the waltz and foxtrot.

Leave was anxiously awaited and quickly organised. The first parties went on disembarkation leave on the 11th November. Men who had less than two years' service received two weeks' leave; those with more than two years were granted three weeks. From the 15th to the 25th November, the camp was closed as the whole battalion was on leave.

In the area near Wimbish Camp there were airfields of the American 8th Air Force as well as other units, many of whom had never been out of the country. The initial relationships were not particularly friendly and problems arose with fighting in the local towns and pubs. Severe warnings were issued that the name of the battalion was being disgraced by this behaviour. Not only the Americans but the civil police were having their problems with the newcomers. Lieutenant Colonel Woods issued orders that all N.C.O.s 'will co-operate with the battalion provost and civil police in arresting those responsible for the unnecessary lack of co-operation with our allies.' Ultimately, it took no less a person that General Eisenhower, the Supreme Commander of the Allied forces, to make a plea that such aggressive tendencies should be turned against the enemy and not against each other.

There was another area of disruption, which affected the brigade's relationship with higher command. 'Bull' was very much the practice of units who had not served abroad, meaning they exemplified 'spit and polish', correct dress, saluting officers and so on. The discipline in the desert was excellent, but it did not rely on correct dress and other 'regimental' activities. In particular, officers and men found themselves in hot water with higher authorities due to the informality of their dress. Gradually these problems were overcome and the battalion settled down to a period of intense training. It was obvious that a role for the division had been found in the forthcoming invasion of Europe. At that time, it was expected that it would be employed as a follow-up division, landing behind an assault division. When it was learned later that General Montgomery wanted his experienced 50th Division to assault Fortress Europe on D-Day, the initial response was one of great anger and disappointment. Many asked, 'Why are we to be first again? Why not send in one of the divisions who had never been out of England and had spent its time training for the invasion?' Men who had survived the severe battles in the Middle East and had seen so many comrades lost, contemplated that the odds against surviving again were very slim. They expected to fight again in Europe – the war had to be won – but another assault against the strongest defences, across open beaches, with an estimated casualty rate of 50 per cent…surely it had to be someone else's turn. However, the grouses quickly disappeared and the division got down to preparing for the greatest invasion in history.

The division had arrived in England with its personal weapons and equipment. It was now to be re-equipped. New vehicles appeared along with anti-tank guns and mortars. New battle tactics had been perfected in English infantry battle schools, which differed in certain aspects from the lessons learnt by the battalion in the desert. These new tactics had to be assimilated into the battle experience of the battalion. Training areas were organised for battalion, brigade and divisional exercises. Lt. Roy Griffiths wrote:

> Lt. Col. Woods, the Commanding Officer, felt that physical fitness was of the essence and all sporting activities were encouraged, with games of football with local soccer sides within the Essex County Football Association and other army units. Major George Lanning arranged rugby fixtures with various colleges at Cambridge. The 8th U.S.A.A.F. provided extremely up-to-date equipment and we were invited to join them in many sporting activities at Debden.

All disembarkation leave was completed by the 6th December. On the 11th, a letter from Gen. Sir John Burnett Stuart, Colonel Commandant of the Rifle Brigade, was published in Part 1 Orders:

> I happened to be here when there appeared in 'The Times' the list of awards for Sicily, including 4 M.C.s and 16 M.M.s won by the Durham Light Infantry and it occurred to me that we would very much like to offer you in the name of the Rifle Brigade, an expression of our admiration and our congratulations on so splendid a performance – and that is the friendly purpose of this note.

Reorganisation followed over the next few days. A draft of 28 other ranks joined on the 12th of the month. On the 21st, the regimental band visited and played for officers and men. On the evening of the 24th December a concert was performed in the camp dining hall by the Hotspots Concert Party from Saffron Walden. The traditional army Christmas was celebrated and the Commanding Officer announced that this day and Boxing Day would be a battalion holiday. On the 27th, the Hotspots returned to perform the pantomime *Cinderella*. Throughout the whole of the time that the battalion spent in this area, the kindness of the local civilian population was considerable.

Training in earnest commenced on the 3rd January 1944. There were conferences and lectures on 'Infantry Co-operation with Tanks' and 'Advance from a Bridgehead'. These were followed by actual training with tanks on the Thetford battle training area. On the 17th of the month, Maj. Gen. S.C. Kirkman C.B.E., M.C. informed the division that he was leaving. The new Commander was Maj. Gen. D.A.H. Graham C.B.E., D.S.O., M.C. On the 31st, Lieutenant Colonel Woods presented a silver bugle to the battalion. On the same day, a draft of eight officers and 26 other ranks joined the unit. Drafts continued to arrive over the next three months. On the 15th January, General Montgomery spoke to the brigade at Haverhill and after praising it once again for past efforts, he announced the division would be given a leading role in the forthcoming invasion already referred to above. This announcement was not received with enthusiasm. The immediate effect was that a number of men overstayed their privileged leave for a day or so. Excuses given on their return included 'missed trains' or 'family illness'. This was not desertion and Commanding Officers dealt with the culprits with understanding and some sympathy for men who had served so long abroad. When the time arrived for the invasion all units were up to full strength and morale was high. On the 23rd of the month, the brigade was inspected at Shudy Camp by H.M. King George VI.

Realism was added to the training by the use of live ammunition. Exercises 'Fox I' and 'Fox II' were carried out on the Stanford battle area. The appearance of heavy bicycles introduced a mobile role for one of the companies, and officers and men rode around the countryside mounted on these heavy beasts, dismounted and attacked 'enemy positions'. On the 12th March, the battalion moved to Southwold in Suffolk. Training here included working with flail tanks, breaching minefields and street fighting. These flail tanks, whilst working on the same principles as the Scorpions at Mareth, were updated and more efficient models. Also introduced to the battalion were some of the 'funnies' of the 79th Armoured Division, A.V.R.Es (Armoured Vehicle Royal Engineers) – an armoured bulldozer designed to cross anti-tank ditches and sea walls and destroy concrete defences. In addition there were 'crocodiles' – armoured flame throwers – and vehicles that could lay a carpet on sand and soft ground to enable tanks and transport to cross.

Towards the end of March, exercise 'Bullshead' was carried out in the Orford training area. In this exercise the battalion had to assault a strongly defended area covered by a deep minefield. The exercise was completed on the 28th. The following day an advance party left Southwold for the tented Toothill camp, which lay between Romsey and Southampton. The full battalion was assembled here by the 7th April. In the early days, the camp was far from comfortable. Heavy rain had made the site extremely muddy and wet. Work was immediately organised to lay duckboards and tidy up the area. Exercise 'Mobcol' – moving the battalion through the assembly area – was carried out on the 13th and 14th April. From the 16th to the 19th of the month, the 50th Divisional exercise 'Smash III' was undertaken. This exercise enabled the division to practice embarking on L.C.I.s (landing craft infantry), sailing out into the Channel and landing on the beaches at Studland. The objective entailed a march of about 16 miles. When reached, the battalion dug in, prepared defences and carried out night patrols. Valuable lessons were learned, particularly on speed of approach. The brigade had taken too long to reach this, largely due to the three battalions advancing along the same axis.

Exercise 'Fabius' was the next major exercise to be carried out. This commenced on the 1st May and involved landing infantry and vehicles on an open beach. Again, the battalion put to sea in American-manned L.C.I.s, with the transport boarding L.C.T.s (landing craft tanks). A landing was made on the beaches of Hayling Island on the 4th May. It was a wet landing, the officers and men wading through waist-deep water to reach the shore. The battalion then marched to Leigh Park where it bivouacked for the night. It rained and there was little comfort, but the whole purpose of the exercise was to simulate battle conditions as near as possible. Further training continued on the 5th and 6th. The battalion returned to Toothill camp on the 7th, and eventually moved to Camp 16 in Nightingale Woods. Conditions here were better: each man had a camp bed and trees and flowers were in full bloom outside the tents. General Eisenhower again spoke to the battalion on the 13th May. He emphasised that efforts be made to get to know the Americans who were their comrades in the great invasion that lay ahead. He knew of the fighting experience and qualities of the division, and knew these would be further enhanced in the fighting to come. He recognised the Africa Star with the number eight (for the Eighth Army), now worn by every man who had served out there and told them that they should be proud to wear it. It was a talk which went down extremely well with all ranks. Maj. H.J. Mogg joined the battalion from the 61st Division Battle School on the 27th May. He never forgot his first encounter with the Geordies:

When I walked through to meet my new C.O., I saw almost every soldier had campaign ribbons on their manly breasts and quite a lot of them had M.C.s, D.C.M.s, M.M.s and I was at a slight disadvantage having not seen a shot fired in anger…I only had a small medal on my chest, which was a Coronation Medal. Apart from that I found I might well have been in a foreign country. I just did not understand the Geordie language. I don't think they understood me. It took me quite a long time to get through to people with this wonderful Geordie accent. Now I can speak Geordie pretty well myself…and I soon got to know the Geordie songs.

The composition of the battalion at the end of May 1944 was as follows:

Battalion Headquarters

Commanding Officer	Lt. Col. H.R. Woods, D.S.O., M.C.
Second in Command	Maj. H. J. Mogg
Adjutant	Capt. R.C. Rickett
Intelligence Officer	Lt. J.D. Reid

Headquarter Company

Officer Commanding	Capt. G. Lanning
Signals Officer	Lt. J.L. Brooker
Motor Transport Officer	Lt. E.N. Hooper
Quartermaster	Capt. A.E. Love M.C.

Support Company

Officer Commanding	Capt. K.M. Wood
Carrier Platoon	Capt. B.J. Gardner
Anti-Tank Platoon	Capt. K.H. Whittaker
Assault Pioneer Platoon	Lt. J.L. Williams
Mortar Platoon	Lt. L.C. Phillips

'A' Company

Officer Commanding	Maj. C.M. D'Arcey-Irvine

'B' Company

Officer Commanding	Maj. J.L. Kennedy

'C' Company

Officer Commanding	Maj. J.H.W. Hudson

'D' Company

Officer Commanding	Maj. L.E.V. Rumble

The camp was sealed on the 26th May. No one could get in or out without permission and a pass. Perimeter guards were provided by the Americans. With the exception of dates and names, final preparations were being made for the invasion. Officers, N.C.O.s and men poured over maps and models of the beaches they were to land on. Defences were examined and landmarks put to memory. Briefings took place daily. Each man was to know the plan of the invasion and his role in it, without revealing specific names and locations. The mighty support of the Royal Navy and the Allied air force was explained. It seemed that little was left to chance. Capt. Roy Griffiths recalled:

> The briefing by the Commanding Officer to all officers was quite concise and precise. Every single support craft of the Navy was itemised to us from the map covering our section of the beach…The beach, with naval support craft from the very large warships right down to the rocket ships, was shown. The three divisions, which were supposedly opposing us on the beach, were each known and a description of each was given to us. The information was then passed to the troops down to rifleman level a very short time before the operation commenced. We still did not know, on our company level, the true date of the assault.

All vehicles had to be waterproofed to enable them to land from the sea. Cpl. Tony Colgan of the Mortar Platoon had to ensure that his carrier was able to land in water, if necessary:

> We had the carriers parked a mile or so away, under a line of trees and in amongst long grass. BOSTIK was the stuff, black, gooey BOSTIK, it stuck to everything, especially as we were using large quantities of it. Each driver had the responsibility of ensuring that his particular carrier was up to the job in hand and we took the job seriously, going over and over every part of the carrier which looked as if it might need some BOSTIK on it. There were large metal panels to be fitted to the front, back and sides, to enable it to go through deep water and these had to be sealed with a heavy cloth which, in turn, had to be BOSTIKED…Whilst we were doing this, our padre painted names on the carriers, mine being AMPHION.

Prior to being sealed into the camp, desertions or absence without leave continued to be a nuisance rather than a worry. Officers understood the need to see loved ones before going into action at the sharp end of the invasion. Obviously it could not be countenanced but the men involved were treated with quite remarkable leniency. Maj. John Mogg recalled:

> The old and the bold who had been through the whole thing, they thought they were perhaps coming back to England to an easier time but not to be selected to be the first ones to be thrown into the invasion…because they had been at it solidly since arriving in the desert until they came out of Italy [Sicily]. They had been fighting practically the whole time. The D.L.I. of all Regiments probably had more battalions fighting than any other regiment. I think I am right in saying that and particularly 6th, 8th and 9th D.L.I. of 151

Brigade. They had been in the thick of everything all the way through…There were quite a lot of deserters, I simply can't remember the figures, but just before we sailed an awful lot of them returned… For being absent without leave in the country, they were treated fairly leniently because we said, 'Alright, we need you back, you know the Battalion.'

Landing Craft Infanctry (L.C.I.) in Southampton Dock – 1–3 June 1944.

Capt. Roy Griffiths also recorded his views on those taking leave without permission:

> In the 9th Battalion, we had three lads who went home to see their mother. They were East Enders and Humph [Lieutenant Colonel Woods] said, 'I'm not going to worry. I know these lads very well. They will be back. They are my three best snipers and they will be back.' And sure enough, it was days before we went on the landing craft, back they came. Humph said, 'Try them and we will give them seven days' C.B. or something.' Then he said, 'What is the point, we're all confined to barracks we can't get out.'

On the 31st May, the Foreign Secretary Sir Anthony Eden visited the brigade and the battalion. His family seat was in County Durham and he was well received by all ranks. The well-rehearsed and organised machine, which would put thousands of men and equipment onto the beaches of Normandy, was set in motion. Operation Bigot Neptune, which dealt with the embarking of troops onto landing craft, the naval and air role and the safe passage across the Channel to the invasion beaches, was a phenomenal undertaking. It dealt with the movement of ships and aircraft on a grand scale and the more mundane objectives of feeding and preparing the soldiers for the crossing and landings. The following appeared in one of the operational orders:

> Relations with Civilians: A high standard of behaviour must be maintained. The reputation of the British Forces and the attitude of liberated countries both during the hostilities and subsequently will depend for a very great extent on the conduct of the military forces and their regard of the rights and property of the local inhabitants.

On the 3rd June, the battalion moved in transport to Southampton docks, less non-fighting vehicles who were scheduled to land on D+4 and D+17. It embarked on three L.C.I.s manned by American crews. At the dock side to see them off was Prime Minister Winston Churchill, Ernest Bevin the Minister of Labour and Field Marshall Smuts. The battalion was divided into three parties. One party was under the Commanding Officer Lt. Col. H.R. Woods and consisted of 'B' Company (Maj. J.L. Kennedy) and half 'H.Q.' Company (Major Lanning) and 'S' Company (Capt. K. Wood). Maj. H.J. Mogg commanded the second party, which consisted of 'C' Company (Major Hudson) and the remainder of 'H.Q.' and 'S' Companies. The third party under the command of Maj. D'Arcy Irvine with 'A' Company and 'D' Company (Major Rumble).

The invasion was postponed for 24 hours due to adverse weather conditions. It was a period of increasing boredom, which the authorities attempted to alleviate by allowing parties of troops ashore and onto the quay. Baths had been organised, recreation activities were available and N.A.A.F.I. goods could be purchased. With the assistance of the American navy, sing-songs were organised in the evening. On the evening of the 5th, after sailing, maps were issued and final briefings took place. The invasion was on for the next day.

At 8 p.m., the L.C.I.s moved down the Solent and reached the open sea half an hour later. During the journey a tremendous ovation was heard from warships they passed. There were ships everywhere, an enormous armada waiting to sail forth. The occasion was not lost on the battalion and officers and men were reassured by the mighty force lying about them. Battalion morale was at a high level, and the 9th was prepared for what lay ahead.

Loading L.C.Is. for D-Day – 1 June 1944. Lt. John Arnold is standing centre right with his back to the camera and his hands in his pockets.

CHAPTER XXII

D-DAY & THE BATTLE FOR NORMANDY

The invasion of Europe on the 6th June, 1944 has been more than adequately covered in many outstanding books and it is not the purpose of this book to go over that ground. Suffice to give the reader an outline of the invasion plans in which to set the role of the 9th Battalion. The invasion area was divided into five beaches to be attacked as follows.

On the west flank, the American 4th Division was to land on Utah Beach, west of the River Vire and on the south-east corner of the Cotentin Peninsula. Omaha Beach lay to the east of the River Vire in the area of Verville-Sur-Mer–St. Laurent–Colville. It was to be assaulted by the American 1st and 29th Divisions. Moving east, the next landing was by the 50th Division on Gold Beach between Le Hamel and La Rivière. The 3rd Canadian Division was to land on Juno Beach on either side of Courseulles. The British 3rd Division was to land on the eastern flank on Sword Beach in the area of Oiustreham. To assist the landings on each flank and secure vital routes out of the beachheads, the American 82nd and 101st Airborne Divisions were to drop in advance of the infantry on the west flank and the British 6th Airborne Division was to be dropped on the eastern flank. The latter's tasks were to secure the bridges and crossings over the River Orne. The 50th Division in XXX Corps would land on a two-brigade front, 231 Brigade on the right and 69 Brigade on the left. No. 56 Brigades and 151 Brigade were the follow-up and would pass through 231 and 69 when they had established the bridgehead. No. 231 Brigade and 56 Brigade would land on Jig Green and Jig Red Beaches, whilst 69 and 151 Brigades would land on King Green and King Red Beaches. The initial landing was timed for 7.25 a.m. on the 6th June. The enemy coastal defences would be pounded by air and naval bombardments prior to the landings. The transport of the 50th Division to France took 520 ships.

The journey was not comfortable. The men were in the bottom of these unwieldy vessels sleeping on bunks. The sea was rough and they were tossed about. Many suffered from seasickness. Maj. John Mogg remembered the journey:

> We got into the Channel. It was a bit poppery and bobbery. Quite a lot of the sailors were feeling a bit sick. The American Lieutenant came to me and said, 'Major I don't think you look too happy.' I said, 'I'm OK, don't worry.' He said, 'I think I have got something that will do you good. Come up to my cabin.' He gave me the strongest Brandy I think I've ever had in my life and on top of it, he put a whole lot of pineapple juice. It was the most extraordinary drink. I said, 'I thought you American ships ought to be dry, you weren't supposed to drink anything.' He said, 'This is purely for medicinal purposes. I

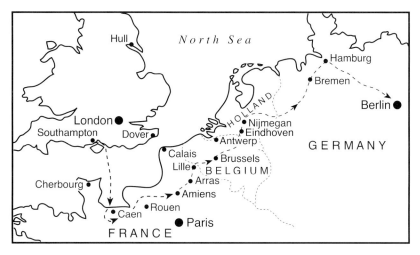

D-Day to Berlin – Route of 9 D.L.I.

don't feel too good myself, so I'll have one too.'

During the crossing there was no sign of enemy craft or air force. The atmosphere was one of considerable seriousness and great purpose. Lt. John 'Darkey' Williams, commanding the Assault Pioneer Platoon, wrote:

> Later I had the opportunity to study the men again when I toured the holds at 'Pipe-down'. I found men putting final touches of oil on their weapons, talking in ardent under-tones of their particular job or of their intentions, i.e. the enemy. (How remarkable that at times like this profanity is non-existent.)
> I could hear always above us the drone of fighters – what a sweet, comfortable sound, One amusing incident, as we were negotiating a lane in the outer enemy minefield…Suddenly, off the port bow a matter of yards, there appeared the ugly spiked shape of a mine. It did not appear to be secured, just floating free on the surface. Our craft heeled steeply over as the helmsman swung sharply to starboard and, as a little chap regained his balance, he called to his friend in a thick Durham accent, 'Look 'Arry, a cow upside down!'

Cpl. Tony Colgan was far from comfortable. He wrote:

> Sleep during the night was limited as we were all keyed up for what was to be the biggest invasion in history. But, of course, the sleeping arrangements were rather primitive. I tried sleeping on the toolbox attached to the front of the carrier. It was only about four feet long and one foot wide. It was unsuccessful. Next I tried sleeping in the driving seat, but it was just not made with that in mind, so all in all, it was a pretty uncomfortable time.

The journey across the Channel was uneventful. There was complete air superiority and no enemy aircraft appeared. At 10.20 a.m. on the 6th June, the battalion landed on its allotted beach on the Normandy coast. Two of the L.C.I.s landed safely though

L.C.I. beached at La Rivière, Normandy, 6 June 1944.

not without incident. The Commanding Officer's boat struck a mine a few yards from the beach. Fortunately, it did no damage. Major Mogg's boat struck a sunken L.C.I., which was broadside onto the beach. This meant that the troops had to clamber over the remains of the L.C.I. and then into about three feet of water to reach the beach. Major Mogg wrote:

The first two shells, which landed in the water fairly near the boat, destroyed any signs of seasickness on us, on any soldiers at all. They wanted to go like mad to get out of it. We had to jump into about three feet of water and wade ashore and there were lots of obstacles to get ashore and we had to climb over them. The only casualties we had, we lost the Signal Sergeant. He jumped into, somehow or other, an enormous, great hole full of water and he went down and never came up again. That was the only casualty we had on the beaches.

It was not so easy to get off the craft. Capt. Eric Hooper recalled:

They'd issued us with some oil-skimmed trousers, which came right up to your chest, gasproof type, same material. They came up to your chest and you tied them with a string in a bow. They dropped the ramps. I was standing on the top of the ramp when we hit an underwater mine and that obviously exploded and blew the ramp up. I got a hell of a shock through my feet though it didn't affect me. I never thought when I went down, with the mine going off, it made a hole in the sand and, of course, I had my map board in one hand and I must have had something in the other hand. I got into the water and I couldn't touch the bottom and I started to float. The air came up, it was compressing the air in the trousers, up to my chest and I started to get buoyant and I was going over. Just then with the pressure of the water it burst the trousers and, of course, I went down. Fortunately by then, I was on the bottom and I could walk ashore. It was a nice feeling that.

'C' Company formed the mobile column. Lt. Donald Taylor wrote:

Our landing on Gold Beach was delayed and, in what for landlubbers, was a nasty swell. We circled for an hour and more until, if not seasick, we were certainly sick of it and glad to get ashore. We had been issued with bicycles to get inland a bit faster. Someone had forgotten his, so I staggered down the ramp with one on each shoulder (and spare under-clothes in my tin hat). Some way on the bikes were piled at the field edge and we marched on.

The men, laden down with their heavy weapons and equipment, waded ashore. Every beach had its beachmaster, whose task it was to get units off the beaches quickly before the arrival of the next wave of troops. Pte. Richard Atkinson recalled:

I remember him [the Beachmaster] shouting, 'Get off my bloody beach!' We replied, 'We don't want to be on your bloody beach!'

Lieutenant Williams was able to get a quick look at what was happening on the beach. He wrote:

In a matter of minutes my chaps were ashore and shedding their waders (a ghastly garment that went over your equipment and completely waterproofed the wearer up to the chest). While my chaps were splashing ashore, I found time to scan the beaches. The 69th Brigade had not found it so very easy. I saw the water lapping the muzzle of a submerged anti-tank gun. The wheels of an armoured car, completely turned over, spinning lazily as the tide struck them. There was an L.C.I. down by the shore to the left of me and there were other signs of resistance at the water's edge.

It struck me suddenly, as I looked about, that all this noise and violence which was in the air, had Jerry on the receiving end. Even as I thought, I saw a mortar bomb fall near

British troops coming ashore from L.C.Is, D-Day, 6 June 1944, heavily laden with equipment and some with bicycles. The latter were quickly dispensed with.

a group of naval ratings and two of them lay down as though they were very tired.

Cpl. Tony Colgan, of the Mortar Platoon, also had a wet landing. He wrote:

We must have landed in about 5 or 6 feet of water. I know I could not see anything through my visor, except water. The carrier commander had to direct me towards the beach. Then, gradually, we saw the light of the sandy beach. 'Everything alright?' I said to the rest of the crew. 'Yes', said Di Boyland, 'I put my finger over the only bit you missed!' Cheek!

Once on the beach, the battalion moved to the assembly area north-east of Meuvaines. The stay here was longer than anticipated and it was not until 4.05 p.m. that orders were received to move forward. A mobile column had been formed comprising 'C' Company on bicycles – quickly dumped – two sections of carriers and the anti-tank gun sections of the battalion, the 288th Anti-Tank Battery, two sections of mortars, a platoon of medium machine guns and Forward Observation Officers for the R.A.F. and artillery. It had been impressed upon all officers of the mobile column, to press ahead at all speed and reach the day's objective astride the Bayeux–Caen road. Similar orders were given to the 6th

Normandy – 6 June – 31 July 1944

274

Battalion, which was moving on a parallel route on the battalion's left. Bold action was called for and artillery support, when required, was laid on. In addition the R.A.F. was on call to give ground support.

The mobile column moved off followed by the main body. There was brief contact with bodies of enemy troops, most of whom were inferior in quality. Most were from the 716th Coastal Defence Division, which comprised two regiments, each of three battalions, and was largely of foreign troops from Germany's conquered countries. The 642nd and 644th Ost Battalions included White Russians, Georgians and other east European nationals, commanded by German officers and N.C.O.s. The move forward was not without incident. Pte. Jim Radcliffe recalled:

> At the briefing back in England we had been told that 'C' Company on bikes, a section of Bren carriers, a section of anti-tank guns (6-pdrs.) and a section of 3" mortars would leave the assembly area and go as fast as we could and occupy this small ridge before the 21st Panzer got to it. We thought this was hilarious, they would have rode all over us. Anyway we set off and we had been going along this road for a few minutes when a dozen Typhoons started bombing and strafing the road a few hundred yards ahead of us. The last plane was coming in for his two-penny-worth when he saw our column. He turned and came straight down at us, his cannons blazing and he dropped a couple of bombs, which lucky for us landed in soft earth in the fields. Back in England we had sewn our aircraft recognition panels into big sheets, so we laid these out. The pilot spotted them on his second run in and veered off, with quite a few shouts to the effect of doubting his parentage ringing in his ears, though he was not really to blame. Only forward troops should display recognition signals but the clowns back on the beaches were doing it.

The advance of the mobile column was not as quick as had been hoped. The long delay in the assembly area did not help the situation. It was found quite difficult to move quickly through the narrow village streets, particularly for carriers and tanks. It was soon obvious that the objective would not be reached before dark and orders were given to dig in short of it but to move quickly the following morning to capture it. The mobile column had reached the Sommervieu area at about 6.30 p.m. and spent the next hour clearing it of the enemy. The main body reached Cauge Ferme, south-east of Sommervieu, and dug in for the night. The first contact with civilians was made and was not always what had been expected. The Allies were not always seen as conquering heroes who had arrived to release the population from an oppressive and cruel invader. By and large, most civilians lived quietly alongside their German overlords and going about their timeless country activities. Over the following days, troops found the welcome at best muted. Pte. R. Atkinson described:

> The civilians really didn't want you there. They weren't too happy because you only brought death and destruction. The Germans treated them well, because they were feeding the Germans and the food was going back to Germany. It was beautiful, lush farming and there were all the cows, legs up in the air. They were all dead. Livestock had been killed in the fields. They didn't want us because we'd killed all their stuff and we were

pinching their wine. The Germans hadn't done anything like that. So there was no love lost at this stage…We wrecked their houses and killed their stock.

Tragically, when help was needed the forward troops, under strict orders to get on as quickly as possible, were not able to assist.

During the night of the 6th/7th, a strong enemy patrol bumped into 'B' Company and the defences around battalion headquarters. A firefight ensued and the enemy were driven off after suffering a number of casualties. The battalion lost one man killed and one wounded.

The Allies were ashore. Fortress Europe had been breached and though many battles were to be fought in the days ahead, Hitler's hold on Europe was broken.

At 6 a.m. on the 7th June, the advance was continued and the battalion reached its final objective of the previous day. The importance of this was obvious as, being on a ridge, the invasion beaches could be clearly seen. With such good observation, enemy artillery would have made a successful landing extremely difficult to achieve. Cachy, south of Bayeux, was reached by the mobile column and the main body came up and the position was consolidated by 8.40 a.m. Five men were killed on the 6th/7th June. Ptes. H. Harmer, who had been with the battalion for 16 months and was a bricklayer from Sussex, E. Cossom from Middlesex, both 'B' Company, W.F. Hartill, C.W. Griffiths and W.F.A. Cronin.

Brigadier Senior had been wounded on the previous day and had a narrow escape from capture by German troops in the area. He had hidden until it was safe to move and then made his way back to the brigade. His wounds were such that he was evacuated. He was replaced by Brig. B.B. Walton, who was wounded on the 16th June. He was replaced by Brig. D.S. Gordon.

The battalion was now entering the Bocage, that area of the Norman countryside that was made up of small fields surrounded by high hedges, which, in turn grew on top of thick banks and were almost impenetrable. It was an area of narrow, twisting lanes, isolated farms and small villages. Each farm, hamlet and village had been turned into a fortress by the enemy. Orchards and woods dotted the landscape. Deeper into the Bocage were the steep hills and narrow river valleys of Suisse Normandy. It was difficult countryside to fight over: easy to defend by a stubborn enemy and yet favoured good infantry tactics. It is during this period that the 50th Division was criticised and it is opportune at this point in the narrative that the reader should understand this in context

The main criticism was that the division, influenced by western desert experience, used the wrong tactics during this part of the campaign. Maj. John Mogg, who had just joined the battalion from battle school, later recalled:

> There is no doubt they were too slow to appreciate it as first class infantry country to be made use of and not feared. At first we were slow to dig slit trenches, we were inclined to use houses, which were apt to become artillery targets and were more frequently booby-

trapped. We were slow to use the ground as infantry country and expected to move behind heavy artillery barrages and air strikes in the nature of the battles in the Western Desert. Carrier platoons were of little value except to help in quick consolidation or dismounted as an extra infantry platoon. The anti-tank platoon had to be content with short fields of fire and the mortars came into their own with a vengeance, learning to fire off maps instead of by direct observation and doing so with deadly effect.

The battalion learnt these lessons quickly under Major Mogg when he succeeded to command during the battle at Lingèvres. However many of the officers and men serving with the division were unable to agree with all of the criticism. Maj. Roy Griffiths of the battalion wrote after the war:

Some books I read after the war about morale of the troops who came back from the desert, that the reason why there was a slow advance in Normandy was because we were rather wary of and inexperienced in the Bocage country because we were so used to the wide open spaces of the desert. But *no one* was experienced in the Bocage country.

There were these high hedges at the sides of the roads and *no one* was experienced and the most people who got the most stick, quite honestly, were the lads in the tanks, because they couldn't see. They could see straight up the roads but couldn't see over the high hedges and what was in the cornfields…It is true to say, that when we achieved our objectives we were never pushed off. What we took we held always and to say that morale was low in 50 Div. or 7th Armed Div. is absolute arrant nonsense and it makes my blood boil.

It seems a fair point that, in the Normandy fighting, all divisions in the Allied armies, British and American, showed inexperience when in the Bocage. These included those divisions which had been training for three years in the United Kingdom and who had the advantage of learning the lessons of the war away from the battlefields and had time to incorporate those lessons into training manuals and exercises. The lessons of the Bocage had to be learnt as the fighting progressed. The lack of appreciation of the problems that fighting in the Bocage would bring was not understood by the planning staffs of the invasion forces. Helmut Wilhelmsmeyer wrote in his article 'From Invasion to Breakout':

The terrain played a big part in the progress of the campaign. Despite their vast planning staffs, the Allies had failed to appreciate the effect that the Normandy Bocage would have upon mobility. The whole countryside was intersected by high solid earth walls topped by dense bushes and trees. Not only was movement impaired but fighting ranges were extremely short – something which the defenders turned to excellent advantage. It was some time before the Americans developed an attachment to go on the front of a Sherman tank which could break through the impenetrable hedgerows.

Patrols were sent out. Enemy tanks, reported to be in the Guéron area, were shelled by British artillery. Ellon was still held by the enemy and infantry and tank activity was reported. At midday a carrier patrol entered Ellon and came back with a prisoner. Ellon was taken by 'C' Company, supported by carriers and artillery, at 7.05 p.m. The battalion remained in this area for the next three days. Patrols reported enemy tanks in the area from time to time, which invariably were engaged and chased off. At 10.30 p.m. on the 12th, the battalion moved to Bernières Bocage where it dug in and sent out patrols. The following day, enemy tanks were again sighted in front of the forward companies' positions. At 10.55 a.m., 'C' Company came under attack from heavy mortar and machine gun fire. It was holding a position south-east of Bernières Bocage. Wounded men were lying out in the open. Pte. John Hibble, a stretcher bearer, moved out without orders and brought in the wounded under heavy enemy fire. He was to repeat these brave deeds on the following day during the attack on Lingèvres. He was awarded the Military Medal.

On a ridge crossing the front of the advancing 50th Division and barring the road to Villers Bocage (an important junction about 20 miles from the coast) lay the Tilly Sur Seulles–Balleroy road and this became the next divisional objective. It was vital that this road be taken quickly. The plan included orders for the 7th Armoured Division to advance towards Tilly Sur Seulles, which commenced on the 10th June. It made only slow progress against pockets of resistance by small groups of enemy infantry armed with anti-tank weapons. On the 12th, its objective was switched and it was ordered to advance and take Villers Bocage and Pt. 213 north-east of the town. With his rear so threatened it was hoped that the enemy would pull back his forces confronting the 50th Division and the country south to Villers Bocage would be cleared. The enemy would be caught between the hammer – the 50th Division – and the anvil of the 7th Armoured Division. Unfortunately, the tanks of the latter were caught by the 2nd Panzer Division that was arriving at the front, and suffered heavy casualties and had to withdraw. The 50th Division could do nothing to help as it was held up on the Tilly–Bayeux road.

The 50th Division plan was for 151 Brigade to advance on the left against the villages of Lingèvres and Verierres and 231 Brigade to advance on the right towards La Senaudière. The 9th Battalion's objective was the village of Lingèvres on the Balleroy–Tilly Sur Seulles road, whilst the 6th Battalion attacked the village of Verrières to the north-east. By the afternoon of the 13th June, the 9th Battalion was south-east of Bernières Bocage. Lieutenant Colonels Woods and Green, commanding 9th and 6th Battalions respectively, were summoned to brigade headquarters for orders. Brigadier Walton ordered that the villages were to be attacked early next day. Major Mogg recalled:

> He [Colonel Woods] didn't say so ever, and he was killed later and he never said so but I heard afterwards that when he had the orders, he said to the Brigadier, 'Brigadier, you know if we do this we shall have a tremendous number of casualties. We ought to do this attack at night and we ought to have some time for reconnaissance.' And the Brigadier said, 'I know that but I have been told this is a desperately important battle. We've got to get this village. We've got to go on so that the breakout can continue from the beachhead

and if we don't do it now, we may well find that the opposition is stiffening up all the time, so we've got to do it.'

On returning to the battalion, Lieutenant Colonel Woods held an 'O' Group and issued his orders for the attack. He showed no concerns about the difficulty of the task or possible casualties – the hallmark of good leadership to always exude confidence. In the time available on the 13th, 'B' Company (Maj. J.L. Kennedy) was ordered to reconnoitre the enemy ground that lay ahead.

It is important to describe the terrain over which the attack was made. The 9th Battalion moved into a wood north of Lingèvres. Between it and its objective was a flat, open cornfield, the corn of which was about three feet high. At the opposite side of the cornfield were woods that screened the village. The church tower showed above the trees along with one or two roofs of the houses. A country road ran down the right side of the cornfield into the village and, just short of the village on the right of the road, was a farm with a walled enclosure. The positions held by the enemy were not known, in depth or in strength. The enemy obviously held the woods and the ditch on its edge, and had excellent observation and fields of fire across the open cornfield. Unknown to

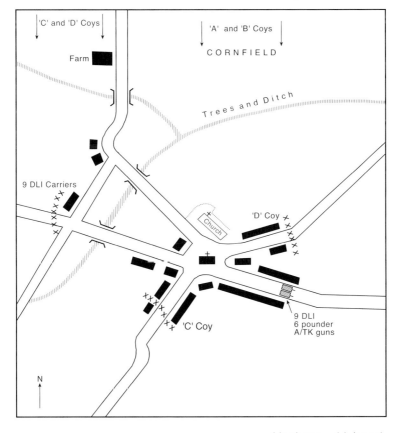

Lingèvres – 14 June 1

the Durhams the enemy had cut the corn about 60 yards short of the woods he held. This was his carefully prepared killing ground.

Maj. C.M. D'Arcy Irvine, commanding 'A' Company, described 'B' Company's reconnaissance:

> In order to estimate or indeed confirm the enemy strength here, it was decided to carry out a reconnaissance in force at almost Company strength, that evening in daylight. 'B' Company (Kennedy) was selected to do this, supported by the Carrier Platoon and a F.O.O. I watched this attack from my Company position and it gave me a fair indication of what we might expect the next day…'B' Company and the carriers were allowed to get right out into the standing corn with only some mortaring and sporadic automatic fire until they were within sixty or seventy yards of the edge of the woods. They were then subjected to withering fire and forced to withdraw very hurriedly suffering considerable casualties. Two German tanks were seen during this attack and one of them was, in fact, brewed up by a tracked anti-tank gun of the Northumberland Hussars, from my Company position. This reconnaissance in force had shown that without doubt the enemy were in strength and probably seasoned and well trained troops, capable of withholding their fire until it would be most effective.

'B' Company's losses were very heavy and included most of its officers. During this Company's action, L/Cpl. Leslie William Smith displayed courage and devotion to duty for which he was awarded the Military Medal. His citation read:

> On the afternoon of the 13th June 1944 near Bernières Bocage, there were two sections of carriers in support of 'B' Company, 9 D.L.I. During the attack the carriers' commander's carrier was hit by an anti-tank shell. In the confusion immediately following, L/Cpl. Smith was conspicuous in rallying the carriers. Eventually the carriers were withdrawn behind 'B' Company's H.Q. L/Cpl. Smith then volunteered to collect the wounded. In face of enemy M.G. fire he drove in front of the enemy's positions four times. He drove the carrier himself and collected the wounded without help other than smoke and supporting fire from a troop of tanks behind him. It was not until he satisfied himself that all that could be done had been done that L/Cpl. Smith returned to his own lines. His example was an inspiration for those who had witnessed him and he showed great devotion to duty and a complete disregard for his own safety.

Patrols were sent out during the night but failed to get a clear picture of the enemy dispositions. It was obvious by now that the enemy was in considerable strength and willing to fight to defend his positions. It was later discovered that the German troops were panzer grenadiers of the Panzer Lehr Division. This division was a training and demonstration division, staffed by veteran officers and N.C.O.s who had seen much action in Russia, Poland and the desert. The troops were young, fit and zealous. It was arguably one of the finest divisions in the German army at that time. It had lost a number of tanks and wheeled vehicles to Allied aircraft, whilst travelling from its base near Chartres. It was still a formidable opponent.

The attack by 151 Brigade on Verrières and Lingèvres was timed to start at 10.15

a.m. on the 14th June. The attack by 231 Brigade was timed for 11.30 a.m. in order for both brigades to benefit from the full force of the artillery support. This support was considerable and comprised the 86th, 90th and 147th Field Regiments (self-propelled), and the whole of the 5th Army Group Royal Artillery of three field regiments, three medium regiments, a heavy regiment and an American artillery battalion. The barrage would fall on the edge of the woods held by the Germans and then roll forward as the Durhams advanced behind it. About 15 minutes before the attack started, Typhoon aircraft would drop an estimated 120 tons of bombs and would fire rockets into the woods. In addition the brigade was supported by Sherman tanks of the 4th/7th Royal Dragoon Guards under the command of Major d'Avigdor-Goldsmid. This support comprised three troops of tanks and had already worked out an efficient system of co-operation with infantry. The battalions carried yellow reflecting panels to mark its position to friendly aircraft. These were tied to the end of rifles and waggled in the air and then pointed in the direction of any concealed enemy positions. The Tank Commanders then took appropriate action. It proved to be a simple but effective system.

At the appointed time prior to the infantry moving off, the artillery opened up and poured a huge weight of fire power on the enemy positions at the edge of and in the woods in front of the village. Then the Typhoons joined in. Lieutenant Williams recalled:

> We were treated to a front seat at a very accurate and sustained 25pdr. barrage and the woods literally jumped and danced in front of of our eyes and not three hundred yards away…The Typhoons, each one, did one dive and each one released two bombs and 10 rockets, straddled and plastered that wood. Surely nothing could live in that now.

At the edge of the woods opposite and across the cornfield, the 9th Battalion formed up along a track that crossed the front of the woods. Lieutenant Colonel Woods attacked with 'A' Company on the left, followed by a much weakened 'B' Company. On the right, 'C' Company led followed by 'D' Company. Lieutenant Colonel Woods moved with the left hand companies and his second in command, Major Mogg, moved with the right hand companies. The axis of the advance was the country road running towards Lingèvres. The companies moved off at 10.15 a.m., in straight lines of two platoons of each company in front, followed by the third platoon. The men moved forward at a steady walk in First World War fashion with rifles held across the chest, bayonets glinting in the sunlight. On the flanks, Sherman tanks of 'A' Squadron 4th/7th Royal Dragoon Guards moved in support. Maj. D'Arcy Irvine, commanding 'A' Company on the left, recalled:

> Initially all went fairly smoothly and we kept very close up behind the barrage. There was a little smoke to begin with but this cleared very rapidly. We had some tanks with us in the early stages, However, when we got within 50 yards of the woods, all hell was let

loose and we could see the Spandaus in enfilade, cutting through the corn all round us.

Lieutenant Williams, Assault Pioneer Platoon, wrote:

Early on the morning of the 14th, Col. Woods sent for me and told me I would accompany him in the attack, in my own carrier, with two men of my platoon (a) to give him protection in the field and (b) to give him a tank-hunting unit once the woods was ours…The C.O. asked me to move along to the right hand platoon of 6 Bn. force in order to 'stop 'A' Coy. people from getting mixed with them – *when* they arrive.' I gathered he was still a little displeased about something though, for the little while I knew him, I still think he was a quiet, gentle, very brave man…For a long time nothing happened (well for about seven or eight minutes, anyway) and then an enemy tank in the left hand corner of the woods fired and set on fire one of the Shermans. The fire was returned with good effect by the remaining two. Another Hun tank opened up from the right hand side of the woods, and then the woods came to life. Our leading troops were now in the middle of the stubble, and were caught there by a withering fire, Spandau and snipers, and still they kept going.

Sgt. Charles Eagles accompanied Lieutenant Williams. He recalled:

Lt. Williams approached me and said, 'Eagles, you and Cpl. Woods come with me, we are to look after Col. Woods, so bale into the second carrier.' We proceeded to fall into the advanced group…We passed over the centre, over the road and entered a large cornfield. The men were well spread out, with rifles at port position, as they waded waist high through the corn. We would be about five hundred yards up the field, which was triangular in shape and were advancing towards the apex when all hell was let loose: withering spandau fire (light machine guns), snipers and mortars caught us in the crossfire. Men were falling left, right and centre and I jumped from the carrier, followed by Jack Williams. We ran over to the other carrier, which had been hit and pulled the Corporal (Cpl. Sowerby) clear. He was screaming in agony as his leg and arm had been blown off. The driver, a young ginger headed lad, was in a terrible state but he was dead – killed immediately. There were dead and dying all around us and gruesome screams filled the air, mingled with the sound of gunfire, which was so intense it was cutting the corn like a scythe.

'A' Company, on the left, suffered heavy casualties and lost all of their officers. Lt. D.S. Taylor was commanding a platoon of this company. He described:

So far as we were concerned, it was a matter of forming up under the cover of the trees on one side of a large field of wheat. Our objective was the tree-lined margin of the far side. The usual artillery stonk lifted and we advanced with almost head-high crops giving an illusion of cover but nought of action opposite until we were within a few yards. Our Company Commander [Major D'Arcy Irvine] fell first with a head wound. Soon after I followed with a lucky one through the chest. Snipers in the trees were the cause of the trouble. One fellow officer wounded and captured, was freed later in the day when the position was taken. Evacuation after being wounded was first by stretcher bearers on Bren carriers, then jeep to a field dressing centre and eventually by boat to Southampton and the local hospital.

Major D'Arcy Irvine recalled the situation immediately before he was wounded:

My left forward platoon (Taylor) reached the woods and quite a considerable number of Germans climbed out of their weapon pits with their hands above their heads. I cannot to this day understand why some of them were not shot but the Geordies paid no attention to them, despite the havoc they had wrought among us and the fact that their compatriots were still keeping up a continuous hail of fire. It was at this stage, just short of the edge of the woods that I was hit.

Lieutenant Colonel Woods followed 'A' Company in his carrier and was seen standing up shouting and urging his men forward. The survivors of 'A' Company had reached the woods. Cpl. R. Cork was amongst them. He wrote:

Lt. Schofield led us through the lanes, with my section in front. When we got to the cornfield, we took up positions in a straight line across the field. I was right hand man of 'A' Coy. with 'C' Coy. on my right. As we went across the cornfield, a shell of our own creeping barrage fell not far in front of me and the left hand man of 'C' Coy. fell. I knelt quickly beside him and thought he had been killed by the blast but I had to carry on. As we came out of the high corn, Spandau machine guns opened up all along our front and many men fell. I was so close to the one nearest me, I saw the dust blown up in little spurts as the bullets left his gun. He was firing straight ahead as I ran forward with sten gun firing towards him. As I got close, the firing stopped and I pulled the gun away. He lay dead in the trench and I hauled his very terrified comrade out. He had to stand on his dead mate. 'Hands on head! Walk!' And, I think he was glad to do so, back across the cornfield, whilst I went to the next trench. On the top lay a pair of binoculars. Something must have told me to keep back. I knocked them into the trench with a couple of shots and went to the next trench but that was also empty but to be certain I fired four shots into each one. I stood back to see what was happening but saw no one else standing. Just then a burst of spandau from deeper in the woods hit me and I fell. I remember one medic, Arthur Hodsman came to me, dressed my wound, asked me if I would like a smoke, which I declined. I said I'd rather have a drink of water but this he couldn't give me as I had internal injuries. He told me about Bill Knox dying and my old pal of 5th Buffs, Bill Dimond. He said he would get him away and he would be back for me. He loaded me onto a stretcher and onto a Bren gun carrier. On the other stretcher I am certain there was another one of our officers, Lt. Taylor. I then lost consciousness and remember nothing until coming to in a large marquee with the wounded lying on many stretchers around me. I now know that in that marquee lay Bill Dimond, Doug Ridpath and Sgt. Major Wase…Bill Wase was wounded as he was talking to Col. Woods when a mortar landed on his vehicle killing him.

Lieutenant Williams continued the story:

A dash and we were in the woods but the Hun had his plentiful Spandaus sited back well inside the edge of the woods, within five minutes the only effective officers were the Col. and his I.O. (Lt. Reed). This clean sweep of leaders was proof enough that snipers were just waiting for a glimpse of a revolver, a pair of binoculars or any visible sign of a key man.

I myself was hit while running back to my carrier after going up to the C.O. to tell him that I had just seen Major D'Arcy Irvine lying in the corn with a nasty head wound and his H.Q. was wiped out.

Sgt. Charles Eagles was with Lieutenant Williams at this time. He wrote:

Jack [Williams] screamed at me, 'This way' as he ran towards Col. Woods' carrier, where the Colonel was standing beside another officer…[He] turned and shouted some order to Jack, who then turned and started to run towards me. Then he started to stagger until he fell at my feet, blood pouring from his thighs. Jack gasped, 'Take a look Eagles – if they've shot my balls off, kill me.' I pretended to look and said, 'You're O.K., then somehow I managed to get him across my shoulders and, how I'll never understand, carried him 50 yards, or maybe 150 yards, I don't know, until I spotted a medic and dropped him at his feet. As the medic attended to his injuries, Jack managed to say, 'I'm O.K. laddie, get yourself back.' Then he fainted. So back I went.

By the time Colonel Woods reached the edge of the woods, he realised that 'A' Company was decimated and 'B' Company passing through was receiving the same treatment. He contacted his Second in Command, Major Mogg, on the radio and was told that this flank of the attack was making progress and receiving fewer casualties. He ordered the Major to push ahead and he would extricate the two left flank companies and swing them round to reinforce 'C' and 'D' Companies.

'B' Company had been ordered to move through 'A' Company and suffered heavy casualties in the process. All of its officers, save one, were killed or wounded. It was at this point that Lieutenant Colonel Woods contacted Major Mogg. The Major remembered this final message:

We are running into terrible trouble here on the left. Most of 'A' Company's officers, in fact all 'A' Companies officers, are casualties. I'm trying to get on with 'B' Company. I will try and see how it happens and if not, if we don't make any ground, you go on with whatever you do with your side of the village. I will try and collect as many of them and try and come round behind you. It's obviously going to be easier at your side.

This was the last message from Lieutenant Colonel Woods as his carrier was hit by a mortar bomb, killing him. His Intelligence Officer, Lt. John Reid, had a miraculous escape and suffered only superficial wounds

It was easier on the right where leading 'C' Company was making steady progress towards the village against strong opposition. Major Mogg was with 'C' and 'D' Companies on this flank. He recalled:

We went through the corn and the Geordies are never very tall guys and the corn that year was extremely high. We marched the whole way across the corn, with still the barrage going on and suddenly you saw the odd Geordie dropping in the corn. You couldn't quite make this out, where it was coming from, when in fact, it was machine gun fire from the edge of the woods and quite a lot of Geordies were dropping in the corn as casualties all the way along. However we advanced…we got into the woods and we discovered afterwards that during the bombardment the Germans had got their machine guns on fixed lines. They had a string attachment to the machine guns so that they could lie at the bottom of their foxholes and then just pull the trigger and then the machine guns shot in enfilade right across the cornfield…'C' Company had lost quite a number of chaps and I had passed 'D' Company through. We got into the village.

One of the difficulties in the early stages of the battle was the loss of the Forward Observation Officers of the 86th Field Regiment. This resulted in a desperate lack of information on the troops' movements and their positions were unknown to the supporting guns. Capt. Roger Turnbull, the F.O.O. with 'A' Company, was killed by a burst of Spandau fire. Capt. Eddie Hall, the F.O.O. with 'C' Company, was also killed in the early stages. His signaller, Lance Bombardier Michley continued to act in his officer's place until he was severely wounded. Fortunately for the battalion, the Sherman tanks of the 4th/7th Royal Dragoon Guards, stayed with the attack every inch of the way. Their support was splendid, particularly when the house-to-house fighting in the village took place and German tanks appeared. The co-operation between infantry and tanks was magnificent, a fact the Germans were to find out to their cost. The right hand companies reached the village just before noon.

Major Mogg, on being informed of the death of Lieutenant Colonel Woods, found himself in command. He recorded:

> By 12 noon, I found myself in command of what was left of 9 DLI in the village of Lingèvres – with 'D' Company fairly strong, 'C' Company at about one platoon strength and the remnants of 'A' and 'B' on their way to reinforce us. Having been well trained at my Battle School, I had a quick 'O' Group.
>
> I ordered 'D' Company to occupy the East and SE edge of the village, facing towards Tilly and 'C' Company of one platoon to look after the approaches from the South. I made a defence fire plan with my gunner, [Major] Ken Swann of 86th Field Regiment. I ordered the support weapons to move forward, putting the carriers to guard the Western approach and set up my Bn. H.Q. in the area of the bridge over the stream just North of the village and on the Bn. axis…
>
> I sited the five remaining Anti-tank guns singly, facing down the road approaches. This was a fatal mistake as in the first counter-attack four of the five were knocked out by advancing tanks coming down the road. It taught me never to site A. Tk guns to fire frontally but always to engage tanks from a flank…luckily no infantry, just enemy tanks.

Sgt. Harry Burton was in command of one of these anti-tank guns sited on the open road. Two enemy tanks approached from down the road and were engaged by his gun. It knocked out the leading tank. Immediately after this success, the anti-tank gun received a direct hit destroying the gun and exploding the ammunition. Sergeant Burton was wounded along with his crew. He withdrew his men and set off to assist other anti-tank guns in the area. He showed a complete disregard for his own safety throughout the action, and was awarded the Military Medal.

Sgt. Robert Hey was also awarded an immediate Military Medal. His platoon occupied a position forward of the village, whilst the rest of the company was on a reverse slope in the rear. His citation described:

> The Platoon was attacked repeatedly for a period of seven hours and eventually had four tanks between themselves and the main position. The Platoon did not waver at any time and continued to fight on when surrounded. This was largely due to Lieut. Dunn, the Platoon Commander. When he was killed, it was due to Sgt. Hey. He showed great personal courage and was an inspiration to the men in the Platoon. By holding his Platoon in this position, he was largely responsible for ensuring the rest of the force to hold on until relieved by another battalion.

The 4th/7th Royal Dragoon Guards played a vital role in repelling the enemy tanks, which now moved on the village from the east, south and west. The Shermans had followed the infantry into the village firing their main armament and machine guns at any targets which presented themselves. Lt. Alistair Morrison, commanding 4th Troop, was ordered to contact the Battalion Commander (Maj. John Mogg) and take his orders from him. This he did and his orders were, 'We've got to capture the village…and when we've got it we must hold it. I want you to give me all the support you can.' The infantry fighting in the houses of the village were supported by the machine guns and 75-mm shells of the three tanks of the troop. Lieutenant Morrison placed his tank in the middle of the village, at the base of the church tower. One of his tanks covered the road from Tilly Sur Seulles and the other watched the road from the south. A third tank was commanded by Sergeant Roberts of the 3rd Troop, who had become separated from his troop. He was given the task of watching any German movement down the road from Verrières where the 6th Battalion was in action. Shortly after noon, Sergeant Roberts destroyed a Panther, which came in from the Verrières road. Trooper MacKillop, in Sergeant Harris' tank, damaged another Panther that raced towards the village down the Tilly Sur Seulles road. Corporal Johnson's tank, watching the road from the south, was destroyed by an armour-piercing shell and he and his crew wounded or killed. Later in the day, it was reported that a group of enemy tanks were on the Belle Epine road to the west of the village. Sergeant Harris' tank, fuel and ammunition replenished, was in position alongside the road and as the enemy tanks raced by his gunner, Trooper MacKillop, destroyed each tank in turn. This magnificent support along with that of the artillery was of great assistance in breaking up enemy counter-attacks which came in throughout the day.

Capt. K.H. Whitaker M.C. was in command of the battalion Anti-Tank Platoon. Early in the action, he was ordered to bring his guns up in support of the right flanking companies, which were moving into the village. He got his guns into position just in time to meet a counter-attack by enemy Tigers and Mark IV tanks. Captain Whitaker

A German casualty being carried to an ambulance after treatement at the Regimental Aid Post – Lingèvres 14 June 1944.

was wounded early in the engagement but repeatedly visited his guns and encouraged his crews to fight off the enemy tanks during a period of seven hours. A total of nine enemy tanks were put out of action or destroyed by the guns and the tank support of the 4th/7th Royal Dragoon Guards. His citation concluded, 'He showed great courage under enemy fire and great endurance when he had every reason to be evacuated as a casualty.' Captain Whitaker won a Bar to his Military Cross.

Lieutenant Morrison witnessed the gallant action of a Bren gun carrier driver who carried the wounded from the village. It is described in *Brightly Shone the Dawn* [Johnson & Dumphie] as follows:

> The wounded – and the dead – were propped up against the hedge and the church wall on the 'home' side of the building to gain what shelter they could from the constant shelling and small arms fire. A Bren gun carrier was in use as a makeshift ambulance, driven by a soldier of the Durhams. He brought the carrier up from the rear, skid-turned it and reversed it under the trees by the church porch. Single-handedly he loaded it up with wounded men and then drove off – slowly so as not to jolt the passengers – back to the first aid post in the large farmhouse by the bend in the road. He was to make the same solitary, dangerous journey many times during the afternoon until towards evening the inevitable end came and his carrier remained stationery in the village centre, its devoted driver and his last cargo still and silent where a chance shell-burst had killed them all.

Not to be outdone and with the survivors of his companies in position, Major Mogg ordered three tank-hunting patrols to seek out enemy tanks. He led one patrol himself, which comprised Capt. Roy Griffiths and Sergeant Jordon of 'D' Company and two other soldiers. He acknowledged later that it was a foolish undertaking due to inexperience as he was, at that point in time, commanding the battalion. He described the action:

> …having crept under bocage banks across four fields and sited the PIAT A. Tk. weapon on top of a bank to fire at a Panther tank, I ordered the gunner to fire. The Geordie said, 'I don't know how this bloody thing works.' He had carried it across the Channel and for seven days in Normandy. A lesson perhaps. In fact the enemy Panther was made a non-

runner by this PIAT [he fired the weapon himself] and the crew baled out.

The Major and his party hot-footed it down the hedgerows and back to their positions before the enemy could retaliate.

Enemy counter-attacks continued throughout the day from elements of the Panzer Lehr Division. Fortunately they were relatively uncoordinated and the battalion, supported by tanks, artillery and Typhoons of the R.A.F, beat them off. 'D' Company was heavily involved. Capt. Roy Griffiths recalled:

I had barely crossed the road to withdraw 18 Platoon under Jimmy Casey, when heavy armoured fire came down into our area and along the road, which we were defending with both platoons. The commander of 17 Platoon was killed, also the Platoon Sergeant and though suffering further casualties were able to reach their allocated defensive box…The Platoon was now getting somewhat fraught…John Mogg decided that once the box defences were complete he required further information from 'A' and 'B' Companies and he sent off Jim Casey to find out what had happened.

Communications were being organised by George Lanning, commanding H.Q. Company. This was an increasingly difficult task, which he did extremely well and kept communications open as far as he was able.…he also arranged supplies of ammunition to fulfil the needs of the forward troops. This he did with great courage and tenacity.

The [17] Platoon Sergeant came down the road and as he passed me he said, 'There are tanks up the road, sir,' and he got a complete H.E. shell to himself. We pulled into a small defensive locality, you couldn't call it anything more than that, a field. Battalion Headquarters, which was John Mogg, the Adjutant Rickards and the M.O. and we had probably about a platoon and a half, not two platoons' worth. Two Platoon Commanders were killed, Jimmy Casey was the only one left.

Pte. Ron Porter was frantically digging in. He recalled:

We were under heavy sniper fire when I had a bullet through the handle of my entrenching tool, while digging a slit trench, and my mate was shot in the shin. 'Lucky bugger,' we said, 'you're going home.' Later that day a Tiger Tank broke out and put two of our anti-tank guns out of action, which had the road covered, and then sprayed the hedgerow with machine gun fire, killing about 10 men. Later that afternoon, we laid them out.

The village was held. The 9th made contact with the 6th Battalion on the left and 231 Brigade on the right. Later that night, the battalion was relieved by a battalion of the Gloucester Regiment, 56 Brigade. The battalion was pulled back to rest and reorganise. Losses had been very heavy. Maj. John Mogg, promoted to Lieutenant Colonel and given permanent command of the battalion, stated:

I discovered then, after a full count, that the number of casualties were 22 officers and 226 other ranks, out of a complement of, I think, about 590. It made a very big hole in 9 D.L.I. People will say, 'Was it worth it?' The only thing I can say, 'We had our orders. We captured the village and, therefore, it was a major strategic and tactical advantage to the division.' I felt terrible that all those young Durham soldiers were lost and when you

Gen. Sir John H. Mogg G.C.B., C.B.E., D.S.O., D.L. Commanding Officer 9th Battalion D.L.I. 1944–45 and Deputy Supreme Allied Commander, Europe 1973 76. One of a long line of fine battalion Commanders throughout World War II.

go to cemeteries there and you look and you are amazed at the ages, 18s, 19s, 20s and the worst thing, in a way, was having two battalions beside each other on this attack. The 6th had quite a few casualties as well. All of them came from, more or less, the same area, such as Newcastle, Gateshead, Sunderland [and by now, due to past heavy losses, from other areas of the country]. I learned a hell of a lot in this first battle, such as, if you are going to do that sort of attack in wooded countryside, the infantry training should have been used a good deal more, and not to adopt a plan, which was very much like the barrage in the desert. And if we'd had more time but, of course we didn't have that time, we should have perhaps insisted on more time in which to discover exactly where the enemy positions were, with much more patrolling at night. I think the attack itself should have been done at night or certainly in the early hours of the morning…A great deal more reconnaissance would have given a much better chance of success…It would have been better to put two companies in at first light and held two in reserve, and you have two companies up your sleeve to reinforce where you were successful. But it is terribly easy to be wise after the event…Infantry tactics dictate you keep a reserve. We had no reserve as all four companies were used.

There are 32 names of men killed on the 14th June, 1944 and recorded in the D.L.I. Book of Remembrance in Durham Cathedral. They include Sgts. W.H.G. Gwilliam and J.W. Young M.M., Cpls. P. Evans and C.B. Simpson M.M., L/Cpls. W. Knox, T. Tedford, J.T. Tranter and G. Watson. Private soldiers who were killed include D.P. Billett, A.W. Brown, A.S. Horton, E.A. Jones, J. Lynch, W.T. Medhurst, A. Mortimer, A.C. Rolfe and L.A. Turner. Lt. H.S. Smith died of wounds on the 15th June as did Cpl. F.W. Hackney and L/Cpl. J. Mitcheson.

Major Mogg was awarded the Distinguished Service Order. His citation read:

Major Mogg took over command of 9 D.L.I. when his C.O. was hit. The 9 D.L.I. withstood all efforts of the enemy to dislodge them from their positions and during the engagement which lasted all day, nine enemy tanks, including Tigers, Panthers and Mark IV Specials, were knocked out and set on fire and heavy casualties inflicted on the enemy. This magnificent achievement was due to skilful handling of his Battalion by Major Mogg and by his cool conduct and example during this fierce attack at a critical time, the Battalion responded so well to his leadership that the enemy eventually retreated in disorder, having been severely mauled.

Lieutenant Colonel Mogg [Later Gen. Sir John Mogg, G.C.B, C.B.E, D.S.O and Bar, D.L.] had joined the battalion as Second in Command a few days before the invasion. He had joined the army in the 1930s and had attended the Royal Military Academy, Sandhurst. Here, he won the Sword of Honour and was commissioned into the Oxford and Buckinghamshire Light Infantry on the 1st January 1937. His first active command in the army in the Second World War was with the 9th Battalion, which he commanded until the end of the war. He was Deputy Supreme Allied Commander, Europe from 1973–76, A.D.C. to H.M. the Queen 1971–74 and Chairman and President of the Normandy Veterans Association from 1982–89.

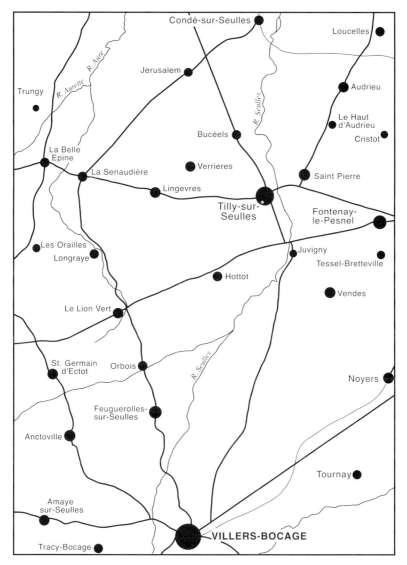

After the battle, there was a desperate need for sleep and rest. The overwhelming feeling was one of relief at surviving the ordeal. Officers were kept very busy reorganising, replacing and checking equipment and materials. Lieutenant Colonel Mogg expressed his opinion of the Durhams in these words:

> I don't know what it is but when the British soldier is really at his lowest, it is then that he is probably at his best. I always found the Geordies were like that. The worse the situation was, the more they reacted and if you could tell them it was going to be bad and it was slightly better, you won a trick. When they were down, they work flat out to get back up again.

There was little time for rest. On the 17th June, the battalion was south of the

Lingèvres–Tilly Sur Seulles road. The objective was now to take Tilly and push on to Hottot. This was true bocage country and the progress over the next few days was painfully slow and bitterly contested. The enemy made clever use of the terrain. Each field, farmhouse, barn and orchard was defended. Roads and hedges were mined, houses were booby-trapped. Tanks had little room to manoeuvre on the narrow twisting roads that were always covered by enemy 88s and anti-tank weapons. This was, indeed, infantry country. Enemy rearguards held up the advance, inflicting casualties and then moving back to the next field or hamlet.

The enemy laid Teller anti-tank mines and 'S' anti-personnel mines in profusion throughout the countryside. 'S' mines, when stood upon, jumped into the air and exploded about waist high. Pte. Jim Radcliffe had a narrow escape:

> I went on an O.P. one day with Sergeant John Farrage, we both got on well together. We were both from the same town and 'spoke' the same language. The O.P. was in a farmhouse bedroom, so we took turns at observing while the other lay on the bed and had a kip. We had been doing this for some time, when a Corporal from the Pioneer Platoon [Corporal Woods], came into the room and said he was looking for booby traps. He knew we had been lying on the bed but he checked it anyway. He called us a lucky pair of buggers. The bed had been booby-trapped; but for the clumsy work of some German soldier we would have been spread all over the bedroom.

The battalion entered Tilly Sur Seulles on the 20th June and settled in just before midnight despite heavy shelling of the area. Over the next few days slight enemy shelling and mortaring continued. The main activity was patrolling, with the object to gain an enemy reaction thus enabling his strength and positions to be identified. A steady advance down the road to Juvigny took place on the 26th of the month. The War Diary entry for this date states that:

> At one time, we actually reached the latter place but had to withdraw as we were in a hopeless tactical position. The area was booby-trapped with made up explosive charges in gaps and hedges.

Casualties continued to mount over the next few days. During the final days of June, the battalion continued to make very slow progress towards Juvigny. During the month, new drafts had been coming into the battalion. These were from a number of regiments and from areas of the British Isles other than the North East of England. Lieutenant Colonel Mogg was impressed by the speed at which they settled in. He described:

> The extraordinary thing was that they came and they all put on a beret with the D.L.I. bugle horn badge and, in no time, as we went on in the battles and we had a few successes, they became more Geordie almost than the Geordies. There was a most wonderful D.L.I. spirit…It's success in battle that really counts. If you are successful in battle and you know that cap badge has been successful, you like that cap badge and you like the

chums who wear that cap badge.

Lt. R. Brewer joined near the end of the month. He recalled:

…the Adjutant interviewed us one day and the C.O. the next. Here was a surprise. During all the rest of my service I had had, in varying degrees, the type of colonel depicted in the film 'Colonel Blimp'. Here was a fellow obviously about my own age and he had the looks and manners that one instinctively liked.

The month of July, 1944, was not one of spectacular advances. For the first half of the month, the battalion inched its way down the road between Tilly Sur Seulles and Juvigny, fighting for every field, hedgerow and building. Extensive patrolling took place daily and a constant pressure was kept up on the retiring enemy but the pace was slow. It was tiring and dangerous work. Every hedge, tree, building or bend in the road might conceal an enemy sniper. Gaps in the hedgerows were soon discovered to be likely places for booby traps as Private Ratcliffe found out on reconnaissance. He describes:

After we had gone further down the road, the officer who was leading decided to turn into a field. This led to some high ground so he thought he could possibly catch sight of the enemy. There was a gap in the hedge and we were going through it. I had an uneasy feeling about this and I said to Sergeant Farrage, did we need to be with the leading section. I explained how I felt and he said, 'OK, we will hang on a minute.' The leading section went through the gap and one of the lads stood on a 'S' mine, these are anti-personnel devices that, when activated, fire a canister up into the air which explodes firing shrapnel in all directions. Very nasty and much feared by the infantry. Quite a few men in the Platoon were hit, including Corporal Cowell who got it in the back.

Enemy shelling and mortaring was experienced on most days. The Germans had turned Juvigny into a 'hedgehog' position, strongly defended by mortars and machine guns. Casualties built up during this period. The battalion snipers became active and caused the enemy some casualties. No. 70 Brigade relieved 151 Brigade on the night of the 7th/8th July. The latter went into divisional reserve, north of Lingèvres, from the 8th to the 12th of the month. Clean clothing was issued, baths were taken and recreational activities included cinema shows and visits to Bayeux where the troops were entertained by the T.T. divisional concert party. Lieutenant Brewer wrote:

I remember the boys teaching a farm girl there how to call in the cattle in basic English! The Padre heard her one day and explained that it was 'pas bon'.

On the 13th July, the battalion was ordered to relieve the 1st Bn. Dorset Regiment north of Hottot. The relief was carried out in the early hours of the following day. On the 15th a tragic event took place when, during the clearing of 75 rusty Hawkins grenades from a track by the Pioneer Platoon, Ptes. J. Martin and G.G. Taylor were killed when the grenades exploded. The Pioneer Officer was instructed that, in future, all grenades or anti-tank mines found in a dangerous condition were to be detonated and not lifted.

The battalion was now operating in the area of Les Le Gallois. Pte. W. Muckleroy was killed by an enemy mortar bomb. On the 17th, a farmhouse in 'H.Q.' Company area was completely destroyed by a tremendous explosion. Lieutenant Looker, the Pioneer Officer, concluded that the explosion was caused by three Teller mines that had been detonated by a timed fuse or by a rat. Fortunately, there were no casualties. On the 18th, a Polish deserter was picked up by 'D' Company. He belonged to the 276th Infantry Division. He provided information that his company had withdrawn four kilometres. A screen of Spandaus had been left in the positions evacuated. He stated that this was normal policy adopted by his battalion. His company was about 50 strong and had suffered considerably from the Allied shelling and mortaring. The 9th and 8th Battalions began to advance during the afternoon of the 18th. It was a slow advance over ground sprinkled with anti-personnel mines and booby traps left behind by the Germans. 'C' Company captured six prisoners of war from the 2nd Company, 987th Grenadier Regiment, 276th Infantry Division. By evening, the two battalions of the Durhams were established on the high ground on the line Le Feugret.

Fighting over such difficult terrain took its toll on the battalion. To add to the constant danger was an all-pervading smell of death, which came off the fields where dead farm animals lay bloated and unattended as it was too dangerous to go and remove them. Pte. Ronald Mallabar joined the battalion about this time. He recalled:

> They were pretty shattered. They had some terrible experiences and I got the impression that they were rather weary. At the same time they seemed to me to be very professional. They seemed to know exactly what they were doing…The Battalion had seen a lot of action and suffered very heavy casualties. It was probably the reason for me being there. They were out of the line when I joined them. The thing I remember about them was that they had a pet goat at Battalion H.Q. and every time a shell started to come over, the goat used to beat everyone into the trenches.

In the early hours of the 19th July, the battalion was established across the Hottot road. This road was found to be blocked with Teller mines and, although some were lifted immediately, others were thought to be booby-trapped and could not be dealt with until daybreak. More prisoners were taken from 276th Division who reported that small groups of the enemy were being left behind to cover the withdrawal of the main body. Other prisoners taken reported that there were a large number of Poles in the division and that morale was very low. Life in the battalion during this period was described by Lt. R. Brewer:

> Maybe I should enlarge a little here on the daily life in this part of the world…it was very close country. There were very few houses anywhere, just an occasional farm house or a very large chateau standing in quite extensive grounds. Civilians were the exception

rather than the rule. We lived in our various holes in the ground, usually in pairs – as much for company as anything – and quite a large part of the day was spent therein, sleeping or reading or writing. From a safety point of view, it was not strictly necessary to remain in all the time but it saved the inconvenience of 'diving for it' if the odd shell did come your way. Shelling, by the way, is not normally as bad as one might imagine, if you keep your head and don't let your imagination run away with you. Except with the high velocity stuff, which is extremely unpleasant – (it is almost all over before you know it's started, it's so fast) – you can always hear the shell coming and get a few seconds warning to get out of the way. Later, with practice, you can even judge pretty accurately, where it will fall and so save yourself a lot of unnecessary 'dives'! So long as you are in some form of trench, barring a direct hit, you stand a very fair chance of survival from shelling.

The battalion had advanced about a mile and a quarter on a front of just over three-quarters of a mile. Two reconnaissance patrols were sent out on the morning of the 21st July as far as the tributary of the River Seulles, due south of Hottot. There was no sign of the enemy. Heavy rain over the last two or three days had made conditions unpleasant. Lieutenant Harling, whilst leading two sections to occupy new positions in a chalk pit, was captured when the party was ambushed by the enemy. The relief by the 6th Battalion was completed on the 26th July. 'C' Company remained in the line under the command of the 6th Battalion. The weather during the day was very good. The battalion rest area was Le Parc de la Mer, Hottot, and the time was spent in cleaning up, reorganising and resting. A cinema show was organised in a farmhouse in the rear area. 'B' Company replaced 'C' Company in the line on the 28th July. The area was not entirely safe as it was subjected to occasional shelling from enemy guns. On the 29th a shell landed in a slit trench occupied by Lieutenant Smith of 'B' Company and his batman. In both cases, their legs were blown off below the knee.

The troops quickly learned the lessons of fighting in the Bocage. Private Mallabar:

If you were fired on on the road, it was difficult to get out as you couldn't scramble through the hedge…There were lots of orchards too. We used to dig in in an orchard. We found that was a mistake because shells or mortar bombs burst among the branches of the apple trees and scattered shrapnel about. We soon found out it was better to dig your hole well out in the open…We were dug in around one of these little Norman fields. We had our trenches round the outside of the field. We were being shelled and our own guns behind were firing at the German batteries and a British spotter plane went up and it was watching the fall of the shot on the German positions, when it came under fire from a German anti-aircraft battery. The pilot immediately dived down into our field and flew round and round just above head height, while the aircraft shells burst amongst us. We wanted nothing more than for this man to go away or climb up a bit higher and get himself killed rather than get us killed…We weren't only hit by German shells, we were sometimes hit by our own when they were falling short.

On the 30th July, it was realised that the enemy was pulling out of Hottot. Orders were issued to all units of the 50th Division that all civilians in the liberated areas were to be sent to brigade collection points, and civilian workers for the Todt Organisation were to be collected together separately. 'D' Company led the battalion advance. Spandaus and snipers were still active and slowed the forward movement. Lieutenant Colonel Mogg decided that, in an attempt to remove the isolated enemy posts which were holding up 'D' Company, a platoon of 'A' Company would move round the enemy's flank. This move succeeded in driving out the enemy and the advance continued. The battalion's positions on the morning of the 31st July were 'A' Company west of Sermentot, 'B' Company at Orbois, 'C' at Beltot, 'D' at Feuguerolles Sur Seulles with a standing patrol at the river bridges south of Feuguerolles. The month of July had been a tough one for the battalions of 151 Brigade. The bocage aided the enemy rearguards but the troops were finding out that the terrain called for good infantry tactics and these were being learnt. An entry in the brigade War Diary summed up the month's activities:

> During the month, no major advance by the Brigade took place but battalions were constantly in action containing and harassing the enemy on their front, whilst the build up of the other forces were taking place. Constant and active patrolling furnished a great deal of valuable information about the enemy dispositions on the front and though a few prisoners were taken, they afforded some very interesting data. This second month since D Day passed with no relief of the Brigade and, as a consequence of this and bad weather for the time of the year, the troops were becoming a little battle weary.

During the month, the enemy dropped leaflets in the battalion area, one of which read:

> Caught Like Foxes in a Trap
> English and American Soldiers!
> Why has Jerry waited ten days after the landings to use his so-called secret weapon behind your back? Doesn't that strike you as queer? It looks very much as though after waiting for you to cross the Channel, he had set a trap for you.
> You're fighting at present on a very narrow slip of coast, the extent of which has been so far regulated by the Germans. You are using up an enormous number of men and huge quantities of material.
> Meanwhile the robot planes, flying low, scatter over London and South-East England explosives, the power and incendiary efficiency of which are without precedent. They spread death and destruction in the towns and harbours, which should be sending you much needed supplies. They are cutting the bridge to your bases...
> How long can you keep up this foolish 'invasion' in these circumstances...

Usually received with much amusement, as this one was, the V rocket raids had started and were to give concern over the following weeks until the bases were overrun.

A brief look at what had been happening elsewhere is now appropriate. On the

18th July, General Montgomery had launched Operation Goodwood aimed at breaking enemy resistance around Caen. The attack was made by VIII Corps, which comprised three armoured divisions, namely, the 7th and 11th and the Guards Armoured, supported by the 3rd British and 3rd Canadian Infantry Divisions. The Germans opposed them with three infantry divisions, the 346th, 16th G.A.F. and 272nd and two armoured divisions, the 21st and 1st S.S. A tremendous aerial bombardment paved the way for the assaulting divisions. The area of the attack was Ranville and south-east of Caen. It had very powerful enemy defences and in spite of valuable ground taken and keeping the main enemy armoured divisions on this front, the attack petered out. On the 25th July, the Americans commenced Operation Cobra which was to lead to the final breakout from Normandy. By the end of the month, Avaranches was in American hands. On the 30th of the month, XXX and XII Corps attacked southwards from Caumont aiming for the Mont Pinçon area. The 50th Division's objective was Amaye Sur Seulles, near Villers Bocage. The 43rd Division on the right was to take Pt. 361 on the western edge of Mont Pinçon, whilst two miles further west, the 15th Division moved to take Pt. 309. On the right flank the 11th Armoured Division was to advance towards the area of St. Martin des Besaces. The 50th Division led off with 56 and 231 Brigades leading. On the 2nd August, Amaye Sur Seulles and the high ground two miles west of Villers Bocage had been taken. The latter was captured on the evening of the 4th August.

The American Third Army was now operating and commenced its spectacular breakout. On the 3rd August, Hitler ordered the counter-attack at Mortain, which failed. The 7th Armoured Division captured Aunay Sur Odon. The 43rd Division took Mont Pinçon on the 8th August. On the eastern flank, the Canadians and British fought towards Falaise and the Allies began to close the gap which became known as the Falaise Pocket, where the Germans were to suffer great loss in men and equipment.

The advance continued. Prisoners of war were falling into the hands of the advancing troops. The main opposition was from isolated numbers of Spandaus and a little shelling and mortaring and, of course, the ubiquitous mines and booby traps. Villers Bocage was bombed by Allied planes. Pte. Jim Ratcliffe witnessed the raid:

> Another vivid memory about this time was watching the R.A.F. bombers destroy Villers Bocage. They came over in a huge bunch, no real formation, and all the bombs seemed to be released at the same time. You could actually see them falling from the planes. Then there was a noise like rolling clap of thunder, a huge column of smoke and that was it, a town wiped out. We went through it after, what a job to get through. There was rubble everywhere. There was supposed to have been Panzers in the place but we never saw any.

On the 7th August, the battalion moved to the area of Aunay Sur Odon in brigade reserve. The objective of the 50th Division was now Condé sur Noireau, an important road centre which, when taken, would cut the main road through which the enemy could retreat from the Falaise Pocket.

No. 151 Brigade's final battle in Normandy was about to take place. The plan was

The D.L.I. moving into the fighting south of Mont Pinçon. Heayv enemy mortar fire greeted their advance as they pushed forward with their tanks along the high ground.

for the brigade to move to the village of Le Plessis Grimault, a village which lay at the foot of Mont Pinçon, and there to advance towards Condé sur Noireau. The 8th Battalion would be on the right and the 6th on the left. The 9th Battalion would remain in reserve at Le Plessis Grimault. Each battalion was supported by tanks of the 13th/18th Hussars and a barrage provided by five field regiments of artillery. The 8th Battalion's objective was La Rivière about four and one-half miles ahead. The 6th Battalion's objective was La Cannardière. The route to the start line, a sunken track on the southern boundary of the village, was over Mont Pinçon and down the road to Le Plessis Grimault. Mont Pinçon had been taken by the 43rd Division after fierce fighting. German observation of the summit of Mont Pinçon and the road leading down to the village was perfectly clear. The Germans were fighting for their main escape route from the Falaise Pocket and would obviously put up fierce resistance to the advance on Condé sur Noireau. The approach road was being heavily and accurately shelled, and the two attacking battalions only just reached the start line in time. By 2.30 p.m., they had reached their objectives. No. 69 Brigade passed through and attempted to capture the high ground. German resistance was fierce and the brigade made little progress. For the following 48 hours, 231 Brigade was brought forward and sought to take the high ground near St. Pierre la Vieille. On the 11th August, it was the 9th Battalion's turn to try and make progress.

The 9th Battalion had been ordered to relieve the 6th Bn. Queens Regiment at Le Plessis Grimault on the morning of the 9th August. Lt. R. Brewer recalled the march over Mont Pinçon and down the open road to the village:

> The road to Plessis led almost over the top of the Mont and was straight and fairly open into the village at the bottom. The plan had been for us to take over the area before first light and the D.C.L.I. and The Queens to be away. That was the plan. The C.O. being relieved had different ideas and our own C.O. had to be downright rude to get him to move at all – 'Six o'clock would be good enough for him', he grumbled. Nobody, it appeared, had any clear idea of the picture where their own troops were, to say nothing of the Jerry positions.
>
> And so dawn found us all lined up on the forward slope of the hill – almost head to tail, like coconuts at a shy. And Jerry wasn't slow to start shying! Everything he could lay

his hands on. It would not have surprised us to see the kitchen sinks being thrown as well. Shrapnel rained down in torrents, so it seemed. Nic [Lieutenant Nichols] and I had the delightful job of wandering round choosing gun positions (those that were already made were useless), going back and getting the guns, leading them in and checking on the progress of the work, when the only place any normal person wanted to be was well underground! We had seven casualties in the platoon that day…That was the only time I really hated being an officer – I had to order men (all credit to them for the way they obeyed) from the comparative safety of the ditch in which they were waiting, on to their carriers and into the hailstorm of death.

Heavy shelling and mortaring of the battalion's positions was experienced over the next two days and some casualties were suffered. The battalion's objectives were two high features – Pts. 249 and 262 – both of which lay south-east of St. Pierre la Vieille and were held in strength by the Germans supported by tanks in St. Pierre. The attack was planned for the 11th August but was postponed till the following day. The plan was for tanks of the 13th/18th Hussars to lead the way, closely followed by the carriers of the 8th and 9th Battalions which, in turn, would be followed by the rest of the battalion. The high ground to the south of St. Pierre was to be attacked by 231 Brigade prior to the Durhams going into the attack. Lieutenant Colonel Mogg planned for the two squadrons of tanks to move ahead with the carriers of the two platoons closely in support. The latter, with their 2-in. mortars and Brens, would attack any opposition which was holding up the tanks. On reaching Pt. 249 there would be a pause allowing the infantry to come up and take over the summit. The tanks and carriers would then move on and take Pt. 262 and hold it until the infantry again came up to consolidate. Zero hour was 1 p.m. The terrain was described by

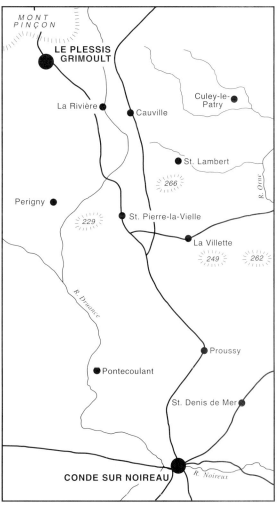

Le Plessis Grimoult – Condé sur Noireau
August 1944

Lieutenant Brewer:

> I must explain the ground first for you to appreciate this attack. On the left of our axis of advance and at right angles to it, was a very narrow, high feature rather like a camel's back – the two humps being Points 249 and 262 (as they were called from their heights – in metres). Jerry was everywhere around us and on the high ground.

The battalion assembled east of St. Pierre la Vieille in the early morning of the 12th. The enemy shelled the start line and casualties occurred. Zero hour was postponed till 1.30 p.m. Point 249 was reached by the tanks at 3 p.m. Communications with the infantry companies were bad and Lieutenant Colonel Mogg and Lt. D.W.R. Bowden, the Intelligence Officer, had to make a reconnaissance to ascertain the positions of the infantry companies. They were found to be coming up to Pt. 249. 'D' Company had taken the village of La Villette and infantry were reported on Pt. 249 at 3.40 p.m. 'D' Company had also reached Pt. 249 as Capt. Roy Griffiths, Second in Command of the company, recalled:

> Shortly after crossing the startline, Dennis Hurst, a New Zealander who commanded the carrier platoon with Jimmy Casey, was killed. We proceeded to our objectives, which were two points on the map – 249 and 262…It was a strange attack. We moved straight forward from the start line and, after short distance, moved out at an angle of 90 degrees to the objective. We came under Spandau small arms fire, being enfiladed, but again our casualties were light. Roy Hill, with his platoon, was allocated 262, with myself and the rest of the Company occupying Point 249. On our right were the remaining rifle companies, which sustained casualties, among who was a very good friend, Peter Farrant, whom I first met in Sicily when he was Liaison Officer with 151 Brigade under the command of Brigadier Ronnie Senior. On reaching our objective, it was reported to me that someone had noticed that the corn sheaves below were moving. I found this hard to believe. However, occupying a position a little forward, I watched through glasses and indeed there was movement in the corn that had been cut and sheaved. Moving back to Point 249, I arranged for a shoot with the Brens and, amongst the corn, several of the enemy appeared carrying on their left arms red-cross armbands but around their shoulders were two belts of Spandau ammunition. I signalled for some artillery support onto their position and the enemy withdrew.

Maj. Lionel E.V. Rumble, commanding 'D' Company, was commended for his leadership of the company as it moved forward under heavy shelling and mortar fire and attained its objective. His courage and leadership at Le Plessis Grimault and, later at Gheel and Bemel, earned him a well-merited Military Cross.

By 4.10 p.m., one squadron of tanks had reached Pt. 262 but was in difficulties. Four anti-tank guns were sent forward to aid the tanks. Lieutenant Colonel Mogg was constantly on the move throughout the attack, making reconnaissance after reconnaissance to the forward positions to ensure that all was going according to his plan. At 5.10 p.m., he found one squadron of tanks on Pt. 262 along with the Carrier Platoon of the 8th Battalion, one section of carriers from the 9th and a platoon of 'A' Company on the way to the summit. C.S.M. Stanley Howe was awarded an immediate Distinguished Conduct Medal. His citation read:

> On the 12th August 1944, near Le Plessis, the 9 D.L.I. were ordered to attack the Pt. 262 feature. C.S.M. Howe's Company was the forward company. The objective was strongly held and throughout the advance the Company was heavily shelled and mortared. On arrival on the objective, one platoon was cut off, both their officers and Platoon Sergeant were killed, whilst C.S.M. Howe, who was forward with the leading platoon, arrived on the objective with 12 men. The situation was serious as it could be seen that a counter attack was imminent. C.S.M. Howe made his way through heavy fire to the other platoon which was cut off. On arrival he reorganised it and with it he fought his way on to the objective. When the enemy counter attacked, it was decisively beaten off.

The two points were now firmly in the hands of the battalion. It had been a brilliantly conceived attack and Lt. R. Brewer may not have been exaggerating too much when he wrote, 'Came August 12th and the attack – impossible on the face of it but outstandingly successful through its improbability and the superb generalship of Lt. Col. Mogg.'

By the early hours of the 13th August, the battalion had been relieved by a battalion of the Shropshire Light Infantry, 43rd Division. It moved into the area of La Gaudine, near Aunay sur Odon where it remained for five days of well-earned rest. Football, baths, visits to the cinema and N.A.A.F.I. and a T.T. concert party filled the leisure time.

Fifteen other ranks were killed on the 12th August. They include Sgt. W.H. Rushforth, L/Sgt. W. Watson, Cpl. A. Ward and Ptes. H. Bailey, C.E. Bradley, S. Hackett, T. Smith, L. Ward and J. Wood.

The daily scenes of the fighting in Normandy witnessed by the soldiers was described by Pte. Ronald Mallabar:

> Burnt-out farmhouses, dead animals, batches of graves, little mounds of earth with a cross on the top, a wooden cross, a rifle with a helmet stuck on top of it. They all seemed to have a little round hole in them, which we didn't like very much. In fact, at this time, the Pioneer Section of the Battalion spent its time making little wooden crosses. It used to be quite worrying seeing them working away at Battalion H.Q. making these crosses in case we had to push anyone under the ground. If anybody was killed, we just had to wrap them in a blanket and bury them and that was that. They had to be fished out later by proper graves people.

For most people there was little thought of death. It could only happen to the other chap as Pte. Mallabar explained:

> It wasn't going to happen to me. Not till I was wounded the first time, it wasn't happening to me. People around me were falling down dead and lying about badly wounded. But it

wasn't me. Not until you're actually wounded yourself, you don't think. At least I didn't. I just made the best of it. When I was eventually wounded, I realised just how mortal I was. I decided that the war would go on forever, until I was killed…Life consisted of the Battalion and when you're away from the Battalion, you want to be back. You feel lost away from it, even though you know you may be going back to be killed. I was in hospital in this country [U.K.] and I was just lying there, longing to get back to the real world, which was the Battalion. It sort of dominated your life. There was nothing else…You had such a bond with the fellows you worked with. You had to rely on them many a time to save your life and the same for them and you loved each other (with a deep brotherly affection). You just wanted to be with them.

On the 17th August, the 50th Division came under XXX Corps along with the 11th Armoured Division and the 43rd Wessex Division. German resistance in Normandy was almost at an end. The enemy had suffered enormous losses in the Falaise Pocket and was now in full retreat. The pursuit was about to begin.

CHAPTER XXIII

THE PURSUIT – BELGIUM & HOLLAND

O n the morning of the 19th August 1944, the 9th Battalion along with 151 Brigade and the 50th Division, all part of the Allied armies, commenced the pursuit of the retreating Germans. The speed of the advance was beyond the most optimistic hopes of any man in the battalion. It was a journey that ended one month later on the Junction Canal in Belgium and saw the destruction of the German Seventh Army and the end of the enemy occupation of Northern France and Belgium. The list of officers, following the losses in Normandy, was:

L. Col. H.J. Mogg D.S.O.	Commanding Officer
Maj. A.E. Hillier O.B.E.	Second in Command
Capt. R.C. Rickett	Adjutant
Capt. J.C. Baily	Intelligence Officer
Maj. W.J.H. Hudson	Officer Commanding 'A' Company
Maj. G.R. Lanning	Officer Commanding 'B' Company
Maj. R.J.H. Callinghan	Officer Commanding 'C' Company
Maj. L.E.V. Rumble	Officer Commanding 'D' Company
Capt. B.T. Gardner	Officer Commanding 'S' Company
Capt. A.T. Shaw	Officer Commanding 'H.Q.' Company
Capt. H.G. Phillips	Mortar Platoon
Lt. T.H. Nichols	Anti-Tank Platoon
Capt. B.J. Gardner	Carrier Platoon
Lt. G.W. Looker	Assault Pioneer Platoon
Lt. J.L. Brooker	Signals Officer
Capt. E. Hooper	Motor Transport Officer
Capt. A.E. Love M.C.	Quartermaster
Capt. A.H. Rea	Medical Officer
Capt. R.W. Kerr (R.A.Ch.D.)	Padre

On the 19th, the battalion commenced its move, at first very slowly as the road was blocked by the columns of other units. St. Honorine la Chardonne, near Condé sur Noireau, was reached at 12.30 p.m. On the following day, it moved over the River Orne and passed through Putanges and Courteilles and arrived at the village of Commcaux. The roads outside Commeaux were filled with enemy transport that had been abandoned or destroyed by the R.A.F. Two villages, Sévigny and Bailleul lying north of Argentan and part of the Forêt de Gouffern, had to be cleared on the 21st, and 15 of the enemy were taken prisoner. These were handed over to the Americans advancing from the south, in view of the battalion's task of clearing the woods. A further 50 prisoners were taken in the woods. The major problem was the fact that almost every by-road was blocked with destroyed enemy vehicles and this made speedy movement difficult. Lieutenant Colonel Mogg and his Intelligence Officer were constantly ahead of the column, reconnoitring a safe route. On the evening of the 21st, he and his I.O. with a squadron leader of the 13th/18th Hussars tried to reconnoitre a route to Chambois, where the battalion was to move to on the following day. The last two miles of the road to this town were completely blocked by German transport. A column of horse-drawn wagons, trucks, half-tracks, motorcycles, trailers, armoured cars and tanks had been caught nose to tail by the R.A.F. and completely wiped out. The death and destruction metered out to the enemy in the Falaise Pocket could now be clearly seen by the advancing troops. Lieutenant Brewer described the scene:

> And what a mess there was there. Death, devastation and destruction was everywhere. Roads were jammed solid with burnt and knocked out transport. Dead were strewn all over the place – hundreds of them – many stark naked and apparently unharmed, killed by blast, sitting as drivers or passengers in their vehicles. It was a horrible, unforgettable sight.

It was believed that the Germans were still in Chambois but this proved not to be the case. The 505 Field Coy. Royal Engineers cleared the road and a precautionary advance guard comprising 'B' Company riding on the tanks of a squadron of 13th/18th Hussars, a section of mortars and one of anti-tank guns led the way into the town. Twenty-one prisoners were taken. In and around the town of Chambois were elements of Americans, Canadians, Poles and Free French and much confusion prevailed. No. 151 Brigade was relieved by 130 Brigade, 43rd Division, and concentrated south of Chambois with orders to prepare to move eastwards and clear the woods east of L'Aigle. No enemy forces were found in the wood. The tactics planned by Lieutenant Colonel Mogg for clearing the wood may be of interest. The War Diary entry for the 23rd August is as follows:

> The plan was for 'D', 'C' and 'B' Coys. to beat the wood with three carrier sections outside the wood as 'stops'. Two troops of tanks moved up the edge of the wood at infantry speed and waited at the far end for the coys. to come out. 'A' Company was mobile reserve. As there were no features to form landmarks for bounds, coys. were to pace 1,000 yds bounds and send up light signals for each bound, first red, second green, third white and fourth red. On leaving the wood, coys. were to R.V. at given points and await orders for move to area Les Brulais.

The move was now to the River Seine at Vernon. The 43rd Division was to make the crossing there and the 50th Division was earmarked to break out from the bridgehead it had created. The battalion arrived in the vicinity of Vernon on the 26th of the month and rested there awaiting the next move forward. On the 30th August, the battalion crossed the River Seine over the 'Goliath Bridge' and through the bridgehead. It was now under the command of the 8th Armoured Brigade and its first specific task was to clear Gisors, its general task to act as flank protection to the Armoured Brigade. The Commanding Officer and his Intelligence Officer went ahead to contact the Commander of the 8th Armoured Brigade. In doing so, the party entered and liberated the village of Neaufles St. Martin, where no Allied forces had yet appeared. Gisors was found to be empty of Germans and the battalion moved on to Beauvais. The leading tanks were delayed for a time due to German resistance in the town. The battalion moved up to the high ground to the west of Beauvais. Anti-tank guns were deployed to cover the east, south and south-east approaches to the town as it was expected that German forces cut off north of Paris would try to break through by Beauvais. The local gendarmes reported that there were about 50 Germans in Goincourt and 'C' Company was sent to clear this village. Four enemy tanks appeared, heading for Beauvais. These were engaged by 17-pdr. anti-tank guns and two were knocked out. Thirty-six prisoners were taken in Goincourt, all from the 148th Grenadier Regiment of the German 49th Division. The battalion entered Beauvais, which was found free of Germans, to a very warm welcome from the inhabitants.

In the early hours of the 31st August, rifle and small arms fire was heard coming from the outskirts of the town. The battalion stood to at 2.45 a.m. At 5 a.m., 30 to 40 Germans attacked 'C' Company. They were driven off and 10 unwounded and six wounded prisoners were taken. Most were from the Fusilier Battalion of the 49th Division and one was from the S.S. Panzer Division (Das Reich). Lieutenant Colonel Mogg met with the local Commander of the F.F.I. (Free French) and arranged for them to provide standing patrols at Noiailles, Auteuil and Anneuil. These would report on any German formations coming up the road towards Beauvais. French reports of enemy tanks and infantry being engaged south of the town proved to be inaccurate. A platoon of 'B' Company investigated a report of Germans in a barracks near the company positions. The platoon fired 2-in. mortars and called upon the enemy were to surrender. As a result 76 prisoners were taken from 148 Grenadier Regiment, 49th Division. Further prisoners were taken during the day. The Guards Armoured Division passed through Beauvais and the battalion followed, moving on to La Flèche. A message was received that the battalion was to press on to Amiens with all speed. The task there was to guard three bridges over the Somme, which had been captured intact.

Through every village and town as the advance continued the local population turned out to welcome their liberators. Lieutenant Brewer described:

> As the breakout from the Normandy bridgehead got underway, so we came across more and more civilians and the greatness of our reception grew and grew. As the last Germans were leaving a place so all the flags and bunting came out of hiding, all ready for our arrival. The most striking thing about it all was the amazing number of British, American and French flags they had. Not shabby ones but beautifully kept ones! Flags out of the windows, across the streets, being waved, flags everywhere. And did some of the Jerries

that had got left behind in the rush look sick about it all! To stop was to be besieged by thousands of people clamouring just to touch the men they had waited so long to see. I was riding a motor-cycle a lot of this time and therefore easier to get at when I slowed down or stopped. Bottles of everything under the sun were produced for 'Tommie' to drink. Flowers were strewn all over the roads, fixed into our jackets, everywhere on all the vehicles. Apples, tomatoes, pears and even hard-boiled eggs in one place, were given to us to eat. And, of course, everyone wanted to kiss us – with some of the pretty Mademoiselles that was two-sided but we had to accept hundreds of 'kisses' to get one Kiss! But it was most gratifying to be liberators to such obviously pleased peoples and, of course, our morale was way up at the top.

The battalion came under the command of 151 Brigade on the 1st September. The stay in Amiens was shorter than expected and on the 2nd, it moved to Doullens. 'B' Company found a flying bomb site at Ransart and 115 prisoners were taken. At the end of the day, the battalion again came under the command of the 8th Armoured Brigade, with orders to follow behind the tanks towards Arras, through this city and on to Lille. German opposition was encountered as they contested the crossing of the Douai-Lille Canal. A bridge was blown at Wingles and the column was diverted to Pont-a-Vendin and Meurchin. 'D' Company was detached to watch the northern flank where the enemy was reported to be in strength. The battalion was now fighting in the area of the World War I battlefields and the inhabitants of this industrial area, with memories of German occupation during the two world wars, were ecstatic.

Lieutenant Colonel Mogg ordered the battalion to move through Seclin and clear the area between this town and Lille. Lieutenant Brewer wrote:

> On the north side of Seclin, we pulled off the road here into a field, by a local railway station called Templemars. The vehicles were spread round the field and the C.O. called his 'O' Group together. He had just started giving his orders when we were rather heavily and unexpectedly shelled from close range. We scattered the vehicles as far as possible and discovered to our horror that the Jerry was but a few fields away! He must have been taken as much by surprise as we were, otherwise we would have been completely wiped out. As it was we had quite a number of casualties in the Battalion and I was kept busy for a while running them back to the hospital at Seclin…The C.O. said later that I had done well and shown great coolness, which pleased me no little – he being so completely fearless himself.

Six other ranks were killed in this shelling. They were Cpl. F.W. Gibbins and Ptes. J. Davidson, K. Duffey, R.B. Knight, A. Linfort and A. Yates. Major Callingham, commanding 'C' Company, was wounded in the left arm and leg. 'B' Company captured Bargues and sent patrols into Noyelles. The main task carried out during the 4th September was to deal with a number of pockets of enemy troops south of Lille. These were identified in and around Noyelles, Houplin, Emmerin and north towards the city. Noyelles was taken by 'D' Company supported by tanks of the 13th/18th Hussars. All indications, during the evening and night, were that the enemy was withdrawing from

Houplin and the surrounding area. On the morning of the 5th, 70 prisoners were taken from the 732nd Grenadier Regiment. Later in the day a further 93 prisoner were taken together with weapons and equipment. Ancoisne and Emmerin were reported clear of the Germans. In the evening a report from the F.F.I. stated that there were S.S. troops in the area north-west of Lille who had been murdering civilians. The battalion War Diary entry for the 5th September stated that the total casualties from the 6th June to date were 10 officers and 91 other ranks killed in action, one officer and seven other ranks killed in accidents, 24 officers and 345 other ranks wounded. Two officers and 42 other ranks were missing. Pte. Jim Ratcliffe lost one of his friends in these actions. He wrote:

> At a place not far from Lille, we had a brush with a German SP gun and they were causing us quite a bit of trouble. Sgt. Farrage had gone out on OP and I was sat at the back of a haystack writing a letter home when a chap from 'B' Coy. came up to me and asked me if I was a mate of Tommy Cooke. I said, 'Yes.' Then he told me he had just been killed and that the same shell had wounded Sgt. Farrage. I felt gutted. Though not in the same company, we managed to see each other whenever possible. I told my mother in a letter what had happened, as she had met him once when we were on embarkation leave. In 1995, Tony Colgan and myself toured the battle sites of WWI. We knew that Tommy had been buried in the London Cemetery at High Wood on the Somme. We had got the information from the Graves Commission. I put a cross on his grave, also a tea bag. Tommy would have liked that. He loved a brew. The last time I saw Tommy alive he had come round to the Mortar lines and we were just brewing up. 'Smashing, I'm just in time', he said.

On the 6th September, the battalion moved up to and through Brussels. The reception here was greater than any experienced so far. The civilians crowded the streets, climbed onto the vehicles and lined the roads so thickly that it was only with the greatest difficulty that the column could pass through. Pte. Jim Ratcliffe described:

> …our entry into Brussels. Talk about hail the conquering heroes, the stuff that was coming into the carrier, bottles of beer, fruit and flowers. We had to keep stopping because of the crowds of people. One time a woman came to the side of the carrier with two absolutely gorgeous young women and asked if I would kiss her daughters…the things a British Tommy has to do for King and Country! Old Batchy, our driver, was doing his nut. He missed all the fun.

The column did get through and the battalion took up positions to cover the eastern approaches to Brussels. 'B' Company was in the area of Nosseghem, 'C' Company at Sterrebeek, 'D' Company with the 8th Battalion on its right and 'A' Company as bridge guard. It was keenly anticipated that the battalion would be staying in these areas for a few days, with the possibility of visits to Brussels. It was not to be. By 6.45 a.m. on the 8th, the battalion marched off on the route Louvain, Herschot and Hersselt and concentrated north of the latter. The next barrier to the advance was the Albert Canal. The main crossing was to be made by the guards division at Beeringen and the

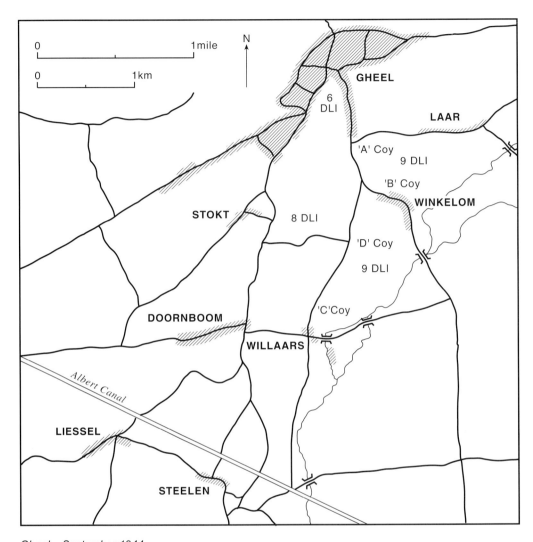

Gheel – September 1944

original plan was for a second crossing to be made by the 8th Armoured Brigade, near Gheel. This brigade would be followed by 151 Brigade, who were then to move towards Turnhout. However, the Germans had decided to make their first serious stand on the Albert Canal and the plan had to be changed. The 8th Armoured Brigade was placed behind the guards at Beeringen to extend the bridgehead at this place. No. 151 Brigade was given the task of establishing the bridgehead at Gheel. The 8th Battalion would make the initial crossing and, at the same time, 69 Brigade would begin to cross further west, near Meulenberg.

At 10.30 a.m. on the 8th September, the battalion concentrated north of Hersselt. The 8th Battalion crossed the canal on the evening of the 8th and established a bridge-head. A Class 9 bridge was constructed by the Royal Engineers. The 6th Battalion was to cross into the bridgehead on the morning of the 9th September behind a squadron of the 61st Reconnaissance Regiment and, if the opposition was light, to push on to the Escaut Canal. The 9th Battalion would follow and be used as the situation demanded. The opposition proved to be anything but light and the plan had to be altered to deal with the new situation. The new plan was for 151 Brigade to capture Gheel and hold it.

At 4 p.m. on the 9th of the month, the battalion was established at Eynthout. Lieutenant Colonel Mogg and his Company Commanders went up to Steelen to look over the ground towards Gheel. Whilst on the embankment by the bridge at Steelen, a German corporal appeared on the far side and surrendered to the party. A patrol was sent out during the night, to investigate the woods north of Eynthout. It bumped into a German post and had to retire, not before its Commander, Lieutenant Reid, was wounded and captured. The new plan was for the 6th Battalion to advance on the left, through Doornboom and Stokt, to the centre of Gheel. The 9th Battalion was to advance on the right, through Willaars and Winkelom to the Laar–Ste. Dymphne area. 'B' Company would lead with the object of taking Laar and consolidate facing north-east. 'D' Company would then pass through 'B' to Ste. Dymphne. 'A' Company would advance to Kievermont and 'C' to Hadschot.

On the morning of the 10th, news was received that the enemy was in strength at Winkelom, De Beindekens and Winkelomsche Heide. The 6th Battalion were fighting fiercely and making slow progress towards Gheel. The Mortar Platoon led the way across the canal, which soon came under fire from enemy mortars.

The plan, revised yet again, was for 'B' Company to take Winkelom and make it a firm base and the other companies to follow. 'B' Company and tactical headquarters crossed the canal. Tactical H.Q. was set up at Willaars. 'B' Company fought its way up the track towards Winkelom against very strong opposition. At 4 p.m., a platoon of the company was held up on the track about 400 yards short of the village. The Platoon Commander, Lieutenant Perelle, had been killed and several of his men wounded. Lieutenant Colonel Mogg went forward to see what the position was. A third platoon, with 'H.Q.' Company, was south of the track and about 200 yards from the village. All were pinned down by heavy enemy machine gun fire. Lieutenant Colonel Mogg arranged for Major Lanning to send up two tanks to assist the platoon assault the village. This was successful and 'B' Company captured the village and held it for the rest of the battle. 'D' Company was ordered forward to take over from the rear platoon of 'B' Company on the track and to dig in and prepare for all-round defence. 'A' Company was ordered forward to hold the area north of Willekom, where the houses of Gheel began. 'C' Company followed with the task of taking Laar. Germans prisoners taken were from the 53rd Flieger Regiment. This regiment was part of General Student's First Parachute Army, which filled the gap between the Seventh Army withdrawing towards the Meuse and Ardennes and the Fifteenth Army in the west. It comprised hardened and fanatical parachute regiments and Luftwaffe ground personnel who, themselves, earned a reputation for tough fighting. The Germans were now truly fighting for the Fatherland, trying to stop the Allies entering their country that lay so close behind them. In addition, the Allies were demanding unconditional surrender. Fierce fighting lay ahead.

At 8.40 p.m. on the 10th September, 'A' Company reported an enemy counter-attack with tanks and infantry. The War Diary entry stated:

> Apparently a force by-passed Gheel to the west and then turned east and overran two coys. of 8 DLI, south of the town. Personnel of 8 DLI warned 'D' and 'C' Coys., who were moving up the track towards 'A' Coy. No tanks were seen and a troop of Shermans was sent up towards 'D' Coy. The counter attack did not cross the Willaars–Winkelmon track but part of the German force moved further south and established itself, with one or two tanks, on and south of the Doornboom X-roads. The C.O. ordered 'C' Coy. to return to the Willaars area and when they arrived (2200 hrs) to make contact with the enemy at the X-roads. The counter attack died down at dark and all coys. were firmly in position. The C.O. visited all coys. during the night.

There was quite severe fighting along the line of the track but 'D' Company stopped the enemy and forced him back. The move of 'C' Company back to Willaars was a wise one as it prevented the enemy from cutting off the whole brigade. His tanks and infantry on the Willaars crossroads were watched throughout the night but neither side was willing to start fighting during the hours of darkness. 'A' Company reported tanks in its area and Lieutenant Colonel Mogg arranged for Sherman tanks to be sent to on the morning of the 11th. At 8.15 a.m. on this morning an enemy force of about 50 attacked 'A' Company. This was broken up and a number of prisoners taken. The enemy also lost about 30 dead. In addition to the 53rd Flieger Regiment, members of the 6th Parachute Regiment appeared on the battlefield – very young, very brave but not well trained. At the Doornboom crossroads, neither side moved for some time. The enemy were shelled but this had little effect. A Sherman tank was destroyed as well as a 6-pdr. gun of the divisional anti-tank regiment. Another Sherman was put out of action later in the morning and the ammunition truck was destroyed but, fortunately, the contents had been removed. Later in the morning, the enemy on the crossroads were seen to be withdrawing but it was too late. In doing so, they met up with a company of 8th D.L.I. and suffered heavy casualties, including the two tanks that were with them. Counter-attacks against the brigade positions continued throughout the day. The 6th Battalion were involved in bitter fighting in Gheel as the Germans strove to drive them out. Attacks against 'A' and 'B' Companies were driven off and an attack against the 8th D.L.I. was met with concentrated artillery fire and failed, and the enemy suffered heavy losses. A prisoner of war reported that the 6th Parachute Regiment had a strength of 2,000–3,000 and had orders to eliminate the bridgehead. Most of the casualties in this regiment were found to be between 17 and 19 years of age. The night passed quietly with patrols out towards Ste. Dymphne and Laars.

On the morning of the 12th September an enemy counter-attack was launched on

'A' Company. A party of the enemy got between 'A' and 'B' Companies. 'A' Company's forward platoon was attacked from three sides and two platoons were cut off. Tanks were sent forward and these helped to stabilise the position and all three platoons were able to disengage and rejoin the company south of the junction of the main road and track. Lieutenant Colonel Mogg ordered that the original position be retaken and this was done by a platoon of 'A' Company. Orders had been received that the battalion would be relieved by the 6th Battalion King's Own Scottish Borderers, 44 Brigade, 15th Scottish Division. The relief of 151 Brigade was completed late at night. The following morning the enemy had withdrawn and 44 Brigade was able to advance unopposed over the ground, which had cost so much to 151 Brigade to take and hold. A report on the action is contained states:

> The battle of the Gheel bridgehead was one of the battalion's sharper actions and, although it was not fought on the main line of the advance, the success gained was vital to the course of the operation that secured the crossing of the Albert and Junction [Escaut] Canals. The Germans planned to start by eliminating the Gheel bridgehead and so open up the flank of the more important Beeringen bridgehead but in this they were denied by the stubborn fighting of 151 Bde. and the troops who should have been deployed against the flank of the Guards, were lost in the three days of counter attacks that all failed to reach the bridge at Steelen…The tank squadron did all that was asked of them and particularly good work with 'A' Coy., in helping to break up the series of attacks on that area. But the real victory belonged to the rifle companies themselves; in three days of almost continuous fighting, against a strong and determined enemy, well supported with tanks and guns and mortars, only one position, once gained, was lost and that was retaken within the hour, by the same company, unaided, that had been driven from it.

Even in the middle of the most severe fighting there is a role for compassion towards one's enemies. Lieutenant Brewer recalled:

> I was in the area of Tac H.Q. I discovered that we had four Jerry prisoners there, one of them wounded and fairly badly. There were no drivers available to take these fellows away so, as I was doing nothing and the platoon jeep was handy, I suggested to the Adjutant that I should take them to Brigade H.Q. where they were going and the R.A.P. [Regimental Aid Post] were both within a few fields distance. We piled on the jeep, including a guard and set off. The R.A.P. was the first call and we all unloaded to take the wounded man in on his stretcher. Suddenly, there was a terrific whistle. A crash and a blinding crash right on the corner, a few yards away. Flames showed that something was on fire. Naturally, instinct is the same whatever nationality you are and when the whistle came. Everyone dived for the ditches on either side of the road but as soon as it was passed, I yelled for the Jerries and everyone reappeared! I cannot help thinking that in similar circumstances, with the positions reversed, British troops would have made a getaway – maybe the prospect of good food was too big an attraction. As we rounded the corner, we found that the blaze was from a carrier that had been hit.

The civilian population, caught in the middle of the fighting, had to find what safe shelter they could. Private Mallabar of the signals section met up with some of them:

> We arrived in a town called Gheel…Gheel took quite a bit of fighting to take it. There was a group of us in a street and we found ourselves in a cellar underneath a house. It was dark and somebody found that one wall of the cellar was lined with shelves on which there were jars of preserved fruit. Well, we'd had nothing decent to eat for weeks, so we opened the fruit and we were eating pears and plums when somebody shone a light and we saw that the other three walls of the cellar were lined with children, old men, women, all sitting with their backs to the wall and their legs stretched out in front of them and absolute terror in their eyes. They didn't know who we were. We could have been the SS for all they were concerned. But, being British soldiers, we were so embarrassed when we saw them that we walked out of the cellar and got on with the war!

Those killed during the period 10th–13th September included Lt. B. de la Perrelle; C/Sgt. H.W. Mitchell and Ptes. C.C. Child, J. Crawford, J.S. Haley, J. Hewitt, F. Hooper, B. Keeling, R. Moscrop, F.W. Pepper and W.J. Ward.

On the 13th September, the battalion moved to Vorst. The stay here was only for a few hours and a move was made to Hulst, where it stayed for two days' rest with baths, cinema, beer and an E.N.S.A. concert. The Brigade Commander, Brig. D.S. Gordon, visited and complemented the battalion on its fighting record since landing in Normandy. Three days later, the battalion moved to Lommel, near the De Groote Barrier Bridge over the Escaut Canal. The Commanding Officer visited XXX Corps headquarters to be informed of the impending airborne attack on the major bridges over the rivers which lay ahead of the British advance and terminated at Arnhem. The battalion was now placed under the command of 231 Brigade with the task of defending the bridge over the Escaut Canal and to relieve the 1st Bn. Dorset Regiment. It took over the defence of the right flank of the De Groote bridgehead. Immediately positions were occupied, patrols were sent out to contact any enemy forces in front.

Field Marshall Montgomery's plans for the airborne action are well documented. On the 17th September the airborne landings began. The Allied Airborne Corps consisted of the American 82nd, 101st Airborne Divisions, the 1st British Airborne Division and the Polish Parachute Brigade. The three divisions were dropped with the task of securing the bridges over the Wilhelmina Canal at Eindhoven and those over the River Meuse at Grave, the River Waal at Nijmegen and the Lower Rhine at Arnhem. XXX Corps, spearheaded by the Guards Armoured Division, was required to advance along the corridor from the Escaut Canal, through Eindhoven, Veghel, Grave, Nijmegen to Arnhem. This long, narrow corridor, not much wider than the main road, was to be protected and widened by the VIII Corps to the east and XII Corps to the west. Such was this daring plan, which was to achieve so much yet fail at Arnhem. On the 17th, the Guards broke out of the bridgehead with massive artillery and air support and set out on the long advance.

The Groote Barrier Bridge was a vital point on the lines of communication for the whole operation. It had to be kept open at all costs. There were quite large numbers of Germans in the woods north-east of the bridge. One prisoner informed the battalion that there were six companies of the 21st S.S. Panzer Grenadier Regiment north of the canal. These were awaiting the arrival of further reinforcements, then they would attack the bridgehead to cut the vital link with the armoured drive. Over the next few days, the enemy put down heavy Spandau and mortar fire on the battalion's positions. Lieutenant Colonel Mogg ordered out patrols by both day and night. A deadly game of 'hide and seek' developed as the patrols sought out the whereabouts of the enemy hiding in the woods. As these were discovered an artillery, mortar and machine gun concentration was brought down with the intention of breaking up any enemy that may attack the bridgehead. Carrier patrols prowled the canal bank to ensure that the enemy did not cross and attack from the flank and rear. The enemy did make two attempts to cross the canal near Neerpelt. These were stopped by aggressive patrolling and the fire of artillery, 4.2-in. and 3-in. mortars and machine guns. On the 18th September, about 10 enemy bombers dropped anti-personnel and incendiary bombs on the battalion's positions. The bridge was undamaged but 'B' and 'C' Companies suffered casualties. 'B' Company headquarters was in a house that was hit and set on fire. One man was killed and three wounded, one of whom was the Commanding Officer, Major Lanning, who was hit in the shoulder. 'C' Company had just sent a platoon out as a fighting patrol. This was caught in the open and had several men wounded, including the Company Commander, Captain Hornsby-Wright, who was with the patrol. As a result of the losses, Lieutenant Brewer was given command of the 15th Platoon. Another Lieutenant was in temporary command of 'C' Company. Lieutenant Brewer wrote:

> He held an 'O' Group directly after breakfast [19th September] to give his plan for dealing with a Spandau that was being troublesome. When he had finished he asked my opinion of it – I told him I was no expert in infantry tactics but it did not sound too healthy. The other two Platoon Commanders, both Sergeants, said quite flatly that it was bloody stupid, so the matter was shelved…The Jerries themselves solved the problem by deciding they were in imminent danger of being cut off and decided that the sooner they pulled out the better…A new C.O. arrived for the Company – one Willy Anderson – ex-Brigade Major, later to be known as the 'Mad Major' for his delight in being as aggressive as possible towards the Germans   he never left them in peace.

On the 19th of the month, the 3rd British Division began an advance north of the canal, from Lille-St.-Hubert. The 6th Bn. Green Howards (69 Brigade) moved into position between Neerpelt and the battalion. These moves eased the situation on the battalion's front and eastern flanks. Patrols reported that the enemy was moving out. The armoured drive north on such a narrow front was running into difficulties. Enemy attacks from both west and east cut the road from time to time behind the armoured spearhead. The urgent task was for this narrow frontage to be widened and the enemy driven off. 50th Division was ordered to drive forward on the route

Eindhoven–Nijmegen–Apeldoorn–Epe–Nunspeet and so widen the corridor and drive off enemy forces. On the 22nd, the division went into army reserve and was told to be ready to move in any direction, as ordered. Orders were received and then counter-manded, until the battalion was finally ordered to move to the village of Bokt, north of Eindhoven. The division had been ordered to clear the area of Veghel where the enemy was reported to have a force of 70 tanks and two battalions of infantry. Bokt was reached on the 23rd September. As enemy attacks were possible, the battalion organ-ised itself for all-round defence. On the following day, a move was made to the woods east of Neinsel. 'D' Company was ordered to relieve a company of the 1st Devons on the canal bank. The 6th Bn. D.L.I. was at Breguel and the 8th at Nunen. There was lit-tle sign of the enemy. Division informed the Commanding Officer that the main axis road had been cut between St. Oedenrode and Veghel. Lieutenant General Horrocks, G.O.C. XXX Corps, was at divisional headquarters and was cut off from his own head-quarters near Nijmegen. Lieutenant Colonel Mogg was ordered to provide a guide and escort to take him via 'D' Company and on to Veghel. This task was given to two sec-tions of carriers with Carrier Platoon Commander Lieutenant Casey, and Intelligence Officer Captain Baily. Capt. Roy Griffiths was with 'D' Company. He recalled:

> We did not expect visitors as we had learned that the road behind us had once more been cut but, sure enough, careering up the road were carriers containing James Casey with his crew, together with the Commander of XXX Corps, Lieutenant General Sir Brian Horrocks. He stopped and spoke to us all and then proceeded to his headquarters at Grave. At Grave Sir Brian addressed the carrier crews, which James Casey commanded, speaking to each and every member.

The 3rd Division was moving up on the right and the overall situation was improving as the main road became more secure. In the afternoon of the 25th, Lieutenant General O'Connor was provided with an escort towards the headquarters of the 101st American Airborne Division. Prisoners of war who were coming in were of poor quality, some even unarmed.

New orders were received and on the 27th September and the battalion moved to Boekel. The tactical situation was no longer urgent and Brigadier Gordon ordered that the battalion should get as much rest as possible. The next four days were spent in maintenance activities, baths, sport and the visit by a French concert party. Sergeant Bland, Anti-Tank Platoon, wrote:

> A stop now at a place called Boekel. We are right next door to a farm, smashing people, do all our cooking for us…Smashing daughter here but the boys are round her like bees round a honey pot – and she likes it.

Whilst at Boekel, news arrived of the failure of the Arnhem operation and the withdrawal of the 1st Airborne Division following a gallant fight against great odds. The barrier of the lower Rhine remained. On the morning of the 2nd October, the battalion, as part of a divisional move, commenced its journey to the Nijmegen area. It was ordered to relieve the 1st Bn. Dorset Regiment, who were holding part of the perimeter covering the Nijmegen Bridge. No. 151 Brigade moved up to join 69 and 231 Brigades in the area between Nijmegen and Arnhem, known as the 'Island'. This was a flat area of ground, rich farming land, intersected by many ditches and canals. It was low-lying and it was impossible to dig a trench as water was met about two feet below the surface. The whole area was overlooked from the high ground behind Arnhem. It proved to be very unpleasant ground to operate within. Enemy shelling was a daily event, the particular target being Nijmegen Bridge over which all essential traffic had to pass to reach the Island. In spite of all of this shelling, the bridge led a charmed life and very little damage was done to it. However, drivers raced across with little thought of damage to their vehicles' springs from the numerous bumps in the road. The main threat to the bridge lay in the east where the enemy held the orchards around Haldaren and the factory at Huize Kamstjatka. One attempt had already been made to dislodge the enemy from this area but this had failed. It was now decided to try again and 151 and 231 Brigades were called upon to make the effort. The attack was planned for the 4th October. Enemy units in the area were identified by patrols as

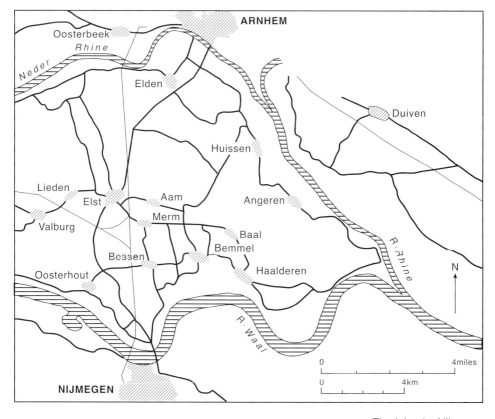

The Island – Nijmegen

being part of the 9th Panzer and 10th S.S. Panzer Divisions.

The plan was for 231 Brigade to attack on the left and 151 Brigade on the right. The latter's orders were to gain and secure the area Baal–Haldaren– Factory. No. 151 Brigade plan was for the 8th Battalion to attack on the right and the 9th on the left. The brigade was supported by machine guns of the 2nd Bn. Cheshire Regiment, anti-tank guns of the Northumberland Hussars, artillery of the 74th Field Regiment, tanks of the 4th/7th Royal Dragoon Guards and Royal Engineers. The 9th Battalion was given the task of taking the village of Baal and the surrounding orchards. Lieutenant Colonel Mogg divided the attack into two phases. In the first, 'D' Company on the right and 'C' Company on the left were to advance to the first objective, the road fork on the Bemmel–Baal road and the orchard running north-west from Mariendaal. In the second phase, 'A' Company was to come up behind 'D' Company and capture the orchard south of Baal. 'B' Company was to pass through 'C' Company and capture Baal itself. Rate of advance was given as 100 yards in three minutes. The battalion carriers were to act as a mobile reserve. The artillery were asked to fire high explosives and smoke on the objectives as the battalion advanced. Heavy mortars were to fire on road and track junctions and orchards. Tanks moved in support of the infantry. Forming-up areas were in the orchards north of Bemel.

The attack commenced at 2 p.m. 'D' Company kept up with the artillery barrage and quickly reached its objective. Forty prisoners were taken. 'C' Company had some trouble with Germans holding the long ditch running south-east from Houtakker and had to ask for the artillery to blast them out and help the company to move forward to its objective, which it did. Sgt. Frederick Andrews was awarded an immediate Military Medal for his part in the capture of the orchard, which was 'C' Company's objective. He led his platoon under heavy enemy fire on to the objective. A lateral road crossed the far side of the orchard and the troops were under orders not to advance over it, as this was the area on which the British artillery bombardment was falling. On reaching the edge of the orchard, enemy machine guns opened up from the area beyond the lateral road and Sergeant Andrew's platoon was cut off from the remainder of the company. The company was suffering heavy casualties from this fire. Sergeant Andrew's citation noted:

> Sgt. Andrews immediately deployed his platoon, leaving a section for fire support, whilst he led the remaining two sections on a dashing assault into the enemy positions. Three of the enemy were killed, ten taken prisoner, the remainder fled.
>
> Had it not been for Sgt. Andrews' outstanding courage and initiative, the company would not have successfully reorganised on the objective.

L/Sgt. Stanley Martin was also awarded an immediate Military Medal:

> At Baal on the 4th October, 1944, L/Sgt. Martin was commanding the reserve section of a leading platoon during the attack by 9 DLI. Just as the platoon made its final assault on

the objective, heavy m.g. and small arms fire came from fresh enemy positions some 50 yds to the left.

L/Sgt. Martin, although his section was weak from casualties, immediately led his men firing his Sten gun as he ran, in a determined charge against the enemy position. He personally jumped into the position killing four of the enemy and taking ten prisoners. Finding fire coming from another position a further 50 yds away, L/Sgt. Martin, undaunted, dashed forward leading the few men he had left and captured a further twenty-six prisoners. L/Sgt. Martin's complete disregard for his own personal safety and his outstanding leadership and determination was an excellent example to all his men.

The second phase had the disadvantage of taking place against an enemy now very alert and prepared to fight hard to retain his positions. 'A' Company endeavoured to move round the left flank of 'D' Company and ran into heavy Spandau fire from a house and orchards. It suffered heavy casualties, including its Commanding Officer, Capt. J.H.W. Hudson who was wounded. All three Platoon Commanders were killed.

The rest of the company, under Capt. P.W.B Thompson, rallied and swung round to the right of 'D' Company and, with the help of a troop of tanks, took its objective. On the left 'B' Company had to fight its way into Baal where it knocked out two half-track vehicles, one towing a 75-mm anti-tank gun. By 4.45 p.m., all companies reported that they were on their objectives.

Lt. R. Brewer of the Anti-Tank Platoon described the scene:

…two fellows came back who had been badly shell-shocked. Awaiting transport to the R.A.P. the poor devils were on the ground crying their hearts out – it was a horrid sight to see grown men in that condition.

When I took the remaining four guns up, the route was strewn with debris, wood from the numerous trees, ripped apart by shelling, an occasional cow or horse in the same condition (Ugh, how they stank!) and bits of buildings. There were also quite a few houses on fire and any amount of Jerry dead and wounded about the place. The infantry were busy digging themselves in and looking after their prisoners, of whom they had quite a haul…I took a couple of guns belonging to the Northumberland Hussars up with me…Mostly all went well and the digging in was soon underway. The exception was the gun on the left flank – I'd only just sited that when an A/P shell cut straight through one of the trail legs, making it a dangerous proposition to fire like that.

And there we stayed…On the fifth day we were relieved by the Royal Welsh Fusiliers…The changeover was not quite uneventful – one of the carriers was hit with shrapnel, as was Sgt. Davies who was in charge of that particular gun. He had quite a lot of pieces in his legs and, though all were small and none serious, it must have been quite painful. He gamely carried on with his job and stayed with the Platoon until we were back in the harbouring area.

Casualties for this attack were 60 in total. At least 12 other ranks were killed. They were Cpl. S. Rowland, L/Cpl. W. Dransfield, Ptes. R.A. Charlton, M.J. Foster, G. Gillespie, A. Hobson, D. McManmon, S.G. Robins, C.J. Russell, J.A. Steadman, J. Thompson, J. Thompstone.

Pte. Richard Atkinson had the task of driving his lorry containing wounded over the Nijmegen Bridge to the medical unit in the town. He recalled:

> I got shelled across there [Nijmegen Bridge]. A few got hit coming across…You panic and put your foot down. Joe Maddison [Motor Transport Sergeant], he shouted, 'Stop! Stop! Stop!' He made me stop. He said, 'Now go into low gear. There's men on the back with blood running out of them.'…He made me drive over dead slow. He was that type of man, cool, calm and collected. I had to drive gently till I got them off the bridge and could get them to the medics. If I'd come charging over hell-for-leather and hit the bridge, they would have been thrown all over the place. I just wanted to be out but he made me take bottom gear and crawl across.

Except for some artillery and mortar fire from time to time, the night of the 4th/5th October was quiet. The battalion held a strong position with all companies close together and linked with the left flank company of the 8th Battalion.

Over the next few days the battalion slipped into what was to become the usual Island routine. Artillery, mortars and machine guns were sited and given defensive fire tasks. Positions were dug and roofed. Observation posts were set up. Patrols went out each night. They were usually of three types, standing patrols in front of the companies positions to give early warning of enemy patrols or a counter-attack, reconnaissance patrols to discover where the enemy front line was and fighting patrols to attack specific targets and capture prisoners. The enemy front lay along the Wettering Canal and usually had standing patrols forward of this line. The canal can best be described as a large drainage dyke and for most of its length consisted of two ditches, each about 12 feet wide, separated by a bank. A typical reconnaissance patrol was sent out between 10 p.m. and midnight on the 5th/6th October. It consisted of Sgt. W. Wright and two other ranks. The Sergeant reported:

> My route from 10 Platoon took me to the canal bank going straight up the gully. Everything was quiet on that route and nothing could be seen. There was activity on the far side of the canal, north-east of the gully, vehicles moving and shouting. We then turned left along the canal for approximately 250 yds, when we turned sharp left again, making for some trees on the left of 10 Platoon position. Our movement was seen after moving in this direction. For approximately 150 yds we were fired at by Spandau, rifles and light mortar fire. We crawled towards the line of trees but still got fired at. We carried on to a gully and turned left into 11 Platoon area and back to Company H.Q. where I made a report.
>
> Conclusions: The first place we were fired on, I should think was by the canal, but the second time it seemed as though he also had a patrol out and was making in the same direction as ourselves.

Any movement by either side brought down shell and mortar fire. On the 5th October, 'C' Company reported that Lt. D.L.W. Bowden had been wounded while out on a reconnaissance patrol and was missing. A second patrol was sent out but he could not be found. At midnight, another patrol was sent out which also failed to find the Lieutenant. He returned to 'C' Company lines at 4.20 a.m. on the 6th, crawling in with a broken leg. Lt. D.L.W. Bowden reported that his patrol had reached the canal. He had crawled up the bank to see if anyone was about, and was there when a grenade was thrown and machine gun fire opened up. The patrol lost contact with the Lieutenant who sustained a broken leg. Alone, he had crawled the 600 yards back to the company lines.

On this day, 231 Brigade on the right was relieved by the 508th Parachute Regiment, 82nd U.S. Airborne Division, who proved to be most helpful and co-operative at all times. The relief by the 4th Bn. Royal Welsh Fusiliers [53rd Division] commenced at 5 p.m. on the 7th October. The movement was spotted by the enemy, who put down a heavy artillery bombardment. Maj. A. F. Douglas-Smith commanding 'B' Company was seriously wounded and died shortly afterwards. With the companies half in and half out of their original positions, an order was received from Brigade to stop the relief, on instructions from 53rd Division. Lieutenant Colonel Mogg, worried about the situation, ordered the companies to move out and concentrate in the area just behind Bemel. An hour later, Brigade revoked the order and the relief was completed.

Four days' rest at Nijmegen followed. The whole battalion was accommodated in the Missehuis. Baths and cleaning up commenced immediately, games and cinema visits were organised. On the 10th of the month, the Commanding Officer with his Company Commanders reconnoitred emergency positions round Bemel, which were to be occupied should the Germans attack from the Reichwald area. The rest ended on the 12th and the battalion relieved the 2nd Devons in Elst. It was positioned around the area of the level crossing north of Elst 'B' Company was in reserve, 'A' Company was on the right in the northern edge of Elst, 'C' Company was on the left round the road and rail bridges over the canal. 'D' Company was behind 'C' facing north-east. Over the next few weeks, the daily routine remained very much the same, and was reminiscent of World War I. Patrols went out, harassing shelling and mortaring occurred from time to time, mines were laid and wire erected. The German positions ran from the railway bridge over the lower Rhine to a point just short of the Laar Straat crossing. It turned here to cross the main road and south along the road to within 200 yards of the Wettering Canal, a stretch where the opposing lines were divided by the width of the road. The line then crossed the open fields for a short distance, then along the canal as far as Haldaren. The British line was a closely woven system of company areas in groups of houses, orchards and the open fields.

'C' Company were in close contact with the enemy. On the 15th, a party of Germans was spotted by L/Cpl. Ernest Jones, Second in Command of a section. The enemy was moving up a ditch on the far side of the main road towards his position. The Lance Corporal took three men and crawled out over 50 yards towards the enemy to get better observation. He found that the party was 15 strong. He sent one of his three men back to the company to report and remained out of sight of the enemy party until it had past him and now lay between him and the rest of his section. The three men attacked the enemy with Sten guns and grenades. The Germans scattered and eight were taken prisoners. During the action, Lance Corporal Jones' men were wounded and lay on the exposed road. Under heavy fire he got them back to the section post. He inflicted further casualties on the enemy as they tried to withdraw. He was awarded the Military Medal for his leadership, initiative and determination. The prisoners, who were with the 37th Fortress Battalion, did not appear fit and were of very low morale. Over the time spent in the Island, many of the prisoners taken came from this unit. Lieutenant Brewer described:

> General Horrocks, our Corps Commander, christened the enemy troops in the area, rather aptly, the 'Duodenal Divisions'. All the dregs of the German Army were reputed to be in that part of the line. On one prisoner captured was a 'chit' from his C.O. excusing him saluting – he was blind in one eye, the sight of the other was defective, making it impossible for him to recognise officers at a distance! On another was found a copy of Company Orders, one of which stated that the sick parades had been far too large in the past and in the future no man under 45 would go sick! They were a very sorry crowd indeed.

The battalion was relieved by the 6th Bn. D.L.I. on the 15th October. On the 17th, it was back in the line and relieved two companies of the 6th Bn. Green Howards and one company of the 6th D.L.I. It had rained for some time and the area was a sea of mud. A report in the regimental museum best describes the conditions:

> The area now taken over included the worst positions in the Island. 'D' Coy. were forward, between De Laar and the railway, with one platoon in a ruined house on the far side of the railway practically in the German FDLs [Forward Defence Locations]. The only way up to the coy was by a muddy track across the fields and all movement had to be restricted to night time, as the greater part of that area was under observation. 'B' Coy. were less inaccessible, in positions south of the orchard at 704729, extending up to the railway but their physical conditions were, if possible, worse, as every trench they dug filled up with water. 'C' returned to their old area round the canal bridges.

A special order was issued on the 18th by Lieutenant Colonel Mogg to the Northumberland and Durham Welfare Association. It read:

> The Commanding Officer, on behalf of all ranks, wishes to thank the Northumberland and Durham Welfare Association for its truly magnificent gift of 90,000 cigarettes.
> It is a great inspiration to the men to know that they are constantly in the thoughts of the people of Northumberland and Durham."

'C' Company lost two men captured by an enemy patrol from an S.S. unit in Arnhem, which got behind the company's forward positions. Deserters coming into the battalion lines were from the 41st Fortress Battalion. Troops of poor quality, they were pleased to be out of the war. As winter came on, the main concern of the units holding the Island was that the Germans might open the floodgates and inundate the area. Lieutenant Brewer recalled:

> Our intelligence kept us informed as to the water level and when it would be ideal for flooding. We also had a plan worked out as to what we'd do if he flooded it anyway – exercise 'Noah'. Certain units were to withdraw to Nijmegen immediately, others were to cover the withdrawal. All roads and tracks had their safe edges marked with high posts painted white so as to avoid unnecessary ditching and DUKWS (those amphibious vehicles) stood at vantage points. Altogether not a very cheerful prospect, especially as our Battalion was holding the covering sector when intelligence said, 'Any minute now!' Luckily we were spared and the night after we left the floods came – finding the 49th Div. instead of 50 Div.

During the afternoon of the 20th October both sides exchanged artillery, mortar and machine gun fire. The German fire increased due to too much movement being observed on the track leading to 'B' Company H.Q. One shell exploded next to company H.Q. and the battalion Second in Command, Maj. A.E. Hillier O.B.E. and Lt. P. Kettle were wounded. Major Hillier died of his wounds. On the 22nd, the battalion was relieved by the 5th Bn. East Yorkshire Regiment and moved into Nijmegen. Again, the whole battalion was billeted in the Missehuis.

Three officers and 20 other ranks went to Antwerp for 48 hours' leave. On the 28th, the battalion moved back into the Island and relieved the III Battalion, 508th Parachute Regiment, U.S. 82nd Airborne Division. The positions taken over were very good, invariably with overhead cover. Companies positions centred round Heuvel. Intermittent shelling and mortaring continued as usual. Patrols were active at night which, on the whole, were quiet except for some Spandau fire on fixed lines. On the 30th, a general readjustment of positions was carried out. 'C' Company positions were taken over by the 1st Bn. Hampshire Regiment, while 'A' and 'B' Companies took over from two companies of 6th D.L.I. American artillery was in support and displayed remarkable accuracy in knocking down houses thought to be used as observation posts.

On the 1st November, the battalion was relieved by the 8th Bn. D.L.I. and moved to Elst for three days. It was in divisional reserve with a counter-attack role should the enemy get into the front line. The 6th Battalion of the regiment was relieved on the 5th November. The positions were in the sector east of Elst and centred around the small village of Aam. A reconnaissance patrol sent out on the night of the 7th November ran into trouble. It had set off an 'S' mine wounding Sergeant Eddy. Lts. A.R. Groves and McClarty were wounded by Spandau fire. Lieutenant McClarty died on the way back to safety. Another patrol up to the canal ran into a German post and Lt. M.C. Hibbert and Pte. J.J. Huntley were killed. Bearings were taken on flying bombs passing overhead in an attempt to locate where they were being fired from. The enemy was quite lively in this area. In addition to shelling, mortaring and machine gun fire, patrols were active and raiding parties appeared from time to time. On the 13th November, the battalion was relieved and moved to Elst. On the 16th, it moved to Ressen.

Unknown to the division, a decision had been taken at the highest level to disband the 50th Division. This was due to the manpower crisis. The 21st Army Group was now running out of reinforcements, particularly infantry, and was faced with a solution which entailed the breaking up of divisions. The 59th Division had already been broken up in the late summer of 1944. With the threat of air raids to Britain now receding, there was less need for anti-aircraft cover and personnel could be drawn from some of the corps, for example the R.A.S.C. These would need retraining and it was decided to set up cadres to retrain men of the R.A. and services such as the R.A.S.C. as infantry. An advance party had been sent to Poperinghe where, it was said, the division would go on its way back to England.

Pte. Jim Ratcliffe was a member of this party. He recalled:

On our first night, Ted Cowell and myself ended up, in a pub called 'Julian's Bar' and we had a great time with a bunch of Belgian WWI veterans…We had been in Poperinghe for about ten days waiting for something to happen when word came through that we were to go back to the Battalion. The powers that be had decided not to break up the 9th but to put us in 131 Lorried Infantry Brigade in the 7th Armoured Division…On our way back we stopped at Ghent and, whilst I was in the toilets, a couple of Jocks from the 51st Highland Division walked in…I thought, 'Here we go, trouble.' The 50th and the 51st did not get on. It all started way back in the desert when, according to the media, the 51st were the only ones doing any fighting. They asked what I was doing around here and I told them that the 50th Division was breaking up. They said, 'It's a bloody shame. What's the Army thinking of?' They were probably thinking who they were going to fight with in the future!

Meanwhile, the division continued with its duties in the Island. A tragic accident happened on the 19th November when a party on a mine-laying task lost three men who were wounded when a box of anti-personnel mines was dropped and exploded. Pte. W.R. Watts died of his wounds. A further six men were wounded when a truck in which they were travelling over the Nijmegen Bridge received a 'near miss' from an enemy shell. All were members of 'C' Company. From the 22nd of the month, the battalion was in brigade reserve. The 8th Battalion was relieved on the 26th and the battalion occupied its final positions in the Island. These were in a corner of the line north and east of Elst. 'C' Company was in its old positions around the canal bridges. 'A' Company was on their right and 'B' Company was separated from the rest of the battalion in orchards between Elst and Aam. 'D' Company was in reserve. On the 28th, 'C' Company reported the loss of two men who had gone back to the cookhouse for rations. These had run into a German patrol and were captured. This patrol, in turn, was shot up by the company's forward patrol and a standing patrol from 'A' Company. Private Anderson got away but was hit twice in the back and arm before getting across the canal. Nothing was heard of Private Nixon, the other man taken prisoner. From time to time groups of Germans were seen moving about and were fired on with Bren guns and rifles. Some of the enemy were seen to fall and be carried away. On the 30th November, the battalion was relieved by the 2nd Bn. South Wales Borderers and moved to back to Nijmegen.

The 50th Division, which had fought with such great distinction in France and Belgium in 1940, the Western Desert in 1942–43, Sicily in 1943 and now Western Europe in 1944, was no more. At Gazala in early 1942, it was the only British infantry division facing the enemy anywhere in the world. Many had been the encounters; many friends had paid the ultimate price. It was retired with honour. Many of the old personnel who had been with it for all or most of the war were to go back to England. Some were found less violent duties in the rear areas. Lieutenant Brewer recalled:

> 50th Division was broken up – a nucleus consisting of some of the old soldiers, who had done their share of the fighting, would go home with the Division. The rest of us would go elsewhere. A Battalion of the Devons and ourselves were joining the 7th Armoured Division – the famous Desert Rats…Before we left Lt/Col. Mogg was given a free hand re-organising our Battalion with the cream of the Brigade – he could throw out anyone. Officers and men alike, that he did not consider to be up to scratch and replace them with the pick from the other battalions…On the 1st December 1944, we bade farewell to 50 Div., in Nijmegen and hail to the 7th Armd. Div. in Kinroy, Belgium.

Capt. G.B. Harrison and Lts. A.M. Moodie, W.S. Carr, A.F. Capstick and P.J.G. Hunt joined from the 6th Bn. D.L.I.

The 9th Battalion followed the same route as its predecessor in World War I. It, too, left the 50th Division before it was broken up in 1918 and under the command of the 62nd West Riding Division, served till the end of that war and entered Berlin as an occupying force.

CHAPTER XXIV

WITH THE 7TH ARMOURED DIVISION

T he battalion had a very short time to re-equip and take on the responsibilities and duties of the infantry arm of an armoured division. The 7th Armoured Division was part of XII Corps and was resting when the battalion joined it. It was fortunate that, in Lieutenant Colonel Mogg, it had a young, intelligent and able Commander. Private Mallabar described what the men of the battalion thought of their C.O:

> The new armoured role seemed to suit him perfectly. He was the ideal commander of a motorised unit and his well known phrase was, 'Crack on!' He would come along the line shouting, 'Crack on !' I remember somebody telling me, I think it was the R.S.M., saying to him, 'Colonel, the centre line's been cut,' meaning the line of advance. 'Never mind,' he says, 'Crack on! Buggar the centre line.' We thought he was great. He was a very, sort of, fair man to deal with. Really very friendly and he also was a brave man. Before we joined the 7th Armoured Division I remember, in Normandy, when we were still in 50 Division, I was crouching in my little trench. there were bullets and shells flying about and there was an ammunition truck burning quite near to me. Colonel Mogg was walking up and down in front of my slit trench with a walking stick saying, 'Keep your head down son, you'll be alright. Keep your head down son' and he was just swinging his walking stick and walking up and down and he's a big target. So, I admired him immensely.

The 9th Battalion replaced the 1st/7th Queens in 131 Brigade. The other battalions in the brigade were 1st/5th Queens and 2nd Devons. The 9th arrived at Kinroy, near Maeseyck, at 3.35 a.m. on the 2nd December. Later in the day a move was made to Dilsen, into uncomfortable billets, though amongst friendly civilians. The feelings of officers and other ranks about the move to 131 Brigade were somewhat mixed. Lieutenant Brewer recalled:

> After spending our first night in a large school at Kinroy, we moved next day to join our Brigade – 131 – at Dilsen in Holland. It seemed a horrible area. (We moved in the mood to find trouble with everything. The esprit de corps in 50 Div. had been exceedingly high and, as one is inclined to do in such cases, we compared all the bad in our new colleagues with the good in our old. Subsequently events proved that, in this particular case, we were not always far wrong as we might have been. – there was little left of the old 7th Armd. of the Desert, bar the name.) As I was saying, the area at Dilsen was not all that it might have been. The houses were few and small and, in consequence, we were pretty cramped. The new Brigadier came to see us – our old one had been very young, keen and intelligent and obviously a man. – This one looked like the 'Fat boy of Peckham' seemed to be playing soldiers in a real 'blimpish' manner and one could almost see the Red Tape oozing out of his ears (or am I being a bit hard?). At any rate, we were not favourably impressed and continued with our ticking – and changing our signs on our uniforms and

vehicles. The T.T.'s were all supposed to have been removed before we moved – for security reasons – but it was amazing how long and [with] how many excuses the old T.T. remained on some vehicles.

On the 4th December, Lieutenant Colonel Mogg attended his first conference at brigade headquarters. Maj. Gen. L.O. Lyne D.S.O. welcomed the battalion to the division and outlined future operations. He also announced that leave to the United Kingdom would commence on 1st January 1945. Orders had been received for the battalion to relieve a Guards Battalion in the Gangelt–Hastenrath–Kievelberg–Vintelen area. This was to take place on the 7th December. This was a very open area of the country, compared to conditions on the Island. Company defence locations were set up based on villages, with the large gaps between covered by fire from weapons. Anti-tank weapons were on a much stronger scale than formerly. Three troops of tanks and two troops of 17-pdr. anti-tank guns were deployed in the battalion area. On the 7th, the battalion took over the new area. 'A' Company moved to Hastenrath, supported by one troop of tanks, a troop of 17-pdrs, a section of medium machine guns and two sections of 3-in. mortars. 'D' Company was at Kievelberg, with four 6-pdr. anti-tank guns and one section of medium machine guns. 'C' Company went to Vintelen, with a troop of tanks, a troop of 17-pdrs and a section of 3-in. mortars. 'B' Company was in reserve in Gangelt and covering the road to Hastenrath. The battalion occupied ground in three countries. The rifle companies were in Germany, 'A' Echelon at Sittard in Holland and 'B' Echelon at Dilsen in Belgium. Due to the danger of German patrol infiltration, orders were issued that no parties of less than four should go out to companies by night and each vehicle should carry an escort of three men, provided by 'B' Company.

The Commanding Officer had a very narrow escape on the 8th. Travelling to Vintelen with Lt. W.L. Carr, Assault Pioneer Platoon, to visit 'C' Company, a shell exploded close to the Dingo vehicle and the Lieutenant suffered a head injury. Several metal splinters hit the car but Lieutenant Colonel Mogg was unharmed. Lieutenant Carr later died of his wounds.

Patrols were sent out each night. Many of these came across trip wires, mines and booby traps. German patrol dogs appeared and had to be dealt with. On the 10th of the month, 'A' Company captured one of these dogs that was lurking in its area. An entry in the War Diary for the evening of the 10th read:

> 1925 hrs – This evening 'A' Company fought another dog war. One went round the platoons and was last seen going up the road having avoided all trip flares laid for it.
> 1945 hrs – Forward posts also heard a whistling noise some way off towards the German lines but if it was meant to call the dog off, it was unsuccessful, as the dog was shot.

The 9th Battalion had a reasonably quiet introduction to life in 131 Brigade and 7th Armoured Division. Shelling and mortaring by the enemy was sporadic. On the

17th of the month, the battalion was relieved by the 3rd Battalion, Irish Guards and moved into divisional reserve at Geleen, south of Sittard. The time in this area was largely spent in erecting defensive positions in Geleen and the high ground south east of Sittard, in case the Germans attacked southwards from Roermond towards Masstricht. These attacks did not take place. Training, daily drills, physical training and sport commenced. Preparations had gone ahead for Christmas and it was celebrated in the traditional army way. A Christmas tree was obtained and erected and the regimental band played for church parades. Lieutenant Colonel Mogg had arranged a party for the officers on Christmas Eve. Lieutenant Brewer recalled:

> For Christmas Eve, the C.O. had arranged a party for the officers…Everyone went mad and enjoyed themselves to the full. The dinner, which started the proceedings, was excellent and to conclude it, instead of speeches the C.O. made everyone in turn get up and recite, sing, tell a story or something…that provided some excellent entertainment…The C.O. the whole time was the absolute life and soul of the party.

Pte. Jim Ratcliffe remembered that Christmas:

> We actually had our Christmas dinner in the canteen of the Limburg Mine, a huge complex, the biggest mine in Europe. The man whose house we were billeted in was the foreman of the mine. We had a smashing dinner followed by sweets, chocolate and fruit. We did not eat this but took it back for the kids. Two of the lads borrowed a motor bike and went back to the village where we had been and shot an Ox. They hacked off one of the back legs and the one on the pillion carried it back across his shoulders. He must have been a powerful lad. They gave it to the people who the platoon was billeted with. We had a great party that night. I remember breaking a wine glass. So we went back in the line. I took a good look round the village and obtained a full set of crystal glasses which I had our dispatch rider deliver to the house where we had been staying.

Lieutenant Colonel Mogg's Christmas message to the battalion read:

> We are spending Christmas Day on the borders of Germany. To some of us it is our first wartime Christmas in the Army, to most of us it is our Sixth. Never before have we been able to expect, with so much confidence, the finish of this war before our next Christmas.
>
> Let us resolve that during the New Year we will put all we can into the final burst to ensure that we will quickly be united with our families and friends at home.
>
> We have a great reputation, which means a tremendous amount. We must treasure that reputation.
>
> I wish each one of you the very best of luck and a happy 1945.
>
> I know that you would like to join me in sending our best Christmas wishes to those of the 9th Battalion who are in hospital, or who are not now with us.

On the 26th December, the battalion relieved the 2nd Devons north of Sittard. Snow, frost and morning mists were now amongst the hazards to be contended. The engine of each vehicle had to be started and warmed up every two hours. White

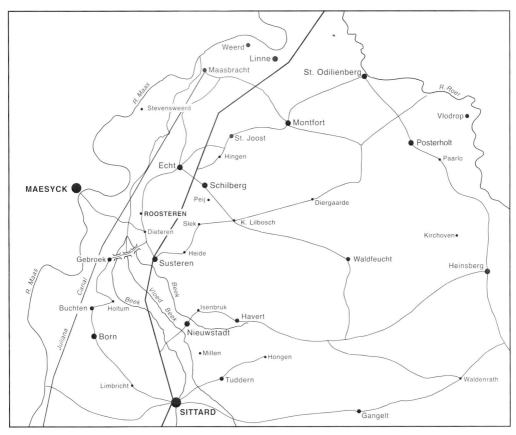

camouflage suits were issued for those going out on patrol. A white blanket of snow covered the landscape, and the enemy mines that were laid in profusion and extremely difficult to detect. 'A' and 'D' Companies occupied Millen and 'B' and 'S' Companies Tuddern. 'C' Company was in reserve, near battalion headquarters in Overhoven. The German forward positions were amongst the woods and houses in front of the Saeffeler Beek. No man's land was quite wide. Owing to morning mists, forward companies had to remain on the alert. Patrols, as usual, went out each night. Intermittent shelling and mortaring from the enemy occurred and prompted a response from supporting guns and mortars. Future plans for an offensive in the Sittard Triangle were being prepared. There was a real need to take an enemy prisoner for identification and information but, try as they might, patrols were just not able to capture any. So 1944 ended with the prospect of much more fighting as the enemy was expected to contest every yard of his homeland but everyone was confident this New Year, 1945, would see the end of the war.

New Year's Day was quite eventful. The largest number of German aircraft for some time was seen flying overhead. These were ME 109s and FW 190s and were returning from a surprise raid on Allied airfields in Belgium. Two of these aircraft were shot down, one near Millen and the other between Tuddern and Hongen. On the 2nd

327

A 9th Battalion patrol in winter snow suits creeps forward at Millen, north of Sittard, January 1945.

January, General Dempsey, G.O.C. Second Army, and Lieutenant General Ritchie, G.O.C. XII Corps, visited the battalion. Patrolling continued at night and shelling and mortaring by both sides flared up on occasions. Sightings of enemy were made from time to time and, whenever possible, artillery fire was brought down upon them.

During the morning of the 8th January, two battalion snipers in snowsuits penetrated almost to Isenbruch. On their return journey they entered a house and shot three Germans sleeping in a ground floor room. Five of the enemy that appeared shortly afterwards round the side of the house were fired upon. The two snipers got away unscathed. It was considered essential to take a prisoner and a raid on Isenbruch was planned. One section of 'D' Company, under Lt. R.H.E. Hill, was to seize a house, half way to the final objective, whilst two platoons of 'C' Company passed through. One of the platoons had to establish a firm base east of Isenbruch and the other was to go through to the village. The jumping-off place was Millen. The supporting artillery fire came down upon Isenbruch, Havert, Schalbruch and known German positions. Mortars and machine guns joined in. There was no retaliation from the enemy and the start line was reached without incident. Unfortunately, at this point, enemy artillery fired on the start line, which caused some men to scatter. Quickly reorganised, the men moved forward. A German mortar fired on the halfway house and Lieutenant Hill was wounded. His section held the house throughout the attack. The leading platoon of 'C' Company advanced through a minefield and suffered casualties. Pte. William Foster was one of three men who succeeded in crossing the minefield. He returned and collected the remainder of his platoon, which consisted of 11 men, and tried to lead them across the minefield. Moving out into an open field they saw a tank and, not knowing it was derelict, withdrew and suffered more casualties on the way back through the minefield. Private Foster had his leg broken and part of his foot blown off. Maj. W.H.M. Anderson, commanding 'C' Company, crossed the minefield three times in an effort to reorganise the company and move around the enemy flank but casualties were heavy and the withdrawal continued. Total casualties in addition to Lieutenant Hill were 20 other ranks killed, wounded or missing. Capt. H.W. Ashton, Second in Command of 'C' Company, went out with a party of stretcher bearers and collected three of the wounded from the minefield. Private Foster came in on the following day. He had heard the rescue party but thought they were Germans and waited to come in on his own, which he did crossing two wide ditches on the way. He was in terrible pain. Whilst crawling back to the lines, a distance of 1,000 yards, he observed parties of Germans moving about, which he reported to his unit on his return. It took Private Foster 12 hours to complete his journey, still dragging his Bren gun with him. He was awarded an immediate Military Medal.

Pte. Ronald Mallabar, Signal Platoon, was on this raid and described the action:

> It was a bigger than usual show, there were four of us signallers went with it instead of the usual one, four of us with 18 Sets. It was in heavy snow [when we] started the advance. It was night-time and as soon as we set off shells began to fall…There was a dyke in front of us, across our front and a ditch about 6 feet deep and about the same across, half-filled with water, which was frozen, of course. So we ran forward and jumped into the ditch to avoid shells and we were standing waist deep in frozen water with these shells falling among us. I was on the radio shouting, 'Lift the stonk! Lift the stonk! Lift the stonk a hundred yards!'…Somebody stuck his revolver in the air and said, 'If you don't shut up, I'll kill you! The Jerries are just over the other side of the dyke.' I must have been shouting louder than usual. Anyway the barrage did lift and moved forward. We clambered out of the ditch and ran straight into a minefield the Germans had laid and the snow had covered it. People started to get their legs blown off…We gave up and went back. I found the way back to Battalion H.Q. The only surviving signaller of the four. I put my radio set down on the ground outside the door and went in. It was a barn and I met the sergeant, my sergeant, who said, 'Is your radio alright?' I'm usually an easy-going fellow but I started shouting, 'I'm the only one of your four signallers who have come back and you want to know if my radio's alright,' and the Colonel pulled me off and gave me a cup of tea and said, 'It's alright son, sit down.'

On the 11th January, the battalion was relieved by the 1st Bn. Gordon Highlanders of the 52nd Lowland Division and moved to Buchten. Preparations were now started for Operation Blackcock, the attack to clear the triangle formed by the Rivers Roer, Wurm and Maas and bring the Allied line up to the River Roer on a front of approximately 12 miles. The enemy units in opposition were the 176th and 183rd German Infantry Divisions, which were dug in supported by self-propelled guns and the dreaded 88s. The 7th Armoured Division would attack on the left flank of XII Corps. Under divisional command were the 8th Armoured Brigade and 155 Brigade from the 52nd Division. The 52nd and 43rd Divisions would advance from the Millen – Gangelt Line up to the Roer at Heinsberg. Three days before the main attack was launched, 1st/5th Queens was to take the village of Bakenhoven, 1,000 yards beyond the front line. They did this supported by the 1st Royal Tanks. An important element on which the planning was based was that the frost would hold and the ground remain firm for the tanks. Unfortunately, a slight thaw took place and this hampered the movement of the tanks and supporting vehicles.

Exercise 'Dryshod' was carried out on the 13th January, and took place near Munstergeleen. This was a rehearsal for the battalion attack that would take place on the 15th. Three sections of canal were dug out by the Royal Engineers and a stream in front of the village answered for the two canals that would have to be crossed in the actual attack. The plan was for an advance on a three-company front. One of these companies was 'A' Company 1st/5th Queens, which came under command in place of 'C' Company, which had lost heavily in the raid described above and was given the task of defending Gebroek. The first problem to be highlighted by the rehearsal was that the white tape used to mark the start line was barely visible when laid on the snow and it was impossible to dye it another colour in time. The kapok bridges gave little trouble but several ladder bridges broke when dropped on the far bank or were too short. It was suggested that ropes be attached to the bank to enable them to be slowly lowered. It was also found that carrying parties from outside companies would be necessary, as too many men were required to do this work.

Heavy enemy counter-attacks were launched on the 1st/5th Queens in the Bakenhoven area and two sections of the battalion The Carrier Platoon was sent up to Gebroek as support. It arrived to find that the situation had been cleared up by the Queens. One platoon of 'D' Company had also been sent up to Bakenhoven. One man in this platoon, L/Cpl. W.C. Sambourne, was killed and two wounded by mortar fire while carrying ammunition. On the 14th, exercise 'Dryshod' was repeated and further improvements were made to the ladder bridges. Parties from 'B' Echelon were used to carry materials and equipment forward and this proved successful.

The plan for the capture of Dieteren by 131 Brigade was for the 9th Battalion to assault the town and cover the bridging of the Vloed Beek and Roode Beek. On this being accomplished, the 1st/5th Queens (less 'A' Company under 9 D.L.I. command) plus one squadron of tanks of 1st R.T.R. were to pass through and capture Susteren, while the 1st Bn. Rifle Brigade advanced up the main road from the south. On Susteren being cleared, the 2nd Devons and tanks of the 1st R.T.R would pass through Dieteren and capture Echt and Schilberg. The 8th Armoured Brigade would occupy the high ground near Waldfeucht and the 22nd Armoured Brigade would pass through into the Linne–Montfort area.

Operation Order No. 7 ordered the 9th Battalion to capture Dieteren. The forward companies in the assault were 'B' Company, right and 'A' Company left, both supported by one section each of the Assault Pioneers. 'B' Company objectives were the eastern exits from Deteren and 'A' Company was to take the northern exits leading from the town. The battalion of the Queens was to follow 'B' Company and capture the concrete works between Dieteren and Susteren. Each advancing company would be supported by four Flail tanks and a barrage of artillery, medium machine guns and 3-in. mortars. Six- and 17-pdr. anti-tank guns were to be prepared to move up quickly in support of the advancing troops. 'A', 'B' and 'D' Companies of the battalion and 'A' Company of the Queens were each given three kapok bridges for crossing the two canals and, with the exception of 'D' Company, carried four 22-foot ladder bridges to cross the first canal and a further four for the second canal crossing. 'D' Company was given two of these bridges. The rate of advance was to be 100 yards every three minutes.

The attack, due to take place on the 15th of the month, was postponed. This decision was received with some relief as it was an extremely dark night and the snow made direction finding far from easy. The attack would now take place on the following morning at 7.30 a.m. It was also decided to cover the advance across the open ground and the canal crossings with smoke.

The advance got underway on time. Almost complete surprise seemed to have been achieved. Enemy retaliatory fire was slight at this stage. Dieteren was reached with little trouble. Both battalions crossed the Vloed Beek and soon crossed the Roode Beek. 'A' Company captured intact the stone bridge that crossed Roode Beek, though it had been prepared for demolition. 'A' Company of the Queens was ordered forward at 8.40 a.m. and 'D' Company came forward. Capt. Roy Griffiths was with 'D' Company. He recalled:

> Part of the equipment we carried in 'D' Company, I think the other companies had the same, were ladders. There were two dykes we had to cross and the bridges had been blown just before Dieteren. We had to cross over on these ladders. We looked like a company of painters and decorators, you know. These bloody great ladders, but they worked. It went very well…Everybody knew what he had to do and where they had to go. Morale was high.

'A' Company reported that it was on its objective at 8.56 a.m. At this time, 'B' Company was moving up the main road into the town and 'Q' Company (Queens) was across the Roode Beek. Two prisoners were taken, each from the 416 Anti-Tank Company 176th Division. They said there were 60 men in Dieteren and 80 in Susteren. Battalion headquarters and 'C' Company had started their move from Gebroek to

Dieteren. 'B' Company reached its final objective in Dieteren at 9.05 a.m. 'Q' Company moved towards the concrete works. Consolidation and mopping up followed. By 10.30 a.m., all companies were in position on their objectives and preparing for the expected enemy counter-attack. The battalion anti-tank guns were sent for. In the afternoon the Germans, now recovered from their surprise, began a systematic and heavy artillery bombardment of Dieteren, the bridges over the canals and the open ground between. The bridging sites were covered by an effective smokescreen laid down by our artillery but this did not deter the enemy guns or lessen their accuracy. 'B' Company came in for particular attention and the company's positions were severely shelled by artillery and mortars. Counter-fire failed to lessen the enemy efforts. A great problem was caused by the failure to build a crossing over the first canal. A single scissors bridge had collapsed after a Flail tank in the act of crossing caused it to cant over to one side. The Royal Engineers were suffering considerable casualties. Two lorry loads of equipment were blown up by a mine on the road out of Bakenhoven. To cap all, a thaw had set in and the ground was being turned into impassable mud.

Communications between the attacking units remained good but contact with the outside world was constantly breaking down. Replacement radio batteries could only be man-handled across the muddy ground. Pte. Thomas Foster was a signaller. He volunteered to go back to the canal area and carry up radio batteries to the forward positions. He crawled and walked the two miles under severe shelling and mortaring carrying batteries and wireless sets urgently required to maintain the vital communications throughout the battalion. He did this on no less than seven occasions, and was awarded an immediate Military Medal. Maj. Anthony G.R. Noble, commanding 'B' Company, was awarded the Military Cross. His citation read:

> On reaching the second canal the leading platoon came under heavy enemy m.g. fire from the far side and was forced to take cover. Realising the momentum of the attack was likely to be stopped, Major Noble, in spite of heavy fire, immediately ran forward and rallied the men. He then led the platoon into and across the canal and charged the enemy. He succeeded in killing two and the remainder fled. He continued the charge on to the final objective with such determination and vigour that the enemy was thoroughly routed, 30 prisoners being taken and more than 20 enemy killed.
>
> A few hours later this company attacked Schilberg during darkness and fierce hand-to-hand fighting developed.
>
> During the whole of the attack however, this officer showed such splendid powers of leadership and command that control was never lost and the action was entirely successful.

No serious German counter-attack materialised during the 16th but the heavy shelling and mortaring continued throughout. Dieteren was firmly held but the enemy was still in Susteren and Oud Roosteren. Supplies could not come up for some time and the men had to rely on their 24-hour packs for food. During the night 16th/17th January, supplies and support began to arrive. Leading the way were the anti-tank guns and carriers with food and ammunition. In their book *A Short History 7th Armoured Division June 1943–July 1945* authors Captains Lindsay and Johnston wrote:

> The salient feature of this battle was the outstanding determination of the Durhams, who faced the enemy and the bitter weather undaunted and by their example inspired all others to make the operation a success.

Casualties on the 16th January included Pte. R. Wood of 'A' Company, who was killed. A further 14 men were wounded.

During the morning of the 17th, the 1st/5th Queens attacked Susteren. The village was captured by late afternoon. Oud Roosteren was captured by the 6th Bn. King's Own Scottish Borderers of the 52nd Lowland Division. Meanwhile, as communications worsened, two companies of the 2nd Devons were brought up to the Gebroek–Bakenhoven area to cover the canal crossings. The Germans now showed their hand and the long awaited counter-attack came in up the line of the Vloed Beek. A platoon of 'C' Company under the command of Capt. H.W. Ashton and Lt. W.O. Slee was sent to a point 200 yards south of the bridge to deal with this situation. Private Mallabar went with this platoon. The move was not without its funny moment, as he described:

> The next message was, 'Enemy m.g. teams have infiltrated behind you. They are firing along the canal and the Engineers can't get on with the bridge building. Send a platoon back to deal with them.' So I went with them…The officer in charge of the platoon was in front, then me, then the riflemen strung out behind us, all in single file a few yards apart. It was still foggy, snow on the ground. Suddenly the officer throws himself to the ground. I couldn't hear a thing for the row in the headphones, so I flung myself on the ground, everybody behind did likewise. The officer gets up and starts walking forward. I get up again cursing because everytime I dived on the ground, up came the radio on my back, knocking my helmet over my eyes and it wasn't very nice and then there was the weight of the thing on my back when I hit the ground. Down he goes again and he gets up again and I get up again. On we go again and then down he goes again. So I lay on the ground. Then I realised he was shaking. So I crawled forward to him and found he was shaking with laughter. I said, 'What's the matter?' and he lifted his water bottle and shook it. The ice in it made a clicking sound like a rifle bolt being operated and he thought he was going to be shot everytime he made a move. So he just lay there and laughed. I didn't feel like laughing. I just had to pass the word back along the line that it was alright. We moved on again.

On reaching the area of the bridge about 60 Germans were observed; 40 of them were moving on the bridge and the other 20 were seen near a barn. Captain Ashton ordered one section to engage the party of 40 Germans whilst he led the other two sections in a bayonet charge against the party near the barn. After a fierce struggle, the enemy fled leaving behind five or six dead and eight prisoners. Captain Ashton was awarded the Military Cross. His citation concluded:

9th Battalion moving up to Echt in Kangaroos – armoured personnel vehicles – January 1945.

> Throughout two very difficult days of continuous fighting this officer led his company with exceptional skill and courage and on several occasions personally led the attack on the enemy positions with the bayonet.

The Queens were being heavily counter-attacked in Susteren by infantry and tanks. At 11 a.m., 'D' Company was sent down to reinforce the Queens. In Dieteren, the afternoon was reasonably quiet. The 2nd Devons, supported by tanks of 'C' Squadron the 1st Royal Tank Regiment and some Crocodiles (flame-throwing tanks) began moving up to attack Ophoven and Echt. By the evening, the 2nd Devons were in Echt but their column moving up the main road was still held up. The road was heavily mined and obstructed by trees that the enemy had felled. 'B' Company was sent forward to support this thrust. The rest of the 9th Battalion was warned that they might be required to follow the western column to Echt. The Devons captured Echt on the morning of the 18th and moved on towards Schilberg. 'D' Company rejoined the 9th Battalion at 7.45 a.m. on the 18th. Later in the morning, the battalion – less 'B' Company – was relieved by the 5th Bn. Kings Own Scottish Borderers and moved up to Echt to relieve the Devons. One company of the K.O.S.B. moved through to occupy Oud Roosteren. Kangaroo troop carriers picked up the battalion, which moved to an assembly area south of Echt. 'A' and 'C' Companies moved to the northern edge of the town and 'D' Company was in reserve. Patrols were sent out to the canal to see if any Germans were holding out on the far side and to find out if any bridges were intact. All bridges had been destroyed and no Germans were found. The situation remained quiet for the rest of the day.

Casualties on the 17th and 18th included the following killed in action: Ptes. L. Jobling, E. Hargreaves and H. Wiles – all 'H.Q.' Company; L/Cpl. R. Barrie, 'D' Company; Cpl. W. Cheese, 'A' Company; Ptes. C. Paterson and E. Hester, 'C' Company. Pte. R. Wills, 'H.Q.' Company, died of his wounds.

At 9.30 a.m. on the 19th January, Lieutenant Colonel Mogg attended a Brigade conference and was informed that the 1st Bn. Rifle Brigade was to clear St. Joost. His battalion, supported by the 11th Hussars, was to advance on Montfort. The 2nd Devons were to help in the capture of St. Joost but being somewhat weak in numbers, 'D' Company of 9 D.L.I. was put under command of the 2nd Devons, its task to cover the eastern flank where the enemy was reported to be in some strength. 'D' Company returned to the battalion in the early afternoon. The remainder of the day was quiet. The road as far as Schilberg crossroads had been cleared by the Devons.

The Rifle Brigade was fighting in St. Joost and the 8th Armoured Brigade was heavily engaged in the area of Koninggbosh–Waldfeught–Bocket with the 52nd Division coming up towards them from the south. It was quite clear that the enemy was intending to fight for this ground, probably to delay the British advance so that the Siegfreid Line could be strongly manned. Two battalions of the German Parachute Regiment Hubner were appearing in the line, one in front of the 8th Armoured Brigade and one to defend Hingen and St. Joost. These were tough, experienced and fanatical troops. Hingen fell on the afternoon of the 20th but the advance was held up in front of St. Joost. A prisoner, taken by the 9th Battalion, stated that about 200 men were in St. Joost with orders to defend it to the last man. The 9th was ordered to provide one company to be prepared to assist the battalions fighting to clear the village and to go through and capture the bridge between St. Joost and Steil. 'C' Company (Maj. W. Anderson) was ordered to carry out this task and it moved up to Schilberg in readiness to attack.

In the plan drawn up, 'C' Company was to by-pass St. Joost on the eastern side and make straight for the bridge. The Rifle Brigade was to hold a firm base in Hingen. Lieutenant Colonel Mogg carried out a reconnaissance of the village but, due to the late arrival of orders, Company and Platoon Commanders were unable to carry out their own reconnaissance in daylight. 'C' Company moved out of Hingen and crossed the Krom Beek and disappeared into the night. Wireless communications broke down almost immediately and no news of the company's progress came back to battalion headquarters. An anxious Battalion Commander and his staff awaited news of the advance. The first information to arrive was carried by two stragglers who returned having lost touch with their platoon when crossing a stream. They were unable to give any information about the rest of the company or the enemy. At 11.40 p.m., the Rifle Brigade reported that its right forward company had made contact with the left-hand platoon of 'C' Company but had since lost touch. Everything appeared to be going according to plan. In reality, this was not the case. Shortly after midnight on the 21st, wireless communication was re-established. No. 13 Platoon reported that they had been split up and needed help. ' B' Company was put on standby to move up to Peij and attack up the main street of the village from there.

Stragglers began to arrive back at battalion headquarters. First, Sergeant Wilson brought in one prisoner from No. 6 Company Hubner Parachute Regiment. Lt. W.O. Slee returned at 3.30 a.m. He had been cut off from his platoon and knocked unconscious by an exploding bazooka rocket fired at a house in which he was sheltering. He was able to make his way back on recovering. Lieutenant Slee was the only officer to return. Altogether about 30 men came back and it was from their accounts that a description of the disaster was pieced together. Very early in the advance, the company had come under exceptionally heavy enemy shelling and mortaring. The company had been split up and sections and platoons killed or captured piecemeal before they had reached the outskirts of St. Joost. Most of the company were prisoners, amongst them Major Anderson. A few men who survived reached some buildings on the edge of St. Joost. Pte. Sidney Webster of 13 Platoon was one of them. He wrote:

> Apart from the Bren, I carried six Bren mags, two 75s and two 36 grenades. The 75s were for the solid ground conditions if we had to dig in anywhere. Everyone was moving. Our Platoon 13 along the canal side…our objectives the houses over the road and on the left. We crossed black like the night itself. We crouched around the outside for a while and with noises coming from the inside, threw 36 grenades in only to kill a couple of horses. Then the trouble began – for a while tracers and machine guns. So up in the loft we went and covered us with straw to keep hidden and also warm…

Cut off from the rest of the company, most of whom had been taken prisoner, Private Webster and the survivors of his platoon remained hidden in the house. He continued:

> We were now on our own…We had a little sleep in turn during the night and we could see white covered ground through the large cracks in the roof. As the day began, three German civilians spotted us in this loft…Within minutes there were shots fired through the roof and I was partly blinded for a minute or two and one of our lads was shot in the arm, Private McCarthy from North Shields. Including Mac, we were down to five, Corporal Wear from Shields, Privates Cliff Holmes, Clarke and myself. …we knew we couldn't stay here very much longer. Within half an hour we heard the sound of tanks. Through a small barred window at the gable end of the building, we noticed a large tank – a Tiger Tank! Our hopes were completely gone…Our artillery started firing next and we laid down behind the wall in this loft and prayed for it to cease. A shell hit the apex and we all wished we had been taken prisoners for a minute… Then I heard groans each side of me, Holmes and Clarke. My legs felt numb. I was covered with bricks and part of an old bike frame that was hanging up in the loft. Corporal Weir pulled the rubbish off

The 9th Battalion fight their way into St. Joost. A Crocodile flame thrower tank is in action in the village.

me…Cliff Holmes kept asking me for water and said his legs felt dead. I could see blood all over…Clarke had almost had it…So the Corporal said, 'We'll give ourselves up to get these lads treated.' While we were looking around for rags [for the wounds], the Germans opened out with tracers and set the straw alight and Holmes and Clarke gripped me, their final grasp before passing away in this loft full of flames and smoke…The three of us were eventually taken prisoner.

Private Webster escaped and hid in a small outhouse containing a boiler. He scrambled into the boiler and hid from the Germans who were continually moving about outside. The battalion, attacking into St. Joost, enabled him to reach safety very tired, wet and dirty. He was able to give information about his own platoon and a body of Germans in a small copse who were dealt with.

At dawn on the 21st, 'B' Company was sent forward to try and reach the survivors of 'C' Company. News had been received of the severe fighting inside the village involving the battalion of the Rifle Brigade. It was held up and had been driven back about 150 yards. It did not auger well for the company's attack. At 5 a.m., 'B' Company launched its attack up the village street; the advance was slow and costly. The enemy were fighting ferociously for every house and garden. By daylight the attack had come to a stop. Lieutenant Colonel Mogg made another plan. 'A' and 'D'

Companies, supported by the tanks of two squadrons of the 8th Hussars and two troops of Crocodiles were ordered to attack. 'A' Company would attack first and 'D' Company would pass through to the bridge. 'A' Company moved off at 10.35 a.m. after a slight delay due to the Crocodiles arriving late. Opposition was, at first, light and the company made good progress. At 11 a.m., 'D' Company reported that their Crocodiles had not arrived. The company was ordered to advance without this support. Off went 'D' Company with the same initial success as 'A' Company. At 11.15 a.m., 'D' Company reported the arrival of its Crocodiles.

By midday, both companies reported that resistance was stiffening considerably. The lack of support from the Crocodiles at this time was most unfortunate. 'A' Company had lost contact with its Crocodiles. 'D' Company reported that their Crocodiles refused to go any further, and none of them had used any flame. The whole of the support had come from the tanks of the 8th Hussars. At 12.40 p.m., 'D' Company was ordered to try and work round the left flank and carry on without their Crocodiles, which were at that time with 'A' Company. It was to no avail as the advance by both companies slowed to a halt in the face of heavy resistance. Maj. S.O. de B. McCartney, commanding 'A' Company, was killed during the afternoon. Lieutenant Colonel Mogg was active moving between both companies and assessing the situation. His anger at the fact that the Crocodiles had failed to act must have been vented upon the appropriate officer, for when 'D' Company put in its sole uncommitted platoon, the Crocodiles moved with it and finally turned the tables on the enemy. As the Crocodiles fired each house in turn, the infantry followed up and cleared the village. It was the end of the resistance in St. Joost. A few of the enemy parachutists were captured and a good many were killed in the cellars. It was reported that two companies of the Hubner Group were almost destroyed. Once they got going, the Crocodiles performed magnificently and 'D' Company reached the bridge, its ultimate objective. The way was now clear for the advance on Montfort.

Lieutenant Colonel Mogg was awarded a Bar to his Distinguished Service Order. The citation concluded:

> Throughout this long and desperate action Lt. Col. Mogg was frequently with his leading companies under heavy shell and small arms fire re-planning and encouraging them on until the village was finally captured.
>
> No praise is high enough for the personal courage, cheerfulness, resource and energy of this young Commanding Officer whose efforts made it possible for the armour to break out for the final capture of Montfort.

Sgt. Thomas Myers was awarded the Distinguished Conduct Medal for his part in the fighting in St. Joost:

> Sgt. Myers was a Platoon Sergeant of a platoon engaged in clearing the village. The platoon had cleared several houses when Sgt. Myers was sent back to Coy. H.Q. to report on the situation. The enemy was at this time on three sides of the Company and the position

338

was confused. After leaving Coy. H.Q. this N.C.O. was informed that approximately twenty Germans were between him and his platoon coming in his direction. He immediately ran some 20yds across bullet swept ground to the corner of a house where he waited for the enemy to appear. He allowed them to approach to within 15yds and then opened fire with his Sten, killing 9, wounding 8 or 9. The remainder took cover behind the house. The N.C.O. waited for developments and saw a German with a machine gun leading the enemy from behind the house. He again waited till they were all in view and then threw 3 or 4 grenades at the party inflicting more casualties and causing the rest to disappear. Sgt. Myers then continued on his way to his platoon. On the way he encountered two more enemy at point blank range whom he shot and killed.

Sgt. Myers thus single handed inflicted over a dozen casualties on the enemy and by his courage and determination fought his way back to his platoon, preventing the enemy from completely encircling his company and enabling them to withdraw and without fighting their way out.

Of many other brave deeds, the majority of which went unrecognised, the award of the Military Medal to Pte. G. Martin was most deserved. He was with his platoon H.Q. fighting in the village when all of the headquarters were killed or wounded except himself. He continued to move forward on his own. On seeing the enemy attempting to cut off the remainder of his platoon, he immediately ran at them firing his Bren gun from the hip. He killed and wounded several of the enemy and the remainder withdrew. The fact that his platoon was able to continue the advance was due to Private Martin's brave action.

In addition to the deaths of Major McCartney and Ptes. A.T. Clarke and C. Holmes described above, Pte. A.J. Holden was killed on the 20th January. Cpls. W. Coombes and F.A. Schofield, L/Cpl. J.S. Maunders and Pte. F.W. Best were killed on the following day. A total of 25 other ranks were wounded and 38 were missing. Of the latter, 35 were from 'C' Company. This company's Commanding Officer, Maj. W.H.M. Anderson was also missing and listed later as a prisoner of war. Lts. E.J. Fitzpatrick, W.F. Ford and W.A. Toomey were wounded. The battalion was relieved by the 2nd Devons on the 22nd January and moved into the area of Peij to relieve the 3rd Commando on the following day. On the same day, a draft of 66 other ranks joined from the 34th Regimental Holding Unit.

Elsewhere, the attack was making good progress. Waldfeucht was taken. Montfort fell on the afternoon of the 23rd to the 1st/5th Queens. On the right, 131 Brigade advanced with the 1st Royal Tanks and the Queens. The objective was Posterholt. In the centre, 22nd Armoured Brigade with the 2nd Devons and 5th Dragoon Guards were to capture St. Odilienberg. On the left 1st Commando Brigade with the 8th Hussars had entered Linne on the evening of the 24th January but withdrew later to a better position slightly to the west. The enemy was now falling back behind the River Roer but not before laying numerous mines to delay the advance. Posterholt and St. Odilienberg fell on the 27th and Paarlo, south of Posterholt, was taken by the 1st/5th Queens on the 29th. On the 31st of the month, the enemy blew up the last bridge over the River Roer, thus signalling the end of Operation Blackcock.

On the 24th January, the battalion moved to Diergaarde. L/Sgt. J. Pascoe, L/Cpl. A. Podgurski and Ptes. H. Osborne and W. Jones were wounded by enemy fire. The Assault Pioneer Platoon were kept very busy checking the area for mines – of which there were many – and clearing and marking safe lanes. The following day, Aandenberg was reached and later, a move was made to Posterholt. L/Cpl. J.F. Ryder of 'A' Company was killed in action. Once established in this area, Lieutenant Colonel Mogg left on a well-earned leave in England and the command of the battalion was handed over to Maj. W.J.R. Scott, the Second in Command. Major Scott was a Territorial Officer whose service with the battalion stretched back to pre-war days.

The area now held was not an easy one to defend. The left flank was covered by the Queens and Devons. The right flank was open as the 52nd Lowland Division had not yet come up to the battalion and Posterholt was open to attack from the south-east. A reconnaissance patrol from this division reported that Karken and Hingen were clear of the enemy but were not occupied by its own troops. Their forward posts held Voorst and the line running south-east to Heinsberg. The German main defences were across the River Roer in the Siegfried Line but they had outposts on the west bank at Vlodrop and Karken. The 27th January was spent in patrolling the area and receiving the odd bout of enemy shelling. Maj. A.G.R. Noble took over as Second in Command from Major Scott. On the 29th, 'A' Company of 1st/5th Queens occupied Paarlo and beat off an enemy counter-attack from across the river. The following day, 'D' Company relieved a company of the Queens in the area of Paarlo. This was a difficult area as the Germans were very close and the road up to the company's positions was under direct observation from the enemy-held bank. Posterholt was shelled and, on one occasion, rocket shells fell in the area itself. A patrol stumbled into a minefield on the 31st January and one man, Pte. R. Turner, was killed and four were wounded. The weather had been very cold. A thaw set in at the end of the month and this turned every road in the area to deep mud.

'D' Company was sent to Echt on the 1st February for a short rest. The senior officers in the battalion at the beginning of February were:

Commanding Officer	Lt. Col. H.J. Mogg D.S.O.
Second in Command	Maj. A.G.R. Noble
Adjutant	Capt. R.J. Somerville
Intelligence Officer	Capt. J.C. Baily
Officer Commanding 'A' Company	Capt. P.W.B Thompson
Officer Commanding 'B' Company	Maj. A.G.R. Noble
Officer Commanding 'D' Company	Maj. L.E.V. Rumble
Officer Commanding 'S' Company	Capt. B.J. Gardner
Officer Commanding 'H.Q.' Company	Capt. E.H. Peace
Motor Transport Officer	Capt. E.H. Hooper

Officer Commanding Mortar Platoon	Capt. H.G. Phillips
Officer Commanding Pioneer Platoon	Lt. J. Pugh
Officer Commanding Carrier Platoon	Lt. J.J.A. Casey
Officer Commanding Anti-Tank Platoon	Lt. R. Brewer
Quartermaster	Lt. R.J.F. Jones
Medical Officer	Capt. A.H. Rea
Padre	Capt. C.E. Hutchinson

'D' Company returned from its short rest on the 3rd February and relieved 'B' Company at the northern end of Posterholt. 'B' Company was taken under the command of the 1st/5th Queens and moved to the village of Paarlo. On the 7th February, the division came under the command of the XVI U.S. Corps. The battalion, supported by an additional platoon of medium machine guns, 'C' Squadron 1st R.T.R., one self-propelled and one troop of anti-tank guns, was now responsible for holding Posterholt, Paarlo and Holst. 'D' Company was relieved by a Composite Company – which was called 'C' Company – raised from the divisional 'B' Echelons. This company was initially commanded by Capt. H.W. Ashton and later by Maj. G.R. Lanning. 'D' Company moved to Holst and 'A' Company moved to Paarlo. In the latter positions, the enemy was in a very strong position over the River Roer, which was about 400 yards away. Trip flares and mines covered the north and west approaches to their position and they had many mines laid in front. Continuous patrolling was carried out at night and clashes occurred with enemy patrols. The battalion was warned to watch for any rise in the water levels, which would indicate the flooding of the Roer. The American Ninth Army was about to start its attack to take the Roer dams. When captured these were found to be damaged and some flooding took place. Lieutenant Colonel Mogg returned from leave on the 9th of the month. On the 12th, the companies holding Holst and Paarlo were relieved by the 2nd Devons. From time to time, Flying bombs were seen to pass overhead. During the afternoon of the 15th, a loudspeaker van from American Psychological Warfare broadcast messages to the enemy on Vlodrop inviting them to send a soldier under a white flag to receive a surrender pass for his unit. No response was received except that the enemy fired a number of leaflets into the battalion's position. The War Diary noted that these leaflets were of 'no particular interest except that some are addressed personally to the 7th Armoured Division and the American Division on our right.' A further entry in the War Diary on the 19th February, announced the arrival of an American Red Cross Canteen driven by, 'two comely American women'. On the 21st, the division was relieved by the 8th American Armoured Division and moved a few miles north of Bree, still under the command of the XVI U.S. Corps. The battalion reached Weert in Holland by mid afternoon.

CHAPTER XXV

OVER THE RHINE

This was the first real rest since Normandy and the battalion looked forward to it. The civilians were extremely friendly and hospitable and many new friends were made. Pte. Jim Ratcliffe wrote:

> We took over this village from the Irish Guards and they had a cow, which we also took over. I used to milk her every night and morning. In fact I was excused 'stand to'. We used to heat a bucket full of this milk and put the section's rum ration in it and then just before you went on guard, you drank a mugful – talk about keeping out the cold.

One month was spent at Weert, relaxing, building up supplies, doing maintenance and training with tanks. Capt. Eric Hooper, Motor Transport Officer, recalled:

> I was very fortunate because I had an M.T. Sergeant who was a motor engineer/fitter and if we were advancing and there happened to be a vehicle which was knocked out, he used to peel off and have a look at this vehicle. If he could get it working he would follow on. I used to have a lot of what they called 'buckshee' vehicles over strength. On one particular time the Colonel asked me how was it after every offensive and we were resting and he wanted a return of M/T vehicles, I was always at full strength. I told him that I had got some good fitters. I didn't tell him what had happened. He [the M.T. Sergeant] used to get these vehicles and he used to cannibalise these vehicles. An order came out that you had-n't to do that but it was done...spare tyres, spare wheels and what have you...His name was Joe Maddison. He was nicknamed, 'The Smokey' and 'Smokey Joe'. He was always covered in diesel and what have you when he had been messing about with vehicles. Going to recover these vehicles, he'd sometimes be away for a couple of days but he came back with an extra vehicle...We used to paint them out [other divisional signs] and put our own signs on.

Training was aimed at crossing a major water obstacle using Buffalo Amphibious Troop Carriers. On the 5th March, Field Marshall Montgomery held an investiture at Bishop's College, Weert. Lieutenant Colonel Mogg received a Bar to his D.S.O. Maj. A.G.R. Noble and Capts. H.W. Ashton and P.W.B. Thompson were invested with the M.C. Sergeant Major Howe and Sgt. T. Myers received the D.C.M. and Lance Sergeant Oliver and Pte. G. Martin the M.M. Sergeant Turner was invested with the B.E.M.

Preparations for the Rhine crossing were underway, though the division's role was to break out of the bridgehead after it was established. Morale was high and there was a feeling that the final days of the war were at hand. The 7th Armoured Division was placed under the command of XII Corps for the drive into Germany. This corps also included the 15th Scottish, 52nd Lowland, 53rd Welsh Divisions and the 1st Commando Brigade. The plan was for the British 6th Airborne Division and the

American 17th Airborne Division to be dropped across the Rhine and ahead of the Allied assaulting divisions. The ground on the far bank of the river north-west of Wesel rose to a height of over 150 feet and was well wooded. This area, known as Diersfordter Wald was the objective for the airborne forces, along with the bridges over the Rivers Ijssel and Lippe. The assault crossing by 21st Army Group was to be covered by 3,000 medium and heavy field guns with the R.A.F bombing towns and villages considered to be enemy strong points in and beyond the bridgehead. The 51st Highland Division of XXX Corps was to assault the area of Rees and 1st Commando Brigade of XII Corps was to cross two miles downstream of Wesel. The 15th Scottish Division was to assault across the river at Xanten. The 9th U.S. Army would cross south of Wesel. The 15th Scottish Division, once across the river, would link up with the 6th Airborne and XXX Corps. The 53rd Welsh Division, supported by the 4th Armoured Brigade along with the 7th Armoured Division, would follow the 15th Scottish once the bridgehead was established. The former was directed on Bocholt and the latter on Borken. There was a profusion of maps and air photographs that covered the areas of the assaults. The air of expectancy was akin to that of D-Day. Everyone was on his toes and eager to get started – and get it over with! The battalion came under the command of the 22nd Armoured Brigade, with orders to co-operate with the 5th Dragoon Guards. The plan was for an advance to be carried out on two routes to Borken, the 5th Dragoon Guards on the right and 5th R.T.R. on the left. The 9th Battalion was to follow the right-hand route mopping up behind the tanks. The main axis of the advance was to be Hamminkeln–Brunen–Raesfeld–Borken.

The enemy units opposite the XII Corps front comprised part of the 2nd Parachute Division, which held the river bank north of Bislich, and the Grenadiers of the 84th Division along the river to Wesel and in the woods behind.

Operation Plunder, the assault across the Rhine, commenced on the night of the 23rd/24th March. By the end of the 24th, the commandos held the greater part of Wesel and the 15th Scottish Division had a foothold in Bislich and was nearly halfway to Wesel. The 51st Highland Division had met strong opposition as it fought its way across the open fields towards Rees and had made slower progress. The 6th Airborne Division had suffered heavy losses but had succeeded in capturing the vital bridges including the one at Hamminkeln two miles beyond Wesel. By the evening of the 26th, the 15th Scottish Division, though still fighting against strong opposition, held a bridgehead about seven miles wide by four and a quarter miles deep. The American Ninth Army, which had crossed at Dinslaken, had linked up with the airborne forces on the Lippe bridges. A tank bridge had been built between Xanten and Bislich and a lighter bridge was in place farther downstream. All was ready for the 7th Armoured to cross the Rhine.

The Brigade Commander, Brigadier Spurling, informed the battalion of the success of the initial crossing of the Rhine. By mid afternoon on the 25th March, the battalion was on the move and left Weert to a great send-off from the local inhabitants.

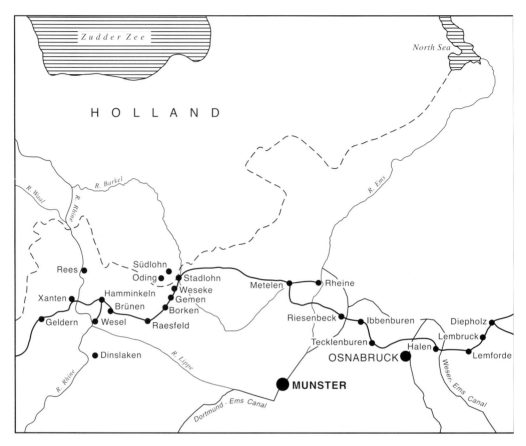

Into Germany – 27 March to 7 April 1944

The German border was crossed east of Venlo and the battalion arrived at its new area near Walbeck before dark, an area devoid of civilians, in marked contrast to what they had left behind. The 26th was a quiet day for the battalion. Lieutenant Colonel Mogg talked to his officers and N.C.O.s about the division's plan. The move commenced on the morning of the 27th. It was a slow journey. Traffic jams were considerable and the column had to halt on a number of occasions. Xanten was reached at 1.20 p.m. and the move across the river commenced at 4 p.m. The battalion was led across the bridge by Captain Peace with a recce party. The C.O. and Intelligence Officer, Capt. J.C. Baily, who followed found the traffic so dense that they had to take to a motorcycle to weave their way through the vehicles. Capt. Baily was riding pillion and was not too happy with the journey, which he found a little hair-raising.

The battalion was ordered to move up through Hamminkeln to an area west of Brünen. The journey was through the area captured by the 6th Airborne Division. Parachutes hung from the trees and lay crumpled on the ground. The concentration of gliders was an impressive sight. Many of the dead and wounded had been collected but it was obvious that the enemy had put up a fight to hold the ground. Prisoners of war

344

were passed making their way to the rear areas. There was little activity, the reason for which became obvious when it was realised that the paratroops had captured the enemy gun lines. The battalion concentrated for the night just short of the ridge in front of Brünen. It was to be ready to move at 6.45 a.m. with the task of mopping up behind the 5th Dragoon Guards. The men were carried in Kangaroo Armoured Troop Carriers.

The division advanced led by the 22nd Armoured Brigade was on a three-regiment front. On the left the 5th R.T.R. was directed on Borken across the wooded plateau to the north of the main road from Brünen to Raesfeld. In the centre, the 5th Dragoon Guards and 9 D.L.I. were to advance along the main road and then turn north at Raesfeld and approach Borken from the south. On the right, the 1st R.T.R. and 1st Bn. Rifle Brigade were to move east to Heiden and then north to Ramsdorf. Up to this point, the centre line had met little opposition. However, the woods in the area provided perfect cover for the enemy to ambush the advancing tanks and infantry. The panzerfaust – a German hand-held anti-tank weapon – came into its own. Increasingly, the advancing troops met extensive minefields, mortar fire, snipers and the occasional 88-mm and self-propelled gun. Every house was bitterly contested and the rubble formed by heavy R.A.F. bombing in the towns and villages became a further source of cover for enemy rearguards to slow the advance and cause frequent casualties.

On the 28th, enemy infantry armed with panzerfausts were met on the west and north-west of the village of Raesfeld. These held up the tanks. Before an assault on the village could be organised, a Brigade Liaison Officer had driven into Raesfeld by mistake and found it empty. 'D' Company was ordered into the village to mop up anyone who may be found there. White flags were flown from the windows of houses and astonished civilians gaped at the huge amount of equipment pouring through their village. The infantry met on this front had been on the Rhine and had had the fight knocked out of them and were not in the mood for further conflict. Prisoners poured in. An American stretcher bearer appeared down the road with 25 prisoners and a further eight were sent back on their own to the cages. Some were Volkssturm – local defence troops of considerable age – but many were from the 84th Division. 'A' Company Rifle Brigade released 'D' Company from the village and the advance was continued from Raesfeld. The advance towards Borken was rapid. The tanks of the 5th Dragoon Guards pressed on up the main road, meeting little opposition on the way. The battalion followed with order to seize the town.

Lieutenant Colonel Mogg's plan for capturing the town was for 'A' Company (Maj. S. Terrell) to move round the right flank by Wansing Bridge and occupy the area of the road junction. 'D' Company (Maj. L.E.V. Rumble) was to go straight up the main road and fork left at the crossroads. 'C' Company (Maj. G.R. Lanning) was to follow and make a firm base in the southern edge of the town. 'B' Company (Maj. A.G.R. Noble), which was still in the woods before the town, was to come up when relieved by a company from the 1st/5th Queens. Roads through the town were completely blocked by the rubble resulting from R.A.F. raids. A way through was found

Infantry of the 9th Battalion advance to Weseke, throught the outskirts of the town – March 1945.

and the town was taken as planned. There was little resistance. Meanwhile the tanks had worked their way round the right flank, via the Wansing Bridge, and ran into opposition at a roadblock at the bridge at Gemen. 'A' Company, when relieved by a company of the 2nd Devons, was ordered to assist the tanks and occupy Gemen. By 9 p.m., 'A' Company had reached its objective and had taken a German hospital in the village. Major Terrell set up an ambush in Gemen and captured four enemy vehicles coming from the west and inflicted heavy casualties on the enemy infantry who were unaware of the speed of the battalion's advance. At one point during the night, the Major posed as a traffic policeman in the centre of the village and directed the enemy traffic into his ambush. The tanks and infantry had covered a distance of 10 miles during the advance.

Battalion casualties had been light. Two men, Ptes. C. Evans and J. Harmison of 'C' Company, were killed in action and seven other ranks were wounded. Total prisoners taken was 87.

On the 29th March, the objectives were Weseke, Südlohn and Stadtlohn. The battalion moved off at 7 a.m. but progress proved to be very slow. Movement off the roads was difficult due to the very soft going, which bogged down tanks and vehicles. The column was held up after four miles by a platoon of enemy infantry supported by four

346

self-propelled guns. Artillery was brought down on the enemy by 'K' Battery, R.A. 'C' Company worked round the right flank and captured Lensing and 'B' Company, in their Kangaroos and with a troop of tanks, charged into Weseke. The enemy was driven off and the four self-propelled guns destroyed or damaged. Eight prisoners were taken by 'C' Company, all of whom were Italians who claimed to be bakers. At 6 p.m., news arrived of a successful carrier attack further south. Some enemy infantry, in woods close to the advance route, had fired on the rear of the column. A section of the Carrier Platoon under Sgt. Andrew Cameron had been ordered out to patrol this flank with the intention of clearing up any opposition or, if proved to be too strong, to contain it until another battalion came up to clear the area. The Sergeant's citation read:

> Sergeant Cameron took the patrol roughly a mile along the road and then came under mortar fire from a house 300yds in front and also rifle and machine gun fire from a large copse on his left flank. He immediately got his crews in dismounted action and for half an hour neutralised the positions with three Brens and 2" mortar. At the end of this period, the enemy ceased fire and Sgt. Cameron on his own initiative, decided to clear the house immediately to his front and then the copse to his left. He ordered the section to return to their carriers and, firing on the move, to make their way to the house, which they did. When close to the house, Sgt. Cameron led one crew dismounted into the house and took five prisoners. On returning to the carriers the enemy again opened up with machine gun fire and wounded two of their own prisoners. Sgt. Cameron then ordered the section to return to the house they had just cleared and make it a firm base. The house by this time was under fire from three sides. The section established themselves in the house and Sgt. Cameron then crawled a hundred yards across the open with a P.I.A.T. covered by the rest of the section. Sporadic machine gun fire was coming from the copse during this time but was silenced when Sgt. Cameron fired two P.I.A.T. rounds at the enemy positions. He then moved across to another house from which the fire was coming and set it on fire with his remaining bomb. He returned to the section and led them through the copse and on to the farmhouse under cover of three Brens, taking in all, one officer and sixty other ranks prisoner, who were all armed with rifles, machine guns, bazookas. By his personal courage, leadership and initiative, Sgt. Cameron cleared the area of a company strength of German infantry with only one carrier section.

The Sergeant was awarded an immediate Military Medal.

The advance on Südlohn and Stadtlohn continued. The progress was slowed by craters in the road and rubble left in Südlohn by the bombing raids. The night of the 29th/30th was spent at the roadside in front of Südlohn with the battalion resting in its vehicles. At 6.15 a.m. on the 30th March, the tanks of the 5th Dragoon Guards bumped into opposition in Stadtlohn and the battalion was called forward to clear the town. 'B' Company was to fight its way to the main crossroads in the centre of the town. 'A' Company was to go to the right of the town and 'D' Company to the left. 'C' Company had the task of working its way through the centre. Initially, the opposition was not great and the companies got into the town without difficulty. The War Diary described the fighting:

When companies got into the town the real fighting began and they settled down to steady house (and rubble heap) clearing, assisted by the C.O. in his armoured car. Opposition was provided by two battalions of 857 Grenadier Regiment detached from 346 Infantry Division. We were afterwards told that this Division was rated by S.H.A.E.F. to be the best formation left on the Western Front and that the Battalion had completely written off at least one of the battalions and much reduced the other.

The street fighting was bloody. The houses and rubble heaps had to be cleared one by one. Enemy snipers were in their element with so much cover available. At noon, 38 prisoners arrived, including three 16-year-old boys from the 3rd Light Flak Battalion Stores Section. The situation in the town improved during the afternoon and first objectives were won and held. The enemy snipers were still active and Maj. A.J.H. Cramsie, Second in Command, was wounded in the leg while entering the town in a jeep. At 4 p.m. 'A' Company who was working towards the bridge called for tank support. 'C' and 'D' Companies achieved their objectives and 'A' Company got a small bridgehead across the river. By 6 p.m. the town was cleared of the enemy and 'C' Company was also across the river. The fighting had been heavy. Maj. G.R. Lanning, Officer Commanding 'A' Company, was awarded the Military Cross. His citation read:

> At Stadtlohn on the 30th March 1945, Major Lanning was ordered to pass through 'D' Company which had captured an objective in the centre of the town and his task was to seize and hold the bridge over the river which runs to the north of the town.
>
> As the town was a mass of rubble from bombing, no tank support was available and the fighting consisted of desperate hand-to-hand combat against two battalions of good German infantry.
>
> Major Lanning handled his Company with so much skill and so effectively that he cleared three hundred yards of which every inch was held very stubbornly by the enemy, taking 30 Prisoners of War and killing or wounding an equal number.
>
> He was always in the thick of the fighting and walking about in such a cool and calm way that he was a great inspiration to all who saw him. He reached a point 150 yards from the bridge with his reserve platoon and found the enemy well dug in around the bridge with 100 yards of open ground to cross.
>
> He decided to make a final assault with his reserve platoon and crawled forward twenty-five yards with a wireless set to where he could obtain observation of the whole area and directed artillery fire on to the enemy near the bridge with some shells falling very close to him. When he finished the shoot he raced back to his platoon, across the open and led them straight on to the bridge at the double before the enemy had time to recover.
>
> He personally killed four of the enemy with his Sten gun and captured the remainder, Without any doubt his great personal courage and skill enabled the bridge to be captured intact and the advance of an Armoured Regiment to continue far earlier than could have been the case if a less vigorous attack had taken place.

The house-to-house fighting was particularly severe. Lt. D.S. Taylor was awarded the Military Cross for his leadership in this action. His citation stated:

348

At Stadtlohn on the 30th March 1945, this officer set a magnificent example to his Platoon by his own personal bravery in leading them from house to house in very heavy street fighting against a determined enemy. Constantly he was the first to come under fire and he pressed home attacks so quickly and vigorously that the enemy eventually found themselves outflanked and suffered some forty to fifty casualties in dead and wounded. Just before the first company objective some twenty of the enemy had made a strong point of a large house which was holding up his platoon. There was a space of a hundred yards of open ground between the platoon and the enemy. Lt. Taylor laid a smoke screen and led an assault at the head of his platoon. His platoon suffered heavy casualties and were pinned to the ground but Lt. Taylor charged the house alone and gave the enemy several bursts with his Sten gun which silenced the fire and the remainder of his platoon advanced and captured twelve of the enemy, the remainder being killed or wounded. After reaching the company objective a further attack was ordered for this officer's platoon to assist two other companies of the battalion. While attacking through Stadtlohn his platoon came under heavy machine gun fire which further reduced his weak platoon to ten men. The coolness of this officer's organisation of the evacuation of his casualties when exposed to enemy fire was only matched by the vigour with which he continued to press on with the attack with his remaining ten men…they encircled the enemy position which enabled the other two companies to advance and eventually link up with this very determined platoon.

Throughout the whole of this day's fighting this officer was an inspiration to all who saw him, by his dashing leadership, initiative and personal courage.

L/ Sgt. Dennis Cross was awarded the Military Medal for his leadership of his section of 11 Platoon during this severe fighting. Lt. J. McNally of 'A' Company had jumped on a tank and made for a wooden bridge, which still spanned the river, and captured it. Though somewhat rickety in appearance it carried the weight of the advancing tanks with the Queens who came through the Durhams' positions to continue the advance beyond the town. Lieutenant McNally was wounded but rejoined the battalion later.

A total of 104 enemy dead were counted. Four officers and 108 other ranks were taken prisoner. Amongst the battalion casualties were five dead: Sgt. R. Eddy, 'D' Company; Cpl. L.A. Ivison, L/Cpl. I. Buttle and Ptes. F. Binmore and C. Hopwood, all of 'A' Company. Three officers, namely Maj. Cramsie and Lts. W.F. Ford and McNally, were wounded, along with 16 other ranks.

Lieutenant Colonel Mogg's tactics helped to break the enemy's resistance after only 24 hours. It was expected to take much longer in view of the enemy's intention of holding the ruined town. David Rissik in his book, *The D.L.I. at War*, explained:

> Instead of the usual drill of holding the enemy frontally and working round the flanks, the C.O. ordered one company to drive a wedge into the centre of the town – which it did – and then two to move to branch off to the flanks in a sort of 'Y-shaped' movement. This surprised the Germans and met with immediate success.

The night was spent in guarding what had been so dearly won. Maj. Noble M.C. took over as Second in Command of the battalion and Capt. H.D. Foster the command of 'A' Company. Captain Foster was one of three Canadians serving with the battalion under the Canloan scheme. On the left flank the 8th Hussars had reached Oding, five miles south-west of Stadtlohn. On the right, 1st R.T.R and 1st Bn. Rifle Brigade had taken Heek.

CHAPTER XXVI

THE FINAL WEEKS

A quiet day was spent in Stadtlohn until, at 11 p.m. on the 31st March, the battalion moved off to link up with the 5th Dragoon Guards at Wüllen. The objective was Rheine, a large town on the River Ems. The 5th Dragoon Guards, 11th Hussars and 9th Bn. D.L.I. led the advance towards Rheine, which was reached after covering 20 miles against little opposition. The move forward continued. Metelen was reached and contact was made with the 11th Armoured Division. The head of the column reached Neuenkirchen and passed through this village, then paused to consider the next stage of the advance. News was received that the 11th Armoured Division had established a bridgehead to the south, across the Ems at Mesum. The plan for the advance on Rhienes was by a combination of tank squadron and infantry company groups. These would move on either side of the main road, 'A' Company on the right and 'C' Company on the left. 'A' Company's objective was the ridge close to the barracks and a wood and from there to the road/railway bridge. If all went well it was hoped to reach the river bridges. Meanwhile, 'C' Company would move round the left by the airfield ridge and work its way into the town from that side. 'B' and 'D' Companies were to be prepared to follow 'A' Company and the Carrier Platoon would work with 'C' Company.

At 3.30 p.m. on the 1st April, fires and explosions were heard and seen on the airfield and at the barracks, where oil and ammunition dumps went up. The advance was slow but steady. Some opposition, mainly snipers, was encountered and shelling from guns on the far side of the river was experienced. 'A' Company reached the ridge without any difficulty. It went on towards the road/railway bridge. As it approached the southern bridge over the river an explosion was heard, indicating that this bridge had been destroyed. 'C' Company advanced against little opposition and a number of prisoners were taken. White flags were being hung from the houses by frightened and confused civilians. It was a fine and warm Sunday and the troops, moving cautiously through the streets and gardens, were amazed to see civilians dressed in their best clothes, going to church.

The enemy held the opposite riverbank in strength. As the river bridges had been blown and the town was effectively blocked by rubble, it was decided that to attempt an immediate river crossing may prove costly and a full-scale infantry attack might be needed. It was decided that 157 Brigade would relieve 131 Brigade in Rheine, and the 9th Battalion was withdrawn. 'A' and 'C' Companies covered the main road into the town; 'B' and 'D' Companies occupied the high ground in the barracks area that dominated the town. The night proved to be quiet. The plan for the 2nd April was for the 7th Armoured Division to cross the River Ems and the Dortmund–Ems Canal by bridgeheads held by the 11th Armoured Division at Mesum. The move was delayed. The terrain across the River Ems, in front of the 11th Armoured Division's bridges, was known as the Teutoburger Wald. It formed a natural defensive line of dense woods climbing up a barrier of hills known as the Tecklenburg Range, an escarpment about 25 miles long and a mile wide. The town of Ibbenburen lay at the north-east end of the Teutoburger Wald at a road junction, which made it an important objective. Its capture was given to the 7th Armoured Division. The task of the division was to cross the river at the bridgehead and advance eastwards from Rheine through these steep wooded hills and over the Dortmund–Ems Canal at Riesenbeck, which was already in the hands of the 11th Armoured Division. The delay to the advance of the 7th Armoured Division was due to the severe fighting which 159 Brigade (53rd Division) was experiencing at the bridgehead. It was estimated that the enemy had the equivalent of seven companies of infantry in the woods and hills. These were well armed and prepared to fight to the last man. The enemy had the considerable advantages of observation and concealment. His forces included cadets and instructors from the Bergen–Hanover Cadet Training School, who were very well trained and skilled men. Their instructors had considerable experience of fighting in Russia and the desert. Over the next few days they were to put up a fanatical resistance to all attempts to break through the narrow valley. No. 159 Brigade had already suffered severe casualties holding on to the bridgehead. At one point the bridgehead became seriously threatened and the 2nd Devons (131 Brigade) were called forward to counter-attack and drive the enemy off. The Germans still held much of the high ground and were covering the gap through the hills to Ibbenburen.

The 9th Battalion had been concentrating at Brochterbeck and at 4 p.m. on the 3rd April moved off towards the crossing. 'C' Company was sent ahead with the Reconnaissance Troop of the 5th Dragoon Guards. The plan was that this company would clear any minor opposition in the gap and the other companies would be ready to move up behind. An enemy party on the western side of the road and in the woods had to be dealt with by tank and infantry co-operation. Resistance stiffened and 'C' Company got involved in a firefight with enemy elements further down the road and north of it. During this action, Sgt. J.F.T. Giles and Pte. G.E. Smith were killed. The positions reached were consolidated for the night.

Heavy fighting took place on the 4th, with an enemy who fought in small groups so that it was extremely difficult to locate them and bring down artillery support. 'A' Company was ordered to pass through 'C' Company and continue the advance towards Ibbenburen; 5th Dragoon Guards were in support. Between the town and the advancing company lay a stream. Early in the advance, 'A' Company was faced with a long row of farmhouses held by the enemy. Each house had to be fought for. Tanks had to destroy each building by shell or flame-throwers but the brave enemy fought in the ruins to the bitter end, firing to the last. German snipers were active at all stages of the action. Tank Commanders and infantry Platoon Sergeants were favourite targets and a number were killed or wounded. Twenty prisoners came into 'A' Company saying that fighting tanks with rifles was a bit too much. The advance continued behind an artillery barrage and the support of the battalion's own 3-in. mortars. At 10.45 a.m., a pause was called to enable the tanks to reorganise and receive ammunition. A bulldozer came forward to clear a roadblock in front of 'C' Company. At 12.30 p.m., 'B' Company came up and passed through 'A' Company. Led by its Canadian Officer, Capt. Hal Foster, this company fought its way to the stream and established a bridgehead on the opposite side. It got to within 600 yards of the bridge over the river, when it was ordered to withdraw slightly and take up a defensive position astride the road. It had been decided that the 52nd Division would attack Ibbenburen and it, also, was to find that this was no easy task. This was the end of the battalion's fighting for Ibbenburen. It was pulled out to return to 7th Armoured Division. It still took another two days of fighting to break the enemy resistance in front of Ibbenburen.

L/Sgt. James M. Nicholson was awarded the Military Medal for his bravery during the fighting. His citation read:

> At Ibbenburen on the 4th April 1945, the Platoon Commander and Platoon Sergeant were wounded and the whole platoon was pinned to the ground over a wide area. Shell fire and accurate sniping and spandau fire was covering the platoon position.
>
> L/Sgt. Nicholson took command and by his personal example in walking round regardless of the danger, managed to rally and reorganise the platoon and led them into cover. As he was no longer in wireless contact with the company he again walked back across the open under fire to a tank troop Commander and reported his position to his Company Commander. On returning he again found his platoon position being fired at by several snipers. He brought the fire of the platoon down which enabled it to advance and he led a final rush onto the objective, killing five snipers and enabling the rest of the company to get on. If it had not been for this N.C.O's inspiring display of coolness and courage, his platoon would have failed to have been effective and this advance would have been held up.

Casualties during the bitter fighting included the following killed in action: L/Cpl. E. Hall of 'B' Company and L/Sgt. J. Hopkinson, Ptes. G. Baker, J. Cox, D. Dickson of 'A' Company and Sgt. J. Giles and Ptes. J. Risidore and G. Smith of 'C' Company. Eighteen other ranks were wounded.

Whilst the heavy fighting had been taking place, forward elements of the 7th Armoured Division had outflanked this difficult area. The 22nd Armoured Brigade had crossed the 11th Armoured Division's bridgehead over the Osnabruck Canal at Halen. It had broken through and a bridge was seized intact over the Ems–Weser Canal by the 5th Royal Tank Regiment. The advance had continued on the 5th April and Diepholz entered on the following day.

Lieutenant Colonel Mogg was not entirely done with the attack towards Ibbenduren. At 7.15 a.m. on the 5th April, he ordered 'B' Company to feel forward down the road towards the bridges to see if any enemy were about. The company reported that it had advanced about 200 yards and met no opposition. On reaching a

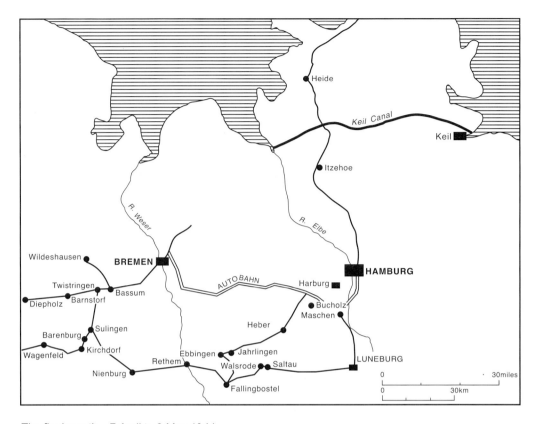

The final month – 7 April to 8 May 1944

roadblock, which they cleared, they could see that the bridge had been blown but the gap was narrow enough to take a scissors bridge. One platoon was able to wade across the stream. As shelling commenced the Commanding Officer ordered 'B' Company to hold the bridge at all costs. The battalion War Diary entry for 12 noon on this day states:

> 'B' Company's capture of the bridge was quite unexpected as the plan was to withdraw us and leave Ibbenburen to 52nd Division. As it was, we had very nearly caused a major change of plan but, as it was thought that the Training Schools were holding the high ground north of the village with at least one battalion, the original plan was kept and we were ordered to withdraw to our old positions.

As a result of this action four men were wounded. The task for the 6th April was to catch up with the rest of the division, which was about 30 miles ahead and advancing on Diepholz. The move was extremely slow due to heavy traffic on the roads and tracks. The battalion reached the village of Barver and concentrated here for the night. All-round defence positions were taken up as the whereabouts of the enemy was unknown, but the night proved to be a quiet one. The task allotted to the battalion on

354

the 7th was to clear the road between Diepholz and Twistringen and to act as flank guard to the rest of the division. At 6 a.m. on the following day, the Carrier Platoon and the Reconnaissance Troop of the 5th Dragoon Guards moved off. The carriers moved west to Rehden and then turned north towards Dickel. The tanks moved up the main road through Donstorf where they found the bridge destroyed and set off to search each flank to find a way round. The carriers reached the Diepholz–Bassum road at Kornau. Here they found that the bridge over the River Hunte was blown but that the railway/road bridge was intact. A change of plan moved the battalion via Sulingen and then north towards Bassum and Twistringen. The first serious opposition was met at Neuenkirchen but this was brushed aside. The enemy were withdrawing slowly but made no serious attempt to delay the advance. The battalion's intention was to put two companies each in Bassum and Twistringen for the night but the enemy had other ideas. On reaching the outskirts of Bassum, the Germans were found to be well dug in along the railway. They were prepared to contest any entry into the town and, as night was falling, it was decided not to attack. By the end of the day, 'C' Company was in touch with the enemy and 'D' Company had moved up behind in support. 'B' Company was in Twistringen. A properly organised attack was planned for the following day.

'D' Company [Major Rumble M.C.] was to make the initial attack against the railway positions. 'A' Company had to be prepared to move through 'D' Company and pass into the town. One squadron of the 5th Dragoon Guards was in support and another was to move west across the main road and come in on the left flank. Artillery and mortar support was laid on. The attack started at 8.15 a.m. and enemy opposition to the advance was strong and stubborn. 'D' Company got up to the railway line west of the level crossing. The left flank attack by the tanks reached the main road and was then held up by an 88-mm gun firing down the road. One platoon of 'D' Company led by its Commanding Officer, Lt. M.H. Ingleton, got beyond the level crossing but came under fire from an 88 and the young Lieutenant and L/Sgt. J.S. Edginton were killed. By 9.30 a.m., 'D' Company had secured its objectives and 'A' Company came up and pushed on into the town. An hour late, the tanks came in from the left flank, having destroyed the 88. By 11 a.m., 'C', 'A' and 'D' Companies were in the town and, except in the south-west area where the enemy was holding out in houses, resistance had been broken. At 1 p.m., the 1st Bn. Rifle Brigade was in Twistringen and moving north-east up the main road to contact the Durhams. By 3 p.m., all companies were established in the town. 'A' Company was covering the roads from the north-west with the Carrier Platoon on their right. 'D' Company was covering the roads from the east and 'C' Company was in reserve. The Rifle Brigade had, by now, made contact. The rest of the battalion moved up to the factory area. A total of 49 prisoners were taken during the day. Killed in action, in addition to the Lieutenant and the Lance Sergeant above, were Pte. A. Hall of 'C' Company and Ptes. J. Horner and P. Russell, both of 'D' Company. Ten other ranks were wounded.

XXX Corps had been fighting on the northern flank of XII Corps front and it was decided to send the 7th Armoured Division to work on the flank of the enemy forces opposing this corps. XXX Corps was advancing on Bremen. The battalion's role in this manoeuvre was to capture Wildeshausen, south-west of Bremen and so cut the main escape route of remnants of the German 15th Panzer Grenadier Division and 1st Parachute Army. The route taken was via Wedehorn, Stelle, Twistringen, Beckeln, Winkelsett, Reckum and Wildeshausen. 'B' Company was picked up at Twistringen and led the column in Kangaroos with a squadron of the 5th Dragoon Guards. The first delay was a roadblock, which was removed by a Sherman bulldozer. A little enemy shelling was stopped by retaliatory fire and the advance continued. At 1.35 p.m., 'B' Company passed through Beckeln. No opposition was met in Winkelsett. On reaching Colnrade, the 5th Dragoon Guards reported that the bridge was blown. A section of carriers, sent out to recce the road east of Winkelsett, was ambushed by a German bazooka party. All of the carriers were destroyed and Sgt. R. Smith of 'S' Company was wounded. By 6 p.m. on the 9th April, 'B' Company had taken up position in the woods in front of Wildeshausen, with a platoon on each side of the road. One troop of tanks was on the road and another was working round the left flank. Enemy parties were in the woods and fighting broke out. Enemy tactics were to operate in small groups, give way against any direct attacks and then appear again in another place. They were tenacious fighters and progress was very slow. As night fell, Lieutenant Colonel Mogg ordered 'B' Company to withdraw as he was concerned it might be outflanked and cut off from the rest of the battalion. The company, supported by artillery that continued to fire into the woods, withdrew successfully. Positions were taken up on the high ground overlooking the approaches to the town. There was no enemy interference during the night.

Lieutenant Colonel Mogg's plan to capture Wildeshausen on the 10th April was divided into three phases. In the first phase, 'A' Company was sent to clear an area of the woods with the support of the Carrier Platoon. In the second, 'D' Company was then to pass through and continue the advance. Finally, 'C' Company was to go through the east end of the town and endeavour to capture the bridges. 'B' Company was in reserve and to be prepared to secure the rest of the town if this should become necessary. The companies went off with considerable élan and quickly reached their objectives. The bridges were found to be passable to tanks. The enemy had beaten a hasty retreat and none was in the town. Tank patrols on the roads leading from the town reported enemy infantry in position and these were engaged. A large quantity of gin was found in Wildeshausen and was quickly confiscated. Although the temptation was great, the battalion saved these spirits for another day. There were signs of enemy counter-attacks coming in, which would require clear heads. At 9.10 p.m., five or six self-propelled guns and about 60 infantry led an attack down the main road from the east. This fell upon 'C' Company. The attack was pushed in with considerable energy and the leading S.P. gun got to within 100 yards of battalion headquarters before being halted. One platoon of 'C' Company and the R.A.P. (Regimental Aid Post) were over-run. The enemy took up position on the outskirts of the town and fighting raged for some two hours. As a result of this action Ptes. C. Faulkner and R. Hodges of 'S' Company were killed and 12 other ranks were missing, believed to be prisoners of war. Amongst these were Sergeant Gray M.M., Corporal Flodman and Privates Bivans, Christie, Foy and Killinor, all of whom managed to escape and rejoin the battalion on the 29th April. A further five men were wounded. The C.O. was visiting Brigade and was cut off from the battalion for some time. Maj. A.G.R. Noble M.C. commanded in his absence and did a magnificent job in a difficult situation.

On the following day, fighting flared up again. Relief by VIII Corps was post-poned whilst these actions continued. It seemed that civilians in the town were passing information to their troops about the battalion's dispositions. 'B' Company pinned the enemy down but was ordered not to get too involved with them as the relief was ordered to go ahead. L/Sgt. Reginald J. Tavener was awarded the Military Medal for his part in this action. His citation read:

> When the company was waiting to be relieved, a strong Boche patrol came on to the company's position amongst the houses at the head of the town and shortly afterwards sniping from mortar bombs, small arms and panzerfausts began…The exact enemy position was not located for some time until this N.C.O. spotted that it was in a house which, owing to its position was difficult to fire at effectively either from a tank or mortar.
>
> L/Sgt. Tavener immediately took the platoon P.I.A.T. and riding on top of a tank over an exposed level crossing to a covered position, from where the tank was unable to help owing to the proximity of enemy panzerfausts, he then fired five P.I.A.T. bombs from various places in adjacent houses at the house and succeeded in driving the enemy out, who were then dispersed by small arms fire from the platoon area…

A battalion of the South Lancashire Regiment took over and the remainder of the battalion withdrew without much difficulty. At 8.30 p.m., the battalion reached Liebenau and settled in for a few days' rest.

The 12th and 13th were spent tidying up and re-equipping as far as possible. Orders were received to cross the River Weser. Plans had been changed. Instead of driving towards Luneburg, the 7th Armoured Division was to break out of the bridge-head at Aller and advance towards the Elbe and Hamburg. The 11th Armoured Division and the 15th (Scottish) Division were to move north through Uelzen and on to Luneburg. The Guards Armoured Division was to come up on the left flank and advance into the peninsula between the Elbe and the Weser. The breakout by the 7th Armoured Division was led by the 8th Hussars and the 1st Royal Tank Regiment. The town of Walsrode was captured on the night of the 15th April. Meanwhile the 9th Battalion and 5th Dragoon Guards were in reserve and stayed in the woods awaiting further orders. Battalion Part 1 Orders reported the award of a Military Cross to Maj. L.E.V. Rumble and Mentions In Despatches for himself, Maj. G.R. Lanning M.C., Lt.

J.J.A. Casey and Cpl. A.D. Johnston. W.O.II D. Bedford was awarded the Croix de Guerre with Silver Star.

On the morning of the 16th April, the battalion crossed the Weser at Rethem. The 8th Hussars had taken a prisoner of war camp at Fallingbostel and released many British and Allied prisoners. Opposition was reported north of Soltau. By 4 p.m., the battalion was positioned just off the road west of Walsrode, ready to move north. It was given the task of protecting the northern flank of the advance and took over from 1st Bn. Rifle Brigade and occupied the villages of Ebbingen and Jahrlingen. 'B' Company went to the former and 'C' Company to the latter village. 'A', 'D' and tactical head-quarters were in Hunzingen. Enemy stragglers came into the positions during the day, mainly from the 2nd Marine Division and the 12th S.S. Training Battalion. They had been broken up in fighting at Rethem and offered little resistance. For several days, the roads were filled with foreign workers and former 'slaves' of the Third Reich – men women and children. Mostly dirty, tired and hungry, they were concentrated into camps and put under the control of the Displaced Persons Units, where they received clothing and food and quickly got cleaned up. The 22nd Armoured Brigade had bypassed Soltau, where enemy resistance was reported, and was striking due north towards the Elbe and Hamburg.

On the 17th of the month, the battalion moved to Frielingen and the Bommelsen–Kleinenhart area, relieving the 2nd Bn. Devonshires. Soltau was captured by 155 Brigade during the night, though fighting continued nearby where the enemy were still active in the woods. On the 18th, the battalion's task was to support the 5th R.T.R. to protect the right flank of the advance and seek to open an alternative route through the woods parallel to the main road. The tanks were met at Heber. A hold-up occurred at a crossroads that held up the tanks; 'A' and 'B' Companies were brought forward with the carriers and mortars to deal with the obstruction. 'A' Company pushed on to Behringen to guard the right flank and secured the bridge site where the Royal Engineers were preparing to build a new bridge. 'B' Company and a squadron of tanks were sent through Tutsberg, Wulfsberg, Neider, Haverbeck and Ehrehrn and east-wards. No opposition was met and the advance was turning into a pleasant country drive in lovely weather. By the evening the battalion had reached Meningen. A halt was called for the night. 'A' Company was in Behringen and took 14 prisoners from the 12th S.S. Training Battalion. 'C' Company moved to the right to hold Undelch and captured a further 18 prisoners. Increasingly, the enemy prisoners were children aged between 13 and 16 and old men who had no wish to continue the fight. 'D' Company and tactical headquarters were in Meningen and 'B' Company occupied Wesel. It was a quiet night and the advance towards Harburg continued on the following day.

The advance lay through a series of ridges covered with forests. The leading tank units of the division attacked Harburg whilst 131 Brigade acted as a protective force on the right flank of the 22nd Armoured Brigade. At 7.30 a.m. on the 19th, the advance got underway. Schierhorn was reached in just over an hour. 'C' Company was in Ollsen a few minutes later. Opposition was light and the leading company and tanks pushed on to Lullau, which was taken with little fight from a demoralised enemy. At 3 p.m., the battalion moved on to Buchholz and 'C' Company was ordered to move up from Hanstedt to Asendorf. Lt. S. Seggie M.C. and his Carrier Platoon entered Bochholz and found it empty of the enemy. During the day, 26 prisoners were taken, one of whom claimed to be a British Secret Service Agent! There is no record that he was able to prove this.

On the following day, tanks of the 5th R.T.R. left Buchholz and turned north towards the autobahn leading into Harburg. Enemy resistance was stiffening and it was thought that he had formed a line covering the approaches to Hamburg and the River Elbe. The task of the 9th Battalion was to advance on a parallel route to the east side of the Aue Valley. One company was sent to support the 5th R.T.R.'s advance on Maschen. 'A' Company and a section of the anti-tank battery were given this task. The towns and countryside teemed with displaced persons recently released from the 'slave' camps. In Buchholz, the civilian population were terrified that once the troops left, the town would be overrun by these people who had suffered so much in the camps. Seeking revenge, it was thought that they would loot, rape and burn down the town if not kept under control by soldiers. A troop of self-propelled guns was left behind to try and keep order.

'A' Company and 5th R.T.R. captured Horst and Maschen during the morning. They captured 34 prisoners most of whom were Hamburg policemen. The 5th R.T.R. Group were through Maschen and Jehrden and approaching Hittfeld. At this point in the advance, enemy resistance stiffened and it looked as though Hamburg would not be taken without a fight. The battalion was ordered to Harmstorf, except for 'C' Company which stayed in Jesteburg. Though not known at the time this was the farthest point reached before the surrender of Hamburg. The advance halted and preparations made for a full-scale attack on the city. Battalion orders were to occupy the high ground north of Hittfeld and hold the town itself. 'D' Company occupied an area south of the level crossing. 'B' Company covered the main road south of Emmelndorf and linked up with the 1st/5th Queens on the left. 'C' Company was in Hittfeld and 'A' Company held Maschen. The only contact with the enemy was on the outskirts of Maschen and in front of 'D' Company. On the right, 11th Hussars had reached Stelle and the Queens, on the left, were in Totensen and linked up with the battalion on the high ground.

For the next few days, the battalion stayed where it was. Aggressive patrolling by day and night, in addition to continuous harassing fire, sought to dominate the enemy. Battalion snipers were active. From time to time, patrols contacted the enemy who proved to be a mixed bag of Regular and Volkesturm [equivalent to the Home Guard] units with little cohesion. All along the line 7th Armoured Division closed up to the Elbe. Prisoners of war were rounded up and sporadic enemy shelling was experienced though no casualties resulted. The civilian population became somewhat difficult as the battalion settled down in one area. Though peaceful, the civilians could not understand why it was impossible for them to continue their peaceful pursuits around the towns and villages and tend to their cattle in the fields. Patrolling and observing enemy positions continued. A report to the regimental newsletter stated:

> During this period 'in the line' – all our administrative staff 'had a go' at standing patrols – even the M.T.O. Eric Hooper had a crack whilst the R.Q.M.S. (unheard of in the British Army) commanded one night patrol.

On the 29th April, the 'top brass' visited the battalion. The Corps Commander, Lt. Gen. N.M. Ritchie C.B., C.B.E., D.S.O., M.C. and Maj. Gen. L.O. Lyne, C.B., D.S.O. appeared along with 131 Brigade Commander, Brig. J.M.K. Spurling D.S.O. A tragic accident occurred on this day when Cpl. L.W. Jones and Pte. G. Barker were killed when grenades they were laying across a track exploded. Pte. W. Prince was wounded in the same explosion. R.Q.M.S. Howard Gibson was awarded the M.B.E. for his dedicated work between the period 1st February and 30th April 1945.

The 1st May was to be a momentous day in the story of the 9th Battalion in World War II. During the morning, Lieutenant Colonel Mogg was called to brigade headquarters. On his return, he called an 'O' Group and informed the assembled officers that preparations were to be made to occupy Hamburg when an expected unconditional surrender was accepted by the enemy. In such an event 9th D.L.I. and 1st R.T.R. were to lead the advance into the city and seize the bridges.

The 9th Battalion The Durham Light Infantry had fought in France in 1940, experienced the humility of Dunkirk, reformed and moved to the Western Desert and had distinguished itself at Gazala, Alamein and Mareth It had taken part in the invasion of Sicily and fought at Primosole Bridge before returning home to land on D-Day. Battles in Normandy, Belgium and Holland added to its reputation. The invasion of Germany followed, where it represented the regiment in the final chapter of the war. Now it was at the centre of history when, on the evening of the 1st May, a car containing the emissaries from Hamburg drove into its positions. The car contained a Major of the German General Staff and a Captain, who claimed to have come to negotiate the safety of hospitals in the city. The vehicle was brought to battalion headquarters by the Intelligence Officer, Captain Baily. In fact, on being transferred to brigade headquarters, they stated that they wished to negotiate a meeting between Major General Lyne and General Woltz, the Commander of Hamburg, and to arrange for the surrender of the city. The terms of unconditional surrender were given to them and they returned with instructions to bring back General Woltz. It was agreed that no aggressive actions would be taken against the garrison unless they attacked. At 10.30 p.m. on the 2nd May, General Woltz arrived at the rendezvous and was escorted by Lieutenant Colonel Mogg to brigade headquarters and then on to Division. In reality, the aim of General Woltz was to arrange a deputation to meet Field Marshall Montgomery to negotiate the surrender of all German forces in North-West Germany. At 9 a.m. on the 3rd, the Battalion Commander met the deputation and escorted them to Brigade. The party included

9 D.L.I. carriers passing the Goods Yard in Hamburg, 3 May 1945

Grand Admiral Von Friedeburg who was representing Admiral Doenitz, General Kinsel who was Chief of Staff to the C. in C., Admiral Wagner and two staff officers. They were taken to Field Marshall Montgomery's headquarters for the final surrender. Meanwhile large parties of enemy troops were marching down the autobahn carrying white flags. Some years later, General Sir John H. Mogg G.C.B., C.B.E., D.S.O. recorded the following memory of this occasion:

> I think it was actually fitting for the 9th D.L.I. that at the first sign of surrender the German Army appeared in front of the D.L.I. lines. I was on the blower...and the platoon commander said to me, 'Colonel, there's a German staff car with a white flag that has arrived and I can't understand what they are saying. They are talking in German.' I went immediately down there in my scout car and there were two staff officers and a German driver. One of the staff officers, in fact, spoke very good English but he didn't admit it to the chap when he was talking to him. I said, 'Where did you learn to speak your English?' He said he had learnt it at Baliol College in Oxford. So I said, 'Well that's very handy.' He said, 'I have a message from General Woltz on the question of surrender and I want to get through to Field Marshall Montgomery'...I then got on to Brigade H.Q. and took this staff car with us...We took it back to Brigade H.Q. and Brigade H.Q. took it on to Monty. The next day there was another great surrender party and we had an escort from 9 D.L.I.

to take them back to Monty's H.Q. So that was really fitting, I think, the 9 D.L.I., who had probably done more fighting than any other single battalion in the British Army, should finish up at Hamburg with the surrender coming through the British lines.

At 3.45 p.m., code word 'Baltic' was received and the battalion prepared to move off into Hamburg. Roadblocks and mines had been removed and the German police cleared the civilians from the roads. There were no aggressive demonstrations and even some civilians reappeared to watch the move into the city. The police, though armed, were helpful and gave no trouble.

The order of march into this great northern city may be of interest. It was 'A' Company, 'B' Squadron Group 1st R.T.R., 4.5 Mortar Platoon, Carrier Platoon, tactical headquarters, 'B' Company ('C' Squadron Group), 'C' Company, a section of Anti-Tank Platoon, Tactical Headquarters 1st R.T.R., Recce Troop 1st R.T.R., 'D' Company and the Medium Machine Gun Platoon. 'B' Company was to take over three bridges, south Elbe and 'C' Company two bridges, in the north Elbe area. Smartness of dress and bearing were strongly stressed. The companies were all in position in the city by 6.30 p.m. on the 3rd May. During the night, 'D' Company had to send a platoon to guard some U-Boats that were under construction and to prevent trouble with displaced persons who were now wandering about seeking revenge on the German civilian population. Pte. Jim Ratcliffe remembered the move into the city:

> It was weird when we were driving through Hamburg because the terms of surrender meant that the German gunners had to stay at their posts and it was a bit off-putting approaching a dirty big 88 mm which is pointing at you, complete with a grim faced crew.

The appalling damage done to the city by the Allied air forces was clearly seen by the troops. Barely a building was undamaged or left standing.

On the 4th of the month, the battalion moved to Tangstedt, north west of Hamburg. The German police had collected all weapons from the large numbers of enemy troops passing through the town and these were placed in the schoolhouse where battalion tactical headquarters was established. At night, 'C' Company was sent to Wedel to take over the guard of a P.O.W. camp from the 11th Hussars. This camp held about 3,000 and included a number of Poles who had been there before and had made their way back as they had nowhere else to go. Whilst officially the war had not ended, it was obvious to all that it was only a matter of time. Many thousands of German troops were coming down the roads into the British lines. The unconditional surrender was accepted on the 5th May and the war against Germany came to an end on the 8th. Pte. Jim Ratcliffe recalled:

> Just then a German soldier came down the road waving his arms, carrying a spandau and shouting to us, 'Kreig Firtish Tommy!' 'War finished.' Our officer, Captain Phillips, said, 'It sounds like its finished,' but he would go up front and get it confirmed. He returned a

short while after and told us that it was true. We all started shaking hands and congratulating each other at coming through it safely. Our officer told us to get off the road and take over the houses nearby, if necessary, throw out people! The one we entered was occupied by two old maiden school teachers. We put them into one room. There was no question of us putting them out onto the street.

Needless to say, the night was one to remember…Some of the rifle company lads got drunk with German troops who, the previous day would have been trying to kill each other. I think everyone, including the German troops, were glad it was over…

On the 6th May, an order was issued that 'all masks will be taken off and full headlights used.' The 8th May 1945 was the official termination of the war and VE day was celebrated with Verey lights, flares, Bofors firing off tracers and bonfires. The report to the regimental newsletter stated: 'Now – having sorted out the German Army in one sense, we are helping to sort it out in another…'

The surrender of the German army was now officially to take place.

CHAPTER XXVII

ARMY OF OCCUPATION

The immediate task of the Allied armies in Germany was to bring about as quickly and as successfully as possible the disarmament and concentration of the German army. The 7th Armoured Division was ordered to screen off the western half of Schleswig Holstein into which the mass of the beaten German army was to be moved and held. On the 7th May, the battalion was ordered to move to an area at the western end of the Kiel Canal. This area was reached early in the evening. A message was received from S.H.A.E.F. that the unconditional surrender had been signed and was to take effect from one minute after midnight on the 9th May. All offensive operations were to cease at once and units were to remain in their present locations. In case the surrender had not reached all German formations, full defensive precautions had to be taken. The battalion moved to the peninsular area north of the mouth of the River Elbe on the morning of the 9th. The task, with the help of the 11th Hussars, was to screen off the peninsular area 'C' into which German army personnel were to be herded and sorted out as they arrived. Area 'C' stretched from Brunsbuttel, north along the main road to St. Michaelis Donn, then west via Barlter to the sea. Companies controlled the roads leading into the peninsular from north, south and east. All German prisoners of war were to be allowed into the sealed-off area but civilians were to be stopped at the stop-lines. Although alterations to the area were made from time to time, the battalion's role remained the same until the beginning of July. It is interesting to take a brief look at the duties and responsibilities laid upon the battalion;

1. Stop-Line: The boundaries of the area was marked by a stop-line. Twenty-four hour checkpoints were set up with the responsibility of stopping all movement into and out the peninsular.

2. Displaced Persons Work: Placing many hundreds of 'slave workers', mainly Poles and Russians, into properly organised and regulated camps. On completion of this work, these unfortunate people came under the control of the Displaced Persons Organisation of the Military Government. The battalion retained the responsibility of locally controlling and feeding them.

3. Local Military Government: The Intelligence Officer became what amounted to a local military governor. Captain Baily had to deal with numerous problems in the first few weeks, helped by two indispensable interpreters.

4. German Troops: German troops poured into the peninsula and the battalion's task was to feed them – usually on bully beef and biscuits.

5. Patrols: Constant patrolling was carried out along the stop-line and throughout the countryside.

In the early weeks, this was an extremely difficult task, not helped by the large numbers of displaced persons running wild throughout the countryside. The companies were, of necessity, scattered with wide gaps between them. It must also be borne in mind that all organisation in Germany had broken down.

Battalion dispositions were as follows. Tactical headquarters was St. Michaelis Donn, which was a small village near the west coast of the peninsular; 'A' Company covered the roads in the northern coastal area; 'B' Company lay astride the main road to Meldorf and south along the railway line to tactical headquarters; 'C' Company was in the Eddelak area and 'D' and 'S' Companies covered the road from Marne. Shortly after arrival, 'D' Company moved to Gudenorf. German troops poured into the area. There were stop-line problems to solve. Enemy arms and ammunition dumps had to be located. The local Nazis were given away to the military by displaced persons and civilians.

On the 13th May, the battalion was moved to the Meldorf area. One of the duties here was to round up all S.S. troops as these were not allowed into the peninsula. Captain Baily, the Intelligence Officer, earned a reputation for sniffing out these people. By the 18th of the month, 44,500 German troops were herded into this area of the peninsula. Pte. Jim Ratcliffe wrote:

> We spent the next few weeks rounding up enemy units. One day we were in a carrier passing a group of Panzers when the track on the carrier broke. The Panzer lads came over to see what the problem was, got stuck in, had it mended and back on while we were thinking about it. Mind you, compared to a track off a Tiger, it was small change.

Most German soldiers were pleased to see the end of the war. The displaced camp at Meldorf was placed out of bounds to all troops due to disease being present among its population. Swimming was organised and unofficial fishing was stopped with this entry in the War Diary: 'Grenades will not be thrown into the Kiel Canal for fishing as they cause severe subsidence to the banks.'

On the 20th May, a further enlargement of the area took place and the battalion moved to police the stop-line on the railway line between Heide and Albersdorf. The 1st Bn. Rifle Brigade were on the left and the 53rd Division on the right. Two days later a move was made to Nordhastedt as overcrowding in the peninsula meant a further extension. German troops, dirty and unkempt, poured into the area, the only transport they had being horse drawn. The battalion had its own canteen, swimming pool and sports fields. A skittle alley was attached to the swimming pool and a cinema provided the latest films. Horse riding became part of the leisure activities. On the 29th, a move was made to a brigade concentration area near Kellinghausen. There were no longer any stop-line duties. Battalion H.Q., 'A' Company and 'A' and 'B' Echelon were in Brockstedt, 'B' Company was in Willenscharen, 'C' Company in Rade and 'S' and 'D' Companies in Fitzbeck. Outings were arranged to Hamburg. All ranks were warned of the danger of contracting V.D. from displaced persons.

The usual duties continued – controlling displaced persons, German army and civilians and all dumps of supplies and ammunition. On the 14th June, the battalion was relieved of all operational duties to prepare for an important ceremonial parade on an undetermined date. 'Bull' became the main activity. Only sport was allowed and battalion sports were arranged on the weekend 15th/16th June. 'H.Q.' Company won by 10 points though an entry in the War Diary doubted the fairness of the result of one event: 'Some dirty work by R.S.M. Mr. Holcroft, won the officers versus W.O.s and N.C.O.s race for the Sergeants Mess!' The 'dirty work' is not recorded. The regimental band arrived and played at various functions. Before leaving for Berlin it broadcast over B.F.N. (British Forces Network) from Hamburg – the first regimental band to do so. A general holiday had been declared for the 14th June to mark the anniversary of the battle at Lingèvres in Normandy. The expected move to Berlin was postponed when Brigade informed the battalion that only two battalions were to go to the capital and the Durhams were not one of them. The battalion was now under the command of the 22nd Armoured Brigade. Though in sole charge of the area and answerable to Division or even Corps H.Q. the battalion also took over the control of the Kreis Segeburg area. Arrangements were being made for the issue of postal votes for the forthcoming general election in Britain.

Victory Parade, 1945

Non-fraternisation orders had been issued since the final days of the war. These had been sweeping, with very little contact being allowed with the civilian population of all ages. Only contact in carrying out of duties was permissible. On the 23rd June, an order was received giving a relaxation of the non-fraternisation laws. In future, troops were allowed to 'talk to and play with children up to eight years of age.' Within a short period of time further relaxation took place and troops were allowed to talk to adults but not enter their homes. Most Germans were proving to be friendly though a small minority remained aloof. On the 24th June, the battalion moved to Segeburg with battalion headquarters, 'H.Q.' and 'S' Companies in the town. 'C' Company was at Brokstedt, 'D' Company at Lentforden and 'B' Company at Nahe.

German troops were now being discharged. This brought with it problems of those men without discharge papers or who held invalid papers. Control of the Wehrnacht was operated through the German Area Commander, Oberst Wepell. Displaced persons continued to create problems, though by now many nationals such as the Russians were being sent to zones occupied by their own troops. On the 30th June, a move was made to the area of Wilster and Itzehoe. All companies were in Wilster except 'C' Company at Beidenfleith and 'S' Company at Wewelsfleith. However, no guards or patrols were necessary, which indicated how the countryside was returning to normal. Around Wilster and Itzehoe there were many entertainment facilities – theatre, swimming, canteen, cinema. The regimental band and bugles arrived to entertain. Yachting and riding were also available. The regimental Colours arrived from England. It was here that the cinema showed the atrocities committed by the Nazis in the concentration camps. Capt. Roy Griffiths wrote:

> In Itzehoe, the Battalion re-grouped and arrangements were made for the townspeople in and around the area to attend a cinema showing the atrocities in many of the concentration camps. At the conclusion of the film some declared that the film was Anglo-American propaganda, others appeared to be genuinely overcome. Those who felt it was a programme of propaganda or 'a joke' were selected for a further showing of the film and returned to the cinema.

On the 20th July, Maj. S. Terrell took a small recce party to Berlin to make arrangements to take over from the Canadian Berlin Battalion. Pte. J. Galbraith remembered the journey and his first look at the German capital:

> About 20 of us were detailed as advance party to Berlin to get the billets ready for the Battalion. It took us about 24 hours, with detours, bridges down, roads blocked and the Russians stopping us at every checkpoint. Anyway, we arrived, I think it was June, a place called Smargendorf, near Hoenzollendamm with a big main street. We were in houses…everything was smashed to pieces, roofs off, walls down and bodies buried in the gardens. Still we got down to it and repaired it the best we could with the Battalion coming in a fortnight.

Also on the 20th July, Maj. Gen. L.O. Lyne, who commanded the 7th Armoured Division, issued the following note to all battalions, from Maj. Gen. John B. Anderson, U.S. Army Commanding XVI U.S. Corps:

> Since the 'Desert Rats' left my command along the Roer, I have followed their activities with great interest and pride – pride that I had the opportunity to have in my command this fine division. Please accept my congratulations on the fine performance of your division. Also I would appreciate being remembered to many fine officers and men whom I met during the brief period of our association…

The main party moved to Brunswick on the 29th and then on to Berlin, arriving on the evening of the following day. It was a climax to an exceptional war record. The report to the regimental newsletter could not have been worded better:

> From Africa to Berlin, first with the honoured 50th Division and finally with the equally honoured 'Desert Rats', France and Dunkirk 1940 – El Alamein to Tunis – Sicily – the beaches of Normandy, through France, Belgium and Holland – from The Rhine to Hamburg and then, at long last, Berlin.

The newsletter continues:

> We are stationed in what was once a fashionable residential area – Wilmersdorf and Schmargendorf. Our barracks were previously occupied by the S.S...We are surrounded by the C.C.G. (Control Commission Germany – more colloquially known as Complete Chaos Guaranteed).
>
> Our chief occupations from a duty point of view are security guards and curfew patrols...The security guards include the Potato Guard – by virtue of the fact that it literally guards potatoes, and other food guards named after the appropriate commodity...V.I.P. Guards include – His Excellency Sir William Strang, Political Advisor to the C in C, General Sir Brian Robertson, the Deputy Commander B.A.O.R. and two of H.M. Judges all of whom live in palatial mansions...Altogether there are just over 100 men on duty every day excluding periodical Guards of Honour.

Private Galbraith wrote:

> Anyway we got settled in doing guards day and night. Everything had to be guarded, mainly food. The 3 million people were starving but if they worked clearing the city, they got a food pass....The army moved heavy equipment in to clear the roads and buildings. You could drive for miles and not see two buildings standing.

The battalion enjoyed very good barracks, plenty of entertainment and recreation with a pretty docile population. The city had suffered hugely from Allied bombing. Eighty per cent of the buildings were uninhabitable. If the Germans were increasingly friendly and co-operative, their smiles failed to hide the considerable danger of starvation and disease. The black market flourished with cigarettes, coffee and food being exchanged for large sums. All Ranks Clubs were established, namely, the Gerboa Club and the Winston Club. German symphony and opera orchestras gave concerts for both the occupying forces and the civilians.

On the 10th August, the Commanding Officer, Lt. Col. H.J. Mogg D.S.O., addressed the battalion before leaving for England. The writer to the newsletter observed:

> The Colonel addressed the Battalion before leaving, to 'endure', as he put it, a course at the Staff College.
>
> Colonel John Mogg was loved and respected by each and every one of us in the Battalion. A finer leader in action one could not wish for, and a better Commanding

Officer one could not find. He was a great commander and whilst we all miss him greatly, we all wish him the very best of luck and success, both in his course and thereafter.

He was succeeded by Lt. Col. A.B. Brown. The battalion command structure in September, 1945, was:

Commanding Officer	Lt. Col. A.B. Brown
Second in Command	Maj. A.R.G. Noble M.C.
Adjutant	Capt. N. Briggs
Intelligence Officer	Capt. J.C. Baily
Officer Commanding 'A' Company	Maj. S. Terrell
Officer Commanding 'B' Company	Maj. F.K. Tonkin
Officer Commanding 'C' Company	Maj. J.R. Lanning M.C.
Officer Commanding 'D' Company	Maj. L.E.V. Rumble M.C.
Officer Commanding 'S' Company	Capt. W.R. Bell
Officer Commanding 'H.Q.' Company	Capt. E.H. Peace
Quartermaster	Lt. (Q.M.) E.J.F. Jones
Motor Transport Officer	Capt. E.H. Hooper
Medical Officer	Capt. E.H. Rea
Padre	Capt. Father J.F. Devine

The Japanese surrender was announced on the 15th August and the following day was given in celebration of the end of the war. Sport and recreation, in addition to normal duties, continued to occupy the battalion's time. On the 7th September, a victory parade was held at the Tiergarten. The King's Colours and regimental Colours of the battalion were carried on parade. A party of 150 from 'A', 'C' and 'D' Companies, commanded by Maj. A.G.R. Noble M.C., took part. The salute was taken by Marshall Zhukov, Lieutenant General Robertson, General Patton and General Koenig. At an investiture on the 10th of the month, Field Marshall Montgomery invested personnel of the 7th Armoured Division in the Olympischer Platz. Maj. G.R. Lanning and Lt. D.S. Taylor received Military Crosses and Sergeants Cameron, Cross and Nicholson received Military Medals. On the 20th, 120 men formed a Guard of Honour for a meeting of the Allied Commanders in the American zone. Major Lanning M.C. was in command, with Capt. Roy Griffiths as Second in Command. The King's Colours and the regimental Colours were carried. Generals Koenig and Eisenhower attended and Field Marshall Montgomery inspected the guard and complemented Major Lanning on the turnout. The Russian representative failed to arrive for the meeting. In the International Sports Meeting held in the Olympic Stadium on the 23rd between American, British and French teams, 11 representatives were from the battalion. Private Courtney was second in the 3,000 metres, Private Stockdale competed in the medley relay team, which was second and Captain Peace and Private Black were in the 4 x 100 relay, which also finished second. The Americans won the competition fairly easily with British team second.

The process of returning officers and men to the United Kingdom prior to demobilisation had already commenced for those who had served the longest. The battalion was to leave the 7th Armoured Division, which was to become a regular division. The Durhams and the 1st/5th Queens were the only non-regular units left and were to be replaced by the 2nd Bn. Essex Regiment and 1st Bn. Oxford and Buckinghamshire Light Infantry. Men in Group 30, who had served the shortest time with the battalion, were to be moved to the regular battalions. The battalion would now join 56 Brigade, 49th Infantry Division. On the 9th November, 'A' and 'S' Companies arrived at Unna. 'A' Company relieved 'A' Company 2nd Essex in Langschede and 'S' Company remained in Unna. 'C' Company arrived on the 11th and relieved 'B' Company 2nd Essex in Frondenberg. 'B' and 'D' Companies arrived on the 13th with 'D' Company taking over in Heeren Werwe and 'B' Company moved to the S.S. Barracks at Unna. A message was received from Brigadier Spurling D.S.O. It read:

> A little less than a year ago you joined the Lorried Infantry Brigade of the 7th Armoured Division, after a long and glorious fighting record with the 50th (Northumbrian) Division.
>
> In the comparatively short time that you have been a 'Desert Rat' you have gained for yourself a record of valour and determination in battle quite unsurpassed, which is a byword in the Division, and the subject of admiration by many outside it.
>
> We, who remain in this Brigade, will also remember you for your good comradeship, for friends we have made and for the high standard of soldier-like bearing you have consistently maintained.
>
> In giving you my sincere thanks for all your help in the victories of the past year, I would like, on behalf of the Brigade, to send each one of you our best wishes for your future, wherever you may be in the coming year.

Duties in this wide new area of villages and scattered farms were very much to do with maintaining order. Day and night patrolling, with occasional sweeps of the area with the object of containing looters, and house checks were carried out. 'D' and 'S' Companies had to look after coal mines. There were four Displaced Persons Camps in the area containing Poles, Jugoslavs and Latvians. The Poles were very troublesome, the other nationals were very quiet. One camp contained 4,000 Hungarians classed as 'disarmed Wehrnacht'. This camp was the responsibility of 'D' Company. In the beginning the camp had to be guarded as no Hungarians were supposed to escape. It was too large to be guarded efficiently and escapes were many. The policy was changed when it was recognised that the Hungarians could not be contained in the camp if they wished to escape. In future, escapes were to be ignored. Occasional assaults and armed robbery took place but on the whole the civilian population was friendly and co-operative. Demobilisation had not affected the battalion too much, though some officers and men had left for England. However, it was becoming more obvious that greater numbers would be leaving the battalion in the next few months. As Christmas approached military and civilians prepared for the festivities. Christmas trees appeared in the villages and towns. Trees were cut down to supplement the fuel shortage. The battalion was given three days' holiday over Christmas. The traditional army Christmas dinner took place with officers and N.C.O.s waiting on the men assisted by English Y.M.C.A. ladies. Concerts were arranged and the Eagle Cinema in Unna put on stage and film shows. As 1945 gave way to 1946, everyone was looking forward to going home.

The 9th Battalion The Durham Light Infantry was raised and prospered in the heavy industrial and coal mining region of North Durham and Tyneside. It is fitting that one of its final acts in Germany touched upon its background and devotion to duty. The following is an extract from the *Civil Affairs and Military Government North-West Europe 1944–46*:

> At midday on the 20th February 1946 an explosion occurred at the Monopol Grimberg mine near Kamen in the Ruhr, trapping 498 men, including three British officers, three thousand feet underground. The force of the explosion was such that it reached the surface, completely destroying shaft equipment and head structures. Trained rescue squads began work at once. Officers of the North German Coal Control including the Deputy Controller-General of Production, directed and took a personal part in the dangerous rescue operations. Men of the 9th Battalion Durham Light Infantry were on duty to preserve order. Many of these were miners in civil life and volunteered to help, but officials would not accept them because there were sufficient German rescue teams familiar with the type of workings in which the disaster occurred…In all 418 persons, including three British Officers lost their lives.

During the months of 1946, officers and men of the battalion came home to demobilisation. Like the battalion of 1914–18, they had served to the very end of the conflict. Their fathers and uncles of World War I must have smiled with pride and muttered a quiet, 'You've done well.'

CHAPTER XXVIII

PARACHUTE BATTALION

The Territorial Army was reformed in 1947. The 9th Battalion left 151 Brigade and was converted to the 17th Battalion The Parachute Regiment (9th D.L.I.) T.A. Light infantry drill and marching pace was retained and the new battalion maintained a close contact with the battalions of 151 Brigade. The first Commanding Officer was Lt. Col. J.C. Slight D.S.O. The Adjutant was Capt. J. Hyde-Thompson M.C., the Quartermaster Captain Runciman, R.S.M. Rafferty and the P.S.I was C.S.M. G. Beddows. Changes occurred in 1948 when Lt. Col. T.H. Birbeck D.S.O. of the Border Regiment succeeded Lt. Col. Slight D.S.O., T.D. Later Commanding Officers included Lt. Cols. R.B. Humphreys, J.R.P. Montgomery M.C., C.F.O. Breese, W.G.S. Mills, R.E. Morton, H. L. Carey T.D. and K.Came O.B.E. A recruitment drive was initiated in December 1948 and this was successful in swelling the ranks of the battalion.

The usual Territorial Army activities continued throughout the ensuing years. There were two drill nights per week, with occasional weekend camps and the annual camp lasting for a fortnight, which was usually held in mid summer or early autumn. Weekend camps enabled the battalion to fire its weapons on the ranges of Whitburn and Bellerby and to jump from captive balloons at Usworth and Thornaby. Final jumps from aircraft were made at Upper Heyford when 'wings' were awarded to those who successfully completed the course. Annual camps enabled officers and men to sharpen their skills as parachutists and practice their role as an infantry assault force. In 1949, the annual camp was held at Hornsea and in succeeding years Fylingdales Moor, Braunton (Devon), Stobs Camp near Hawick, Stanford Battle Area near Thetford, Dibsgate near Shorncliffe and Okehampton. At the Braunton Camp in 1951, the whole brigade dropped on the Westward Ho Golf Course. To these were added more exciting venues abroad. In 1952, for example, the parachute element in the battalion flew to Germany for airborne manoeuvres. The battalion was flown across the Rhine and dropped on a pre-arranged dropping zone and spent three nights and two days in exercises against infantry and armoured formations of the Rhine Army. Leisure breaks activities were found in Bad Oeyenhausen. Private McCarthy had a narrow escape during the parachute drop when his 3-in. mortar barrel failed to drop clear on the way down. He did, however, land safely.

Accidents did occur over the years, usually leg and back injuries. Major A.D. Scott wrote of one fatality:

> One of 17 Para's annual camps in the late 1960's was at Penhale on the north coast of Cornwall. The training included an airborne exercise and the Battalion was split into company groups to carry out different phases using airfields in the south west of England. On arrival at our airfield, we duly drew and fitted 'chutes, packed containers and made

'B' Company, 17th Parachute Battalion 9 D.L.I., Fylingdales Camp 1950.
Back row (standing left to right): Pte. Durkin, Cpl. Robinson, unknown, Pte. Mitchell, Pte. Morton, Pte.
Graves, unknown, unknown, unknown, Pte. Panthaler, unknown, Pte. Perry, Pte. Ford, Pte. Blythe.
Centre row: Cpl. Owens, Sgt. McKenzie, Sgt. Vernon, Lt. Weightman O.C., Lt. Charnley 2/i.c., C/Sgt.
Pragnell, Cpl Wood.
Front row (seated): unknown, L/Cpl. Butterworte, Pte. Huchins, Pte. Parks, unknown, Pte. Sutcliffe,
unknown, Pte. Wilmore, Pte. Brodie, Pte. Bosley, L/Cpl. McCallum.

ready to embark on the Hastings aircraft when it arrived. Unfortunately, and without explanation, it failed to turn up and we stood down.

The next day we learned that the Hastings had crashed and all the crew and instructors on board killed, shortly after it had taken off from RAF Abingdon en route to pick us up. The same Hastings had flown one of the other companies on the previous day. Sadly, amongst those killed was Sgt. Ellis, an APJ1, from 'D' Company. Had the fault that caused the crash happened a little sooner or later the best part of a company would have been lost.

In 1961 and 1965, elements of the battalion flew to North Africa to take part in military exercises. In 1963, the battalion was represented at exercises held in Cyprus.

In addition to the rigorous training of jumps from aircraft and captive balloons, exhibition jumps were put on for several ceremonial and special events held from time to time. In late 1949, a parachute jump display was carried out at Usworth. This was made from a captive balloon and the general public were invited to attend. It was estimated that the huge crowd was 30–50,000. Similar jumps were made at Darlington Air Display in 1950, Carlisle Pageant in 1951 and the Festival of Britain celebrations in July of the same year.

Initially, companies were formed at Gateshead Burt Terrace Drill Hall ('H.Q.' and 'A' Companies) and Felling Drill Hall (Support Company). In 1949 'B' Company was raised at Norton Drill Hall. Thirty-three members were enrolled. The first in this company to be awarded their 'wings' were Second Lieutenant Charnley, Lance Corporals Furness and Brown and Privates Sutcliffe, Coxon and Sudron. 'Wings' awarded to members of the other companies were Captain Trewhitt and Privates Petty, Phillippo, Hockridge, Teasdale, McAndrew, Pickersgill and 'Pablo' Morris. The latter had a flight technique described in the regimental journal as:

> …during the first four jumps of his course was simply to hang on in his harness and at about 50 feet, to shout, 'Oot the way lads, I'm cummen doon' and then hit the deck on all fours like a ruptured crab.

By 1958, the composition of the battalion was:

'A' Company	Fenham Barracks, Newcastle
'B' Company	Norton Drill Hall
'C' Company	Gateshead (1st Platoon at Consett)
'D' Company	West Hartlepool
'S' Company	Felling Drill Hall
'H.Q.' Company	Gateshead

Training included endurance and map reading exercises in more remote areas such as the Lake District. There was also practice acting as the defending or attacking force against infantry battalions of other regiments. In 1956, with the Cold War at its height and fears of an atomic cataclysm between the nations of the Western Europe and Russia and her allies, the battalion undertook a course on atomic warfare. This was held at the Civil Defence Training Centre at Darras Hall and included training in first aid and light rescue.

On the 4th October, 1952, Colours were presented at Brancepeth Castle to the battalion by H.R.H. Princess Royal. The following year, the battalion was represented at the Queen's coronation. The processional party included Maj. I.N.N. Beadle M.C., R.Q.M.S. Curle, C.Q.M.S. Myers and Corporals Parkinson and Bruce. The street lining party included Lt. A. Thompson with the Queen's Colour, Colour Sergeant Pragnell, Sgts. J. Maddison and Freegard, Corporals Barnett, A. Burns and Stones, Lance Corporals George, T. Burns, Hornsby, Kirton, McDonald, Mallinson, Middleton and Mole and Privates Cosgrove, Lavender, Pollett and Robertson. Coronation Medals were awarded to Lt. Col. R.B. Humphreys, Maj. I.N.N. Beadle M.C., Capt. (Q.M.) J.H. Dought, C.S.M. Armstrong, Colour Sergeant Hetherington, Sergeant Helpin and Cpl.

A. Burns. In 1957, 20 N.C.O.s and other ranks under Maj. H.L. Carey represented the battalion at the presentation of the Freedom of Aldershot to the Parachute Regiment. Lts. W.H.W. Swales and J.M. Rowlands carried the Colours in this parade. On the 27th May 1960, a Guard of Honour was provided for the visit of the Queen and the Duke of Edinburgh to Peterlee.

In the same year, the battalion acquired a mascot in the form of 'Geordie', a pit pony. It was found that the pony distinctly disliked marching in front of the band and showed this by pulling, kicking and attempting to break away. When placed behind the band in the marching column it was much quieter and behaved itself.

Sport, always an important element in the battalion's programme of training and fitness, continued over the years with mixed success. Soccer, rugby and boxing were the main sports. Private Readman reached the final of the Territorial Army boxing championships in May 1957. He was awarded the prize for the best runner-up in the light welterweight competition. Lt. Larry L'Estrange was selected for the Ireland rugby union team to play against England at Twickenham. The usual social activities completed the battalion's annual calendar of activities. Dances were held and the annual children's Christmas party took place and was always a great success. Former members of the 9th Battalion were often invited to social events.

In 1967, the Reserve Forces were re-organised and 17th Bn. The Parachute Regiment (9 D.L.I.) was amalgamated with the 12/13th Parachute Regiment to form 4th Parachute Regiment. Two companies of this regiment were provided by the 17th, but 9 D.L.I. had now ceased to exist, the end of a glorious history.

Paras of 'B' Coy. relax duruing a break at camp.

EPILOGUE

The 9th Battalion completed over 100 years of service to the United Kingdom. Few battalions, if any, of other regiments in the British army had served so long in the major conflicts of the 20th century. In the First World War 786 officers and other ranks were killed in action. Many more ultimately died through wounds or gas, were missing or prisoners of war. In this dreadful war, 328 individuals were awarded medals, which included 2 V.C.s, 3 D.S.O.s, 37 M.C.s, 1 M.C. with two Bars, 9 M.C.s with one Bar, 28 D.C.M.s, 197 M.M.s, 3 M.M.s with two Bars, 16 M.M.s with one bar. In the Second World War, awards included 1 V.C., 4 D.S.O.s, 40 M.C.s and more than 190 M.M.s.

The battalion was commanded by a number of fine officers, including Lieutenant Colonels Henderson and Crouch in World War One and Percy, Clarke and Woods in the Second World War. There were two outstanding leaders, one in each war. Lt. Col. Roland Boys Bradford V.C., M.C., 1916–17, became the youngest General in the British army during that conflict and lost his life at Cambrai. In the Second World War, Lt. Col. John Mogg D.S.O., 1944–45, survived the conflict and went on to attain high rank in the post-war army.

In the years following the demise of the battalions of the Durham Light Infantry, many young men of the North-East of England have been recruited into the ranks of the various battalions of the Light Infantry Regiment of the present-day army. They have been found to be worthy successes to their forefathers. Now, at the start of the 21st century, the 'Old and Bold' have diminished in number as time has taken its toll. This year most of the reunions, formerly held annually, have ceased as numbers have diminished. Old Comrades Associations meetings are still held but numbers are falling. However, the legacy of faithful service, courage and sacrifice in the wars of the 20th Century should not be forgotten and, in a small way, this history may help to insure that the memory lives on.

Capt. Bell, O.C. 'S' Coy., stands with a location sign listing the many campaigns of the 9th D.L.I.

APPENDIX

ROLL OF HONOUR 1915–18

Source: *Officers Died in the Great War*

Rank	Name		Date killed or died of wounds
2/Lt.	A.	Little	25. 4. 15
2/Lt.	A.J.	Haughton	23. 6. 15
2/Lt.	O.	Field	18. 7. 15
Capt.	G.H.	Coates	25. 12. 15
Lt.	J.H.	Edgar	24. 2. 16
Lt.	R.E.	Atkinson	25. 2. 16
Capt.	M.H.	Bettison	18. 4. 16
2/Lt.	J.F.G.	Ashworth	25. 6. 16
2/Lt.	D.A.	Brown	23. 7. 16
Capt.	R.	Rutherford	15. 9. 16
2/Lt.	A.	Lawson	16. 9. 16
2/Lt.	J.H.	Tytler	16. 9. 16
2/Lt.	E.A.	Walton	16. 9. 16
Lt.	W.E.O.	Scott	29. 9. 16
2/Lt.	H.	Whiteley	11.10.16
2/Lt.	C.E.	Higginbotham	5.11.16
2/Lt	S.T.	Paxton	5.11.16
2/Lt.	J.	Slater	16.11.16
Capt.	H.J.	Spencer	17.11.16
2/Lt.	H.P.	Tozer (R.F.C.)	16.12.16
2/Lt.	R.	Greenland	13. 4. 17
2/Lt.	R.N.	Bell	14. 4. 17
2/Lt.	F.	Sadler (R.F.C.)	21. 4. 17
2/Lt.	J.G.	Steel	24. 5. 17
2/Lt.	C.J.	Dixon	22. 6. 17
Lt.	H.	Hall	15. 9. 17
2/Lt.	J.	Dick	28.10.17
Capt.	C.F.B.	Simpson	3.12.17
Lt.	W.G.	Wylie M.C. & Bar	28. 3.18
2/Lt.	A.W.	Bell	28. 3.18
2/Lt.	H.M.	Ridley	23. 5.18
Lt.	H.	Strachan	29. 7.18
2/Lt.	E.	Frankland	24.10.18
Lt.	F.W.	Lennox	1. 11.18

Source: *Soldiers Died in the Great War*

Rank	Name		Date killed or died of wounds
Pte.	W.	Garbutt	25. 4. 15
Pte.	T.	Richards	26. 4. 15
Pte.	J.	Berresford	27. 4. 15
Pte.	J.	Brown	29. 4. 15
Pte.	T.S.	Bertram	30. 4. 15
Pte.	H.H.	Smith	30. 4. 15
Pte.	G.A.	Batey	3. 5. 15
Pte.	S.	Hicks	3. 5. 15
Pte.	J.W.	Lightfoot	3. 5. 15
Pte.	J.	Longstaff	3. 5. 15
Pte.	R.	Masterman	3. 5. 15
Pte.	T.	Todhunter	3. 5. 15
Pte.	R.	Vickers	3. 5. 15
Pte.	J.	Walker	3. 5. 15
Pte.	J.C.	Williams	3. 5. 15
Pte.	T.	Carnaffan	11. 5. 15
Pte.	T.	Herron	11. 5. 15
Pte.	J.T.	Hodgson	11. 5. 15
Pte.	J.D.	Hutchinson	11. 5. 15
Cpl.	G.	Lucas	11. 5. 15
Pte.	J.	Batey	12. 5. 15
Pte.	F.	Dixon	12. 5. 15
Pte.	J.	Duffy	12. 5. 15
Pte.	R.	Ridley	12. 5. 15
Pte.	J.	Henderson	13. 5. 15
Pte.	F.	Newby	16. 5. 15
Pte.	Y.R.	Grey	17. 5. 15
Pte.	S.	Cawthorn	18. 5. 15
Pte.	A.	Stewart	18. 5. 15
Pte.	G.W.	Smith	24. 5. 15
Pte.	G.	McKeown	26. 5. 15
Pte.	H.	Heckels	27. 5. 15
Pte.	E.	Scott	27. 5. 15
Pte.	G.	Turnbull	27. 5. 15
Pte.	J.A.	Bell	11. 6. 15
C.S.M.	J.H.	Davidson	22. 6. 15
Pte.	C.H.	Harrison	23. 6. 15
Pte.	C.	Bowman	24. 6. 15
Pte.	W.	Fettes	4. 7. 15
Pte.	H.	Gustard	4. 7. 15
Pte.	M.	Hailes	4. 7. 15
Pte.	C.	Fawcus	5. 7. 15

Pte.	H.	Quinn	5. 7. 15
Pte.	H.	Murray	6. 7. 15
Cpl.	J.	Barker	14. 7. 15
Pte.	C.	Harris	14. 7. 15
Pte.	J.	McGuire	14. 7. 15
Pte.	G.	McLeay	14. 7. 15
Pte.	W.	Towler	14. 7. 15
Pte.	E.W.	Dodd	20. 7. 15
Cpl.	T.	Gunn	21. 7. 15
Sgt.	J.G.	Wheatley	21. 7. 15
Pte.	S.	Caseley	27. 7. 15
Pte.	W.	Pearson	9. 8. 15
L/Cpl.	C.	Houghton	13. 8. 15
Pte.	A.E.	Gamblin	22. 8. 15
Pte.	J.	Bainbridge	28. 8. 15
Cpl.	J.E.	Cain	2. 9. 15
Pte.	J.	Raine	28. 9. 15
Pte.	R.	Renforth	5.10.15
Pte.	E.	Soulsby	10.10.15
Pte.	R.	Clark	14.10.15
Pte.	J.	Lowther	18.10.15
Pte.	W.	Glennon	21.10.15
Pte.	E.	Holloway	27.10.15
Cpl.	J.T.	Reid	27.10.15
Pte.	E.T.	Dixon	31.12.15
Pte.	J.	Tully	10. 1. 16
Pte.	T.W.	Armstrong	21. 1. 16
Pte.	J.	Turbitt	21. 1. 16
Ote.	T.	Evans	5. 2. 16
Pte.	W.	Hawdon	6. 2. 16
Pte.	E.	Thompson	7. 2. 16
Pte.	G.	Turnbull	8. 2. 16
Pte.	W.	Brown	9. 2. 16
Pte.	W.	Curry	9. 2. 16
L/Cpl.	J.	Gardiner	10. 2. 16
Pte.	T.	Horrocks	12. 2. 16
Pte.	J.	McCrystal	12. 2. 16
Pte.	T.	Dixon	13. 2. 16
Pte.	T.W.	Lucas	14. 2. 16
L/Cpl.	J.	Donnelly	23. 2. 16
L/Sgt.	J.H.	Morgan	23. 2. 16
Pte.	W.	Davison	24. 2. 16
Pte.	W.	Dunnett	24. 2. 16
L/Cpl.	H.	Moody	24. 2. 16
L/Sgt.	J.	McNeill	24. 2. 16
Pte.	J.H.	Pearson	24. 2. 16
Pte.	F.	Baggeley	26. 2. 16
Pte.	R.	Carey	26. 2. 16
Pte.	G.	Cook	26. 2. 16
Pte.	W.	Elliott	26. 2. 16
Pte.	J.	Tuff	26. 2. 16
Cpl.	T.	Murray	28. 2. 16
Sgt.	H.	Girdlestone	29. 2. 16
Pte.	T.	Maddison	29. 2. 16
Pte.	J.	Coxon	1. 3. 16
L/Cpl.	J.A.	Drummond	1. 3. 16
L/Cpl.	R.	Edwards	1. 3. 16
Pte.	D.	Graham	1. 3. 16
Pte.	B.	Miller	1. 3. 16
Pte.	W.	Armstrong	2. 3. 16
Pte.	J.W.	Charlton	2. 3. 16
Pte.	A.	Fawcett	2. 3. 16
Pte.	W.	Finlay D.C.M.	2. 3. 16
Sgt.	G.A.	Johnson	2. 3. 16
Pte.	T.	Knight	2. 3. 16
Pte.	G.C.	Morris	2. 3. 16
Pte.	J.	Reed	2. 3. 16
Pte.	N.	Telford	2. 3. 16
Pte.	G.	Thompson	2. 3. 16
Pte.	J.C.	Richardson	3. 3. 16
L/Cpl.	J.	Turnbull	5. 3. 16
Pte.	J.W.	Rawson	13. 3. 16
Pte.	J.	Young	13. 3. 16
L/Cpl.	T.	Carmichael	24. 3. 16
Cpl.	F.H.	Kelly	27. 3. 16
Pte.	L.	Parkin	27. 3. 16
Pte.	R.	Atkinson	28. 3. 16
Pte.	T.	Williams	3. 4. 16
Pte.	J.	Collins	5. 4. 16
Pte.	J.	Brooks	7. 4. 16
Pte.	W.	Cawthorne	7. 4. 16
Pte.	E.	Edwards	7. 4. 16
Pte.	R.	Maddison	7. 4. 16
Pte.	J.	Waugh	7. 4. 16
Pte.	G.	Sowerby	8. 4. 16
Pte.	R.	Doyle	11. 4. 16
Pte.	R.E.	Scott	12. 4. 16
Pte.	W.H.	Parkin	14. 4. 16
Cpl.	R.	Armstrong	15. 4. 16
Pte.	J.	Nunan	16. 4. 16
Sgt.	W.	Whinham	19. 4. 16
Pte.	I	Lamonby	21. 4. 16
Pte.	R.	McRay	27. 4. 16
Pte.	T.	McKenzie	27. 5. 16
Pte.	E.	Redden	29. 5. 16
L/Cpl.	A.	Ferguson	31. 5. 16
Pte.	J.	Moore	6. 6. 16
Pte.	W.	Robinson	6. 6. 16
Pte.	N.	Keating	18. 6. 16
Pte.	J.	Adams	24. 6. 16
Pte.	J.	Alexander	12. 7. 16
Pte.	J.E.	Martin	12. 7. 16
Pte.	W.	Montgomery	16. 7. 16
Pte.	J.	Lawson	17. 7. 16

379

Pte.	J.H.	Smith	25. 7. 16	Pte.	R.	Boyd	16. 9. 16
Pte.	J.	Montgomery	2. 8. 16	Pte.	J.	Buckton	16. 9. 16
Pte.	G.	Waters	4. 8. 16	Pte.	W.	Cassey	16. 9. 16
Pte.	M.	Lewis	6. 8. 16	L/Cpl.	E.	Chilton	16. 9. 16
L/Cpl.	G.	Golightly	8. 8. 16	Pte.	J.W.	Edgar	16. 9. 16
Pte.	E.N.	Nixon	8. 8. 16	Pte.	W.	Fatherly	16. 9. 16
Pte.	W.R.	Greener	9. 8. 16	L/Cpl.	H.	Georgeson	16. 9. 16
L/Cpl.	H.T.	Johnstone	14. 8. 16	Pte.	J.	Gordon	16. 9. 16
L/Cpl.	F.W.	Mumford	28. 8. 16	Pte.	H.	Hann	16. 9. 16
Pte.	T.	Armstrong	15. 9. 16	Pte.	J.	Hutchinson	16. 9. 16
Pte.	T.	Armstrong	15. 9. 16	Sgt.	D.	McKie	16. 9. 16
Pte.	T.	Auckland	15. 9. 16	Pte.	R.	Morton	16. 9. 16
Sgt.	T.	Ayre	15. 9. 16	Pte.	J.S.	Morton	16. 9. 16
Pte.	C.H.	Beaumont	15. 9. 16	Pte.	W.	Murphy	16. 9. 16
L/Cpl.	J.	Brunton	15. 9. 16	Pte.	F.	Murphy	16. 9. 16
L/Sgt.	J.	Carter M.M.	15. 9. 16	Pte.	R.	McKenna	16. 9. 16
Pte.	C.F.	Chambers	15. 9. 16	Cpl.	J.	Purdy	16. 9. 16
Sgt.	R.	Constantine	15. 9. 16	L/Cpl.	W.	Reid	16. 9. 16
Sgt.	T.W.S.	Cowan	15. 9. 16	Pte.	R.	Sweeney	16. 9. 16
Pte.	I	Davidson	15. 9. 16	Pte.	J.	Winder	16. 9. 16
Pte.	A.	Dobbing	15. 9. 16	Pte.	T.	Winter	16. 9. 16
Pte.	E.	Evans	15. 9. 16	Pte.	R.G.	Atkinson	17. 9. 16
Pte.	A.	Graham	15. 9. 16	L/Cpl.	J.	Batey	17. 9. 16
Pte.	M.	Grigg	15. 9. 16	Pte.	J.	Costello	17. 9. 16
Pte.	H.	Grundy	15. 9. 16	Pte.	T.	Ismay	19. 9. 16
Pte.	H.	Hannah	15. 9. 16	Pte.	E.	Temple	20. 9. 16
Pte.	W.	Hawley	15. 9. 16	Pte.	J.	Heslop	26. 9. 16
Sgt.	J.J.	Houghton	15. 9. 16	Pte.	G.	Forbes	28. 9. 16
Pte.	G.	Howe	15. 9. 16	L/Sgt.	J.	Gregory	28. 9. 16
Pte.	A.	Knott	15. 9. 16	Pte.	H.H.	Hampton	28. 9. 16
L/Cpl.	J.	Knox	15. 9. 16	Pte.	T.H.	Hardy	28. 9. 16
Pte.	O.S.	Lynn	15. 9. 16	Pte.	H.	Simpson	28. 9. 16
Ote.	W.	Matthews	15. 9. 16	Pte.	W.	Kelly	29. 9. 16
Pte.	J.A.	Milling	15. 9. 16	Pte.	W.	Lockey	29. 9. 16
Cpl.	R.B.	Miln	15. 9. 16	Cpl.	J.W.	Guy	30. 9. 16
Pte.	J.	McBryde	15. 9. 16	Pte.	T.	Ballantyne	1.10.16
Pte.	E.	Nolan	15. 9. 16	Pte.	P.	Corcoran	1.10.16
Pte.	E.A.	Puddifoot	15. 9. 16	Pte.	F.J.	Dennison	1.10.16
Pte.	A.	Scandle	15. 9. 16	L/Sgt.	H.	Nelmes	1.10 16
Pte.	D.	Swanston	15. 9. 16	Pte.	J.	Turpin	1.10.16
Pte.	T.	Varty	15. 9. 16	Pte.	R.	Brown	2.10.16
Pte.	R.	Walker	15. 9. 16	Pte.	N.	Edminson	2.10.16
Pte.	F.	Walters	15. 9. 16	Pte.	J.	Stewart	2.10.16
L/Cpl.	J.E.	Williams	15. 9. 16	Pte.	G.	Emmerson	3.10.16
L/Sgt.	G.	Williamson	15. 9. 16	Pte.	J.	Hannan	6.10.16
Pte.	S.	Wilson	15. 9. 16	Pte.	R.	Robinson	9.10.16
L/Cpl.	R.	Woods	15. 9. 16	Pte.	W.	Collier	23.10.16
Pte.	A.	Wrightson	15. 9. 16	Pte.	J.	Coleman	4.11.16
Cpl.	F.	Armstrong	16. 9. 16	Pte.	J.	Ainsley	5.11.16
Pte.	J.	Bainbridge	16. 9. 16	Pte.	W.	Alderson	5.11.16
Pte.	T.W.	Beattie	16. 9. 16	Pte.	T.	Ashton	5.11.16
Pte.	E.	Bolton	16. 9. 16	L/Cpl.	J.	Askew	5.11.16

Pte.	J.W.	Bailes	5.11.16	Pte.	J.R.	Pearson	5.11.16
Pte.	W.	Blenkley	5.11.16	Pte.	L.W.	Pointer	5.11.16
Pte.	T.	Bolam	5.11.16	Pte.	A.	Proudfoot	5.11.16
Pte.	R.	Booty	5.11.16	Pte.	L.	Scott	5.11.16
Pte.	W.	Brewis	5.11.16	Pte.	R.A.	Sheraton	5.11.16
Pte.	T.	Brown	5.11.16	Pte.	G.V.	Slater	5.11.16
Pte.	G.	Brown	5.11.16	Pte.	H.	Steward	5.11.16
Pte.	G.	Carlton	5.11.16	Pte.	J.W.	Stokes	5.11.16
Pte.	J.W.	Collings	5.11.16	Pte.	R.	Tench	5.11.16
Pte.	G.	Compton	5.11.16	Pte.	F.W.	Thompson	5.11.16
Cpl.	T.	Davison	5.11.16	Pte.	T.W.	Topham	5.11.16
Pte.	J.S.	Davison	5.11.16	Pte.	T.	Townend	5.11.16
Pte.	J.	Diggle	5.11.16	Pte.	W.	Umpleby	5.11.16
Pte.	G.	Dixon	5.11.16	Pte.	C.	Ward	5.11.16
Pte.	T.	Duke	5.11.16	L/Cpl.	J.	Welford	5.11.16
Pte.	G.	Eastwood	5.11.16	Pte.	W.	Hood	6.11.16
L/Cpl.	A.	Egdell	5.11.16	Pte.	J.	Bell M.M.	6.11.16
Pte.	C.E.	Elliott	5.11.16	L/Cpl.	I	Burton	6.11.16
Sgt.	W.A.	Evans	5.11.16	Pte.	W.	Casey	6.11.16
Pte.	M.	Featherston	5.11.16	Cpl.	T.G.	Lister	6.11.16
Pte.	A.	Firby	5.11.16	Pte.	F.	Owen	6.11.16
Pte.	J.	Foster	5.11.16	Pte.	T.	Sparks	6.11.16
Pte.	W.	Garbutt	5.11.16	Pte.	J.W.	Coverdale	7.11.16
Pte.	H.	Garfit	5.11.16	Pte.	F.	Dickson	7.11.16
Cpl.	D.	Gill	5.11.16	Pte.	T.	Donelly	7.11.16
Pte.	D.	Gillies	5.11.16	Pte.	W.	Eddon	7.11.16
Pte.	H.	Goodey	5.11.16	Pte.	R.	Frazer	7.11.16
Pte.	B.L.	Goose	5.11.16	L/Cpl.	J.C.	Scrowther	7.11.16
Pte.	John	Gray	5.11.16	Pte.	J.	Thompson	7.11.16
Pte.	James	Gray	5.11.16	Pte.	W.S.	Briggs	8.11.16
Pte.	C.T.	Hardwick	5.11.16	L/Cpl.	J.	Cleamson	8.11.16
Pte.	S.J.	Hawkins	5.11.16	Pte.	A.C.	Ninham	8.11.16
Pte.	R.	Hill	5.11.16	Pte.	C.	Russell	8.11.16
Cpl.	J.E.	Hodgson	5.11.16	L/Cpl.	J.	Holliday	10.11.16
Pte.	G.	Hodgson	5.11.16	Pte.	W.	Hirst	11.11.16
Pte.	H.J.	Horsnell	5.11.16	Pte.	A.	Vinton	14.11.16
Pte.	R.G.	Jopling	5.11.16	Pte.	A.	Nelson	15.11.16
Pte.	J.	Kelly	5.11.16	C.S.M.	W.	Raffell	15.11.16
Pte.	F.G.	Kendall	5.11.16	Pte.	E.	Robinson	20.11.16
Pte.	S.J.	Lawrence	5.11.16	Cpl.	G F.	Arrowsmith	26.12.16
Pte.	G.	Loch	5.11.16	Pte.	A.V.	Jackson	31.12.16
Pte.	A.A.	Mallett	5.11.16	Pte.	R.J.	Bryce	3. 1. 17
Pte.	F.	Marshall	5.11.16	Sgt.	G.	Willis	4. 1. 17
Pte.	R.F.	Mason	5.11.16	Pte.	J.E.	Charlesworth	7. 1. 17
Pte.	H.	Mayes	5.11.16	Pte.	J.W.	Hall	7. 1. 17
Pte.	T.	Mayland	5.11.16	Pte.	A.J.	Lusher	9. 1. 17
Pte.	J.	Merritt	5.11.16	Pte.	F.O.	Osterland	9. 1. 17
Pte.	J.	Myers	5.11.16	Pte.	J.W.	Nicholson	10. 1. 17
Pte.	G.	McGurk	5.11.16	Pte.	C.	Starling	10. 1. 17
Pte.	A.	Nicklin	5.11.16	Pte.	J.	Taylor	10. 1. 17
Cpl.	J.	Page	5.11.16	Pte.	A.	Tovey	12. 1. 17
Pte.	R.G.	Pearson	5.11.16	Pte.	J.H.	Dickie	16. 1. 17

Pte.	F.	Easter	16. 1. 17	L/Cpl.	A.C.	Cousons	23. 4. 17
L/Cpl.	W.	Hines	16. 1. 17	Pte.	J.	Dixon	23. 4. 17
Pte.	T.	Hughes	16. 1. 17	L/Cpl.	R.	Hall	23. 4. 17
L/Cpl.	J.	Laverick	16. 1. 17	Pte.	W.	Johnson	23. 4. 17
Pte.	R.	Melrose	16. 1. 17	Pte.	H.	Kelly	23. 4. 17
L/Cpl.	J.	Newton	16. 1. 17	Pte.	G.H.	Kendall	23. 4. 17
Pte.	T.	Standley	16. 1. 17	Pte.	D.W.	Kimber	23. 4. 17
Pte.	R.	Walters	16. 1. 17	Pte.	G.W.	Leggett	23. 4. 17
Pte.	F.	Cooper	18. 1. 17	Pte.	A.	McKinnon	23. 4. 17
Pte.	J.W.	Lockey	18. 1. 17	Pte.	W.M.	Platts	23. 4. 17
L/Cpl.	B.	Thomas	18. 1. 17	Pte.	S.C.	Rackham	23. 4. 17
Pte.	A.	Lambert	20. 1. 17	Pte.	W.S.	Rainbow	23. 4. 17
Pte.	W.	Appleton	25. 1. 17	Pte.	J.	Robson	23. 4. 17
L/Cpl.	J.	Crawley M.M.	4. 2. 17	Pte.	J.A.	Sanderson	23. 4. 17
Pte.	J.R.	Nixon	4. 2. 17	Cpl.	R.	Scott	23. 4. 17
Pte.	E.	Powley	7. 2. 17	Pte.	A.	Stephens	23. 4. 17
Pte.	W.J.	Armstrong	14. 2. 17	Pte.	W.	Stirling	23. 4. 17
Pte.	J.	Bird	14. 2. 17	Pte.	A.E.	Stott	23. 4. 17
Pte.	R.	Moore	14. 2. 17	Pte.	E.	Toole	23. 4. 17
Pte.	W.J.	Kew	23. 2. 17	Pte.	H.	Watson	23. 4. 17
Pte.	H.	Wray	23. 2. 17	Pte.	E.	Williams	23. 4. 17
Pte.	B.	Carr	11. 3. 17	L/Cpl.	C.	Grover	24. 4. 17
L/Cpl.	W.J.	Kemp	14. 3. 17	Pte.	J.	Hill	24. 4. 17
Pte.	T.W.	Lyon	16. 3. 17	Pte.	L.	Polack	24. 4. 17
Pte.	G.W.	Benson	13. 4. 17	Pte.	G.	Hunter	25. 4. 17
L/Cpl.	D.	Binnie	13. 4. 17	Pte.	J.	McCutcheon	25. 4. 17
Pte.	W.H.	Cole	13. 4. 17	Pte.	H.	Nicholls	25. 4. 17
Pte.	J.	Conlon	13. 4. 17	L/Cpl.	W.	Crinnion	27. 4. 17
L/Cpl.	F.	Emmet	13. 4. 17	Pte.	W.	Waugh	27. 4. 17
Pte.	E.W.	Felstead	13. 4, 17	Pte.	T.	Clarkson	30. 4. 17
Pte.	J.f.	George	13. 4. 17	Pte.	G.E.	Colley	2. 5. 17
Pte.	J.	Kelly	13. 4. 17	Pte.	R.	Hudson	3. 5. 17
Pte.	W.	Palmer	13. 4. 17	Pte.	W.	Crowe	5. 6. 17
Pte.	J.	Platford	13. 4. 17	Pte.	T.	Burton	12. 6. 17
Pte.	H.	Routh	13. 4. 17	Pte.	E.R.	Dunn	12. 6. 17
Pte.	H.	Stott	13. 4. 17	Sgt.	A.	Caldwell	14. 6. 17
Pte.	R.	Waller	13. 4. 17			D.C.M., M.M.	
Pte.	J.	Wilson	13. 4. 17	Cpl.	W.E.	Guy M.M.	14. 6. 17
Pte.	J.P.	Binner	14. 4. 17	Pte.	W.L.	Holley	15. 6. 17
L/Cpl.	M	Fodden	14. 4. 17	L/Cpl.	J.	Easterbee	22. 6. 17
Pte.	J.R.	Laws	14. 4. 17	Pte.	R.	Dixon	26. 6. 17
Pte.	R.	Parker	14. 4. 17	Pte.	W.H.	Minnikin	7. 7. 17
Pte.	G.A.	Ryall	14. 4. 17	Pte.	W.	Hart	10. 7. 17
Pte.	A.	Stephenson	14. 4. 17	Pte.	W.E.	Pitcher	13. 7. 17
Pte.	T.	Watson	14. 4. 17	Pte.	F.	Warren	19. 7. 17
Pte.	R.	Drinkald	15. 4. 17	Pte.	J.	Hillery	25. 7. 17
Pte.	E.W.	Weightman	15. 4. 17	Pte.	C.P.	Driver	29. 7. 17
Pte.	F.	Ayre	23. 4. 17	Pte.	T.W.	Davison	30. 7. 17
Pte.	P.	Best	23. 4. 17	Pte.	J.	Renforth	30. 7. 17
Pte.	C.	Brook	23. 4. 17	Pte.	L.	Clark	31. 7. 17
Pte.	A.B.	Coatman	23. 4. 17	L/Cpl.	T.	Bevil	20. 8. 17
Sgt.	J.	Counsellor	23. 4. 17	Pte.	J.	Howarth	20. 8. 17

L/Cpl.	J.	Kelly	20. 8. 17
Cpl.	R.S.	Iredale	21. 8. 17
Pte.	J.W.	Tunstall	6. 9. 17
Pte.	W.	Brownless	15. 9. 17
L/Cpl.	J.	Colgan M.M.	15. 9. 17
Pte.	J.	Dennis	15. 9. 17
Pte.	R.	Hibbs	15. 9. 17
Pte.	W.	Miller	15. 9. 17
Pte.	H.	Westwood	15. 9. 17
Pte.	A.	Williams	15. 9. 17
Pte.	W.	Winchester	15. 9. 17
Pte.	T.	Butt	16. 9. 17
Pte.	W.H.	Birkett	25. 9. 17
Pte.	S.	Hall	28. 9. 17
Pte.	T.F.	Tavener	28. 9. 17
Pte.	J.W.	Russell	7.10.17
Pte.	L.	Donaldson	26.10.17
Pte.	D.A.	Hedley	26.10.17
Pte.	H.E.	Alderson	27.10.17
Pte.	R.	Slater	27.10.17
Pte.	E.J.	Syrett	27.10.17
Pte.	J.	Parkin	28.10.17
Pte.	M.	Raine	28.10.17
Pte.	H.	Sharples	28.10.17
Pte.	W.	Swift	28.10.17
Pte.	J.	Waite	28.10.17
Sgt.	T.	Bell	30.10.17
Cpl.	J.T.	Davies	30.10.17
Pte.	A.	Pearson	31.10.17
Pte.	F.W.	Booth	5.11.17
Pte.	T.	Hodgson	5.11.17
Pte.	G.	Dixon	6.11.17
Pte.	C.	Young	6.11.17
Pte.	J.E.	Clarkson	31.12.17
Pte.	O.	Kendal	28. 1. 18
Pte.	R.W.	Cain	25. 3. 18
Pte.	G.	Atkinson	26. 3. 18
Cpl.	A.	Hall	26. 3. 18
L/Cpl.	R.	Poskett M.M.	26. 3. 18
Pte.	H.E.	Bellerby	27. 3. 18
Pte.	C.S.	Loades	27. 3. 18
Pte.	J.G.	Purvis	27. 3. 18
Pte.	L.	Taylor	27. 3. 18
Pte.	J.	Anderson	28. 3. 18
Pte.	W.	Armstrong	28. 3. 18
Pte.	W.	Carter	28. 3. 18
Pte.	W.	Gratton	28. 3. 18
Pte.	W.	McCallum	28. 3. 18
Pte.	W.	Oddy	28. 3. 18
L/Cpl.	T.	Owens	28. 3. 18
Pte.	F.	Philps	28. 3. 18
Pte.	A.A.	Robson	28. 3. 18
Pte.	J.W.	Smith	28. 3. 18
Cpl.	R.	Stoddart	28. 3. 18
Pte.	T.	Thompson	28. 3. 18
Pte.	M.D.	Wilson	28. 3. 18
Pte.	T.	Knowles	29. 3. 18
Pte.	R.H.	Watson	29. 3. 18
Pte.	P.	Carey	30. 3. 18
Pte.	C.	Burdon	30. 3. 18
Pte.	F.	Gillespie	30. 3. 18
Pte.	F.	Sandy	30. 3. 18
Pte.	C.H.	West	30. 3. 18
Pte.	T.W.	Taylor	11. 4. 18
Pte.	J.	Kenny	12. 4. 18
Sgt.	R.	Lowdon	12. 4. 18
Pte.	G.D.	Graham	16. 4. 18
Pte.	A.S.	Messer	22. 4. 18
L/Cpl.	E	Hindmarch M.M.	29. 4. 18
Pte.	G.A.	Tilton	21. 5. 18
Pte.	G.	Adams	22. 5. 18
Pte.	J.	Martin M.M.	24. 5. 18
Pte.	H.C.	Grass	26. 5. 18
Pte.	R.	Richardson	26. 5. 18
L/Cpl.	G.W.	Greensmith	2. 6. 18
Pte.	J.	Robson	2. 6. 18
L/Cpl.	T.W.	Surtees	2. 6. 18
Pte.	C.	Haslan	3. 6. 18
Pte.	H.	Williams	3. 6. 18
Pte.	A.	Hitchins	9. 6. 18
Pte.	S.	Morris	9. 6. 18
Pte.	G.	Mountford	10. 6. 18
Pte.	J.	Irving	13. 6. 18
L/Cpl.	H.	Wilkinson M.M.	16. 6. 18
Pte.	J.E.	Charlton	19. 7. 18
Pte.	W.	Ramsden	20. 7. 18
L/Cpl.	M.	Barnes	21. 7. 18
Pte.	A.	Beck	21. 7. 18
Cpl.	E.R.	Bell M.M.	21. 7. 18
L/Cpl.	J.	Brooks	21. 7. 18
L/Cpl.	F.J.	Chipchase	21. 7. 18
Pte.	R.	Clark	21. 7. 18
Pte.	G.	Cummersdale	21. 7. 18
Pte.	J.H.	Davidson	21. 7. 18
L/Cpl.	L.	Fossey	21. 7. 18
Pte.	T.	Forster	21. 7. 18
Pte.	P.	Fowlie	21. 7. 18
Pte.	R.	Goodhall	21. 7. 18
Pte.	H.	Grice	21. 7. 18
Pte.	S.	Hampton	21. 7. 18
Sgt.	M.	Hann M.M.	21. 7. 18
Pte.	E.	Hawkes	21. 7. 18
Pte.	G.E.	Hoyle	21. 7. 18
Pte.	J.	Hunter	21. 7. 18

Pte.	C.	Jenkins	21. 7. 18	Pte.	T.W.	Hind	27. 7. 18
Pte.	T.	Leavesley	21. 7. 18	Pte.	C.S.	Reid M.M.	3. 8. 18
L/Cpl.	W.	Marley	21. 7. 18	Pte.	W.	Rawson	28. 8. 18
Pte.	J.	Monfreda	21. 7. 18	Pte.	J.	Black	2. 9. 18
Pte.	J.W.	Montgomery	21. 7. 18	Pte.	A.C.	Cameron	2. 9. 18
Pte.	P.	Morris	21. 7. 18	Pte.	H.S.	Rickayzen	7. 9. 18
Pte.	R.H.	Murphy	21. 7. 18	Pte.	L.	Jones	7. 9. 18
Pte.	P.	McGaban	21. 7. 18	Pte.	A.W.	Ball	12. 9. 18
Pte.	T.	McLaurien	21. 7. 18	Pte.	J.W.	Cannon	12. 9. 18
Pte.	J.G.	Noonan	21. 7. 18	Pte.	J.E.	Christopher	12. 9. 18
Pte.	J.	Norris	21. 7. 18	Pte.	A.	Dudley	12. 9. 18
Cpl.	W.	Park M.M.	21. 7. 18	Pte.	A.	Ford	12. 9. 18
Pte.	F.	Quinn	21. 7. 18	Pte.	A.	Harper	12. 9. 18
Pte.	C.	Raynes	21. 7. 18	Pte.	J.W.	Hayes	12. 9. 18
Pte.	J.W.	Revell	21. 7. 18	Pte.	A.	Innes M.M.	12. 9. 18
Pte.	A.	Rowell	21. 7. 18	Pte.	C.E.	Jepson	12. 9. 18
Pte.	W.	Sandall	21. 7. 18	L/Cpl.	J.	Kendall M.M.	12. 9. 18
Pte.	M.	Stewart	21. 7. 18	Pte.	W.	Laybourn	12. 9. 18
Pte.	H.S.	Storey	21. 7. 18	Pte.	H.	Nichols	12. 9. 18
Pte.	W.	Taylor	21. 7. 18	Sgt.	F.F.	Noble M.M.	12. 9. 18
Pte.	H.	Wall	21. 7. 18	Pte.	A.E.	Stonehouse	12. 9. 18
Pte.	B.	Widdowson	21. 7. 18	L/Cpl.	J.R.	Taylor	12. 9. 18
Pte.	A.	York	21. 7. 18	Pte.	T.	Waugh	12. 9. 18
Pte.	W.	Seaman	22. 7. 18	Pte.	H.M.	Worth	12. 9. 18
Pte.	A.	Smith	22. 7. 18	Pte.	W.	Clark	13. 9. 18
L/Cpl.	A.	Wilson	22. 7. 18	Pte.	S.J.	Harmsworth	13. 9. 18
Sgt.	G.E.	Barrows	23. 7. 18	Pte.	H.	Jagger	13. 9. 18
Pte.	J.	Bellis	23. 7. 18	Pte.	G.A.	Parry	13. 9. 18
Pte.	J.W.	Campbell	23. 7. 18	Pte.	J.T.	Wallace	13. 9. 18
Pte.	A.L.	Chambers	23. 7. 18	L/Cpl.	A.	Williams	13. 9. 18
Pte.	J.	Charlton	23. 7. 18	Pte.	F.	Booth	14. 9. 18
Pte.	F.	Davies	23. 7. 18	Pte.	J.	Croney	14. 9. 18
Cpl.	J.	Dunwoodie	23. 7. 18	Pte.	G.	Hutchinson	14. 9. 18
Pte.	W.H.	Gordon	23. 7. 18	Pte.	W.	Jackson M.M.	14. 9. 18
Pte.	E.	Hunter	23. 7. 18	Pte.	G.H.	Knight	14. 9. 18
Pte.	W.	Ireland	23. 7. 18	Pte.	C.	Nobes	14. 9. 18
L/Cpl.	J.T.	Maine	23. 7. 18	Pte.	W.	Oxborrow	14. 9. 18
Pte.	T.	McDonald	23. 7. 18	Pte.	G.	Skilbeck M.M.	14. 9. 18
Pte.	W.E.	Parsons	23. 7. 18	Pte.	W.	Darlington	15. 9. 18
Pte.	W.	Preston	23. 7. 18	Pte.	J.W.	Rayner	15. 9. 18
Pte.	I.A.	Stocks	23. 7. 18	Pte.	F.O.	Rutland	15. 9. 18
Pte.	J.R.	Storey	23. 7. 18	Pte.	S.	Brown	16. 9. 18
Pte.	S.	Sturgess	23. 7. 18	Pte.	W.	Riley	24. 9. 18
Pte.	T.H.	Thompson	23. 7. 18	Pte.	A.	West	1.10. 18
Cpl.	J.W.	Wearmouth	23. 7. 18	Pte.	R.	Bell	21.10.18
Pte.	D.	White	23. 7. 18	Pte.	E.	Taylor	22.10.18
L/Cpl.	G.	Wilkinson M.M.	23. 7. 18	Pte.	B.	Booth	29.10.18
Pte.	W.	Wright	23. 7. 18	Pte.	T.H.	Bullock	31.10.18
Pte.	J.L.W.	Bennett	24. 7. 18	Pte.	S.	Walker	8.11.16
Pte.	G.A.	Frank	24. 7. 18			Died Germany (P.O.W.)	
L/Cpl.	G.	Stevens	24. 7. 18				
Pte.	W.	Derrick	26. 7. 18				

The following died of illness or wounds at home:

Pte.	C.	Heron	1.10.14
Pte.	J.	Eales	9. 2. 15
Pte.	W.	Chapman	13. 2. 15
Pte.	R.	Turner	6. 5. 15
Pte.	T.W.	Richardson	24. 6. 15
Pte.	W.	Craggs	26. 6. 15
Pte.	C.	Madden	31.10.16
Pte.	G.M.	Harbottle	18. 5. 17
Pte.	W.	Wright	9.10 17
Pte.	G.	Childs	13. 6. 18
Pte.	J.	Reilly	20. 8. 18
Pte.	H.R.	Hughes	8.10.18

WORLD WAR I LIST OF HONOURS & AWARDS TO OFFICERS, N.C.O.S & O.R.S

VICTORIA CROSS

Lt. Col. R.B. Bradford

Pte. T. Young

DISTINGUISHED SERVICE ORDER & MILITARY CROSS

Capt. W.D.B Thompson

DISTINGUISHED SERVICE ORDER & DISTINGUISHED CONDUCT MEDAL

Lt. Col. E.G. Crouch

DISTINGUISHED SERVICE ORDER

Major P.P. Wilson

ORDER OF THE BRITISH EMPIRE

Capt. J.O. Innes

MILITARY CROSS & TWO BARS

Capt. A.C. Scott (R.A.M.C.)

MILITARY CROSS & ONE BAR

Capt.	J.R	Armstrong
Capt.	C.D.	Bowdery
Capt.	T.B.	Jameson
Capt.	H.B.	Johnson
Capt.	C.A.	Marshall
Lt.	H.B.	Plummer
Lt.	W.G.	Wylie

MILITARY CROSS & MILITARY MEDAL

C.S.M. E. Maddison

MILITARY CROSS

Capt.	C.	Bagnall
Capt.	R.	Boys Stones
Capt.	C.H.R.	Gee
Lt.	E.J.	Hampton
Capt.	T.	Harker
Capt.	A.F.	Hebron
Capt.	J.O.	Innes
Capt.	M.	Jolley
Lt. Sir	R.C.	Muir-Mckenzie
Capt.	R.	Mauchlen
Lt.	W.E.	Meikle
Capt.	E.C.	Palmer
Lt.	G.L.	Parkinson
Capt.	J.D.	Rickaby
Capt.	W.H.	Robertson Q.M.
Lt.	J.R.	Swales
Lt.	J.G.	Weightman
Capt.	Rev. J.D.	Wood

2/Lt.	J.F.	Blakey
2/Lt.	F.W.	Cowling
2/Lt.	L.	Dodds
2/Lt.	E.	Dryden
2/Lt.	E.S.	Gibson
2/Lt.	R.	Hall
2/Lt.	W.B.	Little
2/Lt.	J.R.	Thompson
R.Q.M.S.	J.	Taylor
C.S.M.	T.	Sordy

DISTINGUISHED CONDUCT MEDAL, MILITARY MEDAL & BAR

Sgt. T.W. Goffin

DISTINGUISHED CONDUCT MEDAL & MILITARY MEDAL

Sgt.	A.	Caldwell
Pte.	C.W.	Caygill
Pte.	A.F.	Clark
Sgt.	J.W.	Craig
Cpl.	E.	Gill
Pte.	J.	Grundy
Pte.	W.R.	Laskey
Sgt.	T.	Shepherd
Pte.	S.J.	Sterry
L/Cpl.	B.	Wood

DISTINGUISHED CONDUCT MEDAL

C.S.M.	F.H.	Bousfield
L/Cpl.	C.T.A.	Campbell
Pte.	E.	Davison
Pte.	W.	Dixon
Pte.	W.	Finlay
Pte.	J.	Halliday
Pte.	J.	Horan
R.S.M.	W.	Johnstone
Pte.	H.F.	Lee
L/Cpl.	M.	Lee
Sgt.	T.	Mason
L/Cpl.	J.	Masters
L/Cpl.	J.	McDonald
C.S.M.	W.S.	Ridley
Pte.	J.M.	Silcock
Pte.	T.	Thompson
Sgt.	W.	Wilson

MILITARY MEDAL & TWO BARS

| Cpl. | J. | Bee |
| L/Cpl. | G. | Landreth |

L/Sgt.	J.E.	Marsh

MILITARY MEDAL & ONE BAR

L/Cpl.	E.R	Bell
Pte.	E.	Crowther
Pte.	E.	Hindmarch
Sgt.	C.F.	Hutton
Cpl.	A.	Jones
Pte.	C.S.	Reid
Pte.	J.	Richardson
L/Cpl.	W.	Sterling
Pte.	J.	Waitt
Cpl.	H.	Williams

MILITARY MEDAL

Pte.	J.	Adamson
Pte.	W.	Anderson
Pte.	M.	Annable
Sgt.	J.	Appleby
L/Cpl.	J.	Arkless
L/Cpl.	F.	Ashard
Pte.	T.E.	Atkins
L/Cpl.	C.W.	Balls
L/Cpl.	J.W.	Baxendale
Sgt.	J.W.	Beautyman
Pte.	H.	Bell
Pte.	J.	Bell (1279)
Pte.	J.	Bell (1609)
Cpl.	C.	Bickerton
Cpl.	T.	Bilton
Pte.	G.	Bolam
L/Cpl.	J.	Bousfield
L/Cpl.	R.S.	Britton
Pte.	G.W.	Brown
Cpl.	S.	Brown
L/Cpl.	C.	Bryant
L/Cpl.	A.	Burnside
Pte.	T.	Burton
Pte.	F.	Byrne
Pte.	A.	Cameron
Bugler	T.G.	Cameron
L/Cpl.	R.	Carmichael
Sgt.	J.F.	Carr
L/Sgt.	J.	Carter
Pte.	G.	Chambers
Sgt.	T.	Chapman
Sgt.	W.	Chapman
L/Cpl.	H.	Charlton
Cpl.	H.S.	Clay
L/Cpl	C.J	Cobb
Pte.	J.	Colgan
Pte.	J.T.	Coombes
Pte.	J.	Cooper

Sgt.	T.	Counsellor
Pte.	C.	Cranmer
L/Cpl.	P.	Cranney
Pte.	J.	Crass
Pte.	J.	Crawley
Pte.	E.	Crowther
Cpl.	J.	Crozier
L/Cpl.	J.	Cunningham
Pte.	J.	Davidson
Pte.	R.	Davidson
L/Cpl.	B.	Davison
Pte.	G.	Dempsey
Cpl.	M.	Dempsey
Sgt.	J.	Dick
Sgt.	E.	Dobson
Sgt.	T.	Dodds
Cpl.	E.	Edmundson
Pte.	R.	Edwards
L/Cpl.	F.	Fairnington
Sgt.	W.	Farrage
L/Cpl.	L.	Farrow
L/Cpl.	J.	Fenwick
L/Cpl.	M.	Fenwick
L.Cpl.	A.	Flodden
Pte.	T.	Forbes (3183)
Pte.	T.	Forbes (327171)
Pte.	A.	Fortune
Pte.	A.J.	Fox
Pte.	E.	Galley
Sgt.	G.	Gardiner
Cpl.	M.	Garrity
Sgt.	T.	Gibson
Pte.	T.	Gill
Sgt.	B.	Gillings
Pte.	J.	Glanville
Sgt.	F.	Graham
Pte.	G.	Gray
Sgt.	J.	Greenwell
L/Cpl.	W.E.	Guy
Pte.	J.	Hamill
Cpl.	T.H.	Hamilton
L/Sgt.	S.	Hammond
Pte.	M.	Hann
L/Cpl.	J.	Hardy
L/Cpl.	T.	Henderson
L/Cpl.	P.	Henry
Cpl.	W.	Herdman
L/Cpl.	M.	Herron
Pte.	W.R.	Hewitt
L/Cpl.	E.	Hindmarsh
Cpl.	R.	Holborn
Pte.	C.	Holmes

Pte.	J.W.	Howe
Cpl.	J.	Hudson
Pte.	P.	Hunt
Sgt.	G.	Hunter
Pte.	J.R.	Ilderton
Pte.	A.	Innes
Pte.	J.	Jackson
Pte.	J.W.	Jackson
Pte.	W.	Jackson
L/Cpl.	H.	Johnson
L/Cpl.	C.	Johnston
L/Cpl.	W.	Johnston
L/Cpl.	A.E.	Jones
L/Cpl.	J.	Jones
L/Cpl.	C.	Kenny
L/Cpl.	J.	Kendall
Pte.	H.	Kitching
L/Cpl.	J.	Lange
Pte.	A.E.	Laws
L/Cpl.	T.	Leadbitter
Cpl.	T.	Lees
Sgt.	J.	Long
Pte.	W.J.	Lowes
Pte.	J.	McCoy
Pte.	J.T.	McKenna
Sgt.	E.	Maddison (3031)
Pte.	J.	Martin
L/Cpl.	B.	Nimmo
L/Cpl.	J.E.	Moore
Pte.	J.W.	Moore
L/Cpl.	S.	Morgan
Pte.	J.	Morris (2209)
Sgt.	J.	Morris (372)
L/Cpl.	J.	Morris (325497)
Sgt.	J.	Munro
Pte.	P.	Munt
Pte.	F.	Newton
Pte.	J.	Nichol
L/Cpl.	T.	Nicholson
L/Cpl.	B.	Nimo
Pte.	C.	Nobes
Sgt.	F.F.	Noble
L/Cpl.	J.	Norris
Pte.	P.	O'Neill
L/Cpl.	R.	Otley
Cpl.	A.	Outram
Sgt.	D.T.	Padgett
Sgt.	E.	Pallant
Cpl.	W.	Park
L/Cpl.	J.W.	Parker
Cpl.	H.	Pegg
Pte.	J.	Pentland
L/Cpl.	R.	Poskett
Pte.	T.	Prudham
Pte.	J.W.	Purvis
L/Cpl.	R.	Quinn
Pte.	J.	Radford
L/Cpl.	J.W.	Riches
L/Cpl.	T.W.	Robson
Cpl.	W.H.	Scorer
Pte.	A.	Simpson
Pte.	G.	Skilbeck
Pte.	J.	Slack
Pte.	D.	Slater
Cpl.	G.E.	Smith
Pte.	J.	Smith
Pte.	J.W.	Stanton
Sgt.	R.	Stark
Sgt.	W.	Storey
Pte.	W.	Swalwell
Pte.	J.	Taylor
Pte.	H.	Tebb
L/Cpl.	T.	Timothy
Pte.	W.	Todd
Pte.	T.	Vallans
Cpl.	T.	Varity
Pte.	D.	Varty
L/Cpl.	R.P.	Walker
Pte.	G.	Wallace
L/Cpl.	T.	Waters
L/Cpl.	J.W.	Waterworth
Pte.	J.	Watts
Sgt.	E.	Waugh
Cpl.	A.	Wheatley
L/Cpl.	J.	Wildish
L/Cpl.	H.	Wilkinson
Pte.	H.	Williams
Pte.	J.H.	Williamson
Cpl.	R.	Williams
L/Sgt.	W.H.	Wilson
Pte.	H.	Wiseman
Pte.	W.	Wishart
Pte.	S.	Whittaker
Pte	F.	Wright
Pte.	C.	Wood
L/Cpl.	G.	Landreth

MERITORIOUS SERVICE MEDAL

Sgt.	J.M.	Fisher
Sgt.	E.	Attey
Sgt.	B.	Watson
Cpl.	J.	Campbell
Pte.	R.C.	Hughes
Pte.	R.	Jemison

FOREIGN DECORATIONS

Lt. Col. E.G. Crouch
French Legion D'Honneur
Croix de Chevalier

Capt. W.D.B. Thompson
French Croix de Guerre Avec Palm
Capt. J.A.C. Scott (R.A.M.C.)
French Criox de Guerre Avec Palm

Capt. R.C. Palmer   .
French Croix de Guerre Avec Gold Star

C.S.M. T. Sordy
French Croix de Guerre Avec Palm

Sgt. W. Scott Belgium
Croix de Guerre

Sgt. C. Hutton French
Croix de Guerre Avec Gold Star

L/Cpl. G. Landreth
French Croix de Guerre Avec Gold Star

L/Cpl. W. Sterling
French Croix de Guerre Avec Palm

Pte. S. Morgan
French Croix de Guerre Avec Palm

Pte. C.S. Doid
French Medaille Militaire

Pte. E. Sambrook French
Medaille Militaire

The above list is not complete and has been collected from a number of sources. The author apologises for any omissions or errors that may occur. The total number of awards to the battalion are 328 with a further 21 Mentioned In Despatches.

ROLL OF HONOUR 1940–1945

The following Roll of Honour was taken from the book displayed in the Regimental Chapel, Durham Cathedral, and the battalion's own War Diary. This list may not complete and the author apologises for any oversights or omissions.

Rank	Name		Date killed or died of wounds
L/Cpl.	R.W.	Elliott	1. 5. 40
Pte.	E.	Stoker	7. 5. 40
Pte.	J.D.	Ions	10. 5. 40
Pte.	J.	McNeil M.M.	11. 5. 40
Pte.	G.W.	Wharrier	15. 5. 40
Pte.	T.	Young	15. 5. 40
Pte.	V.L.	Longstaff	17. 5. 40
Pte.	T.P.	Howells	18. 5. 40
Cpl.	S.	Smith	19. 5. 40
Cpl.	M.C.	Parker	23. 5. 40
Pte.	J.	Carlton	24. 5. 40
Pte.	W.	Henderson	24. 5. 40
Pte.	K.	Whitfield	24. 5. 40
Capt.	G.G.	Dunn	26. 5. 40
Capt.		Ritchie	26. 5. 40
W.O.11	W.N.	Thompson	26. 5. 40
C/Sgt.	R.	Stonehouse	26. 5. 40
Sgt.	W.	Dixon	26. 5. 40
Sgt.	N.	Edwards	26. 5. 40
Sgt.	G.	Harrison	26. 5. 40
Pte.	R.	Arnold	26. 5. 40
Pte.	T.	Campbell	26. 5. 40
Pte.	J.G.	Chatto	26. 5. 40
Pte.	J. H.	Crame	26. 5. 40
Pte.	S.J.	Devonport	26. 5. 40
Pte.	H.	Haughton	26. 5. 40
Pte.	F.	Heath	26. 5. 40
Pte.	C.S.	Frater	26. 5. 40
Pte.	M.	King	26. 5. 40
Pte.	A.	Laidler	26. 5. 40
Pte.	W.J.	Law	26. 5. 40
Bdsmn.	M.	Leves	26. 5. 40
Pte.	G.W.S.	Mackenzie	26. 5. 40
Pte.	A.E.	Malay	26. 5. 40
Pte.	C.W.	McIntosh	26. 5. 40
Pte.	P.	McLoran	26. 5. 40
Pte.	J.W.	Patterson	26. 5. 40
Pte.	N.	Phillipson	26. 5. 40
Pte.	N.	Sawyer	26. 5. 40
Pte.	F.	Smoth	26. 5. 40
Pte.	G.H.P.	Sunter	26. 5. 40
Pte.	A.G.	Weavers	26. 5. 40
Pte.	R.H.	Smith	26. 5. 40
Pte.	J.	Morton	27. 5. 40
Pte.	W.	Thurlow	27. 5. 40
Pte.	A.	Cook	29. 5. 40
Pte.	J.D.	Morrell	29. 5. 40
Pte.	W.	Robson	29. 5. 40
L/Cpl.	S.	Blackie	30. 5. 40
Pte.	J.A.	Baty	30. 5. 40
Bugler	J.A.	Harrison	30. 5. 40
Pte.	J.A.	Holland	30. 5. 40
Pte.	W.	Renforth	30. 5. 40
Pte.	T.	Slater	30. 5. 40
Pte.	J.H.	Tennick	30. 5. 40
2/Lt.	S.	Cunningham	31. 5. 40
C/Sgt.	G.	Gaul	31. 5. 40
Sgt.	T.	Brown	31. 5. 40
Sgt.	G.H.	Sheader	31. 5. 40
Cpl.	T.C.	Purvis	31. 5. 40
Pte.	R.	Carson	31. 5. 40
Pte.	S.	Letherbridge	31. 5. 40
Pte.	T.	Lunam	31. 5. 40
Pte.	G.W.	Miller	31. 5. 40
Pte.	E.	Nicholls	31. 5. 40
Pte.	F.	Sharpe	31. 5. 40
Pte.	R.E.	Walker	31. 5. 40
Pte.	F.L.	Bowater	1. 6. 40
Pte.	W.J.	Miller	1. 6. 40
Pte.	R.	Minto	1. 6. 40
Pte.	D.	Stewart	1. 6. 40
Pte.	J.E.	Templeton	1. 6. 40
Pte.	W.	Wade	1. 6. 40
Pte.	J.	Miller	17. 6. 40
Pte.	R.	Malkin	18. 6. 40
Pte.	W.	Shaw	23. 6. 40
Pte.	R.	Covell	24. 6. 40
Pte.	E.	Peacey	25. 6. 40
Pte.	P.F.	Latchem	26. 6. 40
Pte.	A.	Forster	28. 6. 40
Pte.	I.	Oxley	30. 6. 40
Pte.	M.	Burrell	8. 8. 40
Pte.	E.	Wilkie	8. 8. 40
Pte.	R.	Harper	28. 8. 40
Pte.	W.	Irving	30. 11. 40
Pte.	F.	Walton	8. 1. 41
Pte.	R.N.	Edgar	28. 4. 41
Pte.	A.	Kidd	1. 5. 41
Pte.	G.	Mooney	15. 5. 41
Pte.	G.R.	Flack	23. 5. 41
Pte.	R.	Hetherington	4. 2. 42

Sgt.	A.	Whistance	21. 3. 42	Pte.	G.	Lawton	27. 6. 42
Pte.	G.S.	Hogg	21. 3. 42	Pte.	A.D.	Macgregor	27. 6. 42
Pte.	J.	Rowan	21. 3. 42	Pte.	E.	Mohn	27. 6. 42
Pte.	T.H.	Wright	21. 3. 42	Pte.	P.M.	Murray	27. 6. 42
Pte.	A.W.	Phipps	22. 3 .42	Pte.	A.S.	Nellist	27. 6. 42
Pte.	W.	Johnson	24. 3. 42	Pte.	S.L.	Onions	27. 6. 42
Cpl.	M.	Forster	10. 5. 42	Pte.	R.	Simm	27. 6. 42
Pte.	F.	Thomason	10. 5. 42	Pte.	J.T.	Tubmen	27. 6. 42
2/Lt.	A.	Robe	1. 6. 42	Pte.	A.H.	Wakenshaw V.C.	27. 6. 42
C/Sgt.	L.	Brennan	1. 6. 42	Sgt.	T.H.	Mason	28. 6. 42
L/Sgt.	F.	Thorburn	1. 6. 42	Cpl.	E.	Davies	28. 6. 42
L/Cpl.	W.T.	McVittie	1. 6. 42	Cpl.	F.	Marshland	28. 6. 42
Pte.	W.L.	Banks	1. 6. 42	L/Cpl.	W.M.	Oliver	28. 6. 42
Pte.	T.	Bennett	1. 6. 42	Pte.	W.H.	Jewkes	28. 6. 42
Pte.	J.	Boxer	1. 6. 42	Cpl.	N.	Ormston	29. 6. 42
Pte.	H.J.	Crookham	1. 6. 42	Pte.	C.	Beaumont	29. 6. 42
Pte.	W.A.	Dunford	1. 6. 42	Pte.	C.	Bell	29. 6. 42
Pte.	W.R.	Elliott	1. 6. 42	Pte.	J.	Burrell	29. 6. 42
Pte.	A.	Halliwell	1. 6. 42	Pte.	A.P.	Price	29. 6. 42
Pte.	A.	Hogg	1. 6. 42	Pte.	J.R.	Smith	29. 6. 42
Pte.	J.	McNally	1. 6. 42	Pte.	J.M.	Stewart	29. 6. 42
Pte.	A.S.	Milburn	1. 6. 42	Pte.	W.B.	Thompson	29. 6. 42
Pte.	A.E.	Price	1. 6. 42	L/Sgt.	R.	Henderson	30. 6. 42.
L/Cpl.	N.V.	Jupp	2. 6. 42	Pte.	L.W.	Spuffard	2. 7. 42
Pte.	W.B.	Atkinson	2. 6. 42	L/Sgt.	R.	Neville	3. 7. 42
Pte.	A.	Winter	2. 6. 42	Pte.	T.	Best	9. 7. 42
Pte.	J.	Ord	5. 6. 42	Pte.	W.E.	Williams	18. 7. 42
Pte.	A.C.	Place	5. 6. 42	Pte.	F.C.	Buck	26. 7. 42
Pte.	A.	Rigby	6. 6. 42	Pte.	J.T.	King	26. 7. 42
Pte.	A.H.H.	Robson	8. 6. 42	Sgt.	G.H.	Forster	27. 7. 42
Sgt.	F.A.	Rasen	9. 6. 42	Pte.	E.H.	Parry	27. 7. 42
Cpl.	R.N.	Scott	10. 6. 42	Pte.	L.	Poole	27. 7. 42
Pte.	J.A.	Appleby	11. 6. 42	Pte.	F.	Thomas	31. 7. 42
Pte.	D.	Bainbridge	15. 6. 42	Sgt.	C.L.	Turner	17. 8. 42
Pte.	E.	Hartley	15. 6. 42	Pte.	J.	Meakins	17. 8. 42
Pte.	G.	Morris	15. 6. 42	Pte.	J.W.	Price	17. 8. 42
Pte.	H.	Ball	16. 6. 42	Sgt.	C.E.	Pennock	5. 9. 42
Pte.	J.	Mould	16. 6. 42	Pte.	L.	Palmer	5. 9. 42
Pte.	H.	Stephenson	20. 6. 42	Pte.	J.	Robinson	5. 9. 42
2/Lt.	H.V.	Braithwaite	25. 6. 42	Pte.	A.	Smallman	5. 9. 42
Pte.	W.E.	Carr	25. 6. 42	Pte.	J.T.	Horton	14. 9. 42
Sgt.	H.S.W.	Jones	27. 6. 42	Pte.	J.A.	Clemmett	25. 9. 42
Sgt.	C.	Lockett	27. 6. 42	Pte.	E.	Grice	25. 9. 42
Cpl.	L.	Howard	27. 6. 42	Pte.	D.	Higgins	25. 9. 42
Pte.	J.H.	Blakesley	27. 6. 42	Pte.	G.	Lomax	25. 9. 42
Pte.	H.	Boardman	27. 6. 42	Lt.	G.	Eldridge	17. 10. 42
Pte.	T.	Brady	27. 6. 42	Pte.	F.	Thornett	17. 10. 42
Pte.	W.	Buckham	27. 6. 42	L/Cpl.	C.	Coils	18. 10. 42
Pte.	J.	Byrne	27. 6. 42	Lt.	D.E.(J.)	Hutchinson	23. 10. 42
Pte.	P.	Crane	27. 6. 42	Lt.	S.G.	Wilkes	23. 10 42
Pte.	M.	Duffy	27. 6. 42	Pte.	F.W.	Jones	1. 11. 42
Pte.	F.E.	Harrison	27. 6. 42	Sgt.	W.N.	Ryle	2. 11. 42

L/Sgt.	D.	Thompson	2. 11. 42	Pte.	B.	Seccombe	22. 3. 43
Pte.	G.	Allen	2. 11. 42	Pte.	R.N.	Snowdon	22. 3. 43
Pte.	A.E.	Carlisle	2. 11. 42	Pte.	C.	Tobin	22. 3. 43
Pte.	G.	Davison	2. 11. 42	Pte.	F.L.	Williams	22. 3. 43
Pte.	A.E.	Fennon	2. 11. 42	Pte.	I.J.	Williams	22. 3. 43
Pte.	J.P.	Fox	2. 11. 42	Capt.	A.R.	Pollard	23. 3. 43
Pte.	E.H.	Fuller	2. 11. 42	Lt.	E.R.	Lacey	23. 3. 43
Pte.	P.	Gouch	2. 11. 42	Pte.	R.	Britton	23. 3. 43
Pte.	L.S.	Heron	2. 11. 42	Pte.	J.	Burns	23. 3. 43
Pte.	W.	Hey	2. 11. 42	Pte.	A.F.	Hardwell	23. 3. 43
Pte.	T.	Holt	2. 11. 42	Pte.	E.	Irlam	23. 3. 43
Pte.	G.C.	Knapper	2. 11. 42	Pte.	G.	Mayers	23. 3. 43
Pte.	J.	Monks	2. 11. 42	Pte.	J.H.	Roberts	23. 3. 43
Pte.	W.A.	Morgan	2. 11. 42	Pte.	E.W.J.	Shelton	23. 3. 43
Pte.	W.	Nicholson	2. 11. 42	Pte.	F.	Whitehouse	23. 3. 43
Pte.	T.	Pollitt	2. 11. 42	W.O.11	E.	Schonewald	26. 3. 43
Pte.	T.	Potter	2. 11. 42	Capt.	T.L.	Megoran	28. 3. 43
Pte.	E.T.	Rourke	2. 11. 42	Cpl.	T.	Smythe	6. 4. 43
Pte.	C.	Stevenson	2. 11. 42	Pte.	G.B.	Cooke	7. 4. 43
Pte.	S.	Tams	2. 11. 42	Pte.	J.W.R.	Hoggarth	9. 4. 43
Pte.	S.J.	Taylor	2. 11. 42	Pte.	P,	McMullen	22. 4. 43
Pte.	B.	Todd	2. 11. 42	Pte.	J.	Brennan	6. 5. 43
Pte.	E.	Whittingham	2. 11. 42	Pte.	G.	Evans	1. 7. 43
Pte.	C.E.D.	Tate	2. 11. 42	Pte.	T.	Allman	5. 7. 43
Pte.	J.A.	Mandley	8. 11. 42	Pte.	H.	Willis	7. 7. 43
Cpl.	J.	Flamson	14. 11. 42	Pte.	H.E.	Robertson	10. 7. 43
Pte.	J.	Rhodes	14. 11. 42	Pte.	F.	Vickers	10. 7. 43
Pte.	R.	Rice	14. 11. 42	Pte.	W.	Rankin	11. 7. 43
Pte.	W.	Foster	15. 11. 42	Sgt.	T.H.	Morris	12. 7. 43
Pte.	C.C.	Fulcher	19. 11. 42	Pte.	W.	Heys	13. 7. 43
Pte.	J.	McIntyre	22. 11. 42	Pte.	K.	Scott	14. 7. 43
Pte.	F.	McMahon	22. 11. 42	Lt.	W.J.R.	Hoyte	15. 7. 43
Pte.	J.W.	Thompson	22. 11. 42	Cpl.	P.	Grace	15. 7. 43
Pte.	L.W.	Smith	2. 3. 43	Cpl.	P.	Garrett	15. 7. 43
Pte.	W.J.	Cardwell	18. 3. 43	Cpl.	R.	Hutchinson	15. 7. 43
L/Sgt.	J.A.	Jones	20. 3. 43	2/Lt.	L.J.	Pleavin	16. 7. 43
Pte.	J.	Bradley	20. 3. 43	Sgt.	I.	Lloyd	16. 7. 43
Pte.	R.	Priestley	20. 3. 43	Sgt.	L.G.	Smith	16. 7. 43
Sgt.	P.B.	Jordan	21. 3. 43	L/Sgt.	G.	Alcock	16. 7. 43
L/Cpl.	A.E.G.	King	21. 3. 43	L/Sgt.	R.J.	Weston	16. 7. 43
Pte.	J.H.	Eason	21. 3. 43	Cpl.	G.	Gibson	16. 7. 43
Pte.	H.	Thompson	21. 3. 43	Cpl.	D.E.	Kennedy M.M.	16. 7. 43
Cpl.	G.L.	Rock	21. 3. 43	Cpl.	J.H.	Kennedy	16. 7. 43
L/Cpl.	J.	Burns	21. 3. 43	Cpl.	J.W.	Parker	16. 7. 43
Pte.	A.G.	Baldwin	22. 3. 43	Cpl.	T.	West	16. 7. 43
Pte.	H.	Benyon	22. 3. 43	L/Cpl.	J.E.	Smith	16. 7. 43
Pte.	H.	Coates	22. 3. 43	L/Cpl.	J.M.	Taylor	16. 7. 43
Pte.	J.	Flanagan	22. 3. 43	Pte.	J.H.	Copleston	16. 7. 43
Pte.	T.	Hall	22. 3. 43	Pte.	H.H.	Crutchley	16. 7. 43
Pte.	J.A.	Hildreth	22. 3. 43	Pte.	T.	Dawson	16. 7. 43
Pte.	T.	Holland	22. 3. 43	Pte.	R.	Degg	16. 7. 43
Pte.	D.	Ivison	22. 3. 43	Pte.	D.	Dixon	16. 7. 43

Pte.	C.	Gilliott	16. 7. 43
Pte.	T.G.	Green	16. 7. 43
Pte.	A.	Guidi	16. 7. 43
Pte.	J.R.D.	Hall	16. 7. 43
Pte.	W.	Howells	16. 7. 43
Pte.	J.T.	Johnson	16. 7. 43
Pte.	D.	Jones	16. 7. 43
Pte.	F.C.A.	Leeke	16. 7. 43
Pte.	J.	Lockett	16. 7. 43
Pte.	H.	Longden	16. 7. 43
Pte.	L.	Mably	16. 7. 43
Pte.	W.H.	Mason	16. 7. 43
Pte.	J.G.	Newton	16. 7. 43
Pte.	Y.	Raine	16. 7. 43
Pte.	C.	Robinson	16. 7. 43
Pte.	T.M.	Rowlands	16. 7. 43
Pte.	H.	Smith	16. 7. 43
Pte.	A.E.	Upcott	16. 7. 43
Pte.	G.J.	Williams	16. 7. 43
Capt.	W.G.	Deacon	17. 7. 43
Lt.	G.	McLoughlin	17. 7. 43
2/Lt.	R.K.	Carr	17. 7. 43
L/Cpl.	R.	Carter	17. 7. 43
L/Cpl.	H.P.	Kaufman	17. 7. 43
L/Cpl.	R.H.	Wild	17. 7. 43
Pte.	J.C.	Andrews	17. 7. 43
Pte.	R.H.	Astrop	17. 7. 43
Pte.	E.	Awford	17. 7. 43
Pte.	F.W.	Bacon	17. 7. 43
Pte.	T.C.	Brown	17. 7. 43
Pte.	W.H.	Bruton	17. 7. 43
Pte.	F.	Dyke	17. 7. 43
Pte.	J.R.	Hardman	17. 7. 43
Pte.	A.	Hamilton	17. 7. 43
Pte.	H.	Holden	17. 7. 43
Pte.	W.	Holden	17. 7. 43
Pte.	A.R.	Kemp	17. 7. 43
Pte.	J.C.H.	Kinson	17. 7. 43
Pte.	H.	Mottram	17. 7. 43
Pte.	E.	Moxon	17. 7. 43
Pte.	L.	Mullen	17. 7. 43
Pte.	G.L.	Oakes	17. 7. 43
Pte.	F.	Smith	17. 7. 43
Pte.	B.J.	Williams	17. 7. 43
W.O.11	R.F.	Diston D.C.M.	18. 7. 43
Pte.	W.	King	18. 7. 43
Pte.	J.	Lynch	18. 7. 43
Pte.	E.	Morgan	18. 7. 43
Pte.	C.	Wood	18. 7. 43
Pte.	B.	Powell	18. 7. 43
Pte.	R.	Dobson	19. 7. 43
Pte.	H.W.	Watson	19. 7. 43
Pte.	R.	Hartley	22. 7. 43
Maj.	W.	Robinson	23. 7. 43
Pte.	S.E.	Smith	28. 7. 43
Pte.	J.	Clarke	5. 8. 43
Pte.	S.	Johnson	5. 8. 43
Pte.	J.	Kirby	7. 8. 43
Pte.	W.S.	Yeo	7. 8. 43
Cpl.	G.E.L.	Speight	8. 8. 43
Pte.	T.	Fox	8. 8. 43
Pte.	A.E.	Friend	8. 8. 43
Pte.	E.	Goddard	8. 8. 43
Pte.	H.T.	Miles	8. 8. 43
Pte.	A.A.	Summerfield	8. 8. 43
Lt.	J.I.	Brett-James	9. 8. 43
W.O.11	F.	Thompson D.C.M.	9. 8. 43
Cpl.	B.	Turner	9. 8. 43
Pte.	S.	Bates	9. 8. 43
Pte.	H.J.	Daglish	9. 8. 43
Pte.	W.	Peel	9. 8. 43
Pte.	A.	Hardy	10. 8. 43
Pte.	L.	Green	12. 8. 43
Pte.	J.D.	Chapman	17. 8. 43
L/Cpl.	A.H.	Broad	20. 8. 43
Pte.	J.	Willan	25. 8. 43
Capt.	P.O.	Johnson	9. 9. 43
Pte.	E.C.	Burt	23. 9. 43
Pte.	F.D.	Phipps	23. 9. 43
Pte.	J.F.	Bradley	1. 12. 43
Pte.	J.	Robson	8. 12. 43
Pte.	L.	Knox	9. 12. 43
Sgt.	W.	Hoole	2. 1. 44
L/Cpl.	S	Burbage	18. 1. 44
Pte.	F.	Lynn	28. 1. 44
Pte.	G.	Hollyhead	6. 2. 44
L/Cpl.	N.	Walker	15. 3 44
Pte.	J.	Mooney	6. 5. 44
L/Cpl.	W.H.	Mears	13. 5. 44
Pte.	J.R.	Roberts	30. 5. 44
Pte.	W.F.A.	Cronin	6. 6. 44
Pte.	W.F.	Hartill	6. 6. 44
Pte.	E.E.A.	Cossom	7. 6. 44
Pte.	C.W.	Griffiths	7. 6. 44
Pte.	H.	Harmer	7. 6. 44
Pte.	R.	Allen	8. 6. 44
Pte.	G.H.	Rylands	9. 6. 44
Lt.	D.M.	Laycock	12. 6. 44
Lt.	J.	Dunn	13. 6. 44
Lt.	I,L,	Roantree	13. 6. 44
Lt.	G.	Schofield	13. 6. 44
Sgt.	C.F.	Cook	13. 6. 44
Pte.	H.	Brownrigg	13. 6. 44
Pte.	A.	Ellis	13. 6. 44

Pte.	E.T.	Hindmarsh	13. 6. 44	Pte.	A.	Cushing	25. 6. 44
Pte.	A.C.	Shields	13. 6. 44	Pte.	G.	Meager	25. 6. 44
Pte.	C.C.	Wraight	13. 6. 44	Pte.	L.W.C.	Weston	25. 6. 44
Sgt.	W.H.J.	Gwilliam	14. 6. 44	Pte.	J.	Casson	27. 6. 44
Sgt.	J.W.	Young M.M.	14. 6. 44	Pte.	W.H.G.	Box	29. 6. 44
Cpl.	P.	Evans	14. 6. 44	Pte.	W.G.	Bishop	11. 7. 44
Cpl.	C.B.	Simpson M.M.	14. 6. 44	Pte.	L.C.	Poole	14. 7. 44
L/Cpl.	W.	Knox	14. 6. 44	Pte.	J.	Martin	15. 7. 44
L/Cpl.	T.	Tedford	14. 6. 44	Pte.	G.G.	Taylor	15. 7. 44
L/Cpl.	J.T.	Tranter	14. 6. 44	Pte.	W.	Muckleroy	16. 7. 44
L/Cpl.	G.	Watson	14. 6. 44	Pte.	F.	Nadin	17. 7. 44
Pte.	D.P.	Billett	14. 6. 44	Pte.	E.A.	Wilgrove	17. 7. 44
Pte.	J.	Bratherton	14. 6. 44	Pte.	F.	Biggar	18. 7. 44
Pte.	A.W.	Brown	14. 6. 44	Pte.	T.P.	Mellor	18. 7. 44
Pte.	C.A.	Coldicott	14. 6. 44	Pte.	J.L.	Miller	18. 7. 44
Pte.	J.	Conlon	14. 6. 44	Pte.	G.	Groome-Laxton	19. 7. 44
Pte.	A.S.	Horton	14. 6. 44	Pte.	A.W.	Burt	21. 7. 44
Pte.	S.	Illingsworth	14. 6. 44	Pte.	T.	Currie	21. 7. 44
Pte.	E.A.	Jones	14. 6. 44	Cpl.	J.	Barrett	22. 7. 44
Pte.	A.	Kitchen	14. 6. 44	Pte.	J.	Woodhall	29. 7. 44
Pte.	W.H.	Lewis	14. 6. 44	Cpl.	E.C.	Higgins	1. 8. 44
Pte.	J.	Lynch	14. 6. 44	Cpl.	R.A.	Jackson	2. 8. 44
Pte.	J.R.	Mahan	14. 6. 44	Pte.	S.E.	Mahoney	2. 8. 44
Pte.	W.T.	Medhurst	14. 6. 44	Pte.	J.R.	Mills	4. 8. 44
Pte.	W.H.	Melhuish	14. 6. 44	Pte.	W.	Mulhern	8. 8. 44
Pte.	A.	Mortimer	14. 6. 44	Pte.	C.	Ware	8. 8. 44
Pte.	J.H.F.	Nicholls	14. 6. 44	Pte.	J.	Lawler	9. 8. 44
Pte.	E.	Quigley	14. 6. 44	Pte.	R.	Middlewood	9. 8. 44
Pte.	W.E.	Roff	14. 6. 44	Pte.	R.B.	Miller	9. 8. 44
Pte.	A.C.	Rolfe	14. 6. 44	Pte.	J.R.	Oliver	9. 8. 44
Pte.	G.W.	Smith	14. 6. 44	Pte.	T.	Parry	9. 8. 44
Pte.	C.H.	Swann	14. 6. 44	Pte.	G.A.	Pyne	9. 8. 44
Pte.	L.A.	Turner	14. 6. 44	Pte.	S.G.	Smart	9. 8. 44
Pte.	J.S.	Vernon	14. 6. 44	Lt.	D.	Hurst (N.Z.)	12. 8. 44
Pte.	T.J.W.	Wrighton	14. 6. 44	Sgt.	W.H.	Rushforth	12. 8. 44
Cpl.	F.W.	Hackney	15. 6. 44	L/Sgt.	W.	Watson	12. 8. 44
L/Cpl.	J.	Mitcheson	15. 6. 44	Cpl.	A.	Ward	12. 8. 44
Lt.	H.S.	Smith	15. 6. 44	Pte.	H.	Bailey	12. 8. 44
Pte.	P.	Brown	16. 6. 44	Pte.	C.G.	Baxter	12. 8. 44
L/Sgt.	P.W.	Harrison	17. 6. 44	Pte.	S.B.	Baxter	12. 8. 44
Cpl.	W.J.	Poxon	18. 6. 44	Pte.	C.E.	Bradley	12. 8. 44
Lt.	D.	Boulton	19. 6. 44	Pte.	O.	Dennison	12. 8. 44
Cpl.	J.	Bell	19. 6. 44	Pte.	S.	Hackett	12. 8. 44
L/Cpl.	J.A.G.	Gant	19. 6. 44	Pte.	R.E.	Neville	12. 8. 44
L/Cpl.	B.	Grocutt	19. 6. 44	Pte.	S.J.	Robbins	12. 8. 44
Pte.	A.	Hill	19. 6. 44	Pte.	T.	Smith	12. 8. 44
Pte.	J.	Jackson	19. 6. 44	Pte.	D.	Walters	12. 8. 44
Pte.	R.A.	Sadler	19. 6. 44	Pte.	L.	Ward	12. 8. 44
Pte.	N.	Meredith	20. 6. 44	Pte.	J.	Wood	12. 8. 44
Pte.	D.A.	Pearce	20. 6. 44	Pte.	F.S.B.	Palmer	13. 8. 44
Pte.	E.J.	Poole	20. 6. 44	Pte.	J.	Robertshaw	14. 8. 44
Pte.	W.	Bates	23. 6. 44	Cpl.	F.W.	Gibbins	3. 9. 44

Pte.	J.	Davidson	3. 9. 44
Pte.	K.	Duffey	3. 9. 44
Pte.	R.B.	Knight	3. 9. 44
Pte.	A.	Linfoot	3. 9. 44
Pte.	A.	Yates	3. 9. 44
Pte.	J.W.	Barker	4. 9. 44
Pte.	T.	Cooke	4. 9. 44
Pte.	A.	Dipalma	4. 9. 44
Pte.	J.G.	Duffin	4. 9. 44
Pte.	N.	Wilson	5. 9. 44
Lt.	B.	de la Perrelle	10. 9. 44
Pte.	C.C.	Child	11. 9. 44
Pte.	J.S.	Haley	11. 9. 44
Pte.	J.	Hewitt	11. 9. 44
Pte.	B.	Keeling	11. 9. 44
Pte.	R.	Moscrop	11. 9. 44
Pte.	W.J.	Ward	11. 9. 44
Pte.	J.	Crawford	12. 9. 44
Pte.	F.	Hooper	12. 9. 44
C/Sgt.	H.W.	Mitchell	13. 9. 44
Pte.	F.W.	Pepper	13. 9. 44
Cpl.	T.H.	Jenkins	16. 9. 44
L/Cpl.	R.W.	Nuttal	16. 9. 44
Pte.	W.	Neill	2. 10. 44
2/Lt.	J.	Birchwood (E. Lancs.)	4. 10. 44
Cpl.	S.	Rowland	4. 10. 44
L/Cpl.	W.	Dransfield	4. 10. 44
Pte.	R.A.	Charlton	4. 10. 44
Pte.	M.J.	Foster	4. 10. 44
Pte.	G.	Gillespie	4. 10. 44
Pte.	A.	Hobson	4. 10. 44
Pte.	D.	McManmon	4. 10. 44
Pte.	S.G.	Robins	4. 10. 44
Pte.	C.J.	Russell	4. 10. 44
Pte.	J.A.	Sreadman	4. 10. 44
Pre.	J.	Thompson	4. 10. 44
Pte.	J.	Thompstone	4. 10. 44
Pte.	A.W.	Rees	5. 10. 44
Pte.	A.A.	Tucker	5. 10. 44
Maj.	A.F.	Douglas-Smith (R. Berks.)	7. 10. 44
Pte.	W.T.	Wagstaff	18. 10.44
Maj.	A.E.	Hillier (N. Staffs.)	20. 10. 44
Pte.	C.	Durrans	20. 10.44
L/Cpl.	H.	Brown	31. 10.44
L/Cpl.	T.	McLarty	8. 11.44
Lt.	M.C.	Hibbert	9. 11.44
Pte.	J.J.	Huntley	10. 11.44
Pte.	W.R.	Watts	19. 11.44
Pte.	M.	Grant	2. 12.44

Lt.	W.L.	Carr	8. 12.44
Pte.	F.	Williams	8. 1. 45
Pte.	S.E.	Eland	9. 1. 45
L/Cpl.	H.	Sockett	10. 1. 45
L/Cpl.	W.C.	Sambourne	13. 1. 45
Pte.	D.Y.	Buchan	14. 1. 45
Pte.	R.	Wood	16. 1. 45
L/Cpl.	R.	Barrie	17. 1. 45
Pte.	H.	Hall	17. 1. 45
Pte.	C.	Hargreaves	17. 1. 45
Cpl.	W.J.	Cheese	18. 1. 45
Pte.	E.S.C.	Hester	18. 1. 45
Pte.	L.	Jobling	18. 1. 45
Pte.	G.N.	Patterson	18. 1. 45
Pte.	D.	Tomlinson	18. 1. 45
Pte.	H.G.	Wiles	18. 1. 45
Pte.	R.	Wills	18. 1. 45
L/Cpl.	W.	Brittain	19. 1. 45
Cpl.	H.	Jordens	19. 1. 45
Pte.	A.J.	Holden	20. 1. 45
Cpl.	W.	Coombes	21. 1. 45
Cpl.	F.A.	Schofield	21. 1. 45
L/Cpl.	J.S.	Maunders	21. 1. 45
Pte.	F.W.	Best	21. 1. 45
Pte.	A.T.	Clarke	21. 1. 45
Pte.	C.	Holmes	21. 1. 45
L/Cpl.	A.	Podgurski	24. 1. 45
L/Cpl.	J.F.	Ryder	25. 1. 45
Pte.	J.W.	Morrell	28. 1. 45
L/Cpl.	P.	Phillips	29. 1. 45
Pte.	R.	Turner	31. 1. 45
Pte.	F.	Dale	4. 2. 45
Pte.	F.J.	Devlin	26. 2. 45
Pte.	G.W.	Roberts	26. 2. 45
Pte.	R.T.	Patrick	11. 3. 45
Pte.	J.	Ellis	21. 3. 45
Pte.	W.P.(J.)	Harmison	28. 3. 45
Pte.	D.E.(C.)	Evans	28. 3. 45
Pte.	J.	Keddie	29. 3. 45
Sgt.	R.	Eddy	30. 3. 45
Cpl.	L.A.	Ivison	30. 3. 45
L/Cpl.	I.	Buttle	30. 3. 45
Pte.	F.	Binmore	30. 3. 45
Pte.	C.	Hopwood	30. 3. 45
Sgt.	J.F.T.	Giles	3. 4. 45
Pte.	J.	Risidore	3. 4. 45
Pte.	G.E.	Smith	3. 4. 45
L/Sgt.	J.	Hopkinson	4. 4. 45
L/Cpl.	E.	Hall	4. 4. 45
Pte.	B.W.G.	Baker	4. 4. 45
Pte.	J.R.	Cox	4. 4. 45
Pte.	D.	Dickson	4. 4. 45

Pte.	A.	Hall	7. 4. 45
L/Sgt.	J.S.	Edginton	8. 4. 45
Pte.	J.L.S.	Horner	8. 4. 45
Pte.	W.(P.)	Russell	8. 4. 45
Pte.	C.	Faulkner	10. 4. 45
Pte.	R.H.	Hodges	10. 4. 45
Pte.	J.	Lowerson	15. 4. 45
Pte.	J.W.	Cook	20. 4. 45
Cpl.	L.W.	Jones	29. 4. 45
Pte.	G.H.	Barker	29. 4. 45
Pte.	T.	Onions	5. 5. 45
L/Cpl.	J.	Hogan	16. 7. 45
Pte.	W.S.	West	18.12. 45
Sgt.	A.C.	Ormston	8. 5. 46
Pte.	H.	Goode	30. 5. 46

OFFICERS FROM OTHER REGIMENTS 1940–1945

The following officers died while in service with the 9th Battalion. This list may not complete and the author apologises for any oversights or omissions.

Rank	Name	Date killed or died of wounds
Capt.	J.M.T.	Ritchie 28. 5. 40 Ox. & Bucks. L.I.
Lt.	G.O.	Eldridge 18. 10. 42 K.S.L.I.
Capt.	R.W.	Henley 1. 11. 42 South Staffs.
Lt.	J.	Handasyde-Dick 2. 11. 42 K.S.L.I.
Capt.	E.R.	Stone 2. 11. 42 R.A.M.C.
Lt.	E.R.	Lacey 21. 3. 43 South Wales Bord.
Capt.	A.R.	Pollard 22. 3. 43 Devonshire Regt.
Lt.	E.A.	Ford M.M. 16. 7. 43 Cameronians
Lt.	W.R.J.	Hoyte 16. 7. 43 Somerset L.I.
Lt. Col.	A.B.S.	Clarke D.S.O. 23. 7. 43 K.O.S.B.
2/Lt.	C.H.	Casey 7. 8. 43 Welsh Regt.
Lt.	J.I.	Brett-James 9. 8. 43 Ox. & Bucks. L.I.
Lt.	D.B.	Thornton 14. 6. 44 Royal Sussex Regt.
Lt. Col.	H.R.	Woods D.S.O. M.C. 14. 6. 44 K.R.R.C.
2/Lt.	K.N.	Black 19. 6. 44 Ox. & Bucks. L.I.
Capt.	H.A.	Wells 19. 7. 44 R.A.M.C.
Lt.	C.F.	Smith 7. 8. 44 North Staffs.
Lt.	P.G.	Farrant 12. 8. 44 Somerset L.I.
Lt.	R.A.	Lear 12. 8. 44 Ox. & Bucks. L.I.
Capt.	D.J.S.	Hurst 12. 8. 44 Queens Regt.
Lt.	J.W.F.	Sutherland 4. 10. 44 Royal N'land Fus.
Lt.	H.N.	Taylor 4. 10. 44 Royal N'land Fus.
Capt.	J.	Birchwood 4. 10. 44 East Lancs.
Maj.	A.F.	Douglas-Smith 8. 10. 44 Royal Berks.
Maj.	A.E.	Hillier O.B.E. 20. 10. 44 North Staffs.
Maj.	S.O.deB.	Macartney 21. 1. 45 Royal Irish Fusiliers
Lt.	M.H.	Ingleton 8. 4. 45 Royal Fusiliers

WORLD WAR II HONOURS & AWARDS TO OFFICERS, N.C.OS. & OTHER RANKS

VICTORIA CROSS

Pte. A. Wakenshaw

DISTINGUISHED SERVICE ORDER & BAR

Lt. Col. H.J. Mogg D.S.O.

DISTINGUISHED SERVICE ORDER

Lt. Col.	A.B.S.	Clarke
Lt. Col.	J.E.S.	Percy M.C.
Maj.	J.C.	Slight
Maj.	E.W.H.	Worrall M.C.

MILITARY CROSS & BAR

| Lt. | W.J.H. | Muir |
| Capt. | K.H. | Whitaker |

MILITARY CROSS

Capt.	H.W.	Ashton
Capt.	G.B.	Beattie
Lt.	C.P.	Donoghue
Lt.	R.H.	Forbes
Capt.	A.R.F.	Hynes
Maj.	G.R.	Lanning
Lt.	A.E.	Love Q.M.
2/ Lt.	E.C.	Medway
Maj.	A.G.R.	Noble
2/ Lt.	A.	Robe
Capt.	J.	Robinson
Maj.	L.E.V.	Rumble
Lt.	D.S.	Taylor
Capt.	P.W.B.	Thompson
Capt.	G.L.	Wood
Maj.	E.W.H.	Worrall

DISTINGUISHED CONDUCT MEDAL

C.S.M.	R.	Diston
Sgt.	E.	Gallon
C.S.M.	S.	Howe
C.S.M.	J.P.	Kemp
Sgt.	T.	Myers
C.S.M.	F.	Thompson

MILITARY MEDAL

Pte.	A.N.	Aldridge
Sgt.	F.	Andrews
Sgt.	H.	Burton
Sgt.	A.	Cameron
L/Sgt.	D.	Cross
L/Sgt.	P.	Daley
Pte.	W.S.	Dixon
Pte.	J.E.	Dunn
Pte.	T.	Forster
Pte.	W.H.	Foster
L/Sgt.	J.B.	Gray
Pte.	J.	Hibble
Sgt.	R.	Hey
Sgt.	J.	Howe
Sgt.	J.W.	Jobson
L/Cpl.	C.P.	Jones
Cpl.	P.B.	Jordan
Cpl.	D.E.	Kennedy
L/Cpl.	A.E.	Lowe
Pte.	J.	McNeil
Pte.	G.	Martin
L/Sgt.	S.	Martin
L/Sgt.	J.M.	Nicholson
L/Cpl.	F.E.	Oliver
L/Cpl.	S.S.	Rose
Pte.	W.W.	Saul
Cpl.	W.A.	Shearer
L/Cpl.	C.B.	Simpson
L/Cpl.	L.W.	Smith
Pte.	C.F.F.	Sollis
Pte.	C.W.	Swatten
L/Sgt.	R.J.	Tavener
Sgt.	L.	Thompson
L/Sgt.	J.W.	Young

MEMBER OF THE BRITISH EMPIRE (M.B.E.)

Capt.	B.S.	Walker
Major	C.M.	D'Arcy-Irvine
R.Q.M.S.	H.	Gibson

FOREIGN AWARDS:

W.O.II D. Bedford

Croix de Guerre with Silver Star

Capt. N.C. Philips

Chevalier of Leopold II and *Croix de Querre with Palm*

ACKNOWLEDGEMENTS

I wish to acknowledge those people without whose assistance this book would never have been written. First and foremost my grateful thanks go to Major I.R. English M.C., T.D., who patiently read and reread successive scripts, pointed out errors and suggested amendments. His continued support and encouragement kept me at my task. I wish to thank him for giving me access to his father's diary and letters, which were an important part of the narrative covering the early months of World War I. I am indebted to the Regimental Trustees, who requested me to write this book and have given me their full support throughout.

My thanks also go to Mr. Stephen Shannon B.A., the manager of the Durham Light Infantry Museum, for his continued assistance throughout the writing of the book. In spite of his involvement in the refurbishing of the Regimental Museum, Stephen always found time to deal with my many queries and make available any material I required. Mr. George Fraser of the museum assisted me in my search for many of the records vital to the completion of the narrative.

I wish to thank the staff of the Sound Records Department of the Imperial War Museum. Ms. Margaret Brooke and her staff were always helpful and gave me permission to use the recorded experiences of veterans of the 9th Battalion, which appear in the text. My particular thanks to Mr. Peter Hart of the Sound Records Department whose help and support made my task easier. I am grateful for permission from the Imperial War Museum's Photographic Records Department for permission to use their photographs, which appear in the book.

Major R. Cross, Regimental County Secretary, and his staff copied the final draft and helped me to overcome many of the hurdles which presented themselves from time to time. Col. R. Walton and Mr. K. Storey supplied me with important information relating to the Volunteers and the early years of the 9th Battalion history. Colonel Walton made available to me his collection of Regimental journals, which contributed to my knowledge of the period when the 9th was a Parachute Battalion. I am indebted to Malcom McGregor for the information on officers killed in World War II.

My thanks are due to the following officers and men who contributed to the successful completion of the book. A number of these have since died:

Sgt. J.L. Williams, Pte. R. Atkinson, Sgt. G. Lambert, L/Cpl. F. Welsh, L/Sgt. J. Clark, Maj. K. Wood M.C., L/Cpl. B. Ridley, Maj. R.H. Forbes M.C., Capt. J. March, Maj. E. Hooper, Sgt. J. Hawkins, Maj. J.L. Kennedy, L/Cpl. J.C. Rodgers, Lt. W.S. White, Pte. J. Everett, Maj. J. Arnold, Sgt. S. Ferguson, Pte. L. Fallows, Cpl. R. Cork, Cpl. A. Colgan, Lt. D.S. Taylor M.C., Gen. Sir H.J. Mogg G.C.B., C.B.E., D.S.O., Lt. J. Williams, Sgt. C. Eagles, Pte. R. Porter, Pte. R. Mallabar, Sgt. W. Wright, Pte. S. Webster, Pte. J. Galbraith, Maj. A.D. Scott.

I am also indebted to the families of the following who made material available to me:

Brig. J.E.S. Percy D.S.O., M.C., Maj. H. Scott-Batey, Pte. E. Kerens, Maj. R. Griffiths, Lt. R. Brewer, Capt. R. Mauchlen M.C.

I apologise for any names which may be missing from the above lists. This is not due to any lack of recognition of them for their support and help.

BIBLIOGRAPHY

Beckett, Ian F.W., *Riflemen Form*, Ogilby Trusts, 1982.

Clay, Major Ewart W., M.B.E., *The Path of the 50th*, Gale & Holden Ltd., 1950.

de Guingand, Major General Sir Francis, K.B.E., C.B., D.S.O., *Operation Victory*, Hodder & Stoughton, 1947.

Delaforce, P., *Churchill's Desert Rats: From Normandy to Berlin with the 7th Armoured Division*, Alan Sutton Publishing, 1994.

D'Este, Carlo, *Bitter Victory: The Battle for Sicily*, 1943.

Durham County Archivist, *Archival Records of the Durham Light Infantry*.

Durham County Archivist, *The Regimental Journals of the Durham Light Infantry 1939–45*.

Durham County Archivist, *War Diaries of the 9th Battalion The Durham Light Infantry WWI and WWII*.

Griffiths, Major R., *Papers of Major R. Griffiths, 1943–45*, County Archivist, County Hall, Durham.

Hastings, Max, *Overlord*, Michael Joseph, 1984.

H.M.S.O., *Official Histories: History of the Second World War*.

H.M.S.O., *Official Histories: Military Operations France & Belgium 1915–1918*.

Johnson, Captain and Dumphie, Captain, *Brightly Shone the Dawn*,

Lewis, Major P., M.C. and Major I.R. English, M.C., *Into Battle with the Durhams*, London Stamp Exchange Ltd., 1990.

Lindsay, Major and Johnston, Major, *A Short History of the 7th Armoured Division 1943–45*.

Montgomery, Field Marshal Bernard L., *El Alamein to the River Sangro*, Barrie & Jenkins, 1973.

————, *Normandy to the Baltic*, Barrie & Jenkins, 1973.

Moore, William, *The Durham Light Infantry*, Lee Cooper Ltd., 1975.

Moses, Harry, *The Faithful Sixth: A History of the 6th Battalion The Durham Light Infantry*, County Durham Books, 1995.

Ogilvie, Capt. George, *Northern Volunteers: Their Rise and Progress*, Andew Dickson Printers, 1888.

Raimes, Major A.L., D.S.O., T.D., *The Fifth Battalion The Durham Light Infantry 1914–1918*, published by a Committee of Past and Present Officers of the Battalion, 1931.

Rissik, David, *The D.L.I. at War: The History of the Durham Light Infantry 1939–45*, The Depot D.L.I., Brancepeth Castle, 1952.

Veitch, Major E.H., M.C., *The Eighth Battalion The Durham Light Infantry 1793–1926*, J.H. Veitch & Sons Ltd.

Verney, Major General G.L., D.S.O., *The Desert Rats*

Ward, S.G.P., *Faithful: The Story of The Durham Light Infantry*, Thomas Nelson & Sons Ltd., 1962.

Westlake, Ray, *The Territorial Battalions; A Pictorial History 1859–1985*, Spellmount Ltd., 1986.

Wilmot, Chester, *The Struggle for Europe*, Collins, 1952.

Wyrall, Everard, *A History of the 50th Division 1914–19*, Percy Lund, Humphreys & Co. Ltd., 1939.

Wyrell, Everard, *A History of the 62nd (West Riding) Division 1914–19, Vols. 1 and 2*.

INDEX

403

Ball, H., 391
Ball, W., 112, 384
Ballantyne, T., 380
Balls, C., 83, 387
Bamford, Lieutenant, 201
Bangalore, 200
Banks, W. L., 176, 391
Bannister, J., 254
Bapaume, 50, 67, 93
Bargues, 306
Barker, G., 360, 396
Barker, J., 379, 395
Barker, John, 28
Barnes, M., 384
Barnes, Matthew, 107
Barnett, C. B., 253
Barnett, Corporal, 374
Barossa Camp, 150
Barrett, J., 394
Barrie, R., 335, 395
Barrows, G. E., 384
Barver, 354
Basseboum, 34
Bassum, 355
Bates, S., 259, 393
Bates, W., 394
Batey, G. A., 378
Batey, George, 16
Batey, J., 378, 380
Battiscombe, C. R., 193
Battiscombe, Sammy, 145
Battle of Frezenberg Ridge, 19
Battle School, 265, 276, 285
Baty, J. A., 390
Bauvin, 141
Bavarian Division, 65
Bavarian Regiment, 55-57, 60
Bavarian Reserve Regiment, 55-56, 60
Bavisiaux, 115
Baxendale, J. W., 104, 387
Baxter, C. G., 395
Baxter, S. B., 395
Bay, West, 151
Bayeux, 276, 293
Bazentin-le-Grand, 52, 63
Bazentin-le-Petit, 51, 63, 71, 73
Bécourt, 50, 61, 63, 73

Beak, Brigadier, 211, 224, 239
Beattie, Chris, 125
Beattie, G. B., 130, 192, 398
Beattie, Geoffrey B., 210
Beattie, Lt. G. B., 130, 398
Beattie, T. W., 380
Beaumont, C., 380, 391
Beaumont, J. W., 133
Beaurains, 78, 138
Beautyman, J. W., 387
Beauvais, 305
Beck, 384
Beckeln, 356
Beckett, 401
Beddows, C. S. M. G., 372
Bedford, 37, 40, 42, 231, 358, 398
Bedford House, 37, 40, 42
Bedford, W. O. II D., 358, 398
Bedouin, 180
Bee, J., 387
Beedom, F., 130
Beeringen, 307-308, 311
Beersheba, 163
Behringen, 358
Beiden, 367
Beit Lid Camp, 163
Belgian Artillery, 135
Belgium, W. Scott, 389
Bell, C., 83, 377, 391
Bell, E. R., 83, 93, 384, 387
Bell, H., 13, 15, 387
Bell, J., 83, 378, 381, 387, 394
Bell, Lt. A. W., 102, 378
Bell, Lt. R. N., 378
Bell, Private, 16, 32
Bell, R., 83, 93, 369, 378, 384, 385, 387
Bell, T., 383
Bell, W. R., 369
Bellerby, H. E., 372, 383
Bellewaarde, 21
Bellis, J., 108, 384
Beltot, 296
Bemel, 300, 316, 319
Benghazi, 166, 213, 238
Benina, 213
Bennett, J. L. W., 384
Bennett, T., 176, 391

Poole, E. J., 394
Poole, L., 193, 391, 394
Poperinghe, 16, 18, 23, 34, 36, 322
Port Said, 159-160, 239
Port Tew, 159
Porter, Capt J., 118
Porter, R., 288, 400
Portsmouth, 151
Poskett, R., 93, 101, 383, 388
Posterholt, 339-341
Postes, 133
Potijze, 12, 14, 16, 18-19, 21, 96-97
Potijze Chateau, 12
Potijze Wood, 19, 21
Potter, T., 209, 392
Potts, Lieutenant, 139
Pourcy, 108
Powell, B., 393
Powley, E., 382
Poxon, W. J., 394
Pragnell, Colour Sergeant, 373-374
Preston, W., 108, 384
Price, A. E., 176, 391
Price, E., 176, 391
Price, J. W., 391
Price, P., 391
Priestley, R., 234, 392
Primosole Bridge, 244-249, 251-257, 259, 261, 360
Prince, W., 360
Prouville, 49
Provin, 140-143, 146
Pru Trench, 51-53, 55-56, 61
Prudham, T., 117, 388
Puddifoot, E. A., 380
Pugh, Lt. J., 341
Puisieux-au-Mont, 99-100
Pulteney, Sir W. P., 76
Punjab Regiment, 163
Purdy, J., 380, 383
Purvis, J. W., 114, 388
Purvis, T. C., 390
Pusieux, 99
Putanges, 303
Puzzilo, 259
Pwllheli, 117
Pyne, G. A., 395

Qattara Depression, 191
Queens Regiment, 298
Quigley, E., 394
Quinn, F., 384
Quinn, H., 379
Quinn, R., 104, 388
R. T. R. Group, 359, 362
Rackham, S. C., 382
Radcliffe, Jim, 275, 292
Radford, J., 114, 388
Raffell, C. S. M. W., 382
Rafferty, R. S. M., 372
Rahman Track, 166, 202, 208
Raine, J., 31, 379
Raine, M., 94, 383
Raine, Y., 393
Raineville, 49
Ramsden, Major General, 178, 192, 195
Ramsden, W., 384
Ramsden, Willie, 106
Ramsdorf, 345
Rankin, W., 392
Ransart, 306
Ranville, 297
Raqabet El Sikka, 183
Ras Chechiban, 172
Rasen, F. A., 177, 391
Ratcliffe, Jim, 255, 257, 262, 293, 297, 307, 322, 326, 342, 362, 365
Ravensworth, 3, 23, 117, 119
Rawson, J. W., 42, 379, 384
Rayner, John William, 113, 385
Raynes, C., 384
Rea, H., 303, 341, 369
Readman, Private, 375
Rebbeck, Lt. W. H., 86
Red Cross, 20, 22, 341
Red Sea, 157
Redcar, 2
Redden, E., 380
Redman, Brigadier, 162
Redman, H., 154
Redshaw, Bob, 191
Reed, J., 379
Reed, Lt., 283
Rees, W., 395
Regent Street, 25

Roermond, 326
Roff, W. E., 394
Rogers, John C., 195
Rolfe, A. C., 290, 394
Rollecourt, 77
Rommel, General, 137
Romsey, 265
Ronville Caves, 79, 99
Roode Beek, 330-331
Rose, Lance Corporal, 248
Rose, S. S., 248, 398
Rothbury, 2-3
Rotherham, 6
Rothwell, R. C., 209
Roubaix, 133
Rourke, E. T., 209, 392
Routh, H., 382
Rowan, J., 172, 391
Rowell, 384
Rowland, S., 317, 395
Rowlands, J. M., 375
Rowlands, T. M., 393
Royal Army Service Corps, 120, 214
Royal Artillery, 150, 281
Royal Dragoon Guards, 281, 285-287, 316
Royal Engineers, 26, 42, 84, 86-87, 114, 200, 202, 216, 218, 223, 225, 236, 241, 244, 265, 304, 308, 316, 330, 332, 358
Royal Fusiliers, 21, 24, 40, 97, 112, 120, 132, 137-139, 317, 319, 397
Royal Irish Fusiliers, 397
Royal Military Academy, 290
Royal Northumberland Fusiliers, 120, 132, 137-139
Royal Scots Fusiliers, 24, 40
Royal Tank Regiment, 202-203, 216, 223, 230, 248, 330, 334, 339, 353, 357
Royal Welsh Fusiliers, 317, 319
Royal West Kents Regiment, 118
Rugeley, 150
Ruhr, 371
Rumble, L. E. V., 130, 236, 254, 266, 269, 300, 303, 340, 345, 355, 357, 369, 398
Rumilly, 113-114
Runciman, Quartermaster Captain, 372
Rushforth, W. H., 301, 395
Russell, C. J., 317, 382, 395

Russell, Captain, 254, 259
Russell, J. W., 383
Russell, P., 355, 396
Russia, 77, 99, 280, 352, 374
Rutherford Alley, 55, 60-61, 63
Rutherford Avenue, 56
Rutherford, R., 54, 124, 378
Rutland, F. O., 385
Ruweisat Ridge, 203
Ryall, G. A., 382
Ryder, J. F., 340, 396
Ryhope, 123
Rylands, G. H., 394
Ryle, W. N., 207, 209, 392
Saarladinghe, 134
Saddler, H., 117
Sadler, Lt. F., 378
Sadler, R. A., 394
Saeffeler Beek, 327
Saffron Walden, 262, 264
Saisseval, 131
Salonika, 3
Saltwell Park, 102, 117
Salvation Army, 62
Sambourne, W. C., 330, 395
Sanctuary Wood, 23-24, 34-37, 46
Sandall, W., 384
Sanderson, H., 212, 250
Sanderson, J. A., 382
Sanderson, Lt., 108, 212, 220, 226, 232
Sandhurst, 290
Sandy, F., 383
Sangro, 401
Sanyet, 193
Sarafand, 161
Saragossa Farm Camp, 93
Sarthe, 128
Saul, W. W., 141, 398
Sawyer, N., 390
Scarborough, 2-3, 117-118
Scarpe, 75, 77, 80
Schalbruch, 328
Schierhorn, 358
Schilberg, 331-332, 334-335
Schleswig Holstein, 364
Schmaltz Battle Group, 245-246
Schmargendorf, 368